# How Languages Work

Language is a highly sophisticated tool we use to communicate with one another in a multitude of different ways.

This new introduction to linguistics presents language in all its amazing complexity, while guiding students systematically through the basics. Students emerge with an appreciation of the diversity of the world's languages, as well as a deeper understanding of the structure of human language, the ways it is used, and its broader social and cultural context.

Chapters devoted to the nuts and bolts of language study – from speech sounds to sound patterns, from sentence structure to meaning – are combined with chapters introducing students to the "functional" aspects of language, such as discourse, prosody, pragmatics, and language contact, helping them gain a better grasp of how language works as speakers use it in daily interaction.

A rich set of Language Profiles helps students explore the world's linguistic diversity and identify similarities and differences between languages, while encouraging them to apply concepts from earlier chapter material. A range of carefully designed pedagogical features fosters student engagement by adopting a step-by-step approach along with study questions and case studies.

Well-chosen illustrations support students in developing their analytical skills; the extensive online material includes multimedia resources for students and instructors.

# How Languages Work

## An Introduction to Language and Linguistics

Editor
**CAROL GENETTI**
*University of California, Santa Barbara*

Assistant Editor
**ALLISON ADELMAN**
*University of California, Santa Barbara*

### Contributors

**Alexandra Y. Aikhenvald**   *James Cook University*
**Ayla Applebaum**   *University of California, Santa Barbara*
**Mira Ariel**   *Tel Aviv University*
**Claire Bowern**   *Yale University*
**Mary Bucholtz**   *University of California, Santa Barbara*
**Wallace Chafe**   *University of California, Santa Barbara*
**Dorothy Chun**   *University of California, Santa Barbara*
**Patricia M. Clancy**   *University of California, Santa Barbara*
**Bernard Comrie**   *University of California, Santa Barbara*
**Guy Deutscher**   *University of Manchester*
**Robert Englebretson**   *Rice University*
**Jan Frodesen**   *University of California, Santa Barbara*
**Matthew Gordon**   *University of California, Santa Barbara*
**Birgit Hellwig**   *La Trobe University*
**Kristine Hildebrandt**   *Southern Illinois University Edwardsville*
**Daniel J. Hintz**   *SIL International*
**Michael Israel**   *University of Maryland, College Park*
**Ritva Laury**   *University of Helsinki*
**Marianne Mithun**   *University of California, Santa Barbara*
**Toshihide Nakayama**   *Tokyo University of Foreign Studies*
**Loretta O'Connor**   *Radboud University Nijmegen*

**CAMBRIDGE**
UNIVERSITY PRESS

# CAMBRIDGE
UNIVERSITY PRESS

University Printing House, Cambridge CB2 8BS, United Kingdom

Cambridge University Press is part of the University of Cambridge.

It furthers the University's mission by disseminating knowledge in the pursuit of education, learning and research at the highest international levels of excellence.

www.cambridge.org
Information on this title: www.cambridge.org/9780521174688

First published 2014
Reprinted 2014
3rd printing 2016

Printed in the United Kingdom by TJ International Ltd. Padstow Cornwall

*A catalog record for this publication is available from the British Library*

*Library of Congress Cataloging in Publication Data*
How languages work : an introduction to language and linguistics / Carol Genetti, Editor, University of California, Santa Barbara; Alexandra Y. Aikhenvald, James Cook University; Ayla Applebaum, University of California, Santa Barbara; Mira Ariel, Tel Aviv University; Claire Bowern, Yale University; Mary Bucholtz, University of California, Santa Barbara; Wallace Chafe, University of California, Santa Barbara; Dorothy Chun, University of California, Santa Barbara; Patricia M. Clancy, University of California, Santa Barbara; Bernard Comrie, University of California, Santa Barbara; Guy Deutscher, University of Manchester; Robert Englebretson, Rice University; Jan Frodesen, University of California, Santa Barbara; Matthew Gordon, University of California, Santa Barbara; Birgit Hellwig, La Trobe University; Kristine Hildebrandt, Southern Illinois University, Edwardsville; Daniel J. Hintz, SIL International; Michael Israel, University of Maryland, College Park; Ritva Laury, University of Helsinki; Marianne Mithun, University of California, Santa Barbara; Toshihide Nakayama, Tokyo University of Foreign Studies; Loretta O'Connor, Radboud University, Nijmegen; Allison Adelman, Assistant Editor; University of California, Santa Barbara.
    pages   cm
Includes bibliographical references and index.
ISBN 978-0-521-76744-6 (Hardback) – ISBN 978-0-521-17468-8 (Paperback)
1. Language and languages–Study and teaching.   2. Linguistics–Study and teaching.   I. Genetti, Carol, 1961– editor of compilation.
P51.H69 2013
400–dc23   2013011956

ISBN 978-0-521-76744-6 Hardback
ISBN 978-0-521-17468-8 Paperback

Additional resources for this publication at www.cambridge.org/genetti

# CONTENTS

# FIGURES

## LANGUAGE PROFILES

# TABLES

## LANGUAGE PROFILES

# PREFACE

*How Languages Work* is designed to be the primary text for a university-level introductory course in linguistics. The audience for the book includes:

- undergraduates taking an introductory linguistics course as a general education requirement;
- beginning linguistics students with limited background in the field;
- linguistics graduate students seeking a helpful reference and introductory discussions of a wide range of sub-disciplines and a range of languages;
- students in related disciplines (such as education, anthropology, writing, or communication) that seek grounding in linguistics; and
- general readers with an avid love of languages.

In addition to courses offered within departments of linguistics, the book might be used in departments of anthropology, education, psychology, communication, applied linguistics, English, or other languages. It introduces the field of linguistics through its subfields, and prepares students for more advanced and specialized coursework.

# ACKNOWLEDGMENTS

This book has been the work of many hands over many years. My sincere thanks go out to the contributing authors, whose combined experience in linguistics can be counted in centuries and whose deep insights into language enrich every page of this book. They have been extraordinarily patient with me as I've pursued this project simultaneously with many others and have graciously accepted deeper editing than they are typically accustomed to as I've strived to bring unity and a consistent voice to these pages. I have greatly appreciated their wisdom, patience, good humor, and sheer hard work.

This book would never have come into existence without the dedicated energy of numerous graduate students in the Department of Linguistics at the University of California Santa Barbara (UCSB). First and foremost, it is my pleasure to acknowledge Allison Adelman, whose meticulous attention to detail and love of good writing have served to improve this book greatly. I strongly doubt that I would ever have brought this to completion if I hadn't had her partnership, flexibility, and cheerful persistence to rely on, and for this she will have my unending gratitude. For the website materials, especially the interactive elements, I enthusiastically thank Carlos Nash and Kobin Kendrick, whose early partnership in this project helped to shape and creatively transform my initial visions, extend them in unanticipated ways, and then elegantly embody them through cleverly concocted lines of code. Other graduate students who have contributed in ways too numerous to mention include Onna Nelson, Nicholas Lester, Rebekka Siemens, Kira Griffitt, Veronica Muñoz LedoYañez, Jennifer Garland, and Mara Henderson. Many UC Santa Barbara undergraduates have commented, corrected, and test-run these materials; I especially note the careful work of Kristin Dunkinson, Kareh Vee, and David Prine.

The Cambridge University Press editorial team has provided constant encouragement and expert advice. Thanks especially to Andrew Winnard, Raihana Begum, Helena Dowson, and Catherine Flack for their encouragement, helpfulness, and impressive expertise.

The book was partly written when I was in residence as a Distinguished Visiting Fellow at the Cairns Institute, James Cook University, in Cairns, Australia. My thanks to Sasha

Aikhenvald and R. M. W. Dixon for their contributions, friendship, and support. UC Santa Barbara has been the home of this book, both intellectually and in financial support. I am grateful to the Division of Humanities and Fine Arts for research funds that have made this project possible. Development of the web materials was supported in part by Instructional Improvement Grants from the Office of Instructional Development.

Finally, I thank Paul, Olivia, and Marcus for their love, support, and uncomplaining patience as I've completed this project.

I dedicate this book to the memory of my parents.

CAROL GENETTI
*Santa Barbara*

# LIST OF GLOSSING CONVENTIONS

| Convention | Meaning |
|---|---|
| 1 | first person |
| 2 | second person |
| 3 | third person |
| A | agentive argument of transitive verb |
| ABL | ablative |
| ABS | absolutive |
| ACC | accusative |
| AD | adessive ("onward") |
| ADJ | adjective |
| ADV | adverbial |
| ADV.DS | adverbial, different subjects |
| ADV.SS | adverbial, same subjects |
| AFFIRM | affirmed evidential knowledge |
| AGT | agentive |
| ALL | allative |
| ALREADY | already |
| ANT | anterior |
| APPL | applicative |
| APUD | next-to locative |
| ASP | aspect marker |
| ASSOC | associative plural |
| AUX | auxiliary |
| AV | active voice |
| AWAY.FROM.RIVER | directional affix |
| BRIEF | brief duration |
| CAUS | causative |
| CLF | classifier |

| | |
|---|---|
| CLT | clitic |
| COM | comitative |
| COMPAR | comparative |
| COMPL | completive |
| COND | conditional |
| CONJ | conjunctive |
| CONJECTURE | evidential |
| CONS | mutual consent |
| CONT | continuous |
| COP | copula |
| DAT | dative |
| DECL | declarative |
| DEF | definite |
| DEM | demonstrative |
| DESIDERATIVE | desiderative |
| DET | determiner |
| DIM | diminutive |
| DIST | distal |
| DISTR | distributive |
| DM | discourse marker |
| DS | different subject |
| DU | dual |
| DUPLICATIVE | duplicative |
| DUR | durative |
| EMPH | emphatic |
| ERG | ergative |
| ESS | essive |
| EVEN | additive |
| EVENT | event |
| EVID | evidential |
| F | feminine |
| FACTUAL | factual |
| FOC | focus |
| FUT | future |
| FUT1>2 | future tense for first-person subject with a second-person object |
| GEN | genitive |
| HABITUAL | habitual |
| HON | honorific |
| I/II/III/IV | gender classes |

| | |
|---|---|
| IE | informal ending |
| ILL | illative |
| IMP | imperative |
| IMPRS | impersonal |
| INC | inceptive |
| INCL | inclusive |
| IND | indicative |
| INDF | indefinite |
| INE | inessive |
| INF | infinitive |
| INST | instrumental |
| INTENSIFIER | intensifier |
| INTR | intrasnsitive |
| IO | indirect object |
| IPFV | imperfective |
| IRR | irrealis |
| ITR | iterative |
| JUST | delimitative |
| LAT | lative |
| LINKER | linking morpheme |
| LOC | locative |
| M | masculine |
| MANIP | manipulative |
| MIDDLE | middle voice |
| MUTUAL | evidential |
| N- | non- |
| NEAR.FUT | near future |
| NEG | negative, negation |
| NMLZ | nominalizer |
| NOM | nominative |
| NUM.CLF | numeral classifier |
| OBJ | objective |
| OBL | oblique |
| OBLIGATE | obligation |
| P/O | patientive argument of transitive verb |
| PASS | passive |
| PFV | perfective |
| PL | plural |
| POSS | possessive |
| POSSEE | possessee |

| | |
|---|---|
| PREP | preposition |
| PRF | perfect |
| PROG | progressive |
| PROX | proximal |
| PRS | present |
| PRT | partitive |
| PST | past |
| PST.PTCP | past participle |
| PTC | particle |
| PTCP | participle |
| PURP | purposive |
| Q | question marker |
| QUOT | quotative |
| REC.PST | recent (past) |
| REM.PST | remote (past) |
| REP | repetitive |
| REPORT | non-personal knowledge |
| S | intransitive subject |
| SBJ | subject |
| SEMBL | semblative |
| SEQ | sequential |
| SG | singular |
| SPEC | specific-indefinite article |
| SS | same subject marking |
| STAT | stative |
| SUB | below locative |
| SUPER | above locative |
| TO | directional affix |
| TOP | topic |
| TR | transitive |
| UNW | unwitnessed |
| UP | up(stream) directional |
| VERBAL.ADJ | verbal adjective |
| WIT | witnessed |
| YET | yet |

# THE BOOK'S APPROACH

This textbook has a distinct theoretical perspective, which has come to be known as "functional," a term that is typically contrasted with approaches labeled "formal" (a contrastive discussion of these two theoretical approaches can be found in Chapters 6 and 14). The central premise of the functional approach is that language is most deeply understood by reference to its function as a tool for the myriad purposes of human communication, which occurs through the medium of discourse. Language is thus shaped by discourse as it is produced in the service of communicative interaction. Since language is a quintessentially human activity, languages are grounded in human physiology and cognition, and are both reflective and creative of human societies and cultures. In addition, languages persist over time and are dynamic and constantly changing. Explaining language – why languages have the structures and properties that they do – requires us to understand this broader context.

Because this book does not present linguistics from a formal perspective, it is an appropriate choice for faculty members who wish to provide their students with an excellent orientation to language and linguistics, but are not interested in the abstract formal models of Generative and related theoretical paradigms, or for those with disciplinary grounding beyond linguistics. However, it is important to emphasize that this book is highly technical and analytical, and requires exacting attention to structural detail. Grammar is presented in significant depth and the material is rigorous and may at times be challenging. However, a major focus of the text is to provide students with explicit direction that will help them acquire analytical skills. In addition, the associated website includes numerous learning aids (such as interactive tutorials) that support this process. The password-protected instructor materials on the website include suggestions for sections to assign (and not assign) for classes with a less technical emphasis.

Importantly, this book is strongly cross-linguistic in its orientation; the focus is not just on *language* but also on *languages*. In exposing readers to languages from across the globe, it serves as an introduction to the world's linguistic diversity. Cross-linguistic comparisons are important not only because they allow us to classify languages, but also because they reveal what a language is or might be. Understanding the similarities and differences between languages is essential to the development of empirically justifiable theories about language, particularly with regards to the relationship between linguistic structures and the communicative needs of their speakers.

In addition, linguistic variety is simply fascinating and fun; it reveals much about humankind, and the thousands of ways that particular communities of speakers have categorized and represented the world around them. For that reason, this book contains a special feature: a set of **Language Profiles**, each written by a linguist who has conducted extensive fieldwork in the community that they write about (with the exception of Guy Deutscher, whose profile is on the long-extinct language Akkadian, which is attested on excavated clay tablets). After a brief introduction to the language and the community in which it is spoken, each language profile provides an overview of the basic structures and then goes into depth on one or more topics that tie in with the primary chapters. The languages were selected so as to represent languages of diverse locations, families, and types. Together, these thirteen short studies serve not only to reinforce and illustrate the main points of the primary chapters, but also to expose the reader to the world's linguistic diversity.

## The book's structure

The book contains fifteen primary chapters and thirteen language profiles. It can fit into academic programs in a number of ways. It provides more than sufficient material for a semester-long introductory course. It can also be used in a shorter academic quarter, with instructors selecting the topics they deem the most crucial for students within their programs. It can also be used across multiple courses; for example, the language profiles can be used in subsequent courses on linguistic analysis, morphosyntax, or languages of the world. Chapters not covered in an introductory course can serve as initial readings in more specialized topic-specific courses (such as one on language acquisition). The material could also be expanded to a two-quarter or year-long course, although in the latter case some supplementary readings would probably be desirable. Further discussion on different ways to structure courses and how to incorporate the language profiles are available on the instructor's portion of the website.

The chapters in this book follow the traditional format of tracing linguistic structure, beginning with the smallest units (sounds), building up to successively larger units, and ending with discourse. Chapters on orthogonal topics – such as semantics, language change, and language acquisition – follow the structural chapters. Because of the functionalist orientation of the book, chapters are included on a variety of topics that are not typically found in introductory textbooks. These include prosody, discourse, pragmatics, and language contact.

The functionalist perspective and broad coverage of this book allow it to fill a niche in the market that is currently not covered by other texts. The contributing authors are practicing linguists and distinguished leaders in their given fields. The editor and each author, while not losing their individual voice, maintain a consistent chapter structure and level throughout, to ensure a smooth reading experience for the student. The text is contemporary and up to date. Most importantly, it presents language in the full richness of its context, as a complex dynamic tool shaped by generations of speakers through discourse interactions, adaptive to the broader social and cultural context in which it is embedded. Readers will develop a deep appreciation of the beauty, complexity, and sheer genius of language, and of humankind to whom it belongs.

#  www.cambridge.org/genetti

The website materials are important companions to the book. The website contains a range of materials that will help instructors teach the course and help students engage with and master the skills of linguistic analysis.

Resources for students include:

- sound files associated with particular examples in the text;
- interactive tutorials on problem solving;
- online flashcards;
- "how-to" guides that take students through steps of linguistic analysis;
- explicit instruction in writing for linguistics;
- study guides;
- self-administered online quizzes on vocabulary and key concepts;
- enriched material about the profiled languages, including interesting cultural information and profiles of speakers.

Resources for instructors include:

- PowerPoint slides for each chapter;
- additional problems and suggested exam questions;
- sample assignments;
- answer keys;
- suggestions on how to structure courses, depending on class goals;
- guide to the language profiles and suggestions on how to incorporate them into classes.

# HOW TO USE THIS BOOK

Linguistics is a highly diverse and interdisciplinary field, taking you from concrete details of physical acoustics to abstract logical argument, from concise grammatical structure to rich observations on culture and society. There are few people for whom all of it comes easily – everyone has their favorite subfields – but it is all essential as every subfield deeply interacts with all others. This book has been designed with the student in mind and has many features to facilitate acquisition of the skills necessary to fully appreciate the complexity of language. What follows is some advice for making the most of these features.

It is important in linguistics to engage with the text. Linguistics is not a field where you read quickly and lightly. It is better not to plan to cover too much at one time and not to hurry through it; take adequate time to fully work through a couple of sections, and then take a break. Throughout the primary chapters, you will find that ***key points have been put in bold italics***. Of course, there are many other important points that you will want to note as well. Textboxes contain case studies and important related side points and should also be read. Be sure to really think about the discussion and make it your own; take time to reflect on your own lifelong experience of language and connect it to what you are learning, and to become conscious of language use as you are immersed in it daily. This practice will take your understanding to an entirely new level.

You will find that the pages are filled with examples taken from languages throughout the world. Most of these are numbered and set off from the text. It is critical that you spend time looking at these in detail, even if you are tempted to skip over them to continue with the main text. They are as important as the text itself: each informs the other and neither can be fully understood in isolation. (See Sidebar 0.1.) You will find that much of the time words from other languages are broken into their component parts and translations of the meaning of each part are provided. Often these translations are abbreviated and put in small caps, for example, SG for singular. Many of these glossing conventions are noted in the sidebars. In addition, each chapter has a list of the glossing conventions used within it positioned just before the exercises. A full list of all glossing conventions can also be found on pages xviii–xxi.

**SIDEBAR 0.1**

Sidebars, such as this one, are helpful in providing important information about the examples and in suggesting ways for you to further engage with the material.

Linguistics has extensive terminology that must be learned to understand the field successfully. The Glossary in the back of the book provides simple definitions and is an important reference tool. All words in the Glossary are presented in **bold** at first mention (as well as later in the book if they haven't been mentioned for a while, as a reminder that a glossary entry is available). Also, each primary chapter has online flashcards to help you memorize terms.

One of the essential features of this book is its focus on linguistic analysis. This is the process by which you take a linguistic expression (a word, a sentence, a stretch of discourse) and figure out all of its parts and subparts and how it contributes to the whole. This fine-grained analysis then leads us to a broader understanding of how languages work, the underlying principles, and how the design of languages both serves and reflects their functions as tools of human communicative interaction.

There are many methods of linguistic analysis, depending on which aspects of language are being studied. For example, determining which aspects of phonetic articulation are meaningful in a language is a very different (though surprisingly not unrelated) exercise from determining whether two languages are members of the same language family, or whether a language differentiates active voice from passive voice. Learning how to apply these methods is central to learning linguistics. In order to make this as easy as possible, methodologies are presented in step-by-step fashion. Sidebars prompt you to apply the methods to further data sets. Each chapter has a set of exercises that allows you to analyze new data. In addition, there are many resources on the *How Languages Work* website that serve as aids for improving your analytical skills. These include interactive tutorials, step-by-step instructions, guides to writing in linguistics, etc.

Another important component of the website is the addition of sound files. By far the majority of instances of language use are spoken, and sound is an integral part of most languages (signed languages being the exception). Throughout this book (and all others) you will see speech sounds represented by letters and other two-dimensional symbols, but keep in mind that these are only *representations* of sounds, not sounds themselves. In moving to the abstraction of representation, considerable richness is lost. To partially address this, especially for those chapters that focus on sound (phonetics, phonology, and prosody), many of the examples are accompanied by sound files accessible on the *How Languages Work* website (see Sidebar 0.2). Take the time to listen to them carefully. Most of the language profiles also have sound files, typically of recorded texts. These provide a tangible sense of the language and its speakers that cannot be otherwise replicated.

**SIDEBAR 0.2**

When sound files are available on the website, they are noted in the sidebars with an icon like this:

One of the most fascinating aspects of studying linguistics is learning about the tremendous variety – and ingenuity – of human languages. Linguistic diversity is both captivating and fun. Languages are inseparable from the people who speak them, and they both embody and reflect the world's cultures and societies. In addition, understanding linguistic diversity is critical to understanding the broader principles that underlie languages, i.e., how languages work, and what languages do. The primary chapters in the book are replete with examples taken from languages across the globe.

In addition, the book contains thirteen language profiles, case studies in shorter chapters that focus on particular languages, written by linguists who have dedicated much of their professional lives to studying and analyzing those languages. These case studies all begin with a brief overview of the language, its situation, and the communities that speak it. They then go on to discuss one or more particular aspects of the language in depth, tying in and reinforcing the concepts and analytical skills of the main chapters. Depending on the length of the class, instructors may or may not require these as reading. If not, they are excellent supplements to the main chapters. As a whole, the set of language profiles will serve to vastly advance one's understanding of linguistics. Not only do they allow the widespread application of linguistic concepts to many different languages, they also illustrate the diversity of language types, especially as regards their grammatical structures. Textbox 0.1 provides a list of the language profiles in relation to the chapters to which they correspond; it is best to read the relevant chapter first.

---

**TEXTBOX 0.1  WHEN TO READ WHICH LANGUAGE PROFILES**

| After Chapter: | Read: |
| --- | --- |
| 3 | Kabardian |
| 6 | Goemai, Manange, Nuuchahnulth, Finnish, Quechua, Bardi, Tsez |
| 7 | Chontal |
| 11 | Indonesian |
| 12 | Seneca, Akkadian |
| 13 | Manambu |

---

My own experience with linguistics is that the farther I climb, the greater the vistas I behold. I hope that students will find their own vistas by exploring the field far beyond this book. To encourage this, every chapter and language profile contains a list of suggested reading with a brief note about each entry; these can provide the next steps toward a deeper understanding of this quintessential aspect of our humanity.

# THE INTERNATIONAL PHONETIC ALPHABET (revised to 2005)

## CONSONANTS (PULMONIC)

| | Bilabial | Labiodental | Dental | Alveolar | Post alveolar | Retroflex | Palatal | Velar | Uvular | Pharyngeal | Glottal |
|---|---|---|---|---|---|---|---|---|---|---|---|
| Plosive | p b | | | t d | | ʈ ɖ | c ɟ | k ɡ | q ɢ | | ʔ |
| Nasal | m | ɱ | | n | | ɳ | ɲ | ŋ | N | | |
| Trill | ʙ | | | r | | | | | R | | |
| Tap or Flap | | ⱱ | | ɾ | | ɽ | | | | | |
| Fricative | ɸ β | f v | θ ð | s z | ʃ ʒ | ʂ ʐ | ç ʝ | x ɣ | χ ʁ | ħ ʕ | h ɦ |
| Lateral fricative | | | | ɬ ɮ | | | | | | | |
| Approximant | | ʋ | | ɹ | | ɻ | j | ɰ | | | |
| Lateral approximant | | | | l | | ɭ | ʎ | ʟ | | | |

Where symbols appear in pairs, the one to the right represents a voiced consonant. Shaded areas denote articulations judged impossible.

## CONSONANTS (NON-PULMONIC)

| Clicks | | Voiced implosives | | Ejectives | |
|---|---|---|---|---|---|
| ʘ | Bilabial | ɓ | Bilabial | ʼ | Examples: |
| ǀ | Dental | ɗ | Dental/alveolar | pʼ | Bilabial |
| ǃ | (Post)alveolar | ʄ | Palatal | tʼ | Dental/alveolar |
| ǂ | Palatoalveolar | ɠ | Velar | kʼ | Velar |
| ǁ | Alveolar lateral | ʛ | Uvular | sʼ | Alveolar fricative |

## OTHER SYMBOLS

| | | | |
|---|---|---|---|
| ʍ | Voiceless labial-velar fricative | ɕ ʑ | Alveolo-palatal fricatives |
| w | Voiced labial-velar approximant | ɺ | Voiced alveolar lateral flap |
| ɥ | Voiced labial-palatal approximant | ɧ | Simultaneous ʃ and x |
| ʜ | Voiceless epiglottal fricative | | |
| ʢ | Voiced epiglottal fricative | | |
| ʡ | Epiglottal plosive | | |

Affricates and double articulations can be represented by two symbols joined by a tie bar if necessary.

k͡p   t͡s

## VOWELS

| | Front | Central | Back |
|---|---|---|---|
| Close | i • y | ɨ • ʉ | ɯ • u |
| | ɪ ʏ | | ʊ |
| Close-mid | e • ø | ɘ • ɵ | ɤ • o |
| | | ə | |
| Open-mid | ɛ • œ | ɜ • ɞ | ʌ • ɔ |
| | æ | ɐ | |
| Open | a • ɶ | | ɑ • ɒ |

Where symbols appear in pairs, the one to the right represents a rounded vowel.

## SUPRASEGMENTALS

| | |
|---|---|
| ˈ | Primary stress |
| ˌ | Secondary stress |
| | ˌfoʊnəˈtɪʃən |
| ː | Long   eː |
| ˑ | Half-long   eˑ |
| ˘ | Extra-short   ĕ |
| ǀ | Minor (foot) group |
| ǁ | Major (intonation) group |
| . | Syllable break   ɹi.ækt |
| ‿ | Linking (absence of a break) |

## DIACRITICS

Diacritics may be placed above a symbol with a descender, e.g. ŋ̊

| | | | | | | | | |
|---|---|---|---|---|---|---|---|---|
| ̥ | Voiceless | n̥ d̥ | ̤ | Breathy voiced | b̤ a̤ | ̪ | Dental | t̪ d̪ |
| ̬ | Voiced | s̬ t̬ | ̰ | Creaky voiced | b̰ a̰ | ̺ | Apical | t̺ d̺ |
| ʰ | Aspirated | tʰ dʰ | ̼ | Linguolabial | t̼ d̼ | ̻ | Laminal | t̻ d̻ |
| ̹ | More rounded | ɔ̹ | ʷ | Labialized | tʷ dʷ | ̃ | Nasalized | ẽ |
| ̜ | Less rounded | ɔ̜ | ʲ | Palatalized | tʲ dʲ | ⁿ | Nasal release | dⁿ |
| ̟ | Advanced | u̟ | ˠ | Velarized | tˠ dˠ | ˡ | Lateral release | dˡ |
| ̠ | Retracted | e̠ | ˤ | Pharyngealized | tˤ dˤ | ̚ | No audible release | d̚ |
| ̈ | Centralized | ë | ̴ | Velarized or pharyngealized | ɫ | | | |
| ̽ | Mid-centralized | e̽ | ̝ | Raised | e̝ ( ɹ̝ = voiced alveolar fricative) | | | |
| ̩ | Syllabic | n̩ | ̞ | Lowered | e̞ ( β̞ = voiced bilabial approximant) | | | |
| ̯ | Non-syllabic | e̯ | ̘ | Advanced Tongue Root | e̘ | | | |
| ˞ | Rhoticity | ɚ a˞ | ̙ | Retracted Tongue Root | e̙ | | | |

## TONES AND WORD ACCENTS

| LEVEL | | | CONTOUR | | |
|---|---|---|---|---|---|
| e̋ or | ˥ | Extra high | ě or | ˩˥ | Rising |
| é | ˦ | High | ê | ˥˩ | Falling |
| ē | ˧ | Mid | e᷄ | ˦˥ | High rising |
| è | ˨ | Low | e᷅ | ˩˨ | Low rising |
| ȅ | ˩ | Extra low | e᷈ | ˧˦˧ | Rising-falling |
| ꜜ | Downstep | | | ↗ | Global rise |
| ꜛ | Upstep | | | ↘ | Global fall |

IPA Chart, http://www.langsci.ucl.ac.uk/ipa/ipachart.html, available under a Creative Commons Attribution-Sharealike 3.0 Unported License.
Copyright © 2005 International Phonetic Association.

PART I

# PRIMARY CHAPTERS

# 1 Introduction: language, languages, and linguistics

**KEY TERMS**
- Linguistics
- Linguist
- Linguistic structure
- The functional nature of language
- Language versus dialect
- Language change
- Linguistic analysis
- Language endangerment
- Language documentation and conservation
- The fields of linguistics

**CHAPTER PREVIEW**

Language plays a crucial role in our lives as a functional system of human communication. It is central to our cultures and societies, and has played a significant role in western intellectual history of the study of philosophy, mind, ancient history, and culture. Linguistics is the scientific study of language. This chapter provides an orientation both to language and to the field of linguistics. It introduces the languages of the world, their distribution and demographics, the important issue of language endangerment and death, and the worldwide effort to document and conserve the world's languages. It then provides an orientation to the field of linguistics and an overview of the major subfields of the discipline.

**LIST OF AIMS**

At the end of this chapter, students should be able to:

- **articulate the importance of language to human lives and society;**
- **discuss the ways in which language is a functional system of human communication;**
- **take an objective, descriptive approach to discussion of language-related issues;**
- **begin to identify fine details of linguistic structure;**

- state basic demographic facts about the world's languages, including issues of language vitality and endangerment;
- state in what ways linguistics is scientific and objective;
- provide a brief overview of the major subfields of linguistics.

## 1.1  Language

### 1.1.1  Language and you; language and us

**Language *is an essential and ubiquitous component of our lives.*** To see that this statement is true for yourself, take a moment to think about your day. Cast your mind back to when you first awoke. What were your thoughts and how were they expressed? Trace the day in your mind and try to count how many people you spoke with, even if it was just a quick "hi" or "thank you." Did you listen to a lecture? Watch television? Talk on the phone? Make an appointment? Sing a song? All of these activities centrally involve language. Now think about what you read today. Perhaps a newspaper, pages on the Internet, e-mail, advertisements, labels, signs, homework assignments? Now move on to thought itself. What thoughts and ideas have passed through your mind? Have you made explicit plans, imagined conversations, debated with yourself? If you are like most people, this brief exercise has revealed that language is both within and around you, a constant part of your internal and external existence. Language is the primary medium which you use to interact with people and institutions in our society. Your particular use of language is also a reflection of who you are as an individual; all of us use language as a means to build and portray our identities in the world around us. We also use language to shape and interpret the great and small experiences of our lives.

Think about the broader world in which we live. Language is the principal means by which societies are constructed and cultures are developed. Think of the size of our society's great libraries, and how the majority of the volumes in those vast collections (14.6 million volumes in the Harvard University Library alone) are language in its written form. The intellectual achievements of humankind are essentially embodied in language. This is not only true of the written works that formally encapsulate our knowledge, but it is also true of the huge body of indigenous knowledge held by the speakers of thousands of languages across the globe, from the Brazilian Amazon to the Mongolian steppes. Some may argue that music and art are non-linguistic, but note that they often incorporate language, as with lyrics. Even works that do not contain language are interpreted and understood through verbal thought, discussion, and critical analysis. Similarly, mathematics could be argued to be non-linguistic, but again language is used to teach, understand, and interpret it.

Beyond the modern world, consider that language has been used by humans for at least 30,000 years, by thousands of groups across the globe, wherever humans have ventured. Speakers of each generation endow their language with their own unique mark, their own contribution, changing it in myriad subtle ways. As language passes from generation to generation, it shifts and adapts to the ever-changing world in which it is embedded.

The preceding paragraphs emphasized that ***language is a pervasive and essential part both of your own life and of who we are as humankind***. The goal of this book is to begin to address the question: *How does language work?* It is a simple question, and one that most people never think to ask. Language is so automatic – almost like breathing – that most people don't realize the complexity that underlies it and the subtle and effortless skill with which they wield it.

The question *How does language work?* may itself be simple but the answer is highly complex. It can be broken down into many smaller questions. To begin with, one must ask: *How do individual languages work?* We really can't understand the nature of language in its broad sense if we don't understand the mechanisms underlying particular languages, preferably of many and diverse kinds. Other key questions include: What are all the pieces of a language? How do the pieces combine and work together to allow for communication to occur? How are languages learned and transmitted? How do languages influence each other? How do languages change over time? These are but a small number of the many questions that define the field of **linguistics**, the scientific study of language. But before discussing the field in more detail, it is important to continue with our exploration of the nature of language.

## 1.1.2 Language is human and all that that implies

***Language is one of the defining traits of humankind.*** Language is tied up with our thought processes, our ability to reason, to self-reflect, and to develop advanced civilizations. Other animal species have developed communication systems, but they pale in comparison to human language. A simple illustration of this is the fact that no system of animal communication appears to be able to communicate events that occurred in the past or events that are imaginary. Neither are there animal communication systems that have adverbs or other devices that allow for detailed descriptions of actions. Animals have nothing comparable in scale, complexity, subtlety, or adaptability to human language.

The fact that language is human has a number of important implications for the nature of language. ***Language is embedded into our physiology, our cognition, and our thought processes.*** Many of the details of linguistic structure are directly dependent on this. For example, the fact that no language makes sounds by curling the tip of the tongue back to touch the uvula (the small appendage hanging down in the middle of the back of the mouth) is directly explainable by the details of human anatomy. Less trivially, anatomical facts are also responsible for a number of features of sound systems, such as the common trend to pronounce a sequence of *t* and *y* as "ch" (e.g., *gotcha* from *got you*). More importantly, language processes are largely resident in the brain and so language shares characteristics with other cognitive functions; for example, language is both learnable and adaptable.

Humans use language for a wide variety of purposes. We communicate everything from urgent warnings to random thoughts, proposals of marriage to complaints. We use it to cajole, threaten, placate, inform, entertain, and command. In other words, ***language is functional***; ***it is a tool of human communication***. The fact that language is used for a wide variety of tasks has direct implications for how it is structured. Linguistic structures are flexible and adaptable, able to express all that humans convey to each other in the course of a conversation, a day, a lifetime, a civilization.

Language is also human in that ***language is a form of human social behavior***. It can be used to build or break social bonds. It serves as a social cue to the formality or informality of a situation, and to the degree of social intimacy or distance among the people speaking. When children acquire language, they do so by using it as a tool of social interaction within particular social settings. The social component of human language is also reflected in how language is used and structured.

Humans use language to interact, and ***using language is an inherently interactional task***. Not only are we listening to our conversational partner and picking up on the many subtleties of word choice, sentence structure, rate of speech, and intonation, we are also constantly assessing when and how to take a turn, and how to communicate our message so that the person to whom we are speaking (the **addressee**) will correctly interpret what we are saying. To take a simple example, I wouldn't say *He is coming for dinner tonight* if I didn't think that the addressee had in mind the person I refer to as *he*. Otherwise, I could use a proper name like *Mike* or a more elaborate phrase like *the guy from across the hall*. I could also start off with an introduction, such as *You know that guy I was telling you about, that owns the cocker spaniels?* All three of these strategies accomplish a similar end of introducing the idea of the person I wish to discuss into the mind of the addressee. Once I am confident that the addressee can identify the correct individual, I can communicate the primary message *He's coming to dinner tonight*. Thus, we see that the interactional component of language is both deep and subtle. The structures of human language reflect our interactional needs.

Humans are creative and ***language is structured to take advantage of human creativity***. All languages are constructed in a way that allows for the creation of novel utterances; any language can produce an infinite number of sentences. Therefore we cannot describe a language by simply making a list of all the possible sentences it contains. Instead, our task is to describe the design principles underlying language that make that infinite number of sentences possible. Obvious instances of human creativity with language include word games, puns, and puzzles. Humans also use language creatively when they innovate new expressions, or use one or more words in a new way. For example, the English word *way* has been used for some time to intensify the meaning of certain types of quantifiers (*way too much, way more than necessary*) or prepositions (*way up, way over*). Younger speakers of some English dialects can now use this intensifier with adjectives; e.g., *way cool*. The use of *way* with adjectives can have specific affective (emotional) implications, e.g., *way unfair*. We don't know who first used *way* to intensify an adjective, but in doing so that person was performing a creative act, using the word in a new grammatical environment. People do this every day. Most of the time grammatical innovations are not repeated, but sometimes particular innovations catch on. Other speakers hear the innovation and use it themselves, spreading it wave-like across a significant portion of the **speech community**, a group of people who share a common language or dialect and cultural practices. If an innovation continues to spread, it could become a regular feature of the language and constitute a **language change**. Many instances of language change are direct reflections of human creativity.

To summarize, just as language is deeply a part of humankind, the human element is deeply a part of language. The structures of language take the form they do because language is instantiated by the human body, as a tool of human communication, and is embedded in human interaction within societies and cultures. Language is at the core of what it is to be human, and humanity is at the core of language.

## 1.1.3   Language is dynamic and adaptable

***Language is in a constant process of change***. The language you speak with your friends today is somewhat different from the way your grandparents spoke to their friends when they were your age. Chances are good that your own grandchildren will probably think that your speech sounds a little old-fashioned. While the difference between grandparents and grandchildren may not be dramatic, over a longer time span, for example, that between oneself and one's grandchildren's grandchildren's grandchildren, the cumulative effect of those generations becomes more noticeable. We can see this in the history of English. Consider the following passage, written by William Shakespeare just over three hundred years ago, and taken from the play *King Henry V*:

> Now, fie upon my false French! By mine honour in true English, I love thee, Kate: by which honour I dare not swear thou lovest me; yet my blood begins to flatter me that thou dost, notwithstanding the poor and untempering effect of my visage.

While educated English speakers will be able to understand this passage, children and adults with less formal education will find it difficult. It is easy to identify the linguistic features that mark this as archaic: the use of the old second-person familiar pronouns, *thee* and *thou*; the inflected verb forms *lovest* and *dost*; and the use of now antiquated words and expressions, such as *fie upon* and *visage*. When we look further back, for example at *The Canterbury Tales*, written by Geoffrey Chaucer more than six hundred years ago, the language becomes even harder to decipher. Consider these lines from "The Wife of Bath's Tale":

> And if thou kanst nat tellen it anon
> Yet shal I yeve thee leve for to gon
> A twelf-month and a day to seche and leere

An answere suffisant in this mateere;
And suretee wol I han, er that thou pace,
Thy body for to yelden in this place.

While some of it seems familiar and suggestive of meaning, much is unclear to the eye of the untrained modern English speaker. The passage is easier to decipher if one learns that *yeve* means 'give,' *seche and leere* means 'search and learn,' *suretee* means 'certainty,' and *yelden* means 'surrender.' Try providing a modern English translation and compare it with that given in Textbox 1.1.

---

TEXTBOX 1.1 **MODERN ENGLISH TRANSLATIONS OF *THE CANTERBURY TALES***

Here is one translation of the excerpt from "The Wife of Bath's Tale," provided by Librarius at the following URL: www.librarius.com/canttran/wftltrfs.htm:

> And if you cannot tell it me anon, then will I give you license to be gone a twelvemonth and a day, to search and learn sufficient answer in this grave concern. And your knight's word I'll have, before forth you pace, to yield your body to me in this place.

Of course, you would never speak this way to someone in a conversation today. A more colloquial current translation might be "And if you can't tell me soon, then I'll give you permission to be gone for a year and a day, to find the right answer to this important question. I'll have you promise as a knight, before you leave, that you will give me your life in this place."

---

***All aspects of language can undergo change.*** Sounds can enter a language or fall out of use. Sentence structures can shift in interesting ways. Words can develop into prefixes, suffixes, or other small linguistic units. Word meanings can be broadened, narrowed, or otherwise shifted. The social implications of using particular words and phrases can change over time, as can larger patterns, such as how we structure and present information.

***Language adapts to the world around it.*** Think of all the vocabulary you use in daily life that your grandparents did not use when they were your age. The words *e-mail, nanotechnology, cell phone,* and *Internet* are just a few of the terms that reflect the technological changes that swept over us in the late twentieth century. In the meantime, words like *hogshead* (a large cask or barrel) and *demijohn* (a narrow-necked bottle enclosed in wicker) are not part of the vocabulary of most people living today (although they might persist in certain subgroups of the population). Changes in vocabulary can reflect social changes as well. The English word *spinster*, meaning an unmarried woman past the age of marrying, has vanished from everyday vocabulary in most of modern society, together with the idea that there is an age of marrying and that marriage and family are the primary goals of a woman's life.

While changes in vocabulary reflecting innovations or social change are probably the most obvious examples of the adaptability of language, languages also undergo adaptations under the influence of **language contact**. When speakers of two distinct languages interact with each other in large numbers over a period of time, one or both languages generally undergo change. An example of a language affected by language contact is English, which adopted huge numbers of words from French after the Norman invasion. Indeed, in the sentence I just wrote, the words *example, adopt, huge, number, French, Norman,* and *invasion* all came into English from French!

Language contact can have a much greater effect than simply adding new vocabulary. Sounds, word structures, and sentence structures can also take on qualities of adjacent languages. For example, in the Tibeto-Burman language family (comprising over three hundred related languages distributed over Southeast Asia, Tibet, and the Himalayan region), the majority of languages place the verb at the end of the sentence. A simplified and translated version of a sentence with this word order might be, for example, *John apple ate*. However, there is one group of Tibeto-Burman languages, the Karenic group, which places the verb in the middle of the sentence. Thus, they would say *John ate apple*. Interestingly, speakers of the Karenic languages have been interacting for centuries with the Thai and the Chinese, and both groups speak languages that put the verb in the middle. It is clear that over the centuries, **bilingual** Karenic speakers matched their sentence structures to those of their neighboring languages. Thus, a significant change to Karenic grammar resulted from language contact through the medium of bilingualism. We see that ***languages adapt not only to the changing technological world, but also to their broader social environment***.

## Language is structured and systematic

When one begins to look closely at language, one is immediately struck by the fact that ***regular and recurring patterns form the basis of linguistic structure***. To begin to explore this aspect of language, take a moment to work through the following small exercise on English grammar:

### Regular patterning of the English past-tense suffix

In English most verbs have a predictable past-tense form. It is written as *-ed* but has different pronunciations. You can discover this in your own speech very easily. Pronounce the following lists of words and listen closely to the sound at the end of each word:

List A: *baked, blessed, heaped, puffed, crashed*
List B: *rubbed, waved, lagged, billed, hummed*
List C: *waited, faded, booted, coded, righted*

If you are a native English speaker and have a sensitive ear, you will have noticed that the words in List A end in <t>, the words in List B end in <d>, and the words in List C end in <ed>. We can now refer to these as the T-List, the D-List, and the ED-List.

Now try pronouncing the following three nonsense words, again listening carefully to how the suffix is pronounced in each word:

Word 1: *smipped*
Word 2: *croomed*
Word 3: *pluted*

Notice that you don't have to think for an instant which sound to put at the end, but that you automatically end Word 1 with <t>, Word 2 with <d>, and Word 3 with <ed>, even though these are nonsense words which you are unlikely to have ever heard or pronounced before.

Take a minute to examine the consonants that directly precede the suffix (i.e., the "pre-suffixal" consonants) in the T-List words. Now compare the pre-suffixal consonants in the D- and ED-List words. Notice that the lists are distinct; you don't find any of the T-List pre-suffixal consonants in D-List words, etc. Now determine which lists Words 1–3 fall into, based on their pre-suffixal consonants.

You will see that Word 1 has a T-List consonant (p) and the suffix is pronounced as <t>, Word 2 has a D-List consonant (m) and the suffix is pronounced as <d>, and Word 3 has an ED-List consonant (t) and the suffix is pronounced as <ed>. You have discovered a systematic fact of English: the pronunciation of the past-tense suffix depends upon the pre-suffixal consonant. ***Even though Words 1–3 are nonsense words, they still follow the systematic patterns of pronunciation*** that form a significant part of the English language. We can state this pattern as follows:

**(1)**   In English, the past tense -*ed* will be pronounced: as <t> following the consonants <k, s, p, f, sh>, as <d> following <b, v, d, l, m>, and as <ed> following <t> or <d>.

> **SIDEBAR 1.1**
>
> The statement in (1) is only part of the pattern, as not all possible consonants are exemplified. The lists for two of the groups are actually much larger than shown here. Can you determine which two groups these are?

This is a statement of a pattern or systematic fact of English (sometimes referred to as a rule). One can predict how the past tense -*ed* will be pronounced on any English verb as long as one knows the pre-suffixal consonant (see Sidebar 1.1).

Once we have observed a regular pattern in language, ***we are led to the question of why this pattern should occur***. This question is critical, because it takes us from recognition and description of a pattern to a search for an explanation of the observed facts. In this case, the explanation is physiological, based on how we produce sounds in our vocal tracts. Since this is a topic covered in the next chapter, we will not go into detail here. The important point is that ***patterns in language can be explained by the role of language as a functional system of human communication***. In this case, the explanation comes from the embedding of language in our human physiologies; in other cases, other aspects of the functional nature of language explain linguistic patterns.

Regular patterns such as this occur in every language many times and at many levels. Some patterns are concerned exclusively with sounds, other patterns are found at other levels, such as word structure or sentence structure. One of the fascinating aspects of language is the interaction of these patterns, which at times can be quite complex. All the patterns in a language that explicitly involve sounds make up the "sound system" or **phonology** of a language; the patterns which involve word structure make up the **morphology**, while the patterns which involve sentence structure make up the **syntax**. Each of these subsystems of language is independent, but each is also interwoven with the others. In the example above, both the phonology (in this case, which sound is pronounced where) and the morphology (the past tense suffix *-ed*) are involved. The morphology and syntax of a language are together referred to as the language's **grammar**. For further discussion of the sub-areas examined in linguistic analysis, see Textbox 1.2.

---

### TEXTBOX 1.2 **LINGUISTIC ANALYSIS**

Many examples of systematicity in language will be presented throughout the following chapters. One of the goals of this book is to teach you how to recognize and analyze systematic patterns in a wide variety of languages, that is, how to perform **linguistic analysis**. This requires learning the common – and sometimes the rare – linguistic categories that are found in the languages of the world, the terminology that accompanies those categories, and the theories underlying them. Linguistic analysis requires logical thought, a clear understanding of linguistic concepts, and concise description and argumentation.

Once linguistic structures are accurately described, the analysis is completed by explanation. *The critical question is: what motivates the linguistic structures to be formed in precisely that way?* This question goes to the very core of linguistic theory. The answer will depend crucially upon the particular structure being explained. There are a number of distinct domains that may contribute to it, including meaning (**semantics**), how the structure is used in context (**function**), factors related to history (**language change**), the physical properties of sound (**phonetics**), and the structure of the human brain and how we learn and process knowledge (**neurology, cognition**).

---

On the other hand, ***no language is perfectly systematic***. Although there are sometimes patterns within patterns within patterns, there are often pieces that don't fit into any regular pattern, but which have idiosyncratic, or irregular, behavior. This is in large part due to language change. The irregularities are leftovers from older patterns that have been obliterated, as new structures emerge and spread through the language.

As an example, consider the English verb *shine*. This verb is a bit irregular as it has two forms of the past tense, *shined* and *shone*. The form *shined* is constructed by adding the regular past-tense suffix to the verb stem and following the rule of past-tense formation we just discovered (*shine* ends in a D-List consonant). The form *shone* is a reflection of an old pattern where past tense was indicated by changing the vowel in a verb's root. This pattern was inherited from an earlier stage in the language. It has largely died out, but traces of it remain in a handful of verbs, especially those that are used frequently and are therefore resistant to change (for example, *take/took, drive/drove*). In the development of English, the marking of past tense by *-ed* gradually spread through the vocabulary, supplanting the older forms. This process has not been completed with the verb *shine*, and both past-tense forms coexist in the modern tongue. Thus, this irregularity of the language has a historical explanation. ***Irregularities in language usually result from language change***.

## 1.2 Languages

### 1.2.1 Languages of the world today

Languages are spoken across the globe. People are spread over the earth from the tip of Tierra del Fuego to the Arctic North, and wherever there are people, there are languages. Think for a minute about each of the continents and their communities. How many languages do you think are spoken in the world?

The question is more difficult than it first appears. The truthful answer is that ***we don't have an exact count, although we are able to make an educated guess***. There are two primary reasons why counting up languages is tricky. One is that ***linguists haven't identified all the languages of the world yet***. There are still speech (and sign-language) communities that follow their traditional ways of life and who have had little interaction with larger population groups or researchers. The languages of these groups are still undescribed. However, there is also a more fundamental problem in counting up languages, which is that ***it is difficult to decide which speech varieties should be counted as languages and which should be counted as dialects of a single language***.

Let's consider possible criteria for distinguishing languages from dialects. One obvious place to start is **mutual intelligibility**: can the speakers of the two language varieties understand each other? The criterion of mutual intelligibility, taken to its logical conclusion, suggests that if they can understand each other, the two varieties are to be considered dialects of a single language; if they cannot understand each other, the varieties are to be considered distinct languages. One problem with this criterion is that there are often multiple varieties of a language, and while speakers of adjacent varieties can understand each other, speakers of geographically separated varieties have a much harder time. This situation is schematized in Figure 1.1:

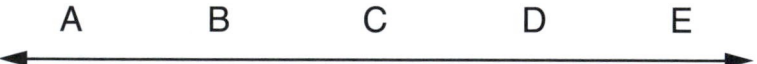

**Figure 1.1** Schematization of language varieties

In Figure 1.1, each letter represents speakers of different varieties and the arrow represents geographic distance. While speakers of A might easily understand speakers of B and C, it might take effort to understand speakers of D, and it might be quite difficult to converse with speakers of E. Similarly, speakers of E might have no problem speaking with those of D and C, but might have more difficulty with speakers of A. So, are A and E different languages? If so, where does one draw the dividing line? This situation is known as a **dialect continuum**, and it represents a common situation throughout the world.

Of course, Figure 1.1 is highly idealized. Communities aren't usually ranged along a straight road with distinct boundaries, and there is often movement and intermarriage between the various groups. However, the problem remains of whether mutually unintelligible A and E should be counted as one or two languages. We can see that the question itself is overly simplistic and obscures the more complex reality of the dispersion of language varieties and their speakers.

***Another problem with the criterion of mutual intelligibility is the word "mutual."*** This implies that speakers of both speech communities are equally at ease or equally perplexed when hearing the speech of the other. However, there are many cases of unidirectional intelligibility, that is, speakers of Group A can understand the speech of Group B, but not the other way around. This situation especially occurs when the Group A variety is spoken by a minority group and the Group B variety is a **standard language**, taught in schools and used in print and broadcast media. In this situation, the Group A speakers have repeated exposure to the B variety and so can understand it. The Group B speakers, on the other hand, may never have heard the speech of Group A, so find it surprising and difficult. It is not always clear whether these varieties are different dialects or different languages.

Another reason why it is difficult to count up languages is that ***there is a complex relationship between language and ethnic identity***. Consider the case of the Newars, an ethnic group which traditionally ruled the Kathmandu Valley in Nepal. While the largest concentration of Newars is in the Kathmandu Valley itself, there are other Newar communities scattered throughout the country. One variety of Newar is spoken in a village called Dolakha, quite a distance to the east. The Dolakha and Kathmandu speech varieties are truly mutually unintelligible. People from these two Newar communities cannot speak to each other in Newar, but must use the national language Nepali to converse. If the question of language versus dialect were to be based solely on mutual intelligibility, then these two varieties would count as separate languages. However, the Dolakha Newars are ethnically Newars in every sense of the word. They have the same customs, social structures, festivals, and traditions, and they intermarry with Newars from other parts of Nepal. Crucially, their language, even though mutually unintelligible with the other varieties, still serves to distinguish the group ethnically from non-Newars, so is a marker of Newar ethnic identity. The language is thus Newar in a very real and relevant sense to the speakers of the language itself. The function of the language as a marker of ethnic identity would suggest that the Dolakha variety is a Newar dialect, not an independent language. The criteria of mutual intelligibility and ethnic identity thus lead us to different conclusions on the question of language versus dialect.

The opposite situation can be found with Swedish and Norwegian, two of the Scandinavian "languages." These two speech varieties are easily mutually intelligible. However, a national boundary and ethnic identity divide the two groups, hence they are considered to speak distinct languages rather than dialects of a single language. Such circumstances motivated the famous quip by the Yiddish linguist

**Figure 1.2** Newars at the temple complex in Patan, Nepal

Max Weinreich: "A language is a dialect with an army and a navy." ***Sociopolitical and ethnic considerations clearly have significant weight in the language/dialect debate***.

While acknowledging that there are inherent difficulties in counting up the languages of the world, we still want to know roughly how many there are. The most current compilation of statistics on the world's languages is found in *Ethnologue: Languages of the World* (available online at www.ethnologue.com). My source for the statistics in the following discussion is the Internet version of the seventeenth edition (Lewis, Simons, and Fennig 2013), which puts ***the total number of known languages at 7,105***. How close was that to your own estimate?

The distribution of languages across continents is given in Table 1.1 (note that "the Americas" include North, South, and Central America, and "the Pacific" includes Australia, New Zealand, and the Pacific Islands). Table 1.1 shows the number and percentage of the world's languages spoken or signed on each continent.

Note that the languages of Europe account for less than 4 percent of the total number of languages of the world, while Asia and Africa have more than 30 percent each.

Table 1.2 presents statistics on the world's languages in relation to the size of the speech communities of native speakers.

**TABLE 1.1** Distribution of languages across continents

| Area | Number | Percentage |
| --- | --- | --- |
| Africa | 2146 | 30.2 |
| The Americas | 1060 | 14.9 |
| Europe | 284 | 4.0 |
| The Pacific | 1311 | 18.5 |
| Asia | 2304 | 32.4 |
| Total | 7105 | 100.0 |

**TABLE 1.2** Number of languages by size of speech community

| Number of speakers | Number of languages | Percentage |
| --- | --- | --- |
| 100 million to 1 billion or more | 8 | 0.1 |
| 10 million to 100 million | 77 | 1.1 |
| 1 million to 10 million | 308 | 4.3 |
| 100,000 to 1 million | 928 | 13.1 |
| 10,000 to 100,000 | 1798 | 25.3 |
| 1,000 to 10,000 | 1984 | 27.9 |
| 100 to 1,000 | 1054 | 14.8 |
| 10 to 99 | 340 | 4.8 |
| 1 to 9 | 134 | 1.9 |
| 0 | 188 | 2.6 |
| Unknown | 286 | 4.0 |

Table 1.2 shows that there are very few languages with very large numbers of speakers; only 5.5% of the world's languages have more than a million speakers. On the other hand, 56% of the world's languages have fewer than 10,000 speakers. When we combine these numbers with population statistics, the results are quite striking. ***Roughly 94% of the world's population speaks only 6% of its languages. The remaining 94% of the languages are spread over only 6% of the population***. Thus, we have a handful of languages with enormous speech communities and a very large number of languages with quite small speech communities.

## 1.2.2  Languages of the world tomorrow

While there are around 7,000 languages spoken or signed on the globe today, not all languages are equally robust. Over time patterns of language use in multilingual communities can shift so that a socially dominant language comes to be used more frequently and less-dominant languages are used in fewer social contexts and among fewer people. Such languages are described as **endangered**, at risk of ceasing to be spoken in the absence of conscious efforts to keep them vital. *According to the Ethnologue, about 45 percent of the world's languages are endangered*.

The endpoint of the language endangerment process is **language death**, which occurs when a language ceases to have speakers and no longer serves as a symbolic marker of identity for the community. Normally the process of endangerment occurs gradually, over three or more generations. It involves a cessation in **language transmission**, the passing on of a language from one generation to the next. When children don't learn the language, the only remaining speakers are adults. That population naturally ages and declines until only a handful of speakers remains. In the absence of community efforts to reverse the trend, the language can cease to be spoken. If it ceases to be a cultural resource for the community, it is classified as dead (or extinct).

---

### TEXTBOX 1.3

Does language death matter? Linguists and members of many speech communities answer with a resounding "yes." Each language is a testament to the ways in which a unique group of people has understood and interacted with their environment and has come to terms with the human condition. Each is a unique inheritance from countless generations of forebears, the encapsulation of their wisdom and knowledge. Each language reflects and instantiates the culture of the speakers. Each contains knowledge, traditions, and history. Each represents what a language can be and so enriches our understanding of this central aspect of our humanity.

"Surely, just as the extinction of any animal species diminishes our world, so does the extinction of any language. Surely we linguists know, and the general public can sense, that any language is a supreme achievement of a uniquely human collective genius, as divine and endless a mystery as a living organism. Should we mourn the loss of Eyak or Ubyky any less than the loss of the panda or California condor?"

*– Professor Michael Krauss*
*Alaska Native Languages Center*

---

There are a number of reasons why languages become extinct. Sometimes the process of language death has been brought about by explicit government policies designed to keep children from learning their native language. However, language extinction is not limited to communities targeted by such policies. *Language endangerment and death appears to be primarily fueled by the broader process of globalization, including a shift from agrarian to urban lifestyles, and the increasing dominance of a small number of languages for the purposes of commerce, education, and the media*. These include both the truly widely spoken languages, like Mandarin Chinese, English, Spanish, Hindi-Urdu, and Arabic, and smaller national languages, like Nepali, Greek, Georgian, and Thai. Often acquisition of such languages is necessary for anyone wanting to pursue an advanced education or a career in modern society. Thus, parents are under pressure to have their children educated in these languages and therefore choose to transmit these languages as opposed to those of the heritage communities.

Another element that can contribute to the loss of a language is the ***loss of the coherence and vitality of the speech community***. If the members of a small speech community become absorbed into a larger group through intermarriage, the community can become dispersed. Where there is no viable speech community, there is little reason to pass the language on to the children; neither will the children hear the language spoken with sufficient frequency to acquire it.

The recognition of the scope of the problem of language endangerment has led to significant work by members of endangered-language speech communities and linguists to record, preserve, and revitalize languages. **Language documentation**, the creation of an extensive record of a language and its community, is an important part of this process. **Language conservation** is also being undertaken in many communities, which are developing materials to be used in the education of children and to promote language use in the speech community. **Language revitalization** is

**Figure 1.3** Members of the Gusii community in Kenya record traditional songs and dances as a component of their documentation of the Ekegusii language and Gusii culture (photo by Kennedy Bosire)

undertaken by speech communities whose language has been entirely lost or significantly reduced. Such projects can do much more than simply teach the language; they can play significant roles in strengthening communities and in promoting the preservation of traditional knowledge, practices, cultural values, and institutions.

## 1.3 Linguistics

### 1.3.1 The scientific study of language

Now that we have learned a bit about language and about the world's languages, we turn at last to the topic of linguistics. ***Linguistics is the scientific study of language***. By "scientific," we mean that the study is both **empirical** (based on observable data) and **objective**. Empirical data is critical for any scientific discipline, as it ensures that others can verify or replicate the findings. The term **linguist** refers to a person who examines the structures and principles underlying languages. Note that this is different from a **polyglot**, a person who speaks many languages. For more on this distinction, see Textbox 1.4.

---

**TEXTBOX 1.4 LINGUIST VERSUS POLYGLOT**

The longer you study linguistics, the more likely it is that someone will ask you the question: "How many languages to do you speak?" This question illustrates the commonly held misconception that linguists are polyglots. It is important to distinguish between the two. A **linguist** is a person who examines the structures of languages and the principles underlying those structures. A **polyglot** is a person who speaks many languages. Many linguists are, indeed, polyglots, but you don't have to be a polyglot to study linguistics. A nice analogy can be made to pilots and airplane mechanics. A pilot knows how to fly an airplane, based both on training and on an instinctive sense of flight and how a plane responds to a particular manipulation of the controls. An airplane mechanic looks inside a plane and knows how each part

contributes to the workings of the whole. One doesn't need to be an airplane mechanic to be a pilot. Neither does one need to be able to fly a plane in order to be a mechanic. A linguist is like a mechanic, looking inside to see how the parts of the language fit together so that the language can function in human communication. The speaker is the pilot, able to use the language efficiently and effectively, but without necessarily knowing how it works.

Probably the best airplane mechanics are also pilots, and in the same way, the most insightful analysis of the language will come from someone who speaks it, but a linguist can make a tremendous amount of headway on the analysis of a language without speaking it.

---

In linguistics, ***empirical data are recordings of spoken or written language, collected into a* corpus**. The nature of the recordings and how they are collected will depend on the goals of the study. For example, if one wishes to study the physical properties of sounds, the best recordings might be those produced in the isolation of a sound booth. If one wishes to study sentence structures and how they are used, the best recordings are likely to be natural conversations or narratives, supplemented by the comments of native speakers that reflect their intuitions about the structures and their meanings in that particular context. If one is studying the language and society, one might choose to make video recordings of authentic interactions. In any case, recorded data, preferably of speech or writing produced in a natural setting, and not constructed by or for a linguist, are the most highly empirical and can be verified by subsequent researchers. This is not to say that this is the only type of useful data in linguistics. Speakers' intuitions about their language, particularly regarding subtle distinctions in meaning, add a depth to our understanding that we could not possibly obtain otherwise.

When we say that a science is objective, we mean that **our analysis is not biased by any preconceived notions, or judgments of "good" and "bad."** Human beings are prone to prejudice, and this can be directed at speakers of languages just as it is directed at ethnicities, religions, sexualities, styles of dress, or any other characteristic by which people are subgrouped. It is not uncommon to find languages described as "primitive," "corrupt," "illogical," "ugly," or just plain "bad." By contrast, other languages can be described as "perfect," "logical," or "beautiful." To take an example from the United States, some speakers of American English believe that the dialect of English spoken in certain African American communities (referred to as African American English, or AAE) is "corrupt" or "ungrammatical." People with this view cite AAE sentences like *She sick* and *She be sick*, and claim that they are "incorrect" since they differ from the Standard American English sentence *She is sick*. In actuality, AAE is making a grammatical distinction in these two sentences that is not marked in the grammar of Standard American English. The sentence *She sick* refers to a present situation; it simply states that the person is sick now. This sentence could be used, for example, to explain why someone is unexpectedly absent. The sentence *She be sick* means that she is often sick or has a long-term illness. The implication is that the illness is ongoing, and lasts for an extended period of time. This meaning distinction between a present state and an ongoing state is systematically made by the grammar of AAE (as well as by many other languages in the world). Of course, speakers of Standard American English can still signal this meaning if they want to, for example, by using an adverb such as *always*, but its use is not grammatically required. This doesn't mean that AAE is any "better" than Standard American English; the two dialects are just different. **Every language or dialect is unique in the types of distinctions it makes. Every language is equally able to convey all of the complex meanings that humans communicate to each other in the course of a lifetime**. Languages differ in which distinctions they grammatically require their speakers to make, and in which meanings can be expressed by other, non-grammatical, means.

An important distinction can be made between **prescriptive** and **descriptive** approaches to language. **A prescriptive approach to language is one that teaches people the "proper way" to speak or write**. Many children are exposed to prescriptive grammar in school, where they are taught, for example, not to split infinitives (e.g., *to boldly go*) or to end a noun phrase with a preposition (e.g., *the man I saw you with*). Prescriptive grammarians choose a set of forms that they enjoin others to adhere to.

These forms represent a (slightly) older stage of the language when the rules were regular, so the establishment of prescriptive rules reflects a resistance to the natural forces of change. In actuality the set of forms chosen for prescription are ultimately arbitrary; ***there is no logical reason why one should not split an infinitive or end a sentence with a preposition***. Prescriptive rules may still have social ramifications, however, and there are environments (such as academic writing) where ignoring these conventions can have negative social consequences (such as lower grades).

***A descriptive approach to language is one that describes how people actually use language***. Descriptivists are not interested in telling people what is right or wrong, but in observing, describing, and explaining actual linguistic behavior. In line with the objective nature of linguistic science, linguistics is a descriptive enterprise.

## 1.3.2  Fields of linguistics

The field of linguistics is as broad and multifaceted as language itself. The following paragraphs provide a very brief orientation to the primary subfields of the discipline. As in the rest of this book, this presentation will take the traditional hierarchical approach to language, beginning with the smallest units and working up to larger and larger levels.

We will begin with the study of speech sounds. The physical properties of sounds – how they are articulated and perceived, and the acoustic signatures of the sounds themselves – are the subject of study in the field of **phonetics**. We will then examine the systematic use of speech sounds in language, or **phonology**. (See Sidebar 1.2 for a brief explanation of the distinction between phonetics and phonology.)

From the study of sounds we move to the study of words themselves. The ways in which words are structured and created are the purview of the field of **morphology**. Morphologists look at all the pieces of words (roots, prefixes, suffixes, etc.), their sounds and meanings, and the principles of their combination. Sidebar 1.3 presents one example of a topic in the area of morphology. The study of how words combine into phrases, clauses, and sentences is the study of **syntax**. Morphology and syntax are tightly integrated and are often referred to as **morphosyntax** or (in some uses) **grammar**.

A critical aspect of language that interacts with all of these levels is **semantics**, meaning in language. The study of semantics includes the study of words (**lexical semantics**) and the study of how meanings combine in clauses and sentences (**propositional semantics**).

When we look at how speakers use linguistic structures in larger stretches of speech, we are studying **discourse**. This

**SIDEBAR 1.2**

Try saying the English words *lack* and *lag*. If you pay attention to your mouth and listen carefully, you will notice that the vowels in these words are produced with the same tongue position, but that the vowel in *lack* is a bit shorter than that in *lag*. This is a phonetic observation, which could be verified by measuring the vowel durations in an acoustic display on a computer screen. Now say *lake/leg*, *pick/pig*, and *lock/log*; you will find that the vowel is always shorter before /k/ and longer before /g/. The same pattern is found before /p/ and /b/ (*lap/lab*) and /t/ and /d/ (*fat/fad*). We see that these sounds pattern in a systematic way. Such systems of sounds form the **phonology** of a language.

**SIDEBAR 1.3**

Languages differ in how they mark negation. In some languages, markers of negation are independent words (English *not*, Italian *non*), while in others they are prefixes (Dolakha Newar *mu-na* 'didn't eat'), suffixes (English *didn't*), or circumfixes (French *n'est pas*). Languages also differ in the number of negation markers they have. Wayampi, a language of northern Brazil, has four markers of negation. The study of the forms, meanings, and uses of these markers falls under the field of morphology.

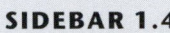

**SIDEBAR 1.4**

You are studying in the library. Two people come in talking loudly. They sit at the table next to you and continue to talk loudly about the party they went to. They ignore your glares and those of other people in the room. Finally you say, *"Hey, could you speak up? I missed that last part."* How is it that the people can interpret this as a request to be quiet? The answer lies in the field of pragmatics.

**SIDEBAR 1.5**

Historical linguistics can tell us much about human pre-history. In many cases, we can trace how populations have migrated across the globe. For example, most of the languages of the Athabascan family are spoken by native communities located between the Yukon region of Alaska down the Pacific coast of North America to northern California. However one branch of the family, which consists of Apache and Navajo, is spoken in the southwest of the United States. Linguists were able to use principles of historical linguistics to discover that the Apachean languages are, indeed, members of the Athabascan family, and to therefore deduce that speakers migrated from the Pacific Northwest to the American Southwest in a prehistoric time period.

field takes into account the interactional nature of language, for example, how speakers need to present their ideas in a way that allows hearers to understand them. With the help of computers, linguists can now look at statistically significant patterns over very large sets, or **corpora**, of discourse data; this methodology is referred to as **corpus linguistics**. The role of the broader context in interpreting linguistic form and meaning is examined in the field of **pragmatics** (see Sidebar 1.4). A large part of the context of speech comes from its embedding in the society and culture of its speakers. This field of study is **sociocultural linguistics**.

The field of **historical linguistics** examines how languages change over time. This historical perspective can be applied to all levels of language: sounds, words, structures, and meanings. Historical linguists are also interested in determining which languages are related and how they have descended from a mother language, which was spoken in the distant past (see Sidebar 1.5 for one such example). But languages don't evolve in isolation. Instead, they often influence each other as their speakers interact over time. The study of such **language contact** is a subfield of historical linguistics.

Our linguistic capabilities are critically embedded in our neurology and our ability to think. The field of **language and the brain** examines the physical and neurological basis of language, while **cognitive linguistics** looks at how language is instantiated by our broader cognitive processes. A related field is **language acquisition**, which studies how language is learned by children (**first language acquisition**) and by adults (**second language acquisition**).

**Computational linguistics** is a field at the intersection of linguistics and computer science that deals with the statistical or rule-based modeling of natural language. It is concerned with applying methods from artificial intelligence and machine learning to problems involving language. The recent acceleration of our technological abilities has led to a greater application of computational methods to a wide range of linguistic questions, such as how languages are learned.

## SIDEBAR 1.6

When we look at sentence structures across languages, we notice that languages differ in the relative ordering of the subject (*Chris* in *Chris ate the apple*), the object (*the apple*), and the verb (*ate*). There are six logically possible orderings of these three categories:

Subject-Object-Verb          Subject-Verb-Object
Object-Subject-Verb          Object-Verb-Subject
Verb-Subject-Object          Verb-Object-Subject

However, all six orderings are not equally instantiated in the world's languages. A famous study of these orderings found that languages which put the subject first are very common, those that put the verb first are much less common, and those that put the object first are very few indeed. Why this should be, and the theoretical implications of this fact, is a question addressed by **linguistic typologists**.

We find languages throughout the world. The field of **typology and universals** looks at how the world's languages are similar and different. See Sidebar 1.6 for an example of this. Typologists are interested in developing a classification of languages based on how they are structured, and in looking for relationships between certain structural language types.

There are many applications of linguistics to situations in the world around us. The field of **applied linguistics** includes a number of subfields, including language teaching and **forensic linguistics**. Recently, there has been a strong move toward **language documentation**, the creation of a record of a language that can be used by speech communities and others in the face of possible endangerment or language death. Of course, linguistics is also a key part of the field of **speech pathology** and **speech and hearing sciences**.

This list of subfields of linguistics is fairly representative but is certainly not exhaustive. While we will not be able to touch on all of these fields in this book, we will cover most of them. The fields are diverse enough that there is usually something to interest everyone, and some readers will find that they are interested by everything. I find that the longer I study linguistics, the more interesting the field becomes. I hope you have the same experience.

## CHAPTER SUMMARY

Human languages are complex, structured, and dynamic systems of human communication, which change over time under a variety of influences. While it is impossible to exactly count the number of languages of the world, our current estimate is in the range of 7,000. However, these are not evenly distributed, as most of the world's population speaks one or more of a small number of dominant languages, while a small percentage of the population speak one of many languages with comparatively few speakers, many of which are endangered.

Linguistics is the scientific study of language. It is empirical and objective. Linguists seek to state succinctly the structural properties of languages, and to understand their interactions, how they change, and how they serve the broader functions of language as a tool of communication that is embedded in human physiology, cognition, interaction, society, and culture. Explaining how individual languages work and how language works more broadly constitutes the aim of linguistic theory.

## SUGGESTIONS FOR FURTHER READING

**Deutscher, Guy**. 2005. *The unfolding of language*. New York: Metropolitan.

This book is an entertaining exploration of how languages change and evolve through the forces that shape human language.

**Harrison, K. David**. 2007. *When languages die: The extinction of the world's languages and the erosion of human knowledge*. Oxford University Press.

This book illustrates the richness of knowledge inherent in human languages, the implications of diverse linguistic systems for our understanding of the mind, and what is lost when a language becomes extinct.

**Lewis, M. Paul**, **Gary Simons**, and **Charles D. Fennig** (eds.). 2013. *Ethnologue: Languages of the world*. 17th edn. Dallas, TX: SIL International. (Online version: www.ethnologue.com)

An excellent reference tool, this is a comprehensive catalog of the known languages of the world, their geographic distribution, demographics, vitality, and status.

**Sapir, Edward**. 1921. *Language: An introduction to the study of speech*. New York: Harcourt, Brace and Company.

A classic and accessible introduction to the study of language by one of the great linguists of the twentieth century.

## EXERCISES

1. On the Internet, go to the British Library website *Learning: Sounds Familiar?* (www.bl.uk/learning/langlit/sounds/index.html). On the map on the homepage of this site, hover your cursor over the icons of people. You will see a label with a location. Listen to the varieties spoken in London, Birkenhead, and Kilmarnock. On a scale of 1 to 5, rank them on ease of intelligibility (with 1 being very easy and 5 being very difficult). Do you consider any one of them to be unintelligible based on your own dialect of English? If so, which one? Would you consider this variety to be a separate language? Why or why not?

2. Find a speaker of a language which you do not speak, and about which you know very little. Ask if the person will help you for a few minutes by talking about his or her language. The goal is to discover some basic facts about the language and to listen to the speaker's experiences, ideas, and attitudes about the language.

   Once you have chosen the language, go to *Ethnologue* online (www.ethnologue.com), browse for the language name, and use this as a resource in providing the following information:

   a. Language name
   b. The country/countries in which the language is primarily spoken
   c. Number of speakers of the language
   d. Speaker's name, age, and occupation
   e. State/province, city, and country of speaker's primary home
   f. Speaker's linguistic history (languages spoken in the home, languages learned in school and at what age, other exposure to languages)
   g. Language(s) in which the speaker is literate
   h. How the speaker decides which language to use when? (Does he or she ever use more than one language with a single person?)

i. Record any further comments about the speaker's thoughts or attitudes about his or her language (e.g., ties to identity, key experiences, or other comments which allow you insight into how the person views the languages, their relation to himself or herself, and their identity).

3. Find a speaker of a language with which you are unfamiliar. (This can be the same speaker as in (2).) Ask this person to translate the following sentence. Be sure to ask for the most natural way to express the meaning, rather than a word-by-word translation of the English.

   *My two aunts will fly back tomorrow and I will meet them at the airport.*

   Ask the speaker to help you sound out the sentence and write it down (you don't have all the skills you need for this yet, but just do your best).

   Compare the English sentence with the sentence in the language of your study. Make a list of any differences that you find between the two languages. For example, they may differ in the number of words used, the order in which they appear, in how they signal future tense, in which words have prefixes or suffixes and what those mean, in the meanings of specific words, in whether or not they use "and" to join sentences, etc.

   In submitting your answer, state the language of study, where it is spoken, your transcription of the sentence in the other language, and list as many differences as you can find.

4. On the Internet, go to www.ethnologue.com and click on "World Languages."
   a. Navigate to the page on Denmark by clicking "Europe," "Northern Europe," and then selecting "Denmark." List the total population of the country and the total number of living languages (in the section called "Language counts"). Now do the same for Papua New Guinea ("World languages" > "Pacific" > "Melanesia" > "Papua New Guinea"). What do these statistics tell you about the relationship of population to language density?
   b. Navigate to the page on the United States. Note the large number of immigrant languages spoken. Do most of the languages in this list look familiar to you? Click on the "Languages" tab and browse through the list. Choose five languages. For each, list the geographic area where the language is spoken, population, and status; also include what it says under "More information" > "Language use" (summarize if the information extensive).
   c. On the US languages page, navigate to "Hawaiian" and browse through the information. Under "language use," Ethnologue states: "1000 under the age of 15; 350 ages 15 to 25." What factors might have contributed to this imbalance in the numbers?

5. Assume you were enrolled in a class that you found frustrating and in which you were not doing well. Write down how you would express this in one or two sentences to your best friend, to your parents, and to your college dean (e.g., on a petition to drop the course). Note down any differences in your choice of words. How is this illustrative of the relationship of language and societal structure?

# 2 Phonetics: physical dimensions of speech sounds

**KEY TERMS**

- Subglottal system
- Voicing
- Voiced vs. voiceless consonant
- Orthography
- Fundamental frequency vs. pitch
- Supralaryngeal vocal tract and its subparts (lips, alveolar ridge, etc.)
- Places of articulation (bilabial, labiodental, etc.)
- Manners of articulation (stop, fricative, etc.)
- Obstruent vs. sonorant
- International Phonetic Alphabet (IPA)
- Vowel
- Co-articulation
- Suprasegmental

**CHAPTER PREVIEW**

*Phonetics is the branch of linguistics that is concerned with the scientific study of speech sounds.* The study of phonetics can provide answers to many questions that you might have wondered about at one time or another. For example, what does it mean to say that someone has a higher-pitched voice than someone else? What makes a tone language like Mandarin Chinese different from a non-tonal language such as English or Spanish? How do English pairs of words such as the verb *import* and the noun *import* differ?

Several areas of phonetics have been the focus of research into the features of speech. **Articulatory phonetics** is concerned with how the vocal organs produce speech. **Acoustic phonetics** deals with the physical characteristics of speech, such as the duration, frequency, and intensity of sounds. **Auditory phonetics** examines the perception of speech by the auditory system. Acoustic, articulatory, and auditory phonetics are all interrelated, since changing the articulatory configuration of the vocal tract results in acoustic changes which in turn potentially influence the perception of a sound. In this chapter, we will consider the first of these areas of phonetic research, providing an overview of the field as well as answers to the questions posed above.

Students will be introduced to the tasks of discerning different speech sounds, describing them in phonetic terms, and accurately recording them using the International Phonetic Alphabet.

### LIST OF AIMS

At the end of this unit, students will be able to:

- **identify the parts of the vocal tract responsible for producing different sounds;**
- **describe the manner and places of articulation of consonants and vowels;**
- **produce the phonetic symbols for English sounds;**
- **transcribe English words using the IPA;**
- **read English words and passages written in the IPA;**
- **use the IPA chart as a reference for sounds in languages other than English.**

## 2.1 The speech organs

***The physical production of speech requires intricate coordination between several parts of the upper body, from the stomach all the way up to the nose***. It is common to divide the speech organs into three subsystems (see Figure 2.1): the subglottal system, the larynx, and the supralaryngeal (or supraglottal) system.

### 2.1.1 The subglottal system

The **subglottal system** includes the lungs and the trachea (or windpipe), which provide the air that the upstream articulators manipulate to produce sound. The lungs function like balloons, recoiling after inspiration and setting the air molecules in the vocal tract in motion.

### 2.1.2 The larynx

Moving up from the lungs and trachea, the **larynx** is the source for many of the sounds produced in speech. It is located behind the thyroid cartilage (or Adam's apple), which is the bump you can feel on the front of the neck if you lean your head back. ***The larynx contains two vocal folds that vibrate during voiced sounds such as z or v***. To feel the vocal folds vibrate, try placing your fingers on the thyroid cartilage in the front of your neck while making a prolonged [zzzzzz] sound. You will feel the cartilage vibrating. Compare this to what happens when you make a long [ssssss] sound. There is no vibration. Vocal fold vibration, otherwise known as **voicing**, does not require any active motion beyond positioning the vocal folds close enough together that the passage of air between them causes them to vibrate. As long as the air pressure below the larynx is less than the pressure above the larynx, you can

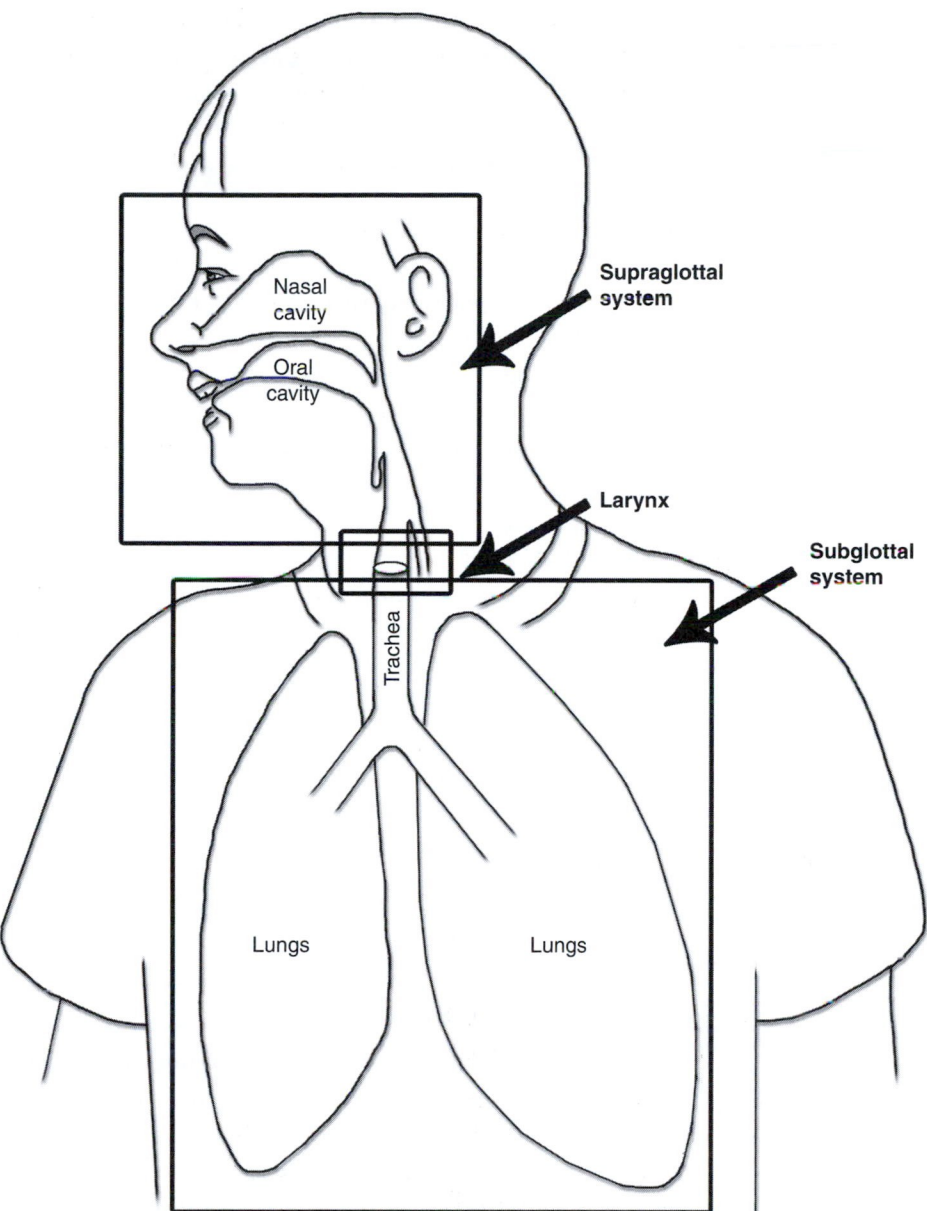

**Figure 2.1** Three subsystems of speech articulation

sustain a voiced sound. When you produce the sound [zzzzz], you are producing a **voiced consonant**.

As you have already learned when you made the [ssssss] sound, it is also possible to make the same sounds without vocal fold vibration, in which case, you produce a **voiceless consonant**. For example, by turning off voicing in *z* you get *s* and by turning off voicing during *v* you get *f*. (See Sidebar 2.1.) Physically, devoicing of these sounds is achieved by opening the larynx wider than for their voiced counterparts.

*In English there are two sounds that only involve the larynx and not any articulators above the larynx*. One is the *h* sound in words like *hat* or *ahead*. The other is the glottal stop found in the middle of the expression *uh-oh*. Try saying *uh-oh* emphatically while your hand is on your larynx and your head is leaned back. You will feel an abrupt stoppage of voicing during the glottal stop between the two vowels as the vocal folds come together to block off all airflow through the larynx. This is called a **glottal stop**, as you stop the airflow by closing the **glottis** (the space between the vocal folds).

*By adjusting the tension of the vocal folds during voicing, you can change the fundamental frequency, and hence the pitch, of a sound*. The fundamental frequency of a sound is commonly referred to as pitch, though the two terms are technically not synonymous. **Fundamental frequency** refers to the physical property of rate of vocal fold vibration, whereas **pitch** refers to the perception of the sound on a scale of low to high. Increasing fundamental frequency also typically increases the pitch. Someone with a relatively high-pitched voice thus has a relatively high fundamental frequency or a fast rate of vocal fold vibration. Conversely, someone with a low-pitched voiced has a relatively slow rate of vocal fold vibration. Try making the sound [ahhhhhh]. Now try raising the pitch of the sound while your fingers are on your larynx. You will feel the larynx tense up and rise. Now try lowering the pitch of the sound. You will feel the larynx relax and lower. In this way, you can see how an individual can easily change the fundamental frequency of his or her voice.

### 2.1.3   The supralaryngeal vocal tract and place of articulation

Above the larynx is the **supralaryngeal vocal tract**, which contains most of the structures that are manipulated in speech. The articulators of the supralaryngeal vocal tract are shown in Figure 2.2. When you use different articulators to produce speech sounds, you are changing the **place of articulation** of the sound.

In discussing different places of articulation, it is useful to move from the front to the back of the mouth (see Figure 2.2), starting with the most visible organs. The lips play an important role in producing many sounds, including *p*, *b*, *m*, *w*, *f*, and *v* in English. Sounds that involve a narrowing or a complete closure of the upper and lower lip are called **bilabials**. The bilabial sounds of English include *p*, *b*, *m*, and *w*. Sounds involving the upper teeth and the lower lip are referred to as **labiodentals**. These include *f* and *v*. For labiodentals, the lower lip is the **active articulator**, since it moves to meet the upper teeth. The upper teeth are thus the **passive articulator**, since they are stationary. Most consonant articulations involve

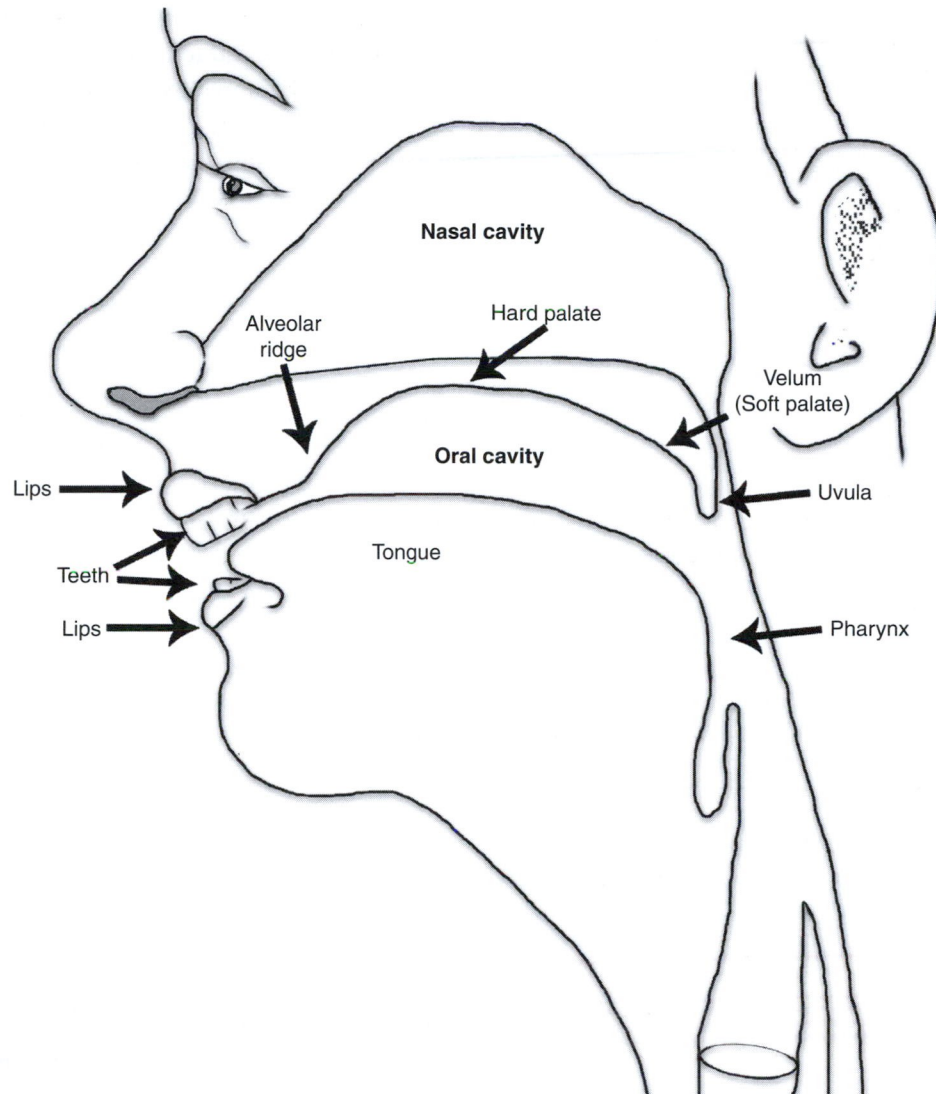

**Figure 2.2** The supralaryngeal vocal tract

both an active and a passive articulator. As we will see, for most consonants, the tongue is the active articulator, while the upper surface of the mouth is the passive articulator.

The structures just behind the lips are relatively immobile compared to the lips. These rigid structures include the teeth, the **alveolar ridge** (the hard ridge just behind the teeth before the upper surface of the mouth becomes more domed in shape), and the **hard palate** (the domed part of the roof of the mouth). The teeth are involved in the production of the English *th* sounds in the words *think* and *this*. These sounds are produced by either sticking the tip of the tongue between the upper and lower teeth, in which case the sounds are said to be **interdental**, or by placing the tip of the tongue against the back of the upper teeth, in which case the sounds are simply called **dentals**. Try saying *think* with an interdental *th* and then with a dental *th*. In order to make the comparison fair, be careful that you are not completing blocking air from leaving the mouth when making the dental *th*. You will not notice much of a difference in the sound from making this small articulatory adjustment.

You may notice that the first sounds of *think* and *this* are different even though they are both spelled as *th*. The two versions of *th* differ in voicing, just as *z* and *s* were shown earlier to do: the *th* in *think* is voiceless, whereas the *th* in *this* is voiced. We will see shortly that there is a system for transcribing speech in which the voiceless and the voiced *th* are represented differently.

> ### SIDEBAR 2.2
>
> You may note that not all of the **alveolar** sounds have the exact same point of contact for your tongue. This type of variation is quite common; in particular, *l* often involves quite a bit of contact with the back of the upper teeth, at least for many speakers of American English. Try making an extended [llll] sound and feel where the tip of the tongue is contacting the upper surface of the mouth. Now try making a [nnnnnn] sound and feel where the contact is. Does it occur at the same place as for the [llllll] sound? Even if there is a difference, you should be aware that it is common for *t, d, n,* and *l* to all be treated as alveolars in discussing the sounds of English.

Just behind the teeth is the alveolar ridge, which is the contact point between the tongue and the roof of the mouth for several sounds, including *t* (a voiceless sound), *d* (voiced), *s* (voiceless), *z* (voiced), *n* (voiced), and *l* (voiced). Another sound *r* (voiced) is also typically assigned to this same group, since *r* is produced with a narrowing in the vocal tract below the alveolar ridge, even though the tongue may only be raised slightly toward the roof of the mouth without touching it. See Sidebar 2.2 for more discussion of alveolar sounds.

There are also sounds that are produced with the tongue contacting the area just behind the alveolar ridge. These are the **postalveolar** (or **palato-alveolar**) sounds, which include the *sh* sound in *ship* (which is a voiceless postalveolar) and the last sound in *rouge* (which is a voiced postalveolar), as well as the first sounds in *jug* (voiced) and *chug* (voiceless). To understand the relationship between alveolars and postalveolars, make an 'sss' sound and then switch to a 'shh' sound. You will feel the tongue sliding backwards along the upper surface of the mouth as it moves from an alveolar to a postalveolar place of articulation.

Sounds involving contact with the roof of the mouth in the center of the hard palate are simply termed **palatals**. English has a single palatal sound: the *y* sound in words like *yellow* and *young*.

Now drag your tongue backwards from the hard palate. You will notice that the upper surface of the mouth becomes softer. This area of the mouth is called the **soft palate**, or **velum**. Sounds produced by contacting the tongue and the soft palate are termed **velars**. These include the *k* (a voiceless velar sound) in words like *cat*, *bucket*, and *crib*, the *g* (a voiced velar) in words like *gas*, *go*, and *bag*, and the final *ng* sound (voiced) in words like *sing* and *lung*. The sound *w* also involves some raising of the back of the tongue toward the soft palate in addition to rounding of the lips; for this reason *w* is often labelled a labial-velar.

The soft palate, or velum, is important for distinguishing sounds involving airflow through the nose and those lacking nasal airflow. Try looking in the mirror while saying *ah* and you will see the velum rise. This raising of the velum ensures that no air escapes through the nose while you are producing the vowel. To see this, hold your finger under your nose while saying *ah*. Now try lowering the velum, holding the same tongue position for *ah* while your finger is still in place under your nose. You will feel air passing through your nose and will hear a nasal-sounding *ahn*, which is found in many languages of the world, such as French.

English also has **nasal** sounds, but they are consonants rather than vowels. Place your finger under your nose while you are making the sounds *m*, *n*, and the *ng* sound in *sing* and *lung*. You will feel air passing through your nose. Nasality is a separate dimension from place of articulation, since sounds can have the same place of articulation but differ in whether they are nasal or non-nasal (i.e., **oral**). The sounds *m* and *b* differ in nasality; both are voiced and both are bilabial, but only *m* is nasal. Try saying an [m] with your finger under your nose and then immediately switch to a [b]. You will feel airflow through the nose during the [m] but not during the [b] even though the lips remain closed throughout both sounds. The sounds *n* and *d* also differ only in nasality; *n* is nasal and *d* is oral. Similarly, *ng* and *g* differ in nasality; *ng* is the nasal member of the pair. Note that it is common to omit the term oral when describing oral sounds, since oral is assumed to be default case. (See also Sidebar 2.3 for a brief discussion of nasals and voicing.)

## 2.2  Manner of articulation

Thus far we have discussed three dimensions relevant for describing speech sounds: the voicing dimension (voiced vs. voiceless), the place of articulation dimension, and the nasality dimension (nasal vs. oral). There is one other dimension that we must consider: the narrowness of the constriction in the vocal tract. Differences in constriction narrowness are referred to as differences in **manner of articulation**.

*Some sounds involve a complete closure of the vocal tract*. These are called **stops**. English stops include *p*, *b*, *m*, *t*, *d*, *n*, *k*, *g*, and the *ng* sound. Of these sounds, *p*, *b*, *t*, *d*, *k*, and *g* are oral stops since there is no nasal airflow, while *m*, *n*, and *ng* are nasal stops. All stops involve two phases: a closure phase, during which the airflow through the mouth is completely blocked, and a release phase, when the constriction is released. To see this, produce just the closure for the voiceless stop *t* without releasing the tongue from the alveolar ridge. You will notice that there is complete silence, since there is no voicing. This means that voiceless stops are only identifiable through their release, which provides crucial information about place of articulation. There is another type of sound in English that resembles an alveolar stop in that it is produced with a complete closure at the alveolar ridge. This sound is called a **flap** and occurs in the middle of words like *pity, butter, lady,* and *ladder.* The key difference between a stop and a flap (sometimes also referred to as a **tap**) is the extreme shortness of the closure for the flap. The tongue briefly taps the roof of the mouth before rapidly returning to position for the following sound.

*It is also possible to produce sounds in which the two articulators are close together, but not so tightly occluded that no air can escape through the mouth*. Sounds produced by a tight narrowing of articulators are termed **fricatives**. Fricatives are characterized by turbulence created through the random collision of air molecules either at the constriction location or, in the case of alveolar or postalveolar fricatives, by funneling air to hit the back of the teeth. Try making an emphatic [sssss] sound while holding your hand palm down against your chin. You will feel air striking the back of your hand because the air is being directed downward after it hits the back of your upper teeth. You will also feel air striking your hand if you produce a prolonged and emphatic *sh* sound. Now try making an [hhhhhh] sound while holding your hand in the same position. You will not feel any air striking your hand. This is because the noise in [hhhhhh] is being produced directly in the larynx and not by directing air against the back of the teeth. You will also notice that the noise of *h* is much quieter than that associated with *s* or *sh*. Sounds like *s* and *sh*, which involve funneling of air against the back of the teeth are particularly noisy. These sounds are called **stridents**.

*There are two sounds in English that are produced by combining a stop with a following fricative in rapid succession*. These are the **affricates**, which include the *j* sound in *jug* (which is voiced) and the *ch* sounds word-initially and word-finally in *church* (which are voiceless). Since affricates have a stop phase, they are often grouped together with other stops.

Additionally, *sounds can be produced through a slight narrowing of the vocal tract, but not enough to cause noise or a complete obstruction*. These sounds are called **approximants**. Approximants in English include the *y* sound in *yellow* and the *w* sound in *water*. Also included in the class of approximants in English is the *r* sound in words like *red, brick,* and *car*.

A final approximant to consider is the sound *l*, which resembles *t* and *d* in involving a complete closure in the middle of the alveolar ridge. There is, however, a crucial difference between *l* and these other sounds (besides the fact that *l* differs from *t* in being voiced). *The l sound is produced with a closure only in the center of the mouth*. At least one side of the tongue (if not both, depending on the speaker) is pulled down slightly, away from the roof of the mouth. The lowering of the side part of the tongue allows air to escape the mouth, whereas the true stops *t* and *d* have a complete closure around the upper surface of the mouth. Try making an [llllll] sound and put your hand first on the left side of the mouth and then on the right side. Is the air escaping from just one or both sides of the mouth? The sound *l* has a **lateral** articulation in opposition to all of the other sounds of English, which have **central** articulations. Note that it is common to omit the term central when describing central sounds, since central is assumed to be default case.

There are a couple of additional useful terms for grouping together certain types of sounds. One of these is the term **liquids**, which includes lateral approximants and *r*-type sounds. Another common descriptor is the term **obstruent**, which refers to the combined set of oral stops and fricatives. Sounds that are not obstruents are the **sonorants**, which include the nasals and all of the approximants, both lateral and central.

It is important to recognize that our discussion of places and manner of articulation has focused on sounds occurring in English. In reality, there are many more sounds found in languages other than English, as you know already if you speak or have studied other languages. Some of these sounds are discussed below.

## 2.3   The International Phonetic Alphabet

Up to now, we have referred to the different sounds of English using the traditional symbols used in English spelling. While this strategy has worked for the most part, ***there are some limitations of using spelling (orthographic) characters to represent sounds***. One problem we have already encountered concerns the English letters *th*, which can represent either a voiceless dental fricative as in *think* or a voiced dental fricative as in *this*. Another issue is the use of two letters to represent a single sound in English. For example, the voiced velar nasal at the end of *sing* is represented by the combination *ng*. Similarly, the voiceless post-alveolar fricative is written as the sequence *sh*. While it is possible to use two letters to represent a single sound, it is more efficient to use a single symbol to represent a sound that behaves phonetically as a single entity. Furthermore, there is the potential for confusion between a single phonetic sound written with two letters and a sequence of two phonetic sounds also written with two letters. For example, if one sees *ng*, how can one be sure without listening to the word, whether *ng* refers to a single voiced velar nasal, or the phonetic sequence *n* (voiced alveolar nasal) plus *g* (voiced velar oral stop), as occurs in a careful pronunciation of the compound *rain gauge*?

There is an even more serious problem with the use of English spelling to represent phonetic sounds. Many individual English letters or combinations of letters represent multiple phonetic sounds depending on the particular word. For example, the letter *x* can represent either a voiced alveolar fricative, *z*, as in *xylophone* or the phonetic sequence of voiceless velar stop, *k*, plus voiceless alveolar fricative, *s*, as in *ox*. Similarly, the letter *o* has three different qualities in the words *ton*, *pond*, and *drone*. Using orthography to represent phonetic pronunciation is thus bound to cause confusion.

Fortunately, this problem is remedied by the existence of a special phonetic alphabet designed to reflect pronunciation: the International Phonetic Alphabet, abbreviated IPA. *A crucial principle guiding the International Phonetic Alphabet is its universal one-to-one correspondence between symbols and pronunciation*. Thus, whenever you see an IPA symbol, you can be sure of its pronunciation, regardless of the language being transcribed. For example, whenever you see an IPA *m*, it will refer to a voiced bilabial nasal stop in any language. The IPA thus provides a useful tool for linguists who are transcribing words and who plan to share these transcriptions with other researchers. It is not the case, however, that all linguistic data are transcribed in IPA at all times; see Textbox 2.1.

---

### TEXTBOX 2.1

As noted, the IPA has been designed to transcribe the sounds of every spoken language. However, it is not the case that all linguists use the IPA at all times. In many parts of the world, the transcription practices of linguists reflect the orthographic practices of the local region. In some cases, particular orthographic practices are widespread in a given region, such as the use of the symbol *š* in the transcription of North American Indian languages for the sound written with "sh" in English spelling and transcribed as [ʃ] in IPA.

In this volume, which takes data from many sources – historical and contemporary – from all over the world, the transcription system of the original source is used. This requires careful attention; transcription notes are provided throughout the book to aid readers in this task. Learning these different systems, and how to interpret a variety of transcription practices, is part of the task of learning linguistics.

---

As it happens, the IPA bears close resemblance to English orthography in many respects. There are only a few major points of departure between the two systems. First, the IPA symbol for a voiceless (inter)dental fricative (as in *think*) is [θ] (IPA symbols will henceforth be written in brackets), while the symbol for its voiced counterpart (as in *this*) is [ð]. The IPA symbol for a voiceless postalveolar fricative (as in *ship*) is [ʃ], while the symbol for its voiced counterpart (as in *rouge*) is [ʒ]. The IPA represents the voiceless postalveolar affricate (as in *church*) as [tʃ] and the voiced postalveolar affricate (as in *jug*) as [dʒ]. The IPA symbol for a voiced velar nasal stop (as in *sing*) is [ŋ]. The IPA symbol for glottal stop, as in *uh-oh* looks like a question mark but with a horizontal base rather than a period [ʔ]. In addition, the IPA symbol for a voiced palatal approximant (as in *young*) is [j], while the symbol for a central alveolar approximant (as in *red*) is an upside-down [ɹ]. Finally, the flap occurring in the middle of words like *city* and *buddy* is represented with the symbol [ɾ].

We are now ready to see the entire list of IPA consonant symbols relevant for describing English in Table 2.1.

In the chart, places of articulation appear as columns across the top of the chart, while manner, nasality, and lateralness are captured in rows. Sounds differing only in voicing appear in the same cell with the voiceless sound on the left and the voiced

**TABLE 2.1** IPA chart for English consonants

| | Bilabial | Labiodental | Dental | Alveolar | Postalveolar | Palatal | Velar | Glottal |
|---|---|---|---|---|---|---|---|---|
| Oral stops | p  b | | | t  d | | | k  g | ʔ |
| Affricates | | | | | tʃ  dʒ | | | |
| Nasal stops | m | | | n | | | ŋ | |
| Flap (tap) | | | | ɾ | | | | |
| Fricatives | | f  v | θ  ð | s  z | ʃ  ʒ | | | h |
| Central approximants | w | | | ɹ | | j | w | |
| Lateral approximants | | | | l | | | | |

**TABLE 2.2** IPA chart for American English vowels

| | | Front | Central | Back |
|---|---|---|---|---|
| High | Tense | i | | u |
| | Lax | ɪ | | ʊ |
| Mid | Tense | e | | o |
| | Lax | ɛ | ə    ʌ | (ɔ) |
| Low | Lax | æ | a | |

counterpart on the right. There are many cells that are empty; this reflects the lack of such sounds in English, but does not mean that they are unattested in other languages. Note that [w] appears in both the bilabial and the velar columns, since, as we have seen, it involves constrictions simultaneously at the lips and at the velum.

 An interactive IPA chart and IPA flashcards to help you learn these symbols is available on the *How Languages Work* website.

There are also IPA symbols for vowels. ***Vowels fundamentally differ from consonants in being produced with a relatively open vocal tract***, though of course there is some movement of the tongue necessary to make different vowel sounds. The IPA chart for American English appears in Table 2.2.

As Table 2.2 shows, the dimensions used to describe vowels differ from those used to classify consonants. ***Vowels can be described in terms of three core dimensions:***

**TABLE 2.3** Example words illustrating the vowels of American English

| Vowel height | Vowel | English words |
|---|---|---|
| High | [i] | beet, bleed, see |
| | [ɪ] | sit, fin, lip |
| | [u] | boot, mood, soon |
| | [ʊ] | foot, could, hood |
| Mid | [e] | late, rain, paid |
| | [ɛ] | red, send, peck |
| | [ə] | (first sounds of) about, ago |
| | [ʌ] | rut, mud, up |
| | [o] | mode, loan, sew |
| | [ɔ] (only some dialects) | caught, dawn, law |
| Low | [a] | hot, mop, rock |
| | [æ] | cat, man, trap |

***backness, height, and tenseness***. In addition, vowels can differ in whether they are produced with lip rounding, as with the vowel in *boat*, or not, as with the vowel in *beet*.

There are three degrees of **height** in English: high, mid, and low. Example words illustrating the vowels of American English are shown in Table 2.3. The mid vowel [ə], also known as **schwa**, is confined to unstressed syllables in English. There is one mid vowel that appears in parentheses in Table 2.2: the vowel [ɔ], which is found only for speakers of some English dialects. Textbox 2.2 describes the regional dialect variation that occurs with American English low vowels.

---

TEXTBOX 2.2 **LOW VOWELS IN AMERICAN ENGLISH**

Many speakers of American English, including most from California, lack the vowel [ɔ]. For speakers who do not have [ɔ], it is because it has merged with the low vowel [a]. Speakers who have undergone this merger typically (at least in California) produce a low central vowel in words like *caught*, *dawn*, and *law*. Speakers who have a contrast between [ɔ] and [a] have pairs of words differing only in the vowel, e.g., *caught* with [ɔ] versus *cot* with [a] and *dawn* with [ɔ] versus *don* with [a]. Try asking several people to say the words *cot* and *caught*. Do any of them have a different vowel in the two words? How does the backness of their vowel in *cot* compare with yours?

Vowels can also be described in terms of **backness**. The back vowels of English are [u, ʊ, o, ɔ], while the central vowels are [ə, ʌ, a]. The vowel [a] varies widely in its backness from speaker to speaker, so you may note that you have a somewhat backer pronunciation than central [a]. The front vowels of English are [i, ɪ, e, ɛ, æ].

Vowels can also differ in terms of their **tenseness**. There are several pairs of vowels in English differing only in tenseness. For example, the pair of vowels [i] as in *seat*, and [ɪ] as *sit* differ along this dimension; [i] is a tense vowel and [ɪ] is a lax vowel. Similarly, [e] is tense and [ɛ] is lax, [u] is tense and [ʊ] is lax, [o] is tense and [ɔ] is lax. All of the central and low vowels in English are regarded as lax. Tense vowels in English are longer than their lax counterparts and also have a slightly more peripheral tongue position (i.e., higher and fronter in the case of front vowels, and higher and backer in the case of back vowels). You can verify this by producing an [i] sound and then changing it to an [ɪ]. You will feel the tongue lowering slightly and retracting. Now try the same exercise by switching from [e] to [ɛ]; you will once again notice the tongue lowering and retracting.

The final parameter along which English vowels can be described is whether they are produced with **lip rounding** or not. The back vowels of English [u, ʊ, o, ɔ] are the rounded vowels, while the front and central vowels are unrounded. To see that *rounding is a separate parameter from tongue height and backness*, try making an [i] sound while looking in the mirror. You will notice that the corners of the mouth are drawn back and that there is no lip rounding. Now without moving your tongue, round your lips by protruding them. The sound you wind up producing is a high tense front rounded vowel, a sound that does not occur in English but that is found in many languages of the world, such as German and French. As a point of interest, this sound is transcribed as [y] in the IPA. This is why we use [j] and not the [y] symbol to transcribe the palatal approximant found in English words like *yam* and *yellow*.

### SIDEBAR 2.4

Students with a careful ear will notice that most pronunciations of the English tense mid vowels [e] and [o] are actually diphthongs, with the tongue moving from the position of [e] to the position of [ɪ] in a word like *lay* or from [o] to [ʊ] in a word like *show*. A **broad phonetic transcription** would transcribe these words as [le] and [ʃo]. A **narrower phonetic transcription**, one which seeks to record as much detail as possible, would transcribe them as [leɪ] and [ʃoʊ].

In addition to the English vowels in Table 2.2, *there are also combinations of vowels in English that function as a single unit in the sound system*. These vowel sequences are called **diphthongs**, in contrast to **monophthongs**, which are produced with a single articulatory configuration. Diphthongs may be regarded as the vocalic equivalent to affricates, since they involve two phases. There are three clear diphthongs in American English. One is [aɪ], which starts off as an [a] and then rapidly sequences into [ɪ]. The diphthong [aɪ] is found in many words in English including *write*, *lie*, and *mine*. The second diphthong is [aʊ], which is found in words like *cow*, *town*, and *bout*. Finally, the diphthong [ɔɪ] occurs in words like *boy*, *soy*, and *toil*. Sidebar 2.4 describes some of the other diphthongs that occur in English, which are a little less clear.

## 2.4   Using the IPA to transcribe words

Now that you are familiar with the IPA, we can try using it to transcribe English words. ***One of the most important aspects of doing phonetic transcription is not to be biased by the spelling of a word.*** Since spelling symbols often differ from IPA symbols, as we have seen, blindly following the English orthography can lead to transcription mistakes. In doing transcription, you may find it useful to first think about how many sounds are in the word you are transcribing. To take a simple example, the English word *do* has two sounds. The first sound is a voiced alveolar stop [d], while the second sound is a high back rounded vowel [u]. (Don't be influenced by the spelling of the vowel as "o.") If we put the two sounds together, we get [du] as the phonetic transcription. Let's take a slightly trickier example now. In the spelling of the word *checks*, there are six letters. In terms of phonetic transcription, however, there are only four sounds. The first sound is the voiceless postalveolar affricate [tʃ]. The vowel is the lax mid front vowel [ɛ]. The final consonant sequence consists of a voiceless velar stop [k] and a voiceless alveolar fricative [s]. (Note that these are only two sounds [k] and [s], even though there are three letters, "cks," in the spelling.) With a little practice, you should be able to phonetically transcribe any English word, or even words in other languages containing sounds that have been introduced in this chapter. It is also possible to go in reverse and sound out the word from the phonetic transcription. For example, if you saw the IPA transcription [tʌf], you would know that it was the transcription for the English word *tough*. Try out the transcriptions in Sidebar 2.5, then check your answers on the following page.

> **SIDEBAR 2.5**
>
> Try transcribing the following English words in the IPA, then check your transcription against the answers in Sidebar 2.6.
>
> 1. yellow
> 2. lamb
> 3. wreath
> 4. beige
> 5. mission
> 6. sixth
> 7. xylophone
> 8. judge

So far we have been considering sounds in isolation, but it is important to recognize that there is overlap between sounds in actual speech. ***While one sound is being pronounced, the speech organs are preparing to produce the next sound***. This articulatory overlap between sounds is termed **co-articulation**. It is easiest to observe co-articulation between adjacent sounds that have different articulators. For example, during the production of a bilabial consonant like [b], the tongue is free to move into position from the preceding vowel into the following vowel, as in the word *reboot*, in which the tongue must move lower to transition from the high front vowel /i/ to the high back vowel /u/. Consonants other than bilabials may even be subject to co-articulation with adjacent vowels. For example, the body of the tongue is relatively free to transition between vowels during alveolar consonants, since alveolars primarily involve the tongue tip but do not involve posterior parts of the tongue, which play a crucial role in producing vowels.

Figure 2.3 contains a sequence of MRI images showing co-articulation between adjacent sounds in the word *leap*, extracted from the phrase *pea leap*. During the first three images, the tongue tip is raised toward the alveolar ridge and the back of the upper teeth to produce the lateral approximant /l/. Already by the fourth image, the middle part of the tongue has begun to rise in preparation for the high vowel /i/ even as the tongue tip is still curled upward for the /l/. (It may be noted that the tongue body is already in a relatively high position for the high vowel preceding the /l/.) The tongue body continues to rise through the fifth frame, reaching its target position by the sixth frame, as the tongue tip gesture for /l/ completely ends. In the seventh frame, while the /i/ is still being articulated, the lips are already starting to close in

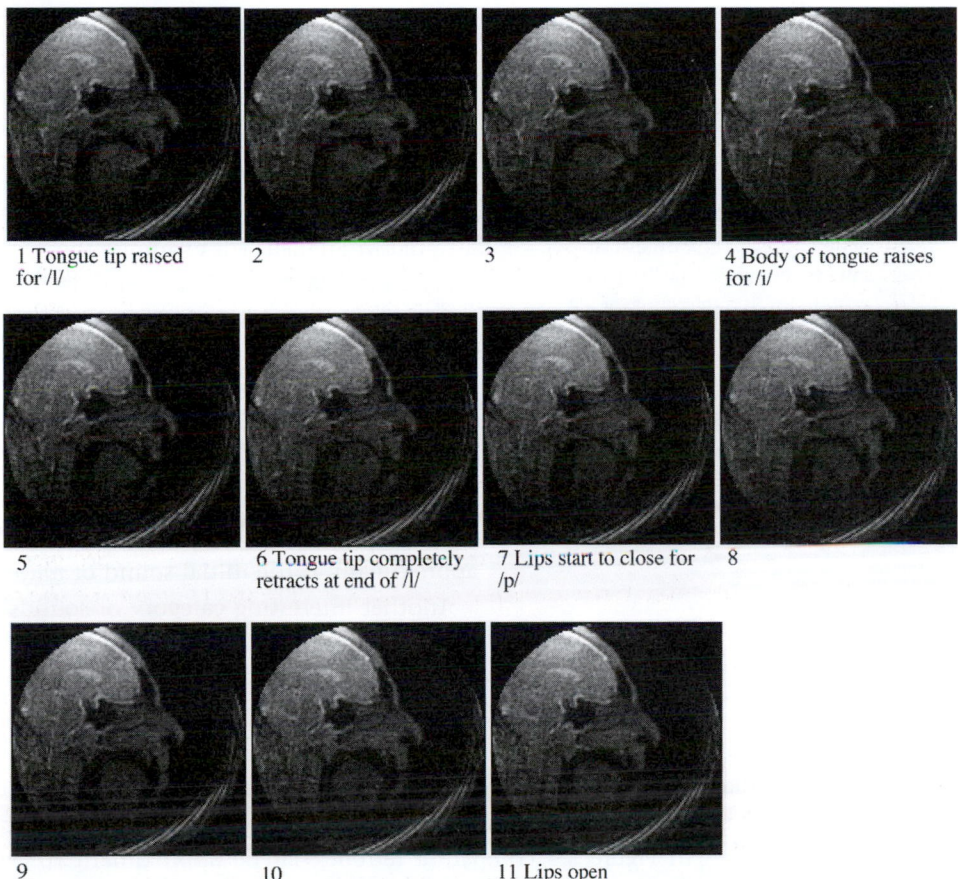

**Figure 2.3** Sequenced MRI images of the word *leap* /lip/ extracted from the phrase *pea leap*. [The MRI images in this chapter were generously made available by Shri Narayanan of the University of Southern California Speech Production and Articulation Knowledge Group (SPAN). More MRI images (in video format with accompanying sound files) for other English sounds are available on SPAN's website: http://sail.usc.edu/span/mri-timit/.]

preparation for the final bilabial stop /p/. The lips make a complete closure by the eighth frame, before gradually opening in the tenth and eleventh frames.

## 2.5  Co-articulation

It is clear from Figure 2.3 that there is substantial co-articulation between adjacent sounds. The tongue body is already preparing for /i/ during the production of /l/, and the lips are already moving into position for the /p/ during the /i/. Co-articulation is an essential characteristic of all speech.

## 2.6  Phonetic typology

***Although English has a relatively large number of sounds, it lacks many sounds that are found in other languages of the world.*** Many of the gaps in the English IPA chart are filled by symbols representing sounds which occur in other languages. See Textbox 2.3 for an example of one such type of sound.

> **SIDEBAR 2.7**
>
> The entire IPA chart is available at the beginning of this book. You can use it as a reference for IPA symbols that you are unfamiliar with. An interactive chart is available on the *How Languages Work* website; you can toggle between a chart with only the sounds of English and a chart with most of the sounds in the world's languages.

On the full IPA chart (see Sidebar 2.7), you will see a number of new symbols that represent sounds not attested in English. For example, the symbol [x] refers to a voiceless velar fricative, as found in the final consonant in the German name *Bach*. There are also places of articulation not found in English. For example, many languages have **uvular** consonants, produced by the back of the tongue coming into contact with or approximating the uvula (the appendage which hangs down in the back of the oral cavity). Uvular consonants are found in many languages, such as French, which has a voiced uvular approximant as the initial sound of *rouge*.

Another interesting category of sounds found in many languages of the world are the **retroflex** consonants, which are often produced with the tip of the tongue curled backwards toward the roof of the mouth behind the alveolar ridge. One language containing this type of retroflex consonant is Tamil, a Dravidian language spoken primarily in southern India. In this language the retroflex consonants are described as "subapical," since the underside of the tongue makes contact with the roof of the mouth. The MRI images in Figure 2.4 compare a retroflex lateral approximant /ɭ/ with a dental /l̪/ (indicated by a subscripted ◌̪ to distinguish it from an alveolar /l/), as produced by a Tamil speaker.

The place of articulation is much farther back in the mouth for the retroflex than for the dental, and the tongue tip is clearly curled back during the retroflex so that the underside of the tongue, rather than the upper surface, makes contact.

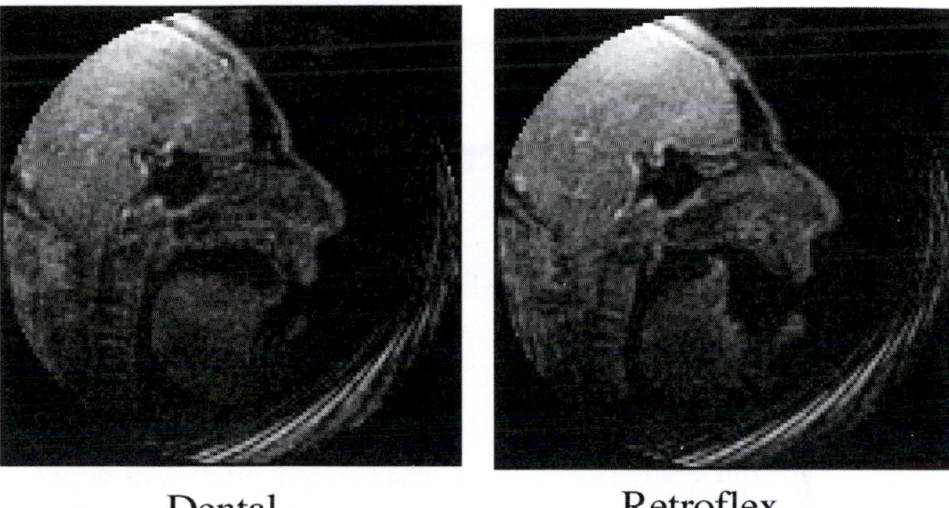

Dental        Retroflex

**Figure 2.4** Dental /l̪/ and retroflex /ɭ/ in Tamil

## 2.7 Suprasegmentals

In addition to describing individual speech sounds, phonetics is also concerned with patterns over groups of sounds. Phonetic properties above the level of individual sounds (otherwise known as **segments**) fall under the heading of **suprasegmentals**.

---

**TEXTBOX 2.3**

**Ejective stops** are common in indigenous languages of North America. For example, Navajo, an Athabaskan language spoken in the southwestern United States, has ejective stops at each place of articulation. 🔊 🎬

To produce the ejective [k'], emphatically say the English word *cake* without releasing the final velar stop. While you are holding the stop closure, close your glottis just as if you were making a glottal stop. Now release the velar closure before releasing the glottal stop and you should hear a popping sound much like in the Navajo velar ejective. Sometimes it takes practice to learn new sounds, so don't be discouraged if you don't produce an ejective on your first try. Everyone finds certain sounds easier to make than others. Ejectives may come naturally to one person while clicks may come more naturally to someone else.

There are many other types of speech sounds in languages. While we cannot introduce all of them here, there are now excellent resources for phonetics on the Internet. If you are interested in hearing other types of sounds from the IPA, the following website (put together by the great phonetician, Dr. Peter Ladefoged) contains links to sound files from languages examined during years of phonetic research throughout the world: www. humnet.ucla.edu/departments/linguistics/Vowels andConsonants

### 2.7.1 Syllables

One unit larger than the segment is the **syllable**. *The syllable is a linguistic grouping that consists of a single peak, which may be flanked on one or both sides by consonants.* The **syllable peak** (or **nucleus**) is so called because it is the most prominent (or loudest) part of the syllable. The syllable peak typically comprises a vowel, the most prominent type of sound. Consonants that precede the syllable peak within the syllable are referred to as the syllable **onset**, while consonants that follow the peak are called the syllable **coda**. Since consonants are less prominent than vowels, syllables typically first increase in prominence (from the onset to the peak), then decrease (from the peak to the coda). Sidebar 2.8 describes the less frequent occurrence of consonants as syllable peaks.

The IPA has a symbol for representing syllable boundaries. It is a period that is positioned between syllables. For example, the name *Mississippi* has four syllables and would be transcribed as [mɪ.sə.sɪ.pi].

> **SIDEBAR 2.8**
>
> Although most syllables have vowels as the peak of the syllable, it is also possible to have consonantal peaks. For example, the words *little* and *butter* each have two syllables, the second of which does not have a true vowel. The syllable peak in the second syllable of *little* is [l] while the peak in the second syllable of *butter* is [ɹ]. Both of these sounds are approximants, the most prominent type of consonant, so are natural syllable peaks. There are two other consonants that can function as syllable peaks in English: [n] as in *button* and [m] as in *prism*.
>
> These types of consonants that function as syllable peaks are known as **syllabic consonants**. In phonetic transcriptions, they are indicated by the symbol [ˌ] appearing under a consonant letter.

### 2.7.2 Stress

Another important suprasegmental property is **stress**. *Stress is the relative prominence of different syllables in a word. Stressed syllables typically have some combination of greater duration, intensity, or fundamental frequency relative to unstressed syllables.* In languages that have stress, there is one syllable per word that carries the main or **primary stress**. For example, the first syllable in *sofa* carries stress, while the second syllable in *relax* is stressed. The IPA symbol for primary stress is [ˈ], which goes above and to the left of the first sound in the primary stressed syllable. The transcriptions of *sofa* and *relax* would thus be [ˈsofə] and [riˈlæks], respectively.

It is also possible for a word, particularly a long word, to have **secondary stresses** that are not as strong as the primary stress but are stronger than completely unstressed syllables. The IPA symbol for secondary stress is [ˌ], which goes below and to the left of the secondary stressed syllable. To take an example of secondary stress from English, the word *Mississippi* has a secondary stress on the first syllable in addition to the primary stress on the third syllable, thus [ˌmɪ.sə.ˈsɪ.pi].

English uses stress to differentiate some pairs of words with different meanings. For example, the word *insight* is stressed on the first syllable while the word *incite* is stressed on the second syllable. English has several noun and verb pairs that differ in the location of stress. For example, the noun *convert* has initial stress while the verb *convert* has stress on the second syllable. Similarly, the noun *import* has stress on the first syllable while the verb *import* has stress on the second syllable. We can see that in English the position of the primary stress cannot be predicted (for more on stress cross-linguistically, see Textbox 2.4).

---

**TEXTBOX 2.4 STRESS SYSTEMS AROUND THE WORLD**

Stress patterns display considerable diversity cross-linguistically.

One of the major distinctions between stress systems is whether stress falls a consistent distance from the word edge across words of different shapes. In many languages, the primary stress of a word falls on a predictable syllable. For example, in Latvian, the first syllable of a word receives primary stress, whereas in Polish, primary stress falls on the second-to-last syllable, also called the "penultimate" syllable, of the word. This type of stress pattern, where the location of stress can be predicted by its position in the word, is called **weight-insensitive stress**. The three most common locations of stress in weight-insensitive stress systems are the initial syllable, the penultimate syllable, and the final syllable, although other stress sites such as the peninitial (second

syllable from the left) and the antepenultimate (third syllable from the right) are also attested. Other languages, such as Yup'ik, display weight-sensitive stress because they preferentially stress intrinsically more prominent (termed "heavy") syllable types, e.g., syllables with long vowels or closed syllables.

Another way in which stress systems differ cross-linguistically is in whether they have only a single primary stress per word or whether they place rhythmic secondary stresses in longer words, as in the English word *Apalachicola*, phonetically [ˌæ.pə.ˌlæ.tʃə.ˈkʰo.lə]. To learn more about the distribution of stress systems cross-linguistically, the interested reader is encouraged to refer to the four chapters and accompanying maps (features 14–17) dealing with stress in the *World Atlas of Language Structures* (http://wals.info/feature).

---

### 2.7.3   Tone

In some languages, stress plays much less of a role than in English. This includes **tone languages** (see Textbox 2.5 for a discussion of the distribution of tone languages worldwide). ***In tone languages, fundamental frequency (or its perceptual correlate, pitch) plays an important part in distinguishing between words with different meanings***. For example, in Dida, a Kru language spoken in the Ivory Coast, Africa, the same string of segments can have different meanings depending on the tone pattern associated with the string. To take one minimal pair, the word [su] with a mid tone means 'tree,' while the same sound sequence with a low tone means 'hot.' (Dida also has other tones besides mid and low tone.) English does not use tone to contrast words. Rather, in English fundamental frequency plays an important role in signaling stress and also in the last of the suprasegmental properties to be discussed here, intonation.

**SIDEBAR 2.9**

Sound files illustrating tonal distinctions in Dida are available on the *How Languages Work* website.

---

**TEXTBOX 2.5 TONE LANGUAGES AROUND THE WORLD**

In some regions of the world the great majority of languages have tone. This is particularly true of China, Southeast Asia, and sub-Saharan Africa. (A discussion of why linguistic features like tone cluster geographically can be found in Chapter 13, section 13.6.) However, tone is not restricted to these regions and, in fact, tone languages are found in many parts of the world. To see the distribution of tone languages, go to the excellent online resource, the *World Atlas of Language Structures*, navigate to the page on tone (http://wals.info/feature/13A), and click on the "show map" button.

Tone languages include: Mandarin, Cantonese, and virtually every other Chinese language; Thai, Vietnamese, Cambodian, and Tibetan in Southeast Asia and the Tibetan Plateau; Zulu, Shona, Igbo, Hausa, and Somali in Africa; Hopi and Cherokee in North America; Mixtec, Huave, and Otomí in Mexico; and Kubeo and Pirahã in South America. Although quite rare in Europe, simple tone systems are found in Norwegian and Latvian. Two tone languages, Manange and Seneca, are described in Language Profiles 4 and 12.

---

### 2.7.4  Intonation

**Intonation** refers to the changes in fundamental frequency (pitch) that occur during a phrase or an utterance. ***All languages (even tone languages) use differences in intonation patterns to mark differences in meaning that are not conveyed by segmental differences***. For example, English statements are typically marked by a pitch fall at the end, while English yes/no questions often have a pitch rise. The English sentence *So, you don't think that'll work* can be uttered with either a rising or a falling pitch pattern, with very different connotations (see Sidebar 2.10). The pitch fall indicates that the speaker is summarizing the opinion of the person he or she is talking to, whereas the pitch rise would be used to question whether the person thinks something will work or not. Intonation patterns and their functions are language-specific, with interesting variations across languages, as illustrated by Chickasaw in Textbox 2.6.

**SIDEBAR 2.10**

Relatively small differences in intonation patterns can dramatically change the connotation of an utterance. Try figuring out the meaning when the sentence *So, you don't think that'll work* is produced with three different intonation patterns. 🎬 🔊

---

**TEXTBOX 2.6**

Most languages of the world have falling pitch as the unmarked intonation contour at the end of declarative sentences. Languages display more variation in whether they employ rising or falling intonation at the end of questions, with the possibility of different types of questions, for example, questions requiring a yes or no answer as opposed to those requiring specific information (such as when something happened) can differ in their intonation within the same language. Chickasaw, a highly endangered American Indian language of Oklahoma, is typologically unusual in that many speakers employ a rise at the end of statements and a fall at the end of questions. 🔊 🎬

Intonation is a very complex area of phonetics since it is used for many functions. These functions may include, among others, to signal that someone has finished speaking or is going to continue speaking after a brief pause, to convey emotions, or to mark emphasis. Intonation is further discussed in Chapter 10, on prosody.

## CHAPTER SUMMARY

In this chapter, we have discussed articulatory phonetics, which deals with how the vocal organs produce speech. The speech organs can be divided into three regions. The subglottal system, which comprises the lungs and the trachea, provides the air that the upstream articulators manipulate to produce sound. The larynx is the gateway to the supralaryngeal system; vibrations of the vocal folds in the larynx produce voicing, which is a key component of many speech sounds. The supralaryngeal system includes the lips, teeth, velum, and tongue, all of which can be moved to produce different speech sounds. These sounds can all be classified according to manner and place of articulation, voicing, and whether they are nasal or oral. We have also learned about the ways in which speech sounds can be transcribed using the IPA. In addition to describing individual sounds, phonetics includes the study of suprasegmental properties such as syllable structure, stress, tone, and intonation. Taken together, the key features of speech production introduced in this chapter on phonetics can be used to describe the sounds of a language; examining the patterns of behavior for sounds within a language falls within the area of phonology, the topic of the next chapter.

## SUGGESTIONS FOR FURTHER READING

**Ladefoged, Peter**. 2005. *A course in phonetics*, 5th edn. Boston: Wadsworth Publishing.

This is the most widely used introduction to phonetics. It introduces the entire International Phonetic Alphabet, including sounds found in a variety of languages other than English.

**Ladefoged, Peter**. 2005. *Vowels and consonants*. Chicago: Wiley-Blackwell Publishers.

This is a somewhat more basic introduction to phonetics than *A Course in Phonetics*.

**Catford, John C**. 2002. *A practical introduction to phonetics*. Oxford University Press.

This introductory book focuses on mastery of phonetics through self-experimentation with one's own vocal tract.

**Ladefoged, Peter**. 1995. *Elements of acoustic phonetics*. University of Chicago Press.

This book provides an informative introduction to the acoustics of speech and techniques for acoustic analysis.

**Johnson, Keith**. 2003. *Acoustic and auditory phonetics*. Malden, Mass.: Wiley-Blackwell Publishers

This book introduces acoustic phonetics and how the auditory system perceives speech.

**Ladefoged, Peter and Ian Maddieson**. 1996. *Sounds of the world's languages*. Oxford: Wiley-Blackwell Publishers.

Drawing on the authors' extensive experience conducting linguistic research on underdocumented and endangered languages, this book is the definitive guide to both acoustic and articulatory properties of sounds found in languages throughout the world.

## EXERCISES

1.  Identify whether or not each of the following transcriptions is a word in American English. If so, write the word. If not, make a change or changes in the transcription to produce an accurate IPA transcription of the American English word that the transcription suggests.

    Note: the symbol [ˌ] under a consonant letter means that it is syllabic; it forms the peak of the syllable, as the orthographic vowel is not pronounced, e.g., the second syllable of *center* [ˈsɛntɻ̩].

    | | |
    |---|---|
    | a. [proˈdus] | k. [ˈkɹiki] |
    | b. [ˈtʃæmpjən] | l. [ˈlək] |
    | c. [ˈkɹɪstl̩] | m. [ˈshɪp] |
    | d. [ˈdʒɪŋgl̩] | n. [sʌppɻ] |
    | e. [ˈspɪtʃ] | o. [ˈʃedz] |
    | f. [əˈlaʊ] | p. [ˈpætʃd] |
    | g. [ɪmˈpeʃɛnt] | q. [ˈkoms] |
    | h. [ˈfɹæntɪc] | r. [ʃʌtl̩] |
    | i. [fʌdge] | s. [kɪttn̩] |
    | j. [heŋɻ̩] | t. [yan] |

2.  Transcribe the following words using the International Phonetic Alphabet: Sound files are available on the website.

    | | |
    |---|---|
    | a. telephone | k. risky |
    | b. yoyo | l. obvious |
    | c. maneuver | m. hopefully |
    | d. phonetics | n. cradle |
    | e. shrink | o. sprinkle |
    | f. forget | p. thank |
    | g. slapped | q. bathes |
    | h. creams | r. feathers |
    | i. baked | s. puppies |
    | j. loudly | t. buoyant |

3.  Mark the positions of primary stress in the following pairs of words:

    | | |
    |---|---|
    | a. electric | electricity |
    | b. tangent | tangential |
    | c. fluid | fluidity |
    | d. pragmatic | pragmatist |
    | e. fortunate | unfortunately |

f. emphasis      emphatic
g. mercury      mercurial
h. constitution      constitutionality
i. industry      industrialization
j. fantastic      fantastical

4. Transcribe the following words using the IPA. Be sure to listen carefully to the words so as not to be misled by standard English orthography. Mark the primary stress.
   Sound files are available on the website.

   | | |
   |---|---|
   | a. paper | n. yearling |
   | b. ride | o. philosophy |
   | c. kitchen | p. chunkier |
   | d. lemony | q. bathes |
   | e. violet | r. bath |
   | f. measure | s. ploughed |
   | g. yes | t. chef |
   | h. honorable | u. thought |
   | i. attacked | v. contribute |
   | j. cupid | w. machine |
   | k. good | x. Celtic |
   | l. crushed | y. whale |
   | m. button | z. jelly |

5. The International Phonetic Alphabet was developed in the late nineteenth century by language teachers in France interested in creating a transcription system for teaching the pronunciation of foreign languages. Since its origination, the phonetic alphabet has been dramatically expanded to include sounds found in languages throughout the world, with the goal of representing all the sounds that are used to differentiate words in all languages. In addition, the group responsible for developing the IPA, the International Phonetic Association, has grown substantially and now has thousands of members throughout the world. Besides developing and maintaining the phonetic alphabet, the International Phonetic Association also produces a journal containing research articles on phonetics and phonetic descriptions of languages. The *Journal of the International Phonetic Association* (or JIPA) was originally published exclusively using the IPA, although it now publishes articles primarily in English. Below is a brief passage (in the IPA) from a fable that has been translated into many different foreign languages in JIPA. Read it aloud and write the passage in standard English orthography.

   ðə nɔɹθ wɪnd ænd ðə sʌn wɹ dəspjurəŋ wɪtʃ waz ðə stɹaŋgɹ, wɛn ə tɹævələ kem əlaŋ ɹæpt ɪn ə waɹm klok. ðe əgɹid ðæt ðə wʌn hu fɹst səksidəd ɪn mekəŋ ðə tɹævələ tek hɪz klok af ʃʊd bi kənsɪɹɹd stɹaŋgɹ ðæn ðə ʌðɹ. ðɛn ðə nɔɹθ wɪnd blu æz haɹd æz hi kʊd, bʌt ðə ɹom hi blu ðə moɹ klosli dɪd ðə tɹævələ fold hɪz klok əɹaʊnd hɪm; ænd æt læst, ðə por nɔɹθ wɪnd gev ʌp ðə ətɛmpt. ðɛn ðə sʌn ʃaɪnd aʊt waɹmli, ænd əmiɹiətli ðə tɹævələ tʊk af hɪz klok. ænd so ðə nɔɹθ wɪnd waz əblaɪdʒd tu kənfɛs ðæt ðə sʌn wʌz ðə stɹaŋgɹ ʌv ðə tu.

6. Find a speaker of a language which you have never spoken or studied and ask if he or she would be willing to pronounce some words for you. Transcribe the words for the parts of the hand: *hand, palm, finger, fingernail, knuckle, wrist*, and any other vocabulary the language might have. (It can be particularly interesting to ask for the words for each finger – pinky finger, ring finger, etc. – as these are often compounds with interesting meanings.) Do your best to transcribe each word in IPA. Be sure to mark any stress, tone, length, and/or nasalization that you hear.
   If you come across a sound you haven't heard before, try to produce it yourself, using the speaker's feedback to improve your pronunciation. Then pay close attention to the positioning of your articulators and describe the sound using the descriptors for place of articulation, manner of

articulation, voicing, vowel height, vowel backness, rounding, and tenseness. You can use the IPA chart in this book and the interactive IPA chart online as an additional resource.

Your report on this study should include the following:

a. Name of the language
b. Name of your speaker
c. One paragraph biography of the speaker (where he or she grew up, schooling, what other languages he or she learned, when)
d. At least ten words transcribed in IPA, with the English translations in single quotation marks.
e. Phonetic descriptions of any sounds that are not also found in English, together with their associated IPA symbols.

Note: This is a challenging exercise for someone who is just beginning to study linguistics. The goal is to expose you to other languages, to give you the experience of working with a speaker of a language that is unknown to you, to teach you to listen carefully, and to begin to train you to hear and produce sounds in other languages. We don't expect perfect accuracy, but do your best! If you go on to study more linguistics, you may have an opportunity to do a fuller study of this type in a course on phonetics.

# 3 Phonology: organization of speech sounds

**KEY TERMS**

- Natural class
- Minimal pair
- Phoneme
- Near minimal pair
- Allophone

- Complementary distribution
- Contrastive distribution
- Phonological rule
- Free variation
- Allomorphy

## CHAPTER PREVIEW

*Phonology is the study of how sounds systematically behave.* We will see in this chapter that sounds often pattern together in groups with respect to where they occur and to how they interact with other groups of sounds. We will learn how to analyze the phonological systems of languages by examining the distribution of sounds in words. We will see that sounds have different statuses in language: some sounds (called **phonemes**) differentiate meanings while other sounds (called **allophones**) do not. These and other complex sound patterns can be represented by formal phonological rules. We will also explore some of the competing phonetic motivations driving phonological patterns. This will allow us to understand the ways in which phonological rules are grounded in both the phonetic and the functional bases of human language.

## LIST OF AIMS

At the end of this chapter, students should be able to:

- **identify natural classes of sounds;**
- **find minimal and near minimal pairs in a data set;**
- **locate sounds in complementary distribution;**
- **describe the environments in which allophones occur;**
- **argue for the phonemic status of sounds of a language;**
- **compare and contrast allophonic and allomorphic variation;**

- recognize common phonological processes;
- discuss functional and phonetic reasons for allophones.

## 3.1   Natural classes

The notion of groups or classes of sounds was introduced earlier in Chapter 2. For consonants, we saw that phonetic features describing voicing and place or manner of articulation can be used to divide sounds into groups. For example, the alveolars of English are [t, d, n, s, z, ɹ, l] while the nasals of English are [m, n, ŋ]. For vowels, phonetic terms for height, backness, tenseness, and rounding can be used to divide vowel sounds into classes. Thus, [i, ɪ, e, ɛ, æ] are front vowels and [i, e, u, o] are tense vowels.

These same phonetic features can be used to describe groups of sounds that behave together in a phonological system. Groups of sounds that pattern together are called **natural classes**. Recall the discussion of the forms of the English past tense from Chapter 1. We saw that the past tense of regular verbs in English is formed through addition of the suffix spelled -*ed* in the orthography. Phonetically, the -*ed* suffix has three realizations. One realization is as a voiceless alveolar stop [t] in such words as *walked* [wakt], *trapped* [tɹæpt], *washed* [waʃt], *laughed* [læft], and *poached* [potʃt]. Another realization is as a voiced alveolar stop in words such as *rubbed* [rʌbd], *wagged* [wægd], *buzzed* [bʌzd], *judged* [dʒʌdʒd], *rhymed* [ɹaɪmd], and *planned* [plænd]. The third realization is to pronounce -*ed* as [əd] in words like *seated* [sirəd], *baited* [berəd], *padded* [pæɾəd], *needed* [nirəd], *rented* [ɹɛntəd], and *landed* [lændəd].

The choice of how to pronounce the past-tense suffix when associated with a particular word is not an arbitrary or unpredictable one that requires rote memorization of the past tense for every English word. ***Rather, there is a pattern that governs the selection of realization***. The [t] realization is used when the base verb form (or root) ends in a voiceless consonant, the [d] realization with verb roots ending in a voiced consonant, and the [əd] variant with verb roots ending in an alveolar stop or flap.

The relationship between the root-final consonant and the selection of a past-tense variant is sensible from a phonetic standpoint. The realization [t] is voiceless, as are the consonants that trigger the [t] past tense; the realization [d] is voiced, as are the consonants that trigger the [d] past tense. The general pattern is thus one of voicing agreement between the root-final consonant and the past-tense suffix. Voicing harmony is one type of **assimilation** process, whereby two sounds come to share some property or cluster of properties. ***Assimilation is the most common type of phonological process and comes in many guises, for example, place-of-articulation assimilation, manner assimilation, nasal assimilation, and rounding assimilation***. Like other assimilation phenomena, voicing assimilation is phonetically motivated. It is articulatorily easier to maintain the same laryngeal setting (either voiced or voiceless) throughout the entire cluster that consists of the root-final consonant and the past-tense suffix than it is to rapidly change from voiced to voiceless or vice versa.

The final realization [əd] also has phonetic grounding. It would be difficult to produce the past-tense alveolar stop immediately after another alveolar stop or flap without an intervening vowel. The schwa [ə] is the perfect "filler vowel" for such cases, because it requires relatively little phonetic effort since it is produced with the tongue near the resting position.

*The variation in the realization of the past-tense suffix illustrates one of the fundamental principles guiding many phonological* **alternations:** *the drive toward minimizing* **articulatory effort**. Both voicing assimilation and schwa insertion reduce the amount of articulatory exertion required to produce the past-tense form of English verbs. As your study of phonology progresses, the attempt to minimize articulatory effort will emerge as a recurring theme in the organization of phonological systems. The goal of the phonologist is not merely to *describe* the patterns found in languages but also to *explain* the forces motivating these patterns, which are often (though not always) phonetically driven.

Given the importance of phonetic considerations in shaping phonological systems, it is not surprising that natural classes play a crucial role in the study of phonology. Consequently, recognizing natural classes is an important analytical skill to develop. *In order for a set of sounds to form a natural class, two criteria must be met: first, the sounds must all share one or more phonetic features; second, the sounds must be the complete set of sounds sharing those features in the given data*. To demonstrate the application of these two criteria, consider the IPA chart for English consonants in Table 3.1.

Keeping in mind the two criteria for a natural class, consider the following sets of consonants and determine whether or not they constitute natural classes.

**TABLE 3.1** The consonants of English

| | Bilabial | Labio-dental | Dental | Alveolar | Post-alveolar | Palatal | Velar | Glottal |
|---|---|---|---|---|---|---|---|---|
| Oral stops | p    b | | | t    d | | | k    g | ʔ |
| Affricates | | | | | tʃ    dʒ | | | |
| Nasal stops | m | | | n | | | ŋ | |
| Flap (tap) | | | | ɾ | | | | |
| Fricatives | | f    v | θ    ð | s    z | ʃ    ʒ | | | h |
| Central approximants | w | | | ɹ | | j | w | |
| Lateral approximants | | | | l | | | | |

1. p t k ʔ
2. m n ŋ
3. t d n ɾ s l ɹ
4. b m

The first group of sounds satisfies the first condition for being a natural class, since all of the sounds are voiceless stops. They also meet the second criterion, since the data set comprises the entire set of voiceless stops in the English IPA chart. Set (1) is thus a natural class. Notice that we need the two phonetic features "voiceless" and "stop" to correctly define this natural class. If we said only that the natural class is the set of voiceless sounds, this would not be adequate since there are many voiceless sounds in the data set that are not in Set (1), e.g., the voiceless fricatives. Nor could we simply describe the natural class as "stops," since Set (1) is missing all of the voiced stops, both oral and nasal.

The second group of sounds also satisfies the first condition since all of the sounds are nasals. Set (2) also meets the second condition, since the sounds constitute the entire group of nasals in the data set.

The third group is a little trickier. It is true that the sounds in Set (3) satisfy the first condition for being a natural class, since they are all alveolars. However, Set (3) is not an exhaustive set of the alveolars in the data: it is missing [z]. For this reason, the third group is not a natural class.

The fourth group is a small set of sounds, which have in common that they are voiced bilabial stops. Set (4) is also the complete set of voiced bilabial stops in English, so we have a natural class. Notice that we need all three descriptive features, "voiced," "bilabial," and "stop," to describe this natural class. The omission of any of these descriptors would mean that the second criterion for being a natural class, that the sounds be an exhaustive set for the given data, would not be met.

The requirement that a natural class be the exhaustive set of sounds sharing the specified features for a given data set means that **the same set of sounds can be a natural class in one language but not in another language**. Consider the inventory of consonants in Chickasaw, an American Indian language spoken in Oklahoma (Table 3.2).

Most of the consonants in Chickasaw also occur in English, with the exception of the voiceless lateral fricative [ɬ]. This sound is similar to the lateral approximant [l], except that [ɬ] is voiceless and is produced with turbulence at the constriction point. It has a sound much like that of English [l] when it occurs immediately after a voiceless stop, such as in the word *play*.

Consider the following set of sounds [p, b, t, k, ʔ]. In English, this set of sounds would not be a natural class; it is missing [d] and [g], which would be necessary to form the complete set of oral stops in English. However, this same set of sounds is a natural class for Chickasaw, since it is the exhaustive set of Chickasaw oral stops.

Now let us consider the set of sounds [t, s]. These sounds have in common that they are voiceless. This is insufficient for describing a natural class in either English or

**TABLE 3.2** The consonants of Chickasaw

|                       | Bilabial | Labio-dental | Alveolar | Post-alveolar | Palatal | Velar | Glottal |
|-----------------------|----------|--------------|----------|---------------|---------|-------|---------|
| Stops                 | p    b   |              | t        |               |         | k     | ʔ       |
| Affricates            |          |              |          | tʃ            |         |       |         |
| Nasals                | m        |              | n        |               |         |       |         |
| Central fricatives    |          | f            | s        | ʃ             |         |       | h       |
| Lateral fricatives    |          |              | ɬ        |               |         |       |         |
| Central approximants  | (w)      |              |          |               | j       | (w)   |         |
| Lateral approximants  |          |              | l        |               |         |       |         |

Chickasaw, however, since there are other voiceless sounds in both languages. If we add the feature "alveolar," we fare better in English at least, since [t, s] is the exhaustive set of English voiceless alveolars. However, [t, s] still does not constitute a natural class in Chickasaw, since Chickasaw has a third voiceless alveolar that English does not, namely the voiceless alveolar lateral fricative [ɬ]. For this reason, [t s] is a natural class in English but not in Chickasaw.

## 3.2 **Phonemic analysis**

### 3.2.1 Phonemes and minimal pairs

***Different kinds of phonological relationships can hold between sounds in a language.*** First, ***some sounds can be used to distinguish words with different meanings.*** For example, the voiceless bilabial stop [p] and the voiceless alveolar stop [t] in English can be used to differentiate words. There are thus many pairs of words such as *pan* vs. *tan*, *pill* vs. *till*, *spill* vs. *still*, *pop* vs. *pot*, and *lip* vs. *lit*, which are differentiated only by whether they have [p] or [t] in a particular position. Sidebar 3.1 gives a further example of this. The occurrence of these sounds is unpredictable and simply an arbitrary property of individual words. In other words, speakers must memorize each word as having either [p] or [t] in the proper place. This is different from the situation with the English past-tense suffixes, where one could predict the past-tense realization based on the root-final consonant. There is no need for speakers to memorize the past-tense form of each word, with the correct variant of the past-tense suffix.

**SIDEBAR 3.1**

In English, [p] and [t] distinguish words with different meanings. Thus, we cannot predict which sound will occur in a particular environment. For example, consider the environment [__ost] (written in IPA). Will this word begin with [p] or [t]?

Both sounds work equally well in this environment. Using [t] will give us *toast*, while [p] will give us *post*. Thus, the occurrence of [p] and [t] is *unpredictable* in English.

Pairs of words like *pan* vs. *tan*, *pill* vs. *till*, *spill* vs. *still*, *pop* vs. *pot*, and *lip* vs. *lit* are called **minimal pairs**. *Minimal pairs consist of two words which have different meanings and differ in only one sound occurring in the same environment*. In this case, the minimal pairs differ only in the presence of [p] or [t] in a certain position in the word. In the first two pairs, *pan* vs. *tan* and *pill* vs. *till*, [p] and [t] occur word-initially. In *spill* vs. *still*, [p] and [t] occur between [s] and [ɪ]. In the last two pairs, *pop* vs. *pot* and *lip* vs. *lit*, [p] and [t] occur word-finally.

Minimal pairs can be found for many different pairs of sounds in English. For example, the minimal pair *rain* vs. *raid* differs only in the final consonant, [n] vs. [d]; the minimal pair *boot* vs. *suit* differs only in the initial consonant, [b] vs. [s]; the minimal pair *seat* vs. *sit* is differentiated only by the vowel, [i] vs. [ɪ]; and the minimal pair *made* vs. *mood* is distinguished only by the vowel, [e] vs. [u].

It is also possible to find minimal triplets, in which three words are distinguished by a single sound, e.g., *made* [e] vs. *mood* [u] vs. *mode* [o]. In English, one can even find quadruplets (e.g., *seat* vs. *sit* vs. *sat* vs. *suit*) as well as sets consisting of even more members that are distinguished by single sounds. All of these **minimal sets** are useful for illustrating that certain sounds in a language are used to differentiate words.

*The requirement that minimal pairs have a single sound difference in the same environment excludes certain pairs of words from constituting minimal pairs*. For example, the pair of words *mat* [mæt] and *mole* [mol] are not a minimal pair. Even though these words have different meanings and even though the first consonant is the same in both words, they differ with respect to *two* sounds: the vowel and the final consonant. The pair of words *slot* [slat] and *late* [let] is also not a minimal pair, since there are two sound differences between the words. The first word has an [s] not present at the beginning of the second word, and the vowels in the two words also

**SIDEBAR 3.2**

Determine whether each of the following pairs of words constitutes a minimal pair:

1. *sled* vs. *slayed*
2. *face* vs. *case*
3. *hot* vs. *shot*
4. *grout* vs. *clout*
5. *remain* vs. *restrain*
6. *singer* vs. *finger*
7. *stamper* vs. *scamper*
8. *devil* vs. *revel*
9. *attack* vs. *aback*

You can check your answers in Sidebar 3.3.

differ. Finally, even though there is only one sound difference between the two words *pat* and *nap*, they are not a minimal pair since the sounds that differ occur in different environments. Try your hand at recognizing minimal pairs by completing the brief exercise in Sidebar 3.2. (The answers are given in Sidebar 3.3.)

*The concept of minimal pairs is important in phonology, since minimal pairs demonstrate the contrastive nature of sounds*. Thus, [p] and [t] are contrastive, as they contrast words with different meanings. The sounds [n] and [d], [e] and [u], and so on, are also contrastive. Sounds that are used to contrast words with different meanings have a special status in phonology: they are called **phonemes**. Phonemes form the building blocks of minimal pairs (or minimal sets of words). For this reason, changing the phonemes in a word often produces completely different words. For example, if you replace the [p] in the beginning of *pile* with a [t], the result is a different

**SIDEBAR 3.3**

Of the nine pairs of words on the previous page, six constitute minimal pairs (Examples 1–3 and 7–9), while three (Examples 4–6) do not. If this was not your answer, perhaps you were misled by English orthography. Try transcribing each word in the International Phonetic Alphabet. You will see that word pairs 1–3 and 7–9 are obviously minimal pairs.

    Word pairs 4–6 are not minimal pairs, since they all differ in terms of more than one sound. *Grout* and *clout* differ in two sounds: both the initial stop and the following liquid; *restrain* has three consonants after the first vowel while *remain* has only one; and *finger* has a distinct voiced velar stop [g] after the velar nasal, while *singer* does not for most speakers of English (a phonetic distinction not represented in the English spelling).

word, *tile*. Phonemes are thus an arbitrary property of individual words: in order to know a word, you must know which phonemes occur in it and how they are ordered.

Given the relationship between minimal pairs and phonemes, we can use minimal pairs to diagnose whether or not sounds are phonemes in a language. If two sounds in question are phonemes, we expect to find minimal pairs differentiated only by the two target sounds. ***In reality, though, sometimes it is not possible to find perfect minimal pairs differentiated by only a single sound for every phoneme. Sometimes it is necessary to settle for* near minimal pairs**. To illustrate the usefulness of near minimal pairs, consider the pair of sounds [ð] and [ʒ] in English. It is difficult to find minimal pairs to demonstrate the phonemic status of these two sounds in English. One possible minimal pair is *bathe* vs. *beige* in which the relevant contrast occurs in final position. However, some speakers pronounce the second word with a voiced post-alveolar affricate [dʒ] rather than the fricative [ʒ]. For these speakers, there are probably no true minimal pairs for [ð] and [ʒ]. Does this mean that these two sounds are not separate phonemes in English? No, because it is possible to find a near minimal pair for the two sounds: *leather* vs. *pleasure*. Clearly, this is not a minimal pair as there is more than one difference between the two words. Not only do the words differ in whether they have a [ð] or a [ʒ], *pleasure* also has an extra sound at the beginning of the word that *leather* does not. Still, *pleasure* and *leather* qualify as a near minimal pair, since the sounds *immediately adjacent* to the target sounds, [ð] and [ʒ], are the same in both words: [ɛ] before the target sound and [ɹ] after it. Like minimal pairs, near minimal pairs are usually sufficient to demonstrate that two sounds are separate phonemes in a language.

### 3.2.2  Allophones and complementary distribution

***Phonemes have different phonetic realizations depending on where they occur***. For example, [p] is not pronounced identically in the words *pin* and *spin*. If you hold your hand in front of your mouth while saying the two words, you will notice that the [p] in *pin* has a very clear puff of air upon release, while the [p] in *spin* largely lacks this salient puff of air. The puff of air associated with the [p] in *pin* is called **aspiration**. The [p] in *pin* is thus an aspirated stop, represented as [pʰ] in the IPA. A [p] occurring immediately after an [s], as in *spin*, on the other hand, is an unaspirated stop and is simply represented as [p].

Aspiration, in fact, is a regular feature of voiceless stops in English when they occur in word-initial position. As with the bilabial stop in *spin*, the alveolar and velar stops [t] and [k] also have variants differing in aspiration depending on context. Thus, we have aspirated stops word-initially in *take* and *come* but unaspirated stops after [s] in *stake* and *scum*.

Crucially, the [p] in both *pin* and *spin* is associated with the same phoneme in English, since there are no minimal pairs differentiated solely on the basis of whether they have unaspirated [p] or aspirated [pʰ] in the same position. ***Rather, the two kinds of [p] are variants of each other that are predictable from the context. When [p] occurs word-initially, it will always be aspirated; when [p] occurs after [s] it will always be unaspirated.*** Therefore, there is no need to memorize whether a given word has an aspirated or an unaspirated [p], since aspiration is predictable from the context. The relationship between aspirated and unaspirated [p] in English is an allophonic one, in which aspirated [pʰ] and unaspirated [p] are **allophones** of the same phoneme. ***Two sounds are allophones if they occur in mutually exclusive environments, i.e., if one allophone occurs in one set of contexts and another allophone occurs in another set of contexts***. Textbox 3.1 illustrates this by demonstrating that the occurrence of allophonic variants is predictable. There is no single environment in which both allophones can occur. This basic criterion for allophones is called **complementary distribution**.

So far we have seen that pairs of sounds may occur in two types of distribution. One possibility is for two sounds to have a **contrastive distribution**, ***meaning that they can occur in the same environment, in words with different meanings***.

---

### TEXTBOX 3.1 **PREDICTABILITY OF ALLOPHONIC VARIANTS**

Can you predict whether the voiceless stops in the following words will be aspirated or unaspirated?

1. *pore*
2. *tore*
3. *core*
4. *pool*
5. *tool*
6. *cool*
7. *spore*
8. *store*
9. *score*
10. *spool*
11. *stool*
12. *school*

You can check your answer by pronouncing each word with your hand in front of your mouth. Notice that words 1–6 all have the puff of air referred to as aspiration while words 7–12 do not.

Now consider two nonsense words: *tobe* and *stobe*. Can you predict which will have an initial aspirated stop and which will have an unaspirated stop? Check your answer by pronouncing each of these two words. If your prediction was that the stop in *tobe* would have aspiration and *stobe* would not, you were right. Any word, even a nonsense word, will conform to the pattern we've established. This is why we say that the presence of aspiration on voiceless stops in English is *predictable*.

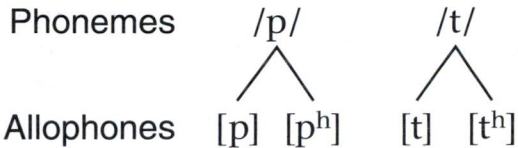

**Figure 3.1** The phonemes /p/ and /t/ and their allophones

This describes the type of distribution found in minimal pairs, which proves that two sounds are separate phonemes. The second type of distribution is **complementary distribution**, *which arises when two sounds occur in a different set of environments from each other*. Complementary distribution indicates that two sounds are allophones of the same phoneme.

In phonology, there are conventions for representing phonemes and allophones. It is customary to represent separate phonemes between slashes // and allophones in brackets []. Brackets are also used in order to remain neutral about whether a sound is a phoneme or merely an allophone; for example, if you are examining new data and haven't yet determined the status of a sound, or if the status of a sound as a phoneme vs. an allophone is not crucial to the point being made.

We may now summarize the relationship between the sounds [p], [pʰ], [t], and [tʰ]. (Notice that I am using the brackets here for a moment in order not to anticipate the conclusion about their phonemic statuses.) We have seen that [p] and [t] are in contrastive distribution since they occur in the same position in minimal and near minimal pairs. We have also learned that aspirated stops are in complementary distribution with unaspirated stops, since they occur in different environments and do not form the basis for minimal pairs. The relationship between the four sounds can thus be represented as in Figure 3.1.

Figure 3.1 shows that the phoneme /p/ (written in slashes) has two allophones: an unaspirated allophone occurring after [s] and an aspirated allophone occurring word-initially. Likewise, the phoneme /t/ has two allophones: an unaspirated allophone occurring after [s] and an aspirated allophone occurring word-initially. Note that it is common for one of the allophones of a phoneme to be identical to the phoneme itself, just as is the case with each of the unaspirated allophones here. The phoneme that is associated with the allophones is often termed the **underlying phoneme**, while the other allophones linked to the phoneme are often called the **surface allophones**. The assumption here is that words are memorized with the underlying phonemes, since this information is unpredictable and must be learned for each word. The surface forms then arise through a process or series of processes that give the underlying phonemes their actual phonetic realizations.

*The phonemic status of the same sound (i.e., whether it is a separate phoneme or an allophone) may differ from language to language*. To demonstrate this, let us consider some data from Hupa, an American Indian language spoken in northwest California (Table 3.3). The sounds whose phonemic status are in question

**SIDEBAR 3.4**

SOME HUPA PHONETIC
SYMBOLS

- An apostrophe after a stop or affricate means that it is an ejective.
- [ʍ] indicates a voiceless labial-velar fricative, like the *wh* that some English speakers pronounce in words like *why* and *which*.
- [ʷ] in 'he is crying' indicates that the preceding sound has lip rounding associated with it.
- [ː] after a vowel indicates that the vowel is pronounced as lengthened.
- [ɬ] indicates a voiceless lateral fricative.

**SIDEBAR 3.5**

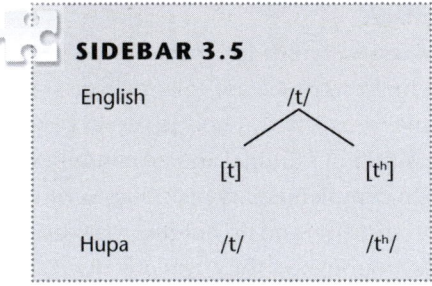

are the pair [t] and [tʰ] and the pair [ɪ] and [u]. Some of the special symbols used are explained in Sidebar 3.4.

First, looking at the pair [t] and [tʰ], it is clear that they are separate phonemes since *your mouth* and *your father* form a perfect minimal pair for these two sounds. Furthermore, *three* and *sweathouse* both form a near minimal pair with *how*, since *three* and *sweathouse* both begin with an aspirated [tʰ] before the vowel [a] and *how* begins with an unaspirated [t] in the same environment. We thus conclude that unaspirated [t] and aspirated [tʰ] are separate phonemes in Hupa, whereas in English, they are allophones of the same phoneme. This difference between the status of the sounds in English and in Hupa is illustrated in Sidebar 3.5.

Turning to [ɪ] and [u], we know that these sounds are separate phonemes in English on the basis of minimal pairs such as *sit* vs. *suit* and *tin* vs. *tune*. In Hupa, however, we do not find minimal pairs differentiated only by these two vowels. Nor are there are any near minimal pairs for [ɪ] and [u] in the data above. This can be determined by creating a chart with the environments in which each of the target sounds occur. In making such a chart, it is important to include both the sound immediately preceding the target sound and the sound immediately following it. A chart for the target vowels [ɪ] and [u] in the Hupa data is given in Table 3.4. The line between the preceding and following sounds is a place holder for the target sound.

**TABLE 3.3** Data from Hupa

| | |
|---|---|
| tʰaːqʼ | 'three' |
| taxʷeːt | 'how' |
| nɪtaʔ | 'your mouth' |
| nɪtʰaʔ | 'your father' |
| ɬɪtʃʼuʍ | 'sand' |
| tʰaːkʲʼuw | 'sweathouse' |
| tʰɪn | 'trail' |
| ʍɪmɪtʼ | 'my belly' |
| tʃʼɪtʃʷʰuw | 'he is crying' |

| ɪ | u |
|---|---|
| **TABLE 3.4** Vowel Environment Chart for [ɪ] and [u] in the Hupa data | |
| n__tʰ | tʃ'__ʍ |
| n__t | kʲʷ__w |
| ɬ__tʃ' | tʃʷʰ__w |
| tʰ__n | |
| ʍ__m | |
| m__t' | |
| tʃ'__tʃʷʰ | |

If there were a minimal or near minimal pair in the data, we would be able to find an environment in Table 3.4 that was identical for the two target sounds; however, this is not the case. ***Therefore, we do not have a contrastive distribution and the two sounds are not separate phonemes; [ɪ] and [u] thus stand in a different relationship in Hupa than in English.*** By process of elimination, this means that [ɪ] and [u] are allophones of the same phoneme in Hupa. If this is in fact true, they should be in complementary distribution, meaning that we should be able to find a different set of environments for each of the two sounds. To do this, we must ask whether there is any environment in which one sound occurs throughout the data, to the exclusion of the other sound. Keep in mind that this environment can involve either the preceding or the following sound, or both, and also that the environment could be expressed in terms of a natural class.

In fact, in Table 3.4, we can see that the [u] always occurs before a labial-velar sound, while the [ɪ] never occurs in this environment. We thus conclude that [ɪ] and [u] are in complementary distribution. It is typically easier to characterize the environment for one of the target sounds than for the other. In this case, it is easier to describe the environment in which [u] occurs, since the positions in which [ɪ] occurs are quite diverse. It is sufficient to give the environment for [u] and to state that [ɪ] occurs "elsewhere," meaning that it occurs in the environments in which [u] does not occur.

As a final step in our analysis, we need to formulate a summary statement of the relationship between the target sounds in the language. This statement might be as follows:

> In Hupa, [ɪ] and [u] are allophones of the same phoneme. [u] occurs before labial-velars and [ɪ] occurs elsewhere.

We might want to take the analysis one step further and decide which of the allophones is the underlying phoneme and which are the surface allophones. It is common to assume that the allophone that occurs in a more diverse set of environments (i.e., in the "elsewhere" set of contexts) is the underlying phoneme, and to derive the other allophone(s) by a rule. For the Hupa data, this would mean that /ɪ/ is the underlying phoneme and that [u] occurs before labial-velars. Our final analysis might thus be expanded as follows:

In Hupa, [ɪ] and [u] are allophones of the same phoneme. /ɪ/ is the underlying phoneme. /ɪ/ becomes [u] before labial-velars.

Once you have an analysis of phonemic data, it is also possible to make predictions about further data that you might not yet have seen. For example, after it has been determined that [ɪ] and [u] are allophones in Hupa and that [u] occurs before labial-velars, we can predict that any new Hupa data should conform to these generalizations. Thus, we should not find any examples of an [ɪ] sound before a labial-velar consonant. In fact, there is an even more interesting prediction that we can make for Hupa. You may recall that Hupa has a labialized velar fricative [xʷ], which occurred in the form [taxʷeːt] 'how.' This sound is similar to the German sound at the end of the composer Bach's name, but also has lip rounding. Given that [xʷ] is both labial and velar, we would expect it to trigger the [u] allophone. This prediction can be easily tested. The name that the Hupa use for themselves is [naːtʰɪnuxʷ], which literally means 'where the trail leads back.' (The root for 'trail' [tʰɪn] appeared earlier in Table 3.3.) As expected, there is an [u] before the final [xʷ], providing further evidence for our assimilation rule and our proposed phonetic explanation for it. This is one example of a local phonological process; some non-local phonological processes are described in Textbox 3.3.

### 3.2.3 Writing phonological rules

The statement about the change from underlying /ɪ/ to surface [u] in Hupa can be written more formally as a rule using features, as in (1).

**(1)**  /ɪ/ → [u] / __ [+labial–velar]

Rule (1) is read as follows: /ɪ/ becomes [u] in the environment before sounds that are labial-velar. It is common in phonology to formalize relationships between phonemes and allophones using rules. The Hupa rule of vowel rounding targets a single sound, the vowel /ɪ/. As we have seen, allophones often refer to sets of sounds that constitute natural classes. The environment that triggers rounding in Hupa is the natural class of labial-velar consonants. Natural classes of sounds targeted by a rule can also be expressed in rules using features. For example, members of the set of voiceless stops in English are realized with aspiration in word-initial position. Aspiration can be written using features as in (2).

**(2)**  [+stop, −voice] → [+aspirated] / # __

Rule (2) targets English sounds characterized by the features [+stop] and [−voice], changing them to their [+aspirated] counterparts in the environment after a word boundary, written with a # sign. Another way to write this rule is to replace the feature [+stop] with the feature [−continuant]. Sounds that are [−continuant] are produced with a complete closure in the oral tract. Sounds fitting this description include both the oral and the nasal stops. If you continue in phonology, you will learn more about the features used by phonologists to write rules. In some instances, as is the case for stops, phonological features differ from phonetic features. The reason for the occasional divergence between phonetic and phonological features lies in the differing goals of phoneticians and phonologists. Phoneticians are primarily interested in providing an accurate and maximally transparent description of sounds, whereas phonologists are focused on describing the patterning of sounds in a language in as succinct a manner as possible.

 It is helpful to become accustomed to reading and writing phonological rules. Further examples of rules are given in Textbox 3.2; other resources are available on the website.

### 3.2.4 Functional and phonetic reasons for allophones

While our analysis of the Hupa vowels may be sufficient for most purposes, it is also worthwhile taking a step back to ponder why this alternation might be taking place. In this case, the motivation is clearly phonetic in nature. Labial-velar sounds are produced with lip rounding, just like the allophone [u]. It is natural for an unrounded vowel to assimilate in rounding to an adjacent consonant with lip rounding. It is also natural for the vowel adjacent to the labial-velar to be pronounced with a backer articulation, since

---

### TEXTBOX 3.2 **EXAMPLES OF PHONOLOGICAL RULES**

Phonological rules are simple notational equivalents of what could be written in prose. They allow for a succinct characterization of phonological patterns and a clear presentation of the essential facts. Several types of rules are given below with their prose equivalents.

/i/ → [j] /_____ V
"The phoneme /i/ is pronounced as a glide before a vowel."

Ø → [p] / [m] _____ [θ]
"A [p] is inserted between an [m] and a [θ]."
(Example: English *warmth*)

V → Ø / # [p] ___ [t]
[−stress]

"Unstressed vowels are deleted between a word-initial [p] and a following [t]."
(Example: English *petition, potato*)

C → [−voice] / _____ #
"Consonants devoice in word-final position."

/t, d/ → [tʃ, dʒ] / _____ [j]
or
[alveolar stops] → [palato-alveolar] / _____ [palatal glide]
"The phonemes /t/ and /d/ are realized as palato-alveolar affricates before a palatal glide."
(Example: English *betcha* from *bet you*)

a labial-velar has a velar component. The conversion from /ɪ/ to [u] before labial-velars in Hupa is thus a phonetically natural process of assimilaton.

Many phonological phenomena such as assimilation seem to be driven by the goal of reducing the amount of work required of the vocal organs. Effort reduction, however, is not the only force behind phonology. Another important consideration is **perceptual salience**; *phonological systems tend to be constructed in a way that increases the perceptual distinctness of sounds from one another*. Perceptual salience plays an important role in driving certain phonological processes, including **dissimilation**, the process by which a sound changes to become less like a nearby sound. For example, in Finnish, when two /ɑ/ (low back unrounded) vowels might otherwise occur in adjacent syllables, the second dissimilates to /o/ when the plural suffix -i is added, as shown in Table 3.5. The two vowels thus become different from each other; the second dissimilates from the first.

Since we are thinking about phonetic motivations, let us ponder whether the aspiration of word-initial stops in English is also phonetically natural. In fact, aspiration may be viewed as a natural kind of strengthening process, called **fortition**. Word-initial position is a common locus of fortition, which can take many forms, such as the change

**TABLE 3.5** Examples of vowel dissimilation in Finnish

| marja | 'berry' | sana | 'word' |
|---|---|---|---|
| marjo-isːa | 'in the berries' | sano-isːa | 'in the words' |
| marjo-ista | 'from the berries' | sano-ista | 'from the words' |

---

## TEXTBOX 3.3 **LOCAL AND NON-LOCAL PHONOLOGICAL PROCESSES**

Most assimilation processes are like the English past-tense voicing assimilation and the Hupa rounding assimilation in that they are conditioned by immediately surrounding sounds. Processes governed by an adjacent environment are called **local**. While most assimilation processes are **local**, there are some that are non-local or **long distance**. One common type of long distance assimilation is **vowel harmony**, which is found in many Ural-Altaic languages, such as Finnish, Hungarian, and Turkish. The most common type of vowel harmony involves assimilation in vowel backness. In a language with prototypical front–back vowel harmony, all vowels in a word must agree in backness. This means that there are multiple forms of suffixes containing a vowel that differ in vowel backness.

To take an example from Finnish, the inessive suffix, which means 'inside,' has two allomorphs. The variant containing a front vowel (−sːæ) occurs after roots with front vowels, e.g., *kylæsːæ* 'in the village,' whereas the allomorph containing a back vowel (-sːɑ) appears after roots with back vowels, e.g., *talosːɑ* 'in the house.' Crucially, the consonants intervening between vowels are typically ignored by vowel harmony. There are other types of vowel harmony systems involving other dimensions, including lip rounding (e.g., in Turkish) and tongue root advancement (e.g., in Akan and other West African languages). Consonant harmony systems are also attested. Some types of harmony affecting consonants include nasality, voicing, and backness.

from a fricative to a stop or the change from an approximant to a stop or fricative. This is probably because word-initial sounds play such an important role in word recognition. The stronger and more perceptible the first sound of a word, the easier it will be for the listener to correctly hear the word. Initial fortition thus seems to be driven by considerations of perceptual salience.

The opposite of fortition is **lenition**, which is a weakening process by which consonants become less consonant-like and more vowel-like. For example, some voiced stops in Spanish weaken to sounds that are more fricative or approximant-like after vowels. Thus, the first "d" in the Spanish word *dedo* 'finger' is a true voiced stop but the second one is pronounced quite similar to the English voiced interdental fricative [ð]. In contrast to fortition, lenition is often driven by considerations of articulatory ease. In the Spanish example, it is easier to produce a fricative or approximant than a full stop when the sound is surrounded by vowels.

The goals of reducing effort and of maximizing perceptual distinctness often conflict, since it takes more effort to make sounds more distinct. To see this, compare the vowel contrast between /i/ and /u/ with another contrast between /ə/ and /ʌ/. The first contrast is perceptually more robust, since /i/ and /u/ sound very different from each other; one vowel is high and front, while the other is high and back. This contrast, however, is relatively difficult to execute articulatorily, since both /i/ and /u/ require tongue positions that are far from the rest position of the tongue in the center of the mouth. The contrast between /ə/ and /ʌ/, on the other hand, is relatively easy from an articulatory standpoint, since both vowels are close to the tongue's neutral rest position in the middle of the mouth. However, this contrast is relatively subtle from a perceptual standpoint, as the two vowels are acoustically quite similar. The perceptual proximity of /ə/ and /ʌ/ is, in fact, easy to verify if you ask someone else to produce the two in isolation and try to guess which one is which.

***The phonological systems of languages are the result of compromise between the two goals of minimizing articulatory effort and maximizing perceptual distinctness.*** The tension between these two goals is described in more detail in Textbox 3.4. One important corollary of this compromise is that languages seek to exert effort only where the perceptual payoff will be greatest. In contexts where the perceptual distinctness is impoverished to begin with, effort will be minimized even if this further reduces perceptual distinctness.

Let us again consider some data from Hupa. Recall that Hupa has a phonemic contrast between aspirated and unaspirated stops. In fact, this contrast is limited to certain contexts; it is not found at the end of roots, a position where there is usually no following vowel. In root-final position, only unaspirated stops occur. This positional restriction against the aspirated vs. unaspirated stop contrast is phonetically sensible; it is difficult to hear whether a consonant is aspirated if it is not released into a following vowel. To make final aspiration audible, a speaker would need to exert additional articulatory effort, such as creating a larger laryngeal opening or using greater subglottal pressure to increase the aspiration noise. Even with this

---

TEXTBOX 3.4 **THE CORRELATION BETWEEN PERCEPTUAL DISTINCTNESS AND ARTICULATORY EFFORT**

The more articulatory effort we put into the production of sounds, the more distinct they become. We need to make distinctions in language so that we can convey the myriad ideas that we use to communicate; the more sounds we distinguish, the easier it will be to differentiate among the thousands of words in a language. The opposite pull – toward routinization, rapidity, and ease of articulation – results in a saving of articulatory effort, but a loss of perceptual distinctness. Thus, we can see that these two forces are correlated:

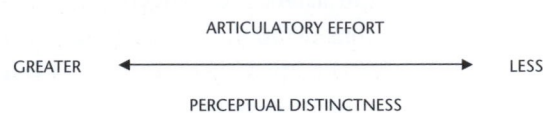

Since we want *greater* perceptual distinctness but *less* articulatory effort, the two forces are in conflict, pulling in both directions and creating tensions that result in complex phonological patterns.

---

additional effort, though, the contrast would still not be as perceptually salient as when the stop is followed by a vowel. Rather than expend all of that articulatory effort for a relatively small increase in perceptual distinctness, speakers have neutralized the contrast between aspirated and unaspirated stops in root-final position. Speakers have thus simplified this aspect of the language, saving articulatory effort in the precise environment where the payoff of perceptual distinctness would be minimal.

### 3.2.5   Free variation

We have seen that sounds can have different relationships in phonology. Some sounds have contrastive distribution and are phonemes, while other sounds are in complementary distribution and are allophones. There is one more type of relationship that sounds can have. ***A single sound can have two different variant pronunciations in the same word.*** For example, there is more than one way to pronounce the final consonant in the word *bad* without any change in meaning. One possible realization of the final [d] is with a release, just like when [d] occurs before a vowel. Another possibility is for the final [d] to lack a release. The IPA symbol for an unreleased consonant is ˺ (written after the unreleased consonant). The two variants for *bad* are thus [bæd] and [bæd˺]. These two possible realizations for word-final [d] are not limited to only the word *bad*, but can occur for any d-final word in English. Moreover, this difference is not only found with [d]; in general, English stops in word-final position may be either released or unreleased. For example, *bag* can be pronounced either [bæg] or [bæg˺], *tube* can be pronounced either [tʰub] or [tʰub˺], *cat* can be realized either as [kʰæt] or [kʰæt˺], etc. ***This situation, in which two different sounds occur in the same environment in the same word, is called free variation.*** We can thus say that released and unreleased stops are in free variation word-finally in English.

### 3.2.6  Allomorphy

We have seen that the English past-tense ending -*ed* has three different phonetic realizations that depend on the final consonant of the root. If the root-final consonant is voiceless, the past tense is realized as [t], e.g., *walked* [wakt] or *sipped* [sɪpt]. If the root-final consonant is voiced, the past tense surfaces as [d], e.g., *robbed* [ɹabd] or *seized* [sizd]. If the final consonant is an alveolar stop or flap, the past tense is realized as [əd], e.g., *rented* [ɹɛntəd] or *waited* [weɹəd]. The past-tense ending, like any suffix, contains information that is crucial to the interpretation of a word. The term for a meaningful part of a word that cannot be further subdivided is a **morpheme**. All roots, suffixes, and prefixes are morphemes, since they contribute meaning to the words in which they appear. Morphemes are discussed further in the chapter on morphology. For our purposes, what is crucial about morphemes is that they often come in several phonetic variants, which are conditioned by context. The morpheme variants that occur in complementary distribution are termed **allomorphs**, just as variants of phonemes that occur in complementary distribution are termed allophones. As we saw earlier for the past tense in English, *allomorphs are often conditioned by the same phonetic motivating forces that govern the occurrence of allophones*.

Suffixes and other affixes are not the only morphemes that may have allomorphs. It is possible for roots to have multiple allomorphs. For example, roots ending in /t/ in English have different allomorphs depending on the context in which they occur. Consider the verb *cite* which ends, when uttered in isolation, in an unaspirated /t/, either released or unreleased, as we just saw in the discussion of free variation. If we add the adjectival suffix -*able* to the root *cite*, the final /t/ changes from an alveolar stop to a flap. Thus, *citeable* is pronounced as [ˈsaɹɾəbl]. The flap is the regular realization of alveolar stops between a stressed vowel and an unstressed vowel. Because the suffix -*able* is unstressed in the word *citeable*, this creates the proper environment for the allomorph of *cite* that ends in a flap. A third allomorph arises when we add the suffix -*ation* to *cite* to produce *citation*, pronounced [saɪˈtʰeʃn]. The /t/ at the end of the root is now realized as an aspirated stop because the suffix -*ation* creates the correct environment for stop aspiration: the position immediately before a stressed vowel. The root *cite* thus has three allomorphs in total, differing in the realization of the final consonant. One, ending in unaspirated [t], surfaces when there are no suffixes. Another, ending in a flap [ɾ], occurs after a stressed vowel and before an unstressed vowel. The third and final allomorph, ending in aspirated [tʰ], occurs before a stressed vowel. The allomorphs discussed here are summarized in Textbox 3.5.

---

**TEXTBOX 3.5  THE THREE ALLOMORPHS OF *CITE***

| | | |
|---|---|---|
| *cite* | [sait] | /t/ is realized as [t] in word-final position |
| *cit-able* | [ˈsaɹɾ-əbl] | /t/ is realized as [ɾ] following a stressed vowel |
| *cit-ation* | [saɪˈtʰ-eʃn] | /t/ is aspirated [tʰ] before a stressed vowel |

It is important to note that all of the rules responsible for the allomorphs of the root *cite* are consistent rules of English that occur even in words for which there are not multiple allomorphs. All voiceless stops are aspirated before stressed vowels (as in words like *peach*, *top*, and *kite*), and all alveolar stops between a vowel and an unstressed vowel become a flap (as in words like *city*, *pity*, and *tornado*). This means that other roots ending in /t/ will also have several allomorphs if they take suffixes with the right shape to trigger rules such as aspiration or flapping. For example, the root *wit* has an allomorph ending in unaspirated [t] when pronounced in isolation, and another allomorph ending in a flap in the suffixed form *witty*. The latter allomorph is the result of a phonological process called lenition. For more on phonological processes, see Textbox 3.6.

---

### TEXTBOX 3.6 **COMMON PHONOLOGICAL PROCESSES**

Allophonic and allomorphic variation are typically triggered by the same phonological processes. This is not surprising since allophones and allomorphs tend to be phonetically motivated and speech physiology varies relatively little across humans, regardless of their language background. Similarly, the compromise between the two goals of minimizing articulatory effort and maximizing perceptual distinctness underlie the phonological systems of all spoken languages, giving rise to the same types of alternations. Some phonological processes are especially common. It is helpful to be familiar with these when doing phonological analysis:

- **Assimilation**: one sound becomes like another sound, e.g., Hupa vowel rounding or /n/ being pronounced as [m] (so labial like the following [p]) in the English word *input*.
- **Palatalization**: a subtype of assimilation in which a velar or alveolar consonant is pronounced in the palatal region when adjacent to a high vowel, a front vowel, or the palatal glide, e.g., *bet you* pronounced as *betcha*, or *did you* as *did-ja*.
- **Dissimilation**: one sound becomes less like another sound, e.g., Finnish vowel rounding, or some pronunciations of the English word *February* as

*Feb[j]uary*, with the first of two /r/ sounds in the word becoming a glide.

- **Metathesis**: two sounds are transposed, e.g., a child's pronunciation of *animal* as *aminal*, or the common pronunciation of football player Brett Favre's name as *Farve*.
- **Deletion**: the loss of a sound, e.g., the loss of the final /n/ in *hymn* (but not in the suffixed form *hymnal*), or the final /b/ in *crumb* (but not in the suffixed form *crumble*).
- **Insertion**: the insertion of a vowel between the two consonants, e.g., in the past tense of English words that end in alveolar stops, such as *betted* and *provided*.
- **Fortition**: the strengthening of a sound, e.g., word-initial aspiration in English or the fortition of [s] to the affricate [ts] in words like English *dance*.
- **Lenition**: the weakening of a sound, e.g., the loss of stop closure intervocalically in Spanish or the realization of English /t/ or /d/ as a flap.
- **Vowel reduction** (a type of lenition): the conversion of unstressed vowels to more schwa-like allophones, e.g., the second vowel in *emphasis*, as compared to *emphatic*, or the fourth vowel in *anticipatory*, as compared to *anticipate*.

---

### 3.2.7   Processes triggered by positioning, stress, and syllable-type

The examples of *cite* and *witty* illustrate another important point: **sometimes phonological processes are triggered by the position of the sound in the word, while other times they are triggered by surrounding sounds**. Word-initial and word-final position often trigger phonological processes. In many languages, syllable position and stress are two additional contexts in which phonological rules apply. For example, consider the word from Chickasaw in (3). In the phonetic transcription, stress is indicated by the IPA symbol ['] and syllable boundaries are represented by periods.

**(3)**  /asabikatok/ 'I was sick'     [a.ˈsaː.bi.ˈkaː.ˈtok]

You will notice that the vowel /a/ is lengthened in the second and fourth syllables. This is a regular phonological process in Chickasaw; vowels are lengthened in stressed syllables, as long as they are not word-final. Thus, we see that both stress and position play roles in this process.

Vowel lengthening in Chickasaw is actually more complicated than this, as the rule does not target all non-final stressed syllables, but only those in **open syllables**, that is, those syllables that end with a vowel. Therefore, the second vowel in [tʃa.ˈlak.ˈkiʔ] 'Cherokee' does not lengthen even though it is stressed. The second syllable in this word is a **closed syllable**, as it ends in a consonant, in this case /k/.

As it turns out, the distinction between open and closed syllables is also relevant for describing the location of stress in Chickasaw. In words that are made up of strings of open syllables, stress will fall on all even-numbered syllables and on the last syllable of the word. We can see this pattern in the word [a.ˈsaː.bi.ˈkaː.ˈtʃi] 'he or she makes me sick.' In contrast, closed syllables in Chickasaw are stressed regardless of whether they are even-numbered or not, e.g., [ˈok.ˈfok.ˈkol] 'type of snail.' Thus, the distribution of stress in Chickasaw depends on both positioning and syllable type.

### CHAPTER SUMMARY

We have learned about the ways in which the sounds of a language pattern together in groups and form systematic relationships. There are three types of relationships that can hold between sounds. One possibility is for two sounds to be in contrastive distribution (the sounds occur in the same position in different words), in which case the sounds are separate phonemes. A second possibility is for sounds to occur in the same position in the same word, in which case they are said to be in free variation. A final option is for two sounds to be in different predictable environments, in which case the sounds are in complementary distribution and are allophones of the same phoneme. Allophones can be conditioned by surrounding sounds, by stress (or lack thereof), by certain positions in the syllable or word, or by some combination of these factors.

The relationships between allophones and their underlying phonemes can be expressed using phonological rules. Phonological rules are motivated by two competing forces: ease of articulatory effort and perceptual distinctiveness, and these give rise to a variety of phonological processes, many of them quite common. Phonological rules are thus grounded in both the phonetic and the functional bases of human language.

In addition to mediating allophonic relationships, phonological rules help determine relationships between allomorphs. The following chapter discusses morphology, including alternations between allomorphs, in more detail.

## SUGGESTIONS FOR FURTHER READING

**Hayes, Bruce**. 2008. *Introductory phonology*. Oxford: Blackwell Publishers.

**Odden, David**. 2005. *Introducing phonology*. Cambridge University Press.

These two books provide a clear and informative overview of phonological theory, focusing on methodological approaches to analyzing phonological data.

**Ohala, John**. 1997. "The relation between phonetics and phonology." In Hardcastle, William and John Laver (eds.), *The Handbook of Phonetic Sciences*. Oxford: Blackwell Publishers. 674–694.

**Kingston, John**. 2007. "The phonetics–phonology interface." In de Lacy, Paul (ed.), *The Cambridge handbook of phonology*. Cambridge University Press. 401–434.

These two book chapters examine the role of phonetics in explaining phonological patterns.

**Blevins, Juliette**. 2004. *Evolutionary phonology: The emergence of sound patterns*. Cambridge University Press.

This book examines historical sound change and the role of phonetics in explaining phonological shifts.

**Vihman, Marilyn**. 1996. *Phonological development: The origins of language in the Child*. Oxford: Blackwell Publishers.

This book provides an overview of the acquisition of phonology by children.

## EXERCISES

1.  Natural classes in Finnish
    The following sounds are the phonemes of Finnish:
    p t d k ʔ m n ŋ s h ʋ j l r i y e ø æ ɑ o u

    State whether the following sets of sounds form natural classes or not. For those that are natural classes, describe that class of sounds using phonetic features.
    (The symbol [ʋ] represents a voiced labiodental approximant.)

    a. p t d k ʔ
    b. t d n s l r
    c. y ø o u
    d. e ø o
    e. k ŋ
    f. ʋ j l
    g. m n ŋ
    h. i y e ø æ o u
    i. d m n ŋ ʋ j l r i y e ø æ ɑ o u
    j. ɑ o u

2.  Examine the following data from Estonian, a Finnic language spoken by approximately 1 million people, primarily in Estonia.

| Estonian | Gloss |
|----------|-------|
| tal:: | 'lamb' |
| lina | 'flax' |
| tal:a | 'of the sole' |
| kan:: | 'jug' |
| lin:a | 'of the town' |
| pak:i | 'of the package' |
| panʲ:: | 'bread' |
| vil:: | 'wool' |
| pala | 'piece' |
| vilʲ:: | 'blister' |
| talʲi | 'winter' |
| lin::a | 'into the town' |
| la::tʲ | 'nature' |
| hal:: | 'frost' |
| talʲ:i | 'stable' |
| palʲ:: | 'ball' |
| sa::t | 'you get' |
| paki | 'gust' |
| pak::i | 'into the package' |

a. Estonian has many palatalized consonants, indicated by the symbol [ʲ]. They sound roughly like an English sequence of a consonant plus [j]. Are the palatalized consonants allophones of their non-palatalized counterparts or are they separate phonemes? Provide evidence for your answer.

b. In addition, Estonian consonants and vowels have three degrees of length phonetically: short; long (indicated by :); and extra-long (indicated by ::). Are any of the length differences allophonic or are all three lengths phonemic? Provide evidence for your answer.

3. Examine the following data from Old Icelandic, the ancestor of the modern West Scandinavian languages Icelandic, Norwegian, and Faroese.

| Old Icelandic | Gloss |
|---------------|-------|
| barn | 'child' |
| barns | 'child' (genitive sg.) |
| bɔrnum | 'children' (dative pl.) |
| barni | 'child' (dative sg.) |
| mɔrkum | 'forest' (dative pl.) |
| marka | 'forest' (genitive pl.) |
| handar | 'hand' (genitive sg.) |
| handa | 'hand' (genitive pl.) |
| hɔndum | 'hand' (dative pl.) |
| dagr | 'day' |
| dags | 'day' (genitive sg.) |
| dɔgum | 'day' (dative pl.) |
| matr | 'food' |
| matar | 'food' (genitive sg.) |
| matir | 'foods' |
| mɔtum | 'food' (dative pl.) |

Describe the alternations affecting the vowels. What is the term for this type of phenomenon? Try writing a rule accounting for the alternations.

4.  Examine the following data from Chickasaw

| Chickasaw | Gloss |
|---|---|
| *sinti?* | 'snake' |
| *ã:sinti?* | 'my snake' |
| *tʃĩ:sinti?* | 'your snake' |
| *fala* | 'crow' |
| *ã:fala* | 'my crow' |
| *tʃĩ:fala* | 'your crow' |
| *paska* | 'bread' |
| *ampaska* | 'my bread' |
| *tʃimpaska* | 'your bread' |
| *iŋkoni* | 'skunk' |
| *aŋkoni* | 'my skunk' |
| *tʃiŋkoni* | 'your skunk' |
| *tali?* | 'rock' |
| *antali?* | 'my rock' |
| *tʃintali?* | 'your rock' |
| *hason* | 'leech' |
| *ã:hason* | 'my leech' |
| *tʃĩ:hason* | 'your leech' |
| *nani?* | 'fish' |
| *ã:nani?* | 'my fish' |
| *tʃĩ:nani?* | 'your fish' |
| *akaŋka?* | 'chicken' |
| *amakaŋka?* | 'my chicken' |
| *tʃimakaŋka?* | 'your chicken' |

Describe the alternations affecting the prefixes meaning 'my' and 'your.' Try writing rules accounting for these alternations.

5.  Writing rules

Here is the phoneme inventory for a language:

p b t d k g m n ɸ β s z ʃ j l i e æ ə ɑ o u

Use rule-writing notation to compose rules corresponding to each of the prose descriptions below. What is the name of each type of process? Hint: Some may have more than one name.

a. /n/ becomes [m] and /d, g/ become [b] before [p, b, m, ɸ, β]
b. /p/ becomes [ɸ], /b/ becomes [β], and /d/ becomes [z] between vowels
c. /b/ becomes [p], /d/ becomes [t], and /g/ becomes [k] word-initially
d. [ə] is added to break up consonant clusters of stop plus nasal
e. /p, t, k/ delete word-finally
f. The clusters /sp, st, sk, ʃp, ʃt, ʃk/ reverse their order of consonants word-finally
g. /s/ becomes [t] before [s]
h. /o/ becomes [e], /u/ becomes [i], and /ɑ/ becomes [æ] after [i e æ]

# 4 Morphology: what's in a word?

**KEY TERMS**

- Morphology
- Morpheme
- Affix
- Compound
- Productivity

- Allomorph
- Lexeme
- Derivation
- Inflection
- Lexicalization

**CHAPTER PREVIEW**

We have seen how groups of sounds pattern in each language as sounds are combined to form words. Morphology is the study of the internal structure of words. This chapter describes the kinds of building blocks used to form words in different languages and the ways they can be combined. Speakers are not usually conscious of the patterns inside of their words, but for most languages, knowledge of such patterns is crucial to the ability to speak. Topics discussed here include the notion of the *word*, the forms morphemes can take, the kinds of meanings they can carry, how to identify and describe them, and what we can learn from the morphological patterns we find. In the process, it introduces core grammatical concepts and analytical skills that will be central to discussions of word classes, syntax, and other topics covered throughout this book.

**LIST OF AIMS**

After reading this chapter, students should be able to:

- discuss ways to identify words in different languages;
- identify basic morphemes in an unfamiliar language;
- identify simple allomorphs and write rules to describe their distribution;
- identify the meanings of basic morphemes;
- define the term "compound" and give examples of compounds;

- explain the difference between possible and actual words;
- define the term "productivity";
- explain what is meant by the terms "lexeme" and "lexicalization."

## 4.1 Introduction to morphology

As speakers, what do we know about our mother tongue? Much of our linguistic knowledge is unconscious. When we start to learn a new language, we often come to appreciate just how much speakers must know in order to talk, whether they are aware of it or not.

It seems obvious that knowing words is a critical part of knowing a language, but what does it mean to know a word? A recent newspaper advertisement claims *Unbelievable weight loss breakthroughs!* Most English speakers recognize each of the words in this phrase as part of the vocabulary of English. They may or may not realize that words can have meaningful parts of their own. The first word, *unbelievable*, has three parts. It is based on the verb root *believe*. With the addition of the ending *-able* we have another word *believ-able* 'able to be believed.' If we add *un-* to that word *believable*, we have yet another word, this one with the opposite meaning: *un-believable* 'not able to be believed.' Each of the meaningful parts of a word, like *believe*, *-able*, and *un-*, is called a **morpheme**. The study of how morphemes are combined to form new words is called **morphology**.

*Morphology is one of the areas in which languages can differ the most from each other*. Compare the two sentences below. The first is from Engenni, a Kwa language spoken in Nigeria. The top line in the example shows the sentence as it was spoken, the second line shows the meaning of each word, and the third line shows a free translation of the whole.

> **SIDEBAR 4.1**
>
> TRANSCRIPTION NOTE
>
> | Engenni symbol | Phonetic description |
> | --- | --- |
> | vowel with grave accent (e.g., ù) | low tone |
> | vowel without an accent | high tone |
> | vowel with acute accent (e.g., Á) | upstepped (extra-high) tone |

(1)  Engenni (Thomas 1978)

| Á | ta | na | wa | ɔmù. |
| --- | --- | --- | --- | --- |
| one | go | to | seek | house |

'Let's go look for the house.'

The second example is from Mohawk, a language of the Iroquoian family spoken in Quebec, Ontario, and New York State. Here again the top line shows the sentence as spoken; note that the whole sentence is expressed in a single Mohawk word. The second line shows the parts (morphemes) of the word. The third identifies the meaning of each morpheme. The fourth provides a free translation of the word as a whole.

(2)  Mohawk
*Teninonhsihsákha.*
te-ni-nonhs-ihsak-ha
you.and.I-two-house-seek-go.and
'Let's go look for the house.'

The Engenni and Mohawk sentences mean roughly the same thing, but the two languages differ considerably in the way they distribute information over their words. In the Engenni example, each word contains just one meaningful part, or one morpheme. In the Mohawk example, all of the same information is packaged into a single word.

## What is a word?

How do we know that the Mohawk sentence in (2) contains just one word? The most obvious way to find out is to ask a speaker. Mohawk speakers have clear ideas about where one word stops and the next begins, whether or not they have ever read or written their language. All would readily agree that (2) is a single word. Let's look at a longer sentence. Compare the Mohawk sentence in (3) with its English translation. The amount of information contained in each word is different in Mohawk and English: the Mohawk sentence contains seven words, and the English translation fourteen. But all Mohawk speakers would again divide the sentence into words in the same way.

**SIDEBAR 4.2**

TRANSCRIPTION NOTE

| Mohawk symbol | IPA |
|---|---|
| *on* | [ũ] |
| *en* | [ʌ̃] |
| : (colon) | [ː] (vowel length) |
| ' (apostrophe) | [ʔ] |
| ´ (acute accent) | high or rising pitch |
| ` (grave accent) | falling tone |

(3)  Mohawk: Konwatsi'tsaién:ni Rita Phillips, speaker

| *Ó:nen* | *ki'* | *iá:ken'* |
|---|---|---|
| ó:nen | ki' | iak-en-' |
| now | in.fact | one-say-s |
| now | in fact | one says |

'Now then, they say,

| *karhá:kon* | *niahatitakhenóntie'* |
|---|---|
| ka-rh-ak-on | n-i-a-ha-ti-takhe-n-ontie' |
| it-tree-be.in-is | there-thither-FACTUAL-they-all-run-to.there-along |
| place in the forest | they started running thither into it |
| they raced off into the forest | |

| *wahonhiákha'* | *sewahió:wane'.* |
|---|---|
| wa-h-on-ahi-ak-ha' | se-w-ahi-owane-e' |
| FACTUAL-they-all-fruit-pick-go.and | one-it-fruit-big-is |
| they went to pick fruit | apple |
| to go pick apples.' | |

In some languages, the boundaries between some words are not as clear. For example, how many words are there in the English term *ice cream* or *ice-cream*? ***All languages change over time, and many aspects of language can change, including the boundaries between words***. When two or more words occur together very frequently in speech, especially when they come to represent a single idea like 'ice cream,' speakers may begin to process them as a single unit, rather than composing the expression anew, word by word, each time they refer to it. The merging of words into a single cognitive unit can occur gradually over time. It is in such cases of change in progress that speakers may be uncertain of word boundaries.

Speaker intuitions usually provide the best indication of boundaries between words (although in some cases standardized spelling conventions can interfere with intuitions). But individual languages may provide additional kinds of evidence. ***In most languages, words can be pronounced alone, but individual morphemes often cannot.*** The Mohawk *-rh-* in 'forest' above would never be pronounced by itself; speakers would not even recognize it if it were. Similarly, if I asked you what English *t* means, you probably would not recognize it as the past tense suffix at the end of *look-ed* [lʊk-t].

Speakers can pause between words: *I . . . don't really want to*. But they rarely if ever pause between the morphemes inside of a word: *Lightn . . . ing was flashing in all direct . . . ions*. This is true for Mohawk as well as for English. If Mohawk speakers are interrupted in the middle of a word, they go back and start over at the beginning. Speakers sometimes insert parenthetical information between words: *I . . . if you want to know the truth . . . don't really want to*. But they do not insert such asides between morphemes: *Lightn . . . really scary . . . ing was flashing*. This suggests that ***words are not usually produced morpheme by morpheme as speakers talk; words are stored as single cognitive units, and selected from memory as wholes for speech***.

***In many languages, it is easy to identify words on the basis of phonological evidence***. Perhaps the most obvious type of phonological evidence is the location of stress. Recall that the term "stress" refers to the relative prominence of a syllable in the word. A syllable with primary stress will often have special pitch, it may be louder, and it may last longer than an unstressed syllable. In some languages, primary stress regularly falls on a certain syllable. In Finnish, for example, stress occurs on the first syllable of each word: *aasi* 'donkey,' *perhonen* 'butterfly,' *välimatka* 'distance,' *valoku-vauskone* 'camera.' In Spanish, primary stress (apart from specific exceptions) falls on the second-to-last syllable: *burro* 'donkey,' *mariposa* 'butterfly,' *biblioteca* 'library.' Mohawk shows the same pattern as Spanish. The accent marks in the Mohawk examples in (2) and (3) above indicate stressed syllables. ***Other types of phonological evidence can provide clues to the boundaries between words as well, though these differ from language to language***.

Does wordhood matter? It can. Often what can be said in one word in a language can also be said, more or less, with multiple words in the same language. But there are usually differences in meaning, although they may be subtle. A number of the morphemes in the Mohawk word in (4a) could be expressed with separate words. If, for example, you and I had been looking for something else beforehand, and I wanted us to shift the goal of our search, it would be more appropriate to name the house separately, as in (4b).

(4)  Mohawk
   a. *Teninonhsihsákha.*          'Let's go look for the house'
      let's go house seek

   b. *Kanónhsote'*                     *tenihsákha.*          'Let's go look for <u>the house</u>'
      it house stands          let's seek

Another example can be seen in Lakhota, a Siouan language of the Plains. Both (5a) and (5b) could be translated 'I made it/them black.'

(5)  Lakhota (Stan Redbird, speaker p.c.)
   a. *Sabwáye.*          'I made it/them black.'
      I blackened

   b. *Sápa*          *wakáǧe.*          'I made it/them black.'
      black          I made

**SIDEBAR 4.3**
TRANSCRIPTION NOTE

| Lakhota symbol | IPA | Phonetic description |
|---|---|---|
| ´ (acute accent) | ['] | primary stress |
| ǧ | [ɣ] | voiced velar fricative |

When asked about the difference, the speaker, Mr. Redbird, explained that if he had just polished his boots he would use (5a). If he had hung a kettle over the fire to start a stew cooking, then returned some time later to find that the flames had come up and eventually left soot on the bottom of the kettle, he would use (5b). The first sentence indicates a single, direct action, while the second is appropriate for a longer string of events and indirect consequences.

## 4.2  Kinds of morphemes

**SIDEBAR 4.4**
HYPHENS

A hyphen on the left of a morpheme, as in the plural -*s*, indicates that that morpheme must attach to something on its left. A hyphen on the right, as in *un*-, indicates that the morpheme must attach to something on its right. Bound morphemes are always written with a hyphen on at least one side.

Morphemes, the building blocks of words, can be classified in several ways. One distinction is between **free morphemes** and **bound morphemes**. *Free morphemes are those that can stand alone as words.* In the English phrase we saw at the outset, the morphemes *believe, weigh, loss, break*, and *through* are all free, because they can be used as words on their own. All of the morphemes in the Engenni sentence in (1) are free: *á* 'one,' *ta* 'go,' *na* 'to,' *wa* 'seek,' and *ọmù* 'house.' In the Mohawk sentence in (3), the words *ó:nen* 'now' and *ki'* 'in fact' are free. ***Bound morphemes are morphemes*** *that never occur as words on their own*. The English morphemes *un-*, *-able*, and *-s* are all bound. Sidebar 4.4 explains the use of hyphens in writing out morphemes.

Another way to classify morphemes is into **roots** and **affixes**. Roots are considered the foundation of the word. *Every word has a root at its core*. The root usually conveys the main meaning of the word. The root of *un-believ-able*, for example, is *believe*. **Affixes are morphemes that attach to roots and modify their meaning in some way**. The morphemes *un-*, *-able*, and *-s* are all affixes. Affixes never stand alone as words; they are bound (see Sidebar 4.5).

Affixes can also be classified according to where they occur: before the root, after the root, on both sides of the root, or inside the root. We can see each of these kinds of affixes in Ilocano, a language of the Austronesian family spoken in the Philippines.

*A **prefix** is a type of affix that appears before the root*, like the English *un-* of *un-believable*. Compare the Ilocano words in the left column in (6) with those on the right.

(6)  Ilocano prefix (Rubino 1997)

|  |  |  |  |
|---|---|---|---|
| *amianan* | 'north' | *taga-amianan* | 'Northerner' |
| *abagatan* | 'south' | *taga-abagatan* | 'Southerner' |
| *bantay* | 'mountain' | *taga-bantay* | 'from the mountains' |
| *ili* | 'town' | *taga-ili* | 'from town' |
| *Amerika* | 'America' | *taga-amerika* | 'American' |

**SIDEBAR 4.6**

TRANSCRIPTION NOTE

| Ilocano symbol | IPA |
|---|---|
| ng | [ŋ] |
| y | [j] |

The prefix *taga-* forms words for origin or nationality from words for places.

*A **suffix** is a type of affix that occurs after the root*, like the English *-able* of *unbeliev-able*. Compare the Ilocano words in the left column in (7) with those on the right.

(7)  Ilocano suffix (Rubino 1997)

|  |  |  |  |
|---|---|---|---|
| *giling* | 'grind' | *giling-an* | 'grinder' |
| *sagat* | 'strain' | *sagat-an* | 'strainer' |
| *balkot* | 'wrap' | *balkot-an* | 'wrapper' |
| *timbeng* | 'weigh' | *timbeng-an* | 'balance, scale' |

Adding the suffix *-an* to a verb can create a noun. Affixes that create nouns are called **nominalizers**. The nouns in (7) designate instruments. This particular suffix can thus be called an instrumental nominalizer.

*An infix is a type of affix that appears inside of the root.*

(8)   Ilocano infix (Rubino 1997)

| | | | |
|---|---|---|---|
| *kuton* | 'ant' | *k-in-uton* | 'ant-infested' |
| *gayaman* | 'centipede' | *g-in-ayaman* | 'infested with centipedes' |
| *ngilaw* | 'fly' | *ng-in-ilaw* | 'fly-infested' |
| *kuto* | 'lice' | *k-in-uto* | 'lice-infested' |

The Ilocano infix *-in-* adds the meaning 'infested.' **When we describe an infix, we always specify where in the root it is inserted**. Here the infix is inserted after the first consonant of the noun: *k-in-uton* 'ant-infested.' (The sequence of letters *ng* is used in the practical spelling system to represent a velar nasal [ŋ], a single consonant.) Infixes are much rarer in the languages of the world than prefixes and suffixes.

**Circumfixes *wrap around the root***, with part occurring before and part after.

(9)   Ilocano circumfix (Rubino 1997)

| | | | |
|---|---|---|---|
| *ragsak* | 'happy' | *pag-ragsak-en* | 'make someone happy' |
| *leddaang* | 'sad' | *pag-leddaang-en* | 'make someone sad' |
| *uray* | 'wait' | *pag-uray-en* | 'make someone wait' |
| *awid* | 'go home' | *pag-awid-en* | 'make someone go home' |

The circumfix *pag-...-en* adds the meaning 'make' or 'cause.' It is called a **causative**. For another example of circumfixes, see Textbox 4.1.

**Words may contain more than one prefix, more than one suffix, or combinations of both**, as in many of the Mohawk words seen earlier.

(10)   Mohawk verb from (3)
*niahatitakhenóntie'*
n-i-a-ha-ti-takhe-n-ontie'
there-thither-FACTUAL-they-all-run-to.there-along
'they started running thither into it'

It is important to note that there are no infixes in this word. The morphemes *n-* 'there,' *i-* 'thither,' *a-* FACTUAL, *ha-* 3 (THIRD PERSON), and *ti-*PL (PLURAL) are all prefixes, because they all occur before the root. No morpheme appears inside of the root *-takhe-* 'run.' Many languages, among them Turkish and the Eskimo-Aleut languages, contain only suffixes. Some others, among them Navajo and other Athabaskan languages, contain only prefixes.

**Words may also contain more than one root**. Such words are called **compounds**. English is particularly rich in compounds. English speakers frequently combine roots, even full words, to create new words, such as *break-through*, *pig-pen*, *hot-dog*, and many more. Frequently used word-formation processes are said to be highly **productive**; this concept is further discussed in Textbox 4.2. Newer compounds are often still written as two words, even when they are pronounced and understood as a term for a single idea. The Mohawk example seen earlier in (4a) is also a compound, built on the noun root *-nonhs-* 'house' and the verb root *-ihsak* 'seek': *teni-nonhs-ihsák-ha* 'Let's go house-hunting.'

## TEXTBOX 4.1 CIRCUMFIXES

Circumfixes, like infixes, are relatively rare among the languages of the world. Often they originated as a combination of a prefix and a suffix that, over time, came to have a meaning of its own. In Example (7) we saw the suffix *-an* that is used to form nouns in Ilocano. Ilocano now has several circumfixes that form terms for places, which must have originated as a combination of some prefix with the nominalizer suffix *-an*. The locative nominalizer *pag- . . . -an* creates names of places from verbs that denote the kind of activity typically done there. The locative nominalizer *ka-. . .-an* creates names of places from nouns referring to objects characteristic of those places.

**TABLE 4.1** Ilocano locative nominalizers (Rubino 1997)

| *adal* | 'study' | *pag-adal-an* | 'school' |
| *langoy* | 'swim' | *pag-langoy-an* | 'swimming pool' |
| *pabuya* | 'show' | *pag-pabuya-an* | 'theater' |
| *sugal* | 'gamble' | *pag-sugal-an* | 'casino' |
| *darat* | 'sand' | *ka-darat-an* | 'sandy place' |
| *ubas* | 'grape' | *ka-ubas-an* | 'vineyard' |
| *pinia* | 'pineapple' | *ka-pinia-an* | 'pineapple field' |
| *mangga* | 'mango' | *ka-mangga-an* | 'mango plantation' |

## TEXTBOX 4.2 PRODUCTIVITY

Productive morphological processes are those that speakers use to create new words. Noun-noun compounding is very **productive** in English: it is a constant source of new words. Some affixes are highly productive as well, like the nominalizer *-ness* of words like *shortsighted-ness*. Others are less productive, like the nominalizer *-hood* in *woman-hood*. Some are no longer productive at all, like the nominalizer *-t* of *weigh-t*. To see just how productive noun-noun compounding is in English, listen to the speech around you for a noun-noun compound that is new to you.

## 4.3  Finding morphemes: morphological analysis

How do we know what the morphemes are in a word? Speakers themselves are rarely conscious of morphological structure unless they have studied grammar. They obviously have some unconscious knowledge of morphology – we see this when they create new words – but few could explain it. If we cannot ask speakers about morphology, how can we discover it in a language?

Morphological analysis is usually done by comparing sets of words, as we did for the Ilocano examples on the last several pages. ***If we find two similar words, one with a particular sequence of sounds and one without it, we can compare the meanings of the words and hypothesize that the additional sequence of sounds adds the additional meaning.*** Consider the following examples from English:

(11)  English word pairs

*happy*      *cool*
*unhappy*   *uncool*

The meanings of the words with *un-* are the opposite of those without. We can hypothesize that English has a prefix *un-* meaning 'not.'

Now examine the pairs of words below from Karo, a language of the Tupi-Guaraní family spoken in the Brazilian Amazon.

(12)  Karo verbs (Gabas 1999)

| | |
|---|---|
| *kə* | 'walk' |
| *takə* | 'make (someone) walk while walking alongside of him or her' |
| *ket* | 'sleep' |
| *taket* | 'put (someone) to sleep and sleep alongside him or her' |
| *noga* | 'eat' |
| *tanoga* | 'feed (someone) while eating with him or her' |

Each of these verbs can occur with or without the element *ta*. The addition of *ta* to the verbs changes their meaning in a systematic way. It looks like we have a morpheme: a recurring sequence of sounds (*ta*) with a recurring meaning. As far as we can tell from the data in (12), this morpheme never appears on its own as a word: it is bound. Since it appears before roots (rather than after them or inside of them), it is a prefix. Semantically, it adds a sense of causation, causing someone to walk, causing someone to sleep, and causing someone to eat. It is thus a causative. But it adds a more specific meaning than the Ilocano causative we saw earlier. Here the causer is also participating in the caused activity: walking, sleeping, or eating. This Karo prefix *ta-* has been termed a comitative causative. These examples illustrate an important principle of morphological analysis. ***We cannot expect that every word in the free translation will correspond to a specific morpheme in the language under analysis.*** Skillful morphological analysis can require the ability to think beyond the translation to imagine what the actual meaning might be. (Linguists generally use the term **gloss** rather than "translation," because they recognize that morphemes and words in

**SIDEBAR 4.7**

GLOSSING CONVENTIONS

We write the gloss of a morpheme in small caps if it is a grammatical term like PLURAL (PL), NEGATIVE (NEG), CAUSATIVE (CAUS), or NOMINALIZER (NMLZ). If it is a translation, we write it between single quotation marks, like for the Mohawk suffix *-ontie'* 'along.' Material in the target language, that is, the language under study, is usually given in italics, or, when handwritten, underlined.

For this chapter (and all subsequent chapters and language profiles) of this book, a full list of the glossing conventions used in each chapter can be found at the end of the chapter, just prior to the Exercises.

one language do not always have perfect semantic equivalents in another. A *gloss* is simply the best approximation to the meaning. See Sidebar 4.7 for glossing conventions.)

In conducting morphological analysis, we may not always find pairs of words like those in (11) and (12): one without an affix and one with it. Fortunately, there is another strategy for detecting morphemes. We may find sets of words that all contain a particular element, or a certain sequence of sounds. We can then compare the meanings of those words to see what they have in common. ***When a recurring form matches up with a recurring meaning, we can hypothesize that we have a morpheme with that form and that meaning***.

Compare the Karo words in (13).

**(13)** Karo verbs (Gabas 1999)

| | |
|---|---|
| *oyaʔwan* | 'I left' |
| *omãmnoy* | 'I saw myself' |
| *owakán* | 'I am angry' |
| *okǝt* | 'I walked' |

All of these words begin with *o*, though otherwise they are different. One involves leaving, one seeing, one being angry, and one walking. One is in the present, and the others are in the past. But all include the meaning 'I.' We can hypothesize that *o-* is a morpheme meaning 'I.'

## 4.4  The meanings of morphemes

Do all languages express the same kinds of meanings in their morphemes? There certainly are similarities. Many languages have noun roots meaning 'head,' 'fish,' and 'house,' just as in English. Many have verb roots meaning 'eat,' 'catch,' and 'kill.'

But languages also show differences in their inventories of roots. Often roots are simply not equivalent. Central Alaskan Yup'ik, an Eskimo-Aleut language spoken in southwestern Alaska, has roots for 'head' (*nasquq*) and 'house' (*ca*), like the languages in Table 4.2. But the Yup'ik root *neqe-* 'fish' also means 'food' and 'eat.' Furthermore, for many Yup'ik roots, there is simply no single equivalent English root. They can be

**TABLE 4.2** Roots in several different languages

**Some noun roots**

| English | head | fish | house |
|---|---|---|---|
| German | *Kopf* | *Fisch* | *haus* |
| French | *tête* | *poisson* | *maison* |
| Engenni | *ùtòmù* | *èsènì* | *ọmu* |
| Mohawk | *-nontsi* | *-itsi-* | *-nonhs-* |
| Ilocano | *ulo* | *ikán* | *bal* |
| Karo | *naká* | *ip* | *ka'a* |

**Some verb roots**

| English | eat | catch | kill |
|---|---|---|---|
| German | *ess-* | *fang-* | *töt-* |
| French | *mang-* | *attrapp-* | *tu-* |
| Engenni | *dhi* | *kunu* | *gbèi* |
| Mohawk | *-k* | *-iena* | *-rio* |
| Ilocano | *kaan* | *tiliw* | *patay* |
| Karo | *'o* | *'ɨy* | *wĩ* |

translated only with a complex explanation. (The Yup'ik material in this chapter comes from the speech of Elizabeth Charles, Elena Charles, and George Charles, and from Jacobson (1985).)

(14)  Some Yup'ik roots

| | |
|---|---|
| *keniq* | 'front part of a parka cover, gathered up and used as a means of carrying things' |
| *ella* | 'world, outdoors, weather, universe, awareness, sense' |
| *pay'u-* | 'to have one's legs so cramped by cold that one cannot move' |
| *qapiar-* | 'to skin a seal or other animal starting from the head and pulling the skin back over the body, rather than splitting the skin' |
| *taarri-* | 'to swat oneself or another in a steambath to tone muscles and stimulate sweating' |
| *caqvir-* | 'having shoes on the wrong feet' |
| *narurte-* | 'to act against accepted standards of behavior' |

---

### TEXTBOX 4.3 **THE MEANINGS OF AFFIXES**

Although different languages can have similar affix categories, languages exhibit interesting differences. Some languages have no affixes that mark past tense, while others have elaborate sets of past-tense affixes, distinguishing degrees of remoteness, such as 'immediate past,' 'recent past,' 'remote past,' and 'mythic past.' Karo has a basic causative prefix *ma-*, as in *ket* 'sleep,' *ma-ket* 'put someone to sleep'; *kət* 'walk,' *ma-kət* 'make someone walk'; *copɨt* 'be fat,' *ma-copɨt*

'make someone fat.' But as we saw, it also has a more specialized kind of causative prefix *ta-* meaning 'cause and participate in the action.' Yup'ik has an unusually rich array of causative suffixes, which differ in sometimes subtle ways. They add meanings such as 'let,' 'allow,' 'permit,' 'cause,' 'compel,' 'force,' 'deliberately or intentionally cause,' 'try to cause,' 'tend to cause,' and 'wait for' (as in 'wait for something to boil').

---

When we compare the meanings of affixes across languages, we find the same kinds of similarities and differences. Some affix meanings show up in language after language. For example, many languages have past-tense affixes, comparable to English -*ed*. Many have plural affixes, comparable to English -*s*. Many have nominalizers, like the Ilocano suffix -*an* we saw in *giling-an* 'grind-er' and the English suffix -*er*. Many have causatives like the Ilocano circumfix in *pag-ragsak-en* 'make someone happy.'

As seen in Textbox 4.3, affix meanings can vary across languages. Look at the meanings of the Yup'ik suffixes in (15).

(15)  Some Yup'ik suffixes

| | | | |
|---|---|---|---|
| *-kuaq* | 'leftover' | *arucetaar* | 'dried fish skin' |
| | | *arucetaar-kuaq* | 'uneaten, leftover dried fish skin' |
| *-kuar-* | 'go by way of' | *imarpig* | 'sea' |
| | | *imarpig-kuar-* | 'go by sea' |
| *-liqe-* | 'be afflicted in' | *ilu* | 'inside, digestive track' |
| | | *ilu-liqe-* | 'have a stomach-ache' |
| *-illiqe-* | 'suffer from lack of' | *murak* | 'wood' |
| | | *mura-illiqe-* | 'suffer from the lack of wood' |
| *-ir-* | 'have cold' | *it'ga-* | 'foot' |
| | | *it'ga-ir-* | 'have cold feet' |
| *-taq* | 'caught object' | *pi* | 'thing' |
| | | *pitaq* | 'caught animal or bird' |
| *-tar-* | 'gather from nature' | *mer* | 'water' |
| | | *mer-tar-* | 'fetch water' |

The verb *mer-tar-* is used, for example, for getting water from a river. For getting water from a faucet or barrel, a different suffix, -*ssaag-*, is used.

---

### TEXTBOX 4.4 **YUP'IK IN USE**

*cucuklillruunga.*
cucuke-li-llru-u-nga
choose-become-PST-IND-1SG
'I voted.'

**Figure 4.1** A sticker that reads "I Voted" in Yup'ik

---

### TEXTBOX 4.5 **MEANINGS IN ROOTS AND AFFIXES**

Meanings are not always distributed between roots and affixes as we might expect. What is expressed by a root in one language might be indicated by an affix in another. Consider the Yup'ik word below, which is a sentence in itself.

*Iruartaa.*
iru-art-a-a
leg-hit.in-TR.IND-3SG/3SG
'She hit him in the leg.'

This verb has just one root, *iru-* 'leg.' We might expect 'hit' to be conveyed by a root as well, but here it is the suffix *-art-*. But how do we know that *-art-* is really a suffix? In Yup'ik, every noun and verb begins with one and only one root. Only roots can occur at the beginning of a word, and they always appear at the beginning. All other morphemes in the word are suffixes. Suffixes never appear at the beginning of a word; they can occur only after a root or another suffix. Yup'ik also has roots meaning 'hit.'

---

### SIDEBAR 4.8
TRANSCRIPTION NOTE (YUP'IK STANDARD ORTHOGRAPHY)

| Yup'ik | IPA | Phonetic description |
|---|---|---|
| e | [ə] | |
| ng | [ŋ] | |
| ll | [ɬ] | voiceless lateral fricative |
| g | [ɣ] | voiced velar fricative |
| q | [q] | voiceless uvular stop |
| r | [ʀ] | voiced uvular trill |

*The affixes that develop in languages are no accident. They grow out of distinctions that speakers have chosen to express most often in daily speech, over generations, centuries, even millennia.* Some affixes reflect concepts that are important to human beings all over the world, like causation. Others reflect the environmental and cultural concerns of individual societies. Textbox 4.5 discusses the meanings expressed by roots and affixes.

## 4.5 The shapes of morphemes

Once we identify a morpheme, can we be confident that it will always show up with the same form? Let's consider English plurals. To form a plural, it looks like we just add -s.

(16) English plurals

| | |
|---|---|
| *newt* | *newt-s* |
| *skink* | *skink-s* |
| *toad* | *toad-s* |
| *frog* | *frog-s* |
| *tadpole* | *tadpole-s* |
| *chameleon* | *chameleon-s* |
| *salamander* | *salamander-s* |
| *iguana* | *iguana-s* |
| *gecko* | *gecko-s* |

But are all of these suffixes really the same? If you pronounce the plural words carefully, you'll notice that they do not all end in the same sound. Some end in voiceless [s], and some end in voiced [z]. Pronounce the plural nouns in (16), checking whether you can hear the difference. Are these just allophones in English, or are they separate phonemes? To find out, we look for minimal pairs. There are plenty of them: *sip* and *zip* are different words, for example, with different meanings. The sounds /s/ and /z/ are thus separate phonemes in English.

If English speakers hear a new noun, they somehow know which form to use for the plural. What word would you use to talk about more than one *swip*? How about more than one *grib*? Speakers automatically use the voiceless /s/ with *swips*, and the voiced /z/ with *gribs*, though they have never heard these words before.

As we saw in Chapter 3, if we look carefully at where each form occurs, we see a pattern. The voiceless plural /s/ comes after nouns ending in *p*, *t*, and *k*. The voiced plural /z/ comes after nouns ending in *d*, *g*, *l*, *n*, *r*, *w*, *y*, and vowels. **We can make a generalization about these contexts**: the form /s/ occurs only after voiceless sounds, and the form /z/ occurs only after voiced sounds. The alternate forms of a morpheme, like the /s/ and /z/ plural here, are called **allomorphs**. (Note that the plural of *allomorph* uses the voiceless /s/, because this word ends in the voiceless sound /f/.) **If we find that a morpheme has allomorphs, we need to mention this in our description of the language, specifying what the various forms are and where they occur.** For our plural allomorphs, we have two forms so far.

(17) -s PLURAL

s used after voiceless sounds

z used after voiced sounds

A description like that in (17) is termed **item and arrangement**: we specify how the items are arranged, that is, where each allomorph occurs.

Allomorphy can be also described in another style, termed **item and process**, using symbols we saw in the chapter on phonology (see Sidebar 4.9). We want to say that the plural suffix becomes voiced after a voiced sound. We begin with the basic sound, here *s*. We then add an arrow → for 'becomes' or 'is pronounced.' To the right of the arrow, we specify how it changed (in this case by becoming voiced). Next is a slash /, which announces that the context is coming up. The blank __ shows us where the sound in question fits into the context.

(18)  *-s*  PLURAL

-s   → [+voiced] / [+voiced] __

-s   becomes voiced in the context after any voiced sound

Are *-s* and *-z* the only allomorphs of the English plural? What about the plural of *grouse?* How about *thrush* and *finch?* How about *partridge?* Even if you can't recognize a thrush, you probably know that its plural would be pronounced with [əz]. We find the same plural with *grouse, finch,* and *partridge.* The voicing rule we worked out in (18) doesn't seem to be working here. Are these erratic exceptions? No, we just need an additional rule. The nouns *grouse, thrush, finch,* and *partridge* all end in hissing fricatives or affricates called **stridents** or **sibilants**. This, too, is systematic. Our new analysis might look something like this.

(19)  *-s*  PLURAL

-s   → əz / [+strident] __

-s   → [+voiced] / [+voiced] __

Anyone who has learned another language after childhood knows that allomorphs can make the task harder. Why would a language have them? Sometimes the answer is hidden in the history of the language, but this time, we can see some reasons. When speakers already have their vocal folds vibrating at the end of a noun (a noun ending in a voiced sound like *b, d, g, v, l, n, r, a, e, o,* etc.), it would take extra work to interrupt the vibration and cut off the voicing in order to produce a voiceless /s/. It is easier to just let the vibration continue to the end of the word. This allomorphy allows speakers to expend less effort. But what about the other allomorph, the /əz/ we find after stridents? If we pronounced the plural of a noun like *grouse* with just /s/, it would be nearly impossible to hear the suffix: [graʊss]. The added vowel helps listeners hear the plural. These are two of the many forces that are always at work shaping the development of languages: ease for speakers and clarity for hearers.

Now what about the plurals *cactus/cacti, phenomenon/phenomena,* and *cherub/ cherubim?* Are these just random irregularities? Not really. They are indeed exceptions to our

**SIDEBAR 4.10**
THE BATTLE OF THE PATTERNS

Not all nouns adopted from Latin into English have *-i* plurals. The plurals of *virus* and *census*, for example, are *virus-es* and *census-es*. How come? Human beings are masters at detecting patterns, in language and elsewhere. The patterns come into play as we speak. The result can be regularization. The plurals of *virus* and *census* have been remodeled in accordance with the major native English pattern of plural formation /-s/~/-z/~/-əz/. Remodeling need not occur all at once. The English plural of *cactus*, for example, is usually *cact-i*, particularly in botanical contexts, but the form *cactus-es* can be heard from native English speakers as well.

rules, but there are reasons they exist. These nouns were brought into English from other languages, specifically Latin, Greek, and Hebrew. The English speakers who originally adopted them knew enough about the donor languages to bring their plural forms along with them. The suffix *-i* in *cact-i* is a Latin plural, the suffix *-a* is a Greek plural, and the suffix *-im* is a Hebrew plural. When enough nouns have been brought into one language from another, and their plural forms have been brought in along with them, speakers may begin to discern this pattern and apply it to new forms they encounter with the same endings. If English speakers want to pluralize a word ending in *-us* (which happens to be a singular ending in Latin), they may decide that it should follow the same pattern as *cactus* and pluralize it with *-i*, even if they have not heard its plural form and don't know whether it came from Latin. Sidebar 4.10 further explains how such patterns may come to be regularized.

We have seen two kinds of allomorphy. The plural allomorphs *-s*, *-z*, and *-əz* are said to be **phonologically conditioned**. The choice of which allomorph to use depends simply on the sound before it: *-əz* is used after stridents, *-s* is used after other voiceless sounds, and *-z* used after other voiced sounds. The plural allomorphs *-i*, *-a*, and *-im* are said to be **lexically conditioned**. One simply has to know the word (lexeme) it is attached to in order to know the plural.

Now let's look at allomorphy in another language. Ilocano has a prefix that can form verbs meaning 'move an object to the location specified by the root.'

(20)  Ilocano verbalizer

| | | | |
|---|---|---|---|
| *sakmol* | 'inside of mouth' | *i-sakmol* | 'put something into the mouth' |
| *ruar* | 'outside' | *i-ruar* | 'take something outside' |
| *ditoy* | 'here' | *i-ditoy* | 'put something here' |
| *ngato* | 'high, up' | *i-ngato* | 'put something up' |
| *baba* | 'down, below' | *i-baba* | 'put something down' |
| *abut* | 'hole' | *y-abut* | 'put something in a hole' |
| *uneg* | 'inside' | *y-uneg* | 'put something inside' |
| *abay* | 'side' | *y-abay* | 'place beside, compare' |

Ilocano seems to have a **verbalizer** prefix *i-*: it turns words into verbs. But when we reach the pair *abut* 'hole,' *yabut* 'put something in a hole,' we see a change in the shape of the prefix. Here the prefix is *y-*. (The letter *y* in the Ilocano spelling system represents a palatal glide, IPA [j].) The forms *i-* and *y-* appear in the same position in

**SIDEBAR 4.11**

ORIGINS OF ALLOMORPHY

Try pronouncing the sequence *i-abay* several times quickly. You will note that with speed, the vowel naturally turns into a glide. This is one of the ways that allomorphs can develop in languages over time.

the word, immediately before the root, and they contribute the same meaning, 'put something somewhere.' These two facts together suggest that we have one morpheme with two allomorphs, that is, two forms of the same morpheme. Sidebar 4.11 illustrates one of the ways in which allomorphy can first arise.

When it appears that we have two (or more) allomorphs, we look to see where each one occurs. When we have phonologically conditioned allomorphs, **the distribution of allomorphs is usually determined by the sounds directly preceding or following them**. Since there is nothing before our prefix here, the most promising place to look is after it. We find:

*i-*     before *s, r, d, ng, b*
*y-*     before *a, u*

(Recall that *ng* is a digraph representing the single consonant [ŋ].) Can we make any generalizations about the context, as we did for the English plural? The *i-* occurs only before consonants, and the *y-* only before vowels. This situation is called **complementary distribution**. In Chapter 3, we saw allophones of a single phoneme in complementary distribution; we now see that allomorphs of a single morpheme can also be in this relationship. The two forms of our prefix never occur in the same context, a confirmation that we do have allomorphs. We can now describe our prefix with its allomorphs.

(21)   *i-*     VERBALIZER
       i → y / __ V

This rule says that the sound *i* is pronounced *y* before a vowel.

Note that roots can have allomorphs as well. Compare *leaf* and *leaves*: /lif/ ~ /liv/.

## 4.6   Are affixes always pieces of words?

Consider the English nouns *mouse/mice* and *man/men*. These plurals seem irregular: they don't match our rules. But they are not random. They are the result of a sequence of developments in the history of the English language, each of which made sense at the time. But how do we describe these plurals today? Do these forms have a plural affix? The answer is yes, but this affix has a different character from the prefixes, suffixes, infixes, and circumfixes we've seen. Here the plural affix could not be described as a piece of a word that is added, but as a change internal to the root. **Sometimes affixes are simply changes in a form, not necessarily pieces added**. This is true of the plurals of *mouse* and *man*: in both, plurality is signaled by a change in the vowel. It is also true of the past tense on verbs like *see/saw* and *run/ran*.

This allomorphy is lexically conditioned, because these changes could not be predicted on the basis of the sounds of the roots alone.

Now compare the Engenni verbs in (22). The marks over the vowels indicate tone. The absence of a mark indicates high tone, and an acute accent (è) indicates low tone.

**(22)** Engenni (Thomas 1978)

*dire*  'cook'
*dìre*  'cooks'
*dirè*  'will cook'

The verb *dire* 'cook' alone has high tone on both syllables (HH). The word *dìre* 'cooks' has low tone on the first syllable and high tone on the second (LH). The future form *dirè* 'will cook' has high tone on the first syllable and low on the second (HL). Here, too, it is easier to describe the tenses as changes made to the root than as pieces of words. The present-tense affix is a LH tone structure, while the future-tense affix is a HL structure.

## 4.7  Words, lexemes, and lexicalization

At the beginning of this chapter, we considered how to identify words in an unfamiliar language. We can now take this question a bit further. Consider the English words *lizard* and *lizards*. We know that they are different words. But we would not expect to find both in a dictionary; we will find only *lizard*. The same is true of the words *talk*, *talked*, and *talking*. They are all different words, but we will find only *talk* in the dictionary. Words like *lizard* and *lizards* are said to belong to the same **lexeme**. Similarly, *talk*, *talked*, and *talking* belong to the same lexeme. The plural suffix *-s* on *lizard* does not form a new vocabulary item; it simply gives us another form of the same one, used for referring to more than one of the item denoted by the word. A **lexeme** is a basic vocabulary item, something we might find as an entry in a dictionary (or in our mental lexicon).

Morphology that does not form a new lexeme, like the plural *-s* on nouns and *-ed* and *-ing* on verbs, is called **inflection**. Inflectional affixes never change the word class of the word that they attach to. *Gavotte* is a noun, and the plural *gavotte-s* is still a noun. Inflectional affixes tend to be highly productive. If we learn a new English count noun like *gavotte*, we expect that it will have a plural, though we may not always be able to predict the form of the plural. ***Inflectional affixes tend to contribute predictable meanings***. If we know that the noun *gavotte* means 'a medium-paced dance popular in the eighteenth century,' we may never have heard it in the plural, but we can predict that *gavotte-s* will mean more than one *gavotte*. For examples of some inflectional affixes in English, see Textbox 4.6.

Languages differ in the meanings expressed in their inflectional morphology, though certain inflectional categories appear in language after language. Plural and tense

---

**TEXTBOX 4.6 SOME INFLECTIONAL MORPHEMES IN ENGLISH**

| -s | PLURAL | *Plums are delicious* |
| -s | 3RD SINGULAR SUBJECT PRESENT | *Sharon changes her car's oil herself* |
| -ed | PAST TENSE | *Voters rejected the measure on the ballot* |
| -ing | PRESENT PROGRESSIVE | *Sarah is riding her bike today* |

These English inflectional affixes can be contrasted with some English derivational affixes, as seen in Textbox 4.8.

---

inflection are both common cross-linguistically. Another common kind of inflectional morphology is **case**. To see what case morphology can do, look at the Latvian sentences given in (23).

(23)  Latvian (Uldis Balodis, p.c.)

a. *Laukā     dzīvo     tārps.*
   field     live.3     worm
   'A worm lives in the field.'

b. *Lauk     ir       liels.*
   field     COP.3     big
   'The field is big.'

c. *Putns     ēd     tārpu.*
   bird     eat.3     worm
   'A bird is eating the worm.'

d. *Putnā     tagad     dzīvo     tārps.*
   bird     now     live.3     worm
   'The worm now lives in the bird.'

e. *Vīrs     ēd     putnu.*
   man     eat.3     bird
   'A man is eating the bird.'

f. *Meža     dzīvo     vilks.*
   forest     live.3     wolf
   'A wolf lives in the forest.'

g. *Mežs     ir     baismīgs.*
   forest     COP.3     terrifying
   'The forest is terrifying.'

h. *Vilks     ēd     vīru.*
   wolf     eat.3     man
   'The wolf is eating the man.'

i. *Vilkā     tagad     dzīvo     tārps.*
   wolf     now     live.3     worm
   'The worm now lives in the wolf.'

---

**SIDEBAR 4.12**

TRANSCRIPTION NOTE: LATVIAN STANDARD ORTHOGRAPHY

| Latvian symbol | IPA |
|---|---|
| *o* | [uə] |
| *ie* | [ɪə] |
| *ž* | [ʒ] |

---

Each of the nouns occurs in several sentences. Now look more closely at the forms of these nouns. Start with the word for 'field.' In (23a) it is *laukā*, but in (23b) it is *lauks*. Look at the words for 'bird.' In (23c) it is *putns*, in (23d) it is *putnā*, and in (23e) it is *putnu*. Take a moment to see whether you can tell why the forms keep changing. The other nouns show similar changes.

Each Latvian noun here contains a suffix that identifies its role in the sentence. These suffixes are what are termed case-markers. The ending *-s* indicates that the noun is the subject.

The word *putn-s* 'bird' is the subject of (23c) 'The bird is eating the worm.' Morphemes that identify subjects, like this *-s*, are called **nominative** case-markers. The word *putn-u* 'bird' is the direct object of (23e): 'The man is eating the bird.' Morphemes that identify objects, like the *-u*, are called **accusative** case-markers. The word *putn-ā* specifies a location in (23d): 'The worm lives in the bird.' The *-ā* is a **locative** case suffix. Case morphology occurs in languages all over the world, though certainly not in every language. Languages that do have case morphology show fascinating variation in the number and functions of their case categories. Latvian itself has other case categories in addition to those shown here. The origins of several of the Latvian words given here are discussed in Textbox 4.7.

---

### TEXTBOX 4.7 **LATVIAN**

Look again at the Latvian words in (23). Do any look like words with similar meanings in other languages that you know? Latvian is spoken at the eastern end of the Baltic Sea, across from Sweden. It is remotely related to English: both are descended from the same ancestral language, Indo-European. Several of the Latvian words in (23) have English cognates that are words descended from the same Indo-European word. The Proto-Indo-European root for 'wolf,' for example, is reconstructed as *wilkʷ-,

nominative form *wlkʷ-os. The Latvian root is *vilk-*, nominative *vilk-s*. The Proto-Indo-European verb root *hed-* is the ancestor of Latin *ed-*, Latvian *ēd*, and English *eat*. The Proto-Indo-European noun *uiHró-* 'free man' developed into Latin *vir* and Latvian *vīr-* 'man.' Proto-Indo-European had case suffixes, which continued into Latin, Latvian, and other languages in the family. English also once had case suffixes, but they have been lost.

---

Not all morphology is inflectional. Morphological processes that create new lexemes are **derivational**. From the root *talk*, a new lexeme was created in the twentieth century: *talk-ie* 'a film with a soundtrack, as distinct from a silent film.' This suffix *-ie* is not fully productive: there are many nouns that speakers would not add it to. Can you imagine a word *window-ie*? ***Derivational suffixes do not necessarily add predictable meaning***. If you only knew the root *talk*, would you be able to predict the meaning of *talkie*? ***Derivational morphology can change the word class of the lexeme it is applied to***, though this is not always the case. (See Textbox 4.8 for some examples of derivational affixes in English.) The nominalizers and verbalizers we saw earlier are derivational affixes. Added to the English verb *govern*, the derivational suffix *-ment* creates a new noun: *government*. Added to the Yup'ik noun *imarpig* 'sea,' the derivational suffix *-kuar-* 'go by way of' creates a new verb: *imarpig-kuar-* 'go by sea.'

Speakers recognize the difference between those words that already exist in their language and those that could but have not yet been created. This knowledge is sometimes referred to as the mental lexicon. English speakers know that the words *joyful* and *peaceful* are part of English, and that *giggleful* and *warful* are not, or at least not yet. Words that *do* exist are called actual words. Words that do not yet exist but could, according to patterns already present in the language, are called potential words. When a speaker first coins a new word through derivation or compounding, listeners will

---

**TEXTBOX 4.8  SOME DERIVATIONAL MORPHEMES IN ENGLISH**

Change the part of speech

| | | |
|---|---|---|
| -ing | verb to noun | *Smoking is bad for your health.* |
| -ly | adjective to adverb | *He sings beautifully.* |
| -er, -or | noun to verb | *He's a baker; she's a director.* |
| -en | adjective to verb | *how to blacken the fish* |
| -able | verb to adjective | *That's understandable.* |
| -ment | verb to noun | *the management* |
| -less | without; noun to adjective | *a hopeless situation* |
| en- | noun or adjective to verb | *enable him to succeed* |

Do not change the part of speech

| | | |
|---|---|---|
| -er | comparative | *Try to be friendlier.* |
| re- | do again | *The old friends were happy to reunite.* |
| pre- | before | *She's taking prenatal vitamins.* |
| in-, un- | not | *He's intolerable; she's unassuming.* |
| -ish | sort of | *The fruit was a reddish color.* |

These English derivational affixes can be contrasted with the English inflectional affixes in Textbox 4.6.

---

often recognize it as an innovation. At this point it is called a **nonce formation**. If other speakers pick it up and use it, it can become an accepted part of the vocabulary or lexicon of the language. This process, by which a morphological formation comes to be recognized as an established word in the language, is called **lexicalization**. A lexicalized word will be understood and learned as a unit, rather than processed as a sequence of individual morphemes. It will have a meaning of its own, which may or may not correspond to the sum of its parts. The word *joy-ful* means 'full of joy' (as we would expect), but *aw-ful* no longer means 'full of awe' (though it once did), and *cup-ful* does not mean 'full of cups.'

## 4.8  Typology

Languages are often classified according to their structural characteristics. The classification of languages according to structural traits is a goal of **linguistic typology**, the study of language types. Perhaps the oldest and still most commonly cited typologies are based on morphological structure. Structures like that seen in the Engenni example at the beginning of this chapter, with words that generally consist of just one morpheme, are called **isolating** or **analytic**. Structures like those in Mohawk are called **polysynthetic**, because words tend to be made up of many (poly-) parts put together (synthetic). This typological dimension, roughly the average number of morphemes per word, is called the degree of synthesis. Languages like English and Japanese are often described as "mildly synthetic", that is, their words may consist of more than one morpheme, but they do not generally show the elaborate morphological complexity of languages like Mohawk.

A second frequently cited typological feature is the degree of fusion. This characteristic pertains to the clarity of divisions between morphemes in a word. Morphological structures with sharp boundaries between morphemes are described as **agglutinating**. The

---

### TEXTBOX 4.9 **MOHAWK IN USE**

Tésta'n
te-s-t-a'n
DUPLICATIVE-2SG.A-stand-INCHOATIVE
change.state-you-standing-become
'Stop!'

**Figure 4.2** A stop sign written in Mohawk

---

English word *understandable* shows agglutinating structure: *under-stand-able*. Morphological structures in which boundaries are not clear are described as **fusional**. The English word *men* consists of the root *man* plus plural marking, but it is difficult to pull the two apart. A language may have both agglutinating and fusional structures, like English, but languages often show general tendencies one way or the other. Quechua, a language of Peru, Bolivia, and Chile (one variety is the subject of a Language Profile) is often cited as an agglutinating language. The second line of the South Conchucos Quechua example below shows the individual morphemes in the word. The top line shows how the word is pronounced. The individual shape of each morpheme remains unchanged.

**(24)**   Quechua (Hintz 2008)
Tsaypitakutitsiya:muru:si
tsay-pita-kuti-tsi-ya:-mu-ru-:-si
return-CAUS-PL-far-PST-I-even
'I made them return.'

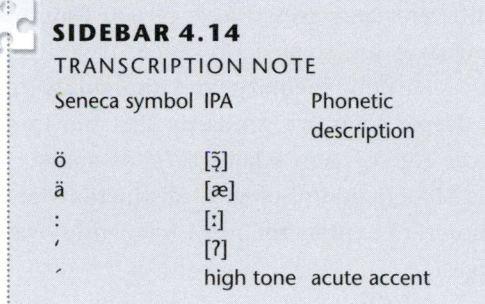

**SIDEBAR 4.13**

TRANSCRIPTION NOTE

| Quechua symbol | IPA | Phonetic description |
|---|---|---|
| : (colon) | [ː] | vowel length |

**SIDEBAR 4.14**

TRANSCRIPTION NOTE

| Seneca symbol | IPA | Phonetic description |
|---|---|---|
| ö | [ɔ̃] | |
| ä | [æ] | |
| : | [ː] | |
| ' | [ʔ] | |
| ´ | high tone | acute accent |

Now compare the Quechua example to the word below in Seneca, an Iroquoian language of present western New York State. (Seneca is also the subject of a Language Profile.) Seneca is more fusional. Again look first at the second line, which shows the shape of each morpheme. Compare this to the top line, which shows what happens when they are combined in a word.

(25)  Seneca (Wallace Chafe, p.c.)
      Ögí:wanä́:go'.
      wa'-wak-rihw-a-nehrako-'
      FACTUAL-me-matter-LINKER-surprise-PFV
      'It surprised me.'

All of the morphemes listed in the second line are present, but a series of historical sound changes have so obscured their boundaries that only people steeped in the history of Iroquoian languages can now decipher them.

## 4.9  Morphology, language, and us

Morphology is connected to both phonology and syntax, but is distinct from each. Some of the patterns we see in phonology have echoes in morphology: just as phonemes can take different forms (allophones) in different contexts, so, too, morphemes can take different forms (allomorphs) in different contexts. (For a discussion of how children learn these forms and contexts, see Textbox 4.10.)

Both morphology and syntax consist of patterns of combining smaller pieces of language to form larger ones: morphemes are combined into words, and words are combined into sentences. But these two levels of structure are not the same. Speakers do not usually exploit their knowledge of morphological patterns, particularly derivational ones, every time they speak. They typically use this knowledge only on certain occasions to invent vocabulary, when they feel the need for a new word.

---

**TEXTBOX 4.10 LEARNING MORPHOLOGY**

Few parents explain affixes and allomorphy to their children. You have probably never heard a parent say: "To make a plural, dear, you must add the suffix -es after sibilants, -s after other voiceless sounds, and -z after other voiced sounds, unless the word requires a special, lexically-conditioned allomorph." Language acquisition occurs naturally, without explicit instruction.

In acquiring language, children often extend regular patterns beyond where they are found in adult speech. For example, children often say *mouses and mans* as the plurals of *mouse and man*. It is clear that the child has learned the regular rule of plural formation and is applying it to all nouns. In time, the child will learn the lexically conditioned forms of the plural and will automatically substitute them for the forms created with the regular plural affix for certain words. Chapter 14 discusses these processes in detail.

Listeners often notice when someone has created a new word, even if the parts are familiar. If I told you my skirt was *unslitable*, you might or might not understand that I cannot make a slit in it, but you would probably realize that you had never heard the term. By contrast, speakers often form new sentences as they speak, on the basis of their knowledge of syntactic patterns. If I told you, *I really want a persimmon-striped umbrella*, your first reaction would probably not be *Gee, I've never heard that sentence before*.

Comparing morphological patterns in different languages reveals certain features characteristic of all human language. Languages are shaped by human cognitive abilities, such as pattern recognition and extension, memory, and the ability to routinize recurring tasks. It is in fact this deeper cognitive similarity that can lead to some of the most interesting differences we see across languages, as speakers automate frequent patterns of expression. Modern morphological distinctions are largely the result of what speakers have chosen to express the most frequently over the course of development of their languages.

## CHAPTER SUMMARY

This chapter has provided a glimpse into the kinds of structures inside words in different languages. We began with the question of how to identify words in an unfamiliar language. The elements that make up words are called morphemes. Morphemes can be classified as bound or free, roots or affixes, prefixes, suffixes, infixes, or circumfixes, and inflectional or derivational. Morphological structure can be discovered in an unfamiliar language, and we can identify and describe alternating forms of morphemes, or allomorphs. Languages can vary widely in their morphological structure: in how much information is typically carried within a word (degree of synthesis) and how clear the boundaries between elements are (degree of fusion). They can also differ in fascinating ways in terms of the kinds of meanings they express. Such differences are not accidental; they grow out of speakers' use of language for everyday communication, and we can see this reflected in how certain words have developed over time. This chapter has begun to reveal the remarkable diversity of linguistic structures; information is packaged and presented in very different ways across languages.

Morphemes are the building blocks of words, and words, in turn, are the building blocks of sentences. How words combine into sentences and the grammatical relationships between words are the central concerns of the field of syntax. But first we'll need to explore in more depth the different kinds of words that one finds in language, and the behaviors and characteristics that allow us to identify word classes.

## TEXTBOX 4.11 **GLOSSING CONVENTIONS USED IN THIS CHAPTER**

| Convention | Meaning | Convention | Meaning |
|---|---|---|---|
| 1 | first person | IND | indicative |
| 2 | second person | LINKER | linking morpheme |
| 3 | third person | NEG | negative |
| A | agent | NMLZ | nominalizer |
| CAUS | causative | PFV | perfective |
| COP | copula | PL | plural |
| DUPLICATIVE | duplicative | PST | past tense |
| FACTUAL | factual | SG | singular |
| INCHOATIVE | inchoative | TR | transitive |

## SUGGESTIONS FOR FURTHER READING

**Aronoff, Mark and Kirsten Fudeman**. 2011. *What is morphology?* (originally published in 2004). Malden, Mass.: Blackwell.

This is a book-length, reader-friendly introduction to morphology, aimed at an audience without prior experience of the field. It covers all of the major topics: wordhood, word classes, inflection and derivation, relations between morphology and phonology, morphology and syntax, morphology and semantics, and productivity.

**Payne, Thomas E**. 1997. *Describing morphosyntax: A guide for field linguists*. Cambridge University Press.

Chapter 2 (on morphological typology) and Chapter 5 (on noun and noun-phrase operations) are especially relevant.

**Sapir, Edward**. 1921. "Form in language: grammatical processes," chapter 4 of *Language: An introduction to the study of speech*. New York: Harcourt, Brace, and World. 57–81.

This little book is a classic, presenting ideas that have captivated linguists for generations. It is well worth reading the whole book through. Chapter 4 discusses morphological structure: compounding, prefixing, suffixing, infixing, internal vocalic change, consonantal change, reduplication, and pitch.

## EXERCISES

1.  Ainu is a language isolate (a language with no known relatives) indigenous to Northern Japan and adjacent Russia. (Data here are drawn from Refsing 1986: 134.)

    | | | | |
    |---|---|---|---|
    | a. *wen* | 'be bad' | *wenno* | 'badly' |
    | b. *pirka* | 'be fine, be good' | *pirkano* | 'well' |
    | c. *esikin* | 'be kind, friendly' | *esikinno* | 'kindly' |
    | d. *araskay* | 'be very able' | *araskayno* | 'successfully' |
    | e. *asin* | 'be new' | *asinno* | 'newly' |

Like many other languages, Ainu does not have a separate adjective category. Qualities are expressed by verbs, like those in the left column above.

Do a complete morphological analysis of the data here.

i. For each lexical category (verb, noun, etc.), provide a list of roots in *italics* with their glosses in 'single quotes.'

ii. For each category, provide a list of affixes (again in *italics*, with appropriate hyphens) with glosses in 'single quotes' for translations, SMALL CAPS for grammatical terms. If you can think of a single-word gloss for your affix(es), use that. If not, provide an explanation of the meaning.

2. The Carib language, a member of the Cariban family, is spoken over the entire coastal area of Guiana. Other members of this language family are found all over northern South America, from Columbia to the mouth of the Amazon and from the coast of Guiana to far into the south and southwest of Brazil. (Data here are drawn from Hoff 1968; colon is used to indicate vowel length, *y* indicates the palatal glide [j], and *ï* represents the high back unrounded vowel [ɯ].)

| | | |
|---|---|---|
| a. *e:ne* | 'see' |
| b. *wose:ne* | 'look at each other' |
| c. *ene:potï* | 'see repeatedly' |
| d. *we:i* | 'become' |
| e. *weipotï* | 'become repeatedly' |
| f. *uxku* | 'try' |
| g. *uxkupo:tï* | 'try again and again' |
| h. *wose:nepo:tï* | 'see each other all the time' |
| i. *ene:kepi* | 'see no longer' |
| j. *se:kapo:ti?ma* | 'tear completely to shreds' |
| k. *wo:mi?ma* | 'go in all together' |
| l. *ema:mï* | 'see day breaking' |
| m. *eka:numï* | 'run' |
| n. *i?ma:tï* | 'run out of' |
| o. *se:kapo:tï* | 'tear to shreds' |
| p. *enï:rï* | 'drink' |
| q. *aki:ma* | 'tease' |
| r. *ema:mï?ma* | 'see dawn turning into daylight' |
| s. *wï:to* | 'go' |
| t. *wo:mï* | 'go in' |
| u. *aki:make:pï* | 'stop teasing' |
| v. *i?matï?ma* | 'run out of completely' |
| w. *enï:rï?ma* | 'drink up' |
| x. *se:ka* | 'tear' |
| y. *wï:topo:tï* | 'go repeatedly' |

Do a complete morphological analysis of the data here.

i. For each lexical category (verb, noun, etc.), provide a list of roots in *italics* with their glosses in 'single quotes.'

ii. For each category, provide a list of affixes (again in *italics*, with appropriate hyphens) with glosses in 'single quotes' for translations, SMALL CAPS for grammatical terms. Different types of affixes (prefixes, suffixes, etc.) should be given in separate lists. If you can think of a single-word gloss for your affix(es), use that. If not, provide an explanation of the meaning.
For the purposes of this problem, ignore vowel length.

3. Daga is spoken in the Owen Stanley Mountains of the Central District of Papua New Guinea. (Data for this problem were drawn from Murane 1974; the orthographic y indicates the palatal glide [j].)

|    |    |    |
| --- | --- | --- |
| a. | *mamana* | 'my father' |
| b. | *inaga* | 'your mother' |
| c. | *yame* | 'his eye(s)' |
| d. | *nanimu* | 'their hands' |
| e. | *goanaya* | 'your livers' |
| f. | *pusinu* | 'our feet' |
| g. | *noga* | 'your mouth' |
| h. | *inana* | 'my mother' |
| i. | *done* | 'its horn' |
| j. | *pusina* | 'my foot, my feet' |
| k. | *yamga* | 'your eye(s)' |
| l. | *evene* | 'his friend' |
| m. | *inase* | 'its tracks' |
| n. | *goanana* | 'my liver' |
| o. | *nonu* | 'our mouths' |
| p. | *yamu* | 'their eyes' |
| q. | *noya* | 'your mouths' |
| r. | *naniga* | 'your hand(s)' |
| s. | *yame* | 'her eye(s)' |
| t. | *inanu* | 'our mother' |
| u. | *mamamu* | 'their father' |
| v. | *inaya* | 'your mother' |
| w. | *goaninu* | 'our younger sibling' |
| x. | *tase* | 'her older sibling' |
| y. | *mamanu* | 'our father' |
| z. | *yamya* | 'your eyes' |

Do a complete morphological analysis of the data here.

i. For each lexical category (verb, noun, etc.), provide a list of roots in *italics* with their glosses in 'single quotes.'

ii. For each category, provide a list of affixes (again in *italics*, with appropriate hyphens) with glosses in 'single quotes' for translations, SMALL CAPS for grammatical terms. Different types of affixes (prefixes, suffixes, etc.) should be given in separate lists. If you can think of a single-word gloss for your affix(es), use that. If not, provide an explanation of the meaning.

iii. Do you have any ideas about whether the roots here are bound or free?

4. Lezgien is a language of the Nakh-Daghestanian family spoken by about 400,000 people in southern Daghestand and northern Azerbaijan in the eastern Caucasus. (Data here are drawn from Haspelmath 1993: 107.)

a. *čajxana*      'teahouse'
b. *ktabxana*     'library'
c. *küčeban*      'idler'
d. *salar*        'kitchen gardens'
e. *quš*          'bird'
f. *sal*          'kitchen garden'
g. *wak'ar*       'pigs'
h. *čaj*          'tea'
i. *qušar*        'birds'
j. *qušarban*     'poultry farmer'
k. *čapxana*      'printing plant'
l. *ktab*         'book'
m. *qahbexana*    'brothel'
n. *nexir*        'herd of cattle'
o. *čap*          'printing'
p. *qahbe*        'prostitute'
q. *nexirban*     'cattle herder'
r. *wak'arban*    'swineherd'
s. *salarban*     'kitchen gardener'
t. *küče*         'street'
u. *čaj*          'tea'

Do a complete morphological analysis of the data here.

i. For each lexical category (verb, noun, etc.), provide a list of roots in *italics* with their glosses in 'single quotes.'

ii. For each category, provide a list of affixes (in *italics*, with appropriate hyphens) with glosses in 'single quotes' for translations, SMALL CAPS for grammatical terms.

5. Samala, also known as Ineseño Chumash, is a Native California language, indigenous to the Santa Inez Valley near Santa Barbara, on the South Coast. It is a member of the Chumashan language family. (Data here are drawn from Applegate 1998. An apostrophe following *p* indicates an ejective bilabial stop.)

**SIDEBAR 4.15**

TRANSCRIPTION NOTE

| Lezgian symbol | IPA | Phonetic description |
|---|---|---|
| č | [tʃ] | |
| š | [ʃ] | |
| x | [χ] | voiceless uvular fricative |
| ü | [y] | |
| k' | [k'] | velar ejective |

a. *salaqwaʔy*    'prepare'
b. *satɨk*        'cure'
c. *suʔinu*       'believe'
d. *siwon*        'play a musical instrument'
e. *sixut*        'burn something'
f. *sukep'*       'give someone a bath'
g. *naʔn*         'go'
h. *alaqwaʔy*     'be ready'
i. *sunaʔn*       'send'
j. *suweʔn*       'put someone to sleep'
k. *atɨk*         'get well'
l. *sutap*        'put something in'

| | |
|---|---|
| m. *ʔinu* | 'be true' |
| n. *iwon* | 'make a sound' |
| o. *kep'* | 'take a bath' |
| p. *sukitwon* | 'take something out' |
| q. *tap* | 'enter' |
| r. *ixut* | 'be on fire' |
| s. *kitwon* | 'emerge' |
| t. *saxkʰit* | 'remember' |
| u. *weʔn* | 'sleep' |
| v. *susaxkʰit* | 'remind' |

Do a complete morphological analysis of the data here.

i. For each lexical category (verb, noun, etc.), provide a list of roots in *italics* with their glosses in 'single quotes.'

ii. For each category, provide a list of affixes (again in *italics*, with appropriate hyphens) with glosses in 'single quotes' for translations, SMALL CAPS for grammatical terms. If there is any allomorphy (changes in the shapes of any morphemes), first explain in words where each allomorph occurs, and then write a rule to describe the situation formally.

6. Burushaski is a language isolate (a language with no known relatives) spoken in Pakistan and India. (Data here come from Lorimer 1935, I:29–34; the orthographic symbol š represents IPA [ʃ] and č represents [tʃ].)

| | sg. | pl. |
|---|---|---|
| a. 'ruler' | *thʌm* | *thʌmo* |
| b. 'crest of spur' | *iriš* | *irišo* |
| c. 'millstone' | *sʌl* | *sʌlo* |
| d. 'lamb' | *ʌčʌs* | *ʌčʌšo* |
| e. 'rope' | *gʌšk* | *gʌško* |
| f. 'bird' | *bʌlʌs* | *bʌlʌšo* |
| g. 'willow shoot' | *ɣʌšk* | *ɣʌško* |
| h. 'boy' | *hilɛs* | *hilɛšo* |
| i. 'hare' | *sər* | *səro* |
| j. 'butterfly' | *holʌlʌs* | *holʌlʌšo* |
| k. 'ox, bull' | *hər* | *həro* |

Do a complete morphological analysis of the data here.

i. Make a list of all roots in each lexical category (nouns, verbs, etc.). Give the roots in *italics*. Give glosses in 'single quotes.'

ii. Make lists of all affixes that occur with each lexical category. Give the affixes in *italics*, with hyphens where appropriate. Give glosses in 'single quotes' if they are translations, and in SMALL CAPS if grammatical terms.

iii. If there are any changes in the forms of any morphemes when they are combined, describe in words the patterns you see. Write a rule or rules describing the changes.

# 5 Word classes: evidence from grammatical behavior

**KEY TERMS**

- Word
- Particular word classes (e.g., noun, verb, etc.)
- Open versus closed class
- Number
- Case
- Head/Dependent
- Paradigm
- Person
- Agreement
- Lexical versus grammatical class
- Particle
- Proximal versus Distal

**CHAPTER PREVIEW**

We have seen that words are constructed by the principled combination of morphemes, and that this gives them internal structures that can be compared and contrasted across languages. This chapter begins the study of how words are then elements in higher-level structures, and how different types of words have different characteristics within such structures. It will describe how words fall into distinct classes, such as noun, verb, adjective, adverb, demonstrative, preposition, and quantifier. It will demonstrate that such classes are determined by the morphological and syntactic behavior of words, not by their meanings. The chapter will present the behavioral properties typical of the most common word classes cross-linguistically. It will further demonstrate the world's remarkable linguistic diversity in showing that not all languages have the same set of word classes; as a result, linguists need to determine which word classes are found in each language independently and which morphosyntactic properties define each class in each language. The ability to understand and identify these behavioral properties of words is a necessary step in conducting syntactic analysis, and will thus be important in later chapters.

**LIST OF AIMS**

At the end of this chapter, students should be able to:

- state why word classes need to be identified by **morphosyntactic behavior**, rather than by meaning;
- identify the most common morphosyntactic properties that characterize the most common word classes in the languages of the world;
- state the major ways in which languages differ with respect to word classes;
- identify the major word classes in sentences in a data set;
- given a data set, present a clear argument that a set of words shares morphosyntactic properties and so constitutes a distinct class.

## 5.1   Words

In this chapter we will move from the study of elements that compose the words of a language to the words themselves. ***A word is an independent, phonologically coherent linguistic unit, containing one or more morphemes, which can fill a particular slot in a sentence***. In a sentence such as *The boy will eat the red apple*, the word *will* can only occur between *boy* and *eat*; moving it can result in a different sentence, *Will the boy eat the red apple?*, or in an ungrammatical sentence: *\*The will boy eat the red apple* (we will follow standard linguistic practice in marking ungrammatical sentences with an asterisk preceding the first word). The word *will* is one member of a class of words, called **auxiliary verbs**, which can only occupy one of two slots in a sentence, the slot directly preceding the verb in a statement (*will eat*), or the slot at the beginning of the sentence in a question (*Will the boy eat?*). In English, all words are restricted syntactically in this way. Try moving the word *red* in the sentence above. You will see that a grammatical sentence occurs only if it is directly preceding a noun. (See Sidebar 5.1.)

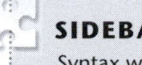

**SIDEBAR 5.1**

Syntax will be presented in detail in the next chapter. Here, we will only refer to the syntactic positioning of words, or how they are ordered with respect to other words in the formation of larger phrases.

### 5.1.1   Identifying word classes

***We can classify words based not only on their syntactic positioning but also on their morphological behavior***. Words such as *red* can be affixed by certain morphemes (*redd-er, redd-est*), but not others (*\*red-tion, \*redd-ed, \*red-ment*). The same morphological behavior is shared by words such as *sweet, hungry, tired, fast, sad, tall*, etc. These words are all members of the same **word class** in English, a class of words that share morphological and syntactic behavior. More specifically, these are members of the word class of **adjectives**.

Many of us were taught in school to identify word classes based on their meanings. For example, I was taught that a noun designates "a person, place, thing, or concept," while verbs are "action words." While these definitions are useful in making children aware of word classes and helping them to develop their linguistic intuitions, ***they are highly problematic as analytical tools used in linguistic analysis***. Take, for example, the word *destruction*. Does this designate an action, a thing, or an abstract concept? How about *flip*? *Flip* is a noun in the sentence *He performed a beautiful flip*, but a verb in the sentence *He flipped the pancakes*. While it is clear that *flip* refers to an action in the latter sentence, it is not clear that it refers to a "thing" or to a "concept" in the former. The flip in the first example seems as much an action as the second.

When we begin to deeply explore the **lexicons** of the world's languages, we encounter many such ambiguous cases. Luckily, we are not restricted to semantic definitions when defining lexical classes. Returning to our *flip* sentences, it is perfectly clear that *flip* is a noun in the first sentence and a verb in the second. To see this, we only need to look at the syntactic positioning and morphological behavior. In the first sentence, *flip* is the head of a **noun phrase**, where it combines with the adjective *beautiful* and the definite article *the*. Only nouns may occur in this syntactic slot. *Flip* can also be made morphologically plural in this phrase, e.g., *beautiful flips*; again, this is behavior only shared by nouns. In contrast to the noun *flip*, the verb *flip* inflects with the past-tense suffix *-ed*. It could also take other verbal suffixes and occur in combination with an auxiliary verb, e.g., *he is flipping the pancakes*; this behavior is only shared by verbs.

**SIDEBAR 5.2**

There are a few languages where the evidence for distinct word classes is not as clear. For example, in some indigenous languages on the northwest coast of North America it is difficult to find morphosyntactic behavioral evidence that differentiates nouns from verbs.

We have seen that while semantic definitions of word classes leave us wanting, morphosyntax provides clear and concrete evidence that allows us to differentiate nouns from verbs in English. ***When we look at languages from all over the world, we find that the vast majority have clear morphosyntactic criteria by which distinct lexical classes are defined*** (but see Sidebar 5.2 for some exceptions). Interestingly, languages differ in the particular set of lexical classes that they have. For example, there are many languages without a lexical class of **articles** (e.g., English *a* and *the*), while English lacks lexical classes of **classifiers** and **evidentials**.

## 5.1.2 Cross-linguistic differences

***Languages differ not only in their inventories of lexical classes but also in the size of each lexical class***. For example, while English has hundreds of adjectives, Jaruwara, an Arawá language of native South America, has only fourteen (Dixon 2004: 75). This does not mean that speakers of Jaruwara cannot express the concepts conveyed by adjectives in English. It is just that they express most of these concepts with verbs or with possessed nouns, rather than with lexical adjectives. Consider the following sentence in Jaruwara and its English translation:

**(1)**   Jaruwara (Dixon 2004: 192)

| *o-tati* | *kone* | *bite* | *nafi* | *sawa–wa* | *kawahake* |
|---|---|---|---|---|---|
| 1SG.POSS-head | hair | small | all | be.white-REDUP | now |

'All the small hairs on my head are white now.'

The English sentence uses two lexical adjectives, *small* and *white*. The Jaruwara sentence uses only one: *bite* 'small.' The concept of 'white' is conveyed with a lexical verb *sawa* 'to be white,' which here has the final syllable repeated or **reduplicated** (marked by REDUP in the morpheme gloss). This process, whereby all or part of a morpheme is repeated to signal a certain meaning, applies to verbs in Jaruwara, but never to adjectives. The fact that *sawa-wa* exhibits reduplication is one piece of evidence that demonstrates that it is a verb.

The example above shows that ***in order to determine the lexical class of a word in a language, we have to determine which grammatical properties characterize each class***. Although no two languages use exactly the same set of criteria to define their lexical classes, there are certain grammatical features that frequently characterize lexical classes in the languages of the world. What follows is a brief cross-linguistic overview of some of the grammatical features that typically characterize common lexical classes. Remember that there is no language that exhibits all the features discussed here, and there are many languages that use criteria not in these lists.

## 5.2 Nouns

***The term* noun *refers to a grammatically defined word class, whose members can function as the heads of noun phrases***. As will be discussed in the next chapter, noun phrases are often linked grammatically to verbs and other elements, and often take on roles such as subject or object. Nouns typically denote entities or concepts. Like verbs, adjectives, and adverbs, ***nouns constitute an* open word class *in most languages of the world***. That is, one can easily incorporate new members into it through **borrowing** and other word-formation processes. Open classes can be contrasted with **closed word classes**, or those that are resistant to new members and whose members are often small in number (e.g., the closed class of articles in English has only two members, *a(n)* and *the*).

***It is common for nouns to inflect (i.e., have different morphological forms) based on the grammatical category of* number**. The majority of languages differentiate only **singular** number from **plural**, as in English *dog* ~ *dogs*. However, some languages also have other number categories, such as **dual** (exactly two), and paucal (a few).

***It is also common for nouns to inflect for* case**, the morphological marking of the syntactic and (in some cases) semantic relationships that hold between the noun

**TABLE 5.1** Declension of Latin *frāter* 'brother'

| | Paradigm for *frāter* 'brother' in Latin | |
|---|---|---|
| | Singular | Plural |
| Nominative (subject) | *frāter* | *frātrēs* |
| Accusative (object) | *frātrem* | *frātrēs* |
| Ablative ('from') | *frātre* | *frātribus* |
| Dative ('to') | *frātrī* | *frātribus* |
| Genitive ('of') | *frātris* | *frātrum* |

---

TEXTBOX 5.1 **CASE**

In many languages, the form of a noun (and sometimes other elements within the noun phrase, such as adjectives or demonstratives) will vary depending on the syntactic and/or semantic relationship that holds between the noun and another word in the sentence (usually the verb). The Latin examples given in Table 5.1 illustrate different case forms of the Latin noun 'brother.' The term **nominative** is used when the noun is the subject of a clause, **accusative** is used when the noun is the object of the clause, **genitive** is used when the noun is a possessor (e.g., *brother's book*) or holds a similar relationship with another noun, and **locative** is used when the noun is a location (*on my brother*), etc. Grammatical relations and semantic case roles are further discussed in the chapter on syntax.

---

phrases and the verb of a sentence (see Textbox 5.1). The paradigm in Table 5.1 illustrates eight distinct case forms of Latin, five in the singular and three in the plural. (The phonological forms that result from case inflections are referred to as **declensions** in traditional grammar.)

Moving on to syntax, ***in many languages a noun must be present in a noun phrase in order for modifiers to be used***. For example, in English we cannot simply say *three very spicy*. We must have a noun in order to use the modifiers, e.g., *three very spicy curries*. In most languages, only a noun can occur in this position, as the **head** of a noun phrase (the modifiers are called **dependents**). The noun and the modifiers together form a single syntactic unit called a noun phrase (discussed in the next chapter). In most languages the ordering of the noun with respect to its modifiers is quite restricted. Thus, in English we cannot move the noun to produce *three curries very spicy* or *curries very spicy three*. There is only one "slot," or position, in the noun phrase in which a noun may occur.

This brief discussion has mentioned only two common inflectional categories of nouns (number and case) and only one syntactic feature (the ability to head a noun phrase). There are many other morphosyntactic properties that can identify the class of noun in the world's languages. When a linguist is studying the grammar of a language, she or he must determine the particular morphological and syntactic features that identify the class of nouns in that language; no two languages will have exactly the same set of features as criteria.

## 5.3 Verbs

*The term verb refers to a class of words that function as predicates, the structural centers of clauses*. Verbs typically denote actions, events, activities, or states. In most languages, the class of verbs is *a large and open lexical class*, with the ability to incorporate new members. Verbs inflect for many different categories in the world's languages. Most typically, verbs inflect for **tense** (e.g., past, present, and future) and the related category of **aspect** (e.g., ongoing versus completed), for properties of their noun-phrase **arguments** (e.g., person, number, and gender), for **negation**, and for **mood** (e.g., declarative and interrogative).

Table 5.2 gives a partial **paradigm** of a verb in Dolakha Newar, a Tibeto-Burman language spoken in Nepal. Note that there are distinct forms for present and future tense. The form of the verb also changes with the person and number of the subject noun phrase. Hence *wāl-a-gi* is used for 'I mix'; *wāl-a-gu* is used for 'we mix,' etc. This type of inflection, in which one word indexes semantic categories of another word, is referred to as **agreement** (see Textbox 5.2). We can say that the Dolakha verb "agrees" in person and number with the subject. In Dolakha Newar, this is true of (almost) every verb and is true only of verbs; agreement is a morphosyntactic feature which uniquely identifies verbs in this language.

**TABLE 5.2** Dolakha Newar verb forms in the present and future tenses

Dolakha Newar present and future tense paradigms for the verb *wāl-* 'mix; knead'

| Subject | Present | Future |
| --- | --- | --- |
| 1st-person singular | *wāl-a-gi* | *wāl-i* |
| 1st-person plural | *wāl-a-gu* | *wāl-i* |
| 2nd-peson singular | *wāl-a-n* | *wāl-i-na* |
| 2nd-person plural | *wāl-a-min* | *wāl-i-nan* |
| 3rd-person singular | *wāl-a-i* | *wāl-e-u* |
| 3rd-person plural | *wāl-a-hin* | *wāl-e-u* |

---

### TEXTBOX 5.2 **AGREEMENT**

When the morphological form of the word varies depending on categories in another word in the same sentence, it is said to agree with that word in that category. In English, demonstratives agree in number with the accompanying noun, e.g., *that boy, those boys*. In many languages, verbs agree in person and number with the subject noun phrase. For example, in French 'I dance' is *je dance* but 'we dance' is *nous dancons*, and 'you (plural) dance' is *vous dancez*. Thus, the form of the verb changes depending on the person and number of the subject. In other words, the French verb agrees with the subject in person and number. There are many types of agreement in the world's languages.

---

There are a number of syntactic properties that can characterize verbs in the world's languages. ***In most languages, verbs occur in a fixed position in a neutral sentence***. For example, in English, the verb comes after the subject and before the object (if there is one), as in the sentence *John broke the lamp*. In many languages, the verb comes at the end of the sentence, as in Japanese:

**(2)** Japanese

| *boku* | *ga* | *tomodachi* | *ni* | *hana* | *o* | *ageta* |
|--------|------|-------------|------|--------|-----|---------|
| 1SG | NOM | friend | DAT | flower | ACC | give.PST |

'I gave flowers to my friend.'

In other languages, the verb comes at the beginning of the sentence, as in Jacaltec, a Mayan language spoken in Guatemala:

**(3)** Jacaltec (Craig 1977: 149)

| *xul* | *naj* | *pel* | *ewi* |
|-------|-------|-------|-------|
| come.PST | CLF | Peter | yesterday |

'Peter came yesterday.'

In many languages, verbs occur in a fixed syntactic position with respect to **auxiliary verbs**. ***Auxiliary verbs form a small and fairly closed subclass of verbs***. They often occur adjacent to the **main verb** (the verb that carries the more concrete semantic information), but can also occur in other positions in the clause. Auxiliary verbs can convey a range of meanings, such as negation, necessity, obligation, and ability. Some auxiliaries, in combination with the main verb, signal whether an event is ongoing, completed, or habitual (these types of distinctions are referred to as **aspect**). The presence of an auxiliary verb sometimes determines the morphological form of a main verb. We can see this by comparing English *should go, had gone*, and *ought to go*. The set of auxiliary verbs in English is given in (4).

**(4)** Auxiliary verbs in English

*has, have, had, do, did, does, shall, will, could,*
*would, may, might, must, can, could, ought*

## 5.4 Adjectives

Adjectives can be either an open class, easily incorporating new members, or a closed class with a finite number of words.

*The lexical class of adjectives in English has two distinct syntactic positions*. Adjectives can occur within a noun phrase where they modify a noun, as in *the sour apple*. They can also occur as the complement to a **copula**, as in *the apple is sour*. This distributional pattern is found with all English adjectives. Sometimes quantifiers have this property (*all the books* ~ *that is all*), but they tend to be considerably more restricted (e.g., *\*the books are several*).

*In many languages, the form of the adjective will vary depending on properties of the noun, such as number, gender, or case*. Thus, adjectives in such languages can be said to agree with the noun. In Russian, adjectives agree with the noun in number, gender, and case, as the paradigm in Table 5.3 shows.

*Adjectives also often have forms for degree*, such as comparative and superlative (e.g., *big*, *bigger*, and *biggest*).

*In many languages, words that express properties of nouns are not members of a lexical class of adjectives but are actually verbs or nouns.* For example, in Dolakha Newar, all color terms are lexical verbs. Consider example (5).

(5) Dolakha Newar
*āmp*                *heŋgar-a*
mango          red-3SG.PST
'The mango became red/reddened.'

In (5), the word for 'red' takes verbal inflection, specifically the suffix for third-person singular past. To produce the noun phrase 'red mango,' a different suffix is needed and the color term is placed before the noun: *hẽga-u āmp*. Note that any verb can be transformed into a noun modifier in this way. For example, compare *mi yer-a* 'the

**TABLE 5.3** Inflection of the Russian adjective *novyj* 'new' (Corbett 2004: 202)

|  | Masculine | Feminine | Neuter | Plural |
| --- | --- | --- | --- | --- |
| Nominative | *novyj* | *novaja* | *novoe* | *novye* |
| Accusative | * | *novuju* | *novoe* | * |
| Genitive | *novogo* | *novoj* | *novogo* | *novyx* |
| Dative | *novomu* | *novoj* | *novomu* | *novym* |
| Instrumental | *novym* | *novoj(u)* | *novym* | *novymi* |
| Locative | *novom* | *novoj* | *novom* | *novyx* |

* These forms depend additionally on animacy.

man came' and *ye-u mi* 'the man who came.' It is clear that the word for 'red' in Dolakha Newar has the same morphological and syntactic patterns as verbs do, and that it is therefore, in fact, a verb.

## 5.5 Adverbs

Like adjectives, the word class of adverb can either be open or closed. ***The term "adverb" is a cover term for words that are not lexical nouns, verbs, or adjectives, but which still have lexical (as opposed to grammatical) content*** (Payne 1997: 69). Semantically, adverbs tend to be modifiers of verbs, clauses, or sentences, or are used to indicate speaker attitude (*Incredibly, she forgot her keys again!*), stance (*Certainly he won't pay!*), or the type or source of evidence (*Apparently they've already left*).

***The extent to which adverbs, or subclasses of adverbs, demonstrate consistent morphosyntactic behavior varies across languages***. Often, they can be defined by their absence of grammatical properties: adverbs usually don't inflect; they don't occur within a noun phrase (unless adjacent to an adjective); and they don't occur with modifiers other than other adverbs. Some adverbs demonstrate considerably more freedom of positioning than do nouns, verbs, or adjectives. We can see this in the English sentences in (6).

**(6)**   *Slowly John opened the envelope.*
*John slowly opened the envelope.*
*John opened the envelope slowly*

No other word class in English has this degree of flexibility in positioning.

## 5.6 Adpositions: prepositions and postpositions

We now move from our discussion of **lexical word classes** (those that signal a vast array of meanings) to a discussion of **grammatical word classes** (those that function grammatically and are more limited in the range of meanings they express). While lexical word classes are open in most languages, ***grammatical word classes are generally closed***, only admitting new members on rare occasion.

Most independent words that function grammatically do not inflect but have a single morphological form; these are referred to as **particles**. There are many types of particles, and particles may be found in a wide variety of grammatical word classes.

***Prepositions and postpositions*** (or **adposition**s) ***are (usually) particles that occur with a noun phrase and that indicate the grammatical, spatial, temporal, or logical relationship of the noun phrase to another element of the clause***. English has prepositions; examples of prepositions in English are *on, of, with, by, under, like*, and *to*.

Prepositions differ from postpositions in their linear ordering with respect to the noun. Very simply, ***prepositions occur before the accompanying noun phrase, while postpositions occur after it***. In the following English examples, the prepositions are underlined and the accompanying noun phrases are in square brackets:

**(7)** *I went to [the beach].*
*The girl with [the umbrella] was still getting wet.*
*You'll find the key under [the mat].*
*He plays like [u professional athlete].*

Now consider the Japanese sentence below:

**(8)** Japanese (Shibatani 1990: 265)

| taroo | wa | tosyokan | ni | itta | ga, | hon | wa | yomanakatta |
|-------|-----|----------|-----|------|-----|------|-----|-------------|
| Taroo | TOP | library | to | go.PST | but | book | TOP | read.NEG.PST |

'Taroo went to the library but did not read a book.'

Note that the word *ni* 'to' follows the noun *tosyokan* 'library,' and is thus a postposition. Thus, Japanese exhibits the opposite ordering than is used in English.

## 5.7 Quantifiers and numerals

***Quantifiers usually occur within the noun phrase where they indicate a quantity of the object denoted by the noun***. Languages differ as to how many quantifiers they have, their structure, and their grammatical properties. Most languages allow only one quantifier in a single noun phrase; the class of quantifiers can then be identified as the set of words which can fill that single syntactic position.

In most languages, **numerals** form a word class distinct from quantifiers. In English, we can note that while two quantifiers cannot co-occur in a single noun phrase (e.g., we cannot say *\*many all boys*), a quantifier and a numeral may co-occur (*all three boys*). Numerals can also take affixes to convert them from cardinal numbers (e.g., *seven*) to ordinal numbers (*seven-th*). This grammatical behavior can distinguish numerals from other quantifiers in the language.

## 5.8 Demonstratives

***Demonstratives form a fairly closed set of words that occur within the noun phrase and which have a deictic ("pointing") function***. Demonstratives can be used to "point" to something in the immediate environment (e.g., *this shirt is really ugly*), to knowledge shared by the speaker and hearer (*That was outrageous last night!*), or to something that has just been said in the discourse (*That's ridiculous! I never want to hear you say that again*).

***Languages differ in the size of the demonstrative class, as well as in the distinctions which they draw***. Perhaps all languages minimally have a distinction between **proximal** demonstratives (e.g., *this*), which indicate things closer to the speaker and hearer, and **distal** demonstratives (e.g., *that*), which indicate things farther from the hearer. Many languages make further distinctions; see Textbox 5.3 for one such example.

---

**TEXTBOX 5.3**

Sinhala, the national language of Sri Lanka, has four levels of demonstratives: one is used if the referent is close to the speaker, another if the referent is close to the hearer, a third if the referent is visible but not close to either one, and a fourth if an object is not visible. These forms are illustrated to the right. Note that the last example is even used if the child is under the table and pulling on the speaker's leg.

| | |
|---|---|
| *meyaa laməyek* | 'this is a child' (in the vicinity of the speaker) |
| *oyə laməyek* | 'that is a child' (in the vicinity of the hearer) |
| *arə laməyek* | 'that is a child' (not near either the speaker or hearer, but visible) |
| *eeya laməyek* | 'that is a child' (not visible to the speaker) |

---

## 5.9 Articles

***Articles form a class of small grammatical particles that obligatorily occur in some noun phrases***. English distinguishes between the **indefinite** article *a(n)* and the **definite** article *the* (see Sidebar 5.3). Articles signal different meanings in different languages.

**SIDEBAR 5.3**

In English, the indefinite article is used when the speaker judges that the hearer will not be able to identify the referent of a noun phrase, e.g., in *A man came in*, there is no assumption that the hearer should know the man. Compare this with the sentence *The man came in*. Here, the hearer is expected to know which man is being referred to. This distinction (referred to as definiteness) will be discussed again in Chapter 9 on discourse.

In some languages, articles take different forms depending on the class of the head noun. The French definite article, for example, has three forms: one used with singular masculine nouns (*le*), one used with singular feminine nouns (*la*), and one used with plural nouns (*les*).

## 5.10 Conjunctions

***Conjunctions are grammatical particles that conjoin two or more words, phrases, or clauses at the same level of structure***. Conjunctions can therefore be identified by their position between two elements of the same syntactic type. For example, the conjunction *and* in English can be used to conjoin words, phrases, and clauses:

(9)  Nouns:          *[Cats] and [dogs] make good pets.*
     Verbs:          *They [eat] and [drink] too much.*

| Adjectives: | My cat is [black] and [white]. |
| Adverbs: | [Slowly] and [carefully] she filled the glass. |
| Noun phrases: | They brought [chocolate cookies] and [filled cakes]. |
| Prepositional phrases: | [Over the river] and [through the woods]. |
| Verb phrases: | We [ate chocolate] and [drank champagne]. |
| Clauses: | [Robin ate chocolate] and [Chris drank champagne]. |

Note that we can't substitute the conjunction *but* into all of the sentences above, only those where verbs are involved.

## 5.11 Pronouns

***Pronouns appear as the sole element of a noun phrase; they do not co-occur with modifiers***, thus they are distinct from nouns (see Sidebar 5.4). Thus in English, the phrases *the you, *big he, and *some us are highly ungrammatical. Pronouns are so called because they may substitute for an entire noun phrase, e.g., *The man with the yellow hat rescued Curious George; he always does.*

Languages have distinct pronouns to refer to the speaker, the hearer, and others. These are referred to as **personal pronouns**. Thus, we consistently find pronouns for **first person** (refers to the speaker: *I, we*), **second person** (refers to the addressee: *you*), and **third person** (refers neither to the speaker nor to the hearer: *he, she, it, they*). Textbox 5.4 describes another type of pronoun distinction as well. As these examples demonstrate, English distinguishes singular from plural pronouns in the first and the third person, but not in the second person (English *you* can refer to one or more). English pronouns also distinguish case to a limited extent. For example, we can contrast the first-person pronouns *I, me,* and *my*. In some languages, personal pronouns distinguish many more cases than these; in others, pronouns do not distinguish case at all.

> **SIDEBAR 5.4**
> NOMINALS
>
> Pronouns and nouns are quite distinct in that nouns can co-occur with modifiers while pronouns cannot. However, they do share the syntactically powerful property of serving as the head a noun phrase. The term **nominal** can be used as a cover term for nouns and pronouns (and sometimes other things beyond the scope of this chapter).

---

**TEXTBOX 5.4 INCLUSIVE AND EXCLUSIVE PRONOUNS**

It is not unusual for languages of the world to contrast the categories of **inclusive** and **exclusive** in the first-person plural pronominal forms. In English, the first-person plural pronoun *we* can either include the hearer (inclusive: *you and I*) or exclude the hearer (exclusive: *She and I, but not you*). In other languages, distinct pronouns can occur.

Dolakha Newar

| | | |
|---|---|---|
| *thiji* | 'we' | (inclusive: you and I and possibly others) |
| *isi* | 'we' | (exclusive: not you, but I and others) |

In addition to personal pronouns, there are also **demonstrative pronouns**. These are simply demonstratives which occur in the syntactic position of pronouns, that is, as the head of a noun phrase without modifiers, as in the sentence *I hate that*.

**Interrogative pronouns** are a subset of the interrogative words (or "question words") of a language that occur in the syntactic position of pronouns. Thus, *who* is an interrogative pronoun in *Who let the dog out?*, while *which* is an interrogative word, but not an interrogative pronoun, in *Which class did you take?*

## 5.12 Other word classes

This chapter has focused primarily on word classes found in English, and has outlined some of the properties of word classes including noun, verb, adjective, adverb, demonstrative, preposition, and quantifier. There are quite a few other word classes in the world's languages that English does not have. For example, some languages have **numeral classifiers**, words that obligatorily occur with a numeral but that vary with semantic properties of the noun (see Textbox 5.5).

---

### TEXTBOX 5.5

In Mandarin Chinese, numeral classifiers are obligatory between a numeral and a noun. Note how the classifier varies with the animacy, size, shape, and function of the noun:

| | | |
|---|---|---|
| *tiáo*: long and skinny things | *sān tiáo yú* | 'three fish' |
| *zhāng*: flat things | *sān zhāng dìtú* | 'three maps' |
| *zhī*: small animals | *sān zhī gǒu* | 'three dogs' |
| *bǎ*: things with handles | *sān bǎ yǔsǎn* | 'three umbrellas' |
| *běn*: volumes | *sān běn shū* | 'three books' |

---

Other languages have **evidentials**, words that express the source of a speaker's knowledge for the content of the utterance and his or her degree of certainty that the information is true. And there are many other word classes as well. A full discussion of all the word classes in the world's languages is beyond the scope of the current chapter; some examples can be found in the language profiles.

### CHAPTER SUMMARY

The world's languages have a wide variety of word classes that reflect the diversity of meanings and relations that people express in language. They are characterized by regular grammatical properties that allow them to act as the building blocks for phrases, sentences, and other utterances. Thus, one must examine these grammatical properties, rather than meanings, to determine the classification of words. Not all languages have the same set of word classes. Each language must be examined independently to determine which word classes it has, and each class must be indentified based on the shared morphological and syntactic properties of the words in the class.

Table 5.4 lists each of the word classes we have discussed, together with some of the morphological and syntactic properties that each class may exhibit.

---

### TEXTBOX 5.6 **GLOSSING CONVENTIONS USED IN THIS CHAPTER**

| Convention | Meaning | Convention | Meaning |
|---|---|---|---|
| 1 | first person | NOM | nominative |
| 3 | third person | POSS | possessive |
| ACC | accusative | PST | past tense |
| CLF | classifier | REDUP | reduplication |
| DAT | Dative | SG | singular |
| NEG | negation | TOP | Topic |

---

**TABLE 5.4** Summary of common morphological and grammatical properties of word classes

| Class | Common morphological categories | Common syntactic properties |
|---|---|---|
| Noun | Number (singular, plural, etc.), gender (masculine, feminine, neuter, etc.), case (nominative, accusative, locative, etc.), person of possessor (my, your, etc.) | May function as head of a noun phrase and so occur with modifiers, such as adjectives (*black cat*), quantifiers (*many years*), and demonstratives (*those books*) |
| Verb | Tense (past, present, etc.), aspect (completed, ongoing, etc.), person/number/gender of arguments, negation, mood (declarative, interrogative, etc.) | Often restricted in position with respect to arguments (e.g., sentence-initial in Jacaltec, sentence-medial in English, sentence-final in Japanese); may occur in combination with auxiliary verbs |
| Adjective | Comparative (*happier*); superlative (*happiest*); number, gender, or case of modified noun | May be found within the noun phrase modifying a noun (*happy people*) or as a complement to a copula (*they are happy*); may co-occur (*big shiny green leaves*) |
| Adverb | Absence of morphological inflection | Some have freedom of positioning |
| Adposition | Usually particles | Precedes (preposition) or follows (postposition) a noun phrase |

**TABLE 5.4** (*cont.*)

| Class | Common morphological categories | Common syntactic properties |
| --- | --- | --- |
| Quantifiers | Sometimes have common nominal morphology, such as case-marking | Like adjectives, some can occur within a noun phrase (*all people*) or as a copula complement (*that is all*), but the latter position can be quite restricted |
| Numerals | Ordinal versus cardinal | Usually within a noun phrase; in some languages, must co-occur with numeral classifiers |
| Demonstratives | Distinguish at least proximal (*this*) from distal (*that*); may inflect for various properties of the noun, such as number (*this ~ these*) | Occur within a noun phrase; may not co-occur |
| Articles | Usually distinguish indefinite (*a*) from definite (*the*) | Obligatorily occur in many noun phrases |
| Conjunctions | Usually particles, so do not vary in form | Occur between syntactic elements of the same type (nouns, noun phrases, etc.) which they conjoin (*apples or oranges*) |
| Pronouns | Distinguish person (1st, 2nd, 3rd), and often distinguish number (singular, plural), case (nominative, accusative, etc.), and other morphological categories of nouns | Occur as the only element in the noun phrase |

## SUGGESTIONS FOR FURTHER READING

**Payne, Thomas**. 1997. *Describing morphosyntax: A guide for field linguists*. Cambridge University Press.

Chapter 3 of Payne (1997), a volume aimed at upper-level undergraduate students, provides a more extensive discussion of criteria for identifying nouns, verbs, modifiers, and adverbs cross-linguistically.

**Aikhenvald, Alexandra**. 2007. "Typological distinctions in word formation." In Shopen, Timothy (ed.), *Language typology and syntactic description*. Cambridge University Press. 1–64.

The "Shopen volumes" contain a variety of classic typological studies on different core topics in morphosyntax. Volume III contains this relevant study.

**Dixon, R. M. W. and Alexandra Aikhenvald**. 2007. *Word: A cross-linguistic typology*. Cambridge University Press.

This volume comprises a set of case studies, each of which presents argumentation for word classes in a different language of the world.

### EXERCISES

1. Each of the following sentences has one word given in bold. State the word class of each bolded word and then give at least two pieces of evidence (morphological or syntactic) that justifies your analysis.

   Example: *I just **oiled** the furniture.*
   Word class: Verb

   Evidence: (i) The verb carries the past-tense suffix *-ed*. (ii) It follows the subject and directly precedes the object. (iii) It is preceded by the adverb *just*.

   a. *My nephew often **drives** to Berkeley.*
   b. *They are planning to make the journey in two long **drives**.*
   c. *The grass is always **greener** on the other side of the fence.*
   d. *He walked onto the **green**.*
   e. ***Usually** she is home by seven.*
   f. *It is the **usual** routine.*

   Now do the same for the following quote, attributed to comedian Groucho Marx:

   *Time **flies like** an arrow; **fruit flies like** a banana.*

   g. ***flies*** in *Time flies like an arrow.*
   h. ***like*** in *Time flies like an arrow.*
   i. ***fruit flies*** in *fruit flies like a banana.*
   j. ***like*** in *fruit flies like a banana.*

2. Consider the following sentences:
   a. *John ran up a bill.*
   b. *John ran up a hill.*

   Note that Example (c) is acceptable, while Example (d) is not:
   c. *John ran a bill up*
   d. *\*John ran a hill up*

   Use what you know about word classes to explain this variation in behavior. Then come up with three similar pairs of sentences that show the same patterns.

3. Consider the following noun phrases in Italian:

   | | |
   |---|---|
   | *un chilo di farina* | 'a kilo of flour' |
   | *una storia sulla infanzia* | 'a story about childhood' |
   | *quei dieci libri verdi* | 'those ten green books' |
   | *quello specchio* | 'that mirror' |
   | *molti problemi difficili* | 'many difficult problems' |
   | *il specchio di mio fratello* | 'my brother's mirror' |
   | *una maglia verde* | 'a green sweater' |

   Provide the English translation of each of the following words:
   *farina*
   *infanzia*
   *verde/verdi*
   *specchio*
   *maglia*
   *storia*

*problemi*
*mia/mio*

a. Is *chilo* a quantifier or a noun? How do you know?
b. *Quei* and *quello* are members of what word class?
c. *Un, una,* and *il* are members of what word class?
d. *Sulla* is a member of what word class?
e. Based on the examples presented, which of the following statements are true?
  i. Possessive expressions precede the noun.
  ii. Demonstratives precede numerals.
  iii. Nouns cannot be modified by both articles and possessive expressions.
  iv. The noun is always the final element in the noun phrase.
  v. Possessive expressions reflect the gender of the following noun.
  vi. Adjectives follow nouns.
  vii. The form of the demonstrative changes with the number of the noun.
  viii. Numerals must directly precede adjectives.

4. Consider the following sentences in Russian (Based on Comrie 1979: 109–111):

a. *rabótnik zaščiščájet žénščinu*    'The workman defends the woman'
b. *rabótniki zaščiščájut žénščinu*    'The workmen defend the woman'
c. *rabótnik zaščiščájet žénščin*    'The workman defends the women'
d. *rabótniki zaščiščájut žénščin*    'The workmen defend the women'
e. *stáryj rabótnik zaščiščájet žénščinu*    'The old workman defends the woman'
f. *stáraja mát' zaščiščájet žénščinu*    'The old mother defends the woman'

  i. List *all* Russian forms for each of the following words.
  'workman'
  'workmen'
  'woman'
  'women'
  'defend'
  'old'
  'mother'
  ii. What is the word class of *zaščiščájet*? When is *zaščiščájet* used, as opposed to *zaščiščájut*? What is the name of this grammatical category?
  iii. Based on the data above, what grammatical category does the Russian noun inflect for?
  iv. Based on the data above, what grammatical category does the Russian adjective inflect for?

5. The following examples illustrate some properties of nouns, verbs, and adjectives in Dolakha Newar. Analyze each sentence, dividing words into morphemes when appropriate. (Note: the form *juu* shortens to *ju* by a rule that is not important for the current problem.)

a. *misāmi ŋila.*    'The/a woman laughed.'
b. *misāmi ŋileu.*    'The/a woman will laugh.'
c. *ŋilgu misāmi*    'The/a laughing woman'
d. *misāmi ḍaktar jura.*    'The/a woman became a doctor.'
e. *misāmi daktar jueu.*    'The/a woman will become a doctor.'
f. *misāmi juu ḍaktar*    'The/a woman doctor'
    (i.e., 'The/a woman who became a doctor.')
g. *misāmi dosari jura.*    'The woman became pregnant.'
h. *misāmi dosari jueu.*    'The/a woman will become pregnant.'
i. *dosari misāmi*    'The/a pregnant woman'

i.  State the properties by which verbs can be identified as a distinct lexical class in this language.
ii. Based on the data given, is there evidence for distinguishing between nouns and adjectives? Why or why not?

Now consider the data in (j) through (m).

   j. *dwākau muca*     'The/a big child'
   k. *cicāu muca*      'The/a little child'
   l. *muca dwākara.*   'The/a child grew.'
 m. *sabun cicāra.*    'The/a soap shrank.'

iii. Based on the data given, are the lexemes for 'big' and 'small' in this language nouns, verbs, or adjectives? Explain.

# 6 Syntax: words in combination

**KEY TERMS**

- Clause
- Constituent
- Phrase: noun phrase, adpositional phrase, verb phrase
- Argument: core vs. oblique
- Transitivity: intransitive, transitive, ditransitive
- Grammatical relations: subject, object, indirect object
- Sentence
- Complex sentence
- Coordination vs. subordination
- Adverbial, complement, relative clause

## CHAPTER PREVIEW

The previous three chapters have shown how sounds are produced and patterned, how they combine into morphemes, and how morphemes combine into words. We now continue up the hierarchy to increasingly complex levels of structure by examining syntax: the combination of words into phrases, clauses, and sentences, and the grammatical principles and relationships that underlie these structures. Syntax is critical to communication as it allows us to talk about events, describe situations, and attribute states, actions, or activities to particular individuals or entities. This is done in part through grammatical relationships between verbs and noun phrases. These relations are grammatically marked and are independent of the semantic relationships between verbs and their arguments. The principles of syntactic organization also allow us to express complex relationships between events or situations. This is done through the combination of clauses into sentences through a variety of means.

Like the previous three units, this chapter emphasizes processes of analysis and argumentation. Each language is unique in the range of grammatical phenomena that can be used to identify and relate elements at every level of the syntax; each language needs to be examined independently, with the syntactic structures justified by the language-particular facts.

## LIST OF AIMS

At the end of this chapter, students should be able to:

- **identify syntactic constituents in a data set;**
- **present arguments for constituency;**
- **differentiate among intransitive, transitive, and ditransitive verbs;**
- **identify core and oblique arguments;**
- **provide evidence that a noun phrase is a subject, object, or indirect object;**
- **state the difference between coordinate and subordinate clauses;**
- **differentiate adverbial, complement, and relative clauses in English.**

## 6.1 Introduction

**Syntax *refers to the set of grammatical structures that allow for the combination of words into phrases and sentences.*** As with other aspects of language, syntactic structures are principled and systematic, with the potential for detailed analysis and description. Words that occur in phrases and sentences can be shown not only to have semantic, or meaningful, relationships to each other, but also to have intricate grammatical relationships to each other. Syntax is important because it provide speakers with a regular structure or framework for conveying relationships between people, things, or ideas and the states, events, or activities that they are involved in. The regularity of this framework within a language allows speakers to quickly produce and process the information. It also allows for the marking of particular grammatical categories that have arisen over time through repeated use by speakers. This process of grammaticalization, as well as the process of syntactic change, will be discussed more fully in Chapter 13. Sidebar 6.1 contains a note about the format of this chapter. Textbox 6.1 introduces a long-standing theoretical debate in the field.

> **SIDEBAR 6.1**
>
> In several places throughout the chapter, you will be directed to apply what you learn to short data sets. Answers are available on the companion website, and indicated by the website icon.
>
> Completing these data sets as you work through the chapter is highly recommended, as it will increase your understanding of the unit and improve your skills of linguistic analysis.

---

**TEXTBOX 6.1 FUNCTIONAL VERSUS FORMAL APPROACHES TO SYNTAX**

This book approaches linguistics from the perspective of **functional discourse-based theory**. Within syntax, functional approaches examine the relationship between particular syntactic structures and how they are used in discourse interaction, and especially seek to explore how the **functions** have shaped the structures. That is, they seek to explain syntactic structures based on how they are used.

A very different perspective is found in approaches to syntax grounded in **formal theory**. These approaches seek to explain syntactic structures independently of function, instead constructing a formal model of linguistic knowledge based on abstract categories, structures, and principles. The model is posited to represent a single Universal Grammar that is considered to be part of humankind's genetic endowment. Language-specific variation is brought about through specific modifications of the model. Radford et al. (2009) is an introductory textbook written from this perspective. See also Chapter 14, section 14.10, for a discussion of formal and functional approaches in the study of how children acquire language.

## 6.2  Constituent structure

*One of the central aspects of linguistic design is hierarchical structure:* units contain units that contain units. We have seen so far that there are units called words that contain smaller units called morphemes, which are made up of smaller units called phonemes. We will now move up from the word level to see that words combine into **phrases**, that phrases combine into **clauses**, and that clauses combine into **sentences**, leading us to progressively more complex structures.

Consider the English sentence in (1):

(1)  *The kids arrived at the house.*

Our intuitions tell us that the two words *the* and *kids* form a single unit. By contrast, *kids* and *arrived*, to the exclusion of *the*, do not. You can sense that there is a natural break between *kids* and *arrived*, as indicated by the symbol | in (2). The starred example, indicating a break between *The* and *kids*, does not seem natural (see Sidebar 6.2).

(2)  a. *The kids | arrived at the house*
     b. *\*The | kids arrived at the house*

**SIDEBAR 6.2**

Remember that when discussing grammar, an asterisk in front of a phrase indicates that speakers find it to be ill-formed or ungrammatical.

Observe that *arrived at the house* forms a unit, as it tells us something about the kids, specifically what they did. We can also note that *at the house* is optional; it can be left off and the result would still be the grammatical sentence *The kids arrived*. Of course, we would have to leave off the entire phrase. We couldn't say, for example, *\*the kids arrived at* and remove only *the house*. So *at the house* appears to be a single unit, separate from *arrived*:

(2)  c. *arrived | at the house*
     d. *\* arrived at | the house*

We are not finished, however, as *the house* is a smaller unit yet, with the definite article *the* pertaining to *house* and not to *at*.

(2)  e. *at | the house*
     f. *\* at the |house*

If we put each of these units within square brackets, we can represent the hierarchical structure visually, as in (2g). The outermost set of brackets encloses the sentence as a whole:

(2)  g.  [[*The kids*] [*arrived* [*at* [*the house*]]]]

*The term* constituent *simply refers to a subpart of a higher unit.* Our sentence contains two major syntactic constituents: [*the kids*] and [*arrived at the house*]. The latter contains two constituents, the verb *arrived* and the phrase [*at the house*]. This in turn contains two constituents: the preposition *at* and the phrase [*the house*].

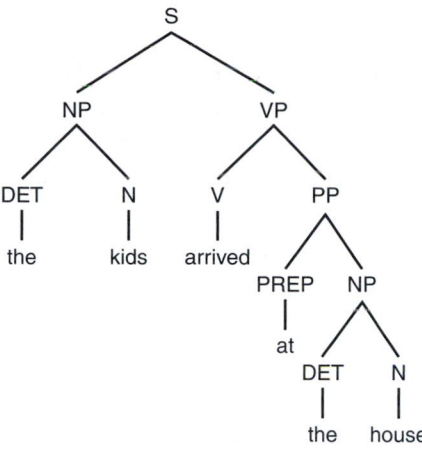

**Figure 6.1** Labeled tree diagram for *The kids arrived at the house*

Finally, [*the house*] has two constituents: the definite article *the* and the noun *house*. Another way to represent the constituent structure of this sentence would be to use a branching **labeled tree diagram**, where every node connecting two branches represents a constituent, labeled for its phrase type and the lexical class of each word. Figure 6.1 presents the labeled tree diagram for Example (2g). Abbreviations used in tree diagrams are given in Sidebar 6.3.

We have arrived at this analysis of the sentence's **constituent structure** largely by using speaker intuition. As scientists, however, it is important to move beyond the level of intuition and to provide argumentation based on the structural facts of the language. We will now provide such evidence for the three major types of **phrasal constituents** that are found in English. These are the noun phrase (NP), the prepositional phrase (PP), and the verb phrase (VP).

### 6.2.1 The noun phrase

*A noun phrase is a grammatically coherent syntactic constituent containing a head noun or a pronoun and optionally one or more modifiers.* The noun or pronoun is the **head** of the noun phrase, or the element that determines the type of syntactic constituent and which is required in order for the modifiers, or **dependents**, to appear. Thus, in English one cannot just say *the three big*, leaving out the head noun. Typical dependents found in the noun phrase include demonstratives, numerals, adjectives, articles, quantifiers, possessors, **adpositional**

**phrases** (such as *with a hammer*), and **relative clauses** (such as *who came late*). Textbox 6.2 gives some further examples of noun phrases in English, with dependent elements underlined.

There are a number of ways to determine that noun phrases are grammatically coherent units. ***In most languages the elements of the noun phrase must form a contiguous group that behaves as a single unit.*** Here we will consider three distinct arguments that illustrate the coherence of the noun phrase and hence its status as a syntactic constituent in English.

First, a noun phrase can appear in any noun-phrase slot in a sentence, providing it fits semantically. When noun phrases switch positions, they do so as complete wholes, as illustrated in (3):

(3)   a. [*My best friend*] *called* [*the doctor*] *for* [*me*].
      b. [*The doctor*] *called* [*my best friend*] *for* [*me*].
      c. [*I*] *called* [*the doctor*] *for* [*my best friend*].

**SIDEBAR 6.4**

Argument 1: When noun phrases are moved, they move as cohesive units.

It is not possible to move only part of a noun phrase. We never find, for example *\*my the doctor called best friend for me*. The fact that the elements of a noun phrase form a cohesive group which acts as a unit (all elements move together) demonstrates that the noun phrase is a syntactic constituent. This argument is summarized in Sidebar 6.4.

**SIDEBAR 6.5**

Argument 2: When a pronoun is used, it replaces an entire noun phrase, not part of it.

A second argument that a noun and its dependent modifiers form a single syntactic constituent is that ***if one chooses to use a pronoun, it replaces not just the noun but all of the dependents as well.*** Consider the sentence in (3a). We can replace the initial noun phrase *my best friend* with the pronoun *she*, i.e., *She called the doctor for me*. However, one can never say *\*my she* or *\*my best she*. This shows that pronouns replace entire noun phrases, not just pieces of them. So again we find evidence that the noun phrase works as a cohesive unit. This argument is summarized in Sidebar 6.5.

---

**TEXTBOX 6.2 DEPENDENTS OF THE ENGLISH NOUN PHRASE**

| Possessors | *my dog; Susan's play* | Prepositional phrases | *the man with one black shoe* |
| Articles | *the truth; an insult* | Relative clauses | *The woman who just arrived* |
| Demonstratives | *those words; that cookie* | | |
| Numerals | *fifty representatives* | | |
| Quantifiers | *some flowers; many nights* | | |
| Adjectives | *blue dress; complex structures* | | |

Note: The English noun phrase can only have one of the following elements: article, demonstrative, possessor. Thus the phrases *\*the your book* and *\*a that flower* are ungrammatical. The cover term for these three categories is ***determiner***.

A third argument for the syntactic unity of the noun phrase is that ***in most languages of the world, the order of elements in the noun phrase is fixed***. For example, in English we say *those three red books on the table*. We cannot shift the order of modifiers to \**three those red on the table books*, or \**red three on the table books those*, etc. The noun phrase thus has internal structuring, a feature of cohesive units. Textbox 6.3 describes English noun-phrase ordering using a syntactic template.

---

## TEXTBOX 6.3 **SYNTACTIC TEMPLATES**

One way to describe the ordering of elements in a syntactic constituent is to use a **template**, which represents the structure of a phrase schematically. It lists all of the elements that could possibly occur in a constituent in the order in which they occur. Optional elements are placed in parentheses. The template for the English noun phrase is as follows:

(DET) (QUANT) (NUM) (ADJ\*) N (PP\*) (REL)

The following abbreviations are standard: NP noun phrase, DET determiner, QUANT quantifier, ADJ adjective, N noun, PP prepositional phrase, REL relative clause. An asterisk placed after the category name indicates that you can have more than one of that type of element in a single phrase. For example, we can have more than one adjective, as in *the big black books*.

---

It is important to note that the ordering discussed thus far is specific to English. Other languages have other set orders of noun-phrase elements. For example, in Mandarin Chinese, noun-phrase elements have the order represented in the template in (4):

(4)   Noun-phrase template for Mandarin Chinese
(DEM) (NUM) (CLASSIFIER) (ADJ)\* (NOMINALIZER) NOUN

A noun phrase of this structure is illustrated in (5a):

(5)   a.   *nà*         *sān*      *dŭo*     *mĕilì-de*            *hūa*
           DIST.DEM    three      CLF        beautiful-NMLZ       flower
           'those three beautiful flowers'

Alternate orders are ungrammatical, as illustrated in (5b):

(5)   b.   \*    *sān*      *dŭo*     *nà*          *hūa*       *mĕilì-de*
                three      CLF       DIST.DEM      flower      beautiful-NMLZ

**SIDEBAR 6.6**

*Argument 3: The order of elements within noun phrases is fixed, showing that noun phrases have internal structure, which indicates that they are grammatical units.*

The fact that the order of noun-phrase elements is fixed reveals that noun phrases have an internal grammatical structure. Such structuring is evidence that noun phrases are cohesive syntactic units. This argument is summarized in Sidebar 6.6.

In some languages, there is other grammatical evidence for the unity of the noun phrase. For example, ***in many***

**SIDEBAR 6.7**

*Argument 4: Elements of the noun phrase can agree for gender, indicating that they are grammatically related members of cohesive units.*

**SIDEBAR 6.8**

For each of the following examples, place brackets around each complete noun phrase and label the category of each word. Answers are available on the website.

Hint: If you are not sure where the boundaries are, try replacing the noun phrase with a pronoun. You can only do this with whole noun phrases, not with parts.

Model:  [*My brother*] *ate* [*those fried green tomatoes*].
         POSS N         DEM ADJ  ADJ   N

Compare the example with pronouns: [*He*] *ate* [*them*]

a. *Her friends brought six chocolate cakes to the party.*
b. *The whole group admired the presents on the table.*
c. *Her favorite present was from her father.*

*languages elements of the noun phrase "agree" for number, gender, or other categories*. In Italian, the indefinite article agrees in gender with the noun it modifies. In other words, the form of the indefinite article depends upon whether the noun is masculine or feminine. The examples in (6) illustrate this agreement:

(6) a.  <u>un</u>        *columbo*        'a male dove'
         INDF.M      male.dove

    b.  <u>una</u>       *columba*        'a female dove'
         INDF.F      female.dove

This pattern of gender agreement applies only to elements within the noun phrase, never to elements outside of it. This behavior shows that the elements in the noun phrase are related grammatically and hence that the noun phrase is a grammatically cohesive unit. This argument is summarized in Sidebar 6.7, and all arguments thus far are reviewed in Textbox 6.4.

Try out the short exercises in Sidebar 6.8 to check your understanding of the noun phrase before moving on to the next section.

**TEXTBOX 6.4 SYNTACTIC ARGUMENTATION**

While it was possible for us to intuitively sense that noun phrases are coherent syntactic units, we have also been able to confirm our intuitions with four arguments based on morphosyntactic behavior:

- **Argument 1**: Noun-phrase elements form a cohesive unit that functions as a group.
- **Argument 2**: When a pronoun is used, it replaces all noun-phrase elements.
- **Argument 3**: Noun-phrase elements have a fixed internal order.
- **Argument 4**: Agreement illustrates that noun-phrase elements are grammatically related.

Since linguists take a scientific approach to language, it is important not to rely solely on intuition – which can be uncertain and variable – but to provide concrete evidence for claims about linguistic structure. Intuition can point in the right direction, but only with argumentation based on linguistic evidence can we reach our goal of a scientific analysis of language.

## 6.2.2    The adpositional phrase

***An adpositional phrase is a syntactic constituent consisting of an adposition (preposition or postposition), which is the head of the constituent, and a dependent noun phrase.*** There are two types of adpositional phrases. In **prepositional phrases** the preposition *precedes* the noun phrase, while in **postpositional phrases** the postposition *follows* the noun phrase. Languages usually have either prepositional phrases or postpositional phrases, but not both. The noun phrase that occurs in an adpositional phrase is called the **object of the adposition**.

In most languages of the world, adpositions cannot occur without an accompanying noun phrase. Thus, while we can easily say *He came from the house* in English, the sentence *\*he came from*, which lacks the dependent noun phrase, is ungrammatical. The same is true in Mandarin Chinese. Example (7a) has a prepositional phrase, set off by square brackets:

(7)  a.  *Wǒ*      *[gēn      tā]*       *chǎojìa     le*
         1SG     with     3SG.M     argue     PFV
         'I argued with him.'

The sentence is not grammatical if either the noun phrase or the preposition is absent, as shown in (7b) and (7c):

(7)  b.  Noun phrase absent
         \*     *Wǒ       gēn       chǎojìa     le*
               1SG     with     argue     PFV

(7)  c.  Preposition absent
         \*     *Wǒ       tā       chǎojia     le*
               1SG     3SG.M     argue     PFV

The same is true of languages with postpositions. Consider Example (8), which illustrates this phenomenon in Japanese. Here there is an **instrumental** postposition, which translates into English as 'with':

(8)  a.  *Taroo     wa      [pen     de]       e          o       kaita*
         Taro     TOP     pen     INST     picture     ACC     draw.PST
         'Taro drew a picture with a pen.'

Again, we see that both the postposition and the noun phrase are required for a grammatical sentence; it is not possible to omit either one:

(8)  b.  Noun-phrase absent
         *\*Taroo     wa      de       e          o       kaita*
          Taro     TOP     INST     picture     ACC     draw.PST

(8)  c.  Postposition absent
         *\*Taroo     wa      pen       e          o       kaita*
          Taro     TOP     pen     picture     ACC     draw.PST

We have seen that adpositions require the presence of a noun phrase to form a syntactically complete unit. Hence the adposition and the noun phrase together form a syntactic constituent.

A second argument for the adpositional phrase as a syntactic constituent is that **the ordering between the noun phrase and the adposition is fixed**. Thus, one can say in English *Hit it with a hammer* but not *\*Hit it a hammer with*. (At this point you might be thinking about some seeming counterexamples to this claim, like the English sentence *Eat it up!* However, *up* in this sentence is actually not a preposition but a verb particle. For more on this, see Textbox 6.5.) Again, this is also true in Mandarin Chinese; *cóng táiběi* means 'from Taipei'; the reverse order which puts the preposition after the noun phrase is ungrammatical: *\*táiběi cóng*. Since elements of the adpositional phrase occur in a fixed order, we see that it is a syntactic constituent.

Another argument for the adpositional phrase as a syntactic unit is that **in most languages the adposition and the noun phrase must be contiguous**; one cannot place other elements between them. For example, in English we cannot say *\*He arrived at suddenly the house*. Even though adverbs like *suddenly* can occur in a number of positions in the sentence, they cannot be placed between the elements of a prepositional phrase. Again this is true for Mandarin: one cannot say *\*cóng kè táiběi*, inserting *kè* 'suddenly' between the preposition and the noun.

**SIDEBAR 6.9**

TEMPLATE FOR THE PREPOSITIONAL PHRASE

The English prepositional phrase has a simple template:

PREP NP

Here PREP is the abbreviation for "preposition" and NP for "noun phrase." The abbreviation of "prepositional phrase" is PP. Prepositional phrases can have many structures, but that is because noun phrases can have many structures; at the higher level of the constituent represented here, the structure is simple.

The template for a postpositional phrase (also abbreviated PP) is simply: NP POST.

## TEXTBOX 6.5 **ENGLISH PREPOSITION OR VERB PARTICLE?**

In English syntax, we have to be careful to differentiate **prepositions**, which head prepositional phrases, from homophonous **particles** that occur in **particle verbs**. Particle verbs are compounds that combine a verb with a particle that historically developed from a preposition, but no longer functions as one. Consider the following English sentences:

a. *Sonia walked out the door.*
b. *Sonia handed out the candy.*

In Example (a) there is a prepositional phrase *out the door*, which contains a preposition *out* followed by a noun phrase *the door*. The preposition indicates the direction of the movement from an inside location outward; it can be simply contrasted with *in the door* which indicates movement in the opposite direction. Now consider example (b). Native English speakers will intuitively know that *out the candy* is not a prepositional phrase in the same way that *out the door* is in (a). Rather, *out* is part of the particle–verb compound *handed out*. We can find syntactic proof for this intuition in the fact that the (b) sentence can be restated with the word *out* positioned after the noun phrase, i.e., *Sonia handed the candy out*. The same is not true of Example (a). The sentence *\*Sonia walked the door out* is decidedly odd, and even if one can think of a context where it would make sense (e.g., bringing a door out by walking it), it is not the semantic equivalent of the sentence in (a).

Also, notice that while substituting *in* for *out* in example (a) simply indicates a change in direction, substituting *in* for *out* in sentence (b) results in a sentence with an entirely different meaning. This is because *hand in* and *hand out* are each unique compounds in the language with meanings that are not simply derivative from the sum of their parts. This is further evidence that *hand out* is a compound and not a verb followed by a preposition.

**SIDEBAR 6.10**

The structure of the English verb phrase can be represented by the following template:

(ADV) V (ADV) (NP) (PP*) (ADV)

Note that adverbs can come in multiple positions.

We have presented three arguments for the syntactic unity of the adpositional phrase: obligatoriness, ordering, and contiguity. Thus, we may conclude that the adposition and noun phrase together form a small but tightly constructed syntactic constituent, the adpositional phrase. Sidebar 6.9 gives templates for both prepositional and postpositional phrases.

### 6.2.3 Other types of syntactic constituents

Most languages of the world have noun phrases and adpositional phrases. However, there are also other types of syntactic constituents that are less universal. ***Each language needs to be examined independently in order to determine which syntactic constituents form the building blocks of the syntax.***

While noun phrases and adpositional phrases are probably the most common types of phrases cross-linguistically, there are other types as well. For example, an adverb and an adjective together can form an adjective phrase (e.g., English *very well*), or in Mandarin, a numeral and classifier can form a classifier phrase (e.g., *sān duǒ* 'three (flowers)').

**SIDEBAR 6.11**

Draw labeled tree diagrams for each of the sentences in Textbox 6.6, labeling the phrase types and word class for each word. Check your work with the answers posted on the website for your learning and skill development.

English has clear evidence for a **verb phrase** (see Sidebar 6.10), ***a syntactic constituent consisting of a verb as the head of the phrase, and optional dependents including adverbs, prepositional phrases, object noun phrases, and indirect objects in prepositional phrases***. Examples of English verb phrases are given in Textbox 6.6; a short exercise to check your understanding appears in Sidebar 6.11.

---

### TEXTBOX 6.6 **ENGLISH VERB PHRASES**

In the following sentences, each verb phrase is put into square brackets and marked as "VP." The major constituents of the verb phrase are labeled with the following abbreviations: NP noun phrase, PP prepositional phrase, ADV adverbial, ADJ adjective.

a. *My parents* [*live in Sonoma* ]$_{VP}$.
         V    PP

b. *She* [*drives to the mountains annually* ]$_{VP}$
      V    PP      ADV

c. *My kids* [*always carve pumpkins at Halloween* ]$_{VP}$
    ADV  V  NP     PP
            Object

d. *My Aunt Helen* [*gave her dog to my mom.*]$_{VP}$
         V  NP    PP
        Object   Indirect object

e. *Carlos* [*is amazing*]$_{VP}$
      V  ADJ

Verb phrases obligatorily contain a **predicate** (in English always a verb), the structural center of the clause. A special type of verb is a **copula**, which denotes a relation between two noun phrases or between a noun phrase and an adjective. The copula in English is *be*. The noun phrase or adjective that follows a copula is called the **copula complement** (sometimes also the **predicate nominal** or **predicate adjective**). In the sentence *Carlos is amazing*, *amazing* is the copula complement (predicate adjective). In the sentence *Kobin is a top scholar*, the noun phrase *a top scholar* is the copula complement (predicate nominal).

We will now explore two arguments for the status of the verb phrase as a syntactic constituent in English. First, the order of elements within a verb phrase is relatively fixed. For example, we cannot place elements other than an auxiliary before the verb, e.g., *\*She with the food drive helps* and *\*Everyone would boxes of chocolates give* are decidedly incorrect. Similarly, placing a prepositional phrase between the verb and a noun phrase results in an ungrammatical sentence: *\*My kids baked for Halloween cookies*. These types of tests constitute clear evidence that the verb phrase is a unit that has internal structure.

A second argument that the English verb phrase forms a syntactic constituent is that it can be replaced with the **pro-verb** *do*. Note that the entire verb phrase is replaced by *do*, not part of it, as the examples in (9) illustrate. (Although some of the starred sentences in the examples below may be grammatical in other contexts, they are not possible utterances in the exchanges given here.)

(9)    a. *Who lives in Sonoma?*
          *My parents do.*
          *\*My parents do in Sonoma.*

       b. *Does she drive to the mountains?*
          *She does.*
          *\*She does to the mountains.*

       c. *My kids baked cookies for Halloween.*
          *They did?*
          *\*They did cookies?*

       d. *Frida gave her dog to Frank.*
          *She did?*
          *\*Did she her dog?*

By replacing the verb phrases with pro-verbs, as in (9), we can see that the verb phrase in English is treated as a single cohesive unit; thus, it is a syntactic constituent.

However, ***not all languages have verb phrases***. The grammatical arguments that illustrate the cohesiveness of the verb phrase in English do not automatically apply to other languages. Every language must be analyzed independently to determine the set of phrasal constituents and their particular grammatical features.

### 6.2.4 Recursive structures in syntax

*One of the interesting design principles of constituent structure is recursion, or the ability for a phrasal constituent to embed another phrasal constituent of the same type within it.* We can see this by examining the templates of the English noun phrase and the English prepositional phrase:

NP: (DET) (QUANT) (NUM) (ADJ*) N (PP*) (REL)
PP: PREP NP

Notice that the noun phrase can contain a prepositional phrase and that a prepositional phrase obligatorily contains a noun phrase. This allows sentences such as (10).

**(10)** *I saw the book on the table by the window in the corner of the room.*

Each prepositional phrase is embedded into the noun phrase containing the noun it modifies. We can represent this by means of a labeled tree diagram. The elements of each phrase are represented on a unique level of the tree, as in Figure 6.2.

We can see that each phrase type is recursively embedded into the other. In principle, this recursion could go on infinitely; however, human cognitive

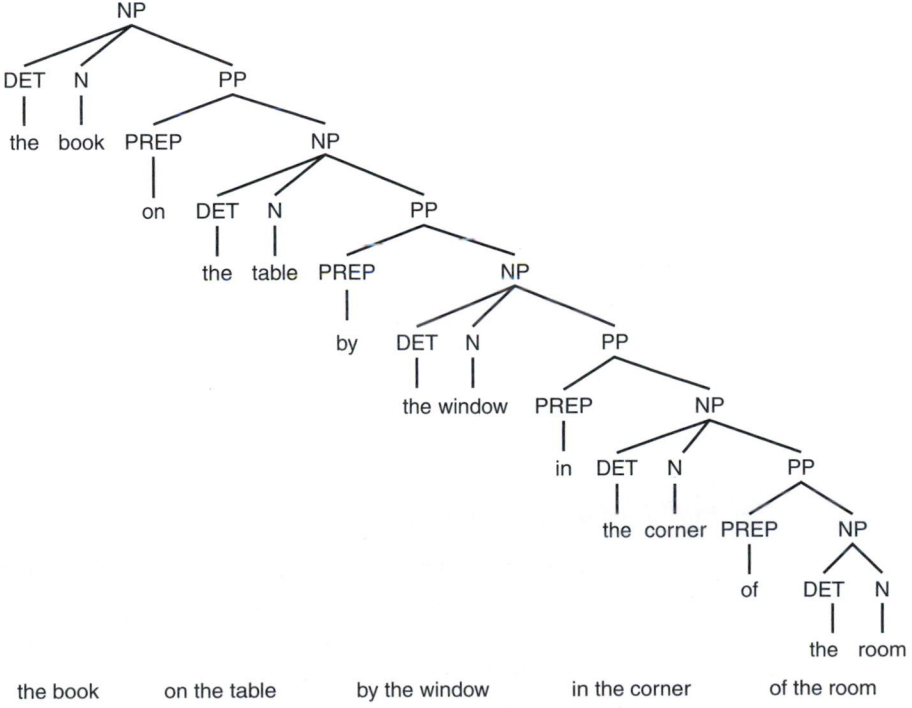

**Figure 6.2** Labeled tree diagram for *The book on the table by the window in the corner of the room*

constraints on memory – as well as physical constraints on production – make excessively long recursive structures impractical as mediums of communication. Nevertheless, ***the ability to embed one complex element into another allows for great structural flexibility and expressive power in human language***.

## 6.3  The clause

We will now move up from the phrase to the next higher level of syntactic organization: the clause. **A clause *can be defined as a syntactic unit typically consisting of a verb (in some languages within a verb phrase), its noun phrase arguments, and optional adverbial elements (usually adverbs and adpositional phrases)***. As with other syntactic units, clauses have internal organization. For example, in most languages the elements of the clause occur in a relatively fixed order. Usually clauses occur as contiguous units; they are not divided by other inserted elements that are not part of the clause. Clauses can also have other restrictions; for example, typically only one tense can be specified per clause.

We can see evidence for these facts in English. For example, the typical order for a verb and its noun-phrase arguments in English is Subject-Verb-Object (SVO), as in (11).

(11)   *The band*   *played*   *my favorite song*

      subject   verb   object

Note that other orderings result in ungrammatical sentences, e.g., *\*played my favorite song the band* is ungrammatical.

We can see the contiguity of clausal elements if we put two clauses together with a conjunction, as in (12).

(12)   *Chris carried the popcorn and Robin carried the drinks.*

The two clauses must occur in a strict linear order: first one then the other. We can't scramble their elements, as shown by the ungrammatical nature of *\*Chris the drinks carried the popcorn and Robin carried* or *\*Chris carried carried the popcorn and Robin the drinks*.

Finally, the fact that clauses in English can have only one tense is illustrated by the inability of the future auxiliary *will* to occur in the same clause as the third-person singular present-tense morpheme *-s*. Thus, while both *Camille will play her violin* and *Camille plays her violin* are acceptable, *\*Camille will plays* is not. This restriction does not hold over separate clauses. So we can say *Camille plays today* *at 4 and she will play again tomorrow.* ***There is a grammatical uniformity within each clause (e.g., the entire clause is in future tense), which we can describe using statements of grammatical regularity, or rules.*** The elements in a clause are grammatically unified, demonstrating that the clause is an important unit in grammar.

We will now look in more detail at the grammatical relationships between elements of the clause, beginning with verbs and their arguments.

### 6.3.1 Arguments and transitivity

***The term* argument *refers to a noun phrase***, but rather than emphasizing its internal constituent structure, the term ***emphasizes the grammatical status of the* argument *in relation to the verb***. There are two types of arguments: **core arguments** and **oblique arguments**. (See Sidebar 6.12 on the meaning of the word *argument*.)

***Core arguments are those that have a grammatical relationship with the verb***; this can be determined by their grammatical behavior, such as the ability to take certain types of affixes, the ability to trigger affixation on the verb, and their ordering in the clause with respect to other elements.

***Oblique arguments do not have a grammatical relationship with the verb***. They may instead be grammatically linked to a preposition or a postposition, although they don't need to be. In many languages, oblique arguments have more freedom of positioning than core arguments. Oblique arguments also convey information external to the strict verbal semantics, such as the location of an event, its time, or the instrument used to carry out an action. Try out the exercise given in Sidebar 6.13 to check your understanding of core versus oblique arguments.

Each argument in the English sentences in (13) has been marked for its core or oblique status:

(13) a. *She ate her french fries with a fork.*
        **core**     **core**     **oblique**

   b. *My mother arrived at the airport this morning.*
        **core**      **oblique**    **oblique**

   c. *The ball hit the goal post.*
        **core**       **core**

---

**SIDEBAR 6.12**

'ARGUMENT'

The word *argument* has both technical and non-technical uses in linguistics and you will see both in this chapter. The technical meaning is that presented here, a noun phrase of a particular grammatical status in relation to a verb. *Argument* is also used in its non-technical sense of advancing evidence in favor of a conclusion. Both terms are used throughout this chapter and beyond.

**SIDEBAR 6.13**

The noun phrases in each of the following examples are underlined. Determine whether each noun phrase is core or oblique. Also note the transitivity of the verb. Answers can be found on the website.

a. *He left with his friends.*

b. *They will meet us at the restaurant.*

c. *Tomorrow I will drive from San Francisco to Los Angeles.*

d. *She gave the letter to her boyfriend.*

d.  *I    gave a dollar  to my son  for ice cream.*
   **core**     **core**     **core**     **oblique**

A brief comparison of the examples in Table 6.1 shows that clauses can differ in the number of core arguments. Some verbs take only one core argument, other verbs take two, and a smaller number of verbs take three. This property of verbs is referred to as **transitivity.** *Verbs that can take at most one core argument are referred to as* **intransitive;** *verbs that can take at most two core arguments are referred to as* **transitive;** *and verbs that can take at most three core arguments are referred to as* **ditransitive**. Verbs of each type are illustrated in Table 6.1, together with the number of core arguments and example sentences with the core arguments underlined.

### 6.3.2  Grammatical relations: subjects

We have seen that verbs have a certain number of core arguments based on their transitivity. Now we will examine how the ***various core arguments have different*** **grammatical relations *with the verb***. We will begin our discussion using English and the grammatical relation of **subject**. Subjects are one type of core noun phrase. In the sentences in (14) – taken from the Santa Barbara Corpus of Spoken American English – the subjects are in bold; while objects are underlined.

(14)  a. ***I** need new filters.* (SBC: 001)
     b. *Do **you** remember the date?* (SBC: 008)

**TABLE 6.1** Examples of intransitive, transitive, and ditransitive verbs and sentences

| Transitivity | Number of core arguments | Example verb | Sample sentence |
|---|---|---|---|
| Intransitive | 1 | 'sneeze' | *I sneezed.* |
| Intransitive | 1 | 'go' | *Sam went to Russia.* |
| Intransitive | 1 | 'grow' | *Tomatoes never grow well here.* |
| Transitive | 2 | 'push' | *Carl pushed the wheelbarrow.* |
| Transitive | 2 | 'build' | *We built our house last year.* |
| Transitive | 2 | 'lift' | *They lifted the table onto the truck.* |
| Ditransitive | 3 | 'give' | *Angelo gave fifty dollars to the foodbank.* |
| Ditransitive | 3 | 'teach' | *He teaches math to high school students.* |
| Ditransitive | 3 | 'tell' | *Mike told that story to my children.* |

c. **She** *wants* <u>*everything*</u> *on her terms.* (SBC: 006)

d. **Me and mom** *always accused* <u>*her*</u> *of being lazy.* (SBC: 001)

Note that the subjects in these sentences consistently precede the verb. This is the usual position for subjects in English statements (although it is possible to change the order for stylistic effect).

Another grammatical feature of English subjects is that they trigger the use of the suffix *-s* on the verb. This suffix is used when the subject is both third-person and singular, as in (14c). Note that we can't use the *-s* suffix when the subject is: first-person, as in (14a); second-person, as in (b); or third-person plural, as in (d). Notice also that the *-s* suffix is not triggered by *her* in (d), even though it is a third-person-singular core argument. This is because *her* is the **object** of the verb *accused*, not the subject (hence the use of *her*, the object form of the pronoun, as opposed to *she*, the subject form). The verb agrees with third-person-singular subjects – rather than objects – in the present tense, as in (c).

From this brief exercise, we have identified two grammatical properties that are shared by English subjects:

i.   English subjects occur before the verb in stylistically neutral statements.

ii.  English subjects trigger third-person-singular agreement in the present tense.

There are a number of other grammatical features of subjects in English. Consider the fabricated sentences in (15), both of which have the subject omitted in the first clause.

(15)  a. *Removing his sunglasses,* **Adam** *watched Sam.*

b. *Removing his sunglasses,* **Sam** *watched* <u>*Adam.*</u>

In each case, it is necessarily the one who is watching (the subject of the second clause) who also removes his sunglasses. When the subject of an initial clause is omitted in this fashion, the omitted subject is necessarily **coreferential** with the subject of the following clause.

We can represent the grammatical relationships between the two subjects as in (16). A null sign is used to indicate that the subject of the initial clause has been omitted.

(16)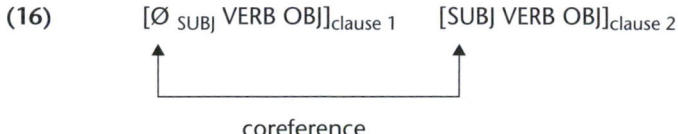

coreference

We have thus uncovered a third property of grammatical subjects in English:

iii. When combining clauses in a certain way, omitted subjects are necessarily coreferential with the subject of the following clause.

***Languages across the world differ in the grammatical properties that define subjects.*** In Nepali, verb agreement indexes the person, number, and – for second and third persons – the honorific status of the subject. The Nepali paradigm in (17) illustrates these various verb forms in the present tense. Note that we find verb agreement with subjects of both intransitive verbs (e.g., *sutnu* 'come') and transitive verbs (e.g., *khānu* 'eat').

| (17) | | *sutnu* 'to sleep' | *khanu* 'to eat' |
|------|------|------|------|
| | 1SG | sut-chu | khān-chu |
| | 1PL | sut-chãũ | khān-chãũ |
| | 2SG | sut-chau | khān-chau |
| | 2PL | sut-chāu | khān-chau |
| | 2HON | sut-nu-huncha | khā-nu-huncha |
| | 3SG | sut-cha | khān-cha |
| | 3PL | sut-chan | khān-chan |
| | 3HON | sut-nu-huncha | khā-nu-huncha |

**SIDEBAR 6.14**

The examples in (20) are taken from recordings of parent–child discourse as part of a larger study on Korean language acquisition by Professor Patricia Clancy, at the University of California, Santa Barbara. The utterances were produced by a child named Wenceng, at age 2 years and 1 month.

**Glossing**

| | |
|------|------|
| NOM | nominative case |
| ACC | accusative case |
| ANT | anterior (marks an event as completed and prior to current time or other event) |
| IE | informal ending (marks an utterance as being informal) |
| DECL | declarative |

In Korean, there is a case-marker *-ka* that is found only on subjects. We find it suffixed both to subjects of intransitive verbs, as in (18a), and to subjects of transitive verbs, as in (b). (See Sidebar 6.14 for a note on these examples.)

(18) a. *mulkoki-ka*          *iss-ta*
       fish-NOM                exist-DECL
       'There's a fish.' (lit. 'A fish exists (there)')

    b. *nay-ka*        *ttwukkeng-ul*      *yel-ess-e*
       1SG-NOM        cover-ACC          open-ANT-IE
       'I opened the cover.'

Case-markers with this distribution are said to mark **nominative** (i.e., **subject**) case. Korean is unlike English in this regard. Korean differs from both English and Nepali in having case-marking, but not verb agreement. It is similar to Nepali, however, in placing the verb at the end of the clause and allowing flexibility in the word order of the subject and the object.

This brief discussion illustrates that ***languages differ in the grammatical properties that define the subject grammatical relation***. While some languages may have a number of grammatical properties that define this relation, others might have only one, or even none. In the latter case, we would say that those languages lacked the subject category.

### 6.3.3 Grammatical relations: objects

Transitive and ditransitive verbs have **objects**. Objects are also a type of core argument, but ***objects have different grammatical properties from***

***subjects***. Consider again our examples of transitive clauses in English; objects are underlined.

(19)  a. *I need <u>new filters</u>.*
      b. *She wants <u>everything</u>.*
      c. *Me and mom always accused <u>her</u>.*
      d. *Adam removed <u>his sunglasses</u>.*
      e. *Sam watched <u>Adam</u>.*

In English, objects directly follow the verb; these are called **direct objects**. We can see that English grammatically distinguishes subjects from direct objects in part by their ordering: in stylistically neutral declarative sentences, subjects precede the verb and objects follow the verb. English is thus described as having SVO (Subject-Verb-Object) constituent order.

English also distinguishes direct objects from **indirect objects**. By definition, ***indirect objects occur only with ditransitive verbs***. In English, indirect objects differ from direct objects in that they can occur in two positions: in prepositional phrases following the prepositions *to* or *for* and in so-called **double-object constructions** where they immediately follow the verb. We can see these two possibilities in the related sentences in (20). *Veronica*, the indirect object, occurs following the preposition *to* in (20a), and in the first position of the double-object construction in (b).

(20)  a. *The Dean gave the prize to Veronica.*
      b. *The Dean gave Veronica the prize.*

In English, only indirect objects have the ability to occur in this pairing of positions. Try out the short exercise in Sidebar 6.15 to check your understanding of direct and indirect objects.

In many languages, case-marking is used to differentiate direct and indirect objects. ***Case-markers that indicate direct objects are called* accusative, *while those that indicate indirect objects are called* dative**. We can see case-marking differentiating these two classes of objects in the Japanese sentences in (21). Note that direct objects occur with the accusative case-marker regardless of whether they are objects of transitive (21a) or ditransitive (21b) verbs (see Sidebar 6.16 for the glossing conventions).

---

**SIDEBAR 6.15**

In each of the ditransitive sentences below, identify the direct object and the indirect object. Then restate the sentence using a double-object construction to confirm your analysis. You can check your answers on the website.

a. *John handed the baby to his mother.*

b. *He taught French to sixth-graders.*

c. *She brought flowers for her sister.*

d. *He told his version of events to the police officer.*

Do the following sentences have indirect objects? How do you know?

e. *He drove me to Portland.*

f. *He worked my shift for me.*

---

**SIDEBAR 6.16**

GLOSSES

| | |
|---|---|
| SG | singular |
| TOP | topic |
| ACC | accusative |
| DAT | dative |
| PST | past |

(21)  a. *watashi*  *wa*  *toofu*  *o*  *tabeta*
         1SG        TOP    tofu    ACC   eat.PST
         'I ate tofu.'

b.  *Erika*  *wa*  *Mika*  *ni*  *hon*  *o*  *kashita.*
    Erika  TOP  Mika  DAT  book  ACC  lend.PST
    'Erika lent a book to Mika.'

**SIDEBAR 6.17**
GLOSSES
| | |
|---|---|
| 3.NOM | 3rd-person nominative |
| PL.OBJ | plural object |
| PST | past |

Nez Perce, a Native American language spoken in eastern Oregon and western Idaho, also has an accusative case-marker, as illustrated in (22).

(The symbol χ indicates a voiceless uvular fricative)

**(22) Nez Perce (Phinney 1934: 368)**

*kaa*  *wéetú*  *núu-ne*  *hi-nées-qicχ-ne*
and   not   we-ACC   3.NOM-PL.OBJ-take.care-PST
'And he didn't take care of us.'

Example (22) also illustrates a verbal prefix *nees-*, which agrees with the direct object in number. Thus in Nez Perce, both case-marking and agreement index the direct object grammatical relation. ***There are many other grammatical properties related to categories of object; each language needs to be examined independently to determine which criteria (if any) distinguish between types of objects***.

### 6.3.4  Other grammatical relations

***While subjects, objects, and indirect objects are familiar from English and most European languages, these are not the only core grammatical relations that are found in the world's languages***. For example, it is quite common to have grammatical properties that pertain only to the "subject" of transitive verbs, but not to the "subject" of intransitive verbs. We refer to this grammatical relation as **ergative**. Discussions of languages with ergative grammatical patters are found in Language Profiles 3 (Manange), 7 (Tsez), and 8 (Bardi).

### 6.3.5  Grammatical relations versus semantic case roles

Up to this point, we have been looking solely at **grammatical relations** between arguments and verbs, that is, the grammatical properties (such as agreement, case, order, etc.) that characterize sets of core arguments. ***It is important to differentiate these grammatically defined relationships from the semantic relationships between arguments and verbs***. Consider the sentences in (25).

(23)  a. *Julie swims at the health club.*
      b. *Julie feels dizzy after breakfast.*

In (23a), Julie is acting intentionally, of her own volition; we say Julie is an **agent** in this clause. In (23b) Julie is not a volitional actor, but someone experiencing a physical state; we say here that Julie is an **experiencer**. In both cases, the noun phrase *Julie* is the grammatical subject of the clause. It occurs before the verb and triggers the third-person-singular agreement marker -*s*. So while the grammatical relationship between *Julie* and the verb is the same in both examples, the semantic relationship is different. ***Grammatical and semantic relationships are independent of each other***.

Now consider the two oblique arguments in (23a) and (b). You will see that while both *the health club* and *breakfast* are oblique (i.e., neither is a core argument), they also differ semantically; *the health club* indicates the location of an activity, while *after breakfast* is temporal, specifying the time that the situation occurs.

***The semantic relationships between verbs and arguments are referred to as* semantic case roles**. The following list gives the most commonly found semantic case roles in the world's languages (see Sidebar 6.18). To illustrate the independence of semantic case roles and grammatical relations, the grammatical relation of each underlined NP will be given in parentheses to the right of each example:

## Case Role

- **Agent**: The volitional instigator of an activity or event.

  | | |
  |---|---|
  | *Andrea carved the pumpkin.* | (subject) |
  | *The dog ate the cake.* | (subject) |
  | *This pumpkin was carved by Andrea.* | (oblique) |

- **Patient**: An entity that undergoes a change of state as the result of an activity or event.

  | | |
  |---|---|
  | *Andrea carved the pumpkin.* | (direct object) |
  | *The dog ate the cake.* | (direct object) |
  | *The pumpkins will be carved by Andrea.* | (subject) |

- **Theme**: An entity undergoing motion or being located.

  | | |
  |---|---|
  | *Shelly took the dog to the vet.* | (direct object) |
  | *Brian is at his mom's house.* | (subject) |

- **Recipient**: An entity that receives a theme.

  | | |
  |---|---|
  | *He speaks Navajo to his children.* | (indirect object) |
  | *She got a letter from an old friend.* | (subject) |

- **Beneficiary**: An entity who benefits from an action.

  | | |
  |---|---|
  | *He substituted for John.* | (oblique) |
  | *He sang songs for the children.* | (indirect object) |
  | *They helped her when she was ill.* | (direct object) |
  | *He benefited from their kindness.* | (subject) |

- **Experiencer**: An entity that experiences a physical or emotional state.

  | | |
  |---|---|
  | *Clifford became delirious.* | (subject) |
  | *Rasheed was tired.* | (subject) |

- **Location**: A static location.

  *Brian slept at <u>his mom's house</u>.*                    (oblique)
  *<u>Each packet</u> contains one ounce of powder.*    (subject)

- **Source**: The beginning point of a motion trajectory.

  *She drove from <u>San Francisco</u> to Los Angeles.*                      (oblique)
  *They left <u>Kenya</u>.*                                                  (direct object)
  *<u>Rotterdam</u> will be next year's starting point for the Tour de France.*    (subject)

- **Goal**: The endpoint of a motion trajectory.

  *She drove from San Francisco to <u>Los Angeles</u>.*    (oblique)
  *He hopes to reach <u>Portland</u> tomorrow.*            (direct object)
  *<u>Seattle</u> is their destination.*                   (subject)

- **Temporal**: A location in time.

  *She comes home during <u>the holidays</u>.*                (oblique)
  *<u>June</u> is when the strawberries are at their best.*   (subject)

- **Instrument**: An entity used to perform an action.

  *She applied the last coat of paint with <u>a roller</u>.*    (oblique)
  *Dad used <u>a small knife</u> to cut open the fish.*        (direct object)
  *<u>This type of key</u> opens several locks.*              (subject)

These examples illustrate the independence of semantic case roles and grammatical relations: each semantic case role is shown in multiple grammatical relations, and each grammatical relation is shown with multiple case roles.

## 6.4  Constructions

Most of the examples cited so far in this chapter have illustrated affirmative, declarative, **active** clauses, which are both the simplest and most prototypical clause types. However, functions like signaling negation, asking questions, giving commands, and highlighting or downplaying the importance of referents in a given discourse context are also critical to human communication. For such tasks, languages have a variety of **constructions**, fixed grammatical patterns associated with particular functions. Consider the five sentences in (24). Although they all convey information about Olivia, a dog, and an event of finding, the sentences have different forms and different functions.

(24)  a. *Olivia found the dog.*       Declarative, affirmative, active
      b. *Did Olivia find the dog?*    Interrogative, affirmative, active
      c. *Olivia didn't find the dog.* Declarative, negative, active
      d. *The dog was found.*          Declarative, affirmative, passive
      e. *Wasn't the dog found?*       Interrogative, negative, passive

| **Active** | Subject | | Verb | | Object |
|---|---|---|---|---|---|
| | Agent | | | | Patient |
| **Passive** | Subject | *be* | Verb$_{\text{past participle}}$ | | (*by* Oblique) |
| | Patient | | | | Agent |

**Figure 6.3** Schemas representing active and passive constructions in English

The sentence in (24b) illustrates a **polar question** (a question that one could answer with a simple "yes" or "no" response). In English, polar questions require an auxiliary verb in the first position of the sentence. This is followed by the subject noun phrase, and then the verb phrase. This is a construction, with the fixed part of it being both the required auxiliary and the strict ordering of the auxiliary, subject, and verb phrase; the function is that of requesting an affirmative or negative response.

English negation, exemplified in (24c), also requires an auxiliary verb, which is followed by the negative morpheme *not* (sometimes contracted into *n't*). In this case, the auxiliary follows the subject, as in the declarative clause. Note that this construction requires the presence of a particular morpheme (the negative) in a particular position.

The **passive** construction exemplified in (24d) requires a particular auxiliary – a form of the verb *be* – and a particular form of the lexical verb (the past participle). In addition, the semantic patient, which would typically be the direct object in an active construction, is the grammatical subject in the passive. These differences can be schematized as in Figure 6.3.

As shown in Figure 6.3, it is also possible for a passive clause to specify the semantic agent in a prepositional phrase as the object of the preposition *by*, e.g., *The dog was found by Olivia*. This is optional, a feature denoted by the parentheses in the schema. The function of the passive is to put noun phrases that denote prominent or important referents into the subject position. For example, if people are discussing a particular lost dog and what happened to it, then keeping NPs referring to the dog in subject position allows for structural continuity with the surrounding discourse. Passive constructions can also be used when speakers want to de-emphasize an agent, or when the identity of an agent is unknown or unimportant. Consider, for example, the ubiquitous passives of the structure [Celebrity name] *was spotted* [e.g., at a local club, with their ex-girlfriend, etc.]. The identity of the person spotting the celebrity is assumed to be unimportant to the reader compared to the celebrity's unexpected appearance in public.

It is important to note that there are cross-linguistic differences in the types of constructions used for a given function. For example, Dolakha Newar signals negation by simply prefixing a negative morpheme to the verb; auxiliaries are not required, as they are in English:

(25)  chana        kehẽ              mo-cõ
      2SG.GEN      younger.sister    NEG-stay
      'your sister isn't staying (at home)'

Polar questions are also constructed differently in Dolakha Newar than in English. They simply involve the addition of a particle (glossed here as Q) at the end of the sentence:

(26)  chin        khã        la-ina            rã
      2SG.ERG     matter     talk-2SG.FUT      Q
      'Will you talk about this matter?'

Without the final question particle, the sentence in (26) would be the affirmative counterpart, i.e., 'you will talk about this matter.'

Interestingly, the range of constructions that are attested in the world's languages for particular linguistic functions (such as asking questions, signaling negation, or giving commands) is usually quite limited. Study of such cross-linguistic variation is the primary focus of **linguistic typology** and can tell us much about how linguistic structures are used to meet speakers' communicative needs.

## 6.5  The sentence

*A sentence **is an integrated syntactic unit consisting of at least one clause and optionally adverbials that have scope over the sentence as a whole.*** The notion of integration is important, because there is a difference between having two adjacent sentences that are not integrated, as in (27a), and having two clauses integrated into a single sentence, as in (27b) or (c).

(27)  a. *The sun came up. It shone in my eyes.*
      b. *When the sun came up it shone in my eyes.*
      c. *The sun came up and shone in my eyes.*

In example (27a), there is nothing that connects the two sentences; each forms a complete syntactic unit that could stand on its own as an independent utterance. By contrast, in examples (27b) and (c), the two clauses have been integrated into a single sentence.

In (27b), the first clause has been marked as **subordinate** by the use of an adverbial conjunction, *when*. Note that this clause could not normally stand on its own; it is providing the temporal frame for the following proposition.

In (27c) the two clauses have been coordinated by the conjunction *and*. The integration of the two is evident from the omission of the subject in the second clause. In English, one typically does not omit the subject in a single-clause sentence.

Thus *Ø *shone in my eyes*, where Ø indicates the position of the omitted subject, is considered ungrammatical.

### 6.5.1 Clause-combining: coordination versus subordination

***A complex sentence is a sentence with more than one clause***. Both (24b) and (c) above are complex sentences. ***Clauses can be combined either by coordinating two independent clauses using a conjunction, thereby creating the larger unit, or by placing one clause inside of another as a dependent (or subordinate) element***. These two structural types can be represented schematically as in Figure 6.4.

With coordination, two (or more) clauses are conjoined at the same level of structure. In contrast, with **subordination**, a main or **matrix clause** has another subordinate clause within it as a dependent element. ***There are three distinct ways by which subordinate clauses are made dependent to a matrix clause, so there are three types of subordinate clauses: adverbial clauses, relative clauses, and complement clauses***.

Many of the world's languages use both coordination and subordination in creating complex sentences. The details of clause combining vary considerably across languages. Here we will restrict the discussion to English.

To begin our exploration, let's consider some examples from *Harry Potter and the Goblet of Fire* by J. K. Rowling. Dependent clauses are underlined.

(28)
   a. *Hermione joined him a moment later and slipped him a butterbeer under his cloak.*
   b. *Harry felt he ought to go, but his curiosity held him in the chair.*
   c. *If Voldemort is really getting stronger again, my priority is to ensure your safety.*
   d. *He sat with Hermione and Ron in the library as the sun set outside.*
   e. *"Dumbledore, you know perfectly well that you did not make a mistake!"*
   f. *She knew he'd passed information to the Death Eaters.*
   g. *Harry watched the dragon nearest to them teeter dangerously on its back legs.*
   h. *Professor Dumbledore was now looking down at Harry, who looked right back at him.*
   i. *Those people whose names come out of the Goblet of Fire are bound to compete in the tournament.*

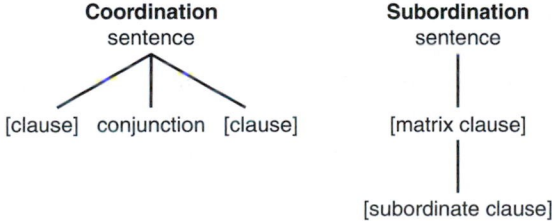

**Figure 6.4** Schematic representation of coordination and subordination

The nine sentences in (28) illustrate four distinct types of clause combining. Examples (a) and (b) illustrate coordination, with clauses combined using a simple conjunction (*and* in (a) and *but* in (b)). Examples (c) and (d) illustrate **adverbial clauses**, marked by the **subordinating conjunctions** (*if* in (c) and *as* in (d)). Examples (e) through (g) illustrate **complement clauses**, where a clause functions as a noun-phrase argument of the verb of the matrix clause. Examples (h) and (i) illustrate **relative clauses**, where a clause is placed within a noun phrase and is a dependent of a head noun. We will now examine each structure in more detail.

### 6.5.2  Clause-combining: coordination versus subordination

**Coordination** *combines two clauses in linear sequence using a conjunction*: typically *and*, *or*, or *but*, or their equivalents in other languages. *Clauses combined through coordination form sentences that behave as single cohesive syntactic units*. There are a number of arguments that support this claim. For example, in English the subject of the second clause in a coordinate structure can be omitted, as in (28a) above. This clause, with the absence of an overt subject argument, would be ungrammatical if it occurred independently, i.e., *\*slipped him a butterbeer under his cloak* is not by itself a complete sentence; it is only grammatical when combined with another clause via coordination.

A second argument that coordinated clauses act as a single cohesive unit is the fact that the unit as a whole can be combined with other clauses. We see this in Example (29), where two conjoined clauses (underlined) function as the complement of a matrix verb.

**(29)**  *Harry watched <u>Cedric pull a knife out of his pocket and cut Cho free</u>.*

### 6.5.3  Adverbial clauses

*Adverbial clauses are dependent clauses that are linked to a matrix clause using either an* **adverbial conjunction** *or an affix that specifies the semantic relationship between clauses*. These conjunctions convey meanings such as condition (*if*), cause (*because*), consequence (*so*), concession (*although*), temporal sequence (*when*, *after*), temporal overlap (*while*), and purpose (*to*, *in order to*).

The subordinate status of adverbial clauses is evident from the fact that they cannot occur independently; for example, *as the sun set outside* cannot stand alone as an independent utterance.

### 6.5.4  Complement clauses

**Complement clauses** *are dependent clauses that function as noun phrase arguments of verbs*. Consider again our "Harry Potter" examples (28e) through (g), repeated here for convenience:

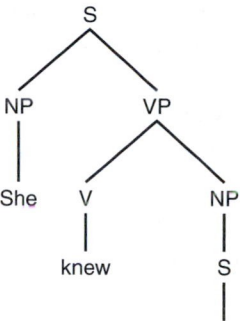

[he'd passed information to the Death Eaters]

She knew [he'd passed information to the Death Eaters]

**Figure 6.5** Labeled tree diagram for a sentence with a complement clause

e. *"Dumbledore, you know perfectly well that you did not make a mistake!"*
f. *She knew he'd passed information to the Death Eaters.*
g. *Harry watched the dragon nearest to them teeter dangerously on its back legs.*

In examples (e) and (f) the verb of the matrix clause is *know* and in (g) it is *watch*; all three are transitive verbs. Rather than having simple noun phrases as objects, however, ***these examples have clauses as objects*** (the underlined portion in each example). These are considered complement clauses as they "complete" the verb by providing one of its core arguments. These complements provide the object of the verb and are thus **object complements**.

The labeled tree diagram of Example (28f) in Figure 6.5 schematically illustrates the relationship between the complement clause and the matrix verb.

The noun phrase preceding the verb phrase is the subject, *she*. The verb phrase consists of the matrix verb *know* and a noun phrase which directly follows the verb, the customary position for objects. In this case, however, the object noun phrase does not consist of a noun and its dependent elements; instead, the noun phrase is realized as an entire complement clause (represented in the tree diagram by S): *he'd passed information to the Death Eaters*.

### 6.5.5  Relative clauses

Relative clauses are similar to complement clauses in that they are embedded as part of a matrix clause. However, relative clauses are not arguments of verbs. Instead ***relative clauses are embedded within noun phrases and function as dependent modifiers of nouns***. Consider sentences (28h) and (i); the relative clauses are underlined.

h. *Professor Dumbledore was now looking down at Harry, who looked right back at him.*
i. *Those people whose names come out of the Goblet of Fire are bound to compete in the tournament.*

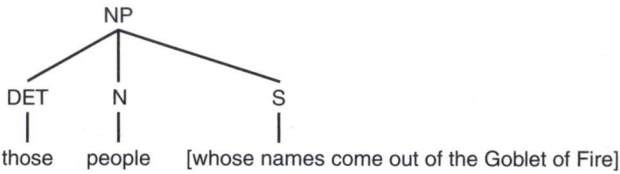

**Figure 6.6** Labeled tree diagram for (i)

In English, relative clauses directly follow the nouns that they modify. ***The noun, relative clause, and any other noun phrase elements together form a single cohesive noun phrase***. We can see this by replacing the subject noun phrase of (i) with a pronoun. This produces *They are bound to compete in the tournament*, with the pronoun replacing not just the demonstrative and noun but also the relative clause. Keeping the relative clause in would produce *\*They whose names come out of the Goblet of Fire*, which is distinctly odd. This shows that the relative clause is part of the same unit as the noun.

The structure of the noun phrase containing the relative clause in (i) is represented in a labeled tree diagram in Figure 6.6.

Comparing this to Figure 6.5, ***we can structurally contrast complement clauses with relative clauses. With complement clauses, an embedded clause is an entire noun phrase, while with relative clauses, an embedded clause is within a noun phrase, following the noun that it modifies***. Within the noun phrase, relative clauses are dependent elements and nouns modified by relative clauses are called **head nouns**.

In describing the English relative clause, it is important to note that there is an obligatory gap in the relative clause, which corresponds to the head noun. In the following examples, the gap is represented by a null symbol:

| | | |
|---|---|---|
| *The guy who Ø came late* | compare | *The guy came late* |
| *The guy I met Ø yesterday* | compare | *I met the guy* |
| *The guy I gave my keys to Ø* | compare | *I gave my keys to the guy* |
| *The guy I was working for Ø* | compare | *I worked for the guy* |

We can see this gapping as a grammatical adjustment for the integration of the relative clause into the noun phrase. It helps to clarify the role of the head noun in the relative clause.

Try out the short exercise in Sidebar 6.20 to check your understanding of coordination and the various types of subordination.

**SIDEBAR 6.20**

For each of the following examples, state whether the structure illustrates coordination or subordination. For subordination, underline the dependent clause and determine whether it is an adverbial, complement, or relative clause. Then check your answers on the website.

a. *Connie read the book that I recommended.*

b. *Connie read the book because I recommended it.*

c. *Connie liked reading the book.*

d. *Connie read the book and wrote a report on it.*

Hints: If a conjunction separates the clauses, it is coordination. If there is an adverbial conjunction (e.g., *if, when,* etc.), it is an adverbial clause. If it directly follows a noun that it modifies, it is a relative clause. If it directly follows a matrix verb, it is an object complement clause.

## CHAPTER SUMMARY

Words combine syntactically into phrases, which combine into clauses, which in turn combine into sentences. At each level there are a variety of structural types:

- Noun phrases, adpositional phrases, and verb phrases are among the phrase types in the world's languages.
- Clauses, containing intransitive, transitive, and ditransitive verbs as their centers, have grammatical relationships with core arguments, including subjects, direct objects, and indirect objects, as well as other categories. Oblique arguments are not grammatically linked to verbs and generally convey information that supplements the verbal semantics.
- Sentences combine clauses either by coordinating clauses at the same level of structure, or by subordinating a clause, through adverbial, complement, or relative clause structures.

Just as with word-class categories, linguistic diversity is reflected in the variety of syntactic categories that are relevant for any particular language. Each language must be examined independently in order to determine the particular syntactic categories that are relevant for that language. To do so, we need to examine patterns of distribution, compare sentences that are minimally distinct, and provide arguments for the existence of structural categories.

Syntax allows us to go beyond the simple naming of things by words and to communicate the multiplicity of situations, events, activities, actions, and complex concepts in which we are engaged. It allows us to state, negate, question, command, and describe. The networks of markings and grammatical relationships mean that words are not simply thrown out randomly in the hopes that others will guess at how they are related, but that they are closely tied to one another in precise and detailed ways. As such, syntax is a central and critical component of linguistic communication.

## TEXTBOX 6.7 GLOSSING CONVENTIONS USED IN THIS CHAPTER

| Convention | Meaning | Convention | Meaning |
|---|---|---|---|
| 1 | first person | ERG | ergative |
| 2 | second person | F | feminine |
| 3 | third person | FUT | future tense |
| ACC | accusative | GEN | genitive |
| ANT | anterior | HON | honorific |
| CLF | classifier | IE | informal ending |
| DAT | dative | INDF | indefinite |
| DECL | declarative | INST | instrument |
| DEM | demonstrative | M | masculine |
| DIST | distal | NEG | negation |

TEXTBOX 6.7  *(cont.)*

| Convention | Meaning | Convention | Meaning |
|------------|---------|------------|---------|
| NMLZ | nominalizer | PST | past tense |
| NOM | nominative | Q | interrogative |
| OBJ | objective | SG | singular |
| PFV | perfective | TOP | topic |
| PL | plural | | |

### SUGGESTIONS FOR FURTHER READING

**Comrie, Bernard**. 1989. *Language universals and linguistic typology*, 2nd edn. Oxford: Basil Blackwell Publishers.

This book is one of the leading introductions to the field of linguistic typology, which encompasses the analysis and classification of the common features and forms of the world's languages. It includes chapters on word order, subjects, relative clauses, case-marking, and causative constructions.

**Dixon, R. M. W.** 2010. *Basic linguistic theory*, Vols. I and II. Oxford University Press.

This book is a sophisticated overview of a theory of grammar that has arisen from extensive typological research.

**Givon, T**. 2001. *Syntax*, Vols. I and II. Amsterdam and Philadelphia: John Benjamins.

These volumes are a cross-linguistic introduction to syntactic structures, with discussion of both structural properties and functional motivations.

**Haspelmath, Martin**, **Matthew S. Dryer**, **David Gil**, **and Bernard Comrie** (eds.). 2005. *The world atlas of language structures*. Oxford University Press. Available online at: http://wals.info/).

This online resource allows you to explore the distribution of linguistic features across the globe.

**Payne, Thomas**. 2006. *Exploring language structure: A student's guide*. Cambridge University Press.

This book provides a detailed introduction to morphology and syntax from a typological perspective.

### EXERCISES

1.  Each of the following English sentences is followed by the label of a particular constituent. Identify that constituent in the sentence, then: (i) write out the entire constituent, (ii) state one structural characteristic that proves it is a constituent of that type, and (iii) provide one argument, based on the reading, that further justifies your analysis.

    **Example:**
    *Marcus is watching football with his dad.*   Prepositional phrase
    i. *with his dad*
    ii. It contains a preposition *with* immediately followed by an NP *his dad*.

iii. Both the preposition and the noun phrase are required. The sentences *Marcus is watching football his dad* and *Marcus is watching football with* are ungrammatical. This criterion of obligatoriness shows that the preposition and the noun phrase are both required to occur, and that the prepositional phrase as a whole is a cohesive syntactic unit.

| | |
|---|---|
| a. *The coat on the back of the chair is still damp.* | Noun phrase |
| b. *Ken put the ice-cream maker in the car.* | Verb phrase |
| c. *I am going for a walk.* | Prepositional phrase |
| d. *The family that moved in across the street keeps their car in the driveway.* | Subject |
| e. *Olivia studied her world-history notes before the exam.* | Object |
| f. *My dog never brings the stick to me.* | Indirect object |

2.  Draw labeled tree diagrams for each of the following sentences. If you are unsure about the constituent structure of an example, use the criteria and arguments discussed in the chapter to test whether the elements are part of the same constituent.

   a. *The team played four games at the youth center.*
   b. *The three girls brought a cake with frosting.*
   c. *Those big dogs down the street always bark at the guy that delivers the mail.*

3.  The following sentence is syntactically ambiguous: there are two possible interpretations, each reflecting a different syntactic structure, although the string of words remains the same. Explain the two meanings and how they differ, and then draw labeled tree diagrams representing the two different possible structures.

   *I watched the birds in the garden.*

4.  Maninka is a Niger-Congo language spoken in West Africa. Tones are not represented in the following data set. (Data are taken from Bird and Shopen 1979.)

   | | |
   |---|---|
   | a. *baba be na* | 'Baba is coming.' |
   | b. *baba be ta* | 'Baba is going.' |
   | c. *a be sigi* | 'S/he is sitting.' |
   | d. *fanta be sunogo* | 'Fanta is sleeping.' |
   | e. *baba be daga sigi* | 'Baba is setting down the pot.' |
   | f. *a be ji sigi* | 'S/he is setting down the water.' |
   | g. *fanta be kini sigi* | 'Fanta is setting down the rice.' |
   | h. *i be daba sigi* | 'I am setting down the hoe.' |
   | i. *an be kini tobi* | 'We are cooking the rice.' |
   | j. *fanta be an fo* | 'Fanta is greeting us.' |

   i. Give the meaning in English of each of the following words. If there appears to be more than one English translation, list both. Can you think of a way to represent a single meaning for these morphemes?

   | | |
   |---|---|
   | *na* | *ta* |
   | *sigi* | *sunogo* |
   | *daga* | *ji* |
   | *kini* | *daba* |
   | *tobi* | *fo* |
   | *an* | |

   ii. What meaning might the word *be* signal?
   iii. What is the order of the noun phrases and the word *be* with respect to the verb in Maninka (in terms of S (roughly subject), O (roughly object), and V (verb))?

5. The goal of this problem is to determine the basic principles underlying the grammatical marking of noun phrases in Nepali, which is an Indo-Aryan language and the national language of Nepal. The answer you turn in should be a coherent analysis of Nepali syntax, based upon the data below. Questions (i) through (vii) are designed to help you work through the data and produce an analysis. Question (viii) tells you what to include in your prose write-up to complete the problem.

Consider the following sentences (in Nepali orthography, *ā* indicates a low central vowel and *a* indicates IPA [ə]):

| | |
|---|---|
| a. *mero āmāle mānchelāi pasalmā heryo.* | 'My mother saw the man at the store.' |
| b. *mero āmāle mānchelāi heryo.* | 'My mother saw the man.' |
| c. *usko āmāle mānchelāi pasalmā heryo.* | 'His mother saw the man at the store.' |
| d. *mero āmāle mero dāilāi pasalmā heryo.* | 'My mother saw my brother at the store.' |
| e. *mero āmāle mero dāilāi pasalmā bhetyo* | 'My mother met my brother at the store.' |
| f. *mero dāile mero āmālāi pasalmā bhetyo.* | 'My brother met my mother at the store.' |
| g. *mero āmā nepālmā āyo.* | 'My mother came to Nepal.' |
| h. *ma nepālmā āẽ.* | 'I came to Nepal.' |
| i. *usko dāi pasalmā āyo.* | 'His brother came to the store.' |
| j. *usko pasal rāmro cha.* | 'His store is good.' |
| k. *mero āmā rāmro cha.* | 'My mother is good/beautiful.' |
| l. *mero āmā calākh cha.* | 'My mother is clever.' |
| m. *mero calākh āmā pasalmā āyo.* | 'My clever mother came to the store.' |

i. Identify the Nepali word for each English meaning by comparing example sentences that differ minimally (as with morphological analysis). If there is more than one form, write them all:

| | |
|---|---|
| 'my' | 'mother' |
| 'his' | 'man' |
| 'store' | 'saw' |
| 'met' | 'good/beautiful' |
| 'brother' | 'came' |
| 'clever' | |

ii. Constituent analysis. Identify the word class of each word. Break each sentence into phrasal constituents. You may want to separate these using square brackets.

iii. Determine whether the verbs for 'saw', 'met', and 'come' are transitive or intransitive. You can do this by counting the number of core arguments in each clause (assume *pasalmā* is oblique).

iv. The verb *cha* is a copula, like English *be*. Copulas are a special type of verb that relate a subject to an adjective or noun phrase. These are referred to as **copula complements**. What type of copula complement is found in Examples 10 through 12 (adjectival or nominal)?

v. Morphological analysis. Compare words with more than one form. Determine the position of morpheme boundaries. List all affixes.

vi. Determine the *grammatical function* of each affix. Under what morphosyntactic conditions does each affix appear? Give a brief statement of the meaning or grammatical function of each affix. Hint: Consider the transitivity of the verbs and the grammatical relations of the arguments.

vii. Based on these data, what is the basic constituent order of the Nepali transitive clause? Use the terms S (subject), O (object), and V (verb) to characterize the order. (E.g., the English sentence *The dog bit the cat* is an SVO sentence: the subject precedes the verb, which precedes the object.)

viii. Now type up the problem, using academic English prose. Be sure that your write-up:
   • states the overall goals of the problem;
   • lists each word, with meanings, broken into morphemes where necessary;

- clearly states the grammatical function of grammatical affixes and *provides evidence* for this by citing the relevant examples;
- clearly states the constituent order of Nepali;
- Provides a complete syntactic analysis of examples (a), (h), (k), and (m), noting the following:
  - The noun or adpositional phrase boundaries, marked with square brackets and labeled
  - The transitivity of the verb
  - The class of each word
  - The core and oblique arguments of each example.

Here are some examples of a complete syntactic analysis of some English sentences; your analysis of Nepali should take this form, but using Nepali words instead of English.

| [My son] NP | eats | [many | cookies] NP | [in | the | afternoon]PP |
|---|---|---|---|---|---|---|
| POSS N | V_trans. | quantifier | N | PREP | ART | N |
| core | | core | | oblique | | |
| [Allison] NP | is | brilliant | | | | |
| NP | V_cop | ADJ | | | | |
| core | | | | | | |

# 7 Semantics: how language makes sense

**KEY TERMS**

- Meaning
- Sense and reference
- Signs: icon, index, symbol
- Connotations and construal
- Propositions: entailments, contradictions, presuppositions
- Semantic anomaly
- Prototype and category structure
- Semantic relations: synonymy, hyponymy, antonymy
- Frames and profiling
- Polysemy
- Metaphor and metonymy

## CHAPTER PREVIEW

***Semantics is the study of meaning in language,*** in particular of those meanings that are conventionally encoded by linguistic expressions. While phonology, morphology, and syntax focus on the formal structure of linguistic expressions, semantics considers their content: the ways they make sense. Utterance interpretation is often an open-ended and idiosyncratic process; a good semantic analysis can offer precise insights as to where the process begins and how to proceed. This chapter introduces students to some basic ways of thinking about the meanings of words and phrases both in terms of their objective (truth conditional) content and in terms of their subjective effects on the imagination of a language user. Important topics include sense and reference, propositional content, entailments and presuppositions, prototypes and category structure, lexical semantic relations, construal, and polysemy.

## LIST OF AIMS

At the end of this chapter, students should be able to:

- **distinguish the encoded (semantic) meanings of expressions from their inferred (pragmatic) meanings;**
- **identify entailments and presuppositions associated with lexemes;**

- identify semantic relations between different lexemes: synonymy, hyponymy, and antonymy;
- distinguish vagueness and polysemy, and identify metaphoric and metonymic relations between the senses of a lexeme;
- distinguish the profile of a linguistic sense from the larger conceptual frame within which it is construed.

## 7.1  The meaning of "meaning"

All human languages allow speakers to talk about the world as it is and as it might be, and to say things which are either true or false, depending on the situation, and with which other speakers can agree or disagree. Languages are useful in these ways because they are meaningful; in other words, they are useful because **linguistic expressions have stable meanings that combine in regular ways to express an unbounded number of imaginable thoughts** (see Textbox 7.1).

Meaning is in many ways the most obvious part of language. Ordinarily, language users are entirely unaware of the intricate rules of phonology, morphology, and syntax that shape their use of language. There is simply too much going on, and at too many levels of organization, for even the most meticulous reader or writer to pay attention to it all at once. In any case, people usually care much more about what is expressed in language than they do about the formal structure of a text or discourse. A text itself is but a means to an end, a vehicle people use to send and receive meaningful messages.

But meaning also seems mysterious and insubstantial, difficult to pin down or define. In fact, the English noun *meaning*, and the verb *mean* from which it derives, have several distinct meanings themselves. In some cases, the verb *mean* doesn't pertain to word, phrase, or sentence meanings at all. In (1), for example, the verb *mean* indicates a relation between a fact and the conclusions one might draw from that fact; and in (2) the verb denotes the relation between an actor and an intended action.

---

### TEXTBOX 7.1  LINGUISTIC EXPRESSIONS AND SEMANTIC CONTENT

Whatever else meaning might be, it is something that attaches to linguistic expressions – both to individual words and morphemes, like *cat* and plural *-s*, and to complex locutions like *cool as a cucumber* and *how do you do*. I will here use the word **expression** broadly for any linguistic form at any level of complexity that has some kind of meaning. An expression is any bit of language, however small or abstract, that can be used to express something. In this chapter, we will call the thing that gets expressed by an expression its **semantic content**, or simply, its **sense**. Like the morphosyntactic forms to which they attach, senses can be very small and abstract (as in inflectional and derivational morphemes, like the English plural *-s* or agentive *-er* suffixes), or very complex and vivid (e.g., in content words like *cat*, *carouse*, *cajole*, and *caboose*, and in multi-word expressions like *shoot the breeze*, *hit the hay*, *go for a ride*, or *take the wheel*).

(1)  a. *The fact that it's raining means you'll get wet if you go outside.*
     b. *These feathers mean there must have been a fight.*

(2)  a. *Something is going on around here and I mean to find out what.*
     b. *I meant to do it, but I didn't have time.*

This chapter is concerned specifically with the kinds of meanings that get associated with linguistic forms. Linguistic meanings are special cases of the more general sorts of meanings above. In (3), for example, the verb *mean* refers to the relation between a linguistic form and the information it normally conveys; in (4), what is "meant" is specifically what someone intended to express in a linguistic utterance.

(3)  a. *The French expression* laissez les bon temps rouler *means 'have a ball!'*
     b. *The English words* haughty *and* supercilious *have very similar meanings.*

(4)  a. *She didn't really mean what she said.*
     b. *When he said he'd try to be there, what he meant was that he wouldn't come.*

The meanings in (3) are **senses**: stable properties of words and phrases, the ideas they conventionally express. But the sentences in (4) describe cases where a speaker says one thing and somehow "means" another: this sort of meaning, **utterance meaning**, is not just a matter of linguistic conventions, but crucially depends on the communicative intentions of a speaker or writer. Inasmuch as meaning is something a speaker does or a hearer understands, it is, in principle, a matter of **pragmatics**, the study of language use and the subject of the next chapter. **Semantics**, on the other hand, considers meanings as stable properties of linguistic expressions: **lexical semantics** studies the senses of individual lexemes and morphemes; **compositional semantics** considers how the sense of a complex expression is related to the senses of its individual parts. ***Semantics studies the meanings directly encoded by linguistic forms, while pragmatics studies the ways people actually use language to accomplish communicative goals***.

When language gets used, even the most mundane utterances tend to express more than just what is literally said: for example, if one morning I say to a friend "I slept badly, and I didn't have any breakfast," she will likely infer that I slept badly *last night*, and I have not had breakfast *today*. The extra meaning seems obvious and is clearly part of what I would communicate with such an utterance. But it is not part of that sentence's **coded content**; it is inferred from the context. Similarly, if my friend responds by saying, "Do you want to go get something to eat?" I would likely take it as a suggestion that we go eat something, though the sentence is literally just a question about what I want.

Normally, of course, the pragmatic meaning of an utterance is closely related to its semantic content: speakers usually try to say more or less what they mean, to line up the conventional content of their utterances with the thoughts they want to communicate. Ultimately, that is what semantic conventions are for. There are other ways one can get an idea across, but semantic conventions make it much easier: they allow people to share information in ways that others will be sure to understand. A **convention**, in general, is just a customary way of doing something in a community, an arbitrary behavior that people adhere to because they expect others to do the same. Semantic conventions, then, are customary ways of interpreting linguistic forms that speakers rely on because they expect others in their community to rely on them as well.

***Because the semantic content of an expression is conventional, it is always at least partly arbitrary***. In principle, any sense that is conventionally expressed one way could just as easily be expressed some other way. If it's a convention, then it could have been different. This, of course, is why languages can differ as much as they do: what in English is called a *tree* is in French called *arbre*, in German *Baum*, and in Swahili *mti*. But the arbitrariness of language is also the reason that words can express concepts at all, rather than just referring to individual items and situations. The word *tree* does not on its own refer to any particular tree or group of trees; rather, it expresses a general idea and so can be used to trigger thoughts about any sort of tree or trees one could ever imagine. Because the link between form and sense is arbitrary, it is trivial for any kind of idea – no matter how abstract or fantastic – to be encoded as a sense; the only real constraints are that an encoded concept must be somehow within the realm of human imagination and something that a speaker might want to express. In fact, the arbitrary nature of the linguistic sign is precisely what makes it so boundlessly powerful.

## 7.2   Kinds of signs: icon, index, symbol

All linguistic **signs** are arbitrary, but just because a sign is arbitrary doesn't mean it can't be motivated as well. The senses of linguistic expressions are often motivated not only by their conventions of use, but also by iconicity, where the form of a sign somehow resembles its sense; and by **indexicality**, where the sense of an expression points to something in its own context of use, like the speaker, the addressee, or the time of speech.

***Signs in general consist of two parts: a meaningful form, the signifier, and its associated interpretation, the signified***. The philosopher Charles Sanders Pierce famously distinguished three basic kinds of signs, based on the different ways a signifier can relate to its signified: in an **icon** the signifier somehow resembles its signified; in an **index** the two are somehow physically or causally connected, so that the presence of the signifier effectively points to, or "indicates," its referent; and in **symbols** the relation is a matter of convention and thus depends on the interpretive habits of those who use the symbol. Diagrams, cartoons, scale models, and acts of impersonation are all icons, because their interpretations depend on some perceived similarity between a signifier and a signified. Footprints and medical symptoms are indices, because they are indications of the things that cause them. Similarly, smoke is an index of fire, puddles an index of rain, and skid marks on a highway are an index of a car's abrupt stop. Such icons and indexes are not conventional.

All words and morphemes are symbols, but not all symbols are linguistic. Coins, stamps, letters, numerals, and national flags are also symbols, as are certain images: the bald eagle is a symbol of the United States; doves are a symbol of peace; and roses are a symbol of love and beauty. Some of these associations are so well established that they feel almost natural, but they are all in fact cultural conventions: roses may be inherently beautiful, but they are a symbol of beauty only to the extent that certain communities habitually interpret them that way.

These three kinds of signs are not, in fact, mutually exclusive; the link between signifier and signified is often motivated in multiple ways. A footprint, for example, both resembles and is causally connected to the foot that made it, and is therefore both an icon and an index. Similarly, a stick figure is a kind of icon, since it resembles the thing it represents, but it is also a conventional way of representing a person and as such is also a symbol.

***All linguistic signs are governed by convention and hence are symbols, but many words and expressions have an iconic or indexical aspect as well.*** Probably all languages have onomatopoetic words for different sorts of sounds, like the English verbs *buzz*, *crackle*, *crunch*, and *tinkle*, or their French counterparts *vrombir*, *crepiter*, *croquer*, and *tintinnabuler*. Words depicting exclamations, like *ow*, *ooh*, *ah*, and *aargh*, and animal sounds, like *woof*, *meow*, *moo*, and *roar*, are also perhaps universally imitative, and therefore iconic. But the particular forms such words take is also a matter of convention and so varies from language to language (see Textbox 7.2).

Finally, ***all languages include an important class of expressions that combine the features of a symbol and an index – forms which conventionally point to a contextually salient referent***. Just as the interpretation of a pointing finger depends on where it is pointing, the interpretation of words like *this*, *here*, *now*, *I*, and *you* depends on the context in which they are used: the pronoun *I* refers to the speaker or writer; *you* refers to the addressee; and *here* and *now* denote the place and time of the utterances in which they occur. Words like these are **deictic expressions**, from the Greek word **deixis**, for 'pointing.' Deictic expressions are symbols, since the association of a linguistic form with a deictic meaning is a convention (different languages have different words for *I*, and even different inventories of deictic expressions); but deictics are also indexical, because their precise significance on any given occasion depends on the context in which they occur.

---

### TEXTBOX 7.2 **ANIMAL SOUNDS IN FIVE LANGUAGES**
(from Wikipedia "Cross linguistic onomatopoeia")

|  | English | French | Spanish | Indonesian | Korean |
|---|---|---|---|---|---|
| Dog | *bow-wow* | *wouf wouf* | *guau guau* | *guk guk* | *meong meong* |
| Pig | *oink oink* | *groin groin* | *oinc oinc* | *grok grok* | *ggul ggul* |
| Rooster | *cock-a-doodle doo* | *cocorico* | *kikiriki* | *kukuruyuk* | *gugugugu* |

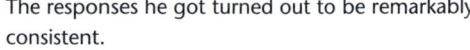

---

## TEXTBOX 7.3 **SOUND SYMBOLISM**

Although linguistic signs are always arbitrary, the link between form and meaning can be at least partially motivated, and some sounds seem to be especially well suited for some meanings. In a famous experiment, the gestalt psychologist Wolfgang Köhler showed subjects two different figures, one like (a), with sharp, jagged edges, and the other like (b), with smooth, sinuous curves. He then asked which of two names *takete* or *baluba* (or in a later version *maluma*) best fit each shape.

The responses he got turned out to be remarkably consistent.

(a) Conduct a survey of some friends. Do people tend to agree in their choices?

(b) What acoustic or articulatory properties in these words do you think might contribute to this effect? Note that the two words have exactly the same length, syllable structure and frequency of use (i.e., zero) in ordinary discourse.

(A)                         (B)

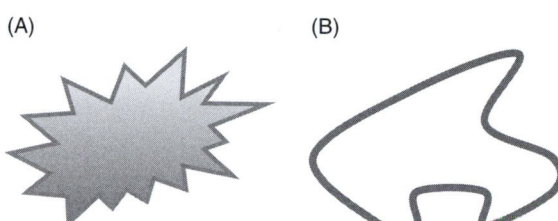

---

## 7.3  Sense and reference

Thus far we have said a lot about the ways meanings can be linked to linguistic forms, but little about just what meanings are. What exactly is it that gets expressed by language? Not surprisingly, there is no simple answer to this question, but there are at least two obvious ways one might think about it. On the one hand, language allows us to talk about things in the world, and so **we might think of meaning directly in terms of reference**, **as the stuff "out there" in the world that we use language to talk about**. On the other hand, and just as importantly, language allows us to express our inner thoughts and to influence those of others, so **we might think of meaning precisely as the stuff of thought, as the** conceptual **contents "in our heads" that trigger and respond to the use of language**. Ultimately a good theory of semantics has to explain both sorts of phenomena.

The idea that meaning is just a matter of reference seems intuitive. The meaning of an expression would just be its reference, the set of things it refers to in the world. So the meaning of *dog* would be the set of all dogs, the meaning of *wet* would be the set of all wet things, and the meaning of a sentence like *The dog is wet* would be a situation in which a particular individual is both wet and a dog. Part of the appeal of an approach like this is that it offers a way of understanding how the meanings of complex expressions like *The dog is wet* are built up from the meanings of their parts. Textbox 7.4 further discusses the idea of composite meanings.

If we only focus on the way words refer to entities in the world, we will miss some important aspects of linguistic meaning. Here are three reasons why there must be more to a word's meaning than just what it refers to.

---

### TEXTBOX 7.4 **THE PRINCIPLE OF COMPOSITIONALITY**

All human language, it seems, obeys a **principle of compositionality**: in general the meanings of complex expressions depend on the meanings of their parts, and individual expressions have stable meanings that combine in regular ways.

If human languages were not at least partly compositional, they would be unlearnable. If word meanings changed randomly from context to context, speakers would not be able to predict the meanings of sentences they had never heard before, like *A penguin explained the commotion.*

But spoken languages need not be, and typically are not, perfectly compositional. Two features of language particularly tend to complicate the picture. First, in most languages, frequent words are often polysemous, i.e., have multiple senses, so the contribution they make will vary from one expression to another. The English verb *run* is polysemous because it can refer either to rapid two-legged motion, the action of a machine, or the action of standing for elected office. Moreover, most languages also include a wide variety of **idioms**, that is, complex expressions the senses of which are not a regular function of their parts. Familiar English idioms include *hang loose, kill time,* and *go fly a kite.*

---

- Reason (1) *Different expressions can refer to the same things but still differ in other aspects of meaning*. For example, the technical term *canine* and the diminutive *doggie* both refer to the same set of things as does the word *dog*, but they do so in very different ways. Words that refer to exactly the same sets of things, but which still differ in meaning, are said to have a common **denotation**, but different **connotations** (see Textbox 7.5).
- Reason (2) *Many expressions – like* unicorn *and* centaur *and the king of Mars – lack any referents in this world*. Some denote things that could exist in another possible world. Others, like *hornless unicorn* and the *intersection of two parallel lines*, seem to denote things that in principle could not exist in any world. At least in this world, such expressions have exactly the same set of possible referents: the set that

---

### TEXTBOX 7.5 **CONNOTATION AND CONSTRUAL**

The term **connotation** generally encompasses all of the non-referential effects that can arise from the use of an expression. Sometimes these form a conventional part of an expression's meaning and contribute to its **construal**, that is, the way a meaning is called to mind. There are in fact many kinds of connotative meanings. The following are just three.

The words *dog, doggie,* and *canine* belong to different **registers** and so tend to occur in different discourse contexts: *dog* is neutral, but *doggie* is used with small children, and *canine* only in certain scientific contexts.

(Register is discussed in more detail in Chapter 11, section 11.2.)

The words *spare* and *deprive* both denote a kind of withholding, but they differ in their **emotive content**: sparing someone sounds like a good thing (emotionally positive), while depriving someone sounds bad (emotionally negative).

Finally, two sentences can refer to exactly the same situation, but present it in very different ways: whether we say of a party *half the guests stayed past 10* or *half the guests left by 10* depends not on the situation itself, but on our **perspective** on it.

has no members, the empty set. But their meanings clearly differ; each makes one think of a very different sort of thing that happens not to exist.

- Reason (3) ***Some important kinds of meaning do not involve reference at all***. Expressions like *if*, *not*, and *maybe* do not help to depict an actual situation; rather, they signal the relation between a possible situation and reality. Many words – like *only*, *very*, *whether*, *not*, *or*, and *maybe* – have big effects on sentence meanings without effecting what a sentence refers to.

For these and other reasons, it makes sense to think of reference as an effect of meaning, rather than a part of it. Ultimately what an expression actually refers to on any occasion of use is a matter of pragmatics. The semantic content of an expression, its **sense**, is not *what* it refers to, but *how* it refers: the concept it activates in one's mind. ***There is thus a three-way relation between a word (or any sign), its sense, and its reference: the word evokes a concept in the mind of a language user, and that concept, which is the word's sense, is what determines its possible referents***.

Figure 7.1 shows the Semiotic Triangle, which illustrates the relationship between reference (a real or imagined cat), linguistic expression (in English, the word /kæt/), and sense (the concept of cat in the mind of a given speaker).

A sense, in effect, is a kind of prompt to imagine something or to compose a thought in a particular way. Senses are thus psychological entities, but since language is a tool for communication, senses are not purely subjective. Senses are experienced subjectively, but like all conventions, ***senses must be shared within a community, and***

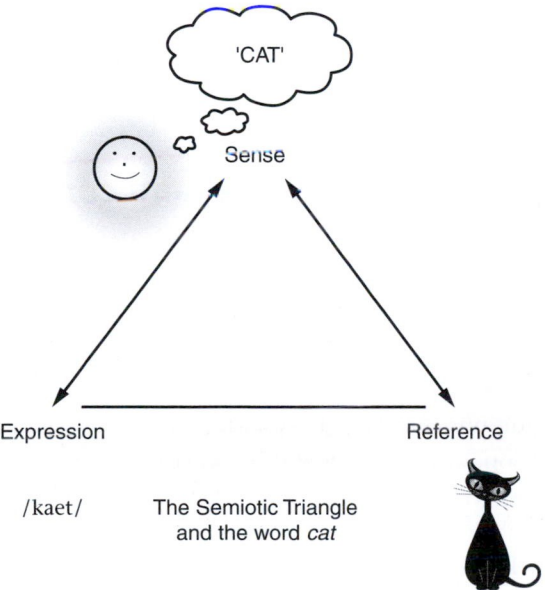

**Figure 7.1** The Semiotic Triangle and the word *cat*

*so they are essentially* **intersubjective** (that is, they are experienced as communal knowledge). Basically, the sense of a word is what an ordinary speaker would expect any other ordinary speaker to expect it to mean.

Most expressions seem to have a fairly clear core sense, often in the form of one or a few properties that define a class of entities. The sense of *unicorn*, for example, is not the set of things that are or could be unicorns, but the set of properties that make something count as a unicorn. The core sense includes at least the features of (i) being a horse [+equine] and (ii) having a horn [+horned]. Other properties – like being mythically pure and gentle and typically white – may or may not be part of the core, but will be widely recognized as typical, if not strictly necessary (judgments here may vary some). Since there are no [+equine, +horned] animals in this world, the word *unicorn* has no referents here. But it is easy to understand why; in fact, it is precisely its sense that makes it not refer.

The distinction between sense and reference is perhaps clearest in the interpretation of deictics like *this*, *here*, *I*, and *you*. As noted above, deictics in general function simultaneously as indices and as symbols: they are symbolic because their meanings are always a matter of linguistic convention; but they are also indexical since their value on any occasion depends on the context of use. Thus, the interpretation of a sentence like *That's the man I saw yesterday* depends on, at least, (i) when it is said, for the meaning of *yesterday*; (ii) who says it, for the meaning of *I*; and (iii) what the speaker is indicating by the use of *that*. But it is only the reference of these words that changes from one context to another; their senses stay the same. Each one always picks out its referent in exactly the same way: *I* always points to the speaker, *yesterday* to the day before the time of speech, and *that* to a contextually salient object of attention. Their senses are thus in effect instructions to find a referent. People use these words to refer, but they succeed in referring because of the words' senses.

## 7.4  Expressing thoughts: entailments and contradictions

The sense of a word or of a sentence is in essence a prompt for thinking. Senses allow us to use language not only to refer to things in the world, but to express all sorts of thoughts. ***The most basic sort of thought is a* proposition: *the sort of thing that can be true or false, possible or impossible; something that one could assert, deny, doubt, or believe*.** Propositions in general are defined by their **truth conditions**: the conditions that have to hold for them to count as true. In order to understand a proposition, one must know what would have to be the case for it to be true. Thus, one basic aspect of a lexical item's sense is its **propositional content**: the contribution to the truth conditions of an expressed proposition. (See Sidebar 7.1 on morphemes which lack propositional content.)

Normally it takes a full clause to express a full proposition. *Paris is the capital of France* says something that could be true or false, but the word *Paris* on its own does not – it

**SIDEBAR 7.1**

DISCOURSE MARKERS

Many meaningful expressions have little or no propositional content. Discourse markers offer some clear examples of expressions with purely **interactional meaning**:

*oh, um, uh, well, like, so, anyway, actually I think, I guess, I mean, you see, you know, know what?*

These are words and expressions that help a speaker to frame an utterance, express an attitude, attend to an audience, or coordinate an audience's attention.

just refers to a place. The smallest sense units (the senses of individual words and morphemes) are always smaller than a full proposition, but they are defined by their effects on propositional meaning.

Simple referring expressions like *Paris* and *France* can pick out individual entities or sets of entities, but relational expressions like *in*, *on*, *own*, *exist* and [*be the capital of* ] allow us to construct predicates – that is, the part of a proposition that is actually *proposed*, "put forth," and predicated about a subject.

Since the semantic and syntactic core of a clause is usually the main verb, let us begin by considering how the verb *kiss* contributes to the meaning of the sentence in (5).

(5)   *She kissed him.*

The words in (5) form a structured syntactic constituent, a sentence (NP+VP), and so express a complex meaning, the structure of which partly mirrors its syntax and partly depends on the lexical meanings of its constituents. Note that this sentence on its own does not express a "complete thought" unless one knows, among other things, who the pronouns *she* and *him* refer to. Typically, the semantic content of a sentence gives only a bare outline of an expressed proposition, along with some pointers (deictic expressions) to salient aspects of the context. Most sentences will not express a full proposition (something that can be true or false) unless they occur in a context that can determine just what its deictic expressions point to.

Words on their own (like *Paris* or *fish*) do not express propositions, but they do have propositional content, and **one can think of the sense of a lexical item as a set of propositions that it contributes to a text or utterance**. One might thus explicate the meaning of *kissed* as having precisely the following four truth conditions:

(6)   For any two individuals, *x* and *y*, *x kissed y* is true if and only if:
      a.  x did something.
      b.  something happened to y.
      c.  x deliberately touched y.
      d.  x used x's lips to touch y.

The four sentences (6a–d) are **entailments** of the word *kiss*. They specify necessary conditions – things that must be true – for something to count as a kiss: that there be (a) an agent (the kisser) who does something; (b) a patient (the kissee), who is affected; (c) a deliberate act of touching; and (d) use of the kisser's lips. For further discussion of truth and meaning, see Textbox 7.6.

The formulae in (6) use variables (x, y) rather than the personal pronouns (*she, he*) in (5), but the effect is the same: these sentences do not express complete thoughts, but

## TEXTBOX 7.6 **TRUTH AND MEANING**

For those unfamiliar with semantic theory, it may seem odd to think about linguistic meaning in terms of truth conditions. After all, the meaning of a sentence does not depend on whether or not the sentence is true: *Pigs can fly* is a perfectly meaningful sentence; it just happens to be false. But part of the reason it is meaningful is that speakers of English can agree on its truth conditions – that is, we know what the world would have to be like for this sentence to be true.

And truth conditions are not just important for factual assertions, but for jokes and stories as well. If someone tells a joke about a panda that walks into a bar, no one is supposed to think such a thing ever actually happened. But to understand the joke, one may at least have to know what the world would be like if a panda did walk into a bar.

There are also many sorts of sentences for which truth seems not to be directly relevant. If someone asks a question like *What is the capital of Texas?* they are not saying anything that is either true or false. Or if someone makes a request like *Get me a doughnut*, it would make no sense to answer, "that's true" or "no, you're lying!" On the other hand, both questions and requests depend on the expression of propositions that do have clear truth conditions. The question about the capital of Texas is, in effect, an attempt to get someone to name the particular city, A, that would make the proposition 'A is the capital of Texas' true. Similarly, with a request like *Get me a doughnut*, the relevant proposition is 'you get me a doughnut,' and the speaker in effect expresses a desire that the addressee should do something to make this proposition true.

Of course, there is more to meaning than just truth conditions, but without truth conditional meaning we could not use language to describe the world as it is or as it might be, to report the news, ask questions, make requests, or even tell lies.

**SIDEBAR 7.2**

SEMANTIC ANOMALY AND HASH NOTATION

Contradiction is a kind of semantic anomaly. A sentence is semantically anomalous if it is structurally (morphosyntactically) well formed, but does not make good sense. Just as the asterisk (*) marks a word or sentence as ungrammatical, the hash sign (#) is used to indicate semantic anomaly.

just the outlines of propositions, which we can call **propositional schemas**. Schemas like these allow us to capture the propositional content of a lexeme without actually expressing a proposition.

One can show that each of the propositional schemas in (6) is an entailment of the word *kiss*. **Narrowly framed, an entailment *is a relation between two propositions, P and Q, such that P entails Q, if (and only if) whenever P is true, Q is also true***. But the term entailment also applies more broadly to any propositional content coded by an expression.

The crucial observation is just that if one calls something a "kiss" and at the same time denies one of the propositions in (6a–d), the result is a kind of nonsense called a **paradox** or contradiction (see Sidebar 7.2), where two propositions are asserted which cannot both be true at once.

**(7)**  a. #*She kissed him, but she didn't do anything.*
   b. #*She kissed him, but nothing happened to him.*
   c. #*She kissed him, but her lips didn't touch him.*

People tend to have strong intuitions about the entailments of lexical items they are familiar with, and they tend to notice when a sentence contradicts itself. So a good way to test whether something is an entailment of a given lexical item is, as in (7), to construct sentences that assert the lexical item and deny the hypothesized entailment. This is the "contradiction test."

Note that the same tests with words like *heard* or *trusted* do not create contradictions. Unlike *kiss* these words lack any entailments about touching or the use of lips (6c and 6d), or even about an actor doing something (6a) or an object being affected (6b). If one trusts or hears another person, one does not necessarily "do" anything, and to be heard or trusted one need not be aware of or changed by the experience.

Furthermore, the contradiction test shows that many things one might expect of a kiss are not part of the word's core sense. Typically, for example, kisses involve two people kissing each other on the lips, or maybe somewhere else on the face, either as a sign of affection or desire. But the fact that none of the sentences in (8) are contradictions shows that none of these are actually entailments of the word.

(8)   a.  *She kissed the ground when she got off the plane.*   'kiss' ≠ 'on a person'
      b.  *She kissed him on the elbow.*   'kiss' ≠ 'on the lips'
      c.  *She kissed him {spitefully/angrily/viciously}.*   'kiss' ≠ 'affection'

This suggests that the core sense of a word like *kiss* may consist of just a few entailments, which together distinguish it from all other English verb senses. Of course, there are many verbs that entail (6a) deliberate action (e.g., *promise, praise, consider, throw*) or (6b) an affected object (e.g., *convince, console, fold, squish*). And there is a substantial group that entails touching (6c), some of which, like *pucker* and *purse*, entail the use of lips (6d). But *kiss* appears to be the only English verb that includes all and only the entailments in (6): other English verbs of kissing (e.g., *smooch, snog, peck*) each have all of these entailments, plus some others, thus limiting them to just some kinds of kissing and not others. To explore entailments further, try the exercise in Sidebar 7.3.

Use the contradiction test to identify the core entailments associated with each verb. Are there verbs that carry all six sorts of entailments listed here? Do the verbs differ much in the number of entailments they encode? Are there particular sorts of entailments that get encoded more than others?

Together the four properties in (6) thus may be sufficient to make something count as a kiss (everything with all these properties is a kiss); and each is individually necessary for something to count as a kiss (every kissing event has all of these properties). If this is the core sense of the verb then in essence a "kiss" really is just a 'deliberate touching with the lips.'

> **SIDEBAR 7.3**
>
> **IDENTIFYING ENTAILMENTS IN VERBS OF 'TOUCHING'**
>
> Like *kiss*, each of the verbs *slap, tickle, pinch, poke, spank*, and *wipe* denotes a kind of touching event in which two individuals, a "toucher" and a "touchee," come into physical contact. For each verb, consider whether its use normally carries any of the following sorts of entailments:
>
> (i) that the toucher act deliberately;
> (ii) that the toucher use a particular body part or instrument;
> (iii) that the touchee have a particular kind of surface;
> (iv) that a particular part of the touchee be affected;
> (v) that the touchee feel something;
> (vi) that the contact occur in a particular manner, either gently or forcefully.

## 7.5  Dictionaries and encyclopedias

But is that really all there is to a "kiss"? The four spare features in (6) may distinguish the verb *kiss* from all comparable verbs in the language, but it's easy to imagine there must be more to its meaning. A sentence like *She kissed him* may call to mind certain kinds of kissing more than others: kissing on the lips, or at least the face, rather than on other parts of the body; people kissing other people rather than rocks or socks or money; kisses of friendship or affection or desire rather than kisses of torture, taunting, or interrogation. But how much of all this gets included in the sense of a word?

In phonology, the distinctive features of a phoneme include just enough information to distinguish it from other phonemes in a language, and the fine-grained details of pronunciation are a matter of phonetics. Perhaps the semantic content of lexical items is similarly sparse, and the rich inferences that people may make on the basis of a word's use are more a matter of pragmatics (see Chapter 8) than semantics. In that case, a speaker's "mental dictionary," or **lexicon**, will indicate certain kinds of common entailments in words, while other sorts of common-sense information about a word's referents are seen as **encyclopedic knowledge**.

It can be hard to know where to draw the line between specialized linguistic knowledge and general world knowledge; ordinary reference dictionaries inevitably include a good deal of encyclopedic information in their definitions. The three definitions of *kiss* in (9), from three widely used English **dictionaries**, all include more than just the four proposed entailments in (6).

(9)  a.  to touch or press with the lips slightly pursed, and then often to part them and to emit a smacking sound, in an expression of affection, love, greeting, reverence, etc. *Dictionary.com*
  b.  to touch or caress with the lips as an expression of affection, greeting, respect, or amorousness. *American Heritage Dictionary*
  c.  to press or touch with the lips (at the same time compressing and then separating them) in token of affection or greeting, or as an act of reverence; to salute or caress with the lips; to give a kiss to. *Oxford English Dictionary*

These dictionaries seem to agree that to understand the word *kiss* one needs to know something about both how they occur, and why. Two offer precise descriptions of the physical act – the labial gesture. All three note typical contexts for people to kiss, thus emphasizing the inherently social nature of the act.

But all three definitions here also resort to just listing different functions of kissing, as in *Dictionary.com*'s "affection, love, greeting, etc." The point of such a list is not to limit the sense of the word with necessary or sufficient conditions, but rather to give some typical examples for people to use in thinking about the category.

---

**TEXTBOX 7.7 MEANING AND PARAPHRASE**

What one finds in a dictionary definition is very different from what can be found in a speaker's mental lexicon. At best a dictionary can paraphrase a word's meaning, using other words to express the same idea. The dictionary helps us understand a meaning by giving us another way to describe that meaning, but this is not at all the same as just having that meaning in mind in the first place.

A paraphrase can be more or less complete or precise, but the actual meaning of a word is the idea itself, not just an alternative way of expressing that idea. As a practical matter, to talk about word meanings, or about any other kind of idea, dictionaries need to use a language or code of some sort. But ordinary thought does not depend exclusively on language: one can imagine a face, for example, without being able to describe it in words.

Ultimately, in studying linguistic meanings we are also trying to understand how words connect to the general, non-linguistic rational abilities, which allow us, with or without language, to think about and react to the world both as it is and as it might be. A theory of semantics must offer some way of describing these abilities, either as a **"language of thought,"** or in a dynamic model of human conceptualization.

---

## 7.6  Prototypes

It may be tempting to think of a word's meaning as a list of simple (binary) features, but that can make it hard to explain some common ways people use and understand language. The problem is that in the ordinary course of events, people often do not – and sometimes cannot – reason about categories in terms of necessary and sufficient conditions. They tend instead to make judgments about category membership (e.g., whether or not something counts as a kiss or a punch or a unicorn) based largely on patterns of resemblance they find to familiar instances of a category. This kind of basic analogical reasoning is what allows us to use words productively, relating new instances to familiar categories.

Generally when one imagines an instance of a category, one does not just think of its most abstract defining properties; instead, one probably begins with fairly rich ideas about what members of that category are like. *These sorts of ideas create* prototype effects, *leading people to recognize and imagine some members of a category more quickly than others*. A single word may have several distinct prototypes. For example, how one imagines a prototypical *kiss* depends a lot on how one imagines the *kissee*, with very distinct images and events for a hurt child, a newlywed, a grandfather, or a bishop's ring.

*Lexical prototypes often include features that are neither necessary nor sufficient for category membership, but still seem to be central to a word's meaning*. Take the word *bird*. Since all animals that have either a beak or feathers are birds, either one of these features alone is sufficient to make something count as a bird. On the other hand, since many animals that are not birds can fly (e.g., bats), and since many birds cannot fly (e.g., penguins), the ability to fly is neither necessary nor sufficient to make something a bird. But most people are very familiar with various

**SIDEBAR 7.4**

PROTOTYPES IN CATEGORY STRUCTURE

Ask several people to imagine examples of each of the following sorts of things (i–v):

(i) something red

(ii) a fruit

(iii) a vehicle

(iv) a game

(v) things to take on a picnic

Next, ask them to imagine examples of each of the following situations (vi–vii):

(vi) a wedding

(vii) a scene with a police officer (*p*), a judge (*j*), and a defendant (*d*).

Are there particular shades of red people tend to think of first and most? What sorts of fruits came first to mind? What sorts of vehicles, games, or weddings? What sorts of things do they imagine *p, j,* and *d* might be doing together or saying to each other?

Can you find any reasons why the sorts of examples people think of first are somehow salient in their experience?

kinds of birds that do fly, and so people can usually expect that other people will think of small, flying, feathered animals, some of which are brightly colored and sing. With the exception of "feathered," none of these features is either necessary or sufficient to make something a 'bird,' but the kinds of birds that share these features tend to be both common and familiar in many parts of the world, and so for many people they form a kind of **prototype** for the category of birds as a whole (see Sidebar 7.4).

Prototypes play an important role in the meanings of many lexical items because people typically reason about things and situations in terms of familiar features and memorable exemplars of similar things. In some cases this sort of reasoning may be viewed as a pragmatic effect of language use. In other cases, whole concepts and categories seem to be organized around one or more salient prototypical examples, in which case prototype effects may be somehow built into the semantics of an expression.

## 7.7   Lexical semantic relations

*Ultimately, the meaning of any lexeme, what it adds to a language, is always partly a function of its relations with other lexemes*: the value of a linguistic expression lies in its potential to contrast with other expressions in the same language.

There are many ways that lexemes can be semantically related, but three in particular seem to stand out: (1) identity of senses, **synonymy**, (2) inclusion of senses, **hyponymy**, and (3) oppositeness of senses, **antonymy**. Synonyms are words with similar or identical meanings, like *amble* and *stroll*. Antonyms are lexemes with (somehow) opposite senses, like *hot* and *cold*. And one lexeme is a hyponym of another if its sense is more specific and it refers to a narrower set of potential referents; thus, *beagle* is a hyponym of *dog*, and *indigo* is a hyponym of *blue*.

Each of these three basic kinds of lexical relations is illustrated in (10), with groups of English adjectives denoting (i) degrees of wealth, (ii) kinds of human figures, and (iii) degrees of hot and cold. (Symbols are explained in Sidebar 7.5.)

**SIDEBAR 7.5**

THE SYMBOLS ⊂ AND ⊃

The symbol ⊂ means "is a subset of," so A ⊂ B means that A is a subset of B, or that A is included in B (A is a hyponym of B).

The symbol ⊃ means "is a superset of," so B ⊃ A means that B is a superset of A, or includes A (B is a hypernym of A).

(10)   a. Synonymy:     i.  *rich – wealthy – affluent*
                            ii.  *slender – slim – sleek – lithe – thin*
                          iii.  *cold – cool – nippy – frosty – frigid*

        b. Hyponymy:     i.  *mega rich* ⊂ *rich*
                            ii.  *slim* ⊂ *thin*
                          iii.  *glacial* ⊂ *cold*

        c. Antonymy:     i.  *rich : poor*
                            ii.  *chubby : slender*
                          iii.  *cold : hot*

These basic semantic relations are usually easy to observe among groups of closely related words, or lexical fields. As a general rule, the more entailments a group of lexemes shares, the more closely related they will be, and languages tend to have many rather densely populated fields of closely related terms. Among verbs of 'touching' for example, we find many hyponyms (e.g., *poke, pat, pet, stroke, kiss*), a few near and partial synonyms (e.g., *feel, reach, contact, abut*), and some opposites (e.g., *shun, separate*).

**SIDEBAR 7.6**

SYNONYMS

Synonyms share a common sense – though the words may differ in their social contexts of use: e.g., *film, movie, flick, motion picture, show*; or, *cat, feline, tomcat, kitty*; or, *coffee, java, joe.*

**Synonyms *are words that share a common sense, having the same – or very similar – entailments*.** In general, if any two words had identical meanings, there would be no reason to have both in the language. Thus, where synonyms can be found in a language, they tend to differ in some small way, either in a nuance of sense or in their typical contexts of use. Still, there are many situations where substituting one word for another will have little or no discernible effect on the meaning of a sentence. (See Sidebar 7.6.)

Since words often have multiple senses, two or more words may overlap very precisely in one or more senses, but still exhibit a very different overall range of uses, as in the following three sets of examples.

Partial overlaps    {*get, take, see, hear, understand*} what someone says
                              {*stand, stomach, put up with, tolerate*} a situation
                              {*want, lack, need, long for*} something

Sometimes the overlap is extensive, resulting in near synonyms:

Near synonyms    *see, watch, look (at), regard, stare*
                          *walk, amble, saunter, stroll, stride, strut*

Teasing apart the semantic differences among near synonyms reveals the fine-grained distinctions lexical items can encode. For example, the 'seeing' verbs, above, seem to **differ in the kinds and quantities of effort or attention** that they entail.

In other cases, **near synonyms may differ not so much in the sorts of situations they depict, but only in what they imply about how the speaker is** *judging the situation*. Thus, the words *spare* and *deprive* both entail that someone is prevented from having or experiencing something, but *spare* makes it sound like a good thing, while *deprive* makes it sound bad. Such *evaluative synonyms* are not uncommon.

Evaluative synonyms    *rapid/hasty; slender/skinny; thrifty/cheap; bold/reckless*

**In other cases, the differences depend on the social context**. Some synonyms are usually used in particular regions, whereas others may vary according to the social context or **register** (see Chapter 11):

Regional variants    *soda, pop, cola, coke*
Register variants    *automobile, motor vehicle, car, wheels, ride*

**SIDEBAR 7.7**

K'iche' Maya seems to lack a broad default like *break*, but the English word *break* does have some vivid hyponyms. Consider words like *splatter, shatter, smash, explode, shred,* and *fracture*. What sorts of entailments do you think these verbs add to those of *break*? How do these entailments differ from those suggested by the glosses for the Mayan verbs?

**Languages can and often do differ in the density of a lexical field.** In English the word *break* applies more or less neutrally to any object that can lose its structural integrity. K'iche' Maya appears to lack any similarly neutral equivalent and instead uses a variety of more specific roots, many of which encode something about the manner of breaking or the type of material that gets broken. The twelve verb roots below come from a list of forty-two different K'iche' Maya "Breaking and Cutting Verbs" reported by Pye (1996) and include all the most common translations for English *break*. (See Sidebar 7.7.)

(11)    K'iche' Maya verbs of 'breaking'

| | |
|---|---|
| *-chiko:j* | 'break a thing by throwing it (e.g., chest, stool, pot)' |
| *-joyopi:j* | 'break a banana from a bunch of bananas' |
| *-mich'* - | 'chop (e.g., a plant); pluck (e.g., feathers, pine needles)' |
| *-paxi:j* | 'break a solid thing (e.g., clay, rock, glass, plate, cup, pot)' |
| *- pi'i:j* | 'break a soft thing (e.g., book tortilla, clay, hardboiled egg)' |
| *-pitz'itz'e:j* | 'crush a soft thing (e.g., clay)' |
| *-q'upi:j* | 'break a hard thing (e.g., bridge, candle, basket, stick, chair, tooth)' |
| *-raqi:j '* | 'smash a hollow thing (e.g., glass, pot, plate, chest, bubble)' |
| *-sak'ij* | 'crack a surface (e.g., wall, melon, plate, glass, skull, tree, board)' |
| *-t'oqopi:j* | 'break/snap a long flexible thing (e.g., rope, wire, string)' |
| *-weqi:j* | 'break/smash a hard thing (e.g., pot, wall, stone griddle, mile post)' |
| *woqi:j* | 'break/shatter a fragile thing (e.g., eggs, vase, light bulb)' |

**Hyponymy** *is a relation between two words, one of which is more specific than the other:* an expression A is a hyponym of another expression B if and only if the denotation of A is a proper subset of the set of entities denoted by B (in which case B is also considered a **hypernym** of A). For example, since a queen is necessarily a woman, and (in the Catholic Church) a pope is necessarily a man, *queen* is a hyponym of *woman* and *pope* is a hyponym of *man*.

In general, hyponyms are both more specific and thus in ordinary assertions more informative, than their hypernyms. Thus, the words *amble, saunter, stride, stroll,* and *march* are all hyponyms of *walk*: each has all the entailments that *walk* does, plus one or two more. Similarly *aged, ancient, antique, decrepit,* and *senile* are hyponyms of *old* since they can all be paraphrased by *old,* but each applies to a much narrower range of referents than does *old.*

For more examples of hyponyms and hypernyms, see Sidebar 7.8. Sometimes hyponymic relationships combine to form taxonomies, as shown in Textbox 7.8.

---

**TEXTBOX 7.8 TAXONOMIES**

Many sorts of lexical fields seem intuitively to be organized by the inclusion relation into a branching hierarchy of groups. Such fields are called **taxonomies**.

Nature      *tiger → carnivore → mammal → vertebrate*
            *emperor penguin → penguin → bird → creature*
Art         *cleaver → knife → tool → thing*
            *spinach → greens → veggies → food → stuff*
Movement    *amble → walk → move*
            *trot → run → locomote*

---

**The familiar term antonym is used both broadly, for any pair of words with opposite meanings**, and more narrowly just for **contrary** (or gradable) **antonyms** – terms that designate opposite regions of a scale with some intermediate range of values between them: e.g., *hot : cold, long : short, fast : slow,* and *big : little* (see Sidebar 7.9). Contraries cannot both be true of the same entity in the same way, but they can both be false. A drink could be neither hot nor cold, a book neither long nor short, and a run neither fast nor slow.

But there are other kinds of 'oppositeness' too. For example, complementarity is an opposition where something is either one way or the other: **complementaries** are pairs of terms, such that wherever one is true the other is false, and wherever one is false the other is true. Typical examples include *dead : alive, odd : even, present : absent, inside : outside,* and *legal : illegal.*

**Reversive antonyms** are terms denoting either movement in opposite directions – for example, *come : go, give : take,* and *raise : lower* – or change between reversible states, like *melt : freeze, dress : undress,* or *cover : uncover.* And **converse antonyms** are terms that denote different participants in a binary relationship, like *husband : wife*, and *student : teacher*, or the same situation from opposite perspectives, as with *in-front-of : behind* and *above : below*.

## 7.8  Sense and imagery

In actual discourse, speakers and writers do not just offer up a series of abstract propositions; they choose propositions based on their communicative goals and formulate them in ways that highlight their relevance, as discussed in the next chapter. To understand the meaning of a word, one has to know its entailments, but one also needs to know how it can be used and what kinds of conceptualizations it can trigger: the **imagery** it evokes and its effects on construal in general. While people tend to think of connotations as loose associations a word might have for some speakers, imagery and construal are core elements of meaning, integral to the way an expression is understood.

*The imagery of a linguistic expression includes not just visual images, but all the tactile, auditory, olfactory, physical-sensory, and motor associations it regularly triggers.* Thus, to sort out the senses of bipedal motion verbs like *amble*, *saunter*, *stroll*, and *traipse*, the relevant images would include not just pictures of people walking, but also motor memories of walking in a leisurely way.

Imagery is just one facet of construal, which includes all aspects of the way an expressed meaning is brought to mind and imagined. *Construal is what explains how two expressions can denote precisely the same set of situations, and yet differ dramatically in their meanings. Usually, it's because they somehow trigger different ways of building up a conceptualization.* And since conceptualization is a complicated process, there are many kinds of construal one could consider.

The phenomenon of **fictive motion** is a good place to start. In (12) the motion verb *ran* presents a static situation as if it were dynamically unfolding.

(12)   a. *A long scar ran from her hip to her knee.*
       b. *A long scar ran from her knee to her hip.*

There is no actual movement except in the virtual gaze of a conceptualizer, and the different wordings in (12) thus correspond to different ways one build can up a mental image or scan an imagined scene.

The contrast in (13), on the other hand, depends on an effect of figure–ground reversal. Here the difference lies not in how the image gets built up in the mind, but rather in where the focus of attention is, on what gets profiled as the primary figure (or **profile**) in a scene and what is left in the background. Thus (13a) profiles a playground and locates it in a shadow, while (13b) profiles a shadow and locates it at a playground. The two expressions describe the same situation, but construe it in different ways.

(13)  a. *the [playground] [in the shadow of the tree].*
      b. *the [shadow] [of the tree on the playground].*

This kind of figure–ground reversal has many manifestations in both thought and language. The contrast between the active and passive sentences in (14) illustrates a similar sort of alternation. Again there is no difference in entailments: it is just a matter of which participant – the kisser or the kissee or both together – stands out as the primary figure in the scene.

(14)  a. *She kissed him.*
      b. *He was kissed by her.*
      c. *They kissed.*

Another important aspect of construal concerns the way an expression's entailments are entered into the discourse. Not all entailments are created equal. A few come out posed in actual assertions or questions or denials, but others may slip in as a kind of background to what is said.

**A presupposition *is a proposition which comes embedded in the use of a construction and so gets expressed without being asserted.*** Since they are not asserted, presuppositions typically survive in questions and under negation, and can be difficult to target in a denial. Thus, for example, the adverb *again* profiles the repetition of an event, but it presupposes the event's prior occurrence. So both *They kissed again* and *They didn't kiss again* presuppose that there was a kiss in the past, but they make contradictory assertions about the occurrence of any later kissing (see Sidebar 7.10).

Presuppositional senses are not at all rare, though where they occur, they are likely to go unnoticed. Normally, as one processes the successive utterances in a discourse, one focuses only on what is new at that moment, and so sentences are usually expressed in ways that highlight new information against the background of what is known or assumed. (This is further discussed in Chapter 9 on discourse.) ***Presuppositions in general thus serve an important role in relating the expressed content of an utterance to information shared by the discourse participants.***

> **SIDEBAR 7.10**
> PARTICLES WITH PRESUPPOSITIONS
> Each of the italicized expressions below contributes a presupposition of some sort. For each sentence, try to identify what propositions are asserted and what is presupposed.
>
> (e.g.) They kissed *again*. (it's happened before)
>  i. They *finally* kissed.
>  ii. They *even* kissed.
>  iii. They kissed *too*.
>  iv. They *already* kissed.
>  v. They are *still* kissing.
>  vi. *The* kiss was brief.

## 7.9  The structure of a sense: profile and frame

Presuppositions represent just one way that the entailments of an expression can be backgrounded. More generally, the sense of any linguistic expression consists of some profiled content construed against a background frame. Profiling is at the heart of word meaning, and of linguistic meaning in general, because linguistic communication is largely a matter of directing the flow of attention.

***A frame is a coherent facet of conceptual structure that provides the basis for understanding one or more semantically related expressions. The profile is that part of an evoked frame that an expression designates.*** Thus, the word *hypotenuse* profiles a line segment within the frame of a particular sort of geometric arrangement, a right triangle. Without this frame, there could be no such thing as a hypotenuse. Similarly, a word like *door* profiles a part of a room, and words like *mother*, *brother*, and *uncle* profile different individuals framed by a network of family relations.

Sometimes the division of labor between profile and frame is obvious. Consider the concept of a 'door.' Thinking of a door, you might imagine a flat object that moves on hinges and covers an entryway, and that can be opened or closed to either allow or prevent access into a room. To imagine a door, one must first imagine an enclosed space, that is a 'room' that one could enter or leave. And to imagine a room, one could also imagine a larger structure of some sort that the room might be part of. Thus, the word *door* profiles an element within the "room" frame, while *room* itself profiles an element in the "building" frame. Ultimately, the word *building* itself also depends on other very general frames (also sometimes called semantic domains) for things like three-dimensional space and human artifacts.

The profile of a word often represents a prominent part of the frame to which it belongs. Thus, a *hypotenuse* is one part of a right triangle; a *lid* is one part of a jar or box; a *finger* is part of a hand. Some words, however, profile an entity or a condition that somehow deviates from the normal background frame. Words like *dent* and *wrinkle*, for example, profile discontinuities in a surface that one might expect to be smooth; similarly, adjectives like *empty* and *absent* profile temporary conditions in which an entity of some sort does not appear where it might have been expected.

Often words with closely related meanings differ only in their profiles. For example, the English word *dream* functions both as a verb – in which case it profiles the process of dreaming as it unfolds in time – or as a noun, in which case it profiles the thing which is envisioned in that process. Similarly, the English agentive suffix *-er* in words like *dreamer* and *runner* switches the profile of a root from the process as a whole to a participant in that process.

***Often a single lexeme on its own can evoke a whole ensemble of culturally specific frames.*** To understand the meanings of terms like *line drive*, *ground ball*, and a *pop fly*, one must know not only that these terms denote ways of hitting a baseball but what a baseball game is in general. And to know what it means to *call*, *raise*, *fold*, *bluff*, or *draw a straight flush*, one needs to know that these are things one can do in a game of poker (see Sidebar 7.11).

SIDEBAR 7.11

**SEMANTIC FRAMES**

Charles Fillmore, a leading figure in semantic theory, stated "to understand what any one member of the group is about is, in a sense, to understand what they are all about" (Fillmore 1985: 223). Consider each of the following lists of words and how the meaning of each word in part depends on the meanings of the others. If you use one word, it is naturally profiled against others within that frame. How would you name the frame represented by each group of words? Which of these frames are culturally specific?

*Monday, Tuesday,*          The _____ Frame
  *Wednesday, Thursday,*
  *Friday*

*tall, grande, venti, trenta*   The _____ Frame

*enroll, attend, study,*        The _____ Frame
  *pass, fail, graduate*

*attack, defend, retreat,*      The _____ Frame
  *defeat, surrender*

*Frames involving knowledge of complex events or scenarios are sometimes called* **scripts.** Common-sense knowledge about restaurants, for example, is organized around the sorts of events that take place in a restaurant: e.g., seating, ordering, eating, clearing, paying, and tipping. Without some background and culturally based knowledge of this complex script, one cannot begin to understand words like *waiter*, *menu*, *tip*, and *reservation*. Scripts in general are useful for describing basic sorts of social knowledge, like how one should behave and what one can expect on a doctor's visit, at a birthday party, on a picnic, or in a linguistics seminar.

Another well-known script, the Commercial Event Frame, provides the conceptual basis for words like *buy*, *sell*, *cost*, and *pay*, among many others. Imagine that Chuck has a beautiful box that he gives to George in exchange for $12. In such a situation, all of the sentences below will be equally true. But while these sentences all depict the same situation, they each have their own distinct meanings because of how they are construed.

(15)  a. *Chuck sold the box to George for $12.*
      b. *George bought the box from Chuck for $12.*
      c. *George paid Chuck $12 for the box.*
      d. *The box cost George $12.*

Evidently, words like *buy* and *sell* describe the same sort of situation with the same sorts of participants engaged in the same basic activities, but they do so in different ways. In order to understand the meanings of these words, one needs to understand that the situations to which they apply always feature certain participants (or **frame elements**) with certain semantic relations (i.e., **case roles**; see Chapter 6) among them. In particular, there has to be a buyer, a seller, some money, and an item to be exchanged; the buyer must give money to the seller, and the seller in return must give the item to the buyer.

One can then analyze the meanings of lexemes like *buy*, *sell*, *cost*, and *pay* as profiling different sorts of entities or relations against the background of the Commercial Event Frame. Thus, *buy* profiles a scene in which the primary figures are the buyer and the goods, and the other participants are left unmentioned or else expressed less prominently in an oblique phrase (i.e., out of the spotlight that falls on the subject and object in a clause). And *sell* denotes exactly the same sort of scene, except it profiles the seller and the goods as the primary figures.

## 7.10  Framing motion events: cross-linguistic differences

As we have seen, words for games, food, art, and clothes can be richly framed. This is also true of more basic sorts of words where the framing involves much more basic aspects of experiences and so can be easy to overlook. Consider a situation in which an entity moves from one place to another. To describe such a situation, one would probably depict the moving entity – or theme – as the primary participant, and the path it moves on – from start to finish – as part of the background frame. But there are many other details one might attend to in a motion event, as can be seen in Textbox 7.9, and different languages tend to present this information in different ways.

---

**TEXTBOX 7.9  PARTICIPANTS AND PROPERTIES OF SIMPLE MOTION EVENTS**

| | | | |
|---|---|---|---|
| **Theme:** | Who is moving? | **Manner:** | What kind of motion is it? e.g., quiet, heavy, sneaky, sudden, etc. |
| **Path:** | What is the route of motion? e.g., a straight line, zigzag, etc. | | |
| **Direction:** | Is the motion towards or away from a reference point? | **Medium:** | Is the motion on land, or through water, air, mud, or something else? |
| **Means:** | What causes the motion? e.g., foot, hoof, wing, car, bus, boat, etc. | **Rate:** | How fast is the movement? |

---

The sentences in (16) are fairly typical of the way motion events tend to be expressed in English. They have a set of fairly standard entailments. In each of these sentences the subject NP denotes a theme, that is, an entity that moves along a path, and the prepositional phrase adjunct depicts a path, while the verbs *slither*, *saunter*, *scamper*, and *crawl* each profile a different manner of motion.

**(16)**  a. *The snake slithered across the floor.*
b. *The actor sauntered out of the room.*
c. *The mouse scampered through the bushes.*
d. *The baby crawled towards the kitten.*

This is the way Chinese, English, and most other Indo-European languages tend to express motion events, with the means and manner expressed in the verb nucleus, while path and direction get specified by phrases and particles lower in the verb phrase, toward the periphery of the clause, as in (17).

**(17)**  a. *The bottle* [$_{manner}$ *floated*] [$_{path}$ *into the cave*].
b. *The children* [$_{manner}$ *jumped*] [$_{path}$ *down the stairs*].

But Romance languages (and many others, including Semitic, Polynesian, Nez Perce, and Caddo) tend to express direction directly in the verb and relegate the manner of motion to the clause periphery. Thus in (18), the French counterparts to (17) have main verbs that express a direction of motion (i.e., *entrer* 'go in' and *descendre* 'go down'), while the manner of motion is optionally specified by a verb at the end of the clause.

(18)  a. *la*      *bouteille*   *est*   *entrée*      *dans*   *la*   *grotte*   *en flottant*
          DET      bottle        AUX     go.into.PST   in       DET   cave       floating

      b. *les*     *écoliers*          *ont*   *descendu*      *l'escalier*        *en sautant*
          DET      schoolchild.PL      AUX     go.down.PST     DET.staircase       jumping

In some other languages, one finds an abundance of motion verbs that entail something about the moving figure. In Atsugewi, an extinct polysynthetic language of Northern California, many verb roots expressing motion or location also have specific entailments about the kind of theme that moves or is located.

(19)  Atsugewi verb roots

|  |  |
|---|---|
| *-lup-* | 'for small shiny spherical objects to move/be-located' |
| *-t'-* | 'for smallish flat objects to move/be-located' |
| *-caq-* | 'for a slimy lumpish object to move/be-located' |
| *-qput-* | 'for loose dry dirt to move/be-located' |
| *-st'aq'-* | 'for runny icky material to move/be-located' |

It is difficult to capture these entailments except by listing the kinds of themes they involve. The *-lup-* root applies to things like round candies, eyeballs, and hailstones; the *-t'-* root is used for things like a stamp, a clothing patch, a button, or a shingle; the *-caq-* root might be used of a toad or a cow dropping; the *-staq-* root covers things like mud, manure, rotten tomatoes, guts, or chewed gum.

*By comparing the semantics of motion verbs across languages, we can see that languages package information differently, with some incorporating particular aspects of the motion event into the core meaning of verb roots, and others indicating these meanings in root-external morphemes or phrases.*

## 7.11  Polysemy: relations between senses

It often happens that two or more words in a language can have the same form, but no real semantic connections. English, for example, has two words *flatter*, one a lexical verb meaning 'to fulsomely praise,' the other the comparative form of the adjective *flat*. These words are **homonyms**, because their formal similarity is just coincidence. But it often happens that a single word in a language will have a number of distinct but more or less closely related senses. Such words are polysemous. **Polysemy** is the property having multiple (*poly-*) meanings (*sem-*s). This is, in fact, the normal condition for most common lexemes.

*In polysemy, the different senses of an expression must be both distinct and related.* For example, the word *hand* occurs both as a noun denoting the part of the body at the end of the arm, or as a transitive verb denoting the action of transferring an object from one person's hand to another. These two senses clearly have something in common, and so *hand* is polysemous.

**SIDEBAR 7.12**
'HANDS' AND 'ARMS'

Body part terms in different languages often differ in their extensions. The *World Atlas of Language Structures* (*WALS*) identifies 228 languages that have a single word for both 'hand' and 'arm,' and 389 that use two or more distinct words for these concepts. For instance, Chai (Nilo-Saharan; Ethiopia) has separate words for 'hand,' *síyó*, 'forearm,' *múní*, and 'upper arm,' *yíró*, but none for 'arm.'

Words that denote both 'hand' and 'arm' can be found in the Oceanic language, Lonwolwol (*va*), Czech (*ruka*), and the Niger-Congo language, Gurma (*nu*). Given that other languages often have separate words here, should these general 'hand/arm' words be analyzed as vague or polysemous? What kinds of evidence might help to decide?

*Polysemy contrasts with vagueness, where a single word encompasses a broad range of referents not because it has multiple senses, but because it has one very general sense.* The noun *thing* and the verb *do* are perhaps maximally vague, since they can be used in reference to almost any entity or action, respectively. But all lexemes, with the possible exception of some proper nouns, are vague in at least some respects. *Chair*, for example, is vague with respect to the color, material, and number of legs an object must have to count as a 'chair.' Similarly, the English word *uncle* is vague in that it refers to a brother either of one's mother or of one's father, though many other languages have distinct terms for these two relations (e.g., in Latin *avunculus*, 'mother's brother,' and *patruus*, 'father's brother'). (See Sidebar 7.12.)

One way to distinguish among the different senses of a word is to look for other words which can substitute for that word in at least some contexts without substantially changing what is said. The following uses of *cry*, for example, require different substitutions, and so arguably involve distinct senses of the word.

(20)  Substitution

    a. She *cried* out in pain.               'yelled (non-verbal)'

    b. "Buttons for sale," she *cried*.      'shouted (verbal)'

    c. She *cried* for hours when the mouse died.    'sobbed, wept'

The substitution test helps us to identify different senses and sub-senses of lexical items, but its results are always open to interpretation. For instance, *cry* could be analyzed as having just one abstract sense encompassing a wide range of vocal behaviors, of which words like *yell*, *weep*, *shout*, and *sob* each profile a specific sort. Or one might argue that *cry* has a specific prototype in the 'weep' sense from which other uses are extended.

When words do have multiple related senses, those senses must be somehow connected, and the most common connections among senses tend to involve either **metaphor** or **metonymy** (or sometimes both). In classical rhetoric, metaphor and metonymy are ways of using an expression that somehow shift the expression away from its original sense. *In metaphor, a term whose sense belongs primarily in* *one semantic frame gets shifted to another frame, often based on some perceived resemblance between the two*: thus, a word like *flower* may be applied to a woman or generally to someone young and beautiful; a word like *path* may apply to any way of achieving a goal; and the word *up* can denote things like happiness, alertness, or increase, in addition to just vertical elevation. **In metonymy, the sense shifts from one element to another within a single frame, based on a principle of contiguity**: classic metonymies include relations of part for whole (*all hands on deck!*), place for event (*remember the Alamo!*), instrument for action (*go bicycling*), and cause for effect (*to suffer minor burns*). If one describes a man as *married to his job*, that is a metaphor, since jobs and marriage are very different kinds of things, but if one locates one's car by saying *I'm parked out back*, that is metonymy, since the speaker (*I*) and the car are very different sorts of things but are saliently connected in the ownership frame.

Often one can find both metaphor and metonymy at work in a single expression. Thus in *lend me your ears*, the association of *ears* with *attention* is metonymic, since ears are for listening and listening is part of paying attention; but *lend* is used metaphorically, since its basic sense of physical transfer is extended to the frame of mental attention (as it is in expressions like *pay attention* and *give a look*).

**Certain patterns of polysemy are so common as to be almost entirely predictable, and such patterns often involve metonymy** of one sort or another. For example, one can use the name of a country, like *France*, to profile: (i) a place (as in *France is a beautiful country*); (ii) a government (as in *France has broken off relations with Belgium*), or other representative entities, like a soccer team (as in *France won the game*).

Similarly, we can use the name of a periodical publication, *P*, like *Time* or *the Washington Post*, to designate the company that publishes it (*P has offices all around the world*), the published content of the periodical (*Jack reads P online*), or the physical publication itself (*Maggie uses P to line her birdcage*).

And the name of a play or novel, like *Hamlet* or *Wuthering Heights*, can be used in reference to a text (as in *She's been studying* Hamlet *for years*), to a physical instance of the text (as in *I left my Hamlet on the train*), or to a theatrical or filmed production of the play. And of course the title *Hamlet* itself is based on another common metonymy, where the name of a main character stands for the whole of a story.

**Certain kinds of metaphorical extensions are also very common in polysemous terms.** For example, color terms are used for emotions (e.g., *He's feeling* blue), perception verbs are used to describe thoughts (e.g., *I see what you mean* or *She felt certain*), spatial terms are applied to time (e.g., *the length of time*), and body-part meanings get extended to spatial relations (e.g., *in back of; the head of the line*).

Many of the most common metaphors are not based on resemblance, but rather on correlations in experience. Thus, we speak of people metaphorically as "warm" or "cold" (that is, 'sympathetic' or 'hostile'), not because sympathy is similar to heat, but because the experience of physical warmth from a human body is an important

> ### TEXTBOX 7.10 **METAPHORS FOR "DIFFICULTY" ACROSS LANGUAGES**
>
> Even very basic concepts may be susceptible to multiple metaphorical construals. The concept of 'difficulty,' for example, can be imagined in terms of heaviness or hardness. In English one speaks of problems as "hard" or "tough" if they are difficult to solve, and as "weighty" or "heavy" if they are severe or important.
>
> In French, similarly the word *dur* is used for both "hard" problems and "hard" objects, and *grave*, *lourde*, and *pesant* are used both for things that are literally heavy, and so difficult to carry, and for abstract things that are difficult to cope with.
>
> The same or similar 'heavy'~'difficult' polysemy can be found in many unrelated languages around the world: for example, Latin (*gravis*), German (*schwer*), Old Irish (*tromm*), Mandarin (*zhóng*), Arabic, (*thaquil*), Hausa (*naunaya*), and Hawaiian (*kaumaha*).

part of some of our most basic experiences of human sympathy: for instance, in a baby's experience of being held and soothed, and in other salient contexts where human warmth and affection are regularly correlated. Because certain aspects of human experience are universal, some metaphors are commonly found cross-linguistically; see Textbox 7.10.

Similarly, for talk about everyday plans and events, we can use the basic vocabulary of space and motion (*come, go, near, far, slow, fast*). Thus, people "set goals," "pass milestones," and "overcome obstacles"; and projects "move forward" or "grind to a halt," but they always "come to an end." Moving around in physical space is one of the first and most important sorts of purposeful activities that humans ever experience, and it seems to provide a useful and adaptable template for thinking about plans and purposes in general.

Often, if not always, ***the metaphors in a language extend the use of a lexical field from relatively vivid and concrete aspects of experience (like lifting and carrying heavy objects) to more abstract sorts of experiences (like making plans or solving problems) or to domains that are otherwise hard to talk about or imagine (like time and emotion)***. This appears to be a robust and consistent feature of the way metaphors are used in everyday language.

Partly because of this, metaphorical expressions often seem like a vivid or colorful way of expressing an otherwise plain idea. But there are many pretty basic ideas that are difficult to think about at all without metaphor. Thus, we tend to use words with basically spatial and physical entailments – e.g., *high/low, rise/fall, peak/abyss* – for speaking and reasoning about very basic, but relatively abstract notions like 'happy' and 'sad,' 'good' and 'bad,' and 'more' and 'less.'

***In these and many other similar cases, the metaphorical use of language seems to reflect a general pattern of thought, that is, a conceptual metaphor in which a complex semantic frame is structured, in whole or in part, by***

*analogy with another semantic frame*. People tend to use language metaphoric-ally precisely because they think metaphorically in general (see Textbox 7.11).

---

**TEXTBOX 7.11 METAPHOR, METONYMY, AND SEMANTIC CHANGE**

Sometimes what starts out as metaphor or metonymy can become a conventionalized sense of a word. If an expression gets used in a way that consistently triggers a metaphoric or a metonymic inference, that inference can become so automatic that it will no longer depend on context to be understood.

---

## CHAPTER SUMMARY

Linguistic signs are prompts to imagine and attend to the world in particular ways. The semantic content of a linguistic expression – its sense – is always only a starting point for the process of interpretation, but it is also what allows us to use language to express our thoughts and to affect the thoughts of others in the first place.

The core sense of any expression, whether a word or a phrase or a larger discourse, typically includes both some propositional content and some constraints on the way that content is construed. An expressed proposition may thus be foregrounded as part of what is said, or backgrounded as a presupposition. In either case, what is actually encoded by an expression is always much less than what it is likely to communicate in context. A theory of semantics needs to explain how people represent these encoded contents and how the encoded meanings of complex expressions are built up from the meanings of their parts. The next chapter turns to pragmatics, and the ways speakers and hearers actually use expressions to express themselves and influence others.

---

**TEXTBOX 7.12 GLOSSING CONVENTIONS USED IN THIS CHAPTER**

| Convention | Meaning | Convention | Meaning |
| --- | --- | --- | --- |
| AUX | auxiliary | PL | plural |
| DET | determiner | PST | past tense |

---

## SUGGESTIONS FOR FURTHER READING

**Croft, William and D. Alan Cruse**. 2003. *Cognitive linguistics*. Cambridge University Press.
Offers a detailed theory of construal operations and the ways they can be encoded in linguistic constructions.

**Cruse, Alan**. 2011. *Meaning in language: An introduction to semantics and pragmatics*, 3rd edn. Oxford University Press.

Provides a broad introduction to linguistic meaning, with very useful discussions of the semantics–pragmatics distinction, lexical semantic relations, polysemy and the problem of delimiting senses, and grammatical semantics.

**Goddard, Cliff**. 1998. *Semantic analysis: A practical introduction*. Oxford University Press.

An introduction to Anna Wierzbicka's Natural Semantic Metalanguage, a theory of lexical meaning based on a small inventory of semantic primes proposed to be shared by all languages. The theory is illustrated with examples from a variety of languages, including English, Polish, Malay, Japanese, and the Australian language Yankunytjatjara, among others.

**Lakoff, George and Mark Johnson**. 1980. *Metaphors we live by*. University of Chicago Press.

A brief yet revealing introduction to the phenomena of conceptual metaphor and metonymy.

**Langacker, Ronald W.** 1991. *Concept, image, symbol: The cognitive basis of grammar*. Berlin and New York: Mouton de Gruyter.

A classic work on the role of semantic imagery in grammar, including essays on case, agreement, the English passive, the Yuman auxiliary, and locative expressions in Cora.

## EXERCISES

1.  **Crafting definitions with prototypes and entailments**
    The contradiction test allows us to figure out which, if any, parts of an expression's sense are strictly entailed and which, if any, are associated with the category without being strictly necessary. Consider at least two words from each of the following lists (i.e., two nouns, two verbs, and two adjectives), and for each try to determine the roles that prototypes and entailments have in their meanings. Base your reasoning on a few constructed (or found) example sentences illustrating what you take to be a normal use of the word in one of its basic senses. Be sure to consider for each word both its precise entailments (if any), and just what sorts of information one should include about it in a dictionary.

    | N | *horse* | *hammer* | *prize* | *bedroom* | *sausage* |
    |---|---------|----------|---------|-----------|-----------|
    | V | *stampede* | *steal* | *admire* | *wrestle* | *memorize* |
    | Adj | *bright* | *happy* | *ancient* | *slippery* | *spoiled* |

2.  **Finding exemplars:** *window*
    The *American Heritage College Dictionary* (3rd edn., 1993) offers the following five senses and subsenses for the noun *window*.
    a.  (i)  An opening constructed in a wall or roof that admits light or air to an enclosure and is often framed and spanned with glass mounted to permit opening and closing.
        (ii)  A framework enclosing a pane of glass for such an opening; a sash.
        (iii)  A pane of glass or similar material in such a framework.
    b.  (i)  An opening that resembles a window in function or appearance.
        (ii)  The transparent panel on a window envelope.
    c.  The area or space behind a window, especially at the front of a shop.
    d.  A means of access or observation.
    e.  An interval of time during which an activity can or must take place.

    Use an online corpus – either the BNC (www.natcorp.ox.ac.uk/), or the COCA (http://corpus.byu.edu/coca/) – to search for the word *window*. Find fifteen to twenty examples of uses of the word *window*, and try to sort your data according to which sense or sub-sense is being used. Can you find cases where a single instance of the word *window* is compatible with more than one of these senses? Can you find uses that these definitions do not seem to cover? And finally, can you think of anything that clearly is *not* a window that one of these definitions might include?

3. Lexical semantic relations

Match the lexical pairs below with the appropriate semantic relations, (a–f). Give evidence for your claims, and briefly discuss one or more examples if they pose any difficulties for analysis.

Semantic relations:

a. Synonyms
b. Hyponyms/hypernyms
c. Complementary antonyms
d. Contrary antonyms
e. Reversive antonyms
f. Converse antonyms

Lexical pairs:

| | | |
|---|---|---|
| *husband* and *wife* | *rich* and *poor* | *long* and *short* |
| *real* and *genuine* | *car* and *sedan* | *say* and *deny* |
| *begin* and *end* | *brother* and *sister* | *animal* and *mineral* |
| *cruel* and *kind* | *bird* and *penguin* | *bread* and *butter* |
| *hard* and *soft* | *hammer* and *tool* | *pure* and *sullied* |
| *couch* and *sofa* | *sad* and *grim* | *girl* and *boy* |
| *true* and *false* | | |

4. Vagueness and polysemy: the case of *school*

Consider the likely referents of the word *school* in each of the following sentences: for example, in (a) the word *schools* refers to physical buildings or campuses, but in (b–f) it refers to various kinds of social constructions. Use the substitution test to identify and describe the range of referents covered by the word *school* in these sentences. What sorts of semantic and pragmatic relationships (propositional, metaphoric, metonymic, etc.) can you observe among the uses of the word *school* here? How can we best explain the wide range of referents this word allows? Are there multiple senses of the word involved, or one very vague sense, or are there other ways to explain this data?

a. Several schools were damaged by the tornado.
b. Sally and Joey went to the game to root for their school.
c. After the game, the whole school gathered to celebrate the victory.
d. The school is considering changes in the code on academic honesty.
e. I can't make it for lunch. I have school from 10 to 4 on Wednesday.
f. School sucks.

5. Frames and profiles

For each of the following lexical items, try to determine (a) what each item designates (its profile) and (b) what sorts of background knowledge it presupposes (its frame). Discuss any problems you may find in drawing these distinctions.

| | | | | |
|---|---|---|---|---|
| *denial* | *departure* | *apology* | *gallop* | *tip* |
| *dent* | *pedal* | *fish* | *mountain* | *bicycle* |
| *hammer* | | | | |

# $8$ Pragmatics: inference for language

**KEY TERMS**

- Context
- Pragmatic inferences
- Linguistic underdeterminacy
- Gricean Maxims
- Particularized conversational implicatures

- The Principle of Relevance
- Contextual implications
- Explicature
- Semanticization
- Semantics/pragmatics division of labor

## CHAPTER PREVIEW

Semantics is one way in which meaning is conveyed through language, but not all meaning is tied directly to linguistic forms. Some of the meaning conveyed through language comes from interpretations based on the broader social, cultural, and interactional contexts; the study of such interpretations makes up the field of pragmatics. Pragmatics is what makes natural discourse coherent and relevant. A major role of pragmatic theories is to explain pragmatic inferences, which are how interlocutors manage to convey much more than their utterances explicitly encode. In producing discourse, speakers routinely provide information that allows addressees to make pragmatic inferences. Addressees base these inferences on contextual assumptions that come in part from the content of the speakers' words, and in part from extralinguistc factors. These processes are informed by some overarching pragmatic principles, which will be discussed throughout this chapter.

## LIST OF AIMS

At the end of this chapter, students should be familiar with:

- **basic concepts in pragmatics, such as: context, contextual assumptions, and pragmatic inferences of various sorts (e.g., particularized conversational implicatures, contextual implications, and explicated inferences);**
- **the two leading pragmatic theories: Grice's theory and Sperber and Wilson's theory;**
- **actual pragmatic analyses that students perform.**

## 8.1  Pragmatics

Consider the following exchange between Maya, a five-year-old, and her mom:

(1)  Maya:  *Aw, they always change it!*
      Mom:    *Really?*
      Maya:  *What, would I lie to you?*

Maya misunderstands her mom, taking her *really?* to indicate that her mom doubted her. But what is it that Maya misunderstands? Clearly it's not the linguistic meaning of *really?* ('is that true?'). Rather, Maya is missing the **pragmatic interpretation** of *really?* in this context (expressing surprise, rather than questioning factuality). But missing this bit creates a communication break between mother and daughter. Next, imagine the very same exchange, but this time, between two adults. In this case, Maya's response would be taken as joking. Surprisingly perhaps, the source for this very different interpretation is exactly the same. While the young Maya was unaware of the pragmatic interpretation of *really?*, the joking Maya pretended it wasn't there. This is not something she could do with the linguistic meaning of the expression. There is a difference between linguistic meanings (observed by both versions of Maya) and pragmatic interpretations (ignored, for different reasons, by both Mayas). Still, pragmatic interpretations play a fundamental role in interaction. What are pragmatic interpretations? How are they derived? How can we tell a pragmatic interpretation from a semantic one? Should we? These are questions that will be addressed in this chapter.

The field of ***pragmatics examines how context supports our use and interpretation of linguistic expressions***. Language is not produced in a vacuum. Linguistic forms must routinely be connected to the interactional, physical, cultural, and social environment in which they are produced. Linguistic behavior is grounded in a particular ***context***, which surrounds, informs, underlies, and shapes a linguistic event. For example, a particular conversation will have a physical context (where the conversation takes place), a social context (the social relationships of the participants), a cultural context (shared knowledge about the culture in which the participants are based), and an encyclopedic knowledge context (specific assumptions shared by speakers and addressees). A particular utterance within a conversation will also have a discourse context, or what was said before the utterance, prompting the speaker to make the utterance and shaping the form it took.

The problem is that context contains a vast number of assumptions. How can we make sure that just the relevant bit of context is accessed? How can we know what use to make of that bit of context on some particular occasion? Pragmatic theories explain how we mobilize our inferential abilities in order to make efficient use of context in the service of communication and how we are able to infer the intended meaning of a linguistic expression, even when that meaning is not made fully explicit. ***Pragmatics is the competence to draw contextually plausible inferences, which complement linguistic meanings***. We will discuss pragmatic theories, different types of pragmatic inferences, and the division of labor between semantics and pragmatics in utterance interpretation.

### 8.1.1 Pragmatics as context-dependent inference drawing

How do you know what a speaker has just communicated to you? Of course, you perform a semantic analysis of his or her words. But it is not enough to just add up the fixed meanings encoded by linguistic expressions in a compositional manner. We have seen that this was insufficient for five-year-old Maya, who based her interpretation of her mother's utterance on word meaning alone, as well as for the adult Maya, who ignored the additional meaning for a special humoristic effect (Example 1). Using and interpreting language crucially relies on something in addition to – and quite different from – the mastery of semantics. ***Utterance meanings are more than the sum of their linguistic parts***. The linguistic system builds on a highly developed inferential system, without which linguistic interactions would not be possible. This ***extralinguistic competence*** is pragmatics.

To appreciate the pervasiveness of pragmatic inferences, consider the following advertisement of the American Lung Association, which was seen on a bus in Santa Barbara, California, in February of 2002:

**(2)**  *Asthma is on the rise. Please double your efforts. Support Christmas Seals.*

As we have seen in other chapters, discourse contains ***stretches of language that are coherently organized***. But what's the connection between asthma being on the rise and doubling our efforts? Which efforts are those? Somehow we need to infer that the efforts are related to the previously mentioned asthma. Since asthma is considered undesirable, we infer that probably what is referred to are efforts towards eliminating or reducing asthma or its effects. Having figured this out, we immediately face another puzzling utterance: How is supporting an organization called Christmas Seals relevant to fighting asthma? Once again, we need to rely on our general knowledge (here, very much culture-dependent) and access the fact that Christmas Seals is a charity that sells stickers used on Christmas cards, and whose profits support fighting lung diseases. In other words, the rather short discourse in (2) is actually interpreted as something like:

**(3)**  *Asthma is on the rise.* [**Therefore,**] *please double your efforts* [**to fight it**]. *Support Christmas Seals* [**because they fight asthma**].

Example (3) is not only clumsy; it feels redundant. Since we can infer the boldfaced information easily, stating it explicitly in this manner is unnecessary. Speakers routinely rely on addressees' cognitive abilities to draw such ad hoc pragmatic inferences. With the help of pragmatics, language production and processing are made more efficient, thus taking less time and effort.

***Human languages are linguistically underdetermined***, that is, they can never encode everything that we actually intend our addressees to understand as the message of our utterances. This is why the ***drawing of pragmatic inferences is critical in making language work as a communicative system***. Consider again Example (3). Although it seems a much more specific version of (2), it still does not explicitly encode every piece of intended information. Aren't the following added interpretations (underlined) also part of the message contained in the advertisement in (2)?

(4)   *Asthma [in the US] is [recently and projected to be in the future] on the rise [(i.e., more people now suffer from it)]. [**Therefore**,] please double your efforts [**to fight it** (and make an effort to fight it even if you haven't in the past)]. Support Christmas Seals [**because they fight Asthma** (and this will constitute YOUR effort in fighting Asthma)].*

Of course they are. And even (4) does not exhaust all the information that goes into interpreting (2). How much is asthma on the rise? We infer that it is rising significantly. How should the addressee support Christmas Seals? Presumably, by buying many Christmas Seals, which support the organization financially (rather than morally, for example). We could enumerate more and more hidden assumptions. There's certainly a lot of interpretation that doesn't meet the semantic eye. It is up to pragmatics to provide it. But how?

## 8.2   Pragmatic theories

Pragmatic interpretations are real and pervasive, but they seem to require mind reading. As difficult as that sounds, this 'mind reading' is a necessary skill for linguistic communication (see Sidebar 8.1). How do we go about reading others' minds in determining the full intended meaning of utterances, given that telepathy is out of the question? This is the task of pragmatic theories.

### 8.2.1   The Gricean Conversational Maxims

Grice views discourse as ***a cooperative endeavor*** (this is his Cooperative Principle). In order to be cooperative participants in discourse, we must abide by the following four maxims (referred to as **Grice's Maxims**):

- The **Quantity Maxim**: speakers must be informative, that is, provide just enough information, neither too much nor too little.
- The **Quality Maxim**: speakers must only assert truthful and well-supported information.
- The **Relevance Maxim**: speakers must be relevant.
- The **Manner Maxim**: speakers must be brief, clear, nonambiguous and orderly.

Consider Marilyn's response in (5). (See Sidebar 8.2 for a note about the examples used in this chapter that come from published corpora.)

(5)   Roy:       *. . . It's dark, how will we see what we're eating.*
      Marilyn:   *. . . Candles* (SBC: 003).

Note that Marilyn's response is just informative enough: it's relevant and short, and we assume she's sincere. It thus obeys all the Gricean maxims. But we must still draw a trivial inference, that the candles will be lit, if the interlocutors are to see what they're eating. In other words, in order to see Marilyn's response as abiding by Relevance, we need to add to her explicit message an implicit assumption.

Inferences such as these, as well as those specified for (2) above and others below, are called by Grice ***Particularized Conversational Implicatures*** (henceforth, implicatures). Implicatures are inferences: the speaker intends the addressee to infer them based on a set of contextually available assumptions. But ***unlike logical inferences (entailments), implicatures are not necessarily true, only plausible***. To see the difference between entailments and implicatures, consider (6):

(6)  a. *He kissed her on the neck.*
     b. *He kissed her.*

In a plea bargain case negotiated in Israel in June of 2007, the defendant's lawyers got the prosecutor to charge him with (b) rather than with (a), although (a) is a faithful description of what happened. Now, of course if 'x kissed y on the neck' then 'x must have kissed y': (a) ***entails*** (b) because if (a) is true, so must (b) be true. Note that the opposite does not hold necessarily. (b) does not entail (a), because he may have kissed her on the cheek, in which case it's true that he kissed her, but it's not true that he kissed her on the neck. Now, why did the lawyers prefer the charge in (b) over (a)? Because of what (a), but not (b) ***implicates***, namely that the kiss was of a sexual nature. Note that this is not a necessary conclusion, though. Perhaps he intended to give her a fatherly kiss on her cheek, but she moved and the kiss accidentally ended up being on the neck, although no sexual intentions were involved. So whereas entailments are necessary inferences, implicatures are not. Thus, if (a) is true, he necessarily kissed her (an entailment), but it's not necessarily true that the kiss was a sexual act (the implicature).

Inferences can be classified as *entailments* (inferences that speakers make based on logical reasoning) and *implicatures* (inferences that are plausible but do not necessarily follow).

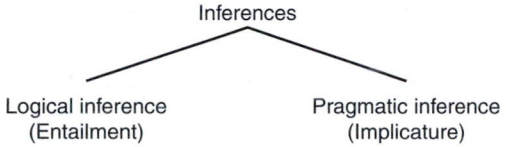

**Figure 8.1** Logical and pragmatic inferences

Now, we've seen that implicatures were needed in (5), even though Marilyn observed the Gricean maxims. On other occasions, **we cannot follow all of the Gricean Maxims, because they happen to clash**. This is another impetus for implicature generation. Suppose someone asks you a question. The Quantity Maxim prompts you to supply a fully informative answer. But what if you can't, because you don't have all the relevant information, or because you're not sure? Observing Quality (truthfulness) forbids you to say something false or unreliable. Look what Rebecca does under such circumstances (Rebecca is the prosecutor and *he* is a defendant in a court case):

(7)  June:        *Is he gonna take the stand?*
     Rebecca:     (H) *He says so* (SBC: 008).

Notice that Rebecca does not explicitly say "yes" (the most informative answer in terms of Quantity). Instead, she provides the evidence she has for an affirmative answer, not wanting to commit to that which she is not sure of. By presenting just the evidence, she lets June infer the likelihood of the man taking the stand. Rebecca violates Quantity, but obeys Quality. The implicatures are: 'maybe he will take the stand'; 'Rebecca is not in a position to know for sure.' They are based on the flouting of Quantity, which Rebecca cannot observe.

Grice's most intriguing observation is that **we sometimes fail to follow one of the maxims not because we can't, but because we choose not to**. Speakers might choose to violate one of the maxims in order to generate an implicature. Let's examine a few examples:

(8)  a. Hebrew (Voice of Israel radio, referring to courtroom testimony)

| *shamati* | *et* | *ha=girsaot* | *ha=shonot* | *shel* |
|---|---|---|---|---|
| hear.PST.1SG | ACC | DEF=version.PL | DEF=different | of |

| *adam* | **ben** | **shmonim** | **ve=tesha**. |
|---|---|---|---|
| person | of | eighty | CONJ=nine. |

'I heard the different versions (testimonies) of an **eighty-nine-year-old person**.'

   b. Hebrew
      Gym teacher:

| *hitayaft* | *klara?* |
|---|---|
| become.tired.PST.2SG.F | Clara |

'Did you get tired, Clara?'

Clara:

**lo**          **nora**
NEG          awfully
'Not too much.'

Gym teacher:

*az*     *kcat*       *klomar*
so     a.little     in.other.words
'So, a little in other words.'

c. Hebrew
   *ze*         *she=nolad*           *li*        **nexed**        **lo**
   prox.dem    that=be.born.PST     to.1SG     grandson        neg

   *omer*     *she=ani*        **savta**
   say        that=1SG         grandmother
   'The fact that **I have a grandson doesn't mean I'm a grandmother**.'

d. Hebrew
   *M*     **yesh**       *lax*         **kalba**      *xola*       **ba=bayit!**
   M       exist       to.2SG.F      dog.F        sick.F      at.DEF=home
   'M, **you have a sick dog at home!**'

e. J:     *How is your tomato?*
   M:     *It's a little ripe.*
   J:     *Yeah, I had to <u>edit it</u>.*

Examples (8a)–(8e) each manifest some maxim violation. Since the speakers are none-theless seen as cooperative, they are taken to have intentionally violated the maxims in order to generate a variety of implicatures. Consider (8a), which refers to the testimony of a person in a court of law. Is the age of a witness relevant? Not in most cases. But here the speaker is trying to tell us more than 'I heard the different versions (testimonies) of a person,' which would have been informative enough under the circumstances. In specifying the age of the person, the speaker provides too much information (contra the Quantity Maxim), thereby implicating that 'an eighty-nine-year-old person, who provides different versions of testimony about some event, is not trustworthy.' This inference is plausible, but does not follow necessarily; therefore it is a particularized conversational implicature.

Now consider Example (8b). Here, too, Quantity is breached, but in a different way. Clara's response is not informative enough. To say that she 'did not get awfully tired' doesn't say anything about how tired she did get. Logically, it even leaves open the possibility that she did not get tired at all ('I didn't get awfully tired; I didn't even get a little tired'). In the context of the utterance, however, the speaker generates the impli-cature that the teacher spells out in the next turn.

In (8c) we have a breach of Quality. A woman who has a grandchild is by definition a grandmother. Obviously, the speaker is therefore a grandmother. Denying this fact appears to be untruthful, and the sentence seems inherently contradictory. Implicatures are crucial, as usual: the speaker, though a grandmother, feels and acts like a young woman. By denying that she is a grandmother, she is implicating a rejection of the (old) image of a grandmother.

Example (8d), which illustrates a violation of Relation, was uttered at a faculty meeting in which the chair, M, had announced that the meeting should be as brief as possible because she had a sick dog to attend to. When M herself seemed to go off topic and cause the meeting to drag on, her colleague produced the utterance in (8d). Although this utterance was irrelevant with respect to the department business being discussed, the intended implicature was, 'stick to the agenda!'

Finally, (8e) shows a Manner violation. It's not immediately clear what it would mean to *edit a tomato*. A speaker abiding by Manner would have used more conventional means to express the same meaning (by saying, for example, *cut out parts of it*). But J chooses an innovative (metaphorical) combination, playfully implicating a similarity between language editing and cutting a tomato.

In all of these cases, the speaker's blatant violation of some maxim is intended to generate a particularized conversational implicature. What is the status of these implicatures? Why don't the speakers express what they mean explicitly? (e.g., "I'm not old"; "Cutting a tomato is like editing a paper"). We have mentioned efficiency in connection with the inferences in (2), and the same applies to (5). But efficiency doesn't seem to be the motivation in the examples in (8). The speakers in (8) aim to make use of the special cognitive and discoursal status of pragmatic inferences.

Implicatures have a cluster of properties that distinguish them from explicitly communicated propositions. We here mention only the main ones. An important difference between semantic meanings and implicatures is that ***implicatures are external to the linguistic meaning***: The proposition explicitly expressed and the implicature generated have separate contents, separate truth conditions. The truth conditions of *I heard the different versions (testimonies) of an eighty-nine-year-old person* specify that 'the speaker heard the different versions of an eighty-nine-year-old person.' The truth conditions of the implicature are quite different, namely that 'an eighty-nine-year-old person is not reliable.' This is why ***implicatures do not affect the truth conditions of the proposition that triggers them***. For example, should it turn out that the implicature 'an eighty-nine-year-old person is not reliable' is not true, this would not render (8) itself a false statement. It may still be true that 'I heard the different versions (testimonies) of an eighty-nine-year-old person.' This is also why, unlike entailments, ***implicatures are cancelable***. Consider example 9, taken from a bumper sticker:

(9)   *I don't suffer from insanity.*
       *I enjoy every minute of it.*

Based on the first sentence in (9), the reader would reason that the author of these words is implicating that he or she is mentally healthy; however, the second utterance cancels this interpretation, rendering the implicature implausible. What's peculiar to implicatures is that denying them does not result in a sense of explicit contradiction. This is what it means to be cancelable. Contrast (9) with a constructed variant (10), where the denial of an explicit meaning ('not suffering from insanity') does create an irresolvable contradiction:

**(10)**   ?? *I don't suffer from insanity. I suffer from insanity.*

Similarly, the speaker of (8d) could continue her 'you have a sick dog at home' with 'but don't stop this interesting discussion.' Only implicatures are cancelable in this way.

     ***Implicatures are only indirectly communicated.*** They are not conventionally and invariably tied to specific linguistic expressions, for they are ***context-dependent***. Compare the use of *really* in (11a) to that in Example (1), here repeated as (11b):

**(11)**   a. LSAC

       A:     *Because nobody's used to rain, it's like schools close.*
       B:     *Really?*
       A:     *Well, I mean, I'm exaggerating here* (LSAC: 1118–01).

      b. Maya:     *Aw, they always change it!*
       Mom:     <u>*Really?*</u>
       Maya:     *What, would I lie to you?*

Unlike in (11b), *Really?* is here used to explicitly question the truthfulness of A's utterance. Since the same expression (*really?*) is involved in (11a) and in (11b), it must be the different context which is responsible for the occurrence or nonoccurrence of the implicature.

    We have seen that Grice's Maxims set up norms, which account for discourse coherence and which guide interlocutors in making pragmatic interpretations. We next review an alternative theory for discourse coherence, and therefore also for how pragmatic interpretations are made.

### 8.2.2  The Principle of Relevance

Sperber and Wilson (1986/1995), in revising Grice's Maxims, have proposed to replace Quantity, Relation, and Manner with a single cognitive principle: ***The Principle of Relevance***. (They also dropped the Quality Maxim altogether.) They argue that people are automatically geared toward searching for maximally relevant information, and that ***linguistic acts specifically come with a presumption of relevance***.

    For an utterance to be Sperber–Wilson ***Relevant***, it must achieve some cognitive effects. Simply put, it must (attempt to) induce some change in the addressee's cognitive state (e.g., by adding or eliminating assumptions he or she holds). However, not every change is Relevant. Imagine that you were Maya's addressee in (1). You would add to your knowledge that 'they always change it.' This would no doubt change your cognitive state, but such an exchange does not meet our expectations for relevance. While you could potentially infer that 'they keep doing the same thing,' this inference is just not relevant enough because we are not told who these *they* are, what *it* is, and why all this matters. For Relevance Theory to account for how natural discourse proceeds, it must define Relevant cognitive effects more narrowly:

- Relevant cognitive effects must be **contextual implications**, i.e., inferences made based on (1) **the content of the utterance** combined with (2) **available contextual assumptions**.
- There must be a **sufficient number of contextual implications** (in order for these implications to have a Relevant cognitive effect).
- Deriving the cognitive effects (i.e., making the inferences) must involve **the most minimal processing effort**.

Let's take these conditions one by one. First, for an utterance to constitute a Relevant contribution, it **must combine with contextual (i.e., background) assumptions to yield further contextual implications** (akin to the Gricean implicatures). Such contextual assumptions may have been mentioned in the preceding discourse, or they may have to be accessed from our encyclopedic knowledge (see Figure 8.2).

Now, the reason why Maya's utterance in (1) couldn't be Relevant to you is that it's hard to imagine what contextual assumptions you could bring to bear on that proposition, such that together, they would yield some implications. For example, how would you know who *they* are and what *it* is. Since no contextual assumptions are involved here, the utterance is not Relevant (for you) in the Sperber–Wilson sense.

In the case of (2), on the other hand, we can combine the explicit proposition (*asthma is on the rise*) with a background assumption (from our general knowledge) that 'asthma is dangerous,' to yield contextual implications such as 'It is alarming that asthma is on the rise'; and 'We should do something to fight asthma.' Since the combination of the content of (2) with contextual assumptions yields contextual implications, the utterance is Relevant. This definition then accounts for our intuitive feeling that relevance entails some connection between an utterance and its context.

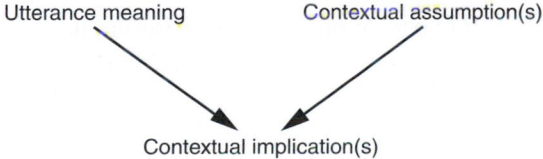

**Figure 8.2** The derivation of contextual implications

Next, ***the more contextual implications there are, the higher the Relevance*** of the utterance. Comparing (6a) and (6b), the former (*He kissed her on the neck*) is more Relevant, for it gives rise to an additional contextual implication that (6b) doesn't, namely that the kiss was sexual. This requirement, however, only specifies that there be a sufficient number of contextual implications, so (6a) may very well be Relevant enough in many contexts.

Third, more is not always merrier. Pretend now that (2) appeared on a bus in Warsaw. Relevance Theory offers an explanation for why the same discourse might not be Relevant/appropriate when in a different context. Cultural differences translate to different contextual assumptions. Polish readers would be able to process the first two sentences, but they would be baffled by the third. Unlike most American addressees, who can easily access the necessary contextual assumptions immediately, non-Americans, who do not know what Christmas Seals are, would have to improvise. They might (correctly) assume that Christmas Seals is an organization that fights asthma. But relying on the Polish addressee to come up with such a culturally foreign contextual assumption as a premise for some conclusion is risky. While speakers do sometimes force addressees to generate contextual assumptions they cannot retrieve from their general knowledge store, such processes are bound to slow the addressee down. This is why Sperber and Wilson's definition of Relevance discourages such uses.

The inappropriateness of the asthma ad in Warsaw is accounted for by defining Relevance as requiring the speaker to balance between contextual effects and processing costs. Although all other things being equal, the more contextual effects, the more Relevant an utterance is, at the same time, the harder it is to derive some contextual implication, the less Relevant that interpretation is. In other words, although we can always add more and more contextual assumptions in order to derive more and more contextual implications, **Optimal Relevance** ***requires a balance between contextual effects and processing effort***. Some contextual assumptions are not easily accessible to us. Others are highly accessible. If so, an utterance that depends on the retrieval of highly accessible assumptions is less effortful. Relevance Theory specifies that the effort exerted on the addressee be minimal: for an utterance to be Optimally Relevant, ***a sufficient number of contextual implications must be derivable by the addressee, and at a minimal processing effort*** (see Figure 8.3). The asthma ad on a Warsaw bus would not be Optimally Relevant, because the processing effort would not be as minimal as it could have been (had another sentence explained what Christmas Seals was).

Here's a case where the processing load is significantly lighter, since the contextual assumption needed is not only part of our common wisdom, it is also stereotypically conjured up in the specific scenario here imagined (starting a fight). It is thus easily available to the interlocutors:

(12)  Jamie:    *Aren't you guys gonna stick up for me?*
                *and beat up on him or something?*
      Miles:    *He's bigger than I am.* (SBC: 002)

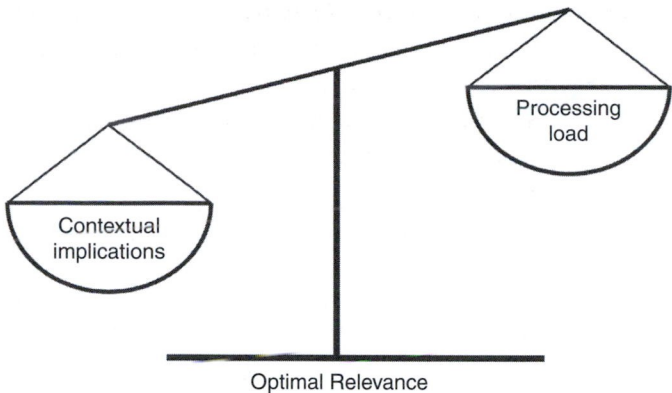

**Figure 8.3** Balancing for Optimal Relevance

When Jamie is (jokingly) asking her friends to beat up on her husband, Miles's relevant response (the contextual implication from his actual utterance) is that 'he won't beat up on the husband.' The interlocutors can reach this conclusion based on an easily accessible contextual assumption, 'it's not advisable to try and beat up on a guy who's bigger than you, because most likely you'll be beaten badly.' This contextual assumption is much easier to retrieve than the assumption that Christmas Seals is an organization that fights asthma (for the Polish addressee).

In sum, both the Principle of Relevance and the Conversational Maxims explain what makes discourse appropriate and coherent. There is an intimate connection between **discourse appropriateness**, the accessing of **contextual assumptions**, and **pragmatic inferences**. Both theories account for the central role of pragmatic inferencing in communication. The total take-home message of some utterance is its **conveyed meaning**, a combination of the semantic meaning and the pragmatic inferences intended by the speaker (see Figure 8.4). For example, for (8d) it is 'You have a sick dog at home' plus 'You should stick to the agenda.'

### 8.2.3 Different pragmatic interpretations for different purposes

So far we have only assumed a distinction between semantic meanings and pragmatic meanings (implicatures). But **pragmatic meanings are not all of one stripe**. Consider again Maya's first utterance in Example (1):

(1)    Maya: *Aw, they always change it!*

What is *it*, and who are *they*? As outsiders we do not know. In order to determine the explicit message that Maya is communicating, her mother must **infer** the referents of these pronouns (based on shared contextual assumptions). **Pragmatic**

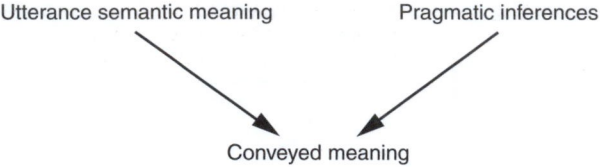

**Figure 8.4** Deriving the conveyed meaning

*inferences are often required to determine even the explicit message of an utterance*, and not just the indirect implicatures intended by the speaker. The underdetermined linguistic meaning must often be developed by pragmatic inferences to make it *a complete proposition, sufficiently specific and understandable*.

The linguistic code enriched by such pragmatic inferences is called (by Sperber and Wilson 1986/1995) the **explicature**. The pragmatic inferences involved in understanding the explicature are then **explicated inferences**. We can illustrate the relationship of semantic meaning, explicated inferences, and the explicature as in Figure 8.5.

Maya's first utterance in (1) is not the only case where an explicit message is incomplete by itself. On the asthma ad, the linguistic expression *Double your efforts* makes no sense if one limits oneself to the semantic meaning alone. Double your efforts for what? Given the contextual assumptions that are salient here, we can derive an explicated inference that the efforts are aimed at fighting asthma. The addressee thus derives the explicature 'Double your efforts to fight asthma,' by combining the linguistic meaning with the explicated inference (see Figure 8.6). Without the added inferred information, the utterance would be conceptually incomplete. Unlike Grice, who considers practically any pragmatic inference to be an implicature, Sperber and Wilson distinguish between implicatures and explicated inferences.

Pragmatics has a far-reaching role in human communication, far more than first envisioned: it is not as if linguistic expressions always provide the main message while pragmatic inferences only provide additional implicit and secondary interpretations, as

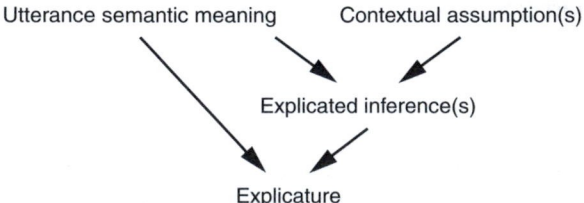

**Figure 8.5** Deriving the explicature

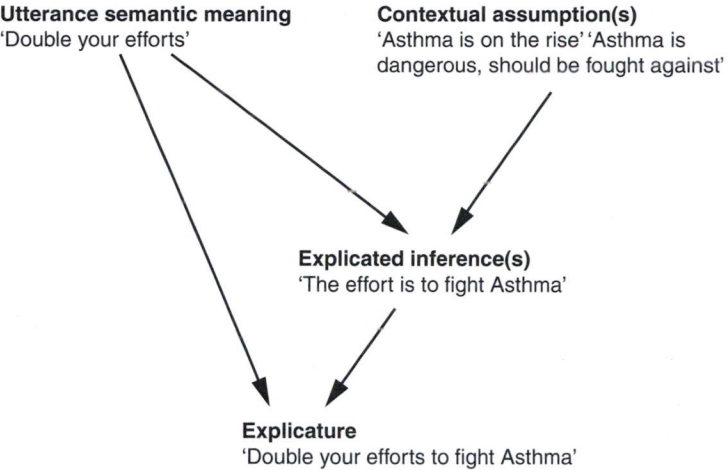

**Figure 8.6** Deriving the explicature of *Double your efforts*

**SIDEBAR 8.3**

Both implicatures and explicated inferences are speaker-intended pragmatic meanings. They differ in that explicated inferences are considered part and parcel of the explicit message; they are directly communicated. Implicatures, in contrast, are indirect. This is why although both are potentially cancelable, explicated inferences contribute to the truth-conditional interpretation of the utterance, while implicatures do not.

in e.g., (8). Rather, *some pragmatic inferences (explicated ones) are an inherent part of the explicit message intended by the speaker* (see Sidebar 8.3). This is the case for *double your efforts* in (2).

According to Relevance Theory, it is the explicature (rather than purely the semantic meaning) that combines with contextual assumptions to yield implicatures. In interactional terms, *it is the explicature that counts as the directly relevant contribution* (rather than the incomplete linguistic meaning). To see that this is the case, consider (13):

(13)   1 J:   *We can walk to Erez,*
       2      *and have breakfast there.*
       3 M:   *But we're having lunch at my parents',*
       4      *and we're going out with R tonight.*
              ((LINES OMITTED))
       5 J:   *Okay,*
       6      *We'll have breakfast another day.*
       7 M:   *Maybe tomorrow.*

Note that when J suggests that they have breakfast another day (line 6), he doesn't mean only that, because it's too trivial: J and M have breakfast every morning. Rather, the explicature from J is 'We'll have breakfast **at Erez** [Cafe] another day.' The same

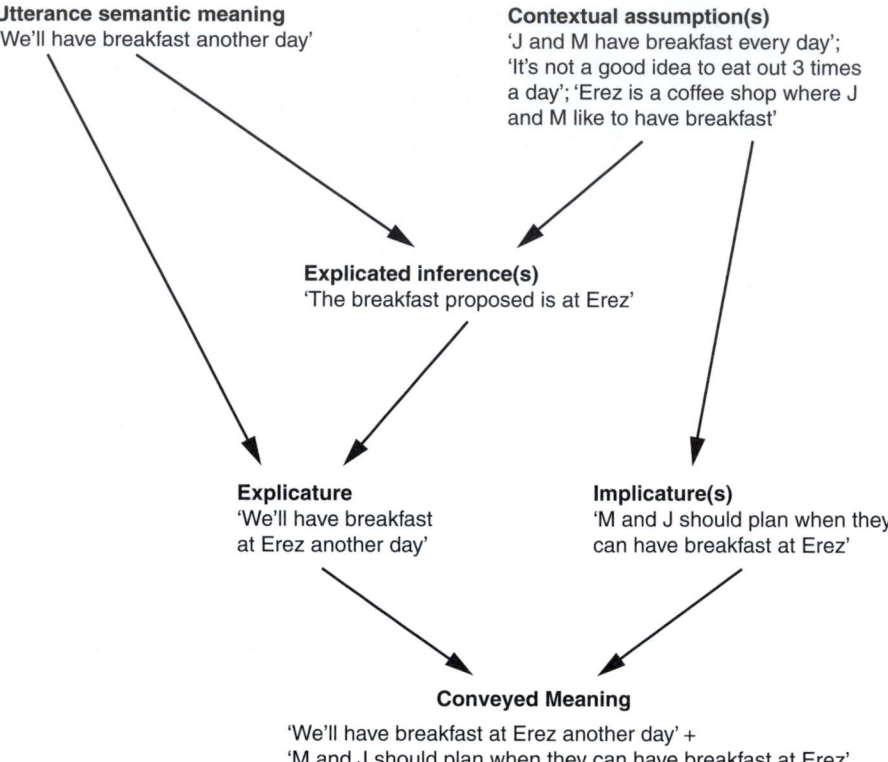

**Figure 8.7** Deriving the conveyed meaning (complete model)

applies to M in line 7. Without the additional explicated inference, neither line 6 nor 7 make any sense. The whole point is whether J and M should eat out that morning. Figure 8.7 shows the complex model we have arrived at, as applied to (13).

All the pragmatic inferences we have considered are speaker-intended, context-dependent, plausible, and cancelable. But whereas implicatures are indirect and external to the speaker's explicit message (the explicature), explicated inferences are part and parcel of it. This is why (14a), rather than (14b) is a faithful report on J's utterance in (13):

(14)  a. *J said that they will have breakfast <u>at Erez</u> another day.*
      b. (i) *J said that they will have breakfast another day, <u>and</u> (ii) <u>in addition he indirectly suggested that it would be at Erez.</u>*

The point is that J did not convey **two separate** messages (as represented in (14b)). J had absolutely no intention of stating that they will have breakfast another day, for that is too trivial a proposition. Rather, he made a single suggestion (as represented by (14a), although part of it was left implicit. Regardless of their different discourse statuses, all pragmatic inferences are crucial to natural discourse.

## 8.3   Semantics versus pragmatics

We have so far treated the semantics/pragmatics division of labor as self-evident. Indeed, ***semantics analyzes conventional, context-invariant meanings***, whereas ***pragmatics accounts for plausible context-dependent inferences***. The implicatures we have reviewed here, in particular, are clearly pragmatic. But not all interpretations are readily classifiable as either semantic or pragmatic. ***It is sometimes difficult to judge whether a given interpretation is the conventional meaning of some form or its pragmatically inferred interpretation***.

For example, I have treated 'questioning factuality' as the semantic meaning of *really?* and 'expressing surprise' as a speaker implicature, which is intended in some but not all contexts. But isn't it possible that *really?* is semantically ambiguous between 'questioning factuality' (its compositional meaning) and 'expressing surprise' (seen as a non-compositional encoded meaning)? If so, perhaps the young Maya in Example (1) simply hasn't yet learned the second ('surprise') meaning of *really?*, and the joking Maya simply ignores this context-appropriate meaning.

The 'surprise' interpretation of *really?* is reasonably inferred from 'questioning factuality.' One may question the factuality of some proposition if it seems surprising. But ***the fact that some interpretation is in principle inferable does not mean that it is actually inferred***. Interpretations associated with certain expressions may undergo a change from having a pragmatic status, where the meaning is contextually inferred, to having a semantic status, where the meaning is conventionally encoded. This ***well-known process, leading to a change from pragmatic status to semantic status, is called* semanticization**, and it has been documented for many expressions. Once some inference (e.g., 'surprise') is frequently derived whenever some specific form (e.g., *really?*) is used, the form–function association may become automatic and gradually conventionally encoded through semanticization.

Has this happened for *really?* It is immaterial for our purposes here whether or not *really?* has in fact crossed the pragmatics/semantics borderline. What is crucial for us is that this borderline can be crossed, and has been crossed many times (Textbox 8.1 provides one such example). ***Many of our current semantic meanings are actually the result of ongoing historical processes of the semanticization of pragmatic inferences***. Therefore, we should only expect to find cases where the ongoing process of semanticization is underway, making it hard to determine whether some interpretation is semantically coded or (still) only pragmatically inferred.

Do such cases mean that the semantics/pragmatics division of labor is useless? Not at all. The great majority of linguistic expressions have fixed semantic meanings, which are pragmatically adapted or enriched in specific contexts, but with no long-term effects on their semantic meanings. Consider (8). Obviously, we would not want to lump the semantic meanings of *the different versions (testimonies) of an eighty-nine-year-old person, you have a sick dog at home!* and *edit a tomato* with the pragmatic contextual interpretations they give rise to here ('unreliable,' 'stick to the agenda,' and 'cut out parts of a tomato,' respectively). On the one hand, ***ad hoc pragmatic inferences are so numerous and context-dependent that it would be pointless to list them as semantic meanings***. On the other hand, ***we need relatively fixed semantic meanings as a basis for constructing specific contextual pragmatic interpretations***. Semantic and pragmatic interpretations are both important, although they serve different functions in language.

---

### TEXTBOX 8.1

The English word *since* is a clear example of an expression for which the semanticization of a pragmatic inference has been completed. Originally, *since* had only a temporal meaning. But in addition to this temporal meaning, speakers using *since* must have frequently generated causal implicatures, which indirectly conveyed a causal relation between events. Observe the following use of the very similar variant *ever since*:

PATRICK:   ... Well **ever since** he heard that I was
                      having problems with my band,
                      you know,
                      he's been calling me a lot more (SBC: 045).

While *ever since* encodes only a temporal relation between *he heard ...* and *he's been calling ...* Patrick here

generates an implicature that it is **because** 'he heard ...' that 'he's been calling ...'. A frequent use of *since* in similar contexts must have paved the way for the semanticization of the causal inference for *since*, so much so, that even in the absence of a temporal connection, a causal interpretation is available:

KATHY:   ... **Since** you have the square root of two on
                    the bottom,
                    ... to make that a square,
                    you have to multiply by the square root of two
                    (SBC: 009).

The semanticization of *since* that allows it to be used in this context has not occurred for *ever since*. Note that *ever since* cannot replace *since* here.

---

### CHAPTER SUMMARY

We have defined pragmatic interpretations as complementary to semantic interpretations. While ***semantic meanings are context-invariant encoded meanings*** specified for particular linguistic expressions, ***pragmatic meanings are nonconventional plausible inferences***, triggered by linguistic expressions only when used in supportive contexts. This is why only pragmatic interpretations are cancelable. We presented two proposals (Grice's Maxims and the Principle of Relevance) that account for the derivation of speaker-intended pragmatic inferences. While differing on many points, both of the approaches view utterance meanings as routinely combining semantic and pragmatic meanings. We further distinguished between types of pragmatic inferences, based on their cognitive and discoursal statuses. Particularized conversational implicatures are external to semantic meanings and indirectly conveyed, while explicated inferences are integrated into the semantic meaning to create a single proposition, the explicature.

We revisited the semantics/pragmatics question in the end, proposing that although pragmatics is very often the source of our current semantic meanings, for the most part, semantic and pragmatic meanings are kept apart. All in all, we cannot overestimate the important role pragmatics plays in interpreting language:

Pragmatics    accounts for ***discourse appropriateness*** (relevance, coherence)
Pragmatics    participates in ***fleshing out the speaker's explicit message*** (explicature)
Pragmatics    explains how ***indirect additional messages*** (implicatures) are derived
Pragmatics    provides ***raw materials for our future grammar*** (semanticization of pragmatic interpretations)

---

### TEXTBOX 8.2 **GLOSSING CONVENTIONS USED IN THIS CHAPTER**

| Convention | Meaning | Convention | Meaning |
|---|---|---|---|
| 1 | first person | F | feminine |
| 2 | second person | NEG | negation |
| ACC | accusative | PL | plural |
| CONJ | conjunctive | PROX | proximal |
| DEF | definite | PST | past tense |
| DEM | demonstrative | SG | singular |

---

### SUGGESTIONS FOR FURTHER READING

**Levinson, Stephen C.** 1983. *Pragmatics*. Cambridge University Press.

This book is the first and classical introductory textbook on pragmatics. It discusses deixis, implicature, presupposition, speech acts and conversational structure.

**Grice, H. Paul**. 1975. "Logic and conversation." In Cole, Peter and Jerry L. Morgan (eds.), *Syntax and semantics*, Vol. III: *Speech acts*. New York: Academic Press. 41–58.

This is the relevant original theory of Grice.

**Sperber, Dan and Deirdre Wilson**. 1986/1995. *Relevance*. Oxford: Blackwell.

This book introduces Relevance Theory.

**Horn, Laurence R.** 1984. "A new taxonomy for pragmatic inference: Q-based and R-based implicatures." In Deborah Schiffrin (ed.), *Meaning, form, and use in context: Linguistic applications* (Georgetown University Round Table on Languages and Linguistics). Washington, DC: Georgetown University Press. 11–42.

This chapter introduces a variant, neo-Gricean theory.

**Ariel, Mira**. 2010. *Defining pragmatics*. Cambridge University Press.

This book is a survey of the field of pragmatics, focusing on how to define and how to do pragmatics.

See also Ariel (2008), Blakemore (1992), Green (1989), Grundy (1995), Huang (2007), and Thomas (1995).

List of sources:

LSAC    The Longman Spoken American Corpus
SBC     The Santa Barbara Corpus of Spoken American English (Du Bois and Englebretson 2004; Du Bois and Englebretson 2005; Du Bois et al. 2000; Du Bois et al. 2003)

## EXERCISES

1. Here are two cases where speakers might seem to contradict themselves. How would you resolve this contradiction? (Hint: Construct the relevant explicatures.)
   a. "I was a composer even before I was a composer and my teacher, composer Abel Erlich, knew it right from the start" (Originally Hebrew, *Haaretz*, July 27, 2007).
   b. At any rate, at this point the arrival in Israel [of the Ethiopian Jews – M.A.] is perceived as incomplete, as one of the interviewees put it: "We've arrived, but we haven't arrived" (Originally Hebrew, *Haaretz*, November 9, 2007).

2. J must have misunderstood M's *D'you know what time it is?* in the following exchange:

   M:    *D'you know what time it is?*
   J:    *What.*
   M:    *No, do you know what time it is?*

   Explain the source of the miscommunication here. Is it the same as in question (1)? (Hint: No.)

3. Using the concepts of particularized conversational implicature, as well as cancellation, can you explain why A's *That's my job* below resembles a punchline in a joke?
   ((The addressee has been very carefully folding up some scotch tape around a picture, so that it won't stick to the wall and damage it))
   A: *You don't have to be such a perfectionist.*
   ((Pause))
   *That's MY job.*

4. Consider Fran's utterances, paying special attention to the underlined expressions, and determine whether their interpretations, provided below, are implicated or explicated:

   Fran:   *and this is a guy <u>like seventy years old</u>,*
           *<u>or something</u>,*
           *he'd been <u>driving a cab for forty years</u>,*
           *and <u>proud of it</u>* (SBC: 051).

   *Like seventy years old, or something* > 'About seventy years old'
   *driving a cab for forty years* > 'driving noncontinuously, whenever he worked', i.e., 'he'd worked as a cab driver for forty years'
   *proud of it* > 'proud of being a cab driver' (not of the cab)

   Here are some questions that might help you decide:
   What if you find out the guy is 50? Or that he drove a cab but not for a living, or that he drove it day and night for 40 years? Or that he was proud of his cab?

5. Consider a few examples with *at the same time* and with *while*. Both are sometimes understood to refer to events or situations that stand in contrast to each other. Based on the following data, what can we

say about the semantic or pragmatic status of 'contrast' for *while* and *at the same time*? Has it semanticized into an encoded meaning or is it only pragmatically inferred in some contexts? Is this status the same for the two expressions? One useful method is to try to exchange the two expressions with each other as well as with *when*, which has roughly the same temporal meaning. Since we're only interested in meaning, you should make syntactic changes as necessary, and then check whether the variants you created are still synonymous. Specifically, check whether the variants convey some contrast, and whether they still convey temporal simultaneity.

(Hints: The less the presence of a contrast interpretation in some variant, the less contrast has semanticized. The less the presence of a temporal interpretation in some variant, the more likely the semanticization of 'contrast' has progressed, to the point that it started ousting the original temporal linguistic meaning.)

Note that the goal here is not to reach the definitive answer regarding these expressions. Rather, to try and construct arguments for a semantic versus pragmatic status.

### *While* examples

a. *I didn't want to have an asthma attack <u>while</u> I was unconscious* (LSAC).

b. Pete: *They were having a drought <u>while</u> I was there* (SBC: 003).

c. Dan:          *... Thank you very much.*
   Jennifer:     *... For what.*
   Dan:          *.. I just took over Iceland.*
   Jennifer:     *.. (TSK) Oh,*
                 ((1 LINE OMMITTED))
                 *.. (H) Right <u>while</u> I was kissing you, you traitor.* (SBC: 024).

d. Randy: *Just take into consideration the type of aircrafts.*
   *It takes the seven-twenty-seven a little b- while to get wound up,*
   *<u>while</u> the seven-thirty-seven'll really go* (SBC: 022).

e. *I haven't done what I would consider to be a good job with this class this quarter.* ((LINES OMMITTED))
   *I feel like, <u>while</u> I'm prepared for class,* ((1 LINE OMMITTED)) *I don't have the hour to just sit and look at the material and go through it and know exactly what it is I'm going to say* (LSAC).

f. *Now they ((crocodiles)) survived <u>while</u> the dinosaurs did not. And one of the theories is because they were so small they were able to hide.*

### *At the same time* examples

a. *He could also do e-mail or write stuff on the computer and either watch television or listen to the radio <u>at the same time</u>* (LSAC).

b. *He was alive <u>at the same time</u> that ah Thomas More was* (LSAC).

c. *Well, I mean, for lunch, what can you bring on like a backpacking trip for lunch that doesn't require any cooking but <u>at the same time</u> is not going* ((LINES OMMITTED)) *to overwhelm you with fat, sugar or salt* (LSAC).

d. Frank: *.. you cannot get a scale for d-*
          ((LINES OMMITTED))
          *distance,*
          *... and <u>at the same time</u> get objects,*
          *that can give you the scale for the size of the planets* (SBC: 019).

# 9 Discourse: language beyond the sentence

## CHAPTER PREVIEW

In the preceding chapters, we looked at linguistic units such as the phoneme, morpheme, phrase, and sentence. Discourse, as described here, is the study of language at levels beyond the sentence, how larger stretches of language are organized, and ways in which this organization influences the shapes of sentences and words. This chapter will particularly focus on the discourse genre of spoken conversation. It will introduce students to conventions for the transcription of conversational speech, and in particular, prosodic features such as intonation. The chapter will look at differences between prosodic and syntactic structuring and how speakers use intonation units to manage discourse goals such as navigating topics of conversation or structuring narratives. It will also introduce the notion of information structure and the concepts of given, new, and accessible information, and will look at how the identifiability of referents is marked in English grammar. At multiple points throughout the discussion, the chapter will illustrate that grammatical structures are employed for discourse purposes.

## LIST OF AIMS

By the end of this unit, the student will be able to:

- **read transcriptions of conversational discourse that indicate prosodic categories;**
- **distinguish between substantive, regulatory, and fragmentary intonation units;**

- identify the functions that intonation units have in navigating a topic of conversation;
- identify the structural elements of a narrative;
- determine whether the activation state of an idea is given, new, or accessible;
- determine whether the referent of a noun phrase is identifiable or non-identifiable;
- articulate why studying discourse contributes to a broader understanding of language and linguistic structure.

## 9.1 Introduction

The term "discourse" is used in a variety of ways. It may, for example, refer to an established way of talking about something, as with "medical discourse" or "feminist discourse." Within linguistics most discourse studies fall into one of two broad categories: investigating ways in which language is used and investigating larger levels of language structure. It is this last use of the term that is discussed here.

It is easiest to understand basic concepts of discourse through examples in one's own language, without the complicating factors of unfamiliar grammatical devices, and with the ability to reflect on one's own discourse practices. For that reason, all of the examples discussed in this chapter are taken from English. Nevertheless, most of what is said in this chapter is true of all spoken languages; only the language-particular details of prosody and grammar differ. Discourse functions are the same across languages because all humans have the same cognitive structures and the same communicative needs in speaking.

## 9.2 Hierarchies of linguistic units

In the field of linguistics there has been a tendency over the years to work gradually upward from smaller units to larger ones. During the period that preceded and immediately followed World War II, much attention was paid to the phoneme, a unit of sound that was regarded as the minimal unit of language. There was also a lively concern for morphology, the structure of words, which were thought to be composed of morphemes, which in turn were composed of phonemes. For example, the word *hunted* was analyzed as a sequence of two morphemes, *hunt* and *-ed*, and each of these morphemes was analyzed as a sequence of phonemes. Around 1960, a great deal of work and effort began to be devoted to syntax, the structure of sentences, which were in turn composed of words. Thus, language at that time was thought to possess a hierarchical structure like this:

sentences
are composed of   words
are composed of   morphemes
are composed of   phonemes.

Beginning around the 1970s, significant attention began to be extended to ways in which sentences combine within still larger stretches of language. ***Language beyond*** *the sentence has been called* **discourse**, and thus a new level was added to the hierarchy:

discourse
is composed of     sentences
are composed of    words
are composed of    morphemes
are composed of    phonemes.

***Discourse studies have led to important revisions in the ways linguists approach language as a whole.*** For example, whereas linguists earlier felt free to invent their own examples of isolated words or sentences, it was impossible to invent larger stretches of language in the same way. Inventing conversations is best left to writers of fiction. ***Discourse studies have thus necessarily emphasized the importance of recording language as it is actually used under natural circumstances. Furthermore, discourse cannot be expected to conform to patterns as clearly defined as those found in morphology or syntax***. The ways people create larger stretches of language are governed by their purposes and the flow of their thoughts, and those processes are not as rigidly structured as words or sentences. In spite of this looser organization, discourse analysts have discovered a variety of ways in which larger stretches of language are organized, and also ways in which discourse factors influence the shape of sentences and words.

## 9.3  Genres of discourse

***Discourse studies have also highlighted the fact that language comes in many varieties, or* genres.** One obvious distinction separates spoken language from written language. Speaking and writing are very different ways of producing and comprehending language, and these differences can lead to significant changes in the language itself.

There are many other genres within spoken and written discourse. For example, spoken language is found in conversations, stories, interviews, speeches, service encounters, and so on. Written language is found in letters, fictional and nonfictional books and articles, news reports, editorials, and e-mail and text messages. ***Each of the many ways language is used follows discourse patterns that are shaped by the needs of that use.***

***Within these varieties, spoken conversations enjoy a special status.*** Early on in human history, people were probably speaking with each other before they developed other ways of using language. People converse often and naturally and with no special training, whereas other uses of language need to be deliberately taught and learned. Written language did not even exist until a few thousand years ago, and until very recently most of the world's population remained illiterate. Because of its priority in these respects, the focus in this chapter will be on spoken conversational discourse.

In one respect analyzing written language is an easier task, because writing has a permanence that allows it to be revisited and analyzed at one's leisure. Spoken language is realized in transient sounds that disappear almost as soon as they are produced. Modern technology has given us the advantage of allowing these evanescent sounds

---

**TEXTBOX 9.1  THE IMPORTANCE OF LISTENING**

Transcriptions of spoken language, even when marking prosodic features such as intonation and loudness, never do justice to the richness of the spoken voice. Try reading Example (1), then listen to the sound file on the website. You'll notice an immediate deepening in your understanding of the conversation and the interaction in which it takes place.

Listening repeatedly, while working though the transcript, is a good habit that will reward you with insights at increasingly fine levels of detail.

---

**TEXTBOX 9.2  DISCOURSE DATA**

Data for spoken discourse typically consists of a set of recordings, accompanied by transcriptions that may be annotated in various ways. The recordings and annotations together are combined into a **corpus** (plural **corpora**) that can be analyzed using a variety of methodologies. The study of discourse benefits from detailed qualitative analyses, of the type introduced here, as well as from quantitative methodologies that reveal patterns over large data sets.

There are a number of publicly available corpora that have been converted into online searchable databases, such as the American Corpus of Contemporary English (http://corpus.byu.edu/coca/). These can be used in a variety of ways. For example, a **concordance** of all of the examples of the word *well* (followed by a comma) in the database produces a list of 2,216,646 examples of *well* in the context in which they occurred, including the eight examples in Figure 9.1 (all from television news shows). One can use this to analyze, for example, how often this *well* was used at the beginning of a speaker's turn, or in expressing a point contrary to that of a previous speaker. This can be done because clicking on each example allows one to see the broader context in which the word appears. One can also query to see how frequently *well*, co-occurs with other words (e.g., *well then* occurs 164 times, while *oh well* occurs ninety times), whether the distributions differ depending on genre, whether there are differences across time, etc.

Linguists from across the world use such corpora to address a wide array of topics in linguistics. The publications page of the American Corpus of Contemporary English (http://corpus.byu.edu/publicationSearch.asp) illustrates the range of this recent work.

of innocence that, to such as can not see into her, may pass **well** enough. MRS. BELVILLE: Nay, my dear, don't say
. BELVILLE: aside like " docility ". to MRS. BELVILLEThe girl's **well** enough for what she is. But let's see what she'll
much grieved for the loss of her. O, how my eyes run! **Well**, but God's will be done. My master said: for my dear
I could not help entertaining a jealousy that she was writing to somebody who stood **well** in her opinion, and my fe
to whom you speak? PAMELA: Yes, I do, sir, too **well**. Well may I forget that I am your servant when you forget wha
you speak? PAMELA: Yes, I do, sir, too well. **Well** may I forget that I am your servant when you forget what belongs
of fire in my attempts to thaw it. MRS. JERVIS comes forward. **Well**, Mrs. Jervis, I know Pamela has your good word
know of? MRS. JERVIS: deeply embarrassedNo indeed, sir. BELVILLE: **Well**, no more of this silly girl. You may only
two miles and a half and a byway to the town, and bring pretty **well** dressed I may come to some harm almost as b
thus you taunt and retort upon me? I will be answered. PAMELA: **Well** then, sir, I will not tell a lie for the world. I

**Figure 9.1**  Some concordance examples from the American Corpus of Contemporary English, based on the word *well*

to be preserved and replayed, greatly improving our ability to analyze speech as it actually occurs. Nevertheless, linguists nearly always begin their analyses by transcribing speech into a written form that they can peruse whenever and however they wish. These transcriptions have their limitations and can never capture everything that is present in the sounds themselves. Thus, their form and content is always determined by the goals of the investigator and by whatever conventions those goals may dictate.

## 9.4  Transcribing conversational speech

Example (1) is an excerpt from a conversation between a mother and daughter. The sequences of two and three dots show shorter and longer pauses. ***The square brackets show overlapping speech***, as in line 7, where the mother's words *but I thought* overlapped with the daughter's words *and then he* in line 6. ***The accent marks show words or syllables that were given special prominence*** with higher pitch, often with louder volume, and sometimes with lengthening. (See Textbox 9.1 for a note on the limitations of transcripts such as this one and the importance of listening, and Textbox 9.2 for a note on discourse data.) A full discussion of prosody is given in Chapter 10.

| (1) | 1 | Daughter: | . . . *Isn't that sád about that kid in the papér?* |
| | 2 | | .. *Who.. who's in a cóma?* |
| | 3 | | *He's a- the star.. baseball player at* BK? |
| | 4 | | . . . *And he got the schólarship to-* |
| | 5 | | . . . *He was the Gatorade player of* the year? |
| | 6 | | .. *Two years ago [and then he-]* |
| | 7 | Mother: | [But I thought] *it was his dád who was.. in the hospital.* |
| | 8 | Daughter: | *Nó it's hím.* |
| | 9 | | .. *He's [in a cóm]a.* |
| | 10 | Mother: | [*Oh.*] |
| | 11 | Daughter: | .. [*He got hit*] *by that drunk driver?* |
| | 12 | Mother: | [*Okay.*] |
| | 13 | Daughter: | . . . *And his younger bróther,* |
| | 14 | | *played at BK on the fóotball team.* |
| | 15 | | . . . *And I gue-* |
| | 16 | | *it was the pa-* |
| | 17 | | *the árticle was about you know how,* |
| | 18 | | . . . *they're all going to-* |
| | 19 | | *all the family's gonna go to the gáme today because,* |
| | 20 | | .. *spórts are very important.* |
| | 21 | | .. *In his [fámily] you know,* |
| | 22 | Mother: | [*Yeah*]. |
| | 23 | Daughter: | *they all used to go watch . . . the older brother play báseball,* |

| | | |
|---|---|---|
| 24 | | *that's what he would want,* |
| 25 | | *is for the family to be at the game,* |
| 26 | Mother: | *Oh* [*really?*] |
| 27 | Daughter: | [*Uh*] *but the coach,* |
| 28 | | *I think it's Tim Beagen.* |
| 29 | | [*And one*] *of the Beagens said you know,* |
| 30 | Mother: | [*Yeah.*] |
| 31 | Daughter: | *if you don't wanna play that's fine,* |
| 32 | | *if you . . . don't wanna,* |
| 33 | | *you could just go out of the play,* |
| 34 | | *. . . you just do whatever,* |
| 35 | | *but it was like aah.* |

One obvious property of spoken language is its production, not as an uninterrupted flow of sound, but as a series of spurts that are usually about one second long. These spurts are sometimes called **intonation units** (IUs), sometimes **prosodic phrases**. They are defined by their **prosody**, a term that includes variations in **pitch**, **volume**, **timing**, and **voice quality**. IUs are represented here in separate lines. There is a tendency for them to decline in both pitch and volume from beginning to end. Figure 9.2 illustrates this declination for line 7, where pitch (more precisely, **fundamental frequency**) is shown at the top, and volume (or **intensity**) at the bottom.

There is also a tendency for IUs to be spoken rapidly at the beginning and more slowly at the end, as in line 1, where the first words *isn't that sad about that* were spoken at an average rate of 90 milliseconds per syllable, while the average rate for the last four words, *kid in the paper*, was a much slower 194 milliseconds per syllable, in large part because of the lengthened pronunciation of the word *paper*. This deceleration is evident at the bottom of Figure 9.3.

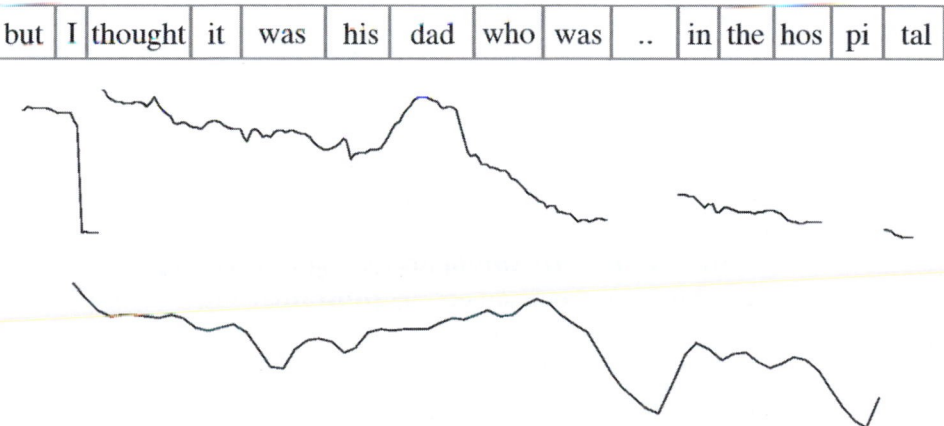

**Figure 9.2** Declining pitch (top line) and volume (bottom) in line 7 of Example (1)

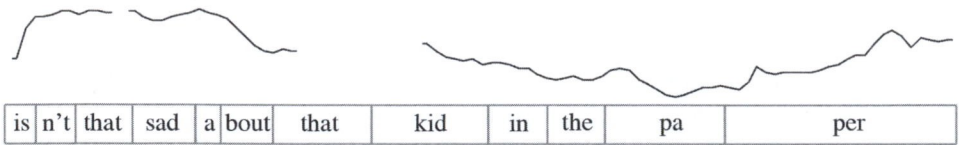

| is | n't | that | sad | a | bout | that | kid | in | the | pa | per |

**Figure 9.3** Pitch and syllable length in line 1 of Example (1)

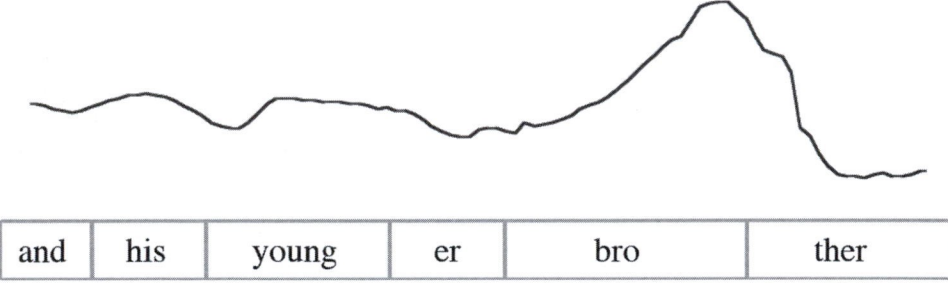

| and | his | young | er | bro | ther |

**Figure 9.4** Line 13 with a low rising terminal contour, indicating more to come

Each intonation unit ends with a **terminal pitch contour** that signals the boundary of the IU as well as the relation of this IU to others (see Sidebar 9.1 for a summary of their transcription conventions). Line 1 ended with a rising pitch on the last syllable of the word *paper*, inviting agreement from the mother. This terminal rise is visible in Figure 9.3; it is represented in the transcription with a question mark. Lines 13 and 14 were closely related, with line 13 introducing the idea of the younger brother and line 14 including him in an activity. Figure 9.4 shows line 13 ending with a very low pitch rise signaling more to come; it is marked in the transcription with a comma. The pitch prominence given to the word *brother* and its lengthened pronunciation are also especially noticeable in this figure.

Line 14 then followed with a terminal falling pitch that signaled the closure of this sequence of closely related ideas; this is marked in the transcription by a period.

Intonation units are sometimes separated by pauses, as can be seen in the two or three dots at the beginnings of lines 1–6, where only line 3 followed immediately without a pause.

*Intonation units can be sorted into three major types according to their function*. Most common are the **substantive** IUs that carry forward the ideas on which the conversation is based. Others serve to regulate the flow of those ideas, and these **regulatory** IUs are usually very short, typically single words of a type known as **discourse particles**. All of the mother's contributions in Example (1), with the exception of line 7, were of this regulatory type, consisting of nothing more than *oh*, *okay*, *yeah*, and *oh really?* The third type consists of **fragmentary** IUs

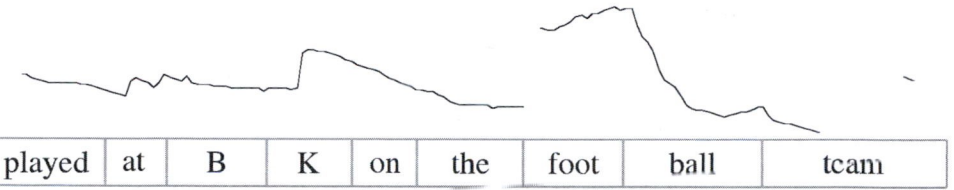

| played | at | B | K | on | the | foot | ball | tcam |

**Figure 9.5** Line 14 with a falling terminal contour

that are broken off before they are finished, as illustrated in lines 4, 6, 15, 16, and 18. They are evidence for the **online creation of natural discourse**, the complex process through which speakers pull their thoughts together and articulate them in real time under the pressures of social interaction. During this process, people often change their minds about what to say or how to say it.

## 9.5 Navigating through a topic: discourse functions of intonation units

*Intonation units cluster within larger units, or* **conversational topics**: extended segments of thought that are too large to be focused on all at once, but that function at a more inclusive level to make discourse coherent and to keep the conversation moving forward. Speakers navigate within a topic using a sequence of ideas expressed in their IUs. This is best seen through a qualitative analysis of the data, where one carefully listens to the speech, analyzing the content, function, and contribution of each IU within the interactional context of the conversation.

In line 1 of Example (1), the daughter introduced a new topic into this conversation, a topic she developed by articulating a succession of ideas all related in some way to the kid who was in a coma. This topic was sustained until its conclusion in line 35. Its progress was determined in part by the interaction between the daughter and her mother, and in part by the daughter's sequential recall of things she had read in the newspaper. *There are a number of ways in which an intonation unit may relate to its topic. One function is to introduce a* **referent**, *the idea of a person, object, or abstract concept that the conversation will discuss*. This can be seen in line 1, where the speaker introduces a new referent and articulates her emotional response to the circumstances in which he is involved. This also establishes a theme of sadness and difficulty. *A second discourse function of an IU is the amplification of an idea that was introduced in a previous IU*, as with line 2 where the identity of the kid was clarified with the relative clause *who's in a coma*.

1    Daughter:      . . . *Isn't that sád about that kid in the papér?*
2                   *.. Who.. who's in a cóma?*

*Intonation units can also serve to clarify the identity of a referent*, as in lines 3 through 6. Line 4 was fragmentary, and whatever the daughter intended to say in line 6 was interrupted by her mother, who is contradicting the daughter's assertion of the identity of the person in a coma.

| 3 | Daughter: | *He's a- the star.. baseball player at BK?* |
| 4 | | *... And he got the schólarship to-* |
| 5 | | *... He was the Gatorade player of the year?* |
| 6 | | *.. Two years ago [and then he-]* |
| 7 | Mother: | *[But I thought] it was his dád who was.. in the hospital.* |

The daughter corrected her mother in the next two IUs, repeating what she had said in line 2. The mother showed her acceptance of the correction with the discourse particle *oh*. **Thus IUs can also correct information and indicate agreement or disagreement with an interlocutor**.

| 8 | Daughter: | *Nó it's hím.* |
| 9 | | *.. He's [in a cóm]a.* |
| 10 | Mother: | *[Oh.]* |

The daughter then explained the reason for the coma, which her mother this time accepted with *okay*. **This is another discourse function of intonation units: elaboration on a topic through the expression of a reason or attendant circumstances**.

| 11 | Daughter: | *.. [He got hit] by that drunk driver?* |
| 12 | Mother: | *[Okay.]* |

Next came a shift in the development of the topic: the introduction of a new **subtopic** where the focus moved from the kid in the hospital to his family. First came the introduction of his brother, who was introduced in line 13 and then treated as the subject of line 14. A sequence of this kind, in which the idea of a person is introduced in one intonation unit that is followed by a second saying something about that person, is evidence for a limit on the amount of information an IU can contain (see below).

| 13 | Daughter: | *... And his younger bróther,* |
| 14 | | *played at BK on the fóotball team.* |

The introduction of the younger brother led to a mention of what the paper said about the entire family attending today's game. **After a referent is introduced, attention shifts from the identity of the referent to the referent's activities**, as with this comment following the introduction of the younger brother. The daughter's language at this point became full of disfluencies, evidence that she was experiencing difficulty in putting her thoughts together and finding the right language to express what she was thinking. She finally succeeded in line 19, and line 20 went on to express the reason the family would attend the game. The mother once more acknowledged her acceptance of this information with a *yeah* before line 20 had been completed.

| 15 | Daughter: | *... And I gue-* |
| 16 | | *it was the pa-* |
| 17 | | *the árticle was about you know how,* |
| 18 | | *... they're all going to-* |
| 19 | | *all the family's gonna go to the gáme today because,* |
| 20 | | *.. spórts are very important.* |
| 21 | | *.. In his [fámily] you know,* |
| 22 | Mother: | *[Yeah].* |

The daughter then amplified the family's reason for attending the game, with the mother's *oh really* expressing surprise at this explanation. ***This response illustrates another function of prosodic units: the expression of the emotion, attitude, or evaluation of the speaker***.

| 23 | Daughter: | *they all used to go watch ... the older brother play báseball,* |
| 24 | | *that's what he would want,* |
| 25 | | *is for the family to be at the game,* |
| 26 | Mother: | *Oh [really?]* |

**SIDEBAR 9.2**

CONSTRUCTED DIALOGUE

Quoting the speech of another person is sometimes called **constructed dialogue**, because it pretends to reproduce a person's language without necessarily repeating the exact words. In this case, the quoted speech provides further elaboration on a major theme of the conversation: the difficulty of the situation.

Next came another subtopic, begun again with the introduction of a person, the coach, whose identity was confirmed by the mother in line 30. In line 29, the daughter attributed the statement that would follow to the coach (or to someone related to him), in an example of constructed dialogue (see Sidebar 9.2).

| 27 | Daughter: | *[Uh] but the coach,* |
| 28 | | *I think it's Tim Beagen.* |
| 29 | | *[And one] of the Beagens said you know,* |
| 30 | Mother: | *[Yeah.]* |
| 31 | Daughter: | *if you don't wanna play that's fine,* |
| 32 | | *if you ... don't wanna,* |
| 33 | | *you could just go out of the play,* |
| 34 | | *... you just do whatever,* |

The topic was finally rounded off when the daughter expressed her emotional reaction to the entire situation by exclaiming *aah*, a sound she emitted with a breathy voice quality that conveyed her depth of feeling.

| 35 | Daughter: | *but it was like.. aah!* |

This exercise has demonstrated that intonation units have a variety of discourse functions with respect to the introduction, construction, and maintenance of a topic. These functions include the introduction of referents, clarification of their identities, the articulation of their activities, amplifying an idea by expressing reasons or other relevant circumstances, expressing agreement or disagreement with a previous point, correcting or contradicting a previous point, and conveying emotions, attitudes, and evaluations. This list is not exhaustive, but it does identify many of the functions that are central to any conversational exchange.

## 9.6  Narratives and their structure

One type of topic that often arises during a conversation is a **narrative**, the recall of a significant and coherent set of events in which the speaker was involved, or which the speaker had learned about from someone else. ***Narratives consist of a sequence of ideas that follow a conventional* narrative schema**, a pattern that captures the way people remember a sequence of events that they find appropriate to relate to others. The narrative schema builds toward a **climax**, something unusual or unexpected that makes the narrative interesting and worth telling. Some or all of the following elements may be included:

a.  Introduction of the narrative
b.  Introduction of the participants
c.  Orientation in space
d.  Orientation in time
e.  Movement toward a climax
f.  The climax
g.  Reaction to the climax
h.  Results of the climax
i.  Coda

We can follow the way this schema was realized in the narrative given in Example (2). The audio for Example (2), together with a complete transcription, is available on the website.

a.  *Introduction of the narrative:* Speakers sometimes say quite explicitly that they are about to tell a story.

**(2)**  1  Alan:  . . . *I got a story to tell you,*
        2         *a shaggy dog story,*
        3         *but as long as we're talking about that recorder and six-hundred dollars,*
        4         *. . . I'll tell you the story.*

b.  *Introduction of participants:* Narratives always involve one or more people, and they are usually introduced near the beginning.

        5   . . . *Oh gosh.*
        6   .. *Uh.*
        7   .. *Ray and I and Sue and Buddy,*

c.   *Orientation in space:* Listeners need to know where something took place.

| 8 | | *... took a trip,* |
|---|---|---|
| 9 | | *... to Mexico City.* |
| 10 | Jon: | *... (sniff)* |

d.   *Orientation in time:* Listeners also need to know roughly when it happened.

| 11 | Alan: | *It must've been,* |
|---|---|---|
| 12 | | *... four to six months after my dad died.* |
| 13 | | *That's how I remember,* |
| 14 | | *he* [*died in*] *sixty-s-* |
| 15 | Jon: | [*Oh yeah?*] |
| 16 | Alan: | *... December sixty-seven so,* |
| 17 | | *... sometime in sixty-eight we took the trip,* |

e.   *Movement toward a climax:* Once a narrator has established the participants, place, and time, the next step is to introduce events that will lead to the climax. This portion is sometimes referred to as a **complicating action**.

| 18 | *it was-* |
|---|---|
| 19 | *.. talked about it for a while,* |
| 20 | *... uh,* |
| 21 | *.. flew down to Mexico City,* |
| 22 | *... uh we,* |
| 23 | *.. couldn't think of the name of the hotel,* |
| 24 | *it wouldn't mean anything now,* |
| 25 | *but we ended up in a ... fabulous hotel,* |
| 26 | *... uh,* |
| 27 | *.. first night,* |
| 28 | *we were very unhappy with our rooms,* |
| 29 | *we went down there,* |
| 30 | *... and the next morning,* |
| 31 | *Buddy who's a ... early riser anyhow,* |
| 32 | *was probably up ... four o'clock,* |
| 33 | *and he went down there,* |
| 34 | *complained to the manager,* |
| 35 | *... so he,* |
| 36 | *.. cause it was not the.. the accommodation we were supposed to have,* |
| 37 | *we checked in about eight o'clock at night so it was,* |
| 38 | *in Mexico that you know is typical.* |

f.   *The climax:* In this case, the size of the accommodations were greater than anything the narrator had expected, especially in contrast to the room that was first assigned. The climax need not be anything wonderfully exciting as long as it conflicts with expectations in some way.

39      *... Well we ended up with a.. corner.. suite.*

40      *... With-*

41      *... It was so big,*

**SIDEBAR 9.3**

TRANSCRIPTION
CONVENTIONS

Laughter is a frequent element of conversational discourse. It is transcribed here with an "@" symbol, with one @ transcribed for each "pulse" of laughter. So what is sometimes written as *ha-ha-ha* would be transcribed @@@.

g.  *Reaction to the climax:* Listeners often respond to a climax by showing their appreciation of its unexpectedness. In this case, Jon laughed, and his two laugh pulses are transcribed with "@" symbols (see Sidebar 9.3).

42      Jon:        *.. @@*

h.  *Results of the climax:* Narrators often amplify the unexpected nature of the climax by providing further information related to it.

43      Alan:       *we could have a party for fifty people and not pressed it.*

44      *.. Three bathrooms in it.*

45      *... Two bedrooms,*

46      *but they had-*

47      *but they had an extra guest bathroom,*

48      *.. a big bar,*

49      *... it was circ-*

50      *open on two sides,*

i.  *Coda:* A story may be summed up or rounded off at the end, as in this case with an explanation of the contrast between the surprising size of the room and what the narrator and his wife actually needed.

51      *course we didn't even have-*

52      *we had the two of us.*

This example demonstrates that **even in spontaneous conversation – which may appear chaotic at first glance – the production of discourse is structured and follows regular patterns**.

## 9.7  The prosodic realization of sentences

Chapter 6 presented evidence for the sentence as a unit of syntax consisting of one or more clauses, which follow regular principles of syntactic structuring. In spoken discourse, sentences are not isolated constructs, but are produced online in the process of meeting the speaker's aims within the social environment. They are also produced with prosody – pauses, intonation, shifts in timing, loudness, and voice quality – which overlays the sequences of words that are structured into phrases, clauses, and sentences.

Typically, in English, the production of an intonation unit, or prosodic phrase, with a falling intonation contour indicates that the speaker has reached a point of closure, while a rising intonation contour indicates that the speaker intends to continue. However, at times the prosodic structuring and the syntactic structuring do not coincide in this way. Consider again the following exchange from Example (1):

| 19 | Daughter: | *all the family's gonna go to the gáme today because,* |
| 20 | | *.. spórts are very important.* |
| 21 | | *.. In his [fámily] you know,* |
| 22 | Mother: | *[Yeah].* |
| 23 | Daughter: | *they all used to go watch . . . the older brother play báseball,* |

Line 20 ended with a falling pitch that suggested the end of a sentence. Syntactically, however, line 21 was a continuation and conclusion of that sentence, in spite of the fact that the rising pitch at the end of it suggested more to come. Between lines 21 and 23, in other words, there was a syntactic sentence boundary but not a prosodic one.

The following sequence from Example (2) shows similar inconsistencies between prosody and syntax. The low rising intonation contour at the end of line 36 suggests continuation, although the sentence is syntactically complete. Line 37 was truncated (unfinished) syntactically, and line 38 was a complete syntactic sentence in itself.

| 31 | *Buddy who's a . . . early riser anyhow,* |
| 32 | *was probably up . . . four o'clock,* |
| 33 | *and he went down there,* |
| 34 | *complained to the manager,* |
| 35 | *. . . so he,* |
| 36 | *.. cause it was not the.. the accommodation we were supposed to have,* |
| 37 | *we checked in about eight o'clock at night so it was,* |
| 38 | *in Mexico that you know is typical.* |

Prosody, more than syntax, mirrors the flow of a speaker's thoughts. The analysis of the syntax and prosody in the production of discourse provides evidence that ***speakers do not always think in well-formed sentences but proceed to articulate a series of ideas until they feel they have reached a point of closure, a point that may or may not coincide with syntactic closure***. At that point, their pitch falls, sometimes prematurely from a syntactic point of view.

This constitutes further evidence that ***sentences are composed online as speakers pull their thoughts together and decide how to verbalize them***. A similar conclusion emerges from examples where the same person talks about the same thing on different occasions. In Example (3), a woman talking about an incident at her apartment introduced her account of it – with continuing prosody after the first line – by saying:

(3)  *. . . I was sitting there in my chair,*
     *. . . just eating my popsicle and-*

On a later occasion, when she told the same story to a different listener, she split these ideas into two prosodic sentences in the opposite order, although syntactically they belonged together, as shown in Example (4).

**(4)**    *I was just eating my popsicle.*
    *.. Sitting there in this chair.*

The ideas expressed in the two IUs were the same, but the way they were distributed across sentences suggested that they had not been stored in the speaker's memory in precisely the form the sentences took.

## 9.8  New, accessible, and given activation states

In producing coherent discourse, speakers must introduce new participants, activities, situations, and concepts, and relate them to what has already been said, and what is assumed to be in the active consciousness of the addressees. ***An idea (a participant, state, event, etc.) is considered given (or activated) if the speaker assumes that the addressee is currently focused on it***; the information is metaphorically "lit up" or active in the person's consciousness. An idea is **new** ***if the speaker thinks it is unlikely that the hearer is focused on it***; the speaker needs to introduce the idea, that is, to activate it, or "light it up" for the hearer. In addition, ***some ideas may not be actively focused on, but may be peripheral in the addressee's consciousness***, for example, an idea that had been mentioned earlier in the discourse. Such an idea would be considered to be **accessible** to the addressee, or "dimly lit" to continue the metaphor. Given, accessible, and new are referred to as **activation states**. Speakers must assess the activation states of ideas in order to determine how to refer to them; the form in which an idea is expressed will depend in part on this assessment.

We have seen that language expresses the flow of a speaker's thoughts and that these thoughts are expressed in a series of IUs, each about one second in length. Each IU conveys the focus of a speaker's consciousness just prior to or during the time the IU is being uttered. When we examine how ideas with different activation states are expressed in a stretch of discourse, we see that ***there is a limit to the amount of new information that can be included during each intonation unit***. We can see this illustrated by the beginning of Example (1).

| 1 | Daughter: | . . . *Isn't that sád about that kid in the papér?* |
|---|---|---|
| 2 | | *.. Who.. who's in a cóma?* |
| 3 | | *He's a- the star.. baseball player at BK?* |
| 4 | | *. . . And he got the schólarship to-* |
| 5 | | *. . . He was the Gatorade player of the year?* |
| 6 | | *.. Two years ago [and then he-]* |

The new information in line 1 was the judgment that the kid's predicament was sad. The remainder of this phrase, *about that kid in the paper*, conveyed an idea that the daughter assumed was already accessible to her mother, who she assumed had read the paper too. Once the idea of *the kid* had been introduced and activated, that idea became given information, so that it could be verbalized with nothing more than the weakly stressed pronoun *he* in lines 3 through 6. Thus, ***given information can be expressed with smaller and less robustly articulated sounds***.

## 9.8.1    Identifiability

In English a noun or a noun phrase is often preceded by a definite or indefinite article: *the* or *a*. At the beginning of Example (2) the noun *story* was preceded by the indefinite article *a* in lines 1 and 2 (in the latter being followed by the modifier *shaggy dog*). When *story* was repeated in line 4, it was preceded by the definite article *the*.

| 1 | Alan: | . . . *I got a story to tell you,* |
|---|---|---|
| 2 | | *a shaggy dog story,* |
| 3 | | *but as long as we're talking about that recorder and six-hundred dollars,* |
| 4 | | . . . *I'll tell you the story.* |

The traditional terms "definite" and "indefinite" are misleading, because the distinction does not involve "definiteness" in its ordinary sense. It is rather a matter of **identifiability**: ***whether or not the idea expressed by the noun is assumed to be already identifiable by the listener***. In line 1, the idea of the story was not shared knowledge and line 2 only amplified that knowledge. However, once it had been introduced in those two lines, its status changed, and by line 4 it could be preceded by *the*, signaling the speaker's assumption that this story could now be identified.

Similarly, line 8 introduced the idea of a trip assumed to be previously unknown to the listener and thus expressed as *a trip*.

| 7 | Alan: | .. *Ray and I and Sue and Buddy,* |
|---|---|---|
| 8 | | . . . *took a trip,* |
| 9 | | . . . *to Mexico City.* |

In contrast, by line 17, the trip was identifiable and could be expressed as *the trip*.

| 17 | Alan: | . . . *sometime in sixty-eight we took the trip,* |
|---|---|---|

The following sequence illustrates greater complexity in this use of the definite and indefinite articles. Alan first said:

| 23 | Alan: | .. *couldn't think of the name of the hotel,* |
|---|---|---|
| 24 | | *it wouldn't mean anything now,* |

He could assume that the listener would know, based on prior mention of a trip to Mexico City, that he and his wife had stayed in a hotel, and also that the hotel undoubtedly had a name. This context made the ideas of both the hotel and its name identifiable. It would have been inappropriate to say *couldn't think of a name of a hotel*, because it would have implied that no hotel had yet been chosen. At this point he might have gone on to say *but the hotel was fabulous*, but what he said instead was,

25        *but we ended up in a . . . fabulous hotel,*

In effect he made a new start by explicitly introducing the hotel as if it had not been mentioned before, letting it now become the setting for the room change that was described in what followed.

In Example (1), a number of ideas were identifiable because they were accessible from the context or from the listener's prior knowledge, as with *the paper*, *the star baseball player*, *the scholarship*, and *the Gatorade player of the year*:

1   Daughter:        *. . . Isn't that sád about that kid in the papér?*
2                        *.. Who.. who's in a cóma?*
3                        *He's a- the star.. baseball player at BK?*
4                        *. . . And he got the schólarship to-*
5                        *. . . He was the Gatorade player of the year?*

Identifiability in English is expressed not only by *the* but also by demonstratives like *that* and pronouns like *he*, both of which are illustrated in this example. Evidently the daughter was able to refer to *that kid in the paper* because the words *in the paper* identified which kid it was, and because she assumed that her mother had already read the article in question.

### 9.8.2   Subjects

The grammatical subjects of clauses usually express ideas that are both identifiable and given, as with the three examples of *he* in lines 3 through 5 above. That is not the whole story, however, as illustrated by the following sequence from Example (1). The grammatical subjects *his younger brother*, *the article*, *all the family*, and *sports* do not qualify as given ideas, but as accessible ones.

13   Daughter:        *. . . And his younger bróther,*
14                        *played at BK on the fóotball team.*
15                        *. . . And I gue-*
16                        *it was the pa-*
17                        *the árticle was about you know how,*
18                        *. . . they're all going to-*
19                        *all the family's gonna go to the gáme today because,*
20                        *.. spórts are very important.*
21                        *.. In his [fámily] you know,*

The ideas of the younger brother and his family were accessible from shared knowledge of the kid's background. The idea of *the article* was accessible from the mention of *the paper* in line 1. The idea of *sports* was accessible from prior mention of baseball and football.

Syntactic subjects, in short, although they are most often given, are sometimes instead accessible, although they are still identifiable. That may be especially true in a conversation between two people who share as much prior knowledge as a mother and daughter. Syntactic subjects, on the other hand, seldom refer to new ideas that are non-identifiable. The study of discourse reveals that ***information of different types receives different grammatical treatments, thus that grammatical structures are used to play particular functions in discourse***.

## CHAPTER SUMMARY

We have seen that language is usually produced in a series of brief spurts or intonation units that are usually restricted to the expression of a single new idea. A larger level of discourse is realized in topics, or coherent idea clusters. Topics are too large to be focused on in their entirety; they are navigated in a series of IUs that express the included ideas. The direction of the navigation may be guided by the interaction between different parties to a conversation, as in Example (1), or by a conventional schema like the narrative schema that was illustrated in Example (2).

Discourse structure influences words and sentences in a variety of ways. Sentences do not always express stable elements of thought but are composed online as a person is talking. Ideas may be new, accessible, or given, thus determining whether they are expressed with prosodically prominent nouns or with weakly stressed pronouns. They may also be identifiable or non-identifiable, as expressed by the presence of the definite or indefinite article. The subjects of clauses are usually both identifiable and given, although sometimes they are accessible from the context or from prior shared knowledge. The study of discourse and the way it is structured demonstrate that syntax cannot be adequately explained in isolation from the larger context in which words and sentences occur.

## SUGGESTIONS FOR FURTHER READING

**Chafe, Wallace**. 1994. *Discourse, consciousness, and time: The flow and displacement of conscious experience in speaking and writing.* University of Chicago Press.

Further discussion of prosodic phrases (intonation units), activation cost, identifiability, topics, and other discourse properties of both spoken and written language.

**Gee, James Paul and Michael Handford** (eds.). 2012. *Routledge handbook of discourse analysis.* London and New York: Routledge.

Discussion of varied approaches to discourse analysis, many of them by authors who are not included in the Schiffrin, Tannen, and Hamilton volume below.

**Schiffrin, Deborah, Deborah Tannen, and Heidi E. Hamilton** (eds.). Forthcoming. *The handbook of discourse analysis*, 2nd edn. Oxford: Blackwell.

Discussions of a variety of approaches to the analysis of discourse by a wide range of authors representing different backgrounds and interests.

### EXERCISES

1. Use the following narrative (slightly edited from a real conversation) as a source of data.

   Last summer I was hiking with my brother in Yosemite, and we were almost to the lake where we were going to go, and the air was pretty thin. And there were two women hiking up ahead of us. We got to a rise, and the lake was right there where we were going to camp. And the two of them got to the rise, and the next minute they just fell over. Totally. (You're kidding.) I guess the stop was just too much, and both of them just totally passed out. They both came to life very quickly, but I guess the hike, and then all of a sudden stopping, and the oxygen thing must have really confused them. It was really odd.

   a. Identify the parts of the narrative schema. (Not all the parts need be present.)
   b. Find all of the examples of the definite article and explain why each noun phrase is identifiable.
   c. Find all of the syntactic subjects and determine whether each of them expresses given or accessible information. Why do you suppose the speaker avoided saying "two women were hiking up ahead of us"?

2. The following narrative is another slightly edited excerpt from a different conversation.

   Steve and I went skiing that day. *Harsh voice:* God! It was really windy! When we get to the top of the chairlift, it was like you were a clapper on a bell you know, when you went to get off, and we had to land like that you know, but a huge gust came by, just as we were landing. We were gonna like- *Falsetto:* Aaah! You know we were coming in like this, you know, and, you know, so we'd wait to- *Shouted:* All right now! Zhoom! We jumped off. *Laughter:* It was great!

   a. Identify the parts of the narrative schema. (Not all need be present.)
   b. Try to imagine the special voice qualities that are suggested by the words added in italics. What do these voice qualities add to the discourse?
   c. There were five occurrences of the phrase *you know*, an expression that occurs very often in modern colloquial conversation. Linguists disagree on its function, but discuss briefly what you think its function might be.

3. Read through the following stretch of conversational discourse (edited from SBC: 003 "conceptual pesticides"):

   | 1 | Roy: | Do you have a particular, um, |
   |---|------|-------------------------------|
   | 2 |      | use for the red peppers, |
   | 3 |      | as opposed to the yellow or green peppers. |
   | 4 | Marilyn: | No, no. |
   | 5 |      | It was all.. salad peppers. |
   | 6 | Roy: | It's all salad peppers. |

| 7 | Marilyn: | Mhm. |
|---|---|---|
| 8 | Roy: | ... In that case I will use a yellow pepper for this evening. |
| 9 | Marilyn: | .. Oh,.. fabulous. |
| 10 | Pete: | What can I do. |
| 11 | Marilyn: | Would you like to ... string the beans? |
| 12 | Pete: | Sure. |
| 13 | Marilyn: | Man that's a big hunk of fish. |
| 14 | Pete: | Where do you want 'em put? |
| 15 | Marilyn: | Shit, it's a huge– |
| 16 | Pete: | Are they just going.. on that? Or... |
| 17 | Marilyn: | Uh... you wanna put 'em in a.. colander, |
| 18 | | and then ... wash 'em? |

a. Give one example each of an intonation unit from this excerpt which is (i) substantive, (ii) regulatory, and (iii) fragmentary.

b. Give one example each of an intonation unit from this excerpt that performs each of the following functions:

   i. Introduction of a topic

   ii. Amplification of an idea

   iii. Clarification of identity of a referent

   iv. Correction/contradiction of a previous point

   v. Indication of agreement or disagreement

   vi. Articulation of activities of referents

   vii. Expression of emotions (like surprise), attitudes, or evaluations

# 10 Prosody: the music of language

**KEY TERMS**

- Segmental properties of speech sounds
- Suprasegmental properties of speech sounds
- Pitch
- Timing
- Intensity

- Fundamental frequency
- Intonation unit (prosodic phrase)
- Voice quality
- Creaky voice
- Harsh voice
- Prosodic styles

## CHAPTER PREVIEW

We have seen that language is typically not produced in sentences isolated from commuicative contexts but is embedded into longer stretches of discourse and social interactions. Within this broader context, speakers need to direct their listeners' attention to particularly important parts of their utterances, and to convey a range of emotions and attitudes.

Speakers do not simply produce language as long sequences of consonants and vowels in monotonous strings of identical timing. Instead, they vary the rate, pitch, and volume of their speech to add nuance and meaning beyond what is conveyed by the words themselves.

Prosody is a cover term for such variations in pitch, volume, timing, and voice quality. These properties accompany the vowels, consonants, and syllables of spoken language. They function to delimit linguistic units like phrases and sentences while signaling relations between them. These properties also make certain portions of our utterances more prominent, and they are basic to the expression of emotion and attitude.

This chapter will present descriptions of various prosodic phenomena in discourse and methods for transcribing them. It explores some of the functions of prosody, including the organization and evaluation of ideas. It also discusses different types of voice qualities and how these, and other prosodic variables, are manipulated by speakers for rhetorical effect.

**LIST OF AIMS**

After reading this chapter students should be able to:

- list the properties of speech that are covered by the term prosody;
- list the four functions of prosody;
- listen to a sample of speech and identify its prosodic properties;
- relate those properties to their functions;
- transcribe a sample of speech and mark some of its prosodic properties;
- judge the effects of prosody in commercials, speeches, or other public uses of language.

## 10.1 Segmental and prosodic properties of speech

***The sounds of spoken language have both segmental and prosodic properties***. These two terms do not refer to different sounds, but to different aspects of the same sound, just as a painting has both form and color at the same time. The term "**segmental**" refers to the way sounds constitute **segments** of language such as vowels and consonants. ***The term prosody refers to variations in four different aspects of sounds: their pitch, volume, timing, and voice quality***. Sometimes these properties have been imagined as "riding on top of" the segments, and thus they have sometimes been called **suprasegmental**.

We begin with an example in which a woman, in the course of a conversation, says the utterance in (1).

**(1)**    *Sure. You've got a real problem.*

The representation of spoken language here is spelled with ordinary English orthography, which is largely restricted to the segmental representation of sounds (see Sidebar 10.1). This way of writing language is familiar to all of us. It captures the bare ideas that were communicated, but leaves open such factors as the timing of those ideas, which ideas were emphasized, how they were related, and the speaker's attitude toward them. To be sure, the fact that the words in (1) were distributed across two separate sentences, both of which ended with a falling pitch, is suggested by the capital letters and the periods, but that is about as far as ordinary writing usually goes in terms of representing prosody.

To know exactly what (1) sounded like when it was spoken, one needs to hear it. Nevertheless, acoustic displays, such as that in Figure 10.1, can be useful in providing visual representations of several kinds of prosodic features. The words at the top are distributed according to their relative timing. We can see that the words *sure* and *problem* occupied more time than

**SIDEBAR 10.1**

The favorable treatment our writing system gives to segmental sounds reflects the fact that they are responsible for conveying *ideas*. A speaker may communicate ideas of events, states, people, and objects by expressing them with linguistic elements like verbs, nouns, and adjectives. In addition to meanings of that sort, language at the same time expresses meanings of other kinds; these meanings are the focus of this chapter.

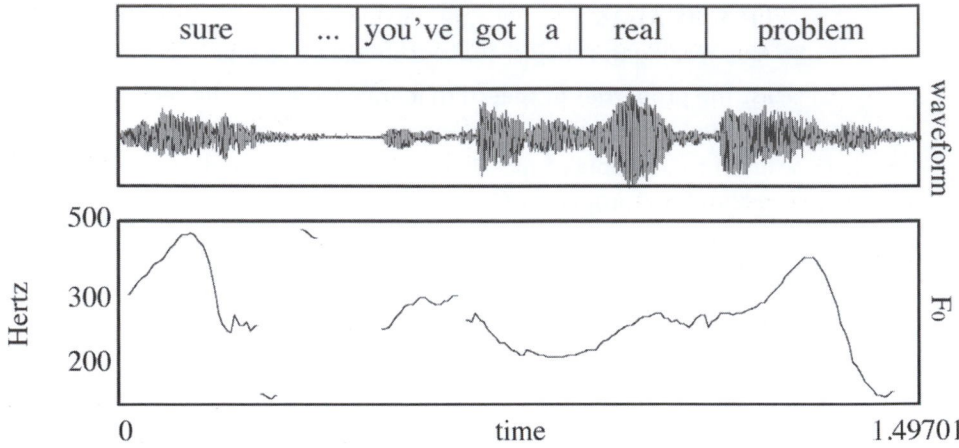

**Figure 10.1** Wave form and fundamental frequency in (1)

the others, whereas the sequence *you've got a* was uttered rapidly. Directly below the words is a **waveform** that shows how positive and negative energy were distributed across the 1.5 seconds occupied by the entire sequence. We can see a pause, shown at the top with three dots and measurable as 123 milliseconds, which intervened between *sure* and what followed. ***The waveform also suggests the relative intensity of these words (perceived as loudness)***, the loudest being *real*, the next loudest *got* and the first syllable of *problem*, the next loudest *a* and the second syllable of *problem*, and the softest being *you've*.

The display along the bottom of Figure 10.1 shows the **fundamental frequency** ($F_0$) of the sound wave, with levels given in Hertz (cycles per second) at the left. ***Changes in $F_0$ are perceived roughly as changes in pitch***. Strictly speaking there is a need to distinguish physical properties such as intensity and $F_0$ from perceptual properties such as loudness and pitch, which refer to the way our brains interpret those physical properties in particular contexts. However, the relation between physical sounds and our perception of them is close enough that we can view Figure 10.1 as a useful approximation to the loudness and pitch that we hear.

In the bottom display we can see that the words *sure* and *problem* were both pronounced with a pitch contour that rose and then fell. Comparing those two rise–fall contours, we can also see that the baseline pitch of *sure* was higher than that of *problem*. The impression given by this raised baseline is that *sure* was an emotionally charged answer to a preceding question, whereas *you've got a real problem* provided more specific information that culminated in an emotionally tinged *problem*. This display also shows that *you've* and *real* were somewhat higher in pitch than *got a*, with those two last words being the least prominent part of the entire sequence in terms of pitch. It is noticeable that *real* was the loudest word in the entire sequence, although *problem* was considerably higher in pitch. The fact that the word *real* functions to intensify the degree of the problem may explain its heightened volume, while the higher pitch on *problem* is consistent with its central role as the carrier of new information.

*There is no universally accepted way of representing prosody in transcripts of speech*; different conventions have been followed by different researchers, depending on their interests and goals. One way of capturing the prosodic features described above was first developed in Berkeley, California, and is now in use in Santa Barbara. It is illustrated in (2), where the sequence is divided into two intonation units that are represented on separate lines. An **intonation unit (IU)** *is a prosodically coherent segment of speech*, a spurt of language whose properties are discussed later in this chapter. In this chapter, a sequence of words within a single intonation unit will be referred to as a **phrase**. The three dots at the beginning of (2b) indicate a pause. The rise–fall in pitch that characterized both *sure* and the first syllable of *problem* is shown using circumflex accent marks over the vowels, while secondary prominences are shown with grave accent marks (`) on *you've* and *real*. The periods at the ends of the lines show the falling pitches at the ends of each of the two intonation units. The arrows at the beginning and end of (2a) capture its raised baseline. A transcript of this sort can help a reader imagine or mimic something that comes close to the way the prosody was actually produced. You can listen to the sound files that accompany the examples in this chapter by going to the website.

(2)  a. ↑*Sûre.*↑
     b. . . . *Yòu've got a rèal prôblem.*

 It is important to note that any given phrase can be produced with many prosodic forms; see Sidebar 10.2.

### 10.1.1  Four visual displays

Figure 10.2 supplements Figure 10.1 by illustrating four different ways the properties of sound can be visually represented for further analysis. You can listen to the utterance of a woman saying *Oh I don't recognize that* in Sound file 10.3 on the website. This utterance, like that in (1), occupies approximately 1.5 seconds. The relative timing display at the top, the waveform below it, and the $F_0$ display are already familiar from Figure 10.1. The graph just below the waveform pools positive and negative energy to give a clearer picture of variations in intensity. We can see that what this woman said was loudest at the beginning, with a peak on the pronoun *I*. After that, the volume gradually declined, only to increase again on the word *that*.

The $F_0$ display illustrates a tendency to perceive elements toward the end of an intonation unit as higher in pitch than they really are. Listening to this phrase, you might find that you hear the word *that* as carrying approximately the same high pitch as the word *I* near the beginning, even though you can see that its fundamental frequency is significantly lower. *I* was characterized by a rising pitch that peaked at 222 Hz, straddling the boundary between *I* and *don't*, at which point the pitch fell steeply. In contrast, the highest pitch during the word *that* was only 173 Hz. (For more on the use of technology to study prosody, see Textbox 10.1.)

## TEXTBOX 10.1

Prosody has been studied in various ways for a long time, but our understanding of it has been greatly enhanced by modern technology. First came the ability to record sounds mechanically and then electronically, and to replay them for further study. But more recent digital technologies have given us analyses of sounds that are more diverse and more accurate than anything that was possible in the past.

In earlier times, pitch, loudness, timing, and voice quality could be studied only through investigators' subjective impressions of what they were hearing, but those impressions could vary considerably with the "ear" and training of the investigator. Although much remains to be understood, technology has brought a new level of objectivity to prosodic research.

Linguist Floyd Lounsbury recording the speech of Cayuga language speaker Lydia Greene in 1960 with the aid of a reel-to-reel tape recorder.

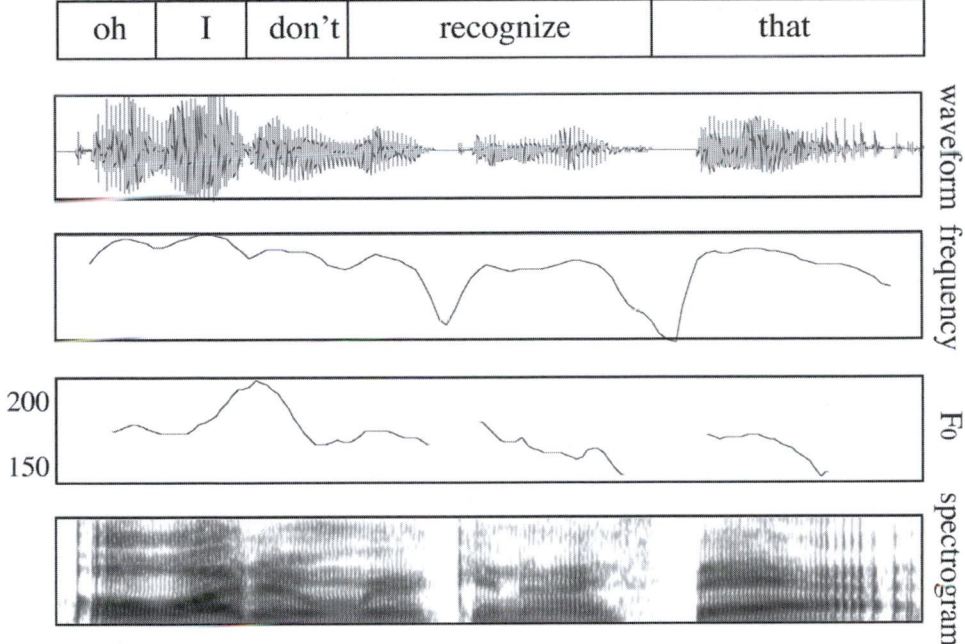

**Figure 10.2** Four ways of visually displaying sound

The display at the bottom of Figure 10.2 is a **spectrogram**, where the relative amount of energy at different frequencies is indicated by degrees of darkness: greater energy is shown with darker shading. This display is useful in showing the timing of segments, the quality of vowels, and other aspects of sound that may include voice quality. In this case the **creaky voice** at the end of the word *that* can be clearly seen in the irregular vertical striations at the right end of the spectrogram, as well as at the end of the waveform at the top. One way in which this utterance might be transcribed is shown in (3), where the creaky voice on the last word is shown using a dotted underline. The circumflex accent (^) shows the rise–fall pitch contour that began on the word *I*. Other prominences are shown with the acute accent marks (´) on the first syllable of *recognize* and on the word *that*.

(3)    *Oh Î don't récognize thát.*

## 10.2  The four functions of prosody

Prosody has several distinct functions, including the delineation of units and their relations, and the expression of prominences and emotions. These four functions are illustrated in Figure 10.3. ***Prosody serves both to organize and to evaluate the ideas that language conveys.*** Organization includes delimiting speech units such as

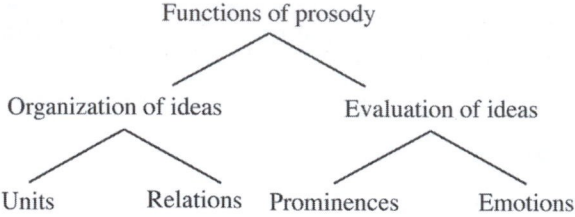

**Figure 10.3** The four functions of prosody

intonation units and sentences while at the same time signaling how those units relate to the flow of ideas. Evaluation includes the assignment of prominences to new and emphasized information as well as the expression of emotions and attitudes. The first three of the four functions at the bottom of Figure 10.3 are observable in any sample of speech, whereas emotion may or may not be evident (though even an absence of emotion can itself be regarded as an attitude).

All four of these prosodic functions are illustrated in the next example, taken from a conversation during which a woman related how she and her husband arrived home from a trip, only to find a stranger stealing lemons from a tree in their backyard. She introduced her story by producing the utterance in (4), which is written using standard English spelling.

**(4)**   *And we're pulling up and I see this girl, who I'd never seen before, sort of dart out of our driveway.*

Although the standard English orthography used in (4) provides only minimal prosodic information, it does contain some clues. The capital letter at the beginning and the period at the end suggest a prosodic contour whose boundaries coincided with the entire grammatical sentence. The commas surrounding "who I'd never seen before" reflect its syntactic status as a **nonrestrictive relative clause**, suggesting that this phrase might have been separated from what came before and after it through the use of pauses and a prosodic contour of its own.

### 10.2.1   The delineation of units: intonation units

As outlined in Figure 10.3, ***one function of prosody is to segment speech into IUs*** like the six that are written in separate lines in (5). (See Sidebar 10.3 for a note on the transcription.) ***It is characteristic of speech to be uttered in brief phrases of this kind, usually approximately one second long and typically containing between three and five words***. Many of these IUs convey substantive ideas, as is true of all except line (a) in this example. In (a) the word *and* links what was to come to the preceding talk about returning from a trip, while the pause filler *uh* helps the speaker hold the floor, both thus regulating the flow of information. ***Intonation units can thus be categorized as either* regulatory *like line (a), or substantive *like all the others***.

**(5)**  a. … ánd uh-
   b. .. we're púlling up;
   c. … and I sèe this gî=rl.
   d. .. (who I'd néver séen before-)
   e. sort of d=árt?
   f. óut of our dríveway.

**SIDEBAR 10.3**

TRANSCRIPTION NOTE

Intonation units are transcribed on separate lines of text. Thus in Example (5), there are six IUs, each transcribed on a separate line. Dots at the beginning of an IU represent preceding pauses; two dots are used for short pauses and three for long pauses.

Figure 10.4 tracks fundamental frequency through the entire sequence. The six intonation units and the intervening pauses are identified at the top. The pauses are shown with two or three dots, suggesting their relative lengths in a rough way. It can be seen that the pitch declines toward the end, and that it peaks during (b) and (c).

***Intonation units are characterized by various properties, not all of which need be present in any particular case. Often there is an initial pause: a period of silence presumably occupied by cognitive activity of some kind before the next IU is uttered***. In Example (5), pauses preceded all but the last two IUs. ***Sometimes pitch and volume decline in the course of an intonation unit, and an IU may begin rapidly and decelerate toward the end***. This deceleration is especially evident in Figure 10.5, which shows the relative duration of the five words in (c). You can see that they becoming progressively longer over the course of the intonation unit.

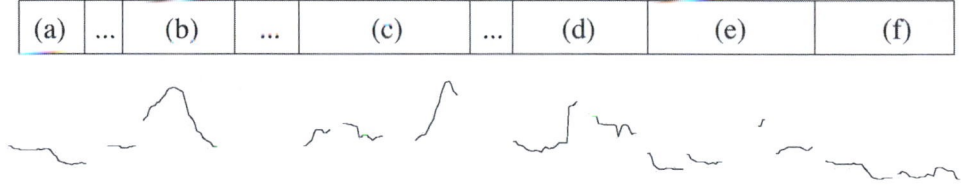

**Figure 10.4** Segmentation into intonation units with overall declining pitch

| and | I | see | this | girl |
|---|---|---|---|---|

**Figure 10.5** Deceleration over the course of an intonation unit

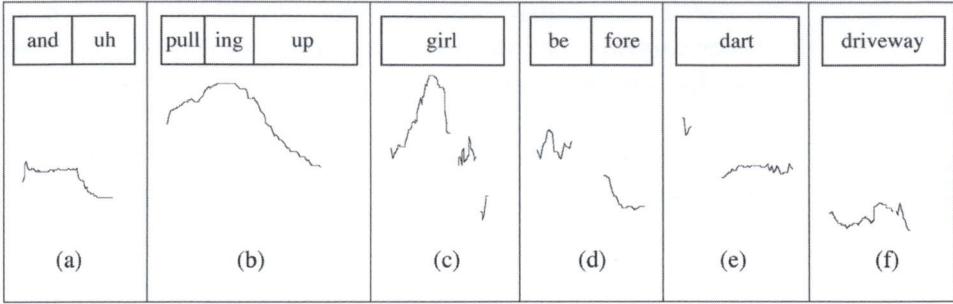

**Figure 10.6** Terminal pitch contours extracted from Figure 10.4

## 10.2.2  Signaling relations: terminal pitch contours

*The most consistent property of an intonation unit is a **terminal pitch contour**, which not only delimits each phrase but also indicates how the phrase relates to the larger context*: whether, for example, there is more to come within the current sequence of ideas, or whether a sequence has been completed. Figure 10.6 extracts the terminal contours from each of the IUs in (5) and lets us compare their shapes.

The terminal contours in (a), *and uh*, and (d), *who I'd never seen before*, both descend to a level pitch, suggesting more to come. Compare this to the transcription in (5), above. You will note that the *more to come* contour is transcribed with hyphen (-) at the ends of these two IUs.

The terminal contour in (b), *we're pulling up*, has a rise on *pull*-and a fall on *-ing up*, also suggesting more to come but conveying a more active emotional involvement with what will follow. In (5) this contour is transcribed with a semicolon (;).

The word *girl* in (c) was also spoken with a rise and fall, but unlike *pulling up* it fell close to the bottom of the speaker's range, suggesting a temporary closure that was transcribed in (5) with a period (.).

The broken trajectory during the terminal contour in (c) reflects a harsh voice quality, expressing in this case a strongly judgmental emotional involvement. The rise–fall during *girl* is transcribed in (5) with a circumflex accent mark (^), and the lengthened pronunciation of this word with an equal sign (=).

In (e) the word *dart* rises slightly to a pitch in the middle of this speaker's range. This contour is typically associated with yes–no questions and thus is transcribed in (5) with a question mark (?). The initial *d* of *dart* is lengthened, and then pronounced with an explosive release that appears as a brief high pitch at the beginning of (e). The lengthening of this consonant is transcribed in (5) with an equal sign (=).

In (f), final closure of the entire sequence is signaled by a fall to the bottom of the speaker's range during *driveway*, transcribed in (5) with a period (.).

In summary, terminal pitch contours are critical parts of IUs. They serve a wide range of important functions: they help delineate IU boundaries, mark relationships between IUs, differentiate questions and statements, and sometimes convey evaluative or emotional content. Particular transcription conventions have been designed to record these and other prosodic features (see Sidebar 10.4).

### 10.2.3 Indicating prominence

We have seen that prosody not only delimits IUs but also signals their relation to the larger context. ***Another function of prosody is to assign degrees of prominence to various linguistic elements at several levels***. At the level of individual words, greater prominence or **stress** is assigned to certain syllables, as illustrated in Figure 10.2 above by the prominence given to the first syllable of the word *recognize*. In that example, the prominence was a matter of higher pitch, whereas loudness remained relatively constant throughout the word. The position of stress in English words is the result of historical processes that took place at different times in the history of the language. Sometimes stress distinguishes different meanings, as the noun *cóntract* (a legal document) is distinct from the verb *contráct* (a disease). In the latter case the lesser prominence of the first syllable has led to a reduced vowel quality as well. In some languages prosodic prominence on certain syllables within words follows a more consistent pattern that serves to delimit the words themselves, as with the first syllable stress in Finnish, the final syllable stress in Armenian, or the pre-final syllable stress in Mohawk.

At a more inclusive level, ***entire intonation units may be more or less prominent with relation to other intonation units***. One way to measure the prominence of an IU is by measuring its **mean intensity**, the arithmetic average of the intensity measurements over the IU. Figure 10.7 plots the mean intensity in decibels of the IUs from

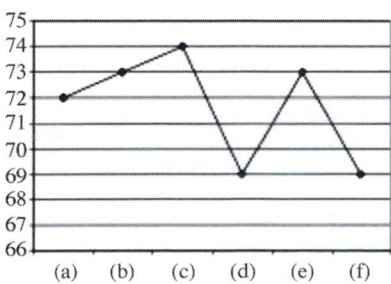

**Figure 10.7** Mean intensity of the intonation units in Example (5)

Example (5). You can see that the IUs (d), *who I'd never seen before*, and (f), *out of our driveway*, are conspicuously less prominent than the others.

Another way to measure relative prominence is with tempo, since more rapid phrases are less prominent than slower ones. Prominence may be expressed by a lengthening of at least some of the segments. Figure 10.8 plots tempo in terms of syllables per second. You can see that (d), *who I'd never seen before*, is uttered more rapidly than the other intonation units. Thus, the reduced prominence of (d) is evident not only in its reduced volume but also in its faster tempo. Its lesser prominence was transcribed in Example (5) by enclosing it in parentheses. It was in fact a parenthetical remark.

***Relative prominence also characterizes parts of intonation units***. Figure 10.9 focuses on IU (b), *we're pulling up*, tracking both pitch (top line) and volume (bottom line). The word *we're* conveys information that was already **given** (the idea of the speaker and her husband), not only because they had already been mentioned in the conversation but also because they were participants in the conversation itself. The **new** idea in this IU is conveyed by the phrase *pulling up*. After the relatively low pitch on *we're*, pitch rises to a peak during the word *pulling*. With respect to volume, the less prominent word *we're* actually begins with the heightened volume that often characterizes phrase-initial words, but then it falls quickly to a low point before beginning to increase with *pulling up*, reaching a maximum during *up*. The decline in pitch during *up*, seemingly at odds with its volume, does not reflect a lack of prominence but was determined by the terminal contour assigned to this intonation unit. Thus, *pulling up*

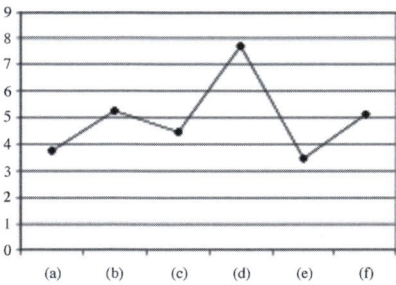

**Figure 10.8** Syllables per second for the intonation units in Example (5)

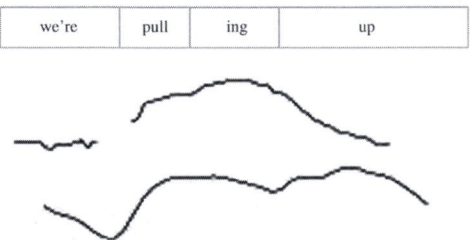

**Figure 10.9** Prominence in pitch (top line) and volume (bottom) in Intonation Unit (b)

can be said to receive the **phrasal accent**, which marks these words as the most prominent phrase in this IU.

Figure 10.10 provides similar information for IU (c), *and I see this girl*. In terms of pitch, the most prominent element was the new idea expressed by *girl*, with a secondary prominence on *see*. Least prominent were *and*, *I*, and *this*. The prominence of *girl* was expressed with heightened volume as well, already anticipated at the beginning of *this*. As in the last example, there was increased volume at the very beginning of this IU.

### 10.2.4  Expression of emotions and attitudes

A major contribution of prosody is the role it plays in expressing emotions and attitudes. In Example (5) there were two places where the speaker's emotional involvement in what she was saying was conspicuously expressed by her prosody. You can hear this in Sound file 10.6 on the website, and can see this in the lengthening of the word *girl* in (b) (see its length relative to the other words in Figure 10.10), and especially in the rise–fall pitch contour of that word, also visible in Figure 10.10 above. The lengthening combined with the pitch pattern express the speaker's emotional attitude toward this girl that might be described as a feeling of disdain.

A different emotional prosody is evident in the word *dart*. Figure 10.11 shows a slight rise to a moderately high pitch on that word, suggesting a questioning attitude.

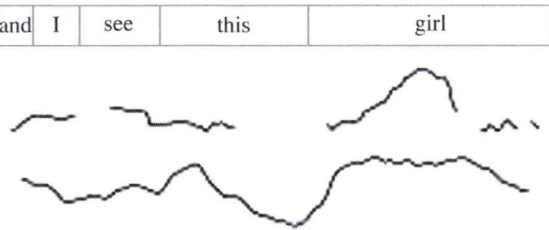

**Figure 10.10** Prominence in pitch (top line) and volume (bottom) in Intonation Unit (c)

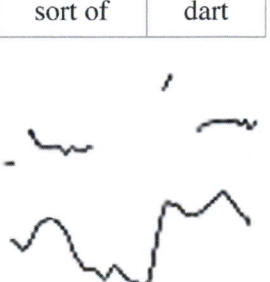

**Figure 10.11** Pitch (top line) and volume (bottom line) in Intonation Unit (e)

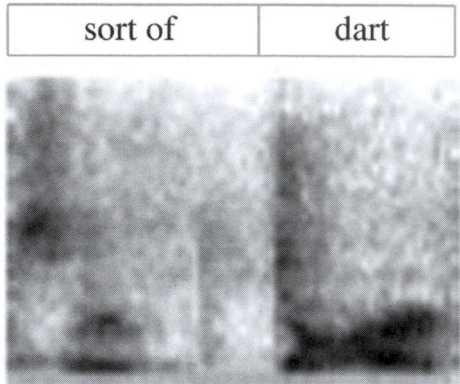

| sort of | dart |
|---------|------|

**Figure 10.12** Spectrogram of Intonation Unit (e)

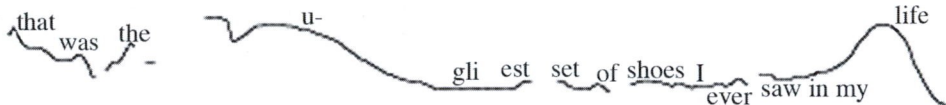

**Figure 10.13** Fundamental frequency in Example (6)

There is also an increase in volume that is evident at the bottom of Figure 10.11. You can see a dual peak of volume, first on the explosive release of the consonant "d" and then on the "art" portion that follows. The special treatment of the "d" is visible in a brief segment of higher pitch at that point, and in the spectrogram in Figure 10.12, where you can see a spike of acoustic energy accompanying the release of the "d." All of these factors reinforce a feeling of sudden swift movement that is conveyed by the word  *dart* itself.

A striking example of the prosodic display of emotion is provided in another conversation, during which one of the participants uttered the sentence in (6).

**(6)**  Thàt was the û==gliest set of shoes I ever saw in my lîfe.

The pitch pattern for (6) is shown in Figure 10.13. The initial vowel of *ugliest* was uttered with extreme lengthening and a very steep rise in pitch at the beginning, followed by a slow fall and leveling off, all of which capture the feeling of disgust this speaker felt toward the shoes. The final contour on the word *life* at the end shows a  second rise–fall pattern, finishing off the entire IU with a continued expression of emotional involvement.

## 10.3  Special voice qualities

At the beginning of this chapter, prosody was defined as a cover term for variations in pitch, volume, timing, and voice quality. Aside from the creaky voice quality in

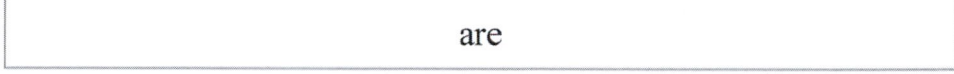

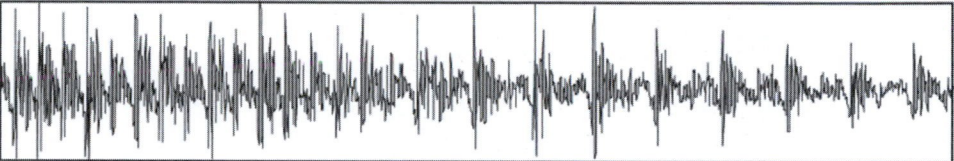

**Figure 10.14** Harsh voice from Example (7)

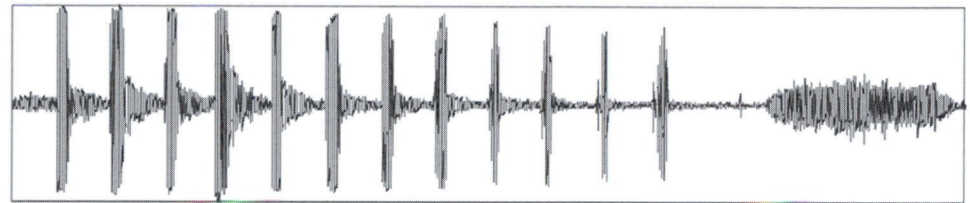

**Figure 10.15** Laughter

Example (3), the examples so far have focused largely on pitch, volume, and timing. *Voice quality is a more diverse feature than the others, involving various ways people modify a normal speaking voice, most often with special effects that are produced in the larynx.* One example is **harsh voice**, produced by irregular vibrations that are superimposed on ordinary voicing. It typically expresses strong emotion, often of anger or fear. In the following example, the speaker is describing a childhood incident in which he was approached by a gang of bullies. When he saw them coming, he expressed his anxiety by saying:

(7)   *Here they â=re.*

The harsh quality of the last word can be heard in Sound file 10.9, and is visible in the waveform in Figure 10.14. Harsh voice resembles creaky voice, but the vibrations are usually at a higher frequency and there is a more extreme irregularity in the sound wave.

   *A different voice quality is laughter, which consists of spasmodic pulses of air that are usually (though not always) voiced as they pass through the larynx.* Laughter comes in many varieties, but Figure 10.15 shows the waveform of a laugh that includes twelve voiced exhalations followed by a prolonged inhalation that serves to replenish the exhaled air. The laugh pulses are paced at a typical rate of slightly more than five per second. The final inhalation is also visible at the end of the waveform.

   Another voice quality is **whispering**, where *the vocal folds in the larynx do not come together as closely as in normal voicing*. In the next example, a man

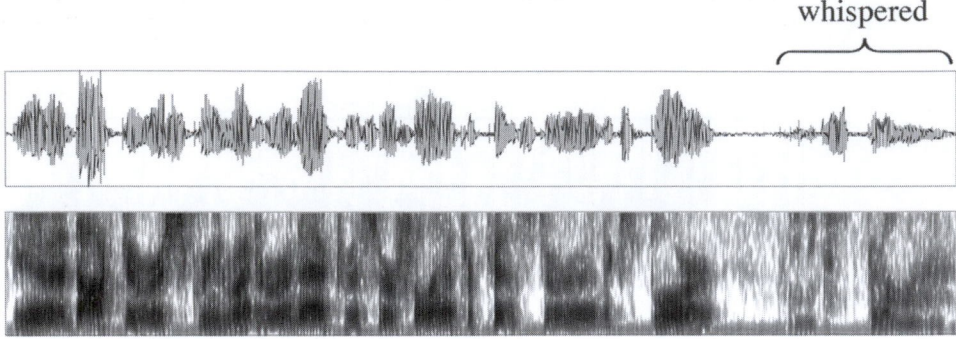

**Figure 10.16** Whispering

(Speaker A) lists possible occupations for his girlfriend (Speaker B), at which point she pauses and whispers to herself, *an explorer!* Her whispering suggests a private emotional involvement in this particular option.

**(8)** a.    *Being a doctor or a screen writer or an actress or a philanthropist or an explorer.*
   b.    (whispered) *An explorer!*

The spectrogram in Figure 10.16 contrasts the man's statement in (8a) with the woman's exclamation in (8b). The final portion shows a diminished waveform, indicating reduced intensity, as well as an attenuation of the acoustic energy that characterizes the normal voice quality of the man's suggestions; this acoustic energy is visible as blackness throughout the spectrogram.

## 10.4  Differing prosodic styles

All the examples so far were taken from recordings of face-to-face informal interactions. ***Conversational language is the most basic of all language uses***. It is the way most of us use language most of the time, and it probably has been the dominant use of language ever since language evolved into its present form. Nevertheless, language is used in many other ways too: in speeches, debates, oral arguments, sermons, and so on, not to mention the many varieties of written language, from shopping lists to newspaper reports to novels. We have already noticed that ordinary writing does not in itself provide very many ways to mark prosody, but prosody inevitably enters the picture whenever written language is read aloud. ***Prosody can be manipulated for different rhetorical effects and can be a significant feature of speech styles***.

In (9) there is a brief excerpt from a famous speech whose written version has been reprinted many times, but whose

**SIDEBAR 10.5**
TRY THIS

As you read the speech excerpt in (9), try to imagine how it sounded. Then listen to Sound file 10.12. How did the prosody you heard differ from what you had imagined based on reading the written words?

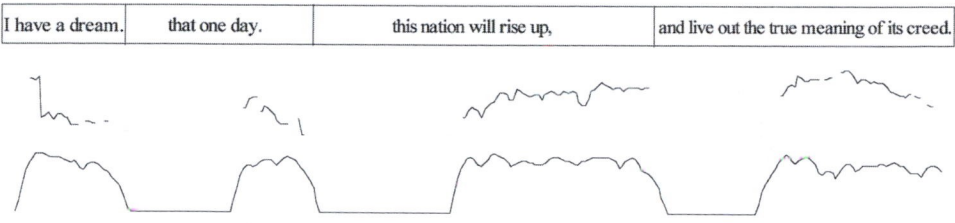

| I have a dream. | that one day. | this nation will rise up, | and live out the true meaning of its creed. |

**Figure 10.17** Dr. Martin Luther King Jr.'s oratorical style

audio and video versions are also easily accessible. The speech is powerful even in written form, but it is much more powerful with access to the sound. The orator's style was inherited from a long tradition in which prosody was exploited to add significantly to the effectiveness of the bare words. See Sidebar 10.5 and try listening  to the audio.

(9)   *I have a dream that one day this nation will rise up and live out the true meaning of its creed.*

Figure 10.17 shows the pitch contours of this excerpt (along the top) and the loudness contours (along the bottom). One obvious feature is the clear separation of the four IUs, separated by pauses of approximately a second and a half. The first two IUs each end with falling pitches that would otherwise be typical of the ends of sentences. The third rises to a higher pitch, and the final IU increases in pitch toward a climax on the words *true meaning*, with a falling pitch at the end.

This distinctive oratorical style was characteristic of a style of preaching widely used in African American churches. The prosodic structure is compelling, powerfully capturing the attention of the listener as it moves from IU to IU.

***The skillful application of prosody is an important component of acting on the stage.*** William Shakespeare, like other playwrights of his time, wrote most of his characters' language in a fixed prosodic style known as iambic pentameter. Their speech was divided into separate written lines, each of which was further divided into five **iambic feet**, which are units composed of a sequence of two syllables, the second of which is stressed. A strict adherence to this pattern would impose the prosody shown in (10) on the beginning of *Henry V*, Act 4, Scene 1.

(10)   a. *Now éntertáin conjécture óf a tíme,*
       b. *when créeping múrmur ánd the póuring dárk,*
       c. *fills thé wide véssel óf the univérse.*

Try reading these lines aloud with strict adherence to the iambic pattern indicated with the accent marks. Notice how such a reading conflicts with a more natural prosody. Then ignore the accent marks and read the same lines again, this time trying to express the meaning of the words. Finally, listen in Sound file 10.13 to what one person did with this passage, and notice the extent to which he departed from iambic pentameter. The transcription in (11) captures some of his interpretation, with extra line breaks used to show variations in his timing. Imagine how dull the play would sound if actors performed it throughout with strict adherence to iambic pentameter.

(11)   a. *Nów=.*
       b. *.. Éntertáin conjécture of a tíme,*
       c. *... when créeping, múrmur,*
       d. *.. and the póuring dárk,*
       e. *... fílls the wí=de véssel of the úniverse.*

**SIDEBAR 10.6**

TRY THIS

Try saying the sentence, "If I were not mad I could have helped you." When you say it, pretend that you wish you were not mad (although you are) because you genuinely want to help the person you love. Are you producing the passage with rising pitch, like Bergman did? How does varying the pitch change the effect of the passage?

Consider next a concluding excerpt from the 1944 movie *Gaslight*. The character played by Ingrid Bergman has discovered that her husband was using a variety of tricks to make her believe she was going mad. His goal was to have her declared insane so that he could acquire full rights to some expensive jewels that had belonged to her aunt, whom in fact he had murdered. In this final scene his treachery has been discovered and his wife taunts him as he is tied to a chair. Try saying these lines aloud or to yourself with a prosody that captures the woman's emotions on discovering her husband's treachery, although she still feels a twinge of regret for this tragic conclusion to their marriage (see Sidebar 10.6).

(12)   *If I were not mad I could have helped you. Whatever you had done I could have pitied and protected you. Because I am mad I hate you. Because I am mad I have betrayed you, but because I am mad, I'm rejoicing with my heart without a shred of pity, without a shred of regret, watching you go with glory in my heart! Mr. Cameron come!* [She opens the door.] *Come Mr. Cameron take this man away! Take this man away.*

Figure 10.18 is a pitch trace of Bergman's voice producing this passage in the movie. The rising pitch conveys Bergman's growing emotional involvement, ending with a final sob on the word *away* that betrays her loss of hope for what she once thought was a loving relationship.

On a more prosaic level, all of us are frequently exposed to language that is read aloud, especially on television or radio. **Speakers vary in their ability to make read speech sound as if it is spontaneous**. This is illustrated by Examples (13) and (14), excerpted from radio announcements.

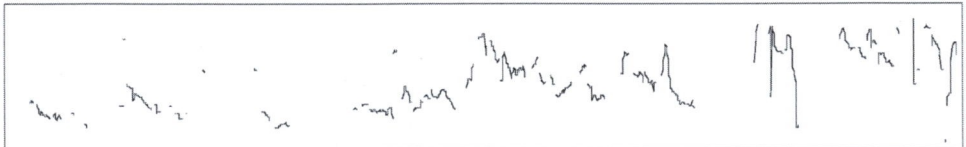

**Figure 10.18** Rising pitch with increasing emotional involvement

**(13)**   a. *This Sáturday.*
           b. *We'll célebrate Présidents Day.*

The prosody of (13) is produced with a restricted pitch range conveying a lack of emotional involvement. Furthermore, both IUs end with sentence-final falling pitches. This prosodic pattern conflicts with the celebratory sense of the phrases. Try saying (13) as if you really meant it, not necessarily dividing it into these two parts. Then listen to how it was actually spoken.

By way of contrast, consider the excerpt in (14). The speaker here was skilled at sounding spontaneous even though he had a script in front of him. He breaks the sentence into three IUs, inserts the pause filler *uh*, and interrupts the third IU with a pause, as if he were searching for words. This final IU shows an expanded pitch range. Again, try saying this sequence yourself before listening to the way it was said by the broadcaster.

**(14)**   a. *Just park wherever you líke,*
           b. *and uh,*
           c. *listen to . . . a free cóncert.*

These examples illustrate the considerable extent to which prosody contributes to the effectiveness of speech. Pitch, volume, timing, and voice quality all play crucial roles in expressing the active involvement of the speaker and in communicating emotional and rhetorical impact to the listener.

---

### CHAPTER SUMMARY

Even detailed written transcriptions cannot fully represent all of the nuances of spoken language; aural information is needed in order to capture the prosody as well. Prosody is a cover term for variations in pitch, volume, timing, and voice quality. Writing systems focus on segmental sounds and show prosody only in an impoverished manner. Prosody is always present as an accompaniment to the segmental vowels, consonants, and syllables of spoken language.

We have seen how prosody has multiple functions, one of which is to delimit linguistic units such as IUs and sentences while signaling relations between them. At the same time it allows speakers to convey a variety of emotions and to direct their listeners' attention to particularly important parts of their utterances, through prosodic distinctions of degrees of prominence. Prosody thus serves both to organize and to evaluate the ideas conveyed by language.

Voice qualities such as creaky voice, harsh voice, laughing, whispering, and sobbing are indicators of various emotional states. Manipulating prosody is an important component of acting, as observable in theater, film, television, radio, and the oral reading of written language of all kinds. Prosodic patterns can be characteristic of particular speech styles and can be used to heighten the effectiveness of oratory. The prosody used in spoken language, as speakers vary the rate, pitch, and volume of their speech, adds nuance and meaning beyond what is conveyed by the words themselves.

### SUGGESTIONS FOR FURTHER READING

**Cruttenden, Alan**. 1997. *Intonation*, 2nd edn. Cambridge University Press.

This book is a useful introduction to prosody in general.

**Edwards, Jane A. and Martin D. Lampert** (eds.) 1993. *Talking data: Transcription and coding in discourse research*. Hillsdale, NJ: Lawrence Erlbaum.

This book discusses various approaches to transcribing spoken language; see especially the chapter by Wallace Chafe titled "Prosodic and Functional Units of Language," pp. 33–43.

**Wennerstrom, Ann**. 2001. *The music of everyday speech: Prosody and discourse analysis*. Oxford University Press.

This book discusses the role of prosody in casual conversations, oral narratives, courtroom testimony, and lectures.

### EXERCISES

1.  Listen to Sound file 10.16, in which a woman is describing the layout of an apartment.

    Here are her words:

    if you go upstairs you're in a hallway and as you start down the hallway to the right it's like a living room and to the left is a bedroom and then if you continue further down there's uh a bathroom on the left and so the hall is real long

    Here is a tracing of her pitch contours, divided into six intonation units. Notice the steep fall to a low pitch that is marked by a very short line near the bottom of four of these segments:

    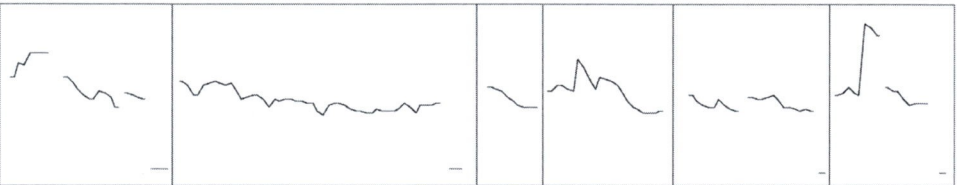

    **Figure 10.19** Pitch contour for Sound file 10.16

    a. Transcribe what the woman says, writing each IU on a separate line.
    b. Mark the terminal contours of each IU, using the transcription conventions given in Sidebar 10.4.
    c. Mark the most prominent syllable in each IU by placing an acute accent mark (´) over its vowel.
    d. After each IU, write S for substantive and R for regulatory.

2.  Listen to Sound file 10.17, in which the speaker is urging people to buy something.

    Here is what he says:

    it's free it's easy and it will save you a ton of money

    Here is a tracing of his pitch contours:

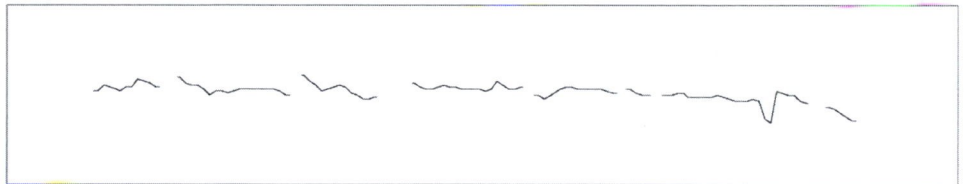

**Figure 10.20** Pitch contour for Sound file 10.17

a. Transcribe what he says, writing each IU on a separate line.
b. Mark the terminal contours of each IU, using the transcription conventions given in Sidebar 10.4.
c. Mark the most prominent syllable in each IU by placing an acute accent mark (´) over its vowel.
d. Imagine how he might have pronounced the last IU using different prosody, and rewrite it to show that prosody.

3. When politicians give a press conference, they usually begin with some prepared remarks before they answer questions from reporters. Sound file 10.18 contains a remark by former President George W. Bush at the opening of one of his press conferences.

Here is what he says:

> The House and the Senate are now considering my supplemental request for operations in Iraq and Afghanistan.

Here is a tracing of his pitch contours:

**Figure 10.21** Pitch contour for Sound file 10.18

Now listen to Sound file 10.19, which contains President Bush's answer to a reporter's question.

Here is what he says:

> Yeah I think it's I think it's a very interesting point you make in your question they're trying to send a warning basically what they're trying to do is is uh cause people to run you know.

Here is a tracing of his pitch contours:

**Figure 10.22** Pitch contour for Sound file 10.19

a. Transcribe each of these selections, dividing them into IUs.
b. Describe one or more differences between reading aloud and speaking spontaneously, as illustrated by these two samples.

# 11 Language in the social world

**KEY TERMS**
- Linguistic feature
- Linguistic repertoire
- Dialect
- Linguistic variety
- Standard

- Code-switching
- Identity
- Language ideology
- African American English
- Style

## CHAPTER PREVIEW

This chapter focuses on how we create our social identities through our use of language. Many of the structural features of language discussed in previous chapters can take on important social functions. Because language is the basis of human communication, it always occurs in a social context, and the use of language both shapes and is shaped by our social relationships and activities.

The chapter begins by surveying the workings of language variation and linguistic diversity. We will then explore the various kinds of social positions that can be taken through language. We will also consider the different levels of language that may be used to do identity work, from languages and dialects to specific linguistic features. In addition, we will examine how ideologies about language and its users may reproduce stereotypes and social inequality. The chapter demonstrates that despite such rigid and inaccurate language ideologies, the identities constructed through language are variable, flexible, and highly socially meaningful to speakers.

## LIST OF AIMS

At the end of this chapter, students will be able to:

- **summarize the different types of identity created through language;**
- **refute language ideologies that value some linguistic varieties over others;**
- **distinguish linguistic and non-linguistic understandings of dialects versus languages;**

- identify key features of African American English;
- distinguish between standard and vernacular;
- distinguish between the phenomena of diglossia, code-switching, interlanguage, and lexical borrowing;
- explain the relationship between language variation and language change;
- identify the forms and social functions of specific linguistic features in language data.

## 11.1  Introduction

*Hello.*
*Hi.*
*G'day.*
*Good afternoon.*
*Hi there!*
*Hey.*
*Howdy!*
*How you doin'?*
*Whassup?*

**SIDEBAR 11.1**

THE SOCIAL MEANING
OF GREETINGS

- Which of these greetings would you use? To whom would you use each one? In what situations?
- What other greetings do you use that do not appear above (especially greetings in languages other than English)? When and to whom do you use each one?
- Which of the above greetings would you never use? Who do you think uses them and in what situations?

*Every day, in every encounter, from the very first moment you begin to speak, you indicate something about yourself, your addressee, and your current situation*. In some sense, each of the utterances listed above "says the same thing": each one functions as a greeting. But from another perspective, these utterances say very different things; they may be used by different kinds of speakers, to different kinds of addressees, and in different speech situations (see Sidebar 11.1).

You probably would not use all of the above greetings to all addressees, and you might use some of them only in special situations. For instance, you might say *Good afternoon* only in a formal context (depending on your age and geographic region), or perhaps you would say *Hi there!* only to a young child. Even *Hello*, which English speakers often think of as the most basic greeting, is likely to be something you use only to strangers or in formal settings (or perhaps on the telephone, usually followed by an addressee-specific greeting once you know who is speaking on the other end). You might use some of the above greetings every day, while you might never use others. And regardless of whether these greetings occur in your own speech, you probably have ideas about the sorts of speakers who use them: perhaps, for example, you associate *G'day* with Australians and *Whassup?* with youth.

In each case, the language that we use indicates to others how we want to be seen: as a member of various social groups based on such factors as age, gender, region, and ethnicity, and as a particular kind of person within those social groups. These examples indicate that language does not only convey information, nor does it only perform interactional functions such as greeting, persuading, requesting, and the like. Our language also indicates how we see others and our relationship toward them: friendly or respectful, similar to us or different from us – imagine, for example, what would happen if you greeted a close friend with a polite *Good afternoon*. Moreover, the way we speak indicates how we understand our current social situation: formal or casual, serious or playful. At the same time that it achieves these purposes, it also serves as a badge of **identity**. With every utterance, we display our own identities and assign identities to our interlocutors. That is, ***through our language use, we constantly socially position ourselves and others***.

The discussion above also suggests that ***we have beliefs, impressions, and expectations about how we ourselves and others use language***. We view certain linguistic forms as characteristic of some social groups and not others (see Sidebar 11.2).

These social expectations are rarely completely accurate and often are entirely wrong. In most cases, the actual language use of individual speakers is far more complex than our ideas about how particular groups speak. For instance, many people may think that women are more likely than men to use more formal greetings, but it is easy to find many counterexamples to challenge this notion. Our beliefs about language and language users are rarely neutral: we tend to perceive some forms of language as "better" – more correct, more pleasant, more intelligent-sounding – than others. For example, we might view greetings like *Howdy* or *How you doin'?* as less "correct" in some way than their counterparts *How do you do?* and *How are you doing?*, but we might also feel that they sound more pleasant or friendlier than a more formal greeting.

> **SIDEBAR 11.2**
> GREETINGS AND SOCIAL EXPECTATIONS
> - What sorts of greetings might be socially expected more from women than men?
> - What sorts of greetings might be socially expected more from working-class speakers than middle-class speakers?

Such beliefs are often strongly held, and they have real-world consequences for how speakers are perceived, but they are based in prescriptive attitudes, not descriptive linguistic facts. From the viewpoint of linguists, all **linguistic varieties** (a cover term that includes languages, dialects, and speech styles and registers) are equally grammatically correct and cognitively complex. In everyday life, however, some forms of language are typically highly prized, while others are devalued. ***Culturally shared ideas about language and its users are known as language ideologies***, ***and they can profoundly shape attitudes toward speakers who do not speak socially prestigious or institutionally powerful linguistic varieties.***

This chapter explores these two different yet intertwined aspects of language as a social phenomenon: language as a resource for displaying identity, and language as a basis for ideology. We will see that even as we use language to communicate about the world and to interact with those around us, we also use it to highlight relevant aspects of the social world at a given moment, such as our own and others' identities, the social situation, and so on. ***The use of language to convey a context-specific meaning is called* indexicality** (*index* literally means 'point to'). Language therefore involves both semantic meaning and social meaning. Moreover, ***the social meaning of language is not assigned arbitrarily, but depends heavily on cultural ideologies about social groups and how they use language***.

## 11.2  Linguistic diversity and language variation

The interdisciplinary field of **sociocultural linguistics** investigates the vast range of interactional, social, and cultural uses and meanings of language (the term *sociolinguistics* is also sometimes used in this broad sense as well as to refer to a more specific set of approaches to the study of language and society). The possibility of endowing language use with social meaning depends on having more than one way of "saying the same thing," and this in turn relies on two fundamental principles of sociocultural linguistics:

(1)  **The principle of linguistic diversity**: ***Many different languages are spoken around the world, and often more than one language is used in a single community or in interactions between communities.***

(2)  **The principle of language variation**: ***Within a single language, variability is inherent based on social, situational, linguistic, and other factors.***

As a result of these two principles, all speakers have available a wealth of linguistic resources for carrying out their social and interactional goals in a variety of cultural contexts.

Obviously, speakers of different languages communicate in different ways, but even when speaking the same language, different kinds of people tend to speak differently, and speakers who may seem to be quite similar socially do not always speak alike. Additionally, every speaker varies her or his speech both across contexts and within the same context, for social as well as linguistic reasons. For example, even in the same conversation a speaker might pronounce the verbal suffix *-ing* sometimes as [ɪn] (as in *I'm doin' homework*) and sometimes as [ɪŋ] (as in *I'm formulating a hypothesis*). In other words, **speakers can differ not only in their use of an entire language or dialect but in their use of individual linguistic features, or specific forms at any linguistic level**. A linguistic feature might be the pronunciation of a specific vowel or consonant (such as the pronunciation of the vowel in words like *half* and *bath* with [ɑː] versus [æ]), the use of a particular grammatical structure (such as *I'm not* versus *I am not* versus *I ain't*), a certain lexical choice (such as *soda* versus *pop*), or a particular interactional practice (such as allowing or avoiding overlap between speaker turns). The task of sociocultural linguistics is to systematically document these different ways of speaking and to explain their interactional, social, and cultural functions and meanings.

### 11.2.1 Linguistic repertoires

One of the primary ways that individuals differ from one another with regard to language is in their **linguistic repertoires**: the full range of linguistic varieties that they are able to use. In some communities most people are **monolingual** (that is, they speak only one language), while in other communities most speakers are **multilingual** (that is, they speak two or more languages). It may seem that those who speak more than one language necessarily have wider repertoires than those who do not, but even monolingual speakers have multiple ways of speaking (see Sidebar 11.3).

> **SIDEBAR 11.3**
> LINGUISTIC REPERTOIRES
>
> - What linguistic varieties are in your own linguistic repertoire? When do you use each one?
> - How does your repertoire compare to that of other members of your family?
> - How does your repertoire compare to that of other residents of your city or region?
> - How has your repertoire changed over time? How is it currently changing?

There may not be an established label for some of the varieties in your repertoire, and you may have resorted to creative labels such as *computerese* or *surfer speak*. Varieties that are associated with the specialized activities of particular groups are often termed **registers**. Some registers are primarily used in professional or other formal settings, such as legal or religious contexts. Extremely informal registers, in contrast, may include the heavy use of **slang**, a set of rapidly changing lexical items often associated with youth and casual social contexts. Many non-linguists incorrectly use the term *slang* to refer to what are correctly termed *dialects* (or better, *varieties*). This misuse frequently reflects a **language ideology** – a culturally shared belief or attitude about language and its users – that devalues those varieties. It is important to recognize that unlike slang, which primarily involves the lexicon, all dialects also include phonology and grammar. Thus, to label a dialect as "slang" ignores its structural complexity and systematicity.

### 11.2.2 Dialects and style shifting

Varieties that are considered to belong to the same language are often divided into dialects. ***Traditionally, the term*** *dialect* ***refers to a variety of a language that is characteristic of a specific group defined on the basis of a factor like geography (e.g., Indian English, the variety of English spoken in India), ethnicity (e.g., Chicano English, the variety of English spoken by many Americans of Mexican heritage), or social class (e.g., Cockney, the working-class variety of English spoken in London). Moreover, dialects are usually considered forms of the same language because they are generally mutually intelligible.*** Linguists' use of the terms *language* and *dialect* therefore differs from the political use of these terms. For example, Serbian and Croatian are now viewed by many people in the Balkan region as separate languages for political reasons, although they are mutually intelligible. Conversely, the languages of China, including Mandarin, Cantonese, and many others, are often called dialects despite being mutually unintelligible in their spoken form, because their speakers are politically unified under a single government and they share a writing system. Thus, the distinction between a language and a dialect may be based on political factors rather than linguistic factors, and even the linguistic criterion of mutual intelligibility is not absolute, as you may have discovered for yourself if you have ever tried to speak to someone with a very different dialect from your own.

Like *slang*, the label *dialect* is often misapplied in ways that reveal negative language ideologies. Non-linguists often erroneously apply the term *dialect* to languages without writing systems, such as many Native American languages and African languages. This usage positions such languages as inferior to those that have a written tradition. In addition, the term *dialect* tends to be used more for some varieties of a language than for others, particularly those that are seen as less prestigious in some way. But in fact ***everybody speaks a dialect***. Speakers often believe they do not speak a dialect because they perceive their way of speaking as simply "normal," but if they visited an area where another dialect is spoken they would quickly discover that they are the ones perceived as speaking a dialect! Moreover, some speakers are **bidialectal** – that is, fluent in two (and sometimes more) dialects. However, no one has mastery over every existing variety of a given language.

It is also important to distinguish dialects from accents. While a dialect is a complete linguistic system that includes phonological, grammatical, and lexical characteristics, an **accent** involves only the phonological characteristics of a given variety. Although we tend to pay special attention to unfamiliar accents, there is no such thing as accentless speech. ***Everyone has an accent*** – that is, everyone's speech has a particular set of phonological features. As with the issue of dialect, it is sometimes said that someone "has an accent" when what is really meant is that the speaker has an accent that is noticeably different from that of the observer or of the surrounding community. Thus, which dialects or accents count as "normal" is a matter of social beliefs, not linguistic facts.

Some languages have a particular dialect that enjoys special status: the standard. The standard is not simply one dialect among others but a different linguistic phenomenon altogether. The **standard *is an artificial* linguistic variety *that has been deliberately engineered to function as the prestige variety and typically also as a wider means of written and spoken communication across social groups that speak different dialects***. Unlike most dialects, which take shape in a "bottom-up" way from their everyday use by speakers, the standard is governed by prescriptive rules that are codified in dictionaries and traditional grammar books and imposed by authorities in a "top-down" way through the educational system and other means. The standard may be based on the speech of elites or it may be constructed out of several existing dialects, but strictly speaking, no one truly speaks the standard, because it is more an idealization than a living variety. One purpose of a standard is to freeze the language in place, but given the principle of language variation, this is an unnatural and impossible goal. In any case, only a tiny minority of the world's languages has established a standard variety. In the United States, a roughly agreed-upon standard has emerged, but if you compare different American English dictionaries and grammar books as well as the speech of elites across the nation (such as members of Congress), you'll find a wide range of variation, especially at the phonological and lexical level. Meanwhile, a number of countries around the world formally enforce and preserve the standard through national language academies. These are generally government entities that monitor language use and issue official pronouncements regarding which linguistic forms are acceptable in institutional contexts such as the media and education. Inevitably, however, in everyday speech these policies are often disregarded. (For a discussion of how Indonesia created its standard language, see Language Profile 11.)

Linguists sometimes distinguish the standard, or prestige dialect, from the vernacular, or a nonstandard dialect. For example, a great deal of sociolinguistic research has found that middle-class speakers use the standard as their primary variety and working-class speakers may use the vernacular. In most situations, however, it is more useful to think of the vernacular and the standard as varieties that are associated not simply with particular social groups but also with particular social situations. This view focuses on the speaker's linguistic repertoire within a given language. From this perspective, ***the vernacular is the variety of a language that a speaker uses for ordinary, everyday interaction, such as with close family members and peers***. One implication of this definition is that, as with dialects and accents, ***every speaker has a vernacular***. For any given speaker, the vernacular may be relatively standard or relatively nonstandard. While the vernacular is used in casual situations, in more formal contexts, speakers may adjust their speech so that it more closely approaches the standard. This phenomenon of ***alternating between different varieties of the same language based on the social context is termed*** **style shifting**.

**SIDEBAR 11.4**

STYLE SHIFTING

- Which context seems to be associated with the most standard speech style? Which context seems to be associated with the most vernacular speech style?
- Which specific linguistic features in the examples would you characterize as more standard and which as more vernacular?
- How can you explain Foxy's style shifting across these three examples?

Example (1) illustrates style shifting between **African American English** (AAE) (see Textbox 11.1 on the next page) and Standard American English in two different interviews with an African American teenage girl from California, who is called Foxy Boston by the researchers who studied her speech, John Rickford and Faye McNair-Knox. In Example (1a), Foxy is speaking to Beth, a European American young adult interviewer whom she has never met before this interview. In Example (1b), Foxy is speaking to a different interviewer, Faye, a middle-aged African American adult woman whom she already knows; Faye's teenage daughter Roberta is present as well. In both (1a) and (1b), the topic of discussion is Foxy's college and career plans. In Example (1c), Foxy is talking to Faye and Roberta about a boy who is interested in her. After examining the data, consider the questions in Sidebar 11.4.

---

## TEXTBOX 11.1 **AFRICAN AMERICAN ENGLISH**

**African American English** (or AAE) is the most widely studied nonstandard variety of American English, and it is also arguably the variety that is the most deeply misunderstood by non-linguists. Despite its name, AAE is not spoken by all African Americans nor only by African Americans, but most of its speakers are of African American heritage, and most African Americans include at least some elements of AAE in their linguistic repertoires, usually along with Standard American English and perhaps other varieties.

Although non-linguists often wrongly label AAE as no more than "bad English" or "slang," it is as rule-governed, systematic, and complex as any other language or dialect. The vast majority of the lexicon, phonology, and grammar of AAE is identical to other varieties of American English, but it has recognizable differences as well, and these have received a great deal of attention from linguists. Researchers are aware that focusing on a few differences runs the risk of overshadowing the substantial similarities between AAE and other English varieties, but they believe it is necessary to call attention to these features so that educators,

speech-language pathologists, and others do not misinterpret elements of AAE as grammatical errors, speech deficits, or indicators of cognitive difficulties. And with good reason: AAE-speaking schoolchildren have been subjected to inappropriate and even harmful educational "remedies" due to outsiders' lack of knowledge of their variety. In fact, far from being linguistically deficient or wrong, AAE contains complex grammatical structures not found in other English varieties that allow for the nuanced expression of meaning and speaker point of view.

Example (1) illustrates a number of the distinctive grammatical features of AAE. Some of these are also found in other nonstandard varieties of English, while others are unique to AAE in their patterning. (Note: Because of the dominance of Standard American English, the terminology for AAE grammatical features typically takes Standard American English as the norm, but this convention should not mislead you into thinking that AAE is simply an "incorrect" version of Standard American English. As the discussion in Textbox 11.2 indicates, AAE has a rich grammatical system in its own right.)

---

(1)  a. Addressee: European American. Topic: College and career plans

*M, she goes to DeAnza's nursing school. And R and T, they're going to, um, CSM, and my friend A, she's going to be with me when I go...*

(Source: Rickford and McNair-Knox 1994: 261; slightly modified transcript)

b. Addressee: European American. Topic: School life

*My teacher, his name is Mr. Segal and he's like, really hard. . . . He teaches us like we're in college, and my um Biology – when I had Biology? This guy named Mr. Cross, I mean he teaches you like you're in college. He gives you, he gives you all your book and he assigns you all this work. It's like so much work . . . and it's, it's done in a week and you're like, "Oh my gosh!"*

(Source: Rickford and McNair-Knox 1994: 244; slightly modified transcript)

c. Addressees: African American. Topic: College and career plans

*Miss R is the one that – [laughter] Miss R the one help me get into this program, and my – and this guy name Mr O at our school, he's Chinese.*

(Source: Rickford and McNair-Knox 1994: 261; slightly modified transcript)

d. Addressees: African American. Topic: Dating and romance

*. . . I be on the telephone and he be going, [breathlessly and fast] "Where you went today? I – I know you wasn't at home! I called you. You wasn't at home! I left a message. You wasn't at home. Where you was at today? Uhn-uhn, uhn-uhn, you got to get a beeper or something so I can page you. You have to call me back. Where was you?!" [laughter] And every day – every day, "Did you go shopping today? What you go buy? You bought this? You bought that? You like it?" And I be going, "Yep, yep, yep."*

(Source: Rickford and McNair-Knox 1994: 244; slightly modified transcript)

---

## TEXTBOX 11.2 **SOME GRAMMATICAL FEATURES OF AAE**

**zero copula**: absence of an overtly expressed copula verb in certain contexts (Ø = absence of a form that occurs in other varieties of English)

*Miss R Ø the one help me get into this program.*
Compare: *Miss R **is** the one* or *Miss R**'s** the one*

**zero auxiliary**: absence of an overtly expressed auxiliary verb in certain contexts

*Where you **went** today?*
Compare: *Where **did** you go today?*

**leveling** of verb forms: use of identical verbal inflection across person and number (e.g., *I go, you go, she go, we go, they go*)

*You **wasn't** at home.*
Compare: *You **weren't** at home.*

**non-inverted question**: *wh*-question in which the subject precedes the verb

*Where **you was** at today?*
Compare: *Where **was you** (at) today?* or *Where **were you** today?*

**habitual *be***: use of uninflected *be* as an aspect marker indicating habitual or repeated activity, rather than as a copula

*And I **be going**, "Yep, yep, yep."*
Compare: *And I **always go**, "Yep, yep, yep."*

Note: Habitual *be* is one of the most widely misunderstood features of AAE. Despite its superficial similarity to the copula in other English varieties, in AAE *be* generally cannot be used as a present-tense copula.

---

You should be able to immediately spot differences between Foxy's speech to Beth in Examples (1a) and (1b) and her speech to Faye and Roberta in Examples (1c) and (1d). In the first two examples Foxy speaks almost entirely in Standard English, while in (1b) she uses some features of Standard English and some features of AAE (compare *Miss R is the one* and *Miss R the one* in her first utterance). Example (1c) shows that even when discussing the rather formal, impersonal topic of school, Foxy uses a somewhat more casual style with her African American addressees, as also indicated by the laughter. But when the topic changes to boys and dating in (1d), Foxy's speech style changes dramatically. Here she uses AAE extensively to narrate and even re-enact her interactions with a boy who often calls her on the phone. ***Systematic style shifting of this kind allows speakers to index the speech situation as formal or informal, distant or intimate, impersonal or highly emotional.***

Many of the grammatical features of AAE are also found in other languages around the world. For example, the use of zero copula in specific grammatical contexts is widespread cross-linguistically, occurring in Ancient Greek, Arabic, Hungarian, Indo-nesian, Mandarin, Quechua, and Russian, among others. Likewise, the rich aspect system of AAE – which includes not only *be* for habitual activity but also grammatical forms indicating completed actions, situations in the distant past, resulting states of being, and more – has counterparts in Atlantic creole languages such as Jamaican Creole, as well as sign languages like American Sign Language, the Austronesian languages of the Philippines, and the Niger-Congo languages of Africa.

### 11.2.3  Multilingualism and code-switching

In addition to variation within a single language, which is characteristic of all languages, the linguistic situation of many communities also involves diversity across languages, with two, three, or more languages in regular use. Typically, these languages are not isolated from one another; rather, individuals in such communities speak more than one language precisely so that they can communicate with the people around them. This situation is by no means unusual – despite the monolingual ideology of a number of countries, including the United States and most other English-speaking nations, Japan, Korea, France, and many others, ***multilingualism is far more typical than monolingualism around the world***, and it is common even in supposedly monolingual nations. India is an example of a highly multilingual nation, with over 400 living languages representing four major language families. In addition to the two official languages, Hindi and English, India officially recognizes twenty-two regional languages. Most speakers know at least two languages, and often more.

Multilingualism introduces an additional set of resources into speakers' linguistic repertoires. In monolingual communities, linguistic repertoires are largely a matter of variation within a single language. ***In multilingual communities, a speaker's repertoire may include two or more languages, and she or he may also have facility in multiple varieties within each of these languages.*** Some US Latinos of Puerto Rican heritage, for example, are able to speak Standard Puerto Rican Spanish, Nonstandard Puerto Rican Spanish, Standard American English, Puerto Rican English, and sometimes other regional or ethnic dialects such as New York English or African American English as well. (Although for analytic purposes linguists may distinguish all of these as separate varieties, they may not be sharply separated from one another in practice, as shown in Example 1b above.) These varieties are all in wide use in Puerto Rican communities in the mainland United States, but individual speakers may have access to some varieties and not others depending on their background; for example, Puerto Ricans educated in the mainland United States who experienced English-only education may lack full fluency and literacy in Standard Puerto Rican Spanish.

In many multilingual communities, speakers use each language in a particular physical context (e.g., English at work, Spanish at home). ***The use of two different languages or dialects according to social domain is called*** diglossia. (Originally, the concept of diglossia was applied only to dialects, but now it is extended to languages as well.) Unlike style shifting, which may occur in a single situation based on topic or addressee, in diglossia, different varieties are used in different situations. In reality, however, the boundaries between domains often blur, and only in a few situations is a language more or less fully circumscribed by a specific domain of use. For instance, languages such as Classical Arabic, Classical Hebrew, and Sanskrit are generally restricted to religious or scholarly contexts. As these examples suggest, in addition to different languages or dialects, diglossic situations also often involve special registers specific to each domain, such as a religious register or a scholarly register.

Multilingual speakers in many communities may have the additional ability to combine the languages they speak through **code-switching**, or *the use of two or more languages within a single interaction or utterance while conforming to the phonological and grammatical system of each language*. Code-switching is often wrongly viewed negatively by monolingual and multilingual speakers alike as "impure" language use, or as a sign that the speaker is not fluent in either language. The truth is that *only speakers who are fluent in two or more languages are able to engage in code-switching*. For this reason and others, extensive code-switching (sometimes called "code-mixing") has been argued to be a separate variety in its own right, distinct from any of the languages involved in this phenomenon. Example (2) presents two illustrations of code-switching between Cantonese and English by young adults in Hong Kong. Because of Hong Kong's history as a British colony, college graduates are typically bilingual in English as well as Cantonese, the primary language of Hong Kong. (Following the 1997 handover of Hong Kong to China, Mandarin has gained in prominence, but it is not widely spoken.)

**(2)**  a. Frank

*ze m hai ngo m hang gong, ji hai ze hou lou sat gong ze e mou di* **moderate** *zung sing di get yan ze dou wui gok dak ngo hai deoi si m deoi jan ze o: zi gei* **personally** *ze o jau hou siu tai pin le ze o m wui*

'Not that I don't want to speak, that is, very honestly speaking, that is without some **moderate** neutral sort of people would all feel that I am speaking of the matter and it is not **personal**. I myself personally I seldom get too biased. I will not'

b. Kelly

*It doesn't matter how you deal with them, it doesn't matter who you are, kei sat **the way that you present yourself by** lei go **language** ji ging bei zo jat zung **arrogant** ge gam gok bei keoi dei le.*

'**It doesn't matter how you deal with them, it doesn't matter who you are**, actually **the way that you present yourself by** your **language** already gives people an arrogant impression'

(Source: Chen 2008: 61; slightly modified transcripts; English is marked in boldface)

**SIDEBAR 11.5**

Can you find an example of each of the following in the data in (2)?

- An insertion
- An alternation
- A tag switch

Note: Bear in mind that code-switching involves switching both from Language A to Language B and from Language B to Language A.

Code-switching is triggered by multiple interactional factors, including the language used by the previous speaker, the speaker's goals (e.g., emphasis, disagreement), and the topic. In addition, code-switching is shaped by complex linguistic factors. Code-switches are of three general types: **insertion** (switching a lexical item within a single clause), **alternation** (switching between entire clauses), and **tag switching** (switching at a **discourse marker**, a lexical item that is independent of the grammar of the clause but performs discourse-level or inter-actional functions). Because so many factors play a role in code-switching, it is difficult to predict when a switch will occur, but it is often possible to explain the function of a switch after the fact (see Sidebar 11.5).

Code-switching should not be confused with types of language mixing that do not require fluent bilingualism. One such phenomenon is **interlanguage**, *a characteristic of nonfluent language learners in which structural elements of the learner's first language and second language are combined due to the learner's incomplete mastery of the second language*. As part of interlanguage, language learners may mix languages because they are unable to sustain speech in their target language (see Chapter 15, section 15.2.3). Both structurally and functionally, code-switching is entirely different from interlanguage. At the structural level, interlanguage often co-occurs with non-native features within the second language. At the functional level, language learners use interlanguage because they lack sufficient knowledge of the target language and must fall back on their first language. By contrast, bilingual speakers code-switch purposefully, if not fully consciously, to achieve a wide variety of communicative goals, including to convey particular nuances of meaning, to create social connection, and to structure their discourse. Bilingual speakers sometimes report that they code-switch because they can't think of the right word in one of their languages, but research demonstrates that this sort of code-switching as a "crutch" is in fact quite rare in fluent bilingual speech. (For more on second language acquisition, see Chapter 15.)

Another phenomenon that must be distinguished from code-switching is **lexical borrowing**, a process of adding new vocabulary to a language that does not require any fluency in the lending language at all (although bilinguals as well as mono-linguals may engage in lexical borrowing). Whereas in code-switching, the phono-logical and grammatical systems of both languages are kept separate as the speaker moves from one language to the other, *in lexical borrowing, the borrowed lexical item is fully integrated phonologically and grammatically into the borrowing language* (for more on lexical borrowing, see Chapter 13, section 13.2). For example, Spanish speakers in the United States often incorporate borrowings or **loanwords** from English into their speech, like *lonche* 'lunch,' *parquear* 'to park,' and *yarda* 'yard.' Conversely, monolingual English speakers use numerous Spanish borrowings with English phonology and grammar, such as *alligator* (from *el lagarto* 'the lizard') or *burrito* (lit. 'little donkey'), pronounced in English as [bəˈɹɪɾoʊ] instead of Spanish [buˈrito]. Borrowing is a common result of linguistic and cultural contact between groups, but unlike code-switching it does not require fluent bilingualism. In order to determine whether the English lexical items in Example (2) above are insertional switches or loanwords, we would ideally need to know whether: (a) they are pronounced according to English or Cantonese phonology; (b) they are adapted into Cantonese grammatical structures; (c) they are understood even by Cantonese monolinguals; and (d) they are considered by the speakers themselves to be English or Cantonese. (As it turns out, according to these criteria, all of the English words in Example (2) are part of code-switching rather than borrowing.)

Finally, it is important to realize that not all bilinguals are able to code-switch, and not all speakers who code-switch do so in the same way. In Example (2a) above, Frank, who was educated in Hong Kong and has a "local" identity, follows the insertional code-switching style typical of most young Hong Kongers. In Example (2b), Kelly, who was educated in the United States during her teen years and then returned to Hong Kong, has a "returnee" identity and combines insertion with alternation and tag switching. This returnee style of code-switching is widely disparaged by local Hong Kongers as pretentious and overly western. In fact, in Example (2b) Kelly is describing the negative ideologies of her local peers toward her returnee speech style. Although she tries to adapt to the local code-switching style in order to fit in and make friends, she is not always fully aware of her switching (as is typical with code-switching in general). And there is another reason why it is difficult for Kelly to abandon her code-switching style: it indexes her identity as a "world citizen," as she puts it.

As Kelly's situation demonstrates, how we use language is intimately tied to our identities, yet the identity we seek to project through language may not be what others perceive, depending on the language ideologies that they hold. This close connection between ideology and identity in language use is also relevant to variation within a single language, as we will see in the next section.

## 11.3  Variation, ideology, and identity

Unlike switching between languages, which is often very noticeable to others, most variability within an individual language is not noticed at all. It is essentially impossible to produce a given utterance, word, or even phoneme in exactly the same way each time we speak, and this constant linguistic variability goes unremarked most of the time. Sometimes, however, a particular social meaning will become attached to a particular linguistic form. *A linguistic feature that varies either across speakers or in the speech of a single speaker is called a* **sociolinguistic variable,** *and the alternate forms that this variable takes in speech are called* **sociolinguistic variants**. Over time, some variants may catch on while others disappear, and as a result the language itself will be different. Through this process, *variation is the source of language change*.

An illustration of the relationship between linguistic variation, language change, and social meaning can be seen in the case of the pronunciation of /r/ after a vowel, or **postvocalic /r/**, in the history of English, as described by researcher Thomas Paul Bonfiglio. This variable has two variants, a **rhotic** variant, in which the /r/ is pronounced as [ɹ], and a **nonrhotic** variant, in which it is pronounced as a vowel, such as [ə] in unstressed syllables, as in *better* ['bɛɾə], and as an offglide or lengthening of the preceding vowel in stressed syllables, as in *car* [kʰɑː]. Although the English spelling system shows that the /r/ was historically pronounced, in the eighteenth century the nonrhotic pronunciation emerged in Cockney, the variety of the London working class. Eventually this pronunciation, though initially stigmatized, gained social prestige among the middle and upper classes of London and surrounding areas, and it was also adopted by American elites on the East Coast and in the South who emulated English fashions.

Until the early twentieth century, the US Midwestern rhotic pronunciation was often seen by nonrhotic speakers as provincial and harsh or aggressive. But with the arrival of Eastern and Southern European immigrants in East Coast cities and the northern migration of African Americans, the nonrhotic pronunciation became associated with these groups and took on a new, negative meaning in the eyes of the middle-class white population. Consequently, the rhotic pronunciation associated with Midwesterners gained status. Today, the nonrhotic pronunciation continues to decline in the United States even among groups that have traditionally used it, such as inhabitants of New York and Boston, elite white Southerners, and African Americans.

The example of postvocalic /r/ illustrates several important points regarding language variation:

1. Contrary to what many non-linguists might expect, it is the speech of non-elite groups, not the elite, that is the primary source of linguistic innovation.
2. Linguistic variation can lead to a systematic change in the language if one sociolinguistic variant gains ground over alternatives.
3. Sociolinguistic variants are often associated with particular social groups, and speakers may adopt variants that allow them to align with a specific group and so to index a desired social identity.
4. A sociolinguistic variant may have different social associations for different groups or in different contexts, and these associations may change over time as new groups take up the variant.

5.  Linguistic forms do not have any inherent social meaning or social value. Instead, they acquire value based on how the speakers who use them are socially perceived and evaluated.

***Language variation and change, then, are closely connected to processes of social identity and cultural ideology.*** (For more on this topic, see Chapter 13.)

The relationship between language and identity has been understood in different ways within different strands of sociocultural linguistics. In one tradition, researchers have sought to discover which linguistic structures correlate with which social groups. From this correlationist perspective, language reflects social identities: we speak as we do because of who we are. For example, linguists have long known that working-class speakers are more likely than middle-class speakers to use [ɪn] rather than [ɪŋ] in verb forms like *talking*, *running*, and *sleeping*. In this approach, a speaker's social category is used to predict which linguistic form she or he will use. ***In the correlationist view, language is seen as reflecting social identities***. The starting point of linguistic analysis in this approach is speakers' social category membership, which is used to explain a given linguistic phenomenon.

However, sociocultural linguists have begun to reverse the relationship between language and identity. Rather than using social categories to explain language, many scholars now use language to explain social identities. By examining how a speaker uses language, we can gain insight into how she or he wants to be perceived by others. ***In the constructionist view, language is seen as creating social identities***. By speaking in particular ways (such as by saying *runnin'* more often than *running*), we index our identities as particular kinds of people (such as working-class rather than middle-class), and those who hear us speak make inferences about our background, our abilities, and even our personalities. These inferences may either support or undermine our own goals for how we wish to be seen. Both speakers and hearers are actively engaged in how language is used and socially interpreted. In addition, language is not understood simply as a mirror reflecting pre-existing categories of identity to which the speaker passively belongs. Instead, ***language is a vehicle for social action, as speakers use linguistic structures to lay claim to a desired set of social characteristics and listeners accept or challenge these identity claims***. In this process, speakers and hearers rely on culturally shared understandings of how various social groups speak.

## 11.3.1  Forms of identity

There are a variety of positions that we can occupy at any given moment within the social world. Perhaps the most obvious of these, because they are the broadest, are demographic categories like gender, age, race and ethnicity, region, and socioeconomic status. Such categories, which have been the focus of most research on sociolinguistic

## TEXTBOX 11.3 "WOMEN'S LANGUAGE": LANGUAGE IDEOLOGY OR LINGUISTIC REALITY?

As women's rights became a central social issue in the 1970s, many linguists began to examine the relationship between language and gender. A much-discussed book by Robin Lakoff originally published in 1975 proposed that women's language is characterized by features of what she considered powerless speech, including the following ([1975] 2004: 78–81):

1. Women have a large stock of words related to their specific interests, generally relegated to them as "women's work": *magenta*, *shirr* (in sewing), *dart* (in sewing), etc.
2. "Empty" adjectives like *divine, charming, cute,* etc.
3. Question intonation where we might expect declaratives: for instance tag questions ("It's so hot, isn't it?") and rising intonation in statement contexts ("What's your name, dear?" "Mary Smith?")
4. The use of hedges of various kinds. Women's speech seems in general to contain more instances of *well, y'know, kinda*, etc.
5. Related to this is the intensive use of *so*. Again, this is more frequent in women's than men's language.

6. Hypercorrect grammar: women are not supposed to talk rough.
7. Superpolite forms: women are supposed to speak more politely than men.
8. Women don't tell jokes.
9. Women "speak in italics" [i.e., use frequent emphatic stress].

Researchers sought to test these claims in the speech of women and men, with mixed results. Language and gender researchers now understand that the notion of **"women's language"** *is not necessarily a description of the speech of all (or most, or any) women, but rather a language ideology regarding how women are expected to speak* – or suffer the social consequences if they do not. Lakoff herself recognized the ideological power of "women's language" in restricting women's behavior and opportunities. It may seem that this decades-old ideology is no longer relevant, and it is certainly true that some of the characteristics of conventionally feminine language use have changed over time, as our cultural ideology of femininity has changed. However, ideologies about how women and men "should" speak and act are still with us.

### SIDEBAR 11.6

CURRENT IDEOLOGIES OF "WOMEN'S LANGUAGE"

- In your opinion, which of the features listed in Textbox 11.3 are currently associated with women? Why does this association persist?
- In your opinion, which of the features have social meanings other than (or in addition to) their association with women? Why might they have these meanings?
- Can you think of linguistic features not listed here that are currently associated with women (or with certain kinds of women)? How might they have come to have this association?

variation, are often viewed as objective facts about an individual and therefore as relatively easy to determine. However, they are not always as straightforward as they first appear. As already discussed, one of the most widely studied linguistic varieties is so closely tied to demography that its very name – African American English – indicates its association with a particular ethnic group, even though not all speakers of AAE are African American and not all African Americans speak AAE. Sociocultural linguists have likewise had a long-standing interest in the demographic category of gender and especially the question of whether women and men speak differently. It seems clear that although we may hold strong beliefs about how women and men speak (or should speak; see Textbox 11.3), there is a great deal of variability in the speech of each gender and a great deal of similarity across the genders (see Sidebar 11.6).

## 11.3.2  Styles and communities of practice

Demographic categories are central to how we are perceived by others, but more important to our own identities and hence to our language use are the social groupings that we ourselves orient to in everyday life. These social groupings are sometimes termed **communities of practice**, or social groups that jointly engage in culturally meaningful activities. Communities of practice include families, friendship groups, teams and clubs, professional and community-based organizations, and any other group that undertakes a shared effort. In accounting for speakers' language use, membership in different communities of practice may override shared demographic membership. In such cases, extensive community-based research is necessary in order to find out which categories matter in how people define themselves and others.

For example, a classic study done by Penelope Eckert in the 1980s in a largely white suburban high school near Detroit, Michigan, found a sharp distinction between the clean-cut "jocks," who dressed in bright or pastel colors and trendy "preppy" styles, were college-bound, and participated in sports, student council, and other school-sponsored activities, and the rebellious "burnouts," who wore non-trendy dark clothing, were disengaged from school, smoked cigarettes, and planned to find jobs in the local community after high school. Linguistically, burnouts used more nonstandard grammar (specifically, **negative concord**, or the marking of negation in more than one possible grammatical position, as in *I didn't never do nothing*), and they also led the jocks in some elements of a sound change in progress in the vowel system of the Detroit area. At the same time, gender interacted with the ethnographic categories of jock and burnout; for example "burned-out burnout girls" (that is, girls who got into the most trouble at school) were also the most advanced participants in some parts of the sound change, particularly the raising of the central vowel in the diphthong /aɪ/. The most extreme raised variant is [ʌɪ], so that *fight* sounds almost like "foight" and *all-nighter* sounds similar to "all-noighter." (*All-nighter* is a slang term used by burnouts to refer to staying out all night partying.)

Figure 11.1 presents in visual form the correlation of combined speaker gender and social category with the extreme raising of /aɪ/. The numbers, derived from statistical calculations that are widely used for analyzing sociolinguistic variation, are probability values for the use of the innovative raised pronunciation by each group of speakers. Numbers above 0.5 indicate that the change is favored in that group; numbers below 0.5 indicate that the change is disfavored in that group. The correlations are all highly statistically significant.

The figure shows that jocks mostly tended not to use the new pronunciation, regardless of gender, and that among the burnouts, most girls had a slight tendency not to use it. Even burnout boys as a group only slightly favored the innovative variant. By contrast, the burned-out burnout girls were the clear leaders in the use of raised /aɪ/. It seems that this variant was especially important for burned-out burnout girls in indexing a tough, rebellious identity.

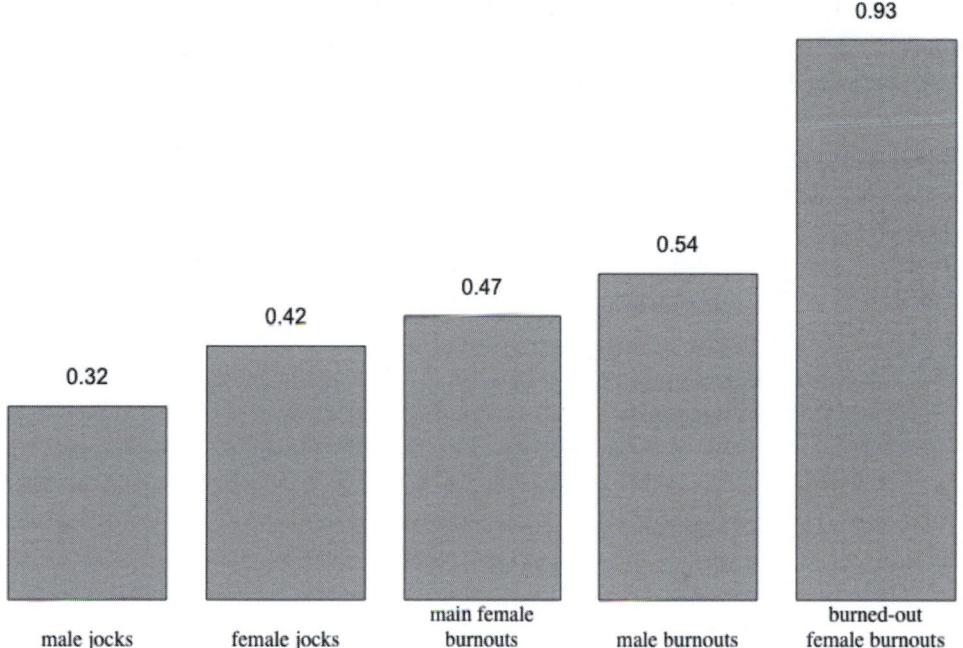

**Figure 11.1** Extreme raising of /aɪ/, combining gender and social category, separating two clusters of burnout girls (adapted from Eckert and McConnell-Ginet 1995: 503)

As we have seen, language use across social groups often involves categories that define themselves partly against those they see as different, such as jocks and burnouts in Michigan and locals and returnees in Hong Kong. Sociocultural linguistic research has also been conducted on other contrasting communities of practice around the world. For example, Qing Zhang has documented local versus cosmopolitan styles of Mandarin among Beijing professionals in the 1990s as China shifted toward a global market economy. State employees tended to use local phonological variants, including adding a rhotic quality to syllable-final vowels, a feature that was ideologically associated with being smooth and streetwise. Meanwhile, employees of transnational corporations used full tones in unstressed syllables, a characteristic of the Hong Kong and Taiwan dialects of Mandarin but not of Beijing Mandarin; this feature was viewed by locals as a "yuppie" way of speaking. And in his study of the speech of two oppositional groups of young working-class men of Castilian descent in Barcelona, Joan Pujolar found that Castilian was used to index a traditionally masculine identity, while Catalan was used to index a politically progressive identity that challenges gender norms. In all of these studies, groups that may seem quite similar based on social categories such as age, gender, and social class turn out to be very different both in their social identities and in their language use. Indeed, it is largely through their language use that they are able to differentiate themselves from one another.

However, oppositional pairs like those discussed above are by no means the only groups in their communities, and every community contains multiple social groupings. Moreover, individuals typically claim membership in more than one group, sometimes simultaneously and sometimes changing their affiliations over time (see Sidebar 11.7).

Linguistic researchers of communities of practice do not simply focus on language use. They also examine such issues as how speakers dress, what they do for fun, their goals and attitudes, and their orientation to larger social and cultural forms, such as school or western culture. In short, they look broadly at the locally available categories of **style**, or socially distinctive ways of doing things. ***Communities of practice are often characterized by distinctive styles***. Although clothing, activities, beliefs, and the like are all important dimensions of style, language is an especially valuable resource for aligning oneself with some social groups and distinguishing oneself from others. Every aspect of the way we talk indexes information about our identities. At the same time, this information is not accessible to everyone. The social meaning of our style often requires insider knowledge – such as residence in a local community or attendance at a particular high school – in order to be correctly recognized and interpreted.

The issue of interpretation is especially important given the multiple social meanings that a linguistic form can index.

### 11.3.3   Roles, stances, and personas

Besides the demographic categories and communities of practice to which we belong, we also position ourselves within specific interactions in a number of other ways, all of which fundamentally rely on language. To begin with, depending on the situation and the other participants, we enact a variety of social and cultural roles, such as teacher, sister, or best friend. The **relational roles** we perform imply a certain set of social rights, obligations, relationships, and areas of expertise that influence the way we speak in particular contexts. Moreover, throughout social interaction we rapidly take up and abandon temporary roles such as narrator, joke teller, or question answerer. These **interactional roles** allow us to engage in specific linguistic activities within social interaction. In addition, each time we speak we also position ourselves toward what we are saying and toward our interlocutors. Such positionings, or **stances**, linguistically enact our attitude at any given moment. Finally, through the way we enact all of these categories, community memberships, roles, and stances we create our own **personas** (or personae). Personas are social types associated with specific personal attributes

**TABLE 11.1** Frequency of falsetto occurrence in Heath's speech across situations (adapted from Podesva 2007: 486)

|  | Barbecue | Phone | Patient |
|---|---|---|---|
| Number of falsetto utterances | 35 | 10 | 15 |
| Total number of utterances | 386 | 260 | 403 |
| Percent falsetto utterances | 9.07 | 3.85 | 3.72 |

and/or broader social groups. For example, we may present ourselves as having attributes such as "bubbly," "aggressive," or "laid-back," and these may be associated with social groups like "cheerleader," "lawyer," or "hippie," which in turn may be tied to locally meaningful styles or broader social categories of race, gender, social class, and the like. Speakers can index many different kinds of identity all at the same time: demographic categories, styles based in local communities of practice, relational social and cultural roles, interactional roles, stances, and personas. This wide range of identity positions necessarily requires speakers to use an equally wide range of linguistic (as well as non-linguistic) resources to index themselves as particular kinds of people in a given situation.

This point is illustrated in a case study of the speech of a gay European American medical student, Heath, conducted by Robert Podesva. Podesva measured Heath's use of a falsetto (i.e., extremely high-pitched) voice quality for expressive purposes in three different social contexts: with his friends at a barbecue, on the telephone with his father, and during a medical consultation with an elderly patient. The results showed that Heath's speech to his friends involved a falsetto voice that was not only more frequent than in other contexts (see Table 11.1), but also of longer duration and of broader pitch variability, and applied to a wider variety of utterance types. Podesva argues that Heath uses falsetto to create a flamboyant "diva" persona but that he does so not simply because he is gay – after all, many gay men do not adopt this sort of persona, and Heath himself does not always do so. Rather, the use of falsetto to construct a diva persona is specific to a particular speaker in a particular context. Identity, then, is not simply a static category but an ever-changing image that we produce through language and other practices. (Another case study – a classic in the field – is discussed in Textbox 11.4.)

*All of the categories, styles, roles, stances, and personas we inhabit, whether temporary or more durable, together constitute our* **identities***, because they comprise the variety of ways that we position ourselves and are positioned by others within the social world.* Thus, although identity is often thought of as a psychological phenomenon, it is more fundamentally a social and interactional process, constructed and negotiated every time we engage with others, based on our own and others' language ideologies. A speaker may say *runnin'* instead of

## TEXTBOX 11.4 **LANGUAGE AND IDENTITY ON A CHANGING ISLAND**

One of the earliest and most influential studies of language and identity was conducted by the pioneering linguist William Labov in the early 1960s for his Master's thesis – not all linguistics graduate students have such a huge impact on the field! Labov studied the speech of local residents on Martha's Vineyard, a small island off the coast of Massachusetts that has been an elite tourist destination for many years. In the distinctive island dialect, words with the /aɪ/ diphthong were pronounced as [ʌɪ] (recall that a similar pronunciation was part of a sound change involving a very different community of practice in the Detroit area, as discussed above). Labov found that in general this pronunciation was disappearing because of the influx of outsiders. But he also discovered that some islanders, especially fishermen, were reversing this trend, using the distinctive island pronunciation at high rates in spite of the social changes on the island. One young man, himself the son of a lobsterman, had grown up on the island and had gone to college on the mainland, but decided to return to Martha's Vineyard to make a living. As his mother told the researcher, "You know, E. didn't always speak that way ... it's only since he came back from college. I guess he wanted to be more like the men on the docks ..." (Labov 1963: 300).

Forty years later, Renée Blake and Meredith Josey returned to Martha's Vineyard to see whether the linguistic trends that had been identified earlier were still under way. They found that the island economy had been transformed into a more heavily service-oriented economy, and the fishing industry was less closely tied to a local island identity. As a result, fishermen no longer led the way in the use of the distinctive pronunciation of /aɪ/, and the islanders are now participating in a large-scale change in the vowel system taking place in many parts of North America.

*running* in order to sound casual but instead be perceived as uneducated; she may swear to convey strong feeling and instead be perceived as unladylike; he may code-switch in order to show solidarity with other bilinguals and instead be perceived as unable to speak either language well. Sociocultural linguistics gives us valuable resources for studying identity as a social accomplishment by offering a wealth of analytic concepts and tools for closely examining language as perhaps the most basic and pervasive way that we display identity.

### CHAPTER SUMMARY

Language is more than a tool for communicating information or accomplishing interactional goals; it is also a resource for creating social meaning, a marker of who we are and how we want to be seen by others. In this chapter, we have seen that the principle of linguistic diversity and the principle of language variation together make possible the numerous social functions that language plays in our lives. Linguistic resources are of many kinds: individual languages and dialects such as Cantonese or African American English; the combination of multiple varieties through practices like diglossia, code-switching, and style shifting; and the use of specific phonological, grammatical, and lexical features, such as raised /aɪ/, habitual *be*, or a slang term like *all-nighter*. All of these may be used to position the speaker as a particular kind of person in a particular social context. Likewise, language may be used to display social identities at multiple levels, from brief interactional stances and roles to more enduring personas and categories. However, speakers are not entirely free to create whatever identity they want using whatever kind of language they want. They are constrained by their own linguistic repertoires, as well as by language ideologies that may lead others to interpret their language use negatively. At the same time, language ideologies are not entirely rigid. As speakers, we can adopt new linguistic varieties or features or work to establish new social meanings for existing elements of our repertoires. In so doing, we create new ways of speaking and new ways of positioning ourselves and others within our social worlds.

## SUGGESTIONS FOR FURTHER READING

**Finegan, Edward and John R. Rickford** (eds.). 2004. *Language in the USA: Themes for the twenty-first century*. Cambridge University Press.

A collection of chapters by leading sociocultural linguists introducing a wide variety of topics concerning language and society; though focused on the US context, the material has implications for many other societies as well.

**Holmes, Janet**. 2013. *An introduction to sociolinguistics*, 4th edn. Harlow: Pearson.

An engaging introductory textbook with a broad international and interdisciplinary perspective.

**Lippi-Green, Rosina**. 2012. *English with an accent: Language, ideology, and discrimination in the United States*, 2nd edn. New York: Routledge.

The second edition of a classic book, with an accessible discussion of how language ideologies are institutionally reproduced in the media, the workplace, and the educational system.

**Llamas, Carmen and Dominic Watt** (eds.) 2010. *Language and identities*. Edinburgh University Press.

A collection of current sociocultural linguistic theory and research on language and identity around the world.

## EXERCISES

1. Classify the following pairs as *different languages*, as *different dialects of the same language*, or as *the same dialect*. Why might non-linguists and linguists come up with different answers in some cases? (You may need to do some research to reach a decision in some cases; the *Ethnologue* is a useful starting point: www.ethnologue.com.)
   a. Castilian and Mexican Spanish
   b. Dutch and Pennsylvania Dutch
   c. Dutch and Flemish
   d. Farsi and Persian
   e. Gullah and Geechee

f. Haitian Creole and French
g. Hindi and Urdu
h. Taiwanese and Mandarin
i. Venetian and Italian
j. Yiddish and German

2. The following examples are taken (and in some cases slightly adapted) from an interview with African American hip hop artist Pharoahe Monch, conducted by H. Samy Alim (2006). Note: In most of this interview, Pharoahe speaks Standard English. Quotation marks below indicate that he is quoting another speaker or himself.

a. Decide whether each of the boldfaced items is slang or an AAE grammatical form. For each slang term, provide your best guess as to the meaning of the term. For each grammatical form, provide the label and give its Standard English equivalent. (You may find it helpful to consult a slang dictionary in your campus library, but bear in mind that online sources such as *Urban Dictionary* often provide unreliable information.)

   i. "When **my album come**, I'm comin better than that!"
   ii. "I wonder if **people gonna view** the same manifestation the way I did when I conceived it?"
   iii. I can't put that full-fledged on my album because that's not me. I would be **frontin** and it would hurt me to **front** to people.
   iv. I have **mad** anxieties.
   v. People around me **be** like, "Yo, man, why you stressin?!"
   vi. My best friends, we **kick it** and it's like therapy for me.
   vii. I appreciate all of that in a MC, you know. . . . Talib is like one of the **illest**.
   viii. If you listen to his albums and **you a MC** and you listen to his lyrics, it kinda makes you be like, "Yo, let me bring some relevance to what I'm saying."
   ix. "Damn! Miles was in the same room with Coltrane and **they was composing** songs together."
   x. (quoting what he hopes others will say about him) "That's one of the main reasons why I like Pharoahe as an MC. Aside from the fact that a lot of the shit that he do is just **tight**!"

b. Given that Pharoahe Monch primarily uses Standard English in the interview, what is the overall function of the use of AAE in the above examples?

3. The following passage is taken from an interview that Carmen Fought (2003: 159) conducted with a 45-year-old bilingual Mexican American man.

a. Classify the type of each code-switch from English to Spanish in the data. (Spanish portions are underlined in the passage.)

   **Original:** But I am the only one that came out *músico*. My- all my brothers were into sports, basketball, baseball, *y todo*, and I couldn't do that. *No me gustaban*. I could, you know, play *y todo, pero a mí me gustaba más la guitarra*.

   **Translation:** But I am the only one that came out a musician. My- all my brothers were into sports, basketball, baseball, and everything, and I couldn't do that. I didn't like them. I could, you know, play and everything, but I liked the guitar more.

   - músico
   - y todo
   - No me gustaban
   - y todo, pero a mí me gustaba más la guitarra

b. Based on the above excerpt, how would you argue against the language ideology that code-switching indicates that the speaker is not fluent in either language?

4. The following data are adapted from unpublished research by Rachel Cranfill and Mary Bucholtz on gender and rising intonation. In the following excerpt, a female undergraduate student, Jennifer, is explaining to a male student, Nathan, how to solve a problem in their calculus homework. (Question marks indicate rising intonation.)

| 1 | Jennifer: | *So you find the gradient of the line?* |
|---|-----------|------------------------------------------|
| 2 | Nathan: | *Uh huh.* |
| 3 | Jennifer: | *And that's,* |
| 4 | | *the vector that you need,* |
| 5 | | *or like the direction?* |
| 6 | Nathan: | *Uh huh.* |
| 7 | Jennifer: | *The directional vector that you need,* |
| 8 | | *to be going from the point to the line?* |
| 9 | Nathan: | *Right.* |

a. What function does rising intonation (marked with a question mark in the transcript) serve in this excerpt?

b. Do the data support Lakoff's claim that rising intonation in "women's language" is an indication of powerlessness?

5. Consider each of the following linguistic features.

a. The choice of an adverbial intensifier (i.e., a word that strengthens the meaning of an adjective) in a sentence like "He's _____ nice."
   - quite
   - really
   - so
   - super
   - totally
   - very

b. The pronunciation of intervocalic /t/ in words like *better*, *pretty*, and *seated* as:
   - [t]
   - [ɾ]
   - [ʔ]

i. List as many aspects of identity as you can that might be associated with each variant. Be sure to consider demographic categories, communities of practice, social and cultural roles, interactional roles, stances, and personas.

ii. Do some forms have more associations for you than others? What language ideologies may underlie some of the associations for a particular form?

iii. Discuss your answers with another student. Do you both agree on the social associations for each form? Do any of the associations seem to be related to one another in some way?

# 12 Language change: the dynamicity of linguistic systems

**KEY TERMS**
- Synchrony and diachrony
- Sound change
- The Great Vowel Shift
- Grammaticalization
- Renewal
- Analogy
- Cognates
- Language families
- Proto-languages
- The Comparative Method
- Linguistic paleontology

## CHAPTER PREVIEW

In previous chapters, we have talked about languages of the world and how they have different ways of expressing similar meanings. We have also examined various specific aspects of linguistic structure, including phonology, morphology, and syntax. But how did these structures within each language come to be? And how do languages come to be so different from each other?

This chapter describes how languages evolve over time: how sounds can shift, how sound systems can be restructured, and how grammar develops. It then discusses **genetic relationships** among languages and how they can be detected. It closes with a glimpse of what reconstructed languages can tell us about their speakers. An important aspect of language change is the fact that it is not arbitrary; it is the result of acts of speakers, as they learn their languages, use them, repair them, and extend them to use in new situations and for new purposes. The investigation of language change can tell us much about why languages are as they are, with all of their seeming irregularities. It can also provide us with a view of the human mind at work, recognizing patterns, and extending them to new situations and uses.

## LIST OF AIMS

After reading this chapter, students should be able to:

- **name and briefly describe some common kinds of sound changes;**
- **give examples of sound changes that have occurred in the development of English;**

- **explain why English spelling can be difficult to learn;**
- **write rules describing simple sound changes;**
- **name and describe processes involved in grammaticalization;**
- **define the term "language family" and name several known families;**
- **apply the steps of the comparative method to a data set, reconstructing proto-forms and stating sound changes.**

## 12.1 Language change

Earlier chapters have shown that languages are tightly patterned, in ways speakers rarely imagine. Because languages seem to operate so smoothly, we might assume they are inert; nothing could be further from the truth. ***All living languages are dynamic, constantly being reshaped by their speakers.*** Most of these adjustments are so gradual that they go unnoticed. Yet when we look carefully at the kinds of changes that occur in language, we can catch glimpses of the human mind at its most creative.

Apart from occasional new technical terms or slang expressions, we are rarely aware of language change. Can you identify the language below? Can you understand it?

> *Sigemunde gesprong æfter dēaðdæge dōm unlytel,*
> *syððan wīges heard wyrm ācwealde, hordes hyrde.*

It is English, but English at an earlier stage of development. This Old English passage is from *Beowulf*, a manuscript written well over a thousand years ago.

(1)  *Beowulf 884–887*

| *sigemunde* | *gesprong* | *æfter* | *dēaðdæge* | *dōm* | *unlytel* |
|---|---|---|---|---|---|
| to.Sigmund | has arisen | after | death.day | glory | great |

'To Sigmund sprang forth great glory after his death,

| *syððan* | *wiges* | *heard* | *wyrm* | *ācwealde* | *hordes* | *hyrde* |
|---|---|---|---|---|---|---|
| Since | of.fight | brave | serpent | killed.off | of.treasure | guardian |

because in brave warfare, he killed the dragon, guardian of the treasure.'

Can you detect any similarities between the language in this passage and modern English? Some of the words are immediately familiar: *æfter* 'after,' *dēað* 'death,' and *dæg* 'day.' Some become identifiable after some consideration. *Unlytel* is 'un-little' or 'not small'; *heard* is the ancestor of modern 'hardy,' *hord* of modern *hoard*, and *hyrde* of modern *herd*, as in *shepherd*. But there are certainly differences between the English of then and now. These differences fall under several types:

- Phonological: The noun *dæg* 'day' has a *g* at the end. The vowel in *heard* is not the same as that of modern *hardy*.
- Morphological: The verb *ge-sprong* has a prefix *ge-*, an old marker of past participles (adjectival forms of verbs). Many of the nouns have case suffixes, which identify their

roles in the sentence. The nouns *wīg* 'fight' and *hord* 'treasure,' for example, end in *-es*, the genitive marker meaning 'of.' The name *Sigemund-e* ends in the dative marker *-e* meaning 'to.' The compound *dēaðdæg-e* 'death day' also ends in the dative *-e*, which identifies it as the object of the preposition 'after.'

- Syntactic: The verb 'sprang' occurs in second position in the first clause, before its subject 'great glory.' This word order is occasionally found in stylized constructions today, but it is rare in everyday conversation. In the second clause, the object 'dragon' occurs before the verb 'killed,' which is not a possible order today. Modern English word order is strongly SVO.
- Lexical: Some of the vocabulary has been replaced by other words in modern English, such as *wīg* 'fight, warfare.'
- Semantic: The meanings of a number of the words have changed. *Dōm* 'glory' has developed into modern *doom*; *wyrm* 'serpent, dragon' into modern *worm*; *cweal-de* 'kill-ed' into modern *quell-ed*.

## 12.2    Sounds

Chapter 3 described ways that speakers alter their pronunciation of sounds. These alternations can result in allophones, discussed in Chapter 3. Over time, the same kinds of processes can result in significant sound change.

### 12.2.1    Here and there: sound change

English spelling is notorious for being difficult to learn. It seems to fit the language badly. There is a reason for this. Old English was written in a version of the Roman alphabet introduced by Irish missionaries. Words were spelled according to their pronunciation at the time, with letters representing their Latin values. ***As sounds changed over the course of the development of English, spelling practices changed too, but not as quickly as pronunciation***. Words now spelled with final *e*, such as *her(e)* and *ther(e)*, were once pronounced with a full final vowel. As time went by, this unstressed *e* underwent **lenition** (weakening). By Chaucer's time in the late fourteenth century, it had become reduced to schwa [ə]. Further lenition resulted in complete **loss**.

Sound changes can be described with rules much like those used in phonology. The term **synchrony** is used to refer to language structures at a single point in time. Synchronic rules, such as those discussed in Chapter 3, are operative at a specific moment, typically the present. The term **diachrony** is used to refer to comparisons of two or more points in time. A **diachronic rule** describes a change in the system between one time and another. We could describe the lenition of the vowel *e* to schwa with a diachronic rule like the one below:

\*e > ə    (The vowel *e* became schwa.)

The asterisk * marks a sound that we infer existed at an earlier time; we have not actually heard it, but we hypothesize what it might have been, in this case on the basis of early documents. Where synchronic phonological rules contain an arrow ➜, diachronic rules usually have the symbol >, which can be read as 'became.' (See Sidebar 12.1 for a note on the differences between rule-writing in historical linguistics and phonology.)

The lenition of *e* to schwa that we saw in *here* and *there* did not occur everywhere in the language. It happened only at the ends of words: it was what is called a **conditioned sound change**. We can specify the context in which it occurred (only at the ends of words), in the same way as in a synchronic phonological rule. We add a slash / to announce that the environment for the change is coming up. We use an underline (a blank) __ to stand for the position of the sound in question. We then specify what sounds occur before it to the left of the blank, and what sounds occur after it to the right. In this case, it does not matter what occurred before the *e*, so nothing appears on the left. The crucial context is what occurred after the *e*, namely a word boundary. This is indicated by the symbol #.

*e > ə / __ #    (The vowel *e* became schwa at the ends of words.)

The weakening or leniting of word-final *e* did not stop at schwa. It continued over time until there was no vowel left at all. We can add this fact to our rule, with a zero:

*e > ə > Ø / __ #    (The vowel *e* became schwa and was then lost at the ends of words.)

There are numerous other examples of lenition that took place during the development from Old English to Modern English. As we saw in (1), the noun 'day' was spelled *dæg*. The final *g* was pronounced at the time, but it later underwent **lenition** to a velar fricative, then was further weakened to just a glide. Sidebar 12.2 provides another example of the lenition of a velar fricative, still reflected in the English spelling system.

### 12.2.2  Trees and leaves: change in the system

***Sound change can have more profound effects; it can result in the remodeling of the sound system.*** The most common way to form a plural in present-day English is to add the suffix *-s* to the basic form of the noun: *tree/tree-s, flower/flower-s*. But not all words follow this pattern. Consider the plurals of *leaf, wife,* and *shelf: leaf/leave-s, wife/*

**SIDEBAR 12.3**

ENGLISH SPELLING

A number of English words begin with the letters *kn*, such as *knee, knight, knit, knead, knave, knife, knock, knot, know,* and *knuckle.* What could explain these spellings? Could you summarize the reason with a diachronic rule? Think about it and compare your answer with that found in Sidebar 12.5.

**SIDEBAR 12.4**

IRREGULARITIES

In English we have singular/plural pairs *knife/knives,* and *self/selves.* Can you imagine why we have *chef/chefs* and not *chef/cheves*? Compare your answer with that found in Sidebar 12.6.

**SIDEBAR 12.5**

ENGLISH PRONUNCIATION

The spelling of English words such as *knee, knight,* and *knit* reflects an earlier pronunciation of these words. They originally began with the consonant cluster /kn/. Over time, the /k/ was lost and the initial cluster was simplified to /n/. This /k/ is still pronounced in other Germanic languages, for example German *Knie* /kni:/, 'knee.'

A diachronic rule for this could be expressed:

*k > ø / # __ n

*wive-s,* and *shelf/shelve-s.* The noun roots change shape: /li:f̠ ~ li:v̠-/, /waif̠ ~ waiv̠-/, /ʃɛlf̠ ~ ʃɛlv̠-/.

As seen in Chapter 3, phonemes may have alternate pronunciations, called allophones. A common process that produces allophones is **assimilation**, whereby a sound comes to be more like its neighbors. Old English originally had just one series of fricative phonemes: /f/, /θ/, /s/, /ʃ/, and /x/. Each of these fricatives had allophones. When a fricative occurred between voiced sounds, it was automatically voiced too. We could write a synchronic phonological rule to describe the allophony at that time. Fricatives assimilated to their neighbors in voicing.

[fricative] → [+voice] / [+voice] __ [+voice]

The voicing was predictable: the fricative [v], for example, occurred only inside of words, between voiced sounds, while [f] occurred everywhere else, that is, at the beginnings of words, at the ends, or next to a voiceless sound. This is a familiar pattern of **complementary distribution**, discussed in Chapter 3.

With the Norman invasion in 1066, French speakers began to arrive in England in significant numbers. As time went by, the influence of their language on English became increasingly apparent. Many French words were adopted into English. The adverb *very,* for example, came into English from the Old French *verrai* (modern French *vrai* 'true'). The ancestors of the present-day English words *veal, veil, venerable, vengeance, venison, venom, vent, vermin, vessel, villain, vine, voyage,* and many more were borrowed from French. The influx of so many words beginning with *v* upset the old pattern of complementary distribution. There were now minimal pairs such as *fine* and *vine*. Voicing was no longer predictable. The result was a change in the phonological system: the addition of a new phoneme /v/. ***Sounds that were originally allophones became separate phonemes***.

### 12.2.3 The moon and the goose: the Great Vowel Shift

Have you ever wondered why the letter *o* is pronounced [o] in words like *so,* but [u] when it is doubled, as in *moon* and *goose*? Vowels are some of the most puzzling aspects of the English spelling system.

As mentioned earlier, when the Roman alphabet was adopted for the spelling of Old English, the vowel letters were used to represent approximately the same sounds as in Latin. Like Latin, Old English had both long and short vowels: long vowels simply lasted longer than short ones, as in *moon* and *keep*. At a certain point, English speakers began to shorten long vowels in certain contexts, a conditioned sound change. One of these contexts was before consonant clusters, as in *monthly* and *kept*. Then, beginning around 1400, vowel sounds began to shift. Long vowels began to rise. Long low vowels (ā, ɔ̄) were pronounced as mid (æ, ō). (English vowel length is traditionally written with a macron, or a bar, over the vowel.) Mid vowels (ē, ō) were pronounced as high (ī, ū). The highest long vowels (ī, ū), which could not rise any higher, broke into diphthongs (əi, əu). These changes, which took place gradually over a period of three centuries, are referred to collectively as the **Great Vowel Shift**. Stages in the process can be seen in Table 12.1.

Because of these shifts, ***the pronunciation of vowels in Modern English is now very different from that in Old English, when the spelling system originated***. This history explains some of the puzzles of modern spelling. The words *moon* and *goose* are spelled with *oo* because they were once pronounced with long *o*. The words *beet* and *beat* are spelled differently because they were once pronounced differently: there was a **merger**. The two vowels ī and ē merged by the time of Wordsworth to ī. The result was a change in the system, from seven long vowels (including diphthongs) to six, and a reduction in the number of long vowels that were not diphthongs.

**TABLE 12.1** *The Great Vowel Shift* (Anttila 1972: 65)

|  | Chaucer (1343–1400) |  |  | Shakespeare (1564–1616) | Wordsworth (1770–1850) | Modern English (present) |
|---|---|---|---|---|---|---|
| *bite* | ī | | *bite* | əi | ai | ai |
| *bete* | ē | | *beet* | ī | ī | ī |
| *bete* | æ | | *beat* | ē | ī | ī |
| *name* | ā | | *name* | æ | ē | ē |
| *foal* | ɔ̄ | | *foal* | ō | ō | ou |
| *fol* | ō | | *fool* | ū | ū | ū |
| *foul* | ū | | *foul* | əu | au | au |

**SIDEBAR 12.7**
ORTHOGRAPHY AND THE GREAT
VOWEL SHIFT
In Table 12.1, the columns for Chaucer and
Shakespeare show both the spelling (on the
left) and the phonetic pronunciation of the
first vowel (on the right). English
orthography changed from the time of
Chaucer to that of Shakespeare, but it has
changed little since then, even though
pronunciation has continued to shift.

The Great Vowel Shift also explains what might seem like senseless allomorphy, such as that of the noun roots in _moon/mon-thly_ and _goose/gos-ling_. The vowels in _moon_ and _goose_ were long, as we can still see from their spelling. During the Great Vowel Shift, they rose from [o:] to [u:]. The vowels in _month_ and _gosling_, on the other hand, had been shortened, because they occurred before consonant clusters. They did not participate in the shift.

Changes in sounds and sound systems are constantly occurring in languages all over the world (see Sidebar 12.7). We cannot predict exactly which changes will occur at a particular time, but we do know about the kinds of changes that tend to occur under particular circumstances. Some of the more common types of sound change are listed in Textbox 12.1.

---

## TEXTBOX 12.1 **SOME COMMON SOUND CHANGES**

Certain types of sound changes occur more often than others, usually because they result in less effort for speakers. Some of the more common types are below.

### 1. Lenition
Speakers often try to put as little energy into pronunciation as possible. Some common kinds of lenition, or weakening, are shifts of voiceless stops to voiced ones (p > b, t > d, k > g), stops to fricatives (p > f, t > s, k > x), oral fricatives to h (f > h, s > h, š > h, x > h), voiced obstruents to glides (b > w, v > w, g > j, dʒ > j), and shifts of vowels toward the center (i > ə, e > ə, a > ə). We saw an example of lenition in the shift of Old English _dæg_ to Modern English _day_.

### 2. Loss
Extreme weakening ultimately results in complete loss of a sound. We saw loss of the velar stop [k] from English words like _knee_ and _knife_, and loss of the velar fricative [x] from English words like _night_ and _right_. The lenition and loss of final [e] is rampant, as in _here_ and _there_.

### 3. Consonant addition: excrescence
Consonants are sometimes added sporadically. Proto-Indo-European *swesr- developed into Proto-Germanic *swestr, with an added t, the ancestor of Modern English

sister. Old English þunrian changed into þundrian, 'thunder,' with an added d. (Compare German Donner.) Such excrescent consonants usually result from tiny shifts in the timing of articulatory movements. Moving from the nasal stop n to the oral continuant r of þunrian, speakers closed off the nasal passage before opening up the mouth, resulting in the oral stop d.

### 4. Vowel addition: prothesis and epenthesis
Vowels are sometimes inserted to break up consonant clusters. Addition at the beginning of a word is termed **prothesis**. A well-known example is the shift of Latin _spiritus_ to Spanish _espiritu_ 'spirit.' Addition within a word is termed **epenthesis**, as in the pronunciation of English _athlete_ as _athalete_.

### 5. Fusion
Two sounds sometimes merge into one. We saw an example of vowel fusion in the shift from Old English _dēað_ to modern _death_, now pronounced [dɛθ].

### 6. Breaking
One vowel sound may separate into two. We saw breaking in the long high vowels affected by the Great Vowel Shift. An example is the vowel of English _foul_, pronounced [u:] in Chaucer's time but [au] today.

---

**TEXTBOX 12.1** (*cont.*)

**7. Assimilation**

Sounds often become more like those around them. The final consonant in English *leaf*, for example, became voiced when it was surrounded on both sides by other voiced sounds, as in *leaves*. This was assimilation in just one feature, voicing. The negative prefix *in-*, as in *in-edible* or *in-tangible*, takes on the point of articulation of a following consonant: *im-possible* [im-p], *in-complete* [iŋ-k]. It shows complete assimilation before a lliquid: *il-legal*, *ir-regular*.

**8. Palatalization**

A very common kind of assimilation is palatalization. Here a consonant takes on the point of articulation of a

following front vowel or glide, becoming palatal. When a stop is palatalized, it often becomes an affricate. Between the time of Proto West Germanic and that of Old English, *\*k* shifted to the affricate *č* before front vowels *i, e*, and the glide *j*. We can hear this in English *church* (Old English *cirice*). Its German cognate *Kirke* still retains the original velar stops *k*.

Numerous other kinds of sound shifts occur as well, some of them gradual and regular, such as the vowel raising of the Great Vowel Shift, and others sudden and sporadic, such as the pronunciation in some dialects of the verb *ask* as *aks*, a kind of change known as **metathesis**.

---

## 12.3 Grammar

It might be tempting to think that since all languages have grammar, often with fairly rigid rules, the grammar we see now has been there from the beginning. ***But like sounds, grammar is constantly evolving***.

### 12.3.1 Grammaticalization processes

Grammatical meanings are typically expressed in languages with small words (e.g., articles, prepositions, auxiliaries, etc.), clitics (e.g., English genitive *'s*, future *'ll*, and negative *n't*), and affixes (prefixes, suffixes, infixes, circumfixes). Some examples of affixes discussed in other chapters are given in (2).

(2)  Some grammatical affixes

| | | | | |
|---|---|---|---|---|
| Manange | *a-khʌ²²* | 'not come' | *a-* | NEG prefix 'not' |
| Goemai | *mòe-jàpnúún* | 'siblings' | *mòe-* | PL prefix '-s' |
| Karo | *o-ya'wan* | 'I left' | *o-* | PST prefix |
| Seneca | *sa-:ayö'* | 'he came back' | [*sa-*] | REP prefix 'again' |
| Chontal | *sago-duy* | 'eating' | *-day* | DUR suffix '-ing' |
| Ilocano | *gilin-an* | 'grinder' | *-an* | NMLZ suffix '-er' |

***The grammatical morphemes that arise in languages are not random. They grow out of what speakers choose to say most often on an everyday basis***. Most grammatical morphemes begin life as full words, usually with relatively general meanings. In some cases, these origins can still be detected. The English grammatical morphemes *beside* and *besides*, for example, developed from Old English phrases *be si:dan* and *be sides* 'by the side' (*OED* 818). The word *be* is the ancestor of our modern preposition *by*. The word *si:dan* is the Old English noun *side*, with the dative case ending (required by the preposition *be*). The word *si:des* is the same noun with the genitive case. Both originally only had a spatial meaning: 'by the side of, near.' The first can still be used that way: *beside the tree*. The second is now used only with more a abstract meaning: 'in addition, moreover.' ***The development of lexical forms to grammatical forms*** (e.g., prepositional phrases to prepositions and adverbs), ***and from grammatical to even more grammatical forms*** (e.g., the abstract adverb *besides*) ***is termed*** **grammaticalization**.

Grammaticalization does not affect single words in isolation. It normally applies to words in particular constructions. As speakers use a certain sequence of words with increasing frequency, it can become automated and processed as a unit. It is a bit like driving to a friend's house in an unfamiliar area. The first time you go, you might think consciously about each stage of the journey: turning off the highway here, continuing for one mile, veering left, passing the fire station, etc. After several visits, you no longer focus on the individual steps; you simply drive to visit your friend. A similar cognitive process occurs with frequent phrases or constructions. Rather than focusing on each word; speakers simply select the whole construction as a chunk. ***Grammar is the product of the*** **cognitive routinization** *of frequently recurring patterns of expression*.

Constructions undergoing grammaticalization are typically extended to more and more contexts. As a result, their meanings tend to become more general and more abstract. We saw an example of such **abstraction** in the shift of the meaning of *besides* from physical location to 'moreover.' (See Sidebar 12.8 for another such example.) In most languages, full lexical items such as nouns and verbs occur with certain inflectional morphemes, such as tense or plural markers. These markers typically disappear during grammaticalization, a process termed **decategorialization**. We can see this in the development of English auxiliaries, which no longer carry person agreement. We can say *She sing-s*, but not *She can-s sing*. Finally, words undergoing grammaticalization within a particular construction tend to lose their individual salience, typically losing their stress and ultimately showing further **phonological erosion**. This, too, we can see in the case of English auxiliaries, such as the erosion of *will* to *'ll*, as in *I'll*.

**SIDEBAR 12.8**

GRAMMATICALIZATION PATHWAYS

Certain types of grammatical developments occur again and again in the world's languages. One common **grammaticalization pathway** is the development of body-part nouns into adpositions. The origins of prepositions in Dhaasanac (a Cushitic language of Ethiopia and Kenya), for example, are still clear: *ʔafu* 'in front of' comes from the noun for 'mouth,' *Bál* 'beside' from 'chest,' *sugu* 'behind' from 'back,' *géere* 'inside' from 'belly' (Tosco 2001, cited in Heine 2010).

Prefixes and suffixes usually develop through similar processes. We can still perceive the origin of some. The English suffix *-ful* in *playful*, *masterful*, and *useful* creates adjectives. In measure terms like *spoonful, cupful*, and *armful*, it creates nouns. The source of the suffix is still obvious: it developed from the adjective *full*, which survives in present-day English. When a word undergoes grammaticalization, the original form may continue in the language with its function. Both the adjective *full* and the suffix *-ful* already existed in Old English. The two have survived alongside each other for over a thousand years.

We can observe processes of grammaticalization occurring in English as we speak. One of the most discussed examples is /aimnə/ (see, e.g., Hopper and Traugott 2004: 2–4). Do you recognize it? Try pronouncing it with a verb: /aimnə it/. This is *I am going to*, as in *I am going to eat*. This construction apparently developed out of constructions like *I am going to see my father*. The original meaning involved a change in physical location for a purpose. A locative adverb could be included: *I am going [to town] to see my father*. The intended action would occur in the future, following the change in location indicated by the motion verb *go*. The current meaning of the construction is simply future tense. This shift in meaning from purpose to futurity is a kind of **metonymic process**, or a change resulting from the frequent association of two elements in the same speech situation. If someone acts in order to bring about some event (*I am going [in order] to see my father*), that event will normally take place in the future (seeing my father). The original construction thus involves both purpose and futurity. Over time, the futurity is reinterpreted as the primary meaning.

Grammaticalization can also have a syntactic side. At a certain point, speakers apparently reinterpreted the syntactic structure of the construction *be going to* from a main clause *I am going* plus a purposive subordinate clause *to see my father* (*I am going [to see my father]*), to a sentence with a future auxiliary phrase *be going to*: *I am going to [see my father]*. This process is called **syntactic reanalysis**. Speakers came to conceive of the syntactic structure in a new way. Such a shift is not immediately obvious. It becomes apparent only when these speakers create new sentences that are incompatible with the old analysis. When one says *I am going to like it*, it is unlikely that motion is intended. The fact that syntactic reanalysis has occurred is confirmed by sentences with a second verb *go*, like *I am going to [go to town]*.

The *be going to* future construction also shows phonological effects that are typical of developing grammatical constructions: the words are losing their individual stress and undergoing further **phonological erosion**. We now hear *I'm going to eat, I'm gonna eat, Imna eat*, and even sometimes *Ima eat*. Note that such reduction does not occur with the original more concrete construction. No one would reduce *I'm going to town* to *I'm gonna town*.

Grammaticalization can involve **metaphorical extension**, or the use of an existing word or construction from one domain to express a concept in another. A frequent metaphorical change involves the extension of markers denoting spatial relations to use for the realm of time. An example can be seen in Cherokee, an Iroquoian language now spoken primarily in North Carolina and Oklahoma. Cherokee contains an ancient verb prefix *ta-* meaning 'hither, toward the speaker.'

(3)   Cherokee cislocative 'hither' (Montgomery-Anderson 2008: 328, 354)

*ta*-kinatansiinooheéli     'He's crawling <u>toward</u> us'
*ta*-àkiiluhcheéli          'He came <u>up to</u> us'

This prefix has now been extended to indicate future tense as well.

(4)   Cherokee future (Montgomery-Anderson 2008: 330–331)

   *ta-yuùhali*      'He <u>will</u> look for it'
   *ta-kintlecheéli*   'He <u>will</u> take revenge on us'

This development suggests a view of the future as something that is coming toward us.

As we look at the kinds of distinctions encoded in grammatical markers in languages around the world, we find that some meanings occur in language after language, such as negation, tense, plurality, and causation. ***The frequency of such grammatical morphemes points to certain universal human concerns, and to concepts that people tend to express often.*** At the same time, we sometimes find surprising grammatical markers, with very specific meanings. The suffixes in (5) are from Nuuchahnulth.

(5)   Nuuchahnulth suffixes (Stonham 2005)

   *-'aḥs*                          'in a vessel or container'
   [*tuw'-aḥs-iƛ*]                 'jumped <u>into the canoe</u>'
   [*tuw'-*]                        'jump'

   *-'ači-*                         'in the bay, gulf, inlet'
   [*ƛii-ʕači-ʔiš*]                'he was shooting <u>in the bay</u>'
   [*ƛii-*]                         'shoot'

   *-at*                            'out of the woods'
   [*wika-at'-as*]                 'she did not come <u>out of the woods</u>'
   [*wika-*                         'come'

   *-ačn'uɬ*                        'from snout to dorsal fin'
   [*hiɬweeʔin suč'iiɬ-ačn'uɬ*]    'it was five fathoms <u>from snout to dorsal fin</u>'
   [*suč'-iiɬ-*]                    'five-fathom'

Nuuchahnulth is a language of the Wakashan family, spoken on Vancouver Island, off the coast of British Columbia. The ocean has been a central part of the lives of Nuuchahnulth people for a long time. Examples like these show that the general processes by which grammatical morphemes and patterns develop are very similar across languages, but the specific distinctions they encode are shaped by the concerns of individual speech communities.

## 12.3.2   Renewal: restoring expressive power

The kinds of processes seen in the previous section are constantly at work in all languages. But if this is the case, shouldn't all languages have eroded to nothing or nearly nothing by now? In fact, there are other processes of change that help to maintain a certain equilibrium.

As frequently used expressions become routine, they can lose their expressive punch: their impact can fade. ***But a primary function of language is communication: speakers use language to convey their thoughts, often in creative ways.*** This creativity can restore freshness and power to the language. An illustration of such a cycle is the development of negative constructions in English. In Old English, negation was usually indicated with a negative particle *ne*: *ic ne wa:t* 'I don't know.' (The verb *wa:t* 'know' has since fallen out of English.) Negation is expressed frequently in all languages, so negative constructions are likely candidates for routinization and erosion over time. Old English *ne* was already a small word. But negation is crucial information. To highlight its importance, speakers often reinforced negative sentences with extra words, such as *wiht* 'something, anything' or *na:wiht* 'nothing, not anything.' Over time, the original negative marker *ne* eroded until it disappeared entirely. As a result, *na:wiht* was left as the only negative marker. With regular use, its emphatic force began to diminish as well. Its phonological form has also eroded to modern *not* and even *n't*.

(6)  English negation (Hock and Joseph 1996: 176)

|   |   |   |   |
|---|---|---|---|
| Stage I | *ic ne wa:t* | 'I don't know' (Old English) | basic |
|   | *ic ne wa:t (na:)wiht* | 'I don't know (no) thing' | emphatic |
| Stage II | *ic ne wa:t* | 'I don't know' | basic |
|   | *ic ne wa:t (na:)wiht* | 'I don't know at all' | emphatic |
| Stage III | *ic ne wa:t na:wiht* | 'I don't know' | basic |
| Stage IV | *I wot(e) not* | 'I don't know' (Shakespeare) | basic |

The cycle of **renewal** continues today. Modern speakers often reinforce what is now the ordinary negative *not* with phrases like *at all* or *a bit*.

## 12.3.3  Analogy: repairing patterns

The human capacity for pattern recognition is crucial for learning and using a language. Not only do humans search for patterns as they learn their mother tongue, and use them as models for creating new utterances; they often go further to repair what they perceive to be irregularities. Language can change both when children make novel hypotheses about the patterns behind the speech they hear, and when speakers attempt to regularize existing patterns.

We saw earlier that sound change can create irregularities in morphology. The most common way to form plurals in English is simply to add a plural suffix to the basic form of the noun: *tree/trees*. But because of various events in the history of English, some nouns change their form in the plural, as in *leaf/leaves* /li:f~li:v-/. Stop here for a moment and listen to how you pronounce the pair *house/houses*. For many English speakers, the noun *house* shows the same kind of allomorphy as *leaf/leaves*: it is /haus~hauz-/. The cause is the same. But for other speakers, in many cases younger ones, the irregularity has been repaired: they use the same form of the noun root in the singular and the plural: [haus̱~haus̱-]. Repairs like this are termed **analogical remodeling**. Speakers perceive a strong pattern among certain pairs of words (*tree/trees, flower/flowers, bird/birds, cloud/clouds*) and, by **analogy** to those pairs, remodel 'exceptions' to make them fit the pattern.

Whether the remodeling occurs when children are first acquiring their language or later in life, once it has occurred, the result simply becomes part of the language. Have you ever thought about the past tense of the verb *dive*? The original form is *dived*, but for many speakers, it is now *dove*. This might at first seem surprising: the most common past tense marker in English is *-ed*. But English also contains robust sets of what are called **strong verbs**. These verbs form their past tenses with a vowel change, a pattern called **ablaut**. One such pattern can be seen in *drive/drove* and *ride/rode*. The past tense of *dive* was apparently remodeled by analogy to such verbs.

In this section we have seen only a sample of the ways languages can evolve. Many more occur, some quite commonly, others more rarely. Most examples here have been taken from English, but all of these processes occur in languages around the world.

## 12.4  Language relationships

Example (7) shows the numerals 'one' through 'five' in a variety of languages. The numerals in (7) are written in standard orthographies or transliterations, rather than the IPA. You may recognize some of the languages. Take a moment to compare them. Can you organize the languages into groups, based on the forms of their numerals? Are there any languages that stand out as not belonging to any group?

**(7)** Numerals in twenty-seven languages

|    | 'one' | 'two' | 'three' | 'four' | 'five' |
|----|-------|-------|---------|--------|--------|
| a. | un | deux | trois | quatre | cinq |
| b. | uno | dos | tres | cuatro | cinco |
| c. | uno | due | tre | quattro | cinque |
| d. | um | dois | três | quatro | cinco |
| e. | un | doi | trei | patru | cinci |
| f. | eins | zwei | drei | vier | fünf |
| g. | een | twee | drie | vier | vijf |
| h. | ein | tsvei | drei | fier | finef |
| i. | en | två | tre | fyra | fem |
| j. | en | to | tre | fire | fem |
| k. | jeden | dwa | trzy | cztery | pięć |
| l. | adín | dva | tri | četírye | pyát |
| m. | jeden | dvě | tři | čtyri | pět |
| n. | eden | dva | tri | četiri | pet |
| o. | e'na | di'o | tri'a | te'sera | pen'te |
| p. | egy | kettő | három | négy | öt |

| q. yksi   | kaksi    | kolme     | neljä   | viisi      |
|-----------|----------|-----------|---------|------------|
| r. bir    | iki      | üç        | dört    | beş        |
| s. satu   | dud      | tiga      | empot   | lima       |
| t. maysá  | duá      | talló     | uppát   | lima       |
| u. wahid  | itsnayn  | tsalatsa  | arbaa   | chams      |
| v. echad  | schnayim | schloschah| arba    | chamischah |
| w. ichi   | ni       | san       | shi     | go         |
| x. -moja  | mbili    | tatu      | nne     | tano       |
| y. énska  | tékeni   | áhsen     | kayé:ri | wisk       |
| z. sga:t  | dekhni:h | sëh       | ge:ih   | wis        |

What could explain the similarities between these numeral words across languages?

Words in different languages may resemble each other for several reasons. One is **onomatopoeia**, or imitation of sounds. Names of birds, for example, are sometimes coined from imitations of their calls, like *whippoorwill* or *chickadee*. Speakers of different languages might come up with similar imitations. This is an unlikely explanation for similarities among numerals. A second possibility is **chance**: only a certain number of sounds can be made with the human mouth, and it is not impossible that the same combination of sounds could have similar meanings in different languages by chance. There is a verb *čʰúw* in Central Pomo, a language indigenous to Northern California, which means 'eat.' It has no relation to English *chew*, however. A third is **language contact**: often speakers adopt words from one language into another. This is the source of much English vocabulary, such as *spaghetti* (Italian), *champagne* (French), and even *tea* (Chinese). But words for the lowest numerals are rarely borrowed. The fourth and perhaps most common reason for lexical similarities across languages is that the languages are descended from the same parent language. The similar words are a **common inheritance** from their ancestor, that is, **cognates**.

*Languages are always changing*. The change typically begins with variation, from speaker to speaker and situation to situation. As long as speakers are communicating with each other, they will not change their speech so radically as to interrupt intelligibility. *When a community splits, however, and the splinter groups no longer interact, their speech will no longer change in parallel*. The longer they are separated, the greater the differences will become. **Dialects** will develop: people may still understand each other but notice differences, as in the case of British and American English. In time, speakers in the different communities will no longer understand each other, as in the case of English and German. At that point, they are said to speak different **languages**. All languages that are descended from a common parent are said to belong to the same **language family**. The languages within a family are often called **daughter languages**. They are said to be **genetically related**.

The languages represented in Example (7) are the following: (a) French, (b) Spanish, (c) Italian, (d) Portuguese, (e) Romanian, (f) German, (g) Dutch, (h) Yiddish, (i) Swedish, (j) Danish, (k) Polish, (l) Russian, (m) Czech, (n) Macedonian, (o) Greek, (p) Hungarian, (q) Finnish, (r) Turkish, (s) Indonesian, (t) Ilocano, (u) Arabic, (v) Hebrew, (w) Japanese, (x) Swahili, (y) Mohawk, and (z) Seneca. Most (a–o) are from the same language family as English, called **Indo-European**. Several, however, are from different families, and their numerals look quite different. Hungarian and Finnish (p, q) are from the Finno-Ugric family. Turkish (r) is from the Turkic family. Indonesian and Ilocano (s, t) are from the Austronesian family. Arabic and Hebrew (u, v) are from the Semitic branch of Afroasiatic. Mohawk and Seneca (y, z) are Iroquoian. Turkish (r), Japanese (w), and Swahili (x) have no relatives on the list.

Among the Indo-European languages, numerals in some languages resemble each other especially closely, such as those in French, Spanish, Italian, Portuguese, and Romanian (a, b, c, d, e); those in German, Dutch, and Yiddish (f, g, h); those in Swedish and Danish (i, j); and those in Polish, Russian, Czech, and Macedonian (k, l, m, n). As far as is known, the original Indo-European speech community separated into over a dozen groups: Romance (a–e), Germanic (f–j), Slavic (k–n), etc. Many of these groups then divided again. The Germanic group split into a North Germanic subgroup (the modern Scandinavian languages), a West Germanic subgroup (English, Dutch, Frisian, German, Yiddish), and an East Germanic subgroup (Gothic). In general, languages that have split the most recently show the most similarities: they have shared a longer history of common development.

### 12.4.1  Family trees

Relationships are often illustrated with what is termed a **family tree** or **Stammbaum** (see Sidebar 12.9). A sample fragment of the Indo-European family tree is given in Figure 12.1.

Indo-European, the language from which English, German, French, Russian, Greek, Albanian, Armenian, Farsi, Hindi, and many other languages are descended, is thought to have been spoken around the fifth millennium BCE. Because there are no written records of it, all that is known is what can be reconstructed by comparing the daughter languages. (See Textbox 12.2 for more on methods used to determine subgroupings.) A reconstructed ancestral language is termed a **proto-language**. The reconstructed ancestor of English and its relatives is called **Proto-Indo-European**.

### SIDEBAR 12.9
#### TREE DIAGRAMS

Family trees are schematic idealizations of language relationships. Splits are rarely as abrupt as the diagrams might suggest. Languages often continue to be influenced by each other and by languages outside of the family. Full versions of the tree seen in Figure 12.1 are available on many websites and can be found by searching online for "Indo-European tree."

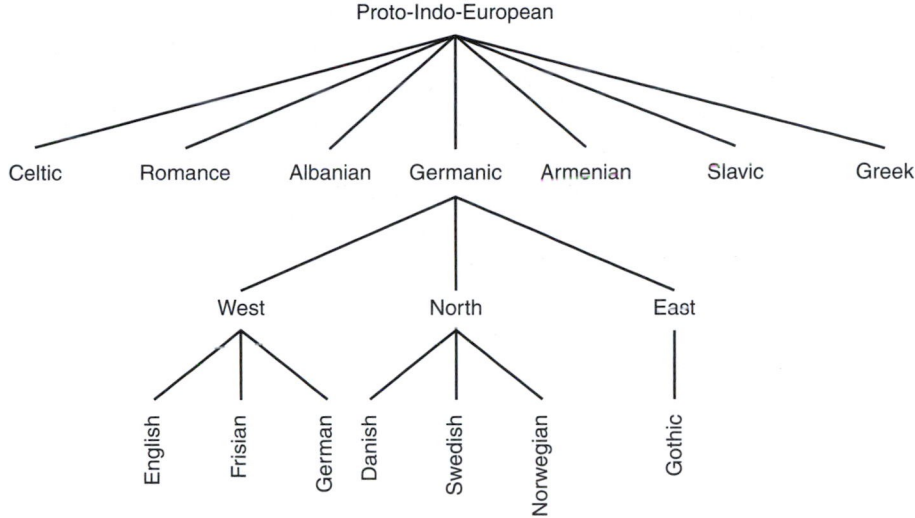

**Figure 12.1** Abbreviated tree of the Indo-European language family

## TEXTBOX 12.2 **CLADISTICS**

Computational methods are also being explored for answering questions about subgrouping, that is, interrelationships among languages already known to have developed from a common ancestor. One method, which comes from work in evolutionary biology, is cladistics. Similarities among languages are calculated in terms of the numbers of features (or "characters") they share, such as lexical cognates, sound changes, and inflectional morphology. A group of languages that share a significant number of features is called a "clade." A clade can be likened to a subgroup in a traditional family tree. But while family trees show a common parent language at the top, with successive splits into subgroups and ultimately

individual languages at the bottom as in Figure 12.1, cladistics first produces networks, or "unrooted trees." Cladograms simply arrange languages in terms of degrees of similarity. An example of a cladogram, from Taylor, Warnow, and Ringe (1998: 400), is below. It shows degrees of similarity among some Indo-European languages, based on a set of forty-six characters.

The lengths of the lines here are meaningful. Note that the line representing the Avestan-Vedic branch is longer than that for the Albanian-Old English branch. This is meant to indicate that Avestan and Vedic underwent more common changes than Albanian and Old English.

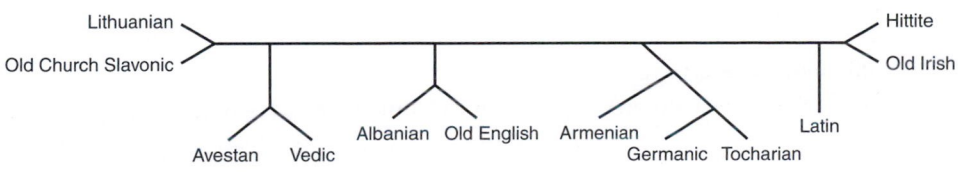

**Figure 12.2** A cladogram showing similarity among some Indo-European languages

## 12.5  The comparative method

To determine that languages are related, we begin by looking for resemblances among basic words, like the numerals above. But **random similarities do not, on their own, constitute evidence of genetic relationship**. The similarities could be due to any of the four factors mentioned above: onomatopoeia, chance, contact, or common inheritance. To uncover genetic relationships, we look for **recurring sound correspondences**. This is done by applying the **comparative method**. The method will be illustrated here with three languages indigenous to northern California: Wintu, Nomlaki, and Patwin.

(8)  Wintu, Nomlaki, and Patwin (Shepherd 2006)

|  |  | Wintu | Nomlaki | Patwin |
|---|---|---|---|---|
| a. | 'ear' | ma:t | ma:t | ma:t |
| b. | 'milkweed' | boq | boq | bok |
| c. | 'frog, toad' | wataqmet | wataq | wata:k |
| d. | 'house' | qewel | qewel | kewel |
| e. | 'bone' | paq | paq | pak |
| f. | 'wild goose' | laq | laq | lak-lak |
| g. | 'play, gamble' | łaqal | łaqal-a | łakal-a |
| h. | 'hole' | holoq | holoq | holok |
| i. | 'hawk' | qačit | qačit | katit |
| j. | 'good, straight' | čal-a | čal-a | tal-o: |
| k. | 'red-tailed hawk' | lad | čeqčeq | tektek |
| l. | 'hurt, sick' | koy-i | koy-a | čoy-i |
| m. | 'be ashamed' | kay-a: | kay-a | čay-i |
| n. | 'enemy' | yuken | yuken | yučen |
| o. | 'body hair' | sekey | sekey | sečey |
| p. | 'climb' | dek-ma | dek-na | det-mu |
| q. | 'woodpecker' | tarak |  | tara:t |
| r. | 'basket root' | se:k | se:k | se:t |
| s. | 'ash tree' | irik-mi |  | irit |
| t. | 'strap, tumpline' | surut | su:t | surut |
| u. | 'belt' | tir-i | ti: | tir-i |

### 12.5.1  Step I: identifying similar morphemes

The first step is to identify potential cognates, or morphemes that are similar enough in form and meaning to be descended from the same morpheme in a common parent language.

Compare the words in (8) to see whether any might not belong. Wintu *lad* (k), a kind of hawk, is completely different in form from Nomlaki *čeqčeq* and Patwin *tektek*. We will not consider it further in our comparison.

Potential cognates must also be similar enough in meaning to have developed from the same word in the parent language. Full semantic details of the words could not be included in (8) for reasons of space; however, some of the words in (8) have exactly the same meanings, such as *ma:t/ma:t/ma:t* 'ear' (a), while others differ. Differences do not mean they cannot be related: meanings can change over time. But the differences must represent plausible semantic change. Nomlaki *yuken* and Patwin *yučen* in (n) are translated 'enemy.' Wintu *yuken* is translated 'dangerous, at war, Shasta.' The Shasta people were the northern neighbors of the Wintu. The semantic relationship between 'enemy' and 'dangerous/Shasta' is sufficient for us to consider them possible cognates. On the other hand, Nomlaki has a word *leni* 'grass,' and Patwin a word *le:ni* 'yesterday.' This difference is too great for them to be cognates.

Finally, it is crucial that specific morphemes be compared. The 'frog' words in (c) are Wintu *wataqmet*, Nomlaki *wataq*, and Patwin *wata:k*. The element *-met* in Wintu is an 'amphibian reptile suffix' (Pitkin 1985: 348). It also appears in Wintu *yir-met* 'mountain lizard' and *yoho:l-met* '(another kind of) frog.' We only need to compare the roots *wataq/wataq/wata:k*. In the forms in (p) for 'climb,' *dek-ma*, *dek-na*, and *det-mu*, only the roots *dek-* are comparable. We do not need to consider the suffixes in our comparison.

Most of this first step has already been done for you in (8). Potential cognates have been assembled, and morphemes have been separated with hyphens.

### 12.5.2    Step II: listing correspondences

When we compare the words *ma:t/ma:t/ma:t* 'ear' in (a), we see that where Wintu has *m*, Nomlaki and Patwin also have *m*. We can summarize this in what is called a correspondence set: *m/m/m*. In the same word we see *a:/a:/a:* and *t/t/t*. In *qačit/qačit/katit* 'hawk' (i), we find the sets *q/q/k*, *a/a/a*, *č/č/t*, *i/i/i*, and *t/t/t*. These sets recur in the data, and with more data, we would see even more. Take a moment now to list all the consonant correspondence sets you find in the data in (8). List each set once, arranging any that share sounds, or are phonetically similar, near each other.

In the words 'tumpline' (t) and 'belt' (u), Nomlaki shows nothing where Wintu and Patwin both show *r*. We write this correspondence using a zero: *r/Ø/r*. Nomlaki words for 'woodpecker' (q) and 'ash' (s) are not available. We represent this gap in the data with a hyphen when first setting up the sets. For the first sound in 'woodpecker,' we write *t/-/t*. Since we have only one other set where this pattern would appear to fit, in this case *t/t/t*, we can assume that *t/-/t* exemplifies this pattern. (On the other hand, if we had two other correspondence sets where the pattern could fit, such as *t/t/t* and *t/d/t*, then we could not make such an assumption.)

| | | | | | | | |
|---|---|---|---|---|---|---|---|
| *p/p/p* | *s/s/s* | *y/y/y* | *m/m/m* | *l/l/l* | *q/q/k* | | |
| *b/b/b* | *h/h/h* | *w/w/w* | *n/n/n* | *ł/ł/ł* | *k/k/č* | *č/č/t* | |
| *d/d/d* | | | | *r/Ø/r* | *k/k/t* | *t/t/t* | |

### 12.5.3    Step III: first pass at reconstruction

We now propose sounds in the parent language, Proto-Wintun, that could be the ancestors of each correspondence set. Each reconstructed sound should be such that:

**a.**  The changes from it to each of its reflexes (descendent sounds) in the daughter language are as plausible as possible, i.e., the kinds of natural changes we know that sounds undergo cross-linguistically. Earlier in this chapter we saw some particularly common kinds of change, e.g., lenition and assimilation.

**b.** The changes are as few in number as possible.

The most likely ancestor of the set *p/p/p*, for example, is *p. This is a hypothesis that Proto-Wintun contained a sound *p that remained unchanged during the several thousand years of development into modern Wintu, Nomlaki, and Patwin. We follow the same procedure for other uniform sets: *b for *b/b/b*, etc. Each has remained the same in the daughter languages.

Proto-Wintun

| | | | | | | | |
|---|---|---|---|---|---|---|---|
| *p | > | p | in W, N, P | *m | > | m | in W, N, P |
| *b | > | b | in W, N, P | *n | > | n | in W, N, P |
| *t | > | t | in W, N, P | *l | > | l | in W, N, P |
| *d | > | d | in W, N, P | *ł | > | ł | in W, N, P |
| *s | > | s | in W, N, P | *w | > | w | in W, N, P |
| *h | > | h | in W, N, P | *y | > | y | in W, N, P |

The same procedure gives us easy reconstructions for the vowels, which are generally identical in the daughter languages. So far things look so simple that we hardly need to write them out.

For the set *r/Ø/r*, a reconstruction of *r is most appropriate, but this entails a change. The data here indicate that *r has disappeared in Nomlaki.

| | | | |
|---|---|---|---|
| *r | > | r | in Wintu, Patwin |
| | | Ø | in Nomlaki |

We next turn to *q/q/k*. Two possible reconstructions spring to mind: *q or *k. A choice of *q entails just one change, *q > k in Patwin. It is a plausible change: shifts from uvular to velar are common cross-linguistically.

| | | | |
|---|---|---|---|
| *q | > | q | in W, N |
| | > | k | in P |

A choice of *k for the *q/q/k* set, however, would entail two changes, *k > q in Wintu and *k > q in Nomlaki. Moreover, this change is much less common cross-linguistically. (It occurs mainly by assimilation to low back vowels.)

### 12.5.4  Step IV: combining sets

We now turn to the sets *k/k/č* and *k/k/t*. A separate proto sound must be posited for each correspondence set, unless there is evidence for combining the sets. A likely ancestral sound for both *k/k/č* and *k/k/t* would be *k. There may have been one original sound, *k, which developed one way in some contexts and another way in others. *k may have developed into Patwin *č* in some contexts, and *t* in others. To determine whether this happened, we investigate the environments where each occurs. (This procedure is similar to that used for finding allophones in complementary distribution.) We can list their contexts as follows. The blank represents the correspondence set in each word. The sound that occurs before it in each language is on the left, in the order Wintu/Nomlaki/Patwin. The sound that occurs after it in each language is on the right.

| /k/č | | k/k/t |
|---|---|---|
| a/a/a __ i/i/i | | e/e/e __ m/n/m |
| #/#/# __ o/o/o | | a/-/a: __ #/#/# |
| #/#/# __ a/a/a | | e:/e:/e: __ #/#/# |
| u/u/u __ e/e/e | | i/-/i __ m/-/# |
| e/e/e __ c/e/e | | |

We do have complementary distribution. The set *k/k/č* always occurs before vowels. In contrast, the set *k/k/t* never occurs before vowels; it always occurs before a consonant or at the end of the word. With this information, we can posit a single ancestral sound *k. This *k remained k in Wintu and Nomlaki. It changed to č (the affricate [tʃ]) in Patwin. This is a plausible sound change, a simple fronting of the obstruent. Before another consonant or at the end of a word, this č was simplified to the stop t. This too is a plausible change.

*k    >    k        in Wintun, Nomlaki
          č        in Patwin
          č > t    / __ C
                   __ #

We are left with the set *č/č/t*. The most obvious reconstruction is *č, a sound not used for our Proto-Wintun consonant inventory so far. It implies just one change, *č > t in Patwin, and, as noted, it is a plausible change.

*č    >    č    in Wintun, Nomlaki
          t    in Patwin

We should check to be certain that there is not complementary distribution between the contexts in which the *č/č/t* and the *t/t/t* correspondences occur. In fact there is not. Both occur, for example, at the beginning of a word before *a*, as in (j) 'good, straight' (*č/č/t*), and (q) 'woodpecker' (*t/t/t*). There is also no complementary distribution between the sets *k/k/t* and *t/t/t*. Both occur after *e* at the end of a word, as in (r) 'root' (*k/k/t*) and (a) 'ear' (*t/t/t*). A check of the contexts for the sets *l/l/l* and *ł/ł/ł* also shows no complementary distribution. Both occur, for example, at the beginning of words before *a*, as in (f) 'wild goose' (*l/l/l*) and (g) 'play, gamble' (*ł/l/ł*).

### 12.5.5    Step V: ordering rules

Each of our rules represents a hypothesis about a sound change that took place in the language. But did they all occur at once? That is unlikely. If not, can we tell anything about the order in which they occurred? Looking back at the last section, we see that we hypothesized the two changes below for Patwin.

*q    >    k
*k    >    č

Our work indicates that the Proto-Wintun word for 'hole' was *holoq. If we assume that the two rules we see there operated in that order (1 before 2), we would have the following sequence of changes:

*holoq      >    *holok      >    holoč
         *q > k              *k > č

If, however, we hypothesize that they occurred in the opposite order (2 before 1), we would have the following sequence of changes:

*holoq          >        holok
(*k > č)      *q > k

Change 2 (*k > č) would not affect the word 'hole,' because at that point the word did not yet contain a *k* (*holoq).

## 12.5.6  Step VI: Inventory check

We now consider the inventory of consonants that we have reconstructed for Proto-Wintun:

*p      *t      *č      *k
*b      *d
        *s              *h
*m      *n
*w      *l      *ł      *r      *y

This is a reasonable, balanced inventory. The absence of *g is noteworthy, but languages with [b] and [d] but no [g] are actually not uncommon cross-linguistically.

## 12.5.7  Step VII: reconstructing words

We are now in a position to reconstruct full words. We will assume that the vowel inventory consists of *i, *e, *a, *o, and *u, with no changes in the daughter languages. Some reconstructions are straightforward:

|            | Wintu | Nomlaki | Patwin | Proto-Wintun |
|------------|-------|---------|--------|--------------|
| a. 'ear'   | ma:t  | ma:t    | ma:t   | *ma:t        |

Others require undoing the sound changes we posited:

| | | | | |
|---|---|---|---|---|
| b. 'milkweed' | boq | boq | bok | *boq |
| i. 'hawk' | qačit | qačit | katit | *qačit |
| t. 'tumpline' | surut | su:t | surut | *surut |

Where the meanings of the cognates in the daughter languages are not identical, we must choose a proto meaning. The words in (f) with their translations are Wintu *laq* 'wild goose,' Nomlaki *laq* 'brant, green-wing teal,' and Patwin *laklak* 'goose species.' The most likely meaning of the Proto-Wintun term is 'goose.'

Comparative reconstruction is one of the primary methods that linguists have used to determine language relatedness and to reconstruct protolanguages.

---

### TEXTBOX 12.3 **INTERNAL RECONSTRUCTION**

There are additional techniques for reconstructing earlier stages of languages. Internal reconstruction takes as a point of departure alternations within a single language. For an example of how it works we can look at Zuni, a language isolate indigenous to the North American Southwest. We cannot apply the comparative method to Zuni, because there are no data from related languages to compare.

Zuni contains a verb prefix *an-* called an *applicative*. The applicative indicates that an additional participant is involved in the situation. Added to the verb 'consent,' it creates a new verb that means 'consent to (someone),' that is, 'permit someone to do something.' Added to a verb meaning 'feel pleasure,' it forms a new verb 'feel pleasure at (something), to enjoy (something).'

| | | | |
|---|---|---|---|
| *sewaha* | 'to consent' | *an-sewaha* | 'to consent to' |
| *ʔeluma* | 'to feel pleasure' | *an-ʔeluma* | 'to enjoy' |

But this prefix does not always appear as *an-*. Before *h* it takes the shape *ah-*; before *l*, it is *al-*; before *w* it is *aw-*; before *y* it is *ay-*.

| | | | |
|---|---|---|---|
| *heye* | 'to defecate' | *ah-heye* | 'to defecate on' |
| *laʔhi* | 'to jump' | *al-laʔhi* | 'to jump at' |
| *weʔa* | 'to burst out laughing' | *aw-weʔa* | 'burst out laughing at' |
| *yučiʔati* | 'to be amazed' | *ay-yučiʔatika* | 'to be amazed at' |

The method of internal reconstruction looks beyond such alternations to the scenario which is likely to have created them. We know that one of the commonest kinds of sound change is assimilation, whereby a sound shifts to become more like its neighbor. The shifting shapes of the Zuni prefix appear to be the result of such changes. We hypothesize that the original applicative prefix was simply *an-*, the most common form. Over time, regular processes of assimilation occurred, resulting in the forms we have today: *ah-* before *h*, *al-* before *l*, *aw-* before *w*, and *ay-* before *y*. We have thus reconstructed a proto form of the prefix, and several sound changes, based only on data in this one modern language.

---

## 12.6  Linguistic paleontology

***Reconstruction of vocabulary in a proto-language can provide glimpses of the world of its speakers***. If, for example, we can reconstruct a term for 'snow,' we can hypothesize that the speakers lived in an area with snow or within sight of snow. We have this term for **Proto-Indo-European**, reconstructed as *sneigwh-*. Watkins

(1981) provides an overview of Indo-European life as seen through reconstructed vocabulary.

The Indo-Europeans apparently lived in an area with wolves (*wl̥p-, *wl̥kwo-), bears (*r̥kso-), beavers (*bhibhru-), and mice (*mūs-). There were salmon or trout (*laks-), eels (*angwhi-), cranes (*ger-), eagles (*er-), thrushes (*trozdos-), and starlings (storos). They knew wasps (*wopsā), hornets (*kr̥s-ro-), flies (*mu-), and bees (*bhei-). They gathered honey (*melit-) and made mead (*medhu-), a honey-based alcoholic beverage. Watkins hypothesizes that the Indo-Europeans oriented themselves by facing east, because the root *deks- 'right' also meant 'south.'

Kinship terms reveal an interesting pattern. There are numerous terms for relatives by marriage on the husband's side, such as 'husband's father,' 'husband's mother,' 'husband's brother,' 'husband's sister,' 'husband's brother's wife,' and 'son's wife,' but none for the corresponding terms on the wife's side. This fact suggests that couples took up residency with the husband's family.

The Indo-Europeans were farmers. They had words for 'grain' (*grəno-, ancestor of our corn), or wheat or spelt, and perhaps rye and barley. They ground it (*melə-, ancestor of meal and mill). They had verbs for 'sow' (*sē-), 'plow' (*plōg-), 'yoke' (*yeug-), and 'gather' (*kerp-, ancestor of harvest). They kept livestock, including cattle (*gwou- 'cow/bull'), sheep (*owi), lambs (*agwhno-), goats (*ghaido-), and pigs (*porko-, ancestor of farrow). They had dogs (*kwon-), and this term was apparently the basis for their word for 'horse' (*ekwo-). The root *peku- meant both 'wealth' and 'cattle.' They could weave (*webh-), sew (*syū-), and produce textiles (teks- 'fabricate, weave'). They knew the wheel (*kʷekʷlo, based on the verb root *kʷel(H)- 'turn').

Indo-European vocabulary was rich in words for ideas, abstractions, and relations. There were numerous terms for mental activity, among them *men- (source of English mind). There were also terms for 'king' (*reg-), a deity (*deiw-), and religious law (*leg- and *yewo, ancestor of Latin jūs), for preaching, praising, and prophesying or singing (*sengwh-).

As we reconstruct Proto-Indo-European vocabulary and draw inferences about the lives of the Indo-Europeans, we cannot help but wonder just where these people lived. There have been many hypotheses, but the puzzle is not yet solved. One approach is to compare the reconstructed vocabulary with what we know about the natural environment and archaeological findings for that period, around the fourth millennium BCE, probably not earlier than 5000 BCE and not later than 2500 BCE. The Indo-Europeans apparently lived where there were wolves, bears, beavers, foxes, otters, hedgehogs, and mice; sparrows, quail, thrushes, cranes, vultures, blackbirds, crows, ravens, eagles, jays, pheasants, and storks; and turtles, frogs, and snakes. But unfortunately most of these animals and birds are ubiquitous through Europe and adjacent Asia, so they do not help us to pinpoint a specific Indo-European homeland.

The term for 'birch' is clearly reconstructible to *bherg'o-. As pointed out by Mallory (1989: 161), it denotes the birch in Indic (bhurja-), Iranian (Ossetic bärz),

Germanic (*birch*), Baltic (Latvian *berzs*), and Slavic (Russian *berëza*). But the Latin cognate *fraxinus* means 'ash,' and there is no cognate in Greek. About half of the tree names reconstructed for Proto-Indo-European show a shift in meaning in Greek. These facts are taken to suggest that the Indo-Europeans originated elsewhere, then later moved into the area, applying original terms to the new trees they encountered.

One possible location of the homeland is the grasslands area north of the Black and Caspian Seas, known as the Pontic-Caspian steppes (Fortson 2004: 41). The reasoning behind this proposal is interesting. We know that the Indo-Europeans had the wheel. Archaeological evidence suggests that wheeled vehicles were invented around 3300–3400 BCE. The Indo-European community could thus not have broken up before this time. At this time, the steppes were inhabited by a group known as the Yamna, who came from the area between the steppes and the nearby forest between the Dnieper and Volga rivers. We know that the Indo-Europeans knew horses. The teeth of horses found in this area from that time show microscopic abrasions, from clamping down on a bit. Additional aspects of culture reconstructed through linguistic paleontology match archaeological findings in the area. But without a written tradition, it is not possible to identify the language of communities uncovered archaeologically. This hypothesis, while promising, must remain just that.

## CHAPTER SUMMARY

We have seen that all aspects of language undergo change. At the phonological level, certain types of sound change are particularly frequent, such as those involving lenition or assimilation. Many of these are motivated by a desire on the part of speakers to reduce the effort necessary for speech. Sound change can have effects beyond the shifting of individual sounds: it can result in the restructuring of the phonological system, with the addition and loss of distinctive features and phonemes. It can also produce seeming irregularities, such as allomorphy. Grammar tends to develop via certain pathways. Grammatical morphemes develop most often from independent lexical items, a process termed grammaticalization. Grammaticalization typically involves a constellation of changes, including cognitive routinization, generalization of meaning, decategorialization, and ultimately phonological erosion. But not all change is reductive. Speakers are constantly reanalyzing the patterns underlying speech, repairing perceived irregularities by analogical remodeling, and renewing constructions that have lost their expressive force.

The fact that languages are constantly changing can result in the differentiation of languages over time. A language family consists of all of those languages descended from a common parent or proto-language. Relationships among these languages are often represented by family tree diagrams. In this chapter we have seen an example of the comparative method, used to establish genetic relationships among languages and to reconstruct aspects of their common parent, such as its sound system and vocabulary. The reconstruction of vocabulary in the proto-language can in turn provide glimpses into the lives of its speakers.

Languages are dynamic systems, constantly changing in all areas of their structure and content. The changes are not predictable, but they are also not random. They are shaped by certain human cognitive faculties such as pattern recognition, the routinization of recurring patterns of expression, and the creative acts of speakers eager to find fresh and powerful ways of conveying their thoughts.

### TEXTBOX 12.4 GLOSSING CONVENTIONS USED IN THIS CHAPTER

| Convention | Meaning | Convention | Meaning |
|---|---|---|---|
| NEG | negation | REP | repetitive |
| PL | plural | DUR | durative |
| PST | past tense | NMLZ | nominalizer |

### SUGGESTIONS FOR FURTHER READING

**Slade, Benjamin** (ed.). *Beowulf on Steorarume*. www.heorot.dk/.

You can find the full text of *Beowulf* by searching for "beowulf" online. A variety of translations are available. You can learn more about the language of the time from an online glossary of all words in the manuscript.

**Gelderen, Elly van**. 2006. *A history of the English language*. Amsterdam: John Benjamins.

This book is an excellent introduction to the history of English.

**Heine, Bernd**. 2010. "Grammaticalization in African languages." In Heine, Bernd and Heiko Narrog (eds.), *The Oxford handbook of grammaticalization*. Oxford University Press. 696–707.

This book features a fascinating but somewhat advanced article on grammaticalization.

**Watkins, Calvert**. 1981. "Indo-European and the Indo-Europeans." *The American heritage dictionary of the English language*. Boston: Houghton Mifflin. 1496–1502.

This book contains further discussion of the Proto-Europeans.

### EXERCISES

In the exercises here, related forms have already been assembled for you. Normally a major part of work in historical linguistics involves this step as well, the discovery of related forms. These exercises provide just enough data for you to be able to detect certain patterns. Normally, one would consider much more data for a solid analysis.

1. French vowels: sound change
   (Thanks to Ben Fortson for expertise on the Romance exercises.)
   For this problem, look only at the stressed syllables. First describe in words what happened to the vowels in these syllables during the development of French. Then write a rule to capture your description.

**SIDEBAR 12.10**

**THE ROMANCE LANGUAGES**
Several of the exercises for this chapter present data from Romance languages. As we saw in Figure 12.2, Romance is one of the branches of the Indo-European language family. Most of the modern languages in this branch are descended from Latin. Among these are French, Italian, Portuguese, and Spanish, as well as Romanian, Provençal, Catalan, Rhaeto-Romance dialects, and more.

**TRANSCRIPTION NOTE**
The transcription here uses the standard spelling systems, with one addition. The symbol ' has been added before the stressed syllable in each Latin word. The brev mark (˘) indicates that a vowel is short.

|          |             | Latin      | French |
|----------|-------------|------------|--------|
| a.       | 'foot'      | 'pĕde      | pied   |
| b.       | 'yesterday' | 'hĕrī      | hier   |
| c.       | 'honey'     | 'mĕl       | miel   |
| d.       | 'holds'     | 'tĕnĕt     | tient  |
| e.       | 'stone'     | 'pĕtra     | pierre |
| f.       | 'hundred'   | 'cĕntu     | cent   |
| g.       | 'wind'      | 'vĕntu     | vent   |
| h.       | 'seven'     | 'sĕpte(m)  | sept   |
| i.       | 'loses'     | 'pĕrdīt    | perd   |
| j.       | 'iron'      | 'fĕrru     | fer    |

2. Greenlandic consonants: sound change
   (Data from Fortescue, Jacobson, and Kaplan 1994)
   Languages of the Eskimo-Aleut family are spoken over a wide area of the Arctic, from Siberia to Greenland. The family consists of two main branches: Eskimoan and Aleut. The language of Greenland, called Kalaallisut, is a member of the first branch.

   The data here show one consonant sound shift. Write a rule to describe this sound change. (The symbol *y* here is used for the IPA [j], while the symbol *c* here represents the IPA [tʃ].)

| **Proto-Eskimoan** |                          | **Kalaallisut (Greenlandic)** |                              |
|--------------------|--------------------------|-------------------------------|------------------------------|
| a. *qayaq          | 'kayak'                  | qayaq                         | 'kayak'                      |
| b. *taciq          | 'spit, sand bar'         | tasiq                         | 'lake'                       |
| c. *kicaq          | 'anchor'                 | kisaq                         | 'anchor'                     |
| d. *uciaʀ-         | 'carry a load'           | usiar-                        | 'carry load on one's kayak'  |
| e. *kənit-         | 'soak'                   | kinit-                        | 'soak in order to soften'    |
| f. *tucaʀ-         | 'hear, understand'       | tusaʀ-                        | 'hear'                       |
| g. *papək          | 'tail'                   | papik                         | 'tail'                       |
| h. *nəqə           | 'food, fish'             | niqi                          | 'meat'                       |
| i. *cayuɣ-         | 'pull or twitch'         | sayuɣ-                        | 'tremble'                    |
| j. *cianəq         | 'lengthwise lathe in kayak' | sianiq                     | 'lengthwise lathe in kayak'  |
| k. *atəq           | 'name'                   | atiq                          | 'name'                       |
| l. *əɣə-           | 'render oil from blubber' | iɣi-                         | 'melt (blubber, snow, ice)'  |

3. Italian laterals: conditioned sound change
   For this problem, look only at the development of the lateral *l* from Latin into Italian. First describe the change in words. Then write a rule that captures what happened.

|          |           | Latin    | Italian  |
|----------|-----------|----------|----------|
| a.       | 'moon'    | lūna     | luna     |
| b.       | 'milk'    | lacte    | latte    |
| c.       | 'freedom' | lībertās | libertà  |

| | | |
|---|---|---|
| d. 'color' | colōre | colore |
| e. 'bad' | malu | malo |
| f. 'thread' | fīlu | filo |
| g. 'mole' | talpa | talpa |
| h. 'much' | multu | molto |
| i. 'false' | falsu | falso |
| j. 'sage' | salvia | salvia |
| k. 'full' | plēnu | pieno |
| l. 'plant' | planta | pianta |
| m. 'flat' | plānu | piano |
| n. 'lead' | plumbu | piombo |
| o. 'to call' | clāmāre | chiamare |
| p. 'key' | clāvis | chiave |
| q. 'to close' | clūdere | chiudere |
| r. 'flame' | flamma | fiamma |
| s. 'flower' | flōre | fiore |
| t. 'river' | flūmen | fiume |
| u. 'white' | blancu | bianco |
| v. 'glacier' | glaciāriu | ghiacciaio |
| w. 'double' | duplu | doppio |
| x. 'example' | exemplu | esempio |

4. French sibilants: conditioned sound change

The earliest documentation we have of French is from the ninth century. The term Old French designates stages of the language from that time up to the fourteenth century. Of course, the language was undergoing change throughout that period.

The French sibilants underwent systematic changes during the thirteenth century. (Look at the IPA transcriptions of Old French and Modern French, rather than their standard spellings. Each of the sequences tʃ, ts, ʤ, and dz represents a single consonant sound, an affricate.)

i. Write rules to describe these changes. Describe in words the changes specified in each rule.

ii. Describe in words any other changes that you notice here.

iii. Can you understand why modern French spelling, in the right hand column, seems to fit modern French pronunciation so badly?

| | Old French | Modern French | Spelling |
|---|---|---|---|
| a. 'field' | tʃaþmp | ʃaþ | *champ* |
| b. 'cow' | vatʃə | vaʃ | *vache* |
| c. 'judge' | ʤyʤə | ʒyʒ | *juge* |
| d. (name) | ʤɔrʤəs | ʒɔrʒ | *Georges* |
| e. 'charge' | tʃarʤjɛr | ʃarʒe | *charger* |
| f. 'hundred' | tsɛþnt | saþ | *cent* |
| g. 'hunt' | tʃatsjɛr | ʃase | *chasser* |
| h. 'shield' | esky | eky | *écu* |
| i. 'sword' | espɛdə | epe | *épée* |
| j. 'our' | nɔstrə | notr | *notre* |
| k. 'islands' | izləs | il | *îles* |
| l. 'taken' | pris | pri | *pris* |
| m. 'have' | avets | ave | *avez* |
| n. 'to the' | alts | o | *aux* |
| o. (name) | fraþntsojs | fraþswa | *François* |

5. Uto-Aztecan: comparative method
   (Data from Sapir 1930; Lamb 1958; Miller 1972; Munro and Mace 1995; assembled in Miller 1988)
   The languages here are all from the Uto-Aztecan family. Shoshone territory stretches over areas of Nevada, Utah, Idaho, and Wyoming; Southern Paiute territory from southeastern California into Nevada, Arizona, and Utah; Mono territory on both sides of the Sierra Nevada Mountains in east central California; and Tübatulabal territory along the Kern River near modern Bakersfield, California.
   A number of developments have occurred since these languages diverged. Some of the words here include morphemes that are not cognate. These are set off by hyphens. You do not need to include those non-cognate morphemes in your analysis.
   For this problem, investigate only the velar stops and any related sounds. Reconstruct a proto-sound or sounds and write rules to describe developments in the various languages.

| | Shoshone | Southern Paiute | Mono | Tübatulabal |
|---|---|---|---|---|
| a. 'fire, heat' | ku- | ku- | ku-na | ku-t |
| b. 'husband' | kuhma | kumma | kuwa | ku:ŋa-n |
| c. 'neck' | kuta | kuta | kutta | kula-:n |
| d. 'firewood' | kuna | kunna | kun(n)a | — |
| e. 'no' | ke | ka | qa-tuʔu | ha-yi |
| f. 'rat' | ka:n | ka: | — | ha-wa:l |
| g. 'jackrabbit' | kammu | kammɨ | qammɨ | — |
| h. 'house' | kahni | kanni | — | hani-:l |
| i. 'wing, feather' | kasa | kasa-p | qassa | — |
| j. 'bite' | kɨ- | kɨ-ʔɨ | kɨ- | kɨ-ʔɨ-t |
| k. 'edge' | kɨma | kɨŋʷa: | kɨwa | — |
| l. 'pat grandfather' | kɨnu | kunnu- | kɨnu | — |
| m. 'come' | kimma | kimma | kimat | — |
| n. 'elbow' | ki:- | ki:-ppɨ | ma-ki:pɨ | — |
| o. 'break, cut in pieces' | — | kapi- | to-qopi | hob-oʔ |
| p. 'face' | kopa-i | kopa- | qope | — |
| q. 'snake' | tokoa | tokoa | toqoqqʷa | — |
| r. 'face' | kopa-i | kopa- | qope | — |

6. Gum languages: comparative method
   (Data from Z'graggen 1980)
   New Guinea is home to a vast number of languages, estimated at over 850. They show tremendous diversity as well. Many are not yet described, or are under-described. The Gum languages are spoken in northeastern Papua New Guinea, in Madang Province.
   For this problem, you will reconstruct just some of the consonants.
   i. Make a list of all correspondence in the data that involve s.
   ii. Make a list of all correspondence sets involving any of the other consonants in these s sets.
   iii. Provide reconstructions for all of your correspondence sets.
      (There is no complementary distribution here.)
      Using rules, list all sound changes that affected your proto consonants in each language.
      Describe in words the rationale for each of your reconstructions.

| | Gumalu | Amele | Bau | Panim |
|---|---|---|---|---|
| a. 'fingernail' | siu | hilo | si | si:lu |
| b. 'vein' | sirima- | hilima- | sirima- | silimʌ- |
| c. 'coconut tree' | asuř | ahul | ʌsur | asul |

|      |                   |         |        |         |        |
|------|-------------------|---------|--------|---------|--------|
| d.   | 'sugar'           | sʌ:     | hʌ     | sʌ      | sʌ     |
| e.   | 'thou (OBJECT)'   | -isɛ-   | -ihi-  | -is-    | -is-   |
| f.   | 'inside (house)'  | famʌn   | hʌmol  | famʌn   | famʌn  |
| g.   | 'plant'           | ɛfɛ-    | ɛhɛ-   | ɛf-     | efe-   |
| h.   | 'pig'             | fo      | ho     | fo      | fo     |
| i.   | 'hold'            | farɛ-   | hɛwɛ-  | fʌl-    | fale-  |
| j.   | 'ear'             | tahi-   | dahi-  | tahi-   | dahi-  |
| k.   | 'throw (stone)'   | tahulɛ- | hɛlɛ-  | dahur-  | hɛlɛ   |

7. Romance labials: comparative method
   (There are additional complexities in the languages beyond those shown in the data here.)
      Provide reconstructions for all of the labial sounds, and then write rules that specify the development of each into the modern language. You may need to compare the phonological environments in which similar correspondence sets occur.

|      |                  | Italian  | Spanish  | Portuguese |
|------|------------------|----------|----------|------------|
| a.   | 'soap'           | sapere   | saber    | saber      |
| b.   | 'bank, shore'    | ripa     | riba     | riba       |
| c.   | 'head'           | capo     | cabo     | cabo       |
| d.   | 'bean'           | fava     | haba     | fava       |
| e.   | 'to prove'       | provare  | probar   | provar     |
| f.   | 'to have'        | avere    | haber    | haver      |
| g.   | 'to owe'         | dovere   | deber    | dever      |
| h.   | 'to wash'        | lavare   | lavar    | lavar      |
| i.   | 'to live'        | vívere   | vivir    | viver      |
| j.   | 'beautiful'      | bella    | bella    | bela       |
| k.   | 'pear'           | pera     | pera     | pera       |
| l.   | 'form, mould'    | forma    | horma    | forma      |
| m.   | 'thorn'          | spina    | espina   | espinha    |
| n.   | 'bath'           | bagno    | baño     | banho      |
| o.   | 'a pound'        | libbra   | libra    | libra      |

8. Takanan Reconstruction
   (Data from Girard 1971)
   The Takanan languages are spoken in northern Bolivia and southeastern Peru. For this problem, you will do a complete reconstruction of the sounds of Proto-Takanan and some vocabulary.

      i. Make a list of sound correspondences.
      ii. Group the correspondence sets by phonetic features so that sets sharing sounds are adjacent.
      iii. Check to see whether any related sets are in complementary distribution.
      iv. Reconstruct a proto-sound for each set or each group of sets in complementary distribution. There should be a different proto-sound for each correspondence set or group of sets in complementary distribution. The proto-sound you choose for each should entail likely sound changes.
      v. With each reconstructed sound, provide rules for its development in the modern languages.
      vi. If any of the sound changes you list in your rules is a recognized kind of phonological process, name that process next to the rule.
      vii. Check to see that you have reasonable consonant and vowel inventories.
      viii. On the basis of your reconstructed sounds and rules, reconstruct the Proto-Takanan word that is the ancestor of each word above.

(The symbol *ñ* represents the palatal nasal: the IPA [ɲ].)

| | Takana | Kavineño | Eseʔeha |
|---|---|---|---|
| a. 'moon' | badi | badi | baʔi |
| b. 'resin' | madi | madi | maʔi |
| c. 'inside' | duhusu | dokoho | doxoho |
| d. 'bat' | bina | bina | biña |
| e. 'grab' | ina- | ina- | iña- |
| f. 'wind' | beni | beni | beni |
| g. 'cook, heat' | sina- | hina- | hiña- |
| h. 'carry' | dusu- | doho- | doho- |
| i. 'to comb' | pesu- | peho- | peho- |
| j. 'liana (plant)' | hunu | kono | xono |
| k. 'watery' | nahi | naki | naxi |
| l. 'papa' | tata | tata | kaka |
| m. 'two' | beta | beta | beka |
| n. 'turtle' | dati | dati | daki- |
| o. 'squash' | hemi | kemi | xemi |
| p. 'sleep' | tawi- | tawi- | kawi- |

9.  Grammaticalization

Each pair of sentences below shows evidence of certain grammaticalization processes within the language. Identify the forms that have undergone any of these processes, and name the processes involved in each development.

1. Bambara

(Data from Donald Lessau, cited in Heine and Kuteva 2002:75)
Bambara is a Mandé language spoken in Mali and Senegal, in West Africa.

a. *ù*      *bέ*      *Nà*
   3PL      AUX      dome
   'They come.'

b. *à*      *bέna*      *Sà*
   3SG      NEAR.FUT      die
   'He will die (soon and/or surely).'

2. Mandarin Chinese (data from Sun 1996: 44, cited in Heine and Kuteva 2002: 153)
(Tones are not represented here.)

a. *ta*      *gei*      *le*      *wo*      *wu-kuai*      *qian*
   3SG      give      ASP      1SG      five            CLF
   'He gave me five dollars.'

b. *wo*      *xie*      *le*      *yi-feng*      *xin*      *gei*      *ta*
   1SG      write      ASP      one-CLF      letter      to      3SG.M
   'I wrote him a letter.'

3. Negerhollands CD

(Data from Stolz 1986: 153, 179, cited in Heine and Kuteva 2002: 158)

Negerhollands is a Dutch-based creole that was once spoken in the US Virgin Islands.

a. *ju       lo:      afo          fa      mi*
   2SG      go      in.front     of      1SG

   'You go in front of me.'

b. *am      a        flig     lo       mi       di       flut*
   3SG      PRF      fly      away     PREP     DEF      flute

   'He flew away with the flute.'

# 13 Language contact and areal linguistics

**KEY TERMS**

- Language contact
- Borrowing
- Calques
- Bilingualism
- Multilingualism
- Pidgin
- Creole
- Interference
- Linguistic area
- Diffusion

**CHAPTER PREVIEW**

The previous chapter introduced the topic of language change and language family. In this chapter, we will explore one type of language change in more detail, the change that occurs when speakers of different languages interact with each other, in other words, when the languages are in contact. This chapter will introduce linguistic borrowing, the incorporation of forms or even meanings from one language into another. It will examine the motivations for borrowing, the range of borrowed elements, factors which promote or impede borrowing, and what happens as borrowed items are incorporated into another language.

The chapter will also discuss correlations between the sociopolitical relationships of language communities and the degree and nature of change from language contact. It will introduce special contact languages, pidgins, and creoles, which come about when groups of people with no language in common must work together or engage in trade. It will conclude by presenting linguistic areas, geographic regions that result from long-term contact between neighboring languages, which results in the sharing of features and structural convergence. This chapter demonstrates that languages are strongly influenced by the larger societal, political, and geographical features that define the speech communities.

**LIST OF AIMS**

After reading this chapter, students should be able to:

- discuss linguistic borrowings and their functions;
- identify linguistic borrowings in English;
- present arguments for language change conditioned by language contact;
- give examples of bilingual and multilingual societies;
- identify features of creoles and distinguish them from pidgins;
- understand the features of koinés;
- understand and define the term "linguistic area";
- discuss sociocultural prerequisites for the formation of linguistic areas.

## 13.1 Language contact and areal linguistics

When you start learning a new language, you may wonder why a word in one language is similar to a word in a language you already know. This situation can result from pure chance. In Latin, 'two' is *duo/dua*. We know this from English words like *dual* or *dualism*. In Malay, the national language of Malaysia, *dua* also means 'two.' This is a coincidence, a curious fact that tells us nothing about the history of these languages, or those who speak them.

Now look at Table 13.1. Color terms in English and in German are very similar to each other. This is no coincidence. The forms and meanings are so similar because these languages come from a single common ancestor, the Germanic subgroup of Indo-European. Their similarities are due to genetic inheritance, as explained in Chapter 12.

Forms and meanings across languages can be similar for yet another reason. Languages and dialects do not exist in a vacuum. ***Speakers of different languages come into contact with each other***: they may trade, intermarry, meet for ceremonies, and so on. ***The languages are then in*** **contact**, with many speakers of one having some knowledge of the other. Speakers cannot help borrowing linguistic features back and forth: habits of pronunciation, significant sounds (phonemes), grammatical categories, vocabulary items, and even some grammatical forms. Thus, ***contact***

**TABLE 13.1** No coincidence: color terms in English and German

| English | German |
| --- | --- |
| *white* | *weiss* |
| *red* | *rot* |
| *green* | *grün* |
| *blue* | *blau* |

*is another source of similarity between languages*, whose speakers adjust their speech habits in line with those of their neighbors.

Every language has been influenced by another, at least to some extent. In English, we find many words that are not native vocabulary. For example, the word *umbrella* comes from Italian *ombrella*, which literally means 'little shade,' and the word *cherries* comes from French *cérise*. The impact of language contact is substantial and easy to identify in some languages. In others, it is not so easy. In contrast to English, Hungarian has very few words taken from other languages; speakers prefer to coin their own words rather than borrow. For example, in English the word *cosmonaut*, literally 'world navigator,' comes from Greek. In Hungarian the word *ür-hajós* ('world navigator') means the same, but all the morphemes are native to Hungarian. Similarly, most languages of Europe use a variant of the word *president* for the head of a company or a republic. Not so in Hungarian: the word for president is *elnök*, which literally means 'first one.'

This shows that *some speech communities purposely reject foreign imports*. Their language ideologies place negative values on foreign words as unacceptable tokens of language mixing. Sometimes government bodies are even set up to ensure that people speak a "pure" language. Recently, the Academy of the French Language became alarmed at how many people are slipping English words into their French (see Textbox 13.1). They established hefty fines for those who fail to use a French word and use an English word instead.

---

### TEXTBOX 13.1 L'ACADÉMIE FRANÇAISE

Established in 1635 and located in Paris, the French Academy is a body of forty elected officials who are experts on the French language. Elected officials hold office for life and are in charge of compiling, editing, and publishing France's official dictionary, *Dictionnaire de l'Académie française*, which includes approving or denying foreign loanwords for use in French and making occasional revisions to the standard orthography. The Academy also awards prizes to French artists and scholars in literature, painting, poetry, theater, cinema, history, and translation. In an effort to keep French "pure," the Academy has taken a stance against English loanwords like *email* and *software* and against local minority languages including Basque, Catalan, and Occitan.

---

## 13.2  Borrowings

When speakers of different languages interact, they borrow forms and meanings. *How much they borrow depends on cultural and social factors*, including the degree of knowledge of each other's languages, speakers' sense of purism, and also on the structure of the languages in contact. Complex morphological patterns in a language can make the incorporation of a foreign word difficult, and thus serve as a natural obstacle to foreign intruders.

**Figure 13.1** L'Académie française, the Academy of the French Language, in Paris

**Borrowing** is one of the primary effects of language contact. A borrowed item is called a **loan**. Some borrowed words are easy to recognize. A person can be said to experience *angst* or *schadenfreude*; a language may have *ablaut*, and a country can be said to engage in *realpolitik*. What we have here, in italics, are **lexical borrowing**: they are words from one language (German) adopted into another (English).

If something is really "cool," an English-speaking youth could refer to it as *über-cool*. The root *cool* is English. But the prefix *über* is German; it means 'super.' This word contains a **grammatical borrowing**, the borrowing of a derivational prefix. Lexical and grammatical forms can be borrowed directly. Or they can come via an intermediate language (See Textbox 13.2).

---

### TEXTBOX 13.2

The preposition *via* 'by way of' comes from the Latin word *via* (the ablative singular form of the Latin noun *via* 'road, channel, course,' literally meaning 'from the road, by the road'). This came into English in about 1779 (Barnhart 2008: 1202).

After South America was colonized by the Spanish and the Portuguese, many words from local languages made their way into English through the intermediaries of these two languages. The word *jaguar* is a legacy of the now extinct Tupinambá language from South America; it came into English through the intermediary of Portuguese.

**TABLE 13.2** Loanwords in English, borrowed from an Arawak language Taino via Spanish.

| Original form | Original meaning | Spanish | English |
|---|---|---|---|
| *barfacoa* | 'raised frame of sticks, a table used for sleeping or cooking' | *barbacoa* (first noted 1655–1665) | *barbecue* (first noted 1697) |
| *hamaca* | 'hammock' | *hamaca* (first noted in 1545–1555) | *hammock* (first noted *c.* 1555) |
| *hurakán* | 'strong wind' | *hurracán* (first noted in 1510–1515) | *hurricane* (first noted *c.* 1650) |

(Sources: Corominas (1961: 83); *The Oxford English Dictionary* (1989); Gastambide Arrillaga (1990: 15); Barnhart (2008: 1202).)

Table 13.2 lists some examples of words from Taino, an Arawak language spoken in the region of what is now Cuba, which were borrowed into Spanish in the sixteenth and seventeenth centuries. These are now common English words.

These words were borrowed as labels for novel items (for instance, a hanging bed, or hammock) or for area-specific phenomena (an unusually strong wind, a hurricane), for which Spanish (and English) had no word. For more on another type of loanword, see Textbox 13.3.

*Sometimes borrowing involves lexical* calquing: *the creation of a new word by translating morpheme-by-morpheme from a source language.* For instance, the German *Ein-drück* 'impression' (lit. 'in-press') has been calqued from Latin *im-pressio*, where each morpheme is translated from Latin into German. The term for 'roof' in Nigerian Arabic translates literally as 'the head of the house' (Owens 1996): this is how speakers of the surrounding Chadic languages refer to a roof.

In addition to lexical calques, *some calques can also be grammatical*. As an example, consider Pennsylvania German (also referred to as Pennsylvania Dutch in the United States), a language spoken by the Mennonite Anabaptists of Swiss-German

---

## TEXTBOX 13.3 PSEUDO-LOANS

Speakers of a language may think they've borrowed a word from another language, when actually that word does not exist in the assumed source language. The German word *Handy* refers to a mobile phone, and many Germans think that it was borrowed from English. It does look English, but there is no such word in English with this meaning. The word *footing* in French means 'jogging' – again, this sounds like an English word, but English does not have it. This is what linguists call **pseudo-loans** (Curnow 2001: 427 discusses this in some detail).

Another example of a pseudo-loan is found in Japanese, where the term *furii daiaru*, borrowed from English *free* and *dial*, means 'toll free,' even though the concept is not expressed this way in English.

origin who left Pennsylvania for Ontario, Canada, after the American Revolutionary War. Most speakers of Pennsylvania German are bilingual in English. Their variety of German is replete with calques. One is the immediate future tense, which is expressed by *geh* 'go,' a development inspired by English *gonna* (Burridge 2006: 183).

***Meanings can also be borrowed.*** This can be seen when the meaning of a word is extended to match the range of meanings found in a neighboring, and often dominant, language. The Lakhota verb *iŋyaŋk* originally meant 'to run,' that is, to describe 'the activity of moving fast on one's legs.' In contemporary Lakhota, due to extensive contact with English, this same verb is commonly used to mean 'to run for election, to function, operate, work as a device, machine, system, concept' (Ullrich 2008: 775). Semantic extensions that arise through borrowing are referred to as **semantic loans**.

***Phonemes can also be borrowed.*** Imagine a language spoken in a geographical area surrounded by languages of a different genetic affiliation. Such a language is likely to develop features atypical for the family it belongs to but shared with its neighbors. This is how Armenian, an Indo-European language, developed glottalized consonants, a feature rarely found in Indo-European; Armenian speakers were in intensive contact with speakers of surrounding Caucasian languages, in which glottalized consonants are ubiquitous (see Chirikba 2008).

Another example is the English phoneme /v/. As noted in Chapter 12, this was originally an allophone of the phoneme /f/ with a predictable distribution, as in *wife* versus *wives*. Then many French words with *v* found their way into English, among them *very*, *valley*, *vain*, and *ravine*. These new words had *v* in a wide range of environments, disrupting the old English pattern of complementary distribution between the allophones [v] and [f]. This caused the two to become different phonemes.

***In addition to words, many languages borrow grammatical forms***, including derivational and inflectional affixes, conjunctions, and discourse markers. For example, speakers of Pennsylvania German freely use English *well* and *I see* in their speech (see Burridge 2006: 189), discourse markers that are commonly used in English. ***Bound morphemes – prefixes and suffixes – are not immune to borrowing***. The prefix *über-*, borrowed from German into English, was exemplified above. Another example is the Spanish plural marker *-s*, which has made its way into Mexicano, a Uto-Aztecan language from central Mexico. The Mexicano word for 'basket' is *chiquihuitl*; to pluralize it, one adds the Spanish suffix *-s*, obtaining *chiquihuite-s* (Hill and Hill 1986: 165). See Textbox 13.4 on the difference between borrowing and code-switching.

## 13.2.1  How do words change through borrowing?

***Once a foreign form is borrowed, it often assimilates to the phonological patterns of the recipient language***. The words *spaghetti* and *gelato* have both been borrowed into English from Italian. In the American English pronunciation of both words, the final syllable begins with an alveolar flap [ɾ], a quick ballistic movement of

---

**TEXTBOX 13.4 BORROWING VERSUS CODE-SWITCHING**

When speakers borrow an expression from another language, they insert it into the structures of their native language so that it is surrounded by native words and fits into native grammatical structures. This practice is distinct from **code-switching**, where a speaker, in a single conversational turn (sometimes even within a single sentence), will switch entirely from one language into another, shifting all phonological, grammatical, and lexical features. Code-switching is further discussed and illustrated in Chapter 11.

---

the tongue against the alveolar ridge. This follows the normal phonological pattern in most American English words – one finds the same sound in the final syllables of *potato* and *convoluted*. But in Italian, these words are pronounced differently: the final syllable of the word *gelato* has a voiceless aspirated stop, and the final syllable of *spaghetti* has a **geminate** consonant, or a lengthened stop, represented in writing by the doubling of the letter *t*. We can say that as these words were borrowed, they were assimilated to the phonological patterns of American English. This is known as **adaptation**: *when a foreign sound in a borrowed word does not exist in the recipient language, it is replaced by the nearest phonetic equivalent*. Words that have been perfectly integrated into the phonological and morphological systems of the language can be difficult to identify as borrowings. It takes a linguist to detect that the English words *cherries*, *very*, and *beauty* are in fact loans, from Old Norman French *cherise*, Old French *verai*, *varai*, *vrai*, and Old French *bealte*, *beaute*, *biaute* respectively.

In contrast, unassimilated loans can stand apart from native words in their phonological make-up. In Mazateco, an Oto-Manguean language from Mexico, all voiceless stops become voiced after nasals; thus we never find the sequence [nt], only [nd]. However, in some Spanish loans, among them *siento* (from Spanish *ciento*), a frequently used word for 'one hundred,' one does find the native Spanish sequence [nt]. Mazateco has been described as having two coexistent phonemic systems – one native, and one for loans (see Fries and Pike 1949).

*If enough loans are unassimilated, new sounds can enter the phoneme inventory.* The case of English /v/ was noted above. Another example is /ʒ/, which was not a phoneme in English prior to contact with French. Like /v/, this sound developed into a separate phoneme in English as a result of numerous loans from French, such as *rouge*. Its adoption reinforced an independent sound change: the palatalization of /zj/ to /ʒ/, as in the word *Asia* (see Campbell 1999: 62).

*Some loanwords are borrowed with their meanings intact, while others undergo semantic shift;* the meanings of loanwords are never fully predictable. We can see this when a single word is borrowed more than once in the history of a language; the different instances of borrowing can develop different meanings in the recipient language, for example, English *chief* and *chef* were both borrowed from the same French word, but *chief* was borrowed into Middle English in the fourteenth century, while *chef* came into Modern English in the nineteenth century.

***Some loans retain morphological features of the source language.*** For example, some Latin borrowings into English require the Latin plural, e.g., the plural of *colloquium* is *colloquia*, whereas others allow either the Latin plural or the English plural, for example, *syllabus* can be pluralized either as *syllabuses* or as *syllabi*. Other borrowed nouns are fully assimilated into the English morphological system and take only the English plural, e.g., *diplomas* as opposed to the original Greek *diplomata*, or *pastas* instead of the Italian plural *paste*.

***Some loans retain syntactic features of loanwords, resulting in the development of new syntactic distinctions.*** An example is Tetun Dili, an Austronesian language spoken in East Timor. This language is currently borrowing many words from Portuguese, a national language. Portuguese nouns, like those of other Romance languages, fall into masculine and feminine gender classes. Articles, adjectives, and other dependent elements in the noun phrase agree in gender with the head noun. Tetun Dili, on the other hand, has no native gender system. However, the Portuguese loanwords are now being borrowed in such great numbers that the genders are being borrowed as well; these nouns require agreement within the noun phrase, as in Portuguese. The result is that Tetun Dili has two systems of nouns, one gendered and one not, with only the former requiring agreement. A similar principle applies to adjectives. For example, the borrowed Portuguese adjective meaning 'pretty, handsome' will have two forms: masculine *bonitu*, from Portuguese *bonito*, and feminine *bonita*, from Portuguese *bonita*. But native adjectives, such as *di'ak* 'good,' will have just one form for both genders (Hajek 2006: 173).

### 13.2.2   Are some forms or some meanings easier to borrow than others?

One of the hardest tasks in comparative linguistics is to tease apart similarities due to genetic inheritance and those due to borrowing and contact. This task would be easier if certain categories of forms or structures were never borrowed, since then similarities in these categories across languages could easily be attributed to shared genetic inheritance. However, ***while some types of forms are more resistant to borrowing than others, no linguistic feature is entirely "borrowing-proof."*** Words of all lexical classes – including possibly surprising categories, such as numerals, personal pronouns, conjunctions, and discourse markers – can be borrowed.

As stated above, ***affixes and grammatical elements can also be borrowed***. We saw above how the German prefix *über* and the Latin preposition *via* have made their way into English. We also find English suffixes of French origin, including *-ment*, as in *develop-ment*, and *-age*, as in *out-age*. In Bolivian Quechua, the Spanish diminutive *-itu* is used with native words, e.g., *rumi-tu* 'little stone.' And the Spanish plural suffix *-s* can appear on native nouns together with the native plural marker *-kuna*: *runa-s-kuna* means 'men,' where *runa* is the native Quechua word for 'man' (see Appel and Muysken 2005: 172–173).

*Some grammatical and features are particularly amenable to borrowing.* About one-quarter of the world's languages have grammatical systems that obligatorily mark how the speaker has come to know the information being expressed. Such systems are said to mark the speaker's information source, or his or her evidence for the facts being conveyed; this is known as **evidentiality**. Getting your information source right is a prerequisite for successful communication in such languages. This is the case in numerous North American Indian languages, including Southern Paiute and Verde Valley Yavapai (Bunte and Kendall 1981). Because the expression of this category is central to their communicative practice, speakers of these languages will sometimes use native evidential markers when they speak English. For example, if a Paiute speaker knows that a woman named Minnie is pregnant because someone told him, he will pass the news onto another by saying *Minnie is pregnant ikm:* the particle *ikm* indicates that the speaker learned this information through a third source, as opposed to learning it through direct observation or by some other means. The fact that evidential meanings – and forms – are prone to borrowing reflects their importance to speakers who have these as part of their linguistic systems; their prevalence in the world's languages shows how important they are in human communication.

### 13.2.3 Why borrow?

There are many reasons why people borrow features from other languages. With loanwords, the most common reason is to fill a gap for an item or a concept that the language has no word for. This explains borrowings such as *hammock* (see above), *umlaut*, from German, or *karma*, from Sanskrit. However, there are also more subtle reasons for borrowing. Borrowing may be motivated by prestige, language attitudes, or civic institutions.

*Borrowing may be motivated by prestige.* Consider the English forms for hooved animals in Table 13.3. The forms in the left-hand column are native, and the ones in the right-hand column are borrowed from French. They belong to an era when French culture dominated the English after the Norman Conquest of 1066, putting emphasis on cuisine and elegant dining (Hock 1991: 385). The terms in the left-hand column refer to animals themselves, the area relegated to peasants who had no exposure to

**TABLE 13.3** Native and borrowed terms for hooved animals in English

| English native forms | Forms borrowed from French |
| --- | --- |
| cow, bull, ox | beef |
| calf | veal |
| pig/hog/swine | pork |
| sheep | mutton |

French, or to elegant life. The terms in the right-hand column belong to the sphere of cuisine, where French influence was strong: this explains why they are of French origin.

The cultural dominance of the French-speaking court in administration and warfare is also reflected in the numerous terms from these lexical fields, such as *justice*, *legal*, *court*, *curfew*, and *grand jury*. In the current era, we see a different direction of borrowing, with many terms related to information technology being borrowed from English into other languages. For an example of this in Spanish, see Textbox 13.5.

***Language attitudes of speakers, sometimes institutionalized through governmental or civic organizations, can determine whether loanwords are acceptable or not***. In many languages, "foreign" importations are rejected tokens of unacceptable "language-mixing." A cultural inhibition against recognizably foreign items and ensuing linguistic purism provides a mechanism for stopping an influx of borrowed forms. Once speakers become conscious of the foreign material in their lexicon – or grammar – they can try to get rid of it. This has happened in the history of various literary languages, including Hungarian, Finnish, and Estonian (see Fodor 1984, Tauli 1984). Such moves towards linguistic purism reflect the association of a group's identity with its own language, in contrast to surrounding, often more dominant, groups (Thurston 1987: 93).

As we have seen, the nature and degree of language contact are reflections of the history, language attitudes, and social interactions of speech communities. They can also reflect the relative political status of each group. A minor language is likelier to borrow forms from a dominant one than the other way around. This is why we find numerous loans from Spanish into indigenous Meso-American and South American languages, and just a handful of loans from indigenous languages into Spanish.

---

### TEXTBOX 13.5 **HOW TO *EMAIL* IN SPANISH?**

The following discussion was recently spied on a blog about the Spanish language. What does this exchange tell us about the role of English in the domain of electronic media?

**Question:** I saw in a sample Spanish sentence recently that you used the word *emails*. First of all, why didn't you use a real Spanish word for email? Second, even if that were a Spanish word, why isn't the plural *emailes* instead of *emails*?

**Answer:** These days, believe it or not, *email* (or *e-mail*) is a Spanish word, very commonly used, although it has not been recognized yet by the Spanish Royal Academy and is considered by many to be an Anglicism. It even has a verb form, *emailear*, that is sometimes used. It is one of those English words that has been adopted into Spanish even though some perfectly good "real" Spanish alternatives exist.

## 13.3  Bilingual communities, diglossia, and language shift

Any individual is a member of a linguistic community. If a community is composed of a number of groups each speaking a different language, an individual may be bilingual or multilingual. ***Bilingualism can be individual***: for instance, some descendants of Swedes in America may still speak some Swedish. ***Or it can be societal***: to be able to communicate within your group, you need to know more than one language. Examples of societal bilingualism include Slovak and Hungarian in the border areas between Slovakia and Hungary, or French and English in French Canada.

***The use of different languages may correlate with different social settings.*** For example, for many years Latin was the language of the Church, and local European languages were used in day-to-day communication. ***Using two varieties of the same language under clearly specified conditions is known as*** diglossia. This is when a more prestigious, and usually more archaic, form of a language is used in "high" functions (such as church, school, literature), and a less prestigious colloquial variety is used in "low" functions (day-to-day oral interaction). For instance, in Arabic diglossia, the "high" language of the Koran coexists with local vernaculars. And in Switzerland, Swiss German (*Schwyzertütsch*) varieties are the language of day-to-day interaction in the German-speaking cantons, with Standard German being the "high" variety.

***In a multilingual situation, the "low" and the "high" varieties are often represented by different languages.*** For many generations, Spanish was a "high" language for Quechua and Aymara speakers, so was restricted to social domains such as religion and government. What may help a minority language survive is its defined role in the society and its special value for the speakers as a repository of heritage and tradition, and a symbol of identity. This is part of what is keeping many Quechua varieties alive.

In a diglossic or multiglossic situation, languages typically influence each other. This usually works in the direction from high to low. For example, three languages are spoken in Sauris, a German linguistic enclave in northeastern Italy (Denison 1971, Lehiste 1988: 53–54): an archaic form of Southern Bavarian German, Italian (the national language), and Friulian (a Romance language closely related to Italian but distinct from it). German is the "low" language: it is used within the family. Italian, the language of organized schooling and religion, is the high language. Friulian is in between high and low; it is the language of communication with the surrounding Friulian speakers, and also serves as a symbol of in-group solidarity among young males who did their secondary schooling in a regional center. Denison noticed that Italian and Friulian elements are acceptable in German (the low language). However, German elements are not introduced into either Italian or Friulian. And Italian – the high language – is also immune from intrusions of the "lower" Friulian. The social relationships between languages and their domains of use correlate with the degree of influence of one onto the other.

In certain types of social situations, the speakers of one language may shift to speaking another, which is typically the language of a socially dominant group. When the majority of a community shifts, it can lead to the **endangerment**, impending **obsolescence**, and **death** of minor languages. ***When a community loses its language as it adopts a dominant one, it is said to have undergone language shift***. The original language may leave its traces on the newly acquired language. For example, the variety of English spoken in Ireland has a distinctive prosodic pattern (colloquially referred to as a "lilt"), which was brought into the language when Gaelic speakers learned English. Like most speakers who acquire a new language as adults, they did not adopt the prosody of the language they are acquiring, but spoke it with their native patterns of rhythm and pitch. Owing to the numerical predominance of Gaelic people in the region, these Gaelic prosodic patterns were adopted by English children, making it a regular feature of the dialect (also see Filippula 2003).

## 13.4   Pidgins and creoles

In the process of European colonization, enslaved or subjugated people from many different linguistic groups were often forced to work closely together. They frequently spoke different languages from their fellow workers and from their employers or overseers; however, they still needed a common idiom for the purpose of business communication. Hence the name "pidgin" which comes from the English word *business*. **Pidgins *are contact languages that are not native to any of those who speak it***. Pidgins are used for fairly limited communication between speakers of different languages who have no other language in common. French, Spanish, Portuguese, English, and Dutch – the major languages of the colonizers – provided the foundation for European-based pidgins.

***Not all pidgins resulted from colonization.*** Trade pidgins also developed outside the world of European colonization. Among them is Chinook Jargon in the Pacific Northwest of North America, Iatmul pidgin in the Sepik area of New Guinea, and various pidgins in the Arctic area (see Jahr and Broch 1996). ***Pidgins are typically limited in their lexicon and simplified in their structure***, compared to the languages they are based on.

As speakers of a pidgin start marrying each other, and the language becomes their primary means of communication, it begins to evolve a more complex structure and richer vocabulary. And for children born of such couples, the pidgin becomes their first language. ***A former pidgin which has acquired native speakers is called a*** **creole**. An example is Tok Pisin, a national language of Papua New Guinea.

---

### TEXTBOX 13.6 **KOINÉS**

When closely related languages, or dialects of the same language, are in constant contact with each other, a need for a common language arises. However, if the varieties may be thought of as having about equal prestige for cultural or political reasons, then a **koiné** can emerge. A koiné is a partly artificial language or dialect devised and employed as a vehicle for supra-regional communication between speakers of closely related languages or dialects.

Swahili and Lingala, two languages of the Bantu family, and the largest national languages in Africa, are also believed to have originated as koinés. They are somewhat simplified compared to other Bantu languages: for instance, they do not have tones.

Koinés are bona fide members of their respective language families (unlike pidgins and creoles). They are somewhat anomalous in that they have features that did not arise as a result of normal historical development.

---

*Pidgins and creoles are generally agreed not to belong to any single language family*: they arise as a makeshift means for filling communicative needs, rather than evolving from natural transmission in the way of regular, non-contact languages. (For an explanation of yet another way a new language can arise, see Textbox 13.6 on Koinés.)

**SIDEBAR 13.1**

SOURCES OF TOK PISIN VOCABULARY

Look at each word in (1) and try to recognize the lexical source of each word and their meanings in Tok Pisin. One word is not from English; can you figure out which one and where it might be from? When you are done, check your answers in Sidebar 13.2 on the next page.

The language of the socially dominant population in a situation of creolization is referred to as the **superstrate** language. As it typically contributes most of a creole's vocabulary, it is also called the **lexifier** language. Minority languages that contribute to the formation of a pidgin or a creole are called **substrate** languages (see Sidebar 13.1). Some vocabulary from the substrate language typically makes it into a creole. In addition, meanings are often influenced by the indigenous languages that provide the substrate. Tok Pisin, which is spoken in new Guinea, is an English-based creole. The vocabulary includes the noun *gras*, from English *grass*, but in Tok Pisin it refers to grass, hair, and fur. This polysemy is the effect of the substrate from Oceanic languages, especially Tolai, that has a noun with these three meanings.

A typical creole looks similar to the lexifier language in terms of its vocabulary, but the grammar is very much unlike it. Consider example (1) from Tok Pisin. You will notice that many – but not all – words are English-based.

(1)   *Mi no save yet sapos bai mi stap long hia o bai mi go long Brisbane long dispela taim*
'I don't know yet if I will be here or if I go to Brisbane at that time'

Example (2) comes from Kristang, a Portuguese-based creole from Malaysia (Baxter 1988: 213). The forms are Portuguese, but the way they are put together (the grammar) is completely different.

(2)    *kora*    *yo*    *ja*    *chegá*    *nali*    *eli*    *ja*    *kaba*    *bai*
      when    1SG    PRF    arrive    DIST    3SG    PRF    finish    go
      'When I arrived there he had gone'

## 13.5   Substratum interference

**SIDEBAR 13.2**

SOURCES OF TOK PISIN
VOCABULARY: ANSWERS

Tok Pisin

| form | English source | Meaning in (1) |
|------|----------------|----------------|
| mi | me | 'I' |
| no | no | NEG |
| yet | yet | yet |
| sapos | suppose | 'if'/'whether' |
| bai | by | FUT |
| stop | stop | 'be at,' 'stay' |
| long | long | location |
| hia | here | here |
| o | or | or |
| go | go | go |
| dispela | this fella | this |
| taim | time | time |

The word from another language is *save* 'know,' from French *savoir*.

If a particular population needs to learn the language of a smaller yet politically dominant group (as is sometimes the case following foreign invasions), they often acquire the **target language** in an incomplete fashion, and so speak it in an altered form. ***The children of the dominant group might then adopt the altered forms of the target-language speakers and so change the target language itself***. Such processes of **substratum interference** have occurred in the history of many languages. Examples include English varieties spoken in Singapore, Papua New Guinea, and other places, or the Afrikaans variety spoken in Zimbabwe.

Majority languages that have dominated indigenous languages in many countries can bear the substrate impact of the minority variety. The English spoken in Ireland has been influenced by the Celtic substrate (see Hilbert 2008; Filppula 2003: 167). The Irish prosodic patterns were mentioned above. Another example is the use of *be* instead of *have* in Irish English, e.g., *They're gone mad* instead of *They've gone mad* (Filppula 2003: 166–167). This structure is parallel to how *be* is used in Gaelic (Irish) and could be attributed to substrate influence.

## 13.6   Linguistic areas

***Borrowings and structural similarities may extend over all or most of the languages in a geographical region, whether they are related or not.*** This results from large-scale linguistic diffusion, which defines the region as a **linguistic area** or a **Sprachbund**. Although languages in these situations are from different families, they become typologically similar: languages may remain different in many of their forms, but their structures will **converge** towards a similar prototype.

    ***A linguistic area is defined as a geographic region including languages from at least two language families, or different subgroups of the same family, sharing significant traits.*** Within a linguistic area, **diffusion**, the spread of linguistic features from one language (or person) to the next, can be unilateral (when it primarily proceeds from one language to the others) or multilateral (when multiple languages exert influence on the others). Languages within an area often share a fair number of features. However, it can be difficult to determine whether those shared features are due to diffusion, as opposed to accidental coincidence, language universals, or genetic factors (if the languages in contact are related).

In an important study of Meso-America as a linguistic area, Campbell, Kaufman, and Smith-Stark demonstrated that not all shared features have the same "weight" in determining whether or not a region is a linguistic area. They state that: "highly 'marked', exotic, or unique shared traits count more than does material that is more easily developed independently, or found widely in other languages" (1986: 535–536). Thus, the best types of evidence for a linguistic area are not traits that are inherited from a common ancestor or due to chance or universals, but those that can be shown to be diffused.

Thus, a highly frequent phenomenon – such as verb-final constituent order, the existence of nasalized vowels, or the presence of a past versus non-past opposition in the tense system – would not be assigned as much weight in determining a linguistic area as would a more exotic, unusual characteristic. An example of such an exotic feature is the marking of evidentiality in the Vaupés area of Brazil; we will return to this shortly.

While a single typologically common trait cannot by itself define a linguistic area, the clustering of traits can be area-specific. When we look at different linguistic areas throughout the world, we see that each is defined by a different cluster of properties. Here are four examples of linguistic areas and the features which define them:

1. Meso-America (Campbell et al. 1986). The languages of this region belong to several different language families, including Mayan, Mixe-Zoquean, Totonacan, and Otomanguean, among others.
   (i) Nominal possession of the type *his-dog the man* ('the man's dog');
   (ii) Body-part nouns being used as markers of spatial relationships (e.g., 'head' for 'on top of');
   (iii) Vigesimal numeral systems (i.e., systems of counting based on twenty as opposed to ten);
   (iv) Basic constituent orders that are not verb final;
   (v) Numerous **lexical collocations**, or ways of expressing particular concepts that are common throughout the Meso-American area, e.g., 'knee' as 'head of the leg,' or 'boa-constrictor' as 'deer-snake.'

2. The Balkan Peninsula. All the languages belonging to the Balkan linguistic area are Indo-European, but from different subgroups. The Slavic languages include Serbian, Croatian, Bulgarian, and Macedonian; there is also Romanian (a Romance language), Greek, and Albanian. Some scholars add to this Romani (the language of the Gypsies, from the Indo-Aryan branch of Indo-European) and Turkish, an unrelated Turkic language.
   (i) A central vowel /ɨ/ or /ə/ (absent from Greek and Macedonian);
   (ii) A single affix that is used for both the dative and genitive cases;
   (iii) Articles that follow the noun (absent from Greek);

(iv) A future tense marked by an auxiliary corresponding to 'want' or 'have' (absent from Bulgarian and Macedonian);

(v) The use of the auxiliary verb corresponding to 'have' in constructions of the type *I have gone* in English (i.e., perfect aspect constructions);

(vi) The absence of infinitives in complement clauses;

(vii) The use of a pronoun in addition to a full noun phrase to refer to an animate object, so that the object is marked twice (Friedman 2006).

3. The Vaupés River Basin in Brazil and Colombia. Languages from this region belong to the genetically unrelated Tucanoan and Arawak families. The area is characterized by obligatory societal multilingualism, based on the principle of **linguistic exogamy**: one can only marry someone who speaks a different language.

(i) Nasalization that occurs on most or all segments in a word;

(ii) Four to five evidential morphemes, which mark the way in which the speaker has acquired the information (whether seen, heard, inferred, assumed, or learned from someone else);

(iii) Numerous **classifiers** used with demonstratives, numerals, and in possessive constructions;

(iv) Small systems of genders in verbal agreement;

(v) Nominative-accusative case-marking;

(vi) A single locative case-marker that indicates direction ('to'), location ('in, at'), and source ('from');

(vii) Numerous lexical collocations, e.g., 'father of goods' = 'rich man.'

4. South Asia (Emeneau 1956; Masica 1976, 2001). This linguistic area is composed of languages from the Indo-Aryan, Dravidian, Munda, and Tibeto-Burman families.

(i) Retroflex consonants, especially stops;

(ii) Dative-subject constructions (where some subject arguments are marked with the dative case);

(iii) A compound verb construction whereby a special auxiliary combines with the immediately preceding main verb and the two verbs referring to a single event;

(iv) The use of an affix to mark causation;

(v) Verb-final constituent order.

It is important to reiterate that no single one of the features is found only in the particular linguistic area, as you can find similar features throughout the world. However, the clustering of the properties is area-specific; it is only in the particular area that the whole set of properties recur in language after language.

In a situation of intensive language contact within a linguistic area, the gradual convergence of languages may result in **structural isomorphism**. In such a case, the grammar and the semantics of one language are almost fully replicated in another. A classic example in the literature is the village of Kupwar in India, where long-standing language contact between Indo-Aryan and Dravidian languages has resulted in extreme convergence (see Gumperz and Wilson (1971); and also Nadkarni 1975)).

Another example of a striking **structural isomorphism** comes from two languages spoken within the Vaupés River Basin linguistic area. Consider the two sentences below, both taken from traditional stories involving a female cannibal. Example (3) is from Tariana, an Arawak language, and (4) is from Tucano, a Tucanoan language, which is in constant contact with Tariana. Compare the content and order of the morphemes in these two examples; you will see that they are almost identical.

(3)  Tariana

*nese*      *pa:ma*         *di-na*
then       one.NUM.CLF.F    3SG.NF-OBJ

*du-yana-sita-pidana*
3SG.F-cook-ALREADY-REM.PST.REPORT
'She had reportedly cooked him already' (reportedly, a long time ago)

(4)  Tucano

*tiíta*     *ni'kó*      *kīī-re*
then       one.NUM.CLF.F    3SG.M-OBJ

*do'á-toha-po'*
cook-ALREADY-REM.PST.REPORT.3SG.F
'She had reportedly cooked him already'

**Figure 13.2** Tariana men from Santa Rosa, who have Tariana as their first language and who also speak Wanano, Desano, and Piratapuya. The women speak Piratapuya, Wanano, Siriano (Tucanoan), and Baniwa (Arawak), but hardly any Tariana. Everyone also knows Tucano, and most people know Portuguese.

Linguistic convergence does not always result in the creation of identical grammars. It is also not the case that categories in language contact always match. Languages in contact often maintain some distinct typological traits. This can be seen from Examples (3) and (4): Tariana maintains its prefixes, and Tucano its suffixes.

Examples of convergence within linguistic areas show that languages may come to be structurally similar due to areal diffusion, notwithstanding the original differences between them.

## CHAPTER SUMMARY

Languages and their speakers do not exist in a vacuum. Different linguistic communities frequently come into contact with each other. Their languages are then in contact, with many speakers of one language having some knowledge of the other. Speakers naturally borrow linguistic features back and forth; habits of pronunciation, significant sounds (phonemes), grammatical categories, vocabulary items, and even some grammatical forms are taken from one language and applied in another.

Here are some of the general principles that have been presented:

- Languages reflect the sociolinguistic history of their speakers. If one language community dominates the other, we expect the language of the dominant group to have more impact than the language of the other group.
- Language contact may result in direct diffusion (borrowed lexical and grammatical forms) and indirect diffusion (borrowed or calqued patterns).
- Language contact may result in the creation of pidgins and creoles. These are non-genetic in their origins, and do not belong to any linguistic family.
- Languages may share features, or combinations of features, as members of an extensive linguistic area.
- Convergence within linguistic areas and contact situations may result in one language adopting the structure of the other. Or it may result in one language adopting new patterns and forms, while at the same time preserving some of its own properties. The outcomes of convergent development depend on the degrees of dominance within each area.

## TEXTBOX 13.7 **GLOSSING CONVENTIONS USED IN THIS CHAPTER**

| Convention | Meaning | Convention | Meaning |
|---|---|---|---|
| 1 | first person | NF | non-feminine |
| 3 | third person | NUM.CLF | numeral classifier |
| ALREADY | already | OBJ | objective |
| DIST | distal | PRF | perfect aspect |
| F | feminine | REM.PST | remote past |
| M | masculine | REPORT | non-personal knowledge |
| | | SG | singular |

## SUGGESTIONS FOR FURTHER READING

**Appel, René and Pieter Muysken**. 2005. *Language contact and bilingualism*. Amsterdam: Academic Archive.

A concise introduction to language contact, with a focus on bilingualism and language acquisition.

**Lehiste, Ilse**. 1988. *Lectures on language contact*. Cambridge, Mass.: MIT Press.

A brief general introduction to language contact, full of insights and generalizations, with an incisive characterization of concepts such as linguistic area and creolization.

**Thomason, Sarah G. and T. Kaufman**. 1988. *Language contact, creolization and genetic linguistics*. Berkeley: University of California Press.

An overview of language contact and contact-induced change, with an emphasis on sociopolitical factors rather than linguistic features in language contact.

**Weinreich, U.** 1953. *Languages in contact*. New York: Linguistic Circle of New York.

A classic work on language contact, with a focus on bilingual communities, and a must-read for any student of language contact.

**Winford, Donald**. 2003. *An introduction to contact linguistics*. Oxford: Blackwell.

An up-to-date introduction to issues related to language contact, with a special focus on the formation of creoles and pidgins.

## EXERCISES

1. When words are borrowed into a language, they can retain their basic meanings but take on different stylistic connotations. This is often the case with French and Latin loans in English.

   A prominent linguist was asked to write a grant proposal for a high-status grant-giving agency. He then was asked to write a popular article for a students' magazine on the same topic as his grant proposal. Two extracts from the grant application and two from the popular article are given below.

   **Extract 1**
   *In similar fashion, scholars have demonstrated the genetic unity of Australian languages.*

   **Extract 2**
   *In exactly the same way, linguists have shown that almost all the languages of Australia belong to one language family.*

   **Extract 3**
   *The documentation of endangered languages is, for a number of reasons, one of the highest priorities facing mankind at the turn of the millennium.*

   **Extract 4**
   *Writing grammars and descriptions of languages that are about to die is, for all sorts of reasons, one of the most important things to be done in the world as we near the year 2000.*

a. Identify which two extracts come from the grant application, and which two come from the popular article. What specific features of each extract served as clues as you considered this?
b. Using a dictionary that provides reliable etymologies (such as the *Merriam-Webster Online*), look up the source language of each of the following words and state whether the word was originally Germanic (i.e., evolved from Old English and is related to Old High German, Old Norse, etc.) or whether it was borrowed into the language from a Romance language (i.e., Latin or French) or Greek.

**Extract 1**
*similar*
*fashion*
*scholar*
*demonstrate*
*genesis* (attested in this extract in the etymologically related word *genetic*)
*unity*
*Austr-* (attested in the word *Australian*)
*language*

**Extract 2**
*exact* (attested in the word *exactly*)
*same*
*way*
*linguist*
*show* (attested in the word *shown*)
*almost*
*all*
*belong*
*one*
*family*

**Extract 3**
*document* (attested in the word *documentation*)
*danger* (attested in the word *endangered*)
*number*
*reason*
*high* (attested in the word *highest*)
*prior* (attested in the word *priority*)
*face* (attested in the word *facing*)
*man*
*kind*
*turn*
*millennium*

**Extract 4**
*write*
*grammar*
*scribe* (attested in the word *description*)
*about*
*die*
*sort*

*reason*
*most*
*important*
*thing*
*do*
*world*
*near*
*year*

   c.  Based on your answers to tasks (a) and (b), what can you say about the relationship of the historical source of vocabulary to academic and popular genres of written English?

**2.**   Identify the origin of each of the following loanwords in English and explain why you think they were borrowed;
   a.  *karma*
   b.  *svastika*
   c.  *cumquat*
   d.  *pajamas*
   e.  *croissant*
   f.  *cockatoo*
   g.  *kangaroo*
   h.  *mutton*
   i.  *canoe*
   j.  *torso*

**3.**   Zulu borrowings (Adopted from Zhurinskij 1995: 33. In Zulu orthography, the trigraph *tsh* represents an aspirated post-alveolar affricate [tʃʰ], the letter *j* indicates a voiced post-alveolar affricate [dʒ], and the letter *y* indicates the palatal glide [j].)

   a.  The following data presents a list of loanwords borrowed into Zulu from English.
      i.  Determine the original English source for each loanword. (Examples (e), (q), and (aa) are proper nouns.)
     ii.  The initial vowel is a separate Zulu morpheme that is added based on the semantics of the loan. What semantic class of noun takes *u-* instead of *i-*?
    iii.  State the phonological rules by which English words are assimilated into Zulu phonology. (Note: It is always better to state a general rule, such as "voiceless stops become voiced," than to state multiple specific rules, such as p>b, t>d, and k>g.)

     A.  *ipulatifomu*
     B.  *isiginali*
     C.  *ipikiniki*
     D.  *ipalagilafu*
     E.  *ifulansi*
     F.  *ikilasi*
     G.  *igilamafoni*
     H.  *iminiti*
     I.  *igilamu*
     J.  *ipulani*
     K.  *ikiliniki*
     L.  *ibizinisi*
     M.  *ujamu*
     N.  *uwisiki*
     O.  *itenisi*
     P.  *ibesiboli*

Q. *ifulentshi*
R. *ipuleti*
S. *idina*
T. *idesiki*
U. *ikoliji*
V. *itsipuni*
W. *ifulemu*
X. *upepa*
Y. *usoda*
Z. *ubiya*
AA. *indiya*

b. How would the following English words sound if borrowed into Zulu?

A. *flat*
B. *cap*
C. *cricket*
D. *globe*
E. *film*
F. *gin*
G. *ginger*
H. *brake*
I. *inch*
J. *juice*

c. What does the proper noun *ingilandi* mean in Zulu?

4. Kikuyu borrowings (Adopted from Zhurinskij 1995: 41. Orthographic *th* represents IPA [ð] and *j* represents the voiced post-alveolar affricate [ʤ].)

a. The words given below are Kikuyu words that were borrowed from English into Kikuyu, as well as the English source word. Make a list of the phonological changes that these words underwent when they were adapted to Kikuyu phonology. Again, generalize where possible.

|       | **Kikuyu**   | **English source** |
|-------|--------------|--------------------|
| i.    | *thukuru*    | *school*           |
| ii.   | *haithukuru* | *high school*      |
| iii.  | *anderethi*  | *address*          |
| iv.   | *raimbarari* | *library*          |
| v.    | *miritari*   | *military*         |
| vi.   | *korenji*    | *college*          |
| vii.  | *thateraiti* | *satellite*        |
| viii. | *mbuku*      | *book*             |
| ix.   | *thonda*     | *soda*             |
| x.    | *mboi*       | *boy*              |
| xi.   | *rumu*       | *room*             |

b. How would the following English words sound if borrowed into Kikuyu?

i. *dresser*
ii. *colour-bar*
iii. *glue*
iv. *agenda*

5. Tok Pisin is a creole language spoken in Papua New Guinea; it was discussed briefly above. The creole is derived from English, but is clearly distinct from it. The excerpts below are taken from a cartoon in a newspaper. They both feature Isuzu trucks; in the second one, the truck is being used as PMV (Public Motor Vehicle) – a type of public transport. Each excerpt is given in Tok Pisin, with an English translation provided.

Make a glossary containing each Tok Pisin word and its English counterpart. Wherever possible, identify the original English word or words that were initially adopted to express each meaning. Finally, note any grammatical features that differentiate Tok Pisin from English.

**Example I (Picture shows men squeezing into a pickup truck)**

Man A:     *Mipela i kam nau long Los Angeles lukim ol profesenel basketbol . . . Ol mai hia i bikpela liklik . . . Tasol mipela inap putim beksait long Isuzu na karim ol i go bek long hotel.*
'We are now coming to Los Angeles to see professional basketball . . . Men here are a bit big. But we can put our backsides into an Isuzu truck and take all back to the hotel.'

Man B:     *Tru tumas, Isuzu em inap . . .*
'Very true, Izuzu can do that/is sufficient . . .'

**Example II (Picture shows a mother dragging a complaining child into a truck, which is being used like a taxi)**

Child to mother:     *Mama, mama, mi no laik . . .*
'Mama, mama, I don't want . . .'

Mother to child:     *yu kam, yu blary hambag..*
'You come, you naughty humbug.'

Driver:     *Mi amamas tru ranim dispela Isuzu PMV. . . Olgeta de mi bungim planti ol naispela pipel. . . Em i gutela wok tru. . .*
'I am happy to run this Isuzu PMV . . . Every day I meet many nice people . . .This is a really good job . . .'

# 14 First language acquisition

**KEY TERMS**

- Longitudinal vs. cross-sectional methodology
- Child-Directed Speech (CDS)
- Phonological error pattern
- Lexical overextension
- Mean length of utterance (MLU)
- Overregularization
- Given vs. new information
- Functional continuity
- Narrative co-construction
- Formal, nativist theory
- Functional, discourse-based theory

**CHAPTER PREVIEW**

Language acquisition holds a central place in linguistics because every linguistic theory must be able to answer the following question: how do children master the basics of their first language spontaneously, without explicit instruction, in a fairly short time, and at a very early age? This chapter will examine the acquisition of many areas that have already been explored in this book, introducing some of the basic research findings in phonology, pragmatics, lexical semantics, morphology, syntax, and discourse. It will also contrast two different theoretical approaches to explaining the everyday yet profound mystery of first language acquisition.

**LIST OF AIMS**

By the end of this unit, students will be able to:

- describe early linguistic developments in several areas;
- identify common research methodologies and their advantages/disadvantages;
- perform basic analyses on first language acquisition data;
- explain some of children's common linguistic errors;
- contrast two different theoretical approaches to language acquisition.

## 14.1  Introduction

*First language acquisition is the process by which young children come to know and use the language(s) of their caregivers*. Over the past fifty years, scholars have produced a large body of research on the acquisition of many languages, but are still far from consensus on how to interpret these findings. The goal of acquisition theory is to articulate explicit explanations for how children master their native language(s), with particular focus on the acquisition of grammar.

First language acquisition has been a controversial area because it forces us to address basic issues about the nature of language itself. Two very different approaches to grammar have dominated research on language acquisition:

- In the formal, nativist approach, grammar is conceptualized as a set of abstract categories, structures, principles, and constraints that are genetically encoded as an innate Universal Grammar (UG). The emphasis in this approach is primarily on linguistic form, and the innate linguistic information in UG is regarded as the basis for adult grammar as well as the acquisition of grammar by children.
- In the functional, discourse-based approach that will be assumed in this chapter, grammar is viewed as a set of forms and functions that are constantly being shaped by the mental processes and communicative needs of speakers and hearers as they use language in everyday talk (discourse). This approach emphasizes the functions (meanings and interactive goals) as well as the forms of grammar, and views discourse as the source of adult grammars and the basis for their acquisition.

While nativist theory assumes that children need innate linguistic knowledge to acquire grammar, discourse-based theory (also known as usage-based theory) assumes that children learn language from discourse, that is, the speech they hear in everyday social interaction. We will return to a more in-depth consideration of these two approaches toward the end of this chapter.

## 14.2  Biological, cognitive, and social foundations of language acquisition

*First language acquisition has a strong biological basis.* The human brain, usually the left hemisphere, is specialized for language, and all normally developing children acquire language on a fairly predictable timetable, similar to patterns of physical and mental growth. Many scholars believe that there is a biologically programmed **sensitive period** during which young children can most readily acquire their first language successfully. Our biological preparation for language also entails a long period for mental and social development during which babies and young children are dependent on their caregivers. In this chapter it will be assumed that *children have universal mental and social capacities that enable them to learn language from the speech that they hear*. These capacities are an important part of our biological adaptation – and of any sensitive period – for language acquisition.

*Language acquisition also has crucial cognitive foundations*. The term **cognition** refers broadly to the mental processes that take in information from the environment, use it to form representations of reality in the mind, and apply this stored knowledge in activities such as thinking, speaking, and remembering. In order to use language, we must be able to perceive, comprehend, plan, produce, and recall linguistic units, such as phonemes, morphemes, words, and sentences. First, the human mind must have powerful cognitive abilities that enable young children to isolate, store, and process these units in the surrounding speech. Secondly, children need to understand something about cause–effect relations in order to use language as a tool for communicating and getting what they want. Thirdly, in order to use words, children must be able to form mental representations of reality; for example, a mental image of a bottle that can be associated with the word *bottle*; such representations allow children to recognize new instances of items when they encounter them and to think about them when they are not in view. Finally, children must be able to discover and use patterns for combining units into larger units, for example, phonemes and morphemes into words, words into sentences, and sentences into narratives, conversations, and other types of discourse.

We know from harrowing stories of abandonment and isolation that *language acquisition has essential social foundations: children need to experience language use in interaction with others in order to acquire language normally*. Infants in normal social environments are naturally motivated to interact and communicate with their caregivers. Long before they can use language, the social basis for language acquisition is established, as infants engage with their caregivers through eye gaze, smiling, gesturing, and vocalizing. The repetitive social routines of young children's daily lives ensure that they will experience the same linguistic forms being used for the same functions again and again. Thus, *children learn the forms and functions of language together, along with relevant social information*, such as who usually says what to whom in particular contexts.

## 14.3  Methodologies in acquisition research

Acquisition researchers use a great variety of methodologies. We can distinguish between **observational studies**, in which the researcher records what the child is saying and doing, and **experimental studies**, in which the researcher manipulates linguistic or contextual features to observe the effect on the child. Observational research has the obvious advantage of naturalness, but the findings are necessarily limited to whatever behaviors occur during the observation. Experiments have the advantage of control but run the risk of eliciting behaviors that happen only in the laboratory and may not be relevant to everyday life. We can also distinguish between **longitudinal research**, which follows one child or a small number of children over time, and **cross-sectional research**, which compares larger numbers of children at different stages of development speaking spontaneously or performing the same experimental task at different stages of development. Observational research is often longitudinal, while **experimental research** typically has a cross-sectional design. Which method is most appropriate depends on what question the researcher is asking and what kind of data is most likely to yield reliable answers to that question.

The original observational method was the diary study, in which the researcher kept a written record of the child's speech. In diary studies, the researcher is often a parent, who has the advantage of constant access to the child. Diaries are selective, however, and tend to be biased toward new or advanced language, while providing little or no information about the speech addressed to the child. Recordings of speech (at first audio, then video) are now the preferred observational methodology (see Sidebar 14.1). Recordings are objective and comprehensive, including all participants' speech; they are also independently verifiable, since transcripts can be checked for accuracy against the original recordings. On the other hand, the types of contexts recorded tend to be limited and the amount of data sparse, usually just a few hours of speech per month. The recent introduction of **dense sampling**, that is, collecting and transcribing at least five hours per week of a child's verbal interactions, is an expensive, labor-intensive methodology, but is one that yields a finer-grained, more reliable record of development (Lieven and Behrens 2012).

Experimental research encompasses a wide range of methodologies and types of tasks. In comprehension experiments, for example, children may be prompted to use toy figures to act out sentences they hear. In production experiments, children may be prompted to tell a narrative using a picture book, describe an event after being taught invented words, such as *Mickey slooped* (= catapulted with a lever) *the ball*, or simply describe an object in tasks designed to elicit particular forms, e.g., *the horse that's wearing a hat*. In judgment tasks, children may be asked to assess the grammaticality of sentences in various ways, for example, by correcting a puppet that makes grammatical errors while attempting to speak English. Ingenious technologies have been used to study infants, as in studies of high-amplitude sucking (infants suck on an artificial nipple faster when they hear a new sound), head turn preferences (infants turn their head to activate one of two audio speakers, e.g., the one that plays their mother's voice vs. that of a different speaker), and preferential looking (infants listening to speech with two screens in view will gaze longer at the one that accurately depicts what they are hearing). Although less natural than spontaneous language use, experiments can yield valuable and sometimes surprising findings that could not have been discovered using observational methods.

TEXTBOX 14.1 **OVERVIEW OF EARLY COMMUNICATION AND LANGUAGE DEVELOPMENT**

| Age | Developmental milestones |
|---|---|
| in utero | • Perception of low-frequency properties of voices, e.g., rhythm, pitch |
| 0–2 months | • Perception of phonetic distinctions between sounds, e.g., [p] vs. [b] |
| 3 months | • Mutual gaze; simultaneous or alternating vocalizations with caregiver |
| | • Social games, e.g., peekaboo |
| 4 months | • Joint attention to objects: follows caregiver's gaze and pointing |
| 6–10 months | • Babbling (reduplicated), e.g., [baba] |
| 8–12 months | • Communicative gestures, e.g., pointing at objects |
| 10–14 months | • Babbling (not reduplicated), e.g., [badida] |
| | • Production of stop consonants, nasals, and [h] |
| 12 months | • Gesture + sound combinations with consistent communicative functions |
| | • First words |
| | • One-word turns in conversational exchanges with caregiver |
| 12–16 months | • Repertoire of several speech acts, e.g., labels, requests, answers |
| 12–18 months | • Gesture + word combinations |
| 18 months | • Two-word combinations |
| | • 50-word vocabulary |
| 1½-4 years | • First 14 grammatical morphemes |
| 2–3 years | • Early grammatical constructions |
| 20–27 months | • Relative clauses |
| 2–2 ½ years | • Conversational skills improve, e.g., frequency of responses increases |
| 2–3 years | • Narratives of personal experience co-constructed with caregiver |
| 2–3 ½ years | • Overregularization of English past tense, e.g., *goed* |
| 3½-4½ years | • Mastery of difficult phonemes, e.g., [ʤ], [ʧ], [θ] |

Sources: Brown 1973; Tomasello and Brooks 1999; Kelly 2003; Diessel 2004; Clark 2009; Hoff 2009; Owens 2012

## 14.4  Overview of language development

How does the process of language acquisition unfold? Textbox 14.1 gives a sample of several developmental milestones. Since individual children vary greatly in the age at which they attain these milestones, the ages and age ranges given in Textbox 14.1 are rough approximations. In the sequence of development, changes take place simultaneously across different areas, from the mastery of speech sounds (phonology) to the construction of narratives (discourse).

Development proceeds incrementally but swiftly; the difference between the linguistic skills of a one-year-old vs. three-year-old is nothing short of astonishing.

## 14.5  Conversational discourse

Face-to-face conversation is the earliest and most common type of discourse and the primary basis for first language acquisition. Despite cross-cultural differences in circumstances, all children raised in normal social environments are surrounded by speech.

### 14.5.1 Early conversations: scaffolding dialogue

Babies are social creatures, eager to interact with their caregivers, but they cannot initially carry on a conversation without adult assistance. In the following famous example, the mother treats her preverbal infant as a conversational partner, creating a turn-taking structure by her responses to the baby's smile, burp, and vocalization.

(1)  Mother and 3-month-old daughter (Snow 1977b: 12)

| | |
|---|---|
| Ann: | (smiles) |
| Mother: | *Oh what a nice little smile! Yes, isn't that nice? There. There's a nice little smile.* |
| Ann: | (burps) |
| Mother: | *What a nice little wind as well! Yes, that's better, isn't it? Yes. Yes.* |
| Ann: | (vocalizes) |
| Mother: | *Yes! There's a nice noise.* |

The adult's words may be incomprehensible to the infant, but such "proto-conversations" communicate emotion, practice the joint attention that is essential for actual conversation, and establish the role of language in the caregiver–child relationship.

As young children begin to understand and use language, the talk addressed to them focuses mainly on the ***here-and-now: the ongoing activities and situations, and the people and objects present in the context***. This type of content engages the child's attention and is readily comprehensible; it also helps the child to see the connection between linguistic forms and their meanings/functions. Once children have begun to talk, caregivers can help them participate in conversation in many ways: using attention-getting forms (e.g., *look!*), introducing here-and-now topics, pausing between turns, asking questions that provide a "slot" in the dialogue for the child's response, and even answering their own questions if the child fails to respond. This kind of behavior is known as **scaffolding**, since it ***provides a temporary structure for children to rely on until they are capable of taking a more active role in the conversation***. The child in the next example is able to introduce a topic on her own, and to sustain it over several turns with some scaffolding from her mother (see Sidebar 14.2 for information about relevant acquisition notation).

> **SIDEBAR 14.2**
>
> ACQUISITION NOTATION
>
> In language acquisition research, a child's age is represented as Years; Months. For example, the notation 1;11 in Example (2) means that the child was 1 year, 11 months old at the time of that recording. Additionally, in this chapter, the URL for examples taken from the *CHILDES* database will be provided with the examples, as in (2).

(2)  Nina (1;11) picks up her doll (Suppes 1974)[a]

| | |
|---|---|
| Nina: | *Big dolly.* |
| Mother: | *Is this a big dolly?* |
| Nina: | *Here.* |
| Mother: | *Nice dolly.* |

| Nina: | *Dress up dolly. Dress up dolly.* |
| Mother: | *Shall we dress up dolly?* |
| Nina: | *Yeah.* |
| Mother: | *Okay. What shall we dress up dolly with?* |
| Nina: | *Clothes. Clothes.* |
| Mother: | *Shall we dress up dolly with a dress?* |
| Nina: | *Yeah.* |

[a] http://childes.psy.cmu.edu/browser/index.php?url=Eng-NA-MOR/Suppes/nina01.cha

While examples like (1) and (2) may seem commonplace, chatting with a preverbal infant or toddler is not regarded as appropriate behavior for an adult in all societies. Among the Kaluli of New Guinea, for example, mothers are more likely to speak *for* rather than *to* young children, holding infants so that they face the addressee and speaking for them in a special high-pitched, nasal voice. Using the form *ɛlɛma* 'say like this,' Kaluli mothers explicitly model assertive speech for young children; for example, one mother told her two-year-old to say, "Is this yours?" to his five-year-old sister, who wanted some of the fruit he was eating (Schieffelin 1990: 71, 88).

In cultures where parents do carry on conversations with very young children, the adult scaffolding seen in Example (2) recedes as the child begins to take a more active role. As children develop cognitively, the content of talk moves away from the here and now and toward encompassing past, future, and even imaginary events. With experience, children learn strategies for gaining the floor, introducing new topics, and collaborating on topics in progress (Ochs, Schieffelin, and Platt 1979; Hoff-Ginsberg 1987). The turn-taking form of conversation can be difficult, especially in multi-party situations; the child must pay close attention to what others are saying in order to formulate a relevant turn, then produce it quickly – before it is forgotten or someone else begins to talk – but without interrupting (Ervin-Tripp 1979). Both the content and form of conversation challenge young children for many years.

### 14.5.2   Child-Directed Speech: talking to young children

In certain societies, adults use a special way of speaking when they address a very young child. This register, called **Child-Directed Speech (CDS)**, has characteristics that attract children's attention, help them understand what is being said, and express positive emotion. CDS also marks the special position of the very young child in society. Textbox 14.2 presents several characteristics of CDS that have been found in English.

Certain features of English CDS seem exquisitely tailored to language learning: prosody that highlights the boundaries of constituents such as noun phrases, simplified grammar, repetitions and paraphrases that offer multiple chances to process the same content, and expansions that model the adult version of what the child is trying to say.

**SIDEBAR 14.3**

In societies that have a CDS register, there may be adults, including parents, who do not believe in using it. If you have come across people with this attitude, what reasons do they give for avoiding CDS?

Cross-linguistic research can shed light on which of these characteristics occur in other languages; high pitch, short utterances, long pauses, and (in mothers) exaggerated prosodic contours have been found in French, Italian, German, and Japanese CDS (Fernald et al. 1989). But not all societies have a special style for speaking to very young children, and even among speakers of the same language, the use and properties of CDS may vary, as well as attitudes toward using CDS (see Sidebar 14.3). While experiencing language use in social interaction is necessary for language acquisition, exposure to CDS per se evidently is not.

### 14.5.3  Early pragmatics: communicating with gestures and words

Before children begin to talk, they rely on gestures and vocalizations to communicate. By about 9–12 months of age, a child will have a small repertoire of communicative behaviors that engage others in interaction and achieve particular goals, for example, to obtain an object that the child wants. Cognitively, the intentional use of gestures and/or sounds to communicate reflects some understanding of cause and effect, and is crucial for the development of **pragmatics**: the use of language in context for communicative functions. Young children's early gestures and vocalizations have important social motivations beyond getting what they want; they will provide useful information (e.g., pointing to an object the addressee is looking for) and will try to convey what they are attending to and feeling simply in order to share their experience with their caregivers (Tomasello 2008: 123). If, for example, a child points at an object and the adult merely looks at it without expressing any interest, the child will continue

---

**TEXTBOX 14.2 CHARACTERISTICS OF CHILD-DIRECTED SPEECH IN ENGLISH**

| | |
|---|---|
| **Prosody:** | • high pitch<br>• exaggerated intonation contours, swooping between high and low pitch<br>• slower rate of speech, with pauses at the end of sentences |
| **Lexicon:** | • special vocabulary featuring reduplicated words and phrases (e.g., *tum-tum* 'tummy,' *din-din* 'dinner,' *go bye-bye* 'go outdoors') |
| **Grammar:** | • short utterances with simple clauses<br>• proper nouns for the pronouns *I* and *you* (e.g., *Mommy* and child's name)<br>• *we* and *let's* for actions performed by the child |

| | |
|---|---|
| **Discourse:** | • vocatives, endearments, and attention-getters<br>• imperatives and questions<br>• repetitions and paraphrases<br>• **expansions**: utterances that provide a fuller, grammatically correct version of the child's prior utterance |

Sources: Broen (1972), Phillips (1973), Cross (1977), Snow (1977a, 1986), Fernald et al. (1989)

gesturing to get a more satisfying response (Liszkowski 2006). Textbox 14.3 presents examples from American children of three common gestures found in preverbal communication.

Such gestures are also often accompanied by sounds; by 12 months a child may have a small set of consistent vocalization + gesture combinations used for particular functions, for example, making a particular sound while reaching for a desired object.

Preverbal gestures and vocalizing set the stage for further pragmatic development. By about 14–20 months, most children can produce a number of **speech acts:** actions that the speaker intends to perform with the utterance, such as a greeting or a request. Textbox 14.4 presents some early speech acts of American children, which may be produced with gestures.

---

### TEXTBOX 14.3 **THREE COMMON GESTURES IN PREVERBAL COMMUNICATION** (adapted from Kelly 2003, 2005)

| Gesture | Description | Examples |
|---------|-------------|----------|
| POINT | Movement of index finger or outstretched hand toward an object while gazing at object or addressee | Caitlin (0;11) points to a child on the other side of the window while gazing at the caregiver. |
| SHOW | Holding out (and sometimes then throwing down) an object while looking at the addressee | Brailey (0;12) holds up a toy telephone while gazing at the caregiver. |
| GIMME | Holding out an open palm as if to receive an object while gazing at object or addressee | Lette (0;12) reaches toward a toy that another child is holding while gazing at that child. |

---

### TEXTBOX 14.4 **SOME COMMON ONE-WORD SPEECH ACTS** (adapted from Snow et al. 1996; examples from *CHILDES*; Bloom 1973; Kelly 2003)

| Speech act | Word (+ Gesture) | Context |
|------------|------------------|---------|
| Verbal move in game | *moo* | With a series of *What's the X say?* queries, mother asks Gerry (1;6) for animal sounds.[a] |
| Notice event | *uh-oh* | Allison (1;4) was sitting on a chair with a doll, when the doll fell to the floor.[b] |
| Statement | *dirty* | Allison (1;4) hands empty cookie bag to her mother.[b] |
| Answer question | *cow* | Looking at toy animals on floor, mother asks Allison (1;4), *Oh, what's that?*[b] |
| Direct attention | *box* [bos][d] + SHOW | Fiona (1;1) holds up a box toward the caregiver.[c] |
| Request | *shoe* [gu] + SHOW | Chera (1;5) holds out her shoe to the caregiver, who is putting shoes on another child.[c] |

[a] http://childes.psy.cmu.edu/browser/index.php?url=Eng-NA-MOR/Cornell/haas1917.cha
[b] http://childes.psy.cmu.edu/browser/index.php?url=Eng-NA-MOR/Bloom73/allison1.cha
[c] Examples from Kelly 2003.
[d] Material in square brackets is in the International Phonetic Alphabet.

Young children's repertoire of speech acts gives an interesting glimpse into their social world, as well as their caregivers' ideology. From the speech acts in Textbox 14.4, for example, we can see that American children quickly learn to act as their parents' conversational partners, answering questions, making comments, and participating in labeling routines (Ochs and Schieffelin 1984). In daycare centers, where the competition is more intense, children must work harder to attract the attention of adults and to get them to perform desired actions.

## 14.6 Phonological development

Once children begin to acquire words, their communicative problems are by no means over, since they have difficulty pronouncing, and sometimes also perceiving, the words correctly. Certain **phonological error patterns** – consistent differences between adult and child pronunciations – are quite common. Textbox 14.5 shows some of the frequent patterns of errors that children make when producing consonants. These patterns create simple sequences of a consonant and vowel (i.e., CV syllables), substitute consonants that are easier to pronounce for more difficult ones, and assimilate sounds to their phonetic environments.

During the babbling period, babies usually produce reduplicated CV syllables, such as [baba]. CV syllables are found in all languages and are regarded as the most natural, basic syllable type. Children's preference for CV syllable structure continues when they begin to produce words. Children create CV syllables by failing to pronounce the final consonant of CVC syllables, e.g., saying [no] for *nose* [noz], and by producing a single consonant instead of a consonant cluster, e.g., [pe] for *play* [ple].

---

TEXTBOX 14.5 **SOME COMMON PHONOLOGICAL ERROR PATTERNS WITH CONSONANTS** (adapted from Dodd et al. 2006; Ingram 1986)

| Phonological error pattern | Word | Adult pronunciation | Child's pronunciation |
|---|---|---|---|
| *Syllable structure patterns* | | | |
| Final consonant deletion | *doll* | [dɑl] | [da] |
| Consonant cluster reduction | *play* | [ple] | [pe] |
| *Sound substitution patterns* | | | |
| Stopping | *see* | [si] | [di] |
| Fronting | *call* | [kal] | [ta] |
| Gliding | *ready* | [ɹɛdi] | [wɛdi] |
| Voicing: | | | |
| Initial voicing | *pie* | [paj] | [ba] |
| Final devoicing | *egg* | [ɛg] | [ɛk] |
| *Assimilation patterns* | | | |
| Consonant harmony | *duck* | [dʌk] | [gʌk] |

Young children also frequently use **sound substitutions**, producing sounds that are easier to articulate instead of more challenging ones. Stops, which are produced with a complete, quick closure and release at the place of articulation, are apparently easier for most children to produce than fricatives or affricates, which involve holding an incomplete closure while the air passes through. Accordingly, a common pattern is **stopping**: using a stop instead of a fricative or other type of consonant, e.g., *see* [si] → [di]. Some children use **fronting**: producing consonants farther to the front of the mouth, for example, pronouncing *car* [kaɹ] as [da] by replacing velar [k] with alveolar [d]. Many children have difficulty with the liquids [l] and especially [ɹ], and rely on **gliding**: substituting the glides [w] or [j] for liquids, so that, for example, *lap* [læp] becomes [jæp]. *Children also tend to use voiceless consonants instead of voiced ones at the ends of words, and voiced consonants rather than voiceless ones at the beginnings of words;* when both **voicing error patterns** are used in the same word, the outcome may confound the listener, as when *pig* [pɪg] becomes [bɪk]. Phonological error patterns can also cause confusion by creating a proliferation of **homonyms**: *words with different meanings that have the same pronunciation.* Thus, the word [ti] in a child's vocabulary could arise from *see* [si] by stopping of the initial consonant, or from *teeth* [tiθ] by deletion of the final consonant, as well as from *T* and *tea*.

Since young children have difficulty moving their articulators rapidly from one place of articulation to another, their errors often involve assimilation: changes in the pronunciation of a sound that are influenced by the phonetic properties of nearby sounds. An interesting type of long-distance assimilation found in children's speech is **consonant harmony**: one consonant is produced with the same place or manner of articulation as a nearby consonant. For example, a child might say [gʌk] for *duck* [dʌk], producing velar [k] instead of alveolar [d] in anticipation of the final [k].

As children's perception improves and they gain motor control over their vocal tracts, their errors gradually disappear, e.g., voicing errors by 3;0 years of age and gliding by 6;5 (Dodd et al. 2006). In the meantime, since *production generally lags behind comprehension*, children may be aware that they are mispronouncing words. In one famous case, a phonologist tried repeatedly to correct his son Amahl, who pronounced *jump* [jʌmp] as *dup* [dʌp], stopping the initial affricate [ʤ] to [d] and reducing the consonant cluster [mp] to [p]; Amahl finally concluded, "Only Daddy can say *dup*." (Smith 1973). In such cases the child can apparently perceive the adult sound correctly, but still lacks the motor control to produce it accurately.

Although the phonological error patterns described in this section have been found in children acquiring several different languages (Ingram 1986; Hua and Dodd 2006), *there are many individual differences in the acquisition of phonology.* Children's individuality is evident in their preference for particular sounds and in their choice of first words; they tend to use words that have the sounds they already learned, and to avoid words with sounds they have yet to master (Schwartz 1988).

## 14.7 Lexical semantics: first words and their meanings

First words offer an interesting window into the cognitive and social world of the young child. ***Words that are used frequently in the child's social interactions are likely to be acquired early***, resulting in a similar list of first words for members of the same social group. Textbox 14.6 gives typical examples found among the first fifty words of English-speaking children. These words evoke an image of the family members, food, clothing, and pets found in the homes of the (usually middle class) children who have been studied, as well as their typical activities, such as playing with toys and reading picture books with their caregivers.

In assessing lexical development, it is important to keep in mind that for the young child, a word does not necessarily coincide with what counts as a single word for an adult; it may consist of unanalyzed or misanalyzed multi-word chunks, e.g., [wəda] *What's that?* and [aba] 'bottle' (from *a bottle*).

***First words and expectations about first words can differ a great deal from one culture to another.*** American parents look forward to hearing *mama* or *dada*, while in Western Samoa parents expect young children, who are seen as willful and cheeky, to start out with the curse *tae* 'shit!' (Ochs 1988:159). Whether adults even recognize their children's first words as such depends on culturally based **ideologies of language acquisition**; the Kaluli in New Guinea do not regard children as having begun to speak until they say *nə* 'mother' and *bo* 'breast,' even if they are using other words (Schieffelin 1990:74). There are also cross-cultural differences in the types of words that children know; for example, Korean mothers use a higher frequency of verbs in active play contexts compared with American mothers, and young Korean children

---

**TEXTBOX 14.6 FIRST WORDS OF ENGLISH-SPEAKING CHILDREN**
(adapted from Nelson 1973; Clark 2009)

| Category | Typical Examples |
|---|---|
| People | *mommy, daddy, baby, grandma, grandpa* |
| Body parts | *eye, nose, ear* |
| Clothes | *shoe, sock, hat* |
| Animals | *dog/doggie, cat/kitty, bird, fish* |
| Food/drink | *juice, milk, cookie, cracker, apple, cheese, banana* |
| Eating/drinking utensils | *bottle, cup* |
| Toys | *ball, block, doll* |
| Vehicles | *car, truck, boat* |
| Household items | *keys, book, clock, light, blanket* |
| Actions/movements | *open, up, down, off, out* |
| Social routines | *bye(bye), hi, peekaboo, thank you* |
| Sounds | *woof, moo, baa baa, vroom* |
| States/situations/sensations | *all gone, uh-oh, ouch* |

tend to have more verbs in their vocabulary than children acquiring English (Choi and Gopnik 1995; Choi 2000).

A vocabulary list may reveal which words a child uses, but what do those words actually mean to the child? Young children with limited vocabularies can get more mileage out of their lexicon by extending a familiar word beyond its normal range, for example, by calling a horse *doggie*. In this type of error, called a **lexical overextension**, a word is used for a larger set of referents than is found in adult speech. The results can be amusing or even poetic, as when a child said *moon* while looking up at a half grapefruit (Bowerman 1978), but may also be distressing, as when *mommy* and *daddy* are overextended to other adults. The opposite error also occurs; **underextensions** apply a word to a smaller set of referents than appropriate, as in the case of the child who said *duck* only when hitting his toy duck off the bathtub, but not in other situations, such as looking at real ducks (Barrett 1986). As Textbox 14.7 illustrates, ***overextensions are often based on a particular perceptual feature that the overextended referents share with the original referent of a word***. Overextensions can also be based on more than one feature of the original referent; for example, one child first used *kick* when kicking a ball, but later also when she was about to throw something, when watching a moth fluttering on a table, and when pushing her stomach against a mirror (Bowerman 1978).

---

TEXTBOX 14.7 **LEXICAL OVEREXTENSIONS BASED ON SHARED PERCEPTUAL FEATURES** (adapted from Clark 1973)

| Child's word | Perceptual basis for overextension | First referent | Child's subsequent set of overextended referents in order of occurrence |
|---|---|---|---|
| baw | shape | ball | > apples > grapes > eggs > squash > bell-clapper > anything round |
| fly | size | fly | > specks of dirt > dust > all small insects > child's own toes > crumbs of bread > a toad |
| koko | sound | cockerel's crowing | > tunes played on the violin > tunes played on the piano > tunes on an accordion > tunes on a phonograph > all music > merry-go-round |
| wau-wau | texture | dogs | > all animals > toy dog > soft home-slippers > picture of old man dressed in furs |
| candy | taste | candy | > cherries > anything sweet |

---

The phenomenon of overextension raises the following question: do children who overextend a word know the difference between the "real" (adult) referent and their own overextended uses? Research has shown that ***comprehension precedes production in lexical development***; at 1;4 years of age, for example, on average children can produce only about 6 words but can understand about 51–100 (Fenson et al. 1994: 66). Happily, then, children usually do know *daddy* from the man next door. Even in production, children overextend only about one-third of their first 75 words; as their vocabularies increase during their third year, overextensions are replaced by more appropriate adult words (Rescorla 1980).

## 14.8 Constructing a grammar

The acquisition of grammar has generated the most research, as well as the most controversy, in the field of language acquisition. This is because linguists who espouse different theoretical frameworks have very different ideas about what grammar is and how sentences should be analyzed.

### 14.8.1 Early word combinations

***For children acquiring English, the production of two-word combinations is usually regarded as the first step in the acquisition of grammar beyond one-word utterances***. Recently, however, it was discovered that the appearance of two-word utterances is preceded – and perhaps facilitated – by changes in the child's word + gesture combinations. First, the word and gesture become temporally synchronized so that they are produced simultaneously; then the word and gesture are used to express distinct elements (Kelly 2003). For example, in the latter stage, instead of reaching toward a banana and saying *banana*, the child will reach toward the banana and say *want*. Two or three months later, the first two-word combinations appear (Kelly 2003; Iverson and Goldin-Meadow 2005). Thus, the acquisition of grammar may have developmental roots in the domain of gesture.

Textbox 14.8 gives examples of typical two-word combinations, with brief characterizations of their functions/meanings and the contexts in which they occurred. Since word combinations with functions roughly equivalent to those in Textbox 14.7 are

---

TEXTBOX 14.8 **SOME EARLY WORD COMBINATIONS IN ENGLISH**
(adapted from Slobin 1979; examples from *CHILDES*[a] (Suppes 1974))
N=Nina (1;11); M=Nina's mother

| Function/meaning | Form | Context |
|---|---|---|
| Label object | *this rabbit* | N and M are "reading" picture book |
| Direct attention | *look rabbit* | N and M are "reading" picture book |
| Disappearance/absence | *horsie gone* | N is looking on shelf for toy horse |
| Demand/desire | *more cookie* | N wants M to give her another cookie |
| Negate | *no fit* | N is trying to place a puzzle piece |
| Possession | *Nina doggy* | M had asked who owns toy dog |
| Locate object | *car leg* | N is putting a toy car on her leg |
| Describe action | *plant tree* | N is "planting" a tree in a toy village |
| Describe object | *red doggy* | N is talking about her toy dog |

[a] http://childes.psy.cmu.edu/browser/index.php?url=Eng-NA-MOR/Suppes/nina01.cha
http://childes.psy.cmu.edu/browser/index.php?url=Eng-NA-MOR/Suppes/nina02.cha

found in many languages, researchers have speculated that these meanings may reflect universals of young children's cognition (Slobin 1970). This may also be due to similarities across cultures in ways of interacting and talking with young children.

Two- and three-word utterances may seem simple, but their implications for the acquisition of grammar have been extremely controversial. In analyzing the development of grammar, **the goal is to capture the child's unconscious grammatical knowledge (i.e., mental representation of grammar) at a given point in time**. Since the child's knowledge is rapidly changing, it is challenging to come up with an analysis that neither under-represents the child's knowledge (failing to attribute to the child knowledge that he or she actually has), nor overrepresents it (attributing adult-like knowledge to the child that he or she does not yet have). The question is, exactly what do children who combine two or three words know about grammar? For example, when Nina says *plant tree*, should we assume that her utterance has internal semantic or syntactic structure, or is she simply placing two words side by side? Textbox 14.9 illustrates some of the analyses that have been proposed.

The first and most concrete analysis in Textbox 14.9, Word + Word, assumes that the child knows only the meaning of the individual words, and the meaning created when they are combined. According to this analysis, when Nina says *plant tree* as she "plants" a toy tree, she knows the meaning of *plant* and of *tree*, as well as the relationship between the action of planting and the tree. (Sometimes one of the words bears a semantically fixed relation to the other, in patterns such as *more* + Word or *no* + Word.) The second analysis in Textbox 14.9 assumes knowledge of broader two- and later three-term semantic relations, such as Agent + Action + Affected Object. The semantic relations may be viewed as arising from the child's

## TEXTBOX 14.9 **ANALYSES OF EARLY WORD COMBINATIONS**

| Sample analysis | What the child is assumed to know: |
|---|---|
| 1. Word + Word | The meaning of individual lexical items and the specific semantic relation between them |
| | (Braine 1976; Tomasello 1992; Lieven et al. 1997) |
| 2. Agent + Action Object + Location, etc. | Case-like relations between general semantic categories, such as Agent, Action, Location, etc. |
| | (Slobin 1970; Schlesinger 1974) |
| 3. S → NP + VP | Word classes (N, V), constituent structure (S, NP, VP), and grammatical relations (Subject, Direct Object) |
| | (Bloom 1970; Pinker 1984) |
| 4. SUBJ VERB OBJ | Constructions: grammatical patterns (e.g., Subject Verb Object) and the meanings they convey (e.g., X acts on Y) |
| X acts on Y | (Tomasello and Brooks 1999; Goldberg and Casinhiser 2006; Tomasello 2006; Lieven 2009) |

cognition, for example, the understanding that agents can cause changes in objects by acting on them. In this analysis Nina's utterance *plant tree* shows that she has acquired the general semantic categories Action and Affected Object, and a rule for combining them in a particular order.

The third analysis in Textbox 14.9 assumes adult-like syntactic knowledge. This analysis reflects the **continuity hypothesis**. that children have the same linguistic categories and rules as adults from the outset (Pinker 1984: 7). According to this analysis, Nina has innate access to the syntactic category Subject NP, which she omits from this utterance since she can only produce two words at a time. She also has an innate VP category, consisting of a Verb and its Direct Object NP; her utterance *plant tree* relies on this innate knowledge, as well as acquisition of the English word order, in which the direct object follows the verb. For those who do not believe in innate grammatical knowledge, this analysis would be regarded as overrepresenting the child's knowledge; for those who espouse the continuity hypothesis, the first and second analyses in Textbox 14.9 would be seen as underrepresentation.

The final analysis in Textbox 14.9 assumes that grammatical constructions pair a particular syntactic pattern (e.g., Subject + Verb + Direct Object) with a particular meaning conveyed by the construction as a whole (e.g., X acts on Y). Researchers in this framework do not assume that the child has adult-like knowledge, so when Nina says *plant tree*, she is showing only partial mastery of the English transitive construction. Her actual degree of knowledge of this construction might be assessed by longitudinal analysis of her speech or by experiments demonstrating whether she can generalize the transitive construction to new nouns and verbs. Recent functionalist approaches to two-word combinations have focused on the first (item-based) and last (construction-based) analyses in Textbox 14.9.

Research using experiments or detailed longitudinal analysis of dense samples of child speech has found that ***children move from specific to general in acquiring grammar***, proceeding from particular Word + Word combinations toward general, adult-like grammatical constructions. The process of **generalization** takes place gradually, with differences in the timing and content of the generalizations made by individual children. This account, in which children construct grammars gradually, learning forms and functions from the speech they hear, is favored by functional, discourse-based theorists. In contrast, formal theorists believe that children have innate knowledge of adult syntactic categories like Subject from the outset, as in analysis (3) in Textbox 14.9. From this perspective, acquiring a grammar is a matter of activating pre-existing knowledge rather than building up knowledge based on experience with discourse.

### 14.8.2  Morphology: adding grammatical bits and pieces

***The early word combinations of English-speaking children typically do not include any grammatical morphemes***. Words with lexical content, such as nouns and verbs, appear in their base (dictionary) form. Grammatical morphemes – both bound morphemes, such as inflectional suffixes, and free morphemes, such as prepositions and articles – are simply missing. ***Children add grammatical morphemes to words and phrases gradually*** rather than suddenly using a morpheme in all contexts where it would be grammatical in adult speech. Children progress at different rates and show different patterns of development as grammatical morphemes are added; thus, one child may use *a* in the phrase *want a + X*, while another child uses *a* in *like a + X* (Pine and Lieven 1997).

Research on the acquisition of English morphemes has shown that although there are individual differences, children tend to acquire their first fourteen grammatical morphemes in a fairly consistent order (Brown 1973; de Villiers and de Villiers 1973). Textbox 14.10 gives the average rank order of emergence in three children acquiring English.

An important question in analyzing morphological development is when a morpheme should be treated as acquired. Using English data, Roger Brown (1973: 258) defined acquisition of a grammatical morpheme as 90 percent use in **obligatory contexts** in which the morpheme is required for grammaticality over three

---

TEXTBOX 14.10 **ORDER OF ACQUISITION OF 14 ENGLISH MORPHEMES** (adapted from Brown 1973; examples from *CHILDES*: Eve 2;3[a])

| Rank order | Morpheme | Example |
|---|---|---|
| 1 | present progressive *-ing* | *I making 'nother one.* |
| 2 | *in* | *Put my pencil in there.* |
| 3 | *on* | *I sitting on my pencil.* |
| 4 | regular plural *-s* | *Please give me two crackers.* |
| 5 | irregular past | *We made a picture.* |
| 6 | possessive *'s* | *I using Fraser's.* (pencil) |
| 7 | uncontractible copula | *Is this mine?* |
| 8 | articles *(a, the)* | *I have a cookie.* |
| | | *Dat's Becky on de (=the) truck.* |
| 9 | regular past *-ed* | *Did you turned it?* (the page) |
| 10 | regular third person singular *-s* | *Gloria sits on our couch.* |
| 11 | irregular third person singular (e.g., *does, has*) | *What / what does. (=That's what it does.)* |
| 12 | uncontractible auxiliary | *Are you having coffee?* |
| 13 | contractible copula | *Papa's a boy.* |
| 14 | contractible auxiliary | *I'm moving the stool.* |

[a] http://childes.psy.cmu.edu/browser/index.php?url=Eng-NA-MOR/Brown/Eve/eve19.cha
   http://childes.psy.cmu.edu/browser/index.php?url=Eng-NA-MOR/Brown/Eve/eve20.cha

consecutive monthly recording sessions. Different criteria may be required with different recording schedules, or if adult use of a morpheme is variable.

Why are certain morphemes acquired earlier than others? The form, function, and frequency of a morpheme are all important factors in explaining its acquisition order. First of all, ***the phonetic form and position of a morpheme affect its perceptual salience***. Morphemes with more phonetic substance, especially vowels, such as *-ing*, *on*, or *in*, are easier to perceive than morphemes consisting of a single consonant, such as plural *-s*. The articles *the* and *a*, with their reduced vowels and lack of stress, are also hard to hear. ***Utterance-final and utterance-initial positions are more salient perceptually than utterance-medial ("sandwich") position***. Possessive *'s* tends to be acquired first at the ends of sentences, e.g., *I using Fraser's*, before appearing between the possessor and possessed, e.g., *Gloria_ ashtray*. Similarly, the uncontractible copula (*Is he nice?*) and auxiliary (*Are they singing?*) are usually acquired before their contractible counterparts (*He's nice* and *They're singing*), which have less phonetic substance and are sandwiched between the subject and main verb.

***Morphemes with simple, semantically transparent meanings tend to be acquired early***. The meanings of *in* and *on* are easy to grasp compared to *the* and *a* – both for children and for linguists! ***Morphemes that are used with high frequency on many different word stems in adult speech, such as plural -s, are likely to appear early***, since their semantic effect is consistent across a large portion of the lexicon. On the other hand, ***semantically complex morphemes encoding multiple distinctions tend to be acquired late***, e.g., third singular *-s*, which encodes person, number, and tense. Finally, morphemes like English past tense, which convey the same meaning through multiple forms (e.g., the regular suffix *-ed*, as well as irregular forms in patterns like *ring–rang*, *feel–felt*, and *hit–hit*), are acquired late and with many errors. In such cases, children may resort to **overregularization**: use of the regular form of a morpheme in cases that require an irregular form. Overregularizations such as *goed* are found well into preschool and beyond, providing support for the notion that children prefer 'one form for one function' in their acquisition of grammar (Slobin 1986).

## 14.8.3   Simple clauses: given vs. new information

Children's early word combinations with verbs generally consist of a simple **clause**: a verb plus its associated arguments – one argument for intransitive verbs, e.g., *Mommy go*, and two for transitive verbs like *hit*, e.g., *She hit the ball*. (See Chapter 6, section 6.3.1.) In these early clauses, the subject is often missing. This happens not only in languages like Spanish and Korean, which allow **ellipsis**, (non-mention) of an argument in adult speech, but also in languages like English, which require overt subjects in most clauses. For example, Nina's utterance *plant tree* as she "plants" a toy tree (Textbox 14.8) omits the subject where doing so is ungrammatical in adult speech.

Why are young children so likely to omit subjects? One reason is that ***subjects often convey*** **given information**: information that is activated in the listener's mind because it has just been mentioned or is obvious in context, e.g., Nina, as she describes her own actions. (See Chapter 9, section 9.8, for additional discussion of given and new.) Since given information is already activated for the listener, it is usually expressed with pronouns in languages like English, or simply left unmentioned in languages like Korean. On the other hand, ***the listener needs an explicit lexical introduction of*** **new information**, that is, information that has not yet been mentioned in the conversation or that is not obvious from the context. Speakers' different treatment of given vs. new information offers a clear case in which linguistic form is sensitive to its discourse context.

Furthermore, ***the grammatical organization of the clause is also sensitive to the distinction between given vs. new information***. In transitive clauses, the subject almost always conveys given information; in contrast, new information usually appears as the direct object of a transitive verb or as the subject of an intransitive verb (Du Bois 1987). Textbox 14.11 describes these patterns, with examples from Nina's speech.

The pattern of presenting given information as the subject of transitive verbs and new information as the subject of intransitive verbs or the object of transitive verbs has proved to be highly robust across languages, and is acquired very early. Figure 14.1 shows the percentage of transitive subjects, intransitive subjects, and direct objects that convey new information in the speech of two Korean children (H and W), aged 1;8–2;10, and their mothers.

---

## TEXTBOX 14.11 **GIVEN VERSUS NEW INFORMATION**

The linguistic forms used for given vs. new information reflect their cognitive functions. **New information** is introduced with a lexical noun phrase because explicit information is needed to activate the new referent in the listener's mind (see Chapter 9, section 9.8). For example, playing with her doll house figures, Nina (2;4) put one in a toy barrel and said, *The man sits in the barrel* (rather than *He*).[a] Moments later, announcing her intention to play with a new toy, she said, *I will find a egg*. If she had said *it* instead of *a egg*, her mother, who had just suggested that she play with a barrel, would not have been able to decipher the intended referent. These sentences illustrate the pattern of new information being introduced lexically, either as the object of a transitive verb or the subject of an intransitive verb.

In contrast, **given information** is typically mentioned with a pronoun. After introducing Nina's toy Easter bunny into the conversation, her mother asked, *What is he pushing?*, and Nina followed up with, *He have a egg?* (The bunny was pushing eggs in a wheelbarrow.) Both sentences use a pronoun to refer to the toy bunny, which is given information, having just been mentioned. And both sentences display the common pattern in which given information appears as the subject of a transitive verb, *push* in the mother's sentence, and *have* in Nina's sentence.

[a] http://childes.psy.cmu.edu/browser/index.php?url=Eng-NA-MOR/Suppes/nina21.cha (Suppes 1974)

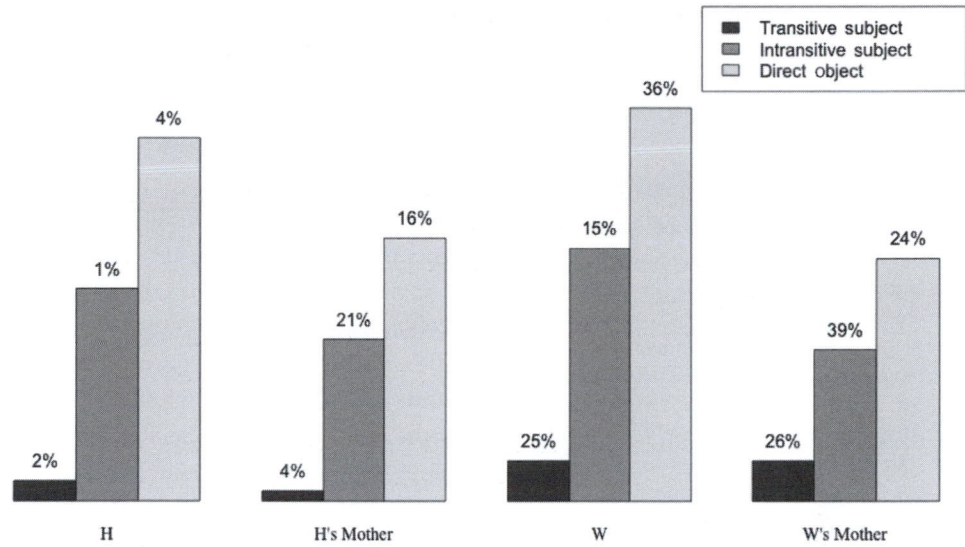

**Figure 14.1** Percentage of transitive subjects, intransitive subjects, and direct objects that convey new information in Korean clauses

As Figure 14.1 shows, although they are very young, the children are already organizing new information in their clauses very much as their mothers do. As expected, the subjects of transitive verbs are usually given; only 2–4 percent convey new information. In contrast, the subjects of intransitive verbs are much more likely to be new, while direct objects have the highest percentage of new referents. As a result, the subjects of transitive verbs are usually left unexpressed, while direct objects and subjects of intransitive verbs are often expressed with lexical nouns. Example (3) illustrates this pattern; the subject (Wenceng) is given information and is not mentioned explicitly, while the direct object (*congi* 'paper') is new and is expressed with a full noun phrase (personal data).

(3)    Her mother has been serving coffee and cookies when Wenceng (1;11) says:
     emma      **congi**      kaci-ko         o-kkey
     mommy     paper       bring-and     come-FUT
     'Mommy, (I)'ll go get paper.'

As the patterns in Figure 14.1 demonstrate, ***grammar functions to convey not only semantic information (who did what to whom), but also pragmatic information (what is new and what is given in the discourse)***. These findings provide powerful support for one of the fundamental tenets of a functional, discourse-based approach to grammar, namely, that ***grammatical form is influenced by discourse function***.

## 14.8.4  Complex sentences: relative clauses

**SIDEBAR 14.5**

COPULA CONSTRUCTIONS
REVIEWED

A copula is a special type of verb that
denotes an identity relation between its
subject, called the **copula subject**, and the
**copula complement**, which cross-
linguistically can be either a noun phrase or
an adjective. In the English example in (4)
the copula *is* relates the first noun phrase *this*
(the copula subject, labeled cs) with the
second noun phrase *the sugar that goes in
there*, the copula complement (cc). (See also
Chapter 6, section 6.2.3.)

At about two years of age, children begin producing syntactic structures that are more complex than a single clause, such as sentences with conjoined clauses, object complements, and relative clauses (see Chapter 6, section 6.5). Relative clauses, like adjectives, are dependent elements that modify the head noun of a noun phrase (NP). Longitudinal research on English (Diessel and Tomasello 2000; Diessel 2004) and Korean (Kim 1987) has found that the earliest and most frequent relative clauses for at least some children occur in copula constructions that have the form illustrated in (4) (relative clauses are underlined). Note that in Korean, relative clauses precede the head noun, and the copula, which attaches to the head noun, comes at the end of the sentence. In both sentences, the relative clause is underlined.

(4)  English and Korean copula constructions with relative clauses compared

a.  English: Setting up a tea party with her mother, Nina (3;0) is putting Play-Doh in a toy sugar bowl (Suppes 1974)[a]

   [*This*] cs *is* [*the sugar that goes in there*] cc

[a] http://childes.psy.cmu.edu/browser/index.php?url=Eng-NA-MOR/Suppes/nina42.cha

b.  Korean: Wenceng (1;11) is looking at a picture of a vacuum cleaner with her mother (Kim 1987: 125)

| [*ike*]cs | [*pupung-hanun* | *ke*]cc | *-ya.* |
|-----------|------------------|---------|--------|
| PROX.DEM | pupung-go.IPFV | thing | -COP.IE |

   '. . . this is the thing that goes "pupung."'

The findings illustrated in (4) raise a question: Why do both English- and Korean-speaking children produce relative clauses in copula constructions so early? The Korean data are especially interesting, since in Korean, the child must first produce the subject of the copula clause, and then the relative clause, before producing the head noun and copula. This is regarded as cognitively challenging for young children, since they must hold the subject of the matrix clause in **working memory** while producing the embedded clause, before they can complete the rest of the matrix clause.

From a functionalist perspective, what is striking about the earliest relative clauses is that they serve to direct the listener's attention to a particular referent with the initial pronoun, often a deictic pronoun like *this* to indicate a referent that is physically close to the speaker and hearer, which the relative clause then describes. As we have seen, there is a long developmental history for this function: at first, pointing gestures that direct adult attention to a present object during the preverbal stage, followed by POINT + label utterances at the one-word stage, and then two-word utterances such as *this rabbit* or *look rabbit*, which focus adult attention with the first word and then add the label for the indicated referent. The sentences in (4) take this line of development one step further, providing more information about the focused referent in the relative clause. ***There is a clear* functional continuity *here, with different forms – from preverbal gesture to relative clauses – being used for the same communicative function of directing attention to a referent*.**

## 14.9   Narrative discourse: telling stories of personal experience

From their earliest vocalizations to complex sentences, ***the goal of children acquiring language is not to have a grammar but to participate in everyday discourse and social interaction***. As we have seen, the earliest type of discourse for young children is face-to-face conversation centered on here-and-now activities, people, and objects. Narrative discourse, on the other hand, requires talking about the "there and then" (Sachs 1983). From a cognitive perspective, the child must be able to move beyond the present moment to talk about past events and absent referents. Children can talk about the past before mastering the past tense or temporal adverbs, but their early narratives of personal experience may be all but incomprehensible to the listener who is not already familiar with the events. The narrative in (5), told by a Japanese boy of only 1;11 years old, is a case in point; his mother immediately recognized the story of the neighbor's dog, which had been hit by a car, but the researcher was completely baffled (personal data).

(5)   Yotchan (1;11) had been asking for another tangerine, when he suddenly said:

| | |
|---|---|
| *wan wan,* | 'Doggie, |
| *tai-tai yoo tte,* | (went) "ow-ow," |
| *paan tte,* | (it went) "bang," |
| *tai-tai.* | ow-ow.' |

Since the story in (5) had probably been told many times, the child was able to introduce the main character and tell a minimal version of the events on his own. Often, however, children under three years of age need adult help to tell stories, and the resulting discourse has the turn-taking form of conversation. Example (6) illustrates this kind of **narrative co-construction**, with the mother asking questions that prompt the child's memory of the events, creating a familiar question–answer format to guide the narration and providing feedback through repetitions, confirmations, and agreements.

(6)   Tara (2;6) and her mother co-construct a story (Miller and Sperry 1988: 300–301)

| | | |
|---|---|---|
| 1 | Mother: | *Tara, Tara.* |
| 2 | Tara: | *What?* |

| 3 | Mother: | *Did we go down to see the fishes?* |
|---|---------|--------------------------------------|
| 4 | Tara: | (nods and tucks thumbs under armpits, elbows askew, gazes intently at her mother) |
| 5 | Mother: | *What'd they look like?* |
| 6 | Tara: | *Fish.* (slowly moves arms, fidgeting with blouse) |
| 7 | Mother: | *What did them fishes –* |
| 8 | Tara: | *I see ... big fish.* (gazes at mother, excited tone) (extends index finger) |
| 9 | Mother: | (laughs) |
| 10 | Tara: | (raises right arm above head) |
| 11 | Mother: | *How big was it?* |
| 12 | Tara: | (turns in circle) *I hold it.* (raises right arm, palms open toward mother) |
| 13 | Mother: | *Was you scared?* |
| 14 | Tara: | *No.* (shakes head negatively) *I holding it.* (arms out at side, palms up) |
| 15 | Mother: | *We seen lobsters. Remember the lobsters? They go* (imitates sounds while making biting, snapping motions with hands) *like that. And that little boy said, 'Ow.'* (pauses) *Cause it bites his finger.* |
| 16 | Tara: | (nods, then shakes head negatively) |
| 17 | Mother: | *Did it bite your finger?* |
| 18 | Tara: | *No. Look, it didn't bite my finger.* (shows finger to mother) |
| 19 | Mother: | *No, it didn't.* |

The mother's contributions in (6) indirectly tell the child what counts as a story worth telling, and what kinds of information a story should include: what happened and how the child felt about it. Her questions support two basic functions of narratives of personal experience: the **referential function**, i.e., recounting who did what to whom in the sequence of events that comprise the plot, and the **evaluative function**, i.e., conveying the significance or point of the story (what makes it worth telling) (Daiute and Nelson 1997; Labov 1997).

Narrators use a variety of verbal and nonverbal **evaluative devices** to convey the point of the story, some of which are given in Textbox 14.12.

In (6), the mother co-constructs the evaluative function by prompting Tara to elaborate on the adjective *big*, by explicitly asking her whether she was *scared* and by quoting the little boy who said *ouch* at the dramatic event of a lobster pinching his finger. The resulting narrative is more than a tale of holding a fish; it is a co-constructed portrayal of Tara as adventurous and unafraid, traits that the working-class mothers in this community value highly and seek to instill in their young daughters. Co-constructing narratives is one way in which *caregivers use language to socialize young children to the ideologies of their social group and to identities shaped by those ideologies*. In telling stories of personal experience, child narrators constantly construct their own identity,

---

**TEXTBOX 14.12 EVALUATIVE DEVICES IN NARRATIVES OF PERSONAL EXPERIENCE** (adapted from Labov 1972, 1997)

a. Expressive phonology (e.g., *noooo!*)

b. Explicit comments (indicating why the events are reportable)

c. Quotation (of the words or thoughts of the narrator or story characters)

d. Dramatic action (such as exciting, reportable events)

e. Intensifiers (e.g., *really, very*)

f. Evaluative adjectives (e.g., *scary, wonderful*)

g. Repetitions (which highlight what the narrator finds significant)

h. Comparators (e.g., *only, even*; adjectives with *more/most* or *-er/-est*; these forms implicitly compare what did happen with what might have happened)

---

**TEXTBOX 14.13 FOUR ESSENTIAL COMPONENTS OF ACQUISITION THEORY**

1. Nature: the child's innate capacities relevant to language acquisition

2. Nurture: the properties of the environment relevant to language acquisition

3. Acquisition mechanisms: the specific means by which the child comes to have and use linguistic knowledge

4. Adult grammar: theoretical assumptions made about the language that the child is in the process of acquiring

---

a constantly evolving version of who they are, through interaction with others (Kyratzis 2000; Bamberg and Georgakopoulous 2008).

## 14.10   Theories of language acquisition

Every linguistic theory must offer some explanation for how children acquire their first language. For decades, the primary focus of theoreticians has been the acquisition of grammar; the longest-standing controversy centers on the relative importance of nature vs. nurture. Textbox 14.13 presents four essential components of any acquisition theory. With respect to nature, the question is: ***what innate endowments does every child bring to the task of language acquisition?*** The nurture component of acquisition theory addresses ***the properties of the environment that are assumed to be relevant***, for example, the language that the child is exposed to. Every theory must postulate specific ***mechanisms that are responsible for how grammatical knowledge is acquired***. The final component – ***the theory's assumptions about adult grammar*** – has the greatest impact on acquisition theory, shaping how the balance between nature and nurture is conceptualized, and what kinds of acquisition mechanisms it makes sense to postulate. As long as scholars have different views of adult grammar, their theories of how children acquire grammar will necessarily differ as well.

Acquisition theories can be viewed as falling into two basic types: formal, nativist theories and functional, discourse-based theories. ***Nativist theories emphasize grammatical form, and assume that* innate linguistic know-ledge *is primarily responsible for children's acquisition of grammar*.** For proponents of nativist theories, the term "innate linguistic knowledge" refers to unconscious knowledge of grammatical categories, structures, and principles that are assumed to be part of the human genetic make-up, that is, of Universal Grammar. In this type of theory, which originated with Chomsky (1965), grammar is conceptualized as an abstract formal system whose form is not affected by the functions it serves in discourse. Just as grammar is viewed as being independent from discourse, language itself is regarded as a unique, self-contained module in the human mind, separate from cognition. Although the child's linguistic envir-onment is recognized as necessary for the acquisition of one language rather than another, in the balance between nature and nurture, ***innate linguistic know-ledge is given much more explanatory weight than environmental factors***.

Chomsky argued that the speech children hear is too filled with grammatical errors and disfluencies to provide an adequate basis for learning grammar. Furthermore, he claimed, children must acquire universal linguistic structures and principles that are too abstract to be learned directly from speech, an argument referred to as the **poverty of the stimulus.** The abstractness of the structures is necessary if the goal is to devise only one set of structures and principles that can apply to all languages. As a solution to the supposed inadequacy of the speech children hear, ***Chomsky proposed that all children are born with such an abstract structure: an innate* Universal Grammar, *which incorporates the linguistic categories, principles, and constraints that provide the foundation for the grammars of all languages*.** Since proponents of UG assume that language cannot be learned directly from the surrounding speech, they reason that it must be acquired by unique mechanisms that are specific to language rather than by general learning mechanisms. ***The acquisition mechanisms that have been proposed include maturation of innate grammatical know-ledge, and triggering by the speech that the child hears of particular innate options***. Textbox 14.14 describes how a nativist approach might explain children's subjectless sentences in terms of triggering, as compared with a func-tional interpretation. In general, in a nativist theoretical framework, the role of learning is minimized, and children's social and cognitive development is viewed as irrelevant to their acquisition of grammar. The dominant metaphor is physical maturation: innate linguistic structure unfolding over time, like puberty, with min-imal environmental influence.

***In* functional discourse-based theory, *grammar is viewed as a system of communication that is shaped by human cognition and communication*.** Grammar is understood to include both structural forms and their discourse

## TEXTBOX 14.14 **SUBJECTLESS SENTENCES: TWO APPROACHES**

Young children often produce sentences without a subject, e.g., Nina's utterance *plant tree*, said while planting a toy tree. While this would be grammatical in certain languages, such as Korean or Spanish, in others, like English, it is not. Both nativist and functional theorists have sought to explain these early subjectless sentences.

An influential nativist account (Hyams 1986), now modified (see Hyams 2011), assumes that there is an innate distinction between languages that allow subjectless sentences, like Japanese, and those that do not, like English. In this account, all children start out with this distinction set to the default option, which is allowing subjectless sentences; children acquiring Japanese or Spanish have the appropriate adult setting. Children acquiring a language like English must switch to the setting that requires subjects; this change is triggered when specific information is encountered in adult speech, e.g., semantically empty subjects, as in the sentence *It's raining*. While other potential triggers have also been proposed, the key point is that learning per se is *not* involved; the two available possibilities are innately specified, and the correct setting is triggered by adult speech, rather than learned from it.

In contrast, **functional discourse-based theories of first language acquisition** have looked to prosodic and discourse factors, as well as learning, to explain children's subjectless sentences. If they are sensitive to the distinction between given vs. new information in discourse, children will not express subjects that convey given information that can be taken for granted in context; this is what both adults and children do in Korean (Clancy 2007). Prosodic factors, such as omitting unstressed pronouns in English, are also involved (Gerken 1991). Even in languages that permit subject-less sentences, their actual frequency in children's speech mirrors that in adult speech, indicating that language-specific learning is playing an important role (Kim 2000).

functions; these forms and functions are subject to the limitations of human cognition and are shaped by the communicative needs of language users. Grammar is not sharply differentiated from discourse; instead, grammatical structure is regarded as "frozen discourse," the crystallization over time of common patterns in talk. In this kind of theory, the ***differences between languages are seen as different responses to one or more functional forces that shape linguistic structure over time***, for example, the communicative motivation to express given information in a reduced way, either with pronouns as in English, or ellipsis (non-mention) as in Spanish. In this theoretical framework, ***the environment – nurture – is accorded a very important role in acquisition***.

Decades of empirical research have shown that ***the speech addressed to young children is grammatical, simple, and fluent***; the here-and-now content of Child-Directed Speech helps children to see the relation between grammatical forms and their functions. No pre-existing innate linguistic knowledge or Universal Grammar is assumed. Instead, ***the innate endowment of the child is considered to be human cognition, which has evolved along with human culture, social interaction, and communication, and therefore includes the cognitive mechanisms necessary for learning and using language***. Thus, both functionalist and nativist theories agree that language acquisition has innate foundations; however, the two approaches differ in their degree of emphasis on innate factors and in how specialized those factors are. Nativist approaches assume that our biological capacity for language is very specifically linguistic (UG), while functionalist theory assumes that non-linguistic (general) cognition is essential to language learning and use. Furthermore, in a functional, discourse-based approach, the endpoint of acquisition is viewed concretely – as knowledge of a particular grammar and how to use it; there is no need to posit that the grammar of any particular language incorporates structures and principles that are so abstract that they could apply to all languages, raising the possibility that children cannot learn them from the speech children hear.

With this view of what needs to be acquired and the kind of information that is available, it becomes plausible to postulate that ***children can learn grammar from everyday talk***. Language acquisition is viewed as learning, and ***the acquisition mechanisms that have been proposed include learning processes that are not necessarily specific to grammar or even to language***, but rather include general cognitive processes such as category formation, pattern recognition, analogy, and the formation of mental representations based on specific instances (exemplars) of language use. The dominant metaphor is construction: children as active learners, building up a grammar based on the speech they hear in order to communicate with the members of their social group.

## CHAPTER SUMMARY

In this chapter, we have explored some of the key theoretical issues and empirical findings in the field of first language acquisition. Building on strong biological, cognitive, and social foundations, one-year-olds begin to communicate using gestures, gesture + word combinations, and one-word speech acts. In developing a lexicon, young children face the cognitive task of figuring out the appropriate extension of each word, in addition to the challenge of constructing a systematic phonology for perceiving and pronouncing words. The acquisition of grammar proceeds gradually, from simple word-based patterns to constructions that relate syntactic structures with clause-level meanings. As they acquire syntax, children are sensitive to the distribution of given and new information within clauses, forging the same powerful links between grammar and discourse found in adult speech. From a theoretical perspective, a functional, discourse-based approach emphasizes that from the earliest gestures and words to the production of complex syntactic structures and narratives, the acquisition process is shaped not by innate knowledge but by the social and cognitive demands of everyday talk.

## TEXTBOX 14.15 **GLOSSING CONVENTIONS USED IN THIS CHAPTER**

| **Convention** | **Meaning** | **Convention** | **Meaning** |
| --- | --- | --- | --- |
| COP | copula | IE | informal ending |
| DEM | demonstrative | IPFV | imperfective |
| FUT | future tense | PROX | proximal |

### SUGGESTIONS FOR FURTHER READING

**Ambridge, Ben**, **and Elena Lieven**. 2011. *Child language acquisition: Contrasting theoretical approaches*. New York: Cambridge University Press.

A comprehensive, critical treatment of acquisition theories that contrasts the same two types of theory as this chapter.

**Bates, Elizabeth, and Michael Tomasello**. (eds.). 2001. *Language development: The essential readings*. Malden, Mass.: Blackwell.

Selected readings that take a functional perspective on several areas of language acquisition.

**Bowerman, Melissa, and Stephen Levinson**. (eds.). 2001. *Language acquisition and conceptual development*. New York: Cambridge University Press.

Selected readings on the relationship between language and cognition in development.

**Clark, Eve V**. 2009. *First language acquisition*, 2nd edn. New York: Cambridge University Press.

Of several useful textbooks on language acquisition, Clark's textbook is the closest in theoretical orientation to this chapter.

**Hoff, Erika**. (ed.). 2012. *Research methods in child language: A practical guide*. Malden, Mass.: Blackwell.

The chapters in this volume survey a range of new technologies and methodologies in acquisition research, as well as the latest advances in well-established approaches to collecting naturalistic and experimental acquisition data.

**MacWhinney, Brian**. 2000. *The CHILDES project: Tools for analyzing talk*, 3rd edn. Mahwah, NJ: Lawrence Erlbaum.

Volume I of the last printed manuals for the CHILDES system covers the transcription and coding conventions (CHAT) and programs for data analysis (CLAN), while Volume II describes the corpora in the CHILDES database. Current versions of these resources are available online at: http://childes.psy.cmu.edu.

**Slobin, Dan I**. (ed.). 1985, 1992, 1997. *The crosslinguistic study of language acquisition*, 5 vols. Mahwah, NJ: Lawrence Erlbaum.

This multi-volume set provides a wealth of information about the acquisition of numerous languages, including theoretical discussion and empirical data.

## EXERCISES

### 1. Phonological error patterns

One two-year-old learning English had many error patterns, resulting in a large number of homonyms in her speech. Below are six phonetic forms – [dak], [dʊk], [dɪk], ['dudu], ['dædæ], and ['mami] – that she used to produce a total of nineteen different words (personal data).

For each of the child's forms, specify which error pattern in Textbox 14.5 accounts for the child's use of that form instead of the correct adult form for the intended word, for example, what error pattern is responsible for the child's use of [dak] for *dog* [dag].

Bonus question: What error patterns are involved in the child's pronunciation of *napkin* ['næpkɪn] as ['mækɪn]?

| Child's form | Intended word | Adult form | Child's form | Intended word | Adult form |
|---|---|---|---|---|---|
| [dak]: | *dog* | [dag] | ['dudu]: | *noodles* | ['nudlz̩] |
| | *tock* | [tak] | | *turtle* | ['tɹɖl̩] |
| | *sock* | [sak] | | *tofu* | ['tofu] |
| | *block* | [blak] | | *tissue* | ['tɪʃu] |
| | *clock* | [klak] | ['dædæ]: | *glasses* | ['glæsəz] |
| [dʊk]: | *book* | [bʊk] | | *carrot* | ['kærət] |
| | *look* | [lʊk] | ['mami]: | *mommy* | ['mami] |
| [dɪk]: | *drink* | [dɹɪŋk] | | *bunny* | ['bʌni] |
| | *kick* | [kɪk] | | *Barney* | ['baɹni] |
| | *stick* | [stɪk] | | | |

### 2. Narrative evaluation

The story below was produced by a four-year-old boy in response to the researcher's question, "Have you ever been to the hospital?" (McCabe 1997: 161)

1   *Only Stevie, when I hit him with the rake one time.*
2   *And he hit me with that big broom.*
3   *And she* (the child's mother) *didn't take <u>me</u> to the hospital.*
4   *Only Steven.*
5   *He hit me with a sharp broom.*
6   *He hit me with that, that hard, hard, that hard,*
7   *ooooohhhhh, I got it in the head.*
8   *He hit me.*
9   *I hit him.*
10  *If he hits me with that once more, that broom once more,*
11  *I'm going to hit him with the rake once more.*

In your opinion, what is the point or significance of this story from the child's point of view? Based on Textbox 14.12, specify four evaluative devices in the story, giving the line number of each device. Comment on how each device contributes to the point of the story. What kind of personal identity do you think the child is constructing for himself and presenting to the listener in this story?

Bonus question: Why do you think the narrator calls the broom that Stevie used to hit him *sharp*?

### 3. Early word combinations

Use the following excerpts from a transcript of Nina at 1;11 to answer questions (a–b):
a. Use the list of functions in the leftmost column of Textbox 14.8 to specify the function of Nina's utterance on each of the following lines: 58, 61, 65, 77, 90.

b. Find and give the line number of one two-word utterance that does not seem to fit any of the functions listed in Textbox 14.8. How would you specify the function of this utterance?

Bonus question: Find two utterances that are longer than two words but serve one of the functions listed in Textbox 14.8. For each utterance, specify its function and describe the development in form that has occurred while functional continuity is preserved.

Transcript: Nina at 1;11 years old (Suppes 1974)

Context: Nina went to visit the San Francisco Zoo the Saturday before this recording. She and her mother spent most of the time in the children's zoo, where the animals were running around loose. Nina really loved it. During this session, Nina (CHI) plays with her toys and then she and her mother (MOT) look at a book from the zoo.

The following excerpts from this transcript, which is available at http://childes.psy.cmu.edu/browser/ index.php?url=Eng-NA-MOR/Suppes/nina03.cha, have been reformatted and renumbered consecutively here for convenience. Asterisks mark places where material from the original transcript has been omitted.

| 1 | MOT: | *you put both the man and the lady in the box, didn't you?* |
| 2 | CHI: | *chicken in my . . . in my box.* |
| 3 | CHI: | *chicken in my box.* |
| 4 | MOT: | *is the chicken in your box?* |
| 5 | CHI: | *chicken my, on my lady.* |
| 6 | MOT: | *the chicken's on your lady.* |
| | | ***** |
| 7 | CHI: | *the lady.* |
| 8 | CHI: | *lady.* |
| 9 | CHI: | *a lady.* |
| 10 | MOT: | *is the lady stuck?* |
| 11 | CHI: | *yeah.* |
| 12 | MOT: | *are you giving me the lady?* |
| 13 | MOT: | *thank you.* |
| 14 | CHI: | *lady.* |
| 15 | CHI: | *man fall down.* |
| 16 | CHI: | *the man too.* |
| 17 | CHI: | *mans.* |
| 18 | CHI: | *many mans.* |
| 19 | CHI: | *many mans.* |
| 20 | CHI: | *many mans.* |
| 21 | MOT: | *are there many men?* |
| 22 | CHI: | *many mans.* |
| 23 | CHI: | *many ladies.* |
| | | ***** |
| 24 | MOT: | *where is the little man?* |
| 25 | CHI: | *in the box.* |
| 26 | CHI: | *little man in the box.* |
| 27 | MOT: | *oh, the little man's in the box.* |
| 28 | MOT: | *I see.* |
| 29 | CHI: | *many box.* |
| 30 | MOT: | *you have many boxes there don't you?* |
| | | ***** |

| 31 | CHI: | *uhoh.* |
|---|---|---|
| 32 | CHI: | *chicken.* |
| 33 | MOT: | *what happened to the chicken?* |
| 34 | CHI: | *fall down.* |
| 35 | MOT: | *he fell down.* |
| 36 | MOT: | *did he get hurt?* |
| 37 | CHI: | *yeah.* |
| 38 | MOT: | *oh, poor chicken.* |

*****

| 39 | CHI: | *play, Mommy.* |
|---|---|---|
| 40 | MOT: | *do you want me to play with you?* |
| 41 | MOT: | *look what I have here.* |
| 42 | MOT: | *this is a book all about the zoo.* |
|  |  | (shows Nina a book from the San Francisco zoo) |

| 43 | MOT: | *did we go to the zoo on Saturday?* |
|---|---|---|
| 44 | CHI: | *zoo Nina.* |
| 45 | MOT: | *did Nina go to the zoo on Saturday?* |
| 46 | CHI: | *picture on the zoo.* |
| 47 | MOT: | *that's a picture of the zoo.* |

*****

| 48 | MOT: | *did you like the zoo?* |
|---|---|---|
| 49 | CHI: | *animals.* |
| 50 | CHI: | *animals.* |
| 51 | CHI: | *animals zoo.* |
| 52 | MOT: | *you saw animals at the zoo?* |
| 53 | MOT: | *what animals did you see at the zoo?* |
| 54 | CHI: | *cow zoo.* |

*****

| 55 | MOT: | *what else did you see at the zoo?* |
|---|---|---|
| 56 | CHI: | *a lion.* |
| 57 | MOT: | *you saw a lion?* |
| 58 | CHI: | *lion zoo.* |
| 59 | MOT: | *you saw a lion at the zoo.* |

*****

| 60 | CHI: | *let's read.* |
|---|---|---|
| 61 | CHI: | *tiger feet.* |
| 62 | MOT: | *those are feet, yeah.* |
| 63 | CHI: | *tiger feets.* |
| 64 | MOT: | *those are the tiger's feet.* |
| 65 | CHI: | *black feet.* |
| 66 | MOT: | *yeah, those are black.* |
| 67 | MOT: | *Nina, when you went to the zoo, did you feed the animals?* |
| 68 | CHI: | *yeah.* |
| 69 | MOT: | *who did you feed?* |
| 70 | CHI: | *feed the llama.* |
| 71 | MOT: | *you fed the llamas?* |

| 72 | CHI: | *feed the llamas with my finger.* |
| 73 | MOT: | *you fed them with your fingers?* |
| 74 | CHI: | *bite my fingers.* |
| 75 | MOT: | *did they bite your fingers?* |
| 76 | CHI: | *yeah.* |

*****

(Nina gets up to pick up her doll.)

| 77 | CHI: | *dolly read.* |
| 78 | CHI: | *read duck.* |
| 79 | CHI: | *dolly take books.* |
| 80 | MOT: | *do you want dolly to see the book about the zoo?* |
| 81 | CHI: | *yeah.* |
| 82 | MOT: | *okay.* |
| 83 | MOT: | *here, dolly, come and look at the book about the zoo.* |
| 84 | CHI: | *dolly look a zoo book.* |
| 85 | CHI: | *lion.* |
| 86 | MOT: | *what's this?* |
| 87 | CHI: | *monkey.* |
| 88 | MOT: | *did you see monkeys at the zoo?* |
| 89 | CHI: | *monkey that.* |
| 90 | CHI: | *that's monkey.* |
| 91 | MOT: | *that's a monkey.* |

*****

| 92 | CHI: | *oh, open that.* |
| 93 | CHI: | *open the pictures.* |
| 94 | MOT: | *what else were there, was there at the zoo?* |
| 95 | CHI: | *ducks play on zoo.* |
| 96 | MOT: | *there were ducks in the zoo.* |
| 97 | MOT: | *what were the ducks doing?* |
| 98 | CHI: | *quack.* |
| 99 | MOT: | *quack.* |
| 100 | MOT: | *what were they doing?* |
| 101 | MOT: | *were they swimming?* |
| 102 | CHI: | *yeah.* |
| 103 | MOT: | *where were they swimming?* |
| 104 | CHI: | *uh, swimming a water.* |
| 105 | MOT: | *they were.* |
| 106 | MOT: | *who else was swimming in the water?* |
| 107 | CHI: | *man swim in the water.* |

4. **Child-Directed Speech (CDS)**

Using the same transcript from Nina as in (3), answer the following questions:

a. Give five examples from the transcript in which Nina's mother uses one of the discourse properties of Child-Directed Speech (see Textbox 14.2). For each example, give the line number and specify which discourse property of CDS Nina's mother is using.

b. In lines 43–59, 67–76, and 94–107 of this transcript, Nina's mother co-constructs a narrative with Nina about their trip to the zoo. Find three examples, other than the ones you have used for (a), in which Nina's mother uses one of the discourse properties of Child-Directed Speech to scaffold

Nina's telling of this story. Give the line number of each example, specify which discourse property of CDS is involved, and briefly describe the role it plays in the co-construction of the narrative.

Note: In answering both (a) and (b), you may use the same discourse property more than once, but try to find different properties if you can, especially for (a).

5. **Morphology**

Using the same transcript as in (3) and (4), answer the following questions:

a. For each of the fourteen grammatical morphemes in Textbox 14.10, indicate whether Nina used that morpheme at least once in the transcript. Give the name of the morpheme and specify either "used" or "not used." If the morpheme was used by Nina, also provide the line number of one correct use.

b. Find five cases in which Nina fails to use a grammatical morpheme from Textbox 14.10 where it is obligatory; for each case, specify the missing morpheme and its line number.

c. Find as many examples of overregularization errors as you can; specify the morpheme that is being overregularized and give the line number of each error.

d. Find two utterances in which Nina uses a preposition incorrectly. For each case, give the line number and indicate which preposition Nina used, as well as which preposition would have been more appropriate.

# 15 Second language acquisition

**KEY TERMS**
- Critical Period Hypothesis
- Communicative competence
- Nativist theories of SLA
- Interlanguage
- Automaticity
- Interaction Hypothesis
- Sociocultural theories of SLA

**CHAPTER PREVIEW**

As we have seen in earlier chapters, language is a complex array of many different components, ranging from individual sounds to the appropriateness of a particular utterance or sentence in a given situation or culture. In this chapter we will look at the issues involved in learning or acquiring a second language as an adolescent or adult learner. The main question with regard to **second language acquisition (SLA)** is: why do people acquire a first language with little conscious effort, while it is so difficult to master all of the aspects of a second language and speak it like a native speaker?

This chapter will first discuss the main linguistic issues concerning how second languages are acquired (e.g., phonology, morphology, syntax, lexicon/vocabulary, pragmatics). It will then describe some of the influences from the field of psychology on the study of second language acquisition and will examine the cognitive processes that differ between first language (L1) and second language (L2) learning. Thirdly, the chapter will consider how social and affective issues of L2 learning have come to the forefront in the last decade of the twentieth century and into the twenty-first century. Finally, interspersed throughout the chapter are discussions of the relationship between current knowledge about how second languages are acquired and the practice of language teaching, including some of the current issues in language teaching, especially those arising from increased globalization.

LIST OF AIMS

At the end of this chapter, students should be able to:

- explain the "nature vs. nurture" argument in terms of second language acquisition;
- explain why learning pronunciation of a second language is more difficult than learning that of one's first or native language;
- describe what developing vocabulary knowledge in a second language involves beyond word definitions;
- explain the distinctions between form, meaning, and use in acquiring grammatical competence;
- give examples of sociolinguistic/pragmatic/cultural differences in a second language that would make the same utterance that one might use in one's native language inappropriate.

## 15.1  Introduction

Many of us grew up hearing and speaking only one language, our "native language," "mother tongue," or **L1**. Others, the lucky ones, heard and spoke more than one language as children (see Sidebar 15.1). As we progress into the twenty-first century, children in many parts of the world, including the United States, grow up speaking more than one language for a variety of reasons (e.g., their community is multilingual, they or their parents are immigrants, they learn foreign languages in school).

No matter how many languages one grew up with, many adults want to learn other languages for various reasons (see Textbox 15.1). As a result, numerous commercial products and websites aim to address this need. Some promise that you can learn a new language effortlessly, without translation, painful memorization, or boring grammar drills. All you have to do is tap your innate language-learning ability, and learning a second language will be as natural and painless as learning your first. But as we will see, ***successful second language learning depends on a complex array of linguistic, social, cognitive, and affective variables***.

**SIDEBAR 15.1**

If you have learned a language other than your mother tongue, at what age did you start? Were you able to learn this second (or third) language as perfectly and with little conscious effort like the first? Which aspects of learning your second language were easy? What was more difficult? Think about how you learned vocabulary, pronunciation, grammar, and knowing how to talk to your friends vs. knowing how to talk with adult strangers. Can you hypothesize why certain aspects of language were easier to learn than others?

## 15.2  Linguistic issues in second language acquisition (SLA)

As adults, most of us do not consciously remember how we learned our first language. It seems that we did not have to memorize vocabulary, learn grammar rules, or think consciously about how to speak politely to our elders. Learning, or acquisition of L1 was effortless (see Textbox 15.2). But learning a second language seems very

---

### TEXTBOX 15.1 **CAREERS IN SECOND LANGUAGE ACQUISITION**

Students interested in linguistics and language learning often consider a career in teaching language. In English-speaking countries such as the United States, Canada, or Australia, there are many types of English as a Second Language (ESL) programs for learners of all ages. In addition, since English has become a global lingua franca, there are numerous opportunities to teach English as a Foreign Language (EFL) in other countries.

Native speakers of English or proficient second language speakers of English might well find opportunities to teach English or work in related areas such as language policy or the development of teaching materials at home or abroad. Or perhaps you are fluent in a language other than English and thus considering foreign language teaching possibilities.

---

### TEXTBOX 15.2 **ACQUISITION VERSUS LEARNING**

Although the words *acquisition* and *learning* are often used interchangeably, there is a tradition within SLA that draws the following distinction between the two: *acquisition* is the process of a child's L1 development in which he or she gradually begins to produce the language without consciously thinking about the rules of grammar, the pronunciation, or the intonation.

In contrast, *learning* occurs with second languages, particularly if the primary source of exposure to the language is a classroom – that is, not a "natural" situation – in which learners must consciously memorize words and rules, deduce patterns in the language, and think about producing sounds and rhythms that are "unnatural" in comparison to the L1.

---

different and much more difficult. Many issues arise for second language learners. The type of explanation that is appropriate for each issue will depend on the aspect of language it involves.

## 15.2.1 Phonology and pronunciation

One of the most interesting questions regarding L2 phonology and pronunciation is why attaining native-like pronunciation presents one of the greatest challenges to second language learners. Almost everyone has known immigrants to their home country who have lived there for many years, and although the grammar and vocabulary of the new language they acquired may be excellent, they may still have noticeable differences in their phonetics and phonology that mark them as non-native speakers. Often most noticeably, these differences are in intonation, timing, and other features of their prosody (Chapter 10). Despite the fact that intonation and rhythm are what infants react to first before they learn words and grammar, these language components are frequently the last that adults acquire.

In linguistics, one common proposal to account for why it is so hard for adolescents and adults to acquire native-like phonological and prosodic patterns (i.e., to "lose their accent," to put it in colloquial terms), while young children are so successful in attaining native pronunciations in their first – and often a second or third language, is the **Critical Period Hypothesis (CPH)** also referred to as the "sensitive period" (see Chapter 14). Proponents of the CPH argue that there is a biologically determined period for language to be learned perfectly, and that only during that period can any language, first or second, be acquired naturally.

Lenneberg (a neurolinguist), proposed in 1967 that certain biological events related to language acquisition can only happen in an early stage of development termed the critical period and that children must receive an adequate and sufficient amount of linguistic input during the critical period in order for language development to proceed normally. He initially hypothesized that this period extends from age 2 to puberty and was based on loss of neural plasticity in the brain. But what are the implications of the CPH for second language acquisition?

There appear to be no simple or definitive answers to this question. A number of studies have shown that the notion of the nature of L2 acquisition changing suddenly and dramatically around the age of 12–13 due to changes in the brain is much too simplistic. There may be different critical periods for different language skills, for example, a critical period for acquiring unaccented speech (suggested to be as early as age 6), which might be different from the critical period for acquiring grammatical competence (which may be closer to puberty) or learning vocabulary. It may be that the exact age of first exposure is not such a central issue, particularly not in a formal learning context. In a recent test of the CPH for SLA, the most compelling finding was that the degree of success in SLA steadily declines throughout the life span (Hakuta et al. 2003). The pattern of decline, however, failed to be marked by a sharp drop at a particular age, which would be the essential hallmark of a critical period.

In L2 research and teaching, there is a trend today toward recognizing **suprasegmentals** (see Chapter 3) as potentially more important than **segments** for speaking comprehensibly and for listening comprehension. Indeed, babies react to **prosody** (as well as facial expressions and gestures) well before they have learned words or language. Studies have shown that L2 learners who have received instruction and training in prosody speak more comprehensibly and fluently than those who have been trained only on segmental accuracy, focused on consonants and vowels (e.g., Derwing, Munro, and Wiebe 1998; Derwing and Rossiter 2003).

Many L2 learners comment that their language classes do not focus much on pronunciation. As a native Russian speaker learning English noted, "My English professors did not give enough attention to pronunciation … after living in the United States for a while, I realized that good pronunciation takes you a lot further than good grammar." It is true that some language teaching approaches have placed little or no emphasis on pronunciation, especially those focused primarily on translation of L2 reading materials and on grammar. This tendency still holds in foreign language contexts where assessment of foreign

**SIDEBAR 15.2**

Communicative competence refers to both a speaker's grammatical competence (including a knowledge of the rules of grammar, vocabulary, pronunciation) and sociolinguistic competence (a knowledge of rules of language use in culturally appropriate ways and the ability to effectively communicate or interact with speakers of the target language).

### SIDEBAR 15.3

As you have probably experienced, when you are trying to communicate meaning, it is very difficult to monitor your sound production at the same time. If you have learned an L2, which types of sounds did you need to practice repeatedly? Were there particular words or expressions you focused on in your practicing? (For example, an English learner practicing /r/ might practice conversational expressions such as *That's right* or *Really*? A Russian learner might practice stringing multiple consonants together at the beginning of a word to say *здравствуйте* [zdravstvujtʲe], 'hello.' And a German learner might practice producing the front rounded vowels marked by an umlaut in the orthography, so as to say *Das ist schön* 'That's nice' or *tschüss* 'bye, so long.')

### SIDEBAR 15.4

Consider a language you have learned. What sounds do you think are difficult for non-native speakers to produce but perhaps not so important from the perspective of intelligibility? A good example might be the *r* sound in many languages. If learners of Spanish, French, German, Farsi, or Arabic simply use the pronunciation of 'r' from their L1 when speaking English, they will probably be understood although noticeably non-native; the phonetic substitution is unlikely to compromise intelligibility. On the other hand, speakers of Japanese, a language that doesn't have a phonemic distinction between /r/ and /l/, can find it difficult to produce English /r/ and /l/ sounds distinctly. Communicative problems may arise because of the many English minimal pairs such as *light/right*, *bled/bread*, etc.

language skills is done largely through written exams. In recent years, however, approaches aimed at developing **communicative competence** have integrated pronunciation into listening and speaking skills (see Sidebar 15.2). In addition to greater emphasis on the intonations and rhythms of a language, recent trends also stress helping learners develop strategies to improve pronunciation outside the classroom, such as extensive listening to gain familiarity with intonation and stress, as well as intensive practice on diagnosed problem areas along with monitoring of progress (see Sidebar 15.3).

Although communicative language teaching approaches have de-emphasized "skill and drill" exercises, pronunciation is one area in which repeated practice can be beneficial, leading to automaticity.

In the teaching of English pronunciation, another recent development is the recognition that in this age of global Englishes, a variety of accents is acceptable. At the beginning of the twenty-first century, approximately three of every four users of English worldwide was a non-native speaker (Crystal 2003). We can assume, then, that much communication in English occurs among L2 speakers with different first languages and not between native and non-native speakers. A language put to this type of use is known as a lingua franca. While descriptions of English as a lingua franca (ELF; not to be confused with EFL, English as a Foreign Language) can include grammar, the lexicon, and pragmatics, pronunciation for ELF is of particular interest to those involved with language teaching and language policy. The notion of "correct pronunciation" based on accepted standards becomes less of an issue than describing what constitutes intelligible communication (see Sidebar 15.4). For example, researchers have pointed out that some English sounds that are difficult for L2 speakers to produce, such as the *th* sounds (ð and θ), are not really necessary for intelligible global communication (Seidlhofer 2005).

*In addition to English there are, of course, many other languages used as lingua francas throughout the world.* For example, Standard Cantonese is a lingua franca in Singapore and Malaysia as well as in Hong Kong and the Guangdong province of China. Urdu is an official language of India and a lingua franca of Pakistan.

## 15.2.2   Lexicon/vocabulary

Many people believe that vocabulary may be the most important aspect of any language that is being learned; if you don't know enough words, no amount of grammar knowledge will allow you to speak, read, or write the language. But how much vocabulary does one need to know in order to speak an L2? It depends on the purpose. Some estimate that for everyday conversation or for the purposes of reading a newspaper in English, we need to know approximately 2,000 words (Lightbown and Spada 2006); however, it depends on the content of the conversation and on the newspaper. Many first-year language textbooks claim to teach 2,000–3,000 words (see Sidebar 15.5), but most of us have had the experience of being *unable* to hold a basic conversation or read a newspaper in an L2 even after studying the L2 for a year (at the college level). For English, it is estimated that the 2,000–3,000 most frequent words make up as much as 80–90 percent of most non-technical texts. But in typical L2 classrooms, particularly after the first year of instruction, much of the vocabulary that is taught is from literary works or for relatively specialized topics. Based on what typical students are able to read and say after two years of L2 study in the classroom, it is likely that learners actually need to know several thousand English words (4,000 perhaps) in order to converse about more than the weather, one's family, and the most basic of everyday activities.

**SIDEBAR 15.5**

A quick look at some first-year Spanish and German L2 textbooks used in the USA reveals that their glossaries contain between 1,500–6,300 words!

For many languages, researchers have determined which words are most frequently used in spoken and written discourse; the lists resulting from such analyses are used for teaching materials and self-study. For example, consider the sentence groups below taken from two Productive Levels Tests for English. The learner's task is to complete the partially spelled-out words.

2000-word level:
1. The rich man died and left all his we_____ to his son.
2. Teenagers often adm____ and worship pop singers.
3. La___ of rain led to a shortage of water in the city.

5000-word level:
1. This is a complex problem which is difficult to compr__.
2. We do not have adeq_____ information to make a decision.
3. She is not a child, but a mat_____ woman. She can make her own decisions.
   (Nation 2001: 425–427)

When learners try to guess the words, they undoubtedly use contextual cues: associated words (e.g., *rich* associates with *wealth*) or words that tend to occur with others (e.g., *lack of rain, adequate information*). In fact, to know a word means not just understanding individual meanings but knowing which words "go together" or collocate with others. Because theories of SLA are placing increasing importance on such **collocations** for developing proficiency, *L2 vocabulary teaching materials increasingly emphasize the learning of groups of words as sets, including collocations* (e.g., *light lunch, slight chance, endless supply, pretty much, right now*) *and lexical bundles* (*by the way, give me a break, I'd be happy to*). With the development of **corpus linguistics**, we now have a great deal of information about how words combine with other words in English as well as in many other languages. In addition, **corpus** analyses show which groups of words are common in different registers, such as casual conversation vs. academic prose. For example, analysis of a large corpus of conversational English identified the most frequent **lexical bundles**, defined as "recurrent expressions, regardless of their idiomaticity, and regardless of their structural status" (Biber et al. 1999: 990). Here are a few examples that begin with the personal pronoun *I: I'm going to get, I'll have a look, I can't be bothered, I'll see what you, I can't remember what.* As you might imagine, the learning of lexical bundles and other word combinations such as collocations helps to produce idiomatic speech and to avoid odd pairings of words (e.g., *big solution, make a vacation, make a party*) that may result from L1 to L2 translation or from a limited L2 vocabulary.

One other area in which corpus linguistics has contributed greatly to vocabulary study is showing us how vocabulary and grammar interact, often referred to as lexico-grammatical structure. Furthermore, these interactions often differ depending on the registers of language. Table 15.1 gives examples from Biber et al. (1999: 478) of the most frequent verbs used in English passive voice in three different registers: conversation, journalism, and academic prose.

**TABLE 15.1** Frequency of lexical verbs with the passive

| Register | Lexical verb | Occurrences per million words |
| --- | --- | --- |
| Conversation | *be done* | over 100 |
| | *be called* | over 40 |
| | *be put* | over 40 |
| Journalism | *be expected* | over 200 |
| | *be said* | over 100 |
| | *be held* | over 100 |
| Academic prose | *be made* | over 300 |
| | *be used* | over 300 |
| | *be seen* | over 300 |

As Table 15.1 indicates, both the lexical verbs and the frequencies of passive verbs vary across registers. For example, while *be done* (as in *It's gotta be done*) is the only verb in conversational English to occur more than 100 times per million words, passive verbs in academic prose (e.g., *This procedure should be repeated*) occur with much greater frequency. In fact, several other lexical verbs not listed here occurred more than 300 times per million words in the academic prose data. And most verbs listed for the journalism and academic prose registers were rarely used in passive form in conversational English. In sum, ***developing vocabulary knowledge involves not only word meanings but also awareness of grammatical forms in language use***.

As for learning L2 vocabulary, linguists have different views regarding which methods are most effective (see Sidebar 15.6). Some believe that extensive reading (especially for pleasure, because it is more motivating) is the best way to learn vocabulary because the words are encountered in context (e.g., Krashen 1989). Others believe that learners would need to encounter the same word between six and ten times in order to actually learn the word (Zahar, Cobb, and Spada 2001), and therefore specific and targeted study/memorization/use of vocabulary is necessary. Another issue to consider, according to studies, is that in order to read fluently (without constant, focused, painstaking effort), one needs to understand the meaning of between 90–95 percent of the words in a text! If learners need to look up every other word in assigned L2 texts, the size of their vocabulary may simply not be large enough, not to mention the fact that looking up so many words may be disruptive to comprehension. SLA researchers are continually studying the role that L2 vocabulary plays in the L2 reading process.

**SIDEBAR 15.6**

You might have opinions about effective methods for learning vocabulary, based on your personal experiences. For example, in your L2 classes, did you have to memorize long lists of (unrelated) vocabulary? Was it an effective way of increasing your vocabulary? Which ways of increasing your L2 vocabulary have worked best for you?

Of course, ***how much and what kind of vocabulary a learner needs depends on his or her learning goals***. If someone is learning Chinese for business purposes, particular terms related to the profession would be important as well as general vocabulary appropriate for "small talk" topics and a range of polite expressions to be used in social situations. In fact, there are special vocational language programs that focus on the vocabulary needed in professions such as nursing. Consider a person interested in learning German only to read scientific articles or someone studying Japanese only to study literature. These learners have very different vocabulary needs than someone who is learning, say, "survival" language for travel. Young people are often very interested in learning the current idioms and slang expressions of an L2 in order to communicate with others their own age; they don't want to sound like a textbook. Consider, for example, an oft-taught question in L2 classes: *What do you do in your free time?* (in German: *Was machst du in deiner Freizeit?*). A learner of German who asked this question on a trip to Germany was laughed at because it sounded stilted and unnatural. Clearly, an important part of vocabulary learning and teaching in any language is considering the contexts and purposes of language use.

### 15.2.3  Grammar

In our discussion of vocabulary learning, we pointed out that the grammar of a language is not something that can be clearly separated from meanings in actual communication (see Textbox 15.3). The essential role of grammar in learning an L2 was emphasized by applied linguist Henry Widdowson, who stated, "Language learning is essentially grammar learning and it is a mistake to think otherwise" (1988: 154).

While many language learners associate the word *grammar* with language rules that characterize prescriptive usage, **current approaches to the teaching and learning of L2 grammar emphasize not rules but rather meaningful and dynamic language systems that change over time**. What constitutes "correct" or appropriate grammar depends on a number of communicative variables. Thus, learners need not only to acquire grammatical forms but also to gain understanding of the meanings and uses of grammatical structures (see Sidebar 15.7). To borrow an example from our last section, a learner of English acquiring the passive voice must know not only the forms of the structure in various tenses (e.g., *is written, is being written, has been written*) but also how the structure is used in written or spoken English, such as to put focus on the semantic **patient** (see Chapter 6) that is **given**, meaning the referent is already being discussed in the discourse (e.g., *The burglar was arrested yesterday*) or to avoid mentioning who is to blame for an action by omitting reference to the semantic **agent** (e.g., *Mistakes were made*). As another example, the modal verb *may* in English is an easy form to learn, but has several meanings, including permission (*you may leave*) and possibility (*it may rain*). Further, an English learner may

**SIDEBAR 15.7**

If you have learned or studied a language other than your mother tongue, think about how you learned or were taught the grammar of that language. What were some of the most difficult things to learn about that language's grammar? How similar was the language to your L1, or if you have learned multiple L2s, how similar are the L2s to your L1 or to each other? These are some of the questions that will be discussed here. Just how does one go about learning the grammatical system of an L2?

---

**TEXTBOX 15.3**

Chapter 14 included a discussion of **nativist** versus **functional discourse-based** theories of first language acquisition. Nativist theories are based upon the view that innate grammatical structures (Universal Grammar, or UG) are required to explain certain facts, such as the child's ability to produce utterances that he or she has never before heard. A functional discourse-based theory, by contrast, would attribute such behavior to more general processes of human cognition, such as learning and analogy. The same theoretical debate is found with regard to second language acquisition, and this motivates interesting questions in both fields. If one assumes the existence of UG, to what extent are these structures still available to someone learning a second language, particularly when the learner is no longer a child, but an adolescent or an adult? Or, if one assumes there is no UG, then how do human cognitive abilities allow for the acquisition of the second language, and what is the role of interactional discourse in this process?

discover that speakers in informal contexts often use another modal, *can*, and not *may*, to ask permission: *Can we go when we've finished our exam?* As these examples illustrate, acquiring the grammar of an L2 involves not just learning the forms, but also multiple meanings and appropriate uses of structures in communicative contexts.

Sensitivity to the communicative context is only one important factor in successful L2 acquisition. Another factor is the first language that the learner brings to the process. L2 learners frequently make errors that can be attributed to transfer from L1. For example, native speakers of Chinese or Korean learning English may omit the *-s* inflection for English plural nouns since their L1s do not normally mark for plural (e.g., *\*I bought two book*). Word order differences between languages account for many such errors. A speaker of Farsi learning English, for example, might transfer that language's subject, object, verb ordering as well as the ordering of adjectives after nouns in producing English utterances (e.g., *I man old saw* for *I saw an old man*). A native speaker of English learning French may incorrectly place some adjectives, such as those denoting colors, before nouns instead of after them (e.g., *\*la blanche maison* for 'the white house'). It is also the case, however, that **many grammatical errors made by L2 learners are not caused by interference from L1 but are specific to the particular L2 being learned**. For example, in English some lexical verbs, such as *enjoy*, are followed by complement clauses in which the verb is in the *-ing* (**gerund**) form, as in *I enjoy **reading** mysteries*, and do not take complements in which the verb is in the infinitive (*\*I enjoy **to read** mysteries*). Many learners of English, regardless of their L1s, will make errors in using the wrong complements after such verbs until they acquire the correct structures.

Further evidence that the L1 is not the only factor contributing to errors in L2 production is that **L2 learners, regardless of their mother tongue, master certain grammatical morphemes in the same order as children learning that same language as an L1**. For example, L2 English learners in early stages of acquisition typically use the word *no* or *not* to negate utterances, placing it at the beginning of the utterance, as in *No have dog*; later they may use other forms combined with auxiliaries such as *don't*. The same pattern is attested in L1 acquisition of English. Another example is that learners of English may extend the regular past tense rule to irregular verbs, producing *teached* or *putted*, or apply the regular plural formation to irregular nouns, producing forms such as *teeths*. Again, these patterns are frequently found in the speech of children acquiring English. Native speakers of English make similar types of mistakes when learning other languages. For example, learners of Japanese sometimes apply the regular morphological rules of verbal negation (using the morpheme-*nai*) to the separate word class of adjectives, leading to forms like *atsui-nai* or *atsu-nai* for 'not hot' as opposed to the correct form *atsu-kunai*. Such mistakes are also found in the speech of children acquiring Japanese.

Another way that L2 acquisition can mirror processes of development of L1 is that acquisition does not always proceed in a linear fashion. Sometimes learners experience **U-shaped learning**, first producing a correct form, perhaps by imitation, then later producing an incorrect form after learning the grammatical system, and finally producing the correct form again once the exceptions to the rules have been learned or the grammatical system has been mastered. For example, in L1 acquisition, a child might produce the sequence: *I have more than you* (2 yrs.); *I have many-er than you* (3 yrs.); *I have more than you* (4 yrs.). Similarly, in adult L2 acquisition, a learner may say *She taught me English* early on, based on having heard the form *taught*; then later, after learning to form the past tense with *-ed*, the learner might produce *She teached me English*; and finally, after learning that the verb *teach* is irregular, he or she will say *She taught me English*.

The over-generalization of grammatical rules and the observation of U-shaped learning patterns led to the development of an important concept in linguistic approaches to SLA, namely that of **interlanguage**, which *is the L2 language system created by a learner; this interlanguage is neither the L1 system nor the native-like L2 system, but something in between*. A learner's interlanguage is constantly changing and is continually revised based on new words, forms, or structures that enter the system. It can be thought of as a continuum of a learner's evolving L2 language system, or even as a third language, with its own grammar, lexicon, and phonology. The key point is that the learner's language at any given time is an internalized system, created as that learner imposes structure on the available linguistic input. As such, a learner's interlanguage can be seen as an important intermediate stage that is part of the language-learning process rather than as a system that is considered deficient. This allows greater tolerance for errors, as mistakes are considered to be steps in the evolving process of L2 mastery. Learners often experience, when learning an L2, that certain errors persist when they speak or write the language. This is called **stabilization** or **fossilization**, a phenomenon that may prevent the learner's L2 system from becoming native-like.

### 15.2.4  Cross-cultural issues and pragmatic interpretation

Chapter 8 introduced pragmatics as extralinguistic competence, the ability to draw correct inferences based on the context of an utterance. *Culture is a critical part of the extralinguistic context, and there are many culturally based expectations for how utterances should be interpreted*. This fact is (often keenly) felt by second language learners – and speakers of the target language who interact with them – when utterances intended in one way are interpreted in quite another.

This can be true of conventionalized interactions, such as the exchange of greetings, where different greetings have different implications about the level of formality of the interaction and the social relationship between interlocutors. For example in the United States, the following greetings and responses are common:

| | | |
|---|---|---|
| *How are you today?* | *How're ya doin'?* | *What's up?* |
| *I'm fine, thanks.* | *I'm good.* | *Not much.* |

*How are you?* can be used in more formal situations, resulting in the more formal and polite *I'm fine, thanks*, whereas *How's it going?* or *How're ya doin'?* are less formal and are often answered with *I'm good*. In the most informal settings, e.g., on college campuses, you might hear *What's up?* (and even *'Sup?*), with a reply like *Nothin'* or *Hey*. Speakers immersed in the cultural context know that the question itself is often used as a greeting and is not intended to be interpreted as a true question about how the other person actually is; likewise, the responses are rather formulaic as well. An L2 hearer lacking this cultural context may not realize that the "question" is a standard greeting, but rather interpret it as a request for information. When coming from a stranger, e.g., a store cashier, he or she may either feel affronted by the question or proceed to give a full and complete answer about how he or she really is doing that day, surprising the cashier! A similar mistake can be made by American speakers in other cultural contexts. For example, in Spain, when people ask *¿Qué tal?* ('How are things/What's up?') they are often using it as a genuine request for information and expression of interest in the other person, so when an American answers *Nada* ('nothing'), the response could be perceived as cold, rude, and insensitive.

Missed interpretations can also occur in other conventionalized interactions, such as the giving and receiving of compliments, or the acceptance or refusal of a date. People draw inferences about intended meanings based on the interactional norms of their native cultures, and they respond accordingly, sometimes in ways that are inappropriate or misinterpreted in the foreign cultural context. The following examples, taken from observations by students in the United States, illustrate typical cases:

- Japanese: When a Japanese teacher complimented an American student, the student said *Thank you!* but later realized that this was an inappropriate response to a compliment in a Japanese context, where it is considered polite to deny compliments, as the speaker then appears more humble.
- Persian: When a Persian student said to an American, *Wow, you've gotten big/fat*, it was intended as a compliment, meaning 'You look healthy/good.' The culturally based intended interpretation is that fat indicates a lack of illness. In the US cultural context, however, being fat is often considered to be unhealthy and unbecoming, so the statement was interpreted as an insult.
- Hungarian: When a Hungarian woman was invited to go on a date by an American man, she said *No, I can't; I'm busy*. He said, *Okay, maybe next time*. But in Hungarian culture, he was supposed to keep asking and trying to persuade her to go out with him. She expected him to interpret her utterance in that way and was disappointed when he didn't persist.
- Japanese: A Japanese man asked an American woman if she liked a certain food. It was his way of asking her out, following cultural norms in Japan. Lacking this

extralinguistic cultural context, she responded honestly to the linguistic meaning of the utterance, saying *No, I don't like that food*. Not knowing that she did not understand his pragmatic intention, he assumed from her response that she did not want to go out with him.

Missed interpretations based on different cultural assumptions are not limited to conventionalized interactions. This is especially true when people prefer to be indirect:

- Japanese: A student arrived late to Japanese class, and when the teacher commented *You seem to be very busy*, she was expecting the student to offer an explanation as to why the student was late. Without the shared cultural background that would indicate this was an indirect request for explanation, the student found the comment to be confusing.
- Italian: An American student's Italian roommates kept asking her *Aren't you hot?* whenever she wore boots and jeans during the summer. They were trying to imply that she was inappropriately dressed, based on their cultural assumptions about seasonally appropriately clothing, which she did not share. She was not able to interpret their questions as suggestions that she dress differently.

***One aspect of language use where people frequently encounter difficulty has to do with determining the appropriate level of formality***. Speakers who want their linguistic forms to be interpreted as polite and well-meaning may mistakenly appear either overly formal and cold, or overly informal and presumptuous. We can see this in the examples below, from L2 writers sending emails to the editors of a scholarly journal; some were overly formal and others were far too informal:

- L1 Arabic: *It honours me to send my manuscript to consider for publication in your estimable journal.*
- L1 Korean: *Dear editors, if you possibly find a time to review my attached file and give a feedback to my current concern above, it would really be appreciated, sir.*
- L1 Persian: *I entreat you to consider my humble paper as an attachment for publication. I hope these few lines find you in the best of your health.*
- L1 Persian: *i have written an article . . . and now I wanna submit it in one ELT journals. how can I submit it in your journal? plz send some information.*
- L1 Chinese: *Dear Editor, Please check this article.*
- L1 Chinese: *Dear Professor, Thank you very much for your immediate response and your exciting website. Wish you a healthy body and a happy life.*

One recent development in the teaching of pragmatics for L2 learners is a greater emphasis on the bicultural or multicultural identities that many speakers of other languages possess. That is, although learners need to be aware of practices that are potentially offensive or off-putting to people of the L2 culture, as illustrated in some of the examples above, speakers do not necessarily need to adopt all L2 communicative norms when speaking the L2. One example might be the response to compliments. An American woman might respond to a compliment about a personal item such as clothing with a comment like *Oh, yes, I just love it!* In another cultural context, such a response might be interpreted as bragging or in another unintended way. A woman who feels uncomfortable responding in such a way should not feel she needs to give up her L1 norm of responding, as long as it is not objectionable and does not elicit interpretations that she did not want to make. Or she might combine some part of an L2 manner of response with that of her L1. Thus, learning the pragmatics of an L2 becomes an additive experience rather than one that replaces L1 with L2, creating a more complex (in the good sense) and richer identity for the language learner. However, ideally, the learner should be making conscious choices about appropriate forms to use in social situations and not "default" L1 forms resulting from a lack of knowledge about the L2.

## 15.3  Cognitive processing issues in SLA

First and second language acquisition are important fields of study not only within linguistics but also within the field of psychology. The term **psycholinguistics** is used to indicate the intersection of these fields, including the acquisition of language. Since language acquisition is a cognitive process, it is also of great interest to those who study **cognitive linguistics**. Different people use different cognitive strategies in the process of L2 acquisition. For example, some people consciously think through nearly everything they are going to say before saying it, mentally translating from their L1 into the L2 before speaking or writing, thus monitoring their production. Others may use "chunks" of language or grammatical formulas in the construction of sentences. These represent different learning processes that can vary across individuals or that can be used by a single individual at different points in the L2 acquisition process. There are also different ways in which language is comprehended, including "top-down" processing where learners are able to reach a basic level of comprehension of an utterance without understanding every word, and "bottom-up" processing where comprehension proceeds more slowly as learners focus on individual words or morphemes, which can be an obstacle to the comprehension of the whole. It is interesting to consider the implications of these differences and what they reveal about learning and about human cognition.

Before considering these implications, it is important to understand the historical context out of which the field of psycholinguistics developed. Until the middle of the twentieth century, **behaviorism** was a dominant theory within the field of psychology. With regard to L1 learning, it was thought that children learn the language of their environment by imitating, needing to communicate, and being reinforced and rewarded when they are understood and have successfully gotten their message across. Applied to L2 learning, the theory suggests that if a learner hears a stimulus in an L2 and repeats the word or sentence enough times, it will become a habit and can then be used to communicate successfully. However, as theories of psychology evolved in the late twentieth century, there was a reaction against behaviorist theories. In SLA, this entailed a movement toward cognitive theories, including a shift in focus from the learner's *external* environment to the individual's *internal* thought processes. ***In the cognitive tradition, the focus is on the central role of the human mind in processing linguistic data that is heard or received as input, with a reduced role for repetition and habit formation***.

Some psychologists and psycholinguistics who study cognition and learning (in particular, information processing) theorize that L1 learning is just another cognitive skill that humans are able to master (like learning to play the piano or learning math). ***They believe that language learning involves general cognitive abilities and basic information-processing mechanisms in the brain***. SLA is viewed as the acquisition of complex skills, and, like learning to play a sport or a musical instrument, the role of **automaticity** is of great importance. The goal of SLA is for the learner to be able to process linguistic input and output quickly, unconsciously, and effortlessly, that is, automatically, without having to think about each word or step in the process. To do this, the learner begins with controlled processing, in which the associations have not yet been built up by repeated use and so require conscious attention. With time and experience, learners begin to use language more automatically. Language processing is also believed to be highly dependent upon input frequency, with frequency effects found in the processing of phonology, lexis, grammaticality, syntax, and formulaic language production (Ellis 2002). The effects of frequency of exposure and input have been studied in first and second language acquisition (see Textbox 15.4), and help explain, for example, the variance of morpheme acquisition order. But ***the main question is how learners move from knowledge of the examples received as input to automatically producing language; for SLA, this question remains unanswered***.

There seem to be a number of different mechanisms at work as learners automate their L2 production. Two important mechanisms proposed in the SLA literature are the **monitor** and the **affective filter**. The monitor is the learner's cognitive "watchdog"

---

TEXTBOX 15.4

The influence of frequency can be investigated from many perspectives. Corpus linguists, for example, might count and analyze patterns in the L2 learners' input. Psycholinguists would want to study these patterns in language processing, or the relationship between input frequency and memory.

TEXTBOX 15.5 **MONITORING L2 SPEECH**

Just as the affective filter mechanism might differ greatly from one L2 learner to another, some learners monitor themselves better than others. The disadvantage of monitoring too closely or carefully is that speakers may not say as much as they would like. Perhaps even worse, speakers might take so much time to think about their correct L2 usage that the conversation may have moved on to another topic before they have the chance to utter a sentence!

**SIDEBAR 15.8**

In thinking about your L2 learning experiences, do you ever feel self-conscious about speaking the L2? Do you worry about sounding stupid? Do you know gregarious people who will gab in an L2 "fluently" while making lots of grammatical mistakes?

that consciously reviews what the learner has said in the L2 and *monitors* it for correctness (see Textbox 15.5). The affective filter is the emotional component of an L2 learner's conscious learning process, which involves how comfortable or uncomfortable he or she is when speaking an L2. When trying to speak a foreign language, many learners have the experience of not wanting to sound stupid. In acute cases of discomfort, the affective filter would be "high" and the learner would find it difficult to communicate in the language (see Sidebar 15.8).

Another mechanism that learners use in the process of SLA is **negotiation for meaning**, a specific type of interaction where L2 learners explicitly signal that they do not understand something and the interlocutor provides input as an attempt to clarify and facilitate their understanding. This is part of a broader theory known as the **Interaction Hypothesis**, proposed by Long (1996); see Sidebar 15.9. These kinds of interactions are important for developing communicative competence and are interrelated with the social aspects of SLA, to be discussed in the next section.

Many examples of negotiation can be found in transcripts of computer-mediated communication. For example, in a negotiation between a native speaker of Spanish and a learner of Spanish, the learner (Speaker Y) did not understand the Spanish word *común*, which the native speaker (Speaker X) used (Blake 2000: 125):

X:  *Cuales son en común?*
    [What are in common?]
Y:  *como se dice comun en igles? no comprehende*
    [How do you say "common" in English?. . . no understand]
X:  *común es cuando algo y una otra algo son el mismo; entiendes mi explicacion?*
    ["Common" is when something and another thing are the same; do you understand my explanation?]
Y:  *si, gracias . . .*
    [Yes, thank you.]

**SIDEBAR 15.9**
THE INTERACTION
HYPOTHESIS
The Interaction Hypothesis states
that: "*Negotiation for meaning,
and especially negotiation work
that triggers interactional
adjustments by the [Native
speaker] or more competent
interlocutor, facilitates acquisition
because it connects input, internal
speaker capacities, particularly
selective attention, and output in
productive ways*" (Long 1996:
451–452).

In addition to such mechanisms, a host of individual learner differences are also factors in acquisition and learning. Among them is a wide array of differences in cognitive styles (e.g., verbal vs. visual vs. auditory vs. kinesthetic learners), learning styles (inductive vs. deductive), personality (e.g., introvert vs. extrovert), aptitude, age, motivation (e.g., instrumental vs. integrative), and affect (e.g., insensitive vs. empathetic). Some of these factors will be discussed in the next section.

In sum, this section has introduced some of the cognitive mechanisms that facilitate L2 comprehension and production. SLA learning processes vary across individuals, share features with other types of learning, and are both embedded in and mediated by social interaction. We turn to a fuller exploration of the latter in the next section.

## 15.4 Sociocultural and affective aspects of SLA

Because language is inherently interactional, the social and affective aspects of communication are significant factors in the process of L2 learning. This section will consider the importance of social interaction for SLA, sociocultural theories as applied to SLA, and individual differences among learners, such as personality differences, willingness to take risks, and opinions about language learning.

As seen in the preceding section, the Interaction Hypothesis posits that social interaction is an important factor in SLA. Many important pedagogical methods rely on social interaction as a medium of teaching and learning. Since the late 1970s, the input-interaction-output theory of SLA has been central in providing many insights into second language learning and teaching, or "instructed SLA." Simply put, the model proposes that language acquisition is strongly facilitated by learners using the target language in interaction. In particular, when learners actively negotiate meaning in an L2 with a communicative partner, they benefit from experience with both comprehensible input and output through interaction. Input includes all language that a learner hears or reads through either informal or formal learning; output is simply the language that the learner produces, either speaking or writing. Many L2 classroom activities draw on this model, such as those in which students are given tasks to complete that require meaningful verbal interaction. In collaborative tasks, learners are assigned a goal and must communicate using whatever linguistic or extralinguistic resources they have to achieve the intended outcome.

In the mid 1990s some scholars moved to a more enriched theoretical approach to SLA, believing that the input-interaction-output model did not sufficiently explain how second languages are learned in that it was rooted in cognitive and interactionist SLA theory. Sometimes referred to as the "social turn in SLA," these enriched approaches were based in large measure on the **sociocultural linguistic** theories of Vygotsky and Bakhtin. The underlying premise of these theories is that language is predominantly a social tool and as such is developed through interaction between and among communicators. The key notion is that language use does not take place in a vacuum but in real social contexts. When applied to SLA, the implication is that language instructors must allow L2 learners to become active participants in the target-language culture, while SLA theorists should investigate how participation in a variety of sociocultural contexts affects the learner's L2 ability.

**SIDEBAR 15.10**

Based on your own language-learning experience, how important do you think it is to interact with native speakers of an L2? How important has it been for you to have conversations with others in the L2 (e.g., in an L2 class)? Was it helpful for you to speak with other L2 learners, or were you worried that you would hear and learn their mistakes?

It is important to note that cognitive, linguistic, and social factors *all* play significant roles in linguistic use, choice, and development. An L2 learner's interlanguage is a variable linguistic system and is ***created by the interaction of both social factors and cognitive processes*** (see Sidebar 15.10). Consider for a moment that when speaking an L1, we do not speak in the same way with all of our conversation partners. We might even speak differently to our mothers than we would to our fathers, not only in terms of the topics we discuss, but possibly also in our choice of vocabulary, tone of voice, or intonation. Similarly, for L2 learners, social variables such as who the interlocutor is (instructor vs. classmate; native vs. non-native speaker of the L2), the topic of discussion (everyday conversation vs. literary discussion), the social situation surrounding the discourse (classroom setting vs. authentic encounter), and the interactional norms of a given community or type of communication (what is expected in a service encounter in different countries, e.g., the extent to which a store clerk offers help or advice), *all* have an influence on our choice of linguistic forms.

Finally, we would be remiss if we did not mention the role of culture in L2 teaching and learning at least briefly. It's safe to say that most language learners and teachers believe that developing an understanding of the L2 culture is an integral part of language learning. The following excerpt from a student's language-learning history supports this belief:

> The [Chinese] professors incorporated a lot of authentic materials to generate interest in the language and culture we were studying. This included samples of authentic foods to mark special occasions on the Chinese calendar and teaching us folk songs. My French teachers also adopted this approach by teaching us songs, having us read newspaper articles, and introducing us to classic art and cinema.
>
> Meredith, native English speaker

During the past few decades, however, applied linguists have challenged many of the traditional ways of teaching culture in language classrooms, pointing out that "culture" is a much more complex topic than merely introducing different kinds of food, holidays, popular songs, or points of interest in different countries. They have raised questions as

**SIDEBAR 15.11**
Considering other languages and cultures with which you are familiar, can you think of cultural differences between subgroups of speakers of the language? What aspects of the culture would you choose to teach in a second language classroom?

to how we can teach the culture of countries which themselves have such great diversity. If, for example, we are teaching about American culture, how do we deal with the tremendous variety involving different ethnic groups, age groups, parts of the country (e.g., the Deep South vs. the Pacific Northwest), different lifestyles (e.g., urban vs. rural culture), and so on.

In addition to the dangers of stereotyping or misrepresenting cultures, some theorists of foreign language teaching believe that how much L2 culture should be taught depends on the learners' goals (see Sidebar 15.11). McKay, an applied linguist who has been concerned with the teaching of English as an international language, stresses that language teachers abroad need to be aware of the learning needs and native cultures of the students. She suggests that some aspects of an L2 culture may be uninteresting or irrelevant to learners. As an example she discusses a textbook lesson concerned with garage sales, and questions whether this is useful to learners in countries where people do not sell their used possessions in this way. Language teachers also need to be aware that English as an international language, by its very definition, does not belong to a single culture, so it is difficult to decide which culture should be taught (McKay 2000). This does not mean that culture is not an important part of language learning but that the teaching of it requires sensitivity and respect.

**CHAPTER SUMMARY**

Anyone who has ever tried to learn a language has probably experienced the excitement of being able to understand and communicate with speakers of that language. Most of us have also experienced the difficulties and frustrations of not being as fluent or proficient in an L2 as we are in our native language. The field of second language acquisition is relatively new (only about a half-century old) and is still grappling with the questions of how learners create a new language system (their interlanguage) with only limited exposure to an L2, what parts of an L2 are learned, and what is not learned or is more difficult to learn. Since language is a complex human phenomenon, with physical, cognitive, and sociocultural dimensions, understanding language learning will require us to take all of these dimensions into account, although some may be more relevant for the explanation of particular phenomena than others. As we have seen, the main approaches to the study of SLA have been influenced by linguistics, psychology, and most recently, by sociocultural theory, but the process of SLA is complex and there are still no definitive answers as to why most people do not master other languages as well as their first. Nevertheless, linguistic research continues to deepen our understanding of the processes of first and second language acquisition, and the field of applied linguistics continues to act upon this growing knowledge base in order to develop approaches and materials that will facilitate SLA.

### SUGGESTIONS FOR FURTHER READING

**Brown, H. D.** 2009. *Principles of language learning and teaching*, 5th edn. New York: Pearson Longman.

This is a thorough introduction to second language teaching and learning that also includes chapters on first language acquisition, individual differences in second language learning, sociocultural factors and cross-linguistic influences, and theories of SLA.

**Lightbown, P. and N. Spada**. 2006. *How languages are learned*, 3rd edn. Oxford University Press.

This is a very readable introduction to second language acquisition that also discusses learning and teaching in the second language classroom.

**Saville-Troike, M.** 2012. *Introducing second language acquisition*, 2nd edn. Cambridge University Press.

This is a concise and clear introduction to the basic principles of second language acquisition and contains activities at the end of each chapter to check learners' comprehension.

### EXERCISES

1. With one or more classmates, take turns interviewing each other about your language-learning experiences using the questions raised in the sidebars of this chapter, either in class or on a class website. If one of you has not studied another language, you could consider the questions in regard to someone you know, such as a relative or friend.

2. Think of the most effective foreign language teacher you have ever had.

   a. What were the most effective things the teacher did to help you learn?
   b. What were the most important/effective things in the textbook or course materials?
   c. What did *you* have to do in order to learn the language?

3. Phonology/pronunciation
   Identify an L2 speaker of a language that you speak well. Record him or her either talking in a conversation or narrating a brief story. Describe any phonetic differences that mark the speech as non-native, including reference to vowels, consonants, melody, rhythm, and stress.

4. Lexicon/vocabulary
   Search the internet for a list of the 2,000 most common words in one of the languages that you have studied or learned. About how many of these words do you know? How proficient do you feel in this language? Do you feel that your proficiency can essentially be measured by the number of vocabulary words that you know, or are other factors involved?

5. Grammar/morphology
   In the transcript below, an adolescent learner of English is telling a story to a listener, using the book *A Boy, a Dog, a Frog and a Friend*, which has illustrations but no words. What grammatical errors can you identify? If you were an ESL tutor for this learner, what types of things might you focus on for a language lesson?

   One day a little boy went to the lake and he was fishing. Suddenly he felt something fall into the lake and he was pulled into the lake and he falled into water. And his dog and his friend frog also jumped into the lake. And then he found . . . other side of the lake he met a big turtle. And they followed the turtle. His friend, the dog? I don't know if that's the thing. He was talking to the turtle and they . . . the turtle was so . . . the turtle and the dog fought each other and turtle bite dog's foot. The turtle couldn't open mouth, open his mouth and boy tried to help dog. But, turtle never open his mouth so they decided to take the turtle with his dog. And the boy and dog and frog, and they went back the other side of the lake. And the turtle was disappears. The turtle was in the water but again the turtle bite bites the dog's tail and the dog falled fall into the water again.

6. Pragmatics

A special area of pragmatics research, called L2 developmental pragmatics, considers how learners develop the ability to respond in an L2 to social situations such as ones involving making requests, complaints, and apologies. One study (Beebe and Waring 2005) asked English adult learners how they would respond to insults in several situations. The researcher asked their subjects to write down what they "thought they would say" using actual words, not descriptions, in response to rudeness. In one situation, "the bookstore situation," the customer is told by a rude clerk, *If you want to browse, go to the library*. The following are responses that two subjects gave. Which do you think was stated by the lower proficiency learner and which by the higher proficiency learner? Why? How would you characterize these very different responses? Could factors other than proficiency level explain the difference?

Response A:     *Of course I have the right to have a look before I buy it. But now I changed my mind. I am not going to buy anything from your store.*
Response B:     *I see. I am going to the library.*

7. Psychological/cognitive issues in SLA

Think of the L2 you have learned most recently. Do you mentally translate word for word from your L1 into your L2 before speaking or writing? Do you find it easier to learn "chunks" of language or to learn grammar rules so that you can construct your own sentences? Look at your textbook to see how much of the vocabulary is taught in "chunks" or "collocations" and how much is taught in lists. How are vocabulary lists organized, by part of speech, by topic, or otherwise? Is this organization helpful for your learning style, or would a different strategy be better?

8. Here are several more excerpts from language learning histories written by college students. Discuss each in terms of concepts or principles you learned about in this chapter, such as the importance of learning contexts (e.g., classroom vs. "real-world" settings), the distinction between learning and acquisition, negotiated learning, or other concepts you think are relevant. How do these experiences compare with any you have had?

**Excerpt 1 (Learner of Spanish, native speaker of English)**

[N]othing helped me as much with my fluency as when my friend and I vacationed in Chile last year. The country has a low English-speaking population and my companion spoke no Spanish, so I was responsible for reading the signs and menus, and speaking with people for directions. Just walking through the airport gave me opportunies to interact with native speakers in ways I never had before – finding baggage claim, renting a car, and finding the hostel. Even though I had not spoken Spanish regularly in almost two years, after only a few days in Chile, I began to notice that I was thinking directly in Spanish and was no longer relying on English as my crutch.

**Excerpt 2 (Learner of Swedish, native speaker of English)**

When I studied abroad in Sweden for four months, I was given an amazing opportunity to learn a language in its native country . . . My hallmates . . . encouraged my Swedish and taught me slang terms and other necessary vocabulary, but the language that comes most naturally and comfortably to me now is what I used in daily life when I was alone or trying out my Swedish on unsuspecting clerks.

**Excerpt 3 (Learner of English, native speaker of Arabic)**

A few months after I graduated from high school I had the opportunity of a lifetime . . . I was issued a visa to come to the USA . . . my best friends at the time were English dictionary and grammar books; I have to say they didn't help me get that far away. I needed the type of language that would help me survive and get things done in the real world. A few weeks later I got a job as a cook in a fancy restaurant. I had to improve my listening comprehension to properly take orders from waiters, and to improve my reading speed to go quickly through the cook book. Basically, I had no time to write everything I hear, and definitely no time to analyze the perceived and produced English. I had to take the language as it is, with no further analysis.

PART II

# LANGUAGE PROFILES

**LANGUAGE PROFILE 1**

# Kabardian

## 1.1  Introduction

In this language profile, we will apply what we have learned in Chapters 2 and 3 on phonetics and phonology in order to examine the phonology of Kabardian, an endangered Northwest Caucasian language spoken predominantly in the Kabardino-Balkar republic in the Caucasus mountain region of southern Russia and in Turkey (see Figure LP1.1). We will focus here on a variety of Kabardian spoken in Turkey; the second author of this profile grew up speaking the language there.

According to *Ethnologue* (17th edn, online version), there are approximately 520,000 ethnic Kabardians; it is unknown how many are speakers. About one-third reside in Turkey following a mass exodus from Russia that occurred after a long period of war in the nineteenth century. Most of the remaining speakers still live in Russia, though smaller communities are found in other countries, such as Syria, Lebanon, Georgia, Germany, and the United States. While there is still a large Kabardian-speaking community in Russia, the survival of Kabardian outside of Russia is very uncertain. In Turkey, which is home to over 200,000 ethnic Kabardians, there is no formal instruction in Kabardian available to students and the number of people speaking Kabardian at home has steadily declined due to several factors. These include intermarriage with non-Kabardians and movement of speakers into large cities where Kabardian is not perceived as a socioeconomically viable language. Turkish laws that actively discouraged the use of minority languages (e.g., prohibitions against the publication of materials in languages other than Turkish, a ban on non-Turkish surnames, and laws against the use of languages other than Turkish in schools) have only recently been liberalized. Knowledge of Kabardian is unusual in urban areas, and the prolonged period of decreased social value placed on Kabardian has led many Kabardian-speaking couples to speak only Turkish to their children. Most Kabardians in Turkey speak Turkish as a first language.

Kabardian belongs to the Circassian branch of the Northwest branch of the Caucasian language family. The Circassian branch also includes three other languages:

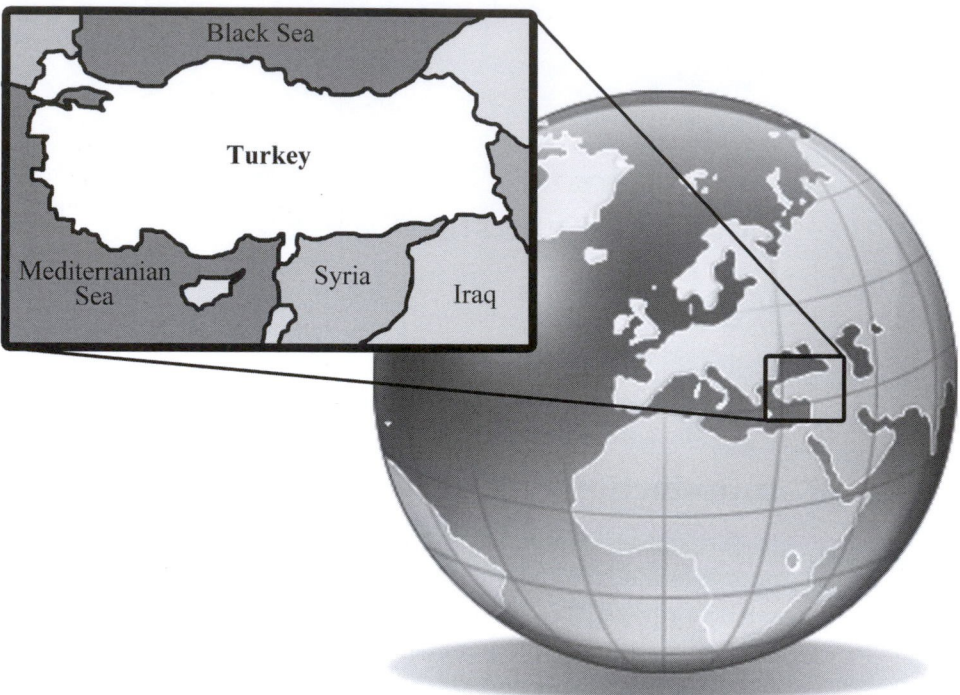

**Figure LP1.1** Map of the Black Sea region

Ubykh, a highly endangered language of Turkey, and the two closely related varieties of Abkhaz and Abaza. The Circassian languages are commonly divided into two branches: East Circassian, including Kabardian and the closely related Besleney, and West Circassian, including Adyghe and its associated dialects. A family tree depicting the relationships between Northwest Caucasian languages is given in Figure LP1.2.

In this language profile we explore the phonological system of the variety of Kabardian spoken in Turkey. By employing the methodology introduced in Chapter 3, we will discover which sounds are separate phonemes and which are allophones of the same phoneme. We will begin the discussion with the consonants, and then move on to the vowels. In addition, we will briefly examine syllable structure and stress in Kabardian.

## 1.2 Consonants

### 1.2.1 Stops

Kabardian has aspirated and unaspirated voiceless stops, just as English and Hupa do (as presented in Chapter 3 on phonology). Recall from our discussion of English that aspirated and unaspirated stops are in complementary distribution, with the aspirated

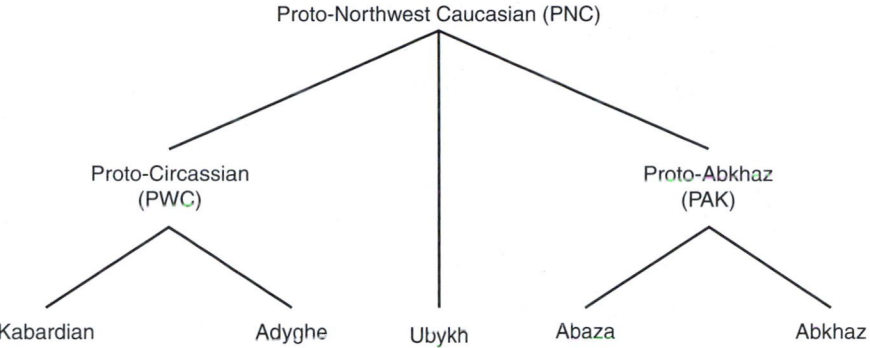

**Figure LP1.2** The Northwest Caucasian family of languages

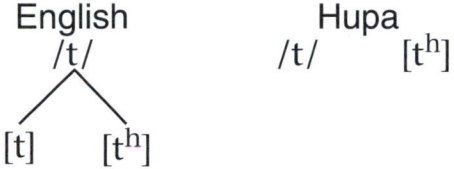

**Figure LP1.3** Alveolar stops in English and Hupa

allophone occurring word-initially in words like *pin* and *tab* and the unaspirated allophone occurring after [s] in words like *spin* and *stab*. In Hupa, on the other hand, we discovered **minimal pairs** differentiated solely on the basis of whether a stop was aspirated or not and thus concluded that aspiration is a phonemic, or contrastive, property of stops in Hupa. The relationship among alveolar stops in these languages was represented as in Figure LP1.3.

Let's now ask whether aspirated and unaspirated stops are separate phonemes in Kabardian, as in Hupa, or whether they are merely allophones, as in English. To tackle this question, consider the Kabardian words in (1).

(1)

| | |
|---|---|
| [pɐ] | 'many' |
| [pʰɐ] | 'nose' |
| [pamɐ] | 'stench' |
| [tamɐ] | 'wing' |
| [tɐ] | 'nut, seed' |
| [tən] | 'sew' |
| [tʰən] | 'give a present' |
| [tʰanɐ] | 'young bull' |
| [tanɐ] | 'silk' |

As these words show, Kabardian has minimal and near-minimal pairs that are differentiated only on the basis of aspiration. For example, the pair [pɐ] 'many' and [pʰɐ] 'nose' differ solely in whether the initial stop is aspirated or not. Likewise, the pair [tanɐ] 'silk'

**SIDEBAR LP1.1**

Note that the vowel [ɐ] is virtually identical to the vowel found in English words like *but* and *sub*, which is often transcribed as the IPA symbol [ʌ] in descriptions of English.

and [tʰanɐ] 'young bull' are distinguished by the aspiration, or lack thereof, on the initial consonant. (See Sidebar LP1.1 for a note on the vowel [ɐ].)

As it turns out, there are two other series of stops in Kabardian. One of these is the **ejective** series and the other is the voiced series. Ejective stops, discussed in regards to Navajo and Hupa in Chapters 1 and 3, are created by closing the glottis and compressing the air behind the stop's closure position. When the stop is released, it makes a characteristic popping sound. Voiced stops, which are familiar from English, contrast with voiceless stops in pairs such as *buy* and *pie* or *rankle* and *wrangle*. Ejective stops are one type of **glottalization**, the production of a glottal constriction in conjunction with one or more non-glottal segments.

***Whenever there are four series of stops, we need to determine if they are all phonemic, or if the members of one series are allophones of another series.*** Let's investigate whether ejective stops and voiced stops in Kabardian are separate phonemes, allophones of each other, or allophones of the voiceless unaspirated and voiceless aspirated stops. The data in (2) will help determine the phonemic status of ejective and voiced stops in Kabardian.

(2)  [p'ɐ]       'bed'
  [pɐ]        'many'
  [pʰaʃɐ]     'leader'
  [pʰɐ]       'nose'
  [p'aʃ'ɐ]    'thin'
  [paʃ]       'stick'
  [sabɐ]      'dust'
  [napɐ]      'face'
  [jap'ɐ]     'their bed'
  [tʰanɐ]     'young bull'
  [tanɐ]      'silk'
  [tʰənʃ]     'easy, comfortable'
  [t'ə]       'ram'
  [tɐ]        'nut, seed'
  [tədɐ]      'very'
  [ʃatɐ]      'cream'
  [nadɐ]      'hollow, lacking a seed'
  [jat']      'their ram'

There are several minimal and near-minimal triplets in (2), revealing a three-way contrast in stops at both the bilabial and the alveolar places of articulation. In word-initial position, the minimal triplet [p'ɐ] 'bed,' [pɐ] 'many,' and [pʰɐ] 'nose' shows that ejectives, voiceless unaspirated, and voiceless aspirated stops are contrastive at the bilabial place of articulation. Similarly, the near-minimal triplet [tʰənʃ] 'easy, comfortable,' [t'ə] 'ram,' and [tədɐ] 'very' shows the same three-way contrast for alveolars.

(3) Kabardian three-way contrasts in word-initial position

| [pʼ] | [pʼɐ] | 'bed' | [tʼ] | [tʼə] | 'ram' |
| [p] | [pɐ] | 'many' | [t] | [tədɐ] | 'very' |
| [pʰ] | [pʰɐ] | 'nose' | [tʰ] | [tʰənʃ] | 'easy, comfortable' |

In word-medial position, there is also a three-way contrast at both places of articulation. However, the nature of the contrast differs somewhat from the contrast in word-initial position. In medial position, the contrast is between ejectives, aspirated stops, and voiced stops, as in the triplet [sabɐ] 'dust,' [napʰɐ] 'face,' and [japʼɐ] 'their bed.'

(4) Kabardian three-way contrast in word-medial position

| [pʼ] | [japʼɐ] | 'their bed' |
| [b] | [sabɐ] | 'dust' |
| [pʰ] | [napʰɐ] | 'face' |

Notice that, ***even though both voiced stops and voiceless unaspirated stops occur in Kabardian, there is no contrast between voiced and voiceless unaspirated stops in either initial or medial position***. Voiceless unaspirated stops occur word-initially and voiced ones are found word-medially.

In fact, there is an alternation in the realization of one of the stops, depending on its position in the word. The first sound in the word [tɐ] 'nut, seed' is a voiceless unaspirated stop, whereas the same sound surfaces as a voiced stop when a prefix is added to form the word [na-dɐ] 'hollow, lacking a seed.' On the basis of this active alternation and the overall distribution of the two types of stops, we can conclude that voiceless unaspirated stops and voiced stops are in **complementary distribution** and are therefore **allophones** of the same phoneme. This phoneme contrasts with ejectives and voiceless aspirated stops, which each occur both word-initially and word-medially. The relationship between phonemes and allophones for the four types of bilabial stops in Kabardian can be represented as in Figure LP1.4 (analogous patterns are found for the alveolars).

Both voiceless aspirated stops and ejectives have a single allophone each, whereas the voiceless unaspirated stop has two allophones: a voiceless unaspirated one in initial position and a voiced one in medial position.

So far we have focused on only two places of articulation, bilabial and alveolar. Kabardian also has stops at other places of articulation. Two of these, velar stops and the glottal stop, are familiar from our discussion of English. In addition, Kabardian has **uvular** stops, which are produced by raising the back of the tongue up to touch the uvula (see Chapter 2 for more on uvular sounds).

Kabardian allows for further modifications to its stops in the form of **secondary articulations**, which involve an additional articulatory gesture overlapping with the primary stop constriction. The velar, uvular, and glottal stops have secondary articulations with lip rounding, as described in Textbox LP1.1.

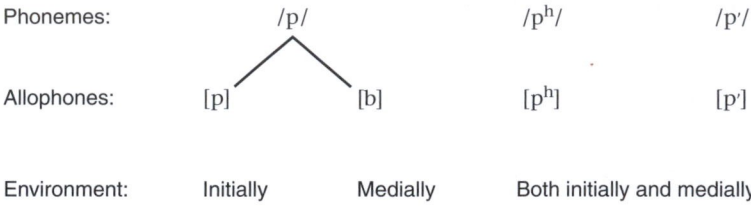

Phonemes:                /p/                    /pʰ/              /p'/

Allophones:      [p]              [b]           [pʰ]             [p']

Environment:     Initially     Medially     Both initially and medially

**Figure LP1.4** Bilabial stops in Kabardian

---

**TEXTBOX LP1.1**

The closest English equivalent to stops with secondary lip rounding in Kabardian are clusters like [kw] in words like *quick* and *quiet*. These English clusters differ from the Kabardian rounded stops, however, in their degree of articulatory overlap between the stop and the rounding gestures. In English, the stop and the rounding are produced more or less in sequence, whereas in Kabardian, they are almost completely overlapped.

---

The other type of secondary articulation in Kabardian is palatalization, which can accompany velar stops. Palatalization involves raising the sides of the tongue simultaneously with the stop closure. Auditorily, palatalization sounds like a stop plus a palatal glide, as in the casual pronunciation of the name *Keanu*, where the combination of the initial [k] and the first vowel sound almost like the sequence [kj].

In addition to stops, Kabardian also has a series of affricates, occurring at the alveolar place of articulation; these affricates sound similar to clusters of an alveolar stop plus an alveolar fricative in English words such as *cats* and *kids*. The voiceless affricate also occurs as aspirated [tsʰ] and as an ejective [ts'].

**SIDEBAR LP1.2**

TRANSCRIPTION OF SECONDARY ARTICULATIONS

Secondary articulations, such as labialization, glottalization, and palatalization, are seen as additional articulations overlapped with the primary consonant. In order to indicate their secondary status, they are written as superscripts:

[ʷ]    labialization
[']    glottalization
[ʲ]    palatalization

The words in (5) illustrate the stop and affricate phonemes of Kabardian. It may be noted that none of the places of articulation behind the alveolar place of articulation makes a three-way contrast between voiceless unaspirated, voiceless aspirated, and ejective stops. In addition, Sidebar LP1.2 explains some of the transcription conventions used for secondary articulations.

(5)   /p/        [padzɐ]      'fly'
       /pʰ/       [pʰasɐ]      'early'
       /p/        [p'ɐ]        'bed'
       /t/        [tamɐ]       'wing'

| | | |
|---|---|---|
| /tʰ/ | [tʰanɐ] | 'young bull' |
| /t'/ | [t'at'ɐ] | 'watery' |
| /ts/ | [tsanɐ] | 'naked' |
| /tsʰ/ | [tsʰə] | 'animal hair' |
| /ts'/ | [ts'ɐ] | 'name' |
| /gʲ/ | [gʲanɐ] | 'shirt' |
| /kʲ'/ | [kʲ'apsɐ] | 'rope' |
| /kʷʰ/ | [kʷʰɐbʒɐ] | 'gates' |
| /kʷ'/ | [kʷ'asɐ] | 'fugitive' |
| /qʰ/ | [qʰɐ] | 'cemetery' |
| /qʷʰ/ | [qʷʰafɐ] | 'boat' |
| /q'/ | [q'alɐ] | 'city' |
| /qʷ'/ | [qʷ'aʒɐ] | 'village' |
| /ʔ/ | [səjʔɐ] | 'my hand' |
| /ʔʷ/ | [ʔʷɐxʷ] | 'work' |

## 1.2.2    Fricatives

Kabardian also has a large number of fricative phonemes: eighteen in total. While many of these are found in English, including [f, v, s, z, ʃ, ʒ, h], others are not. Kabardian has a voiceless palatal fricative [ç], voiced and voiceless velar and uvular fricatives (some of which are accompanied by lip rounding), as well as a voiceless pharyngeal fricative [ħ] and a lateral fricative [ɬ].

First, let's look at the places of articulation found in the Kabardian fricative inventory. We are already familiar with velars and uvulars from our discussion of stops, but we have not yet encountered palatal fricatives, pharyngeal consonants, or lateral fricatives. The voiceless palatal fricative [ç] has an equivalent English sound in the initial consonant in the words *human* and *hue*. Pharyngeal fricatives are produced by retracting the root of the tongue toward the back of the throat to create a constriction, which gives the auditory impression of a noisy [h] sound. We are already familiar with lateral approximants, such as [l], from our discussion of English. Lateral fricatives are produced by raising the middle of the tongue slightly while maintaining the closure with the tip of the tongue. The result will be a noisy fricative, which can be either voiced or not. The voiceless lateral fricative [ɬ] of Kabardian sounds quite similar to the allophone of [l] found after the aspirated stop in English words like *clay* and *plea*, where the aspiration noise overlaps with the [l].

Another interesting type of fricative in Kabardian is the ejective fricative. Kabardian has three: [f', ʃ', ɬ']. These are quite rare in the languages of the world. In a cross-linguistic survey of phoneme inventories, Maddieson (1984) reports that ejective fricatives occur in only 10 out of 317 languages. Ejective fricatives are produced much like their stop counterparts, by compressing air in a chamber between the glottis and the oral constriction. In the case of fricatives, the oral constriction is not complete but is merely tight enough to produce noise. This requires a delicate balancing act, since the fricative opening allows the escape of some of the air that is necessary to create the pressure increase for the ejective's characteristic release burst.

Examples of words illustrating the fricatives of Kabardian appear in (6).

(6)  /v/      [vaqʼɐ]        'shoe'
     /f/      [fadɐ]         'drink'
     /fʼ/     [fʼatɐ]        'hoe'
     /z/      [zawɐ]         'fight'
     /s/      [sabɐ]         'dust'
     /ɬ/      [ɬaqʷʼɐ]        'foot'
     /ɬʼ/     [ɬʼɐ]          'dead'
     /ʃ/      [ʃatʰɐ]        'cream'
     /ʒ/      [ʒan]          'bright'
     /ʃʼ/     [ʃʼalɐ]        'young'
     /ʒ/      [ʒawɐ]         'umbrella'
     /ç/      [çamɐ]         'foreign'
     /xʷ/     [xʷabɐ]        'warm'
     /ɣ/      [ɣən]          'powder'
     /ɣʷ/     [taɣʷɐ]        'good'
     /ʁ/      [ʁatçɐ]        'spring'
     /ʁʷ/     [ʁʷazɐ]        'target'
     /χ/      [χarzənɐ]      'good'
     /χʷ/     [χʷapsɐ]       'envy'
     /ħ/      [ħadɐ]         'corpse'
     /h/      [pʼɐha]        'beds'

### 1.2.3  Sonorants

The remaining Kabardian consonant phonemes are also found in English. Kabardian has two nasals [m, n], a palatal approximant [j], a labial-velar approximant [w], and a lateral approximant [l]. It also has a tap [ɾ], which does not occur word-initially and is often realized with some noise, particularly when devoiced in final position. The tap is grouped here with the sonorants because in Kabardian it shares phonological behavior with the other sonorants, suggesting that it is part of the sonorant natural class in this language. Words exemplifying [m, n, j, l, ɾ] appear in (7).

(7)  /m/      [mazɐ]         'moon'
     /n/      [napʰɐ]        'face'
     /j/      [jatʼɐ]        'mud'
     /w/      [wasɐ]         'price'
     /l/      [lalɐ]         'very soft'
     /ɾ/      [taɾij]        'satin'

**TABLE LP1.1** The consonants of Turkish Kabardian

| | Labial | Denti-alveolar | Palato-alveolar | Palatal | Palatalized velar | Velar | Uvular | Pharyngeal | Laryngeal |
|---|---|---|---|---|---|---|---|---|---|
| Stops | p pʰ p' | t tʰ t' | | | kʲ kʲ' | kʷʰ kʷ' | qʰ q' qʷʰ qʷ' | | ʔ ʔʷ |
| Affricates | | ts tsʰ ts' | | | | | | | |
| Fricatives | f f' v | s z | ʃ ʃ' ʒ | ç | | xʷ ɣ ɣʷ | χ ʁ χʷ ʁʷ | ħ | h |
| Nasals | m | n | | | | | | | |
| Laterals | | ɬ ɬ' l | | | | | | | |
| Tap | | ɾ | | | | | | | |
| Glides | (w) | | | j | | w | | | |

## 1.2.4  Summary of Kabardian consonants

Table LP1.1 summarizes the consonant phonemes found in the variety of Kabardian spoken in Turkey. There are a total of forty-five consonants. This far exceeds the average number of consonants found in the world's languages, which is twenty-one according to Maddieson's survey of 317 languages. The Kabardian inventory also dwarfs the twenty-five consonants found in American English.

## 1.3  **Vowels**

On the surface, Kabardian seems to have many different vowels, just like English. The words in (8) illustrate some of the vowel qualities found in Kabardian.

(8)  
[panɐ]    'thorn'  
[pɐn]    'coffin'  
[pən]    'offspring, kids'  
[jaʒɐ]    'their mouth'  
[jaʒə]    'their wind'  
[lɐʒa]    'work (past interrogative)'  
[pamɐ]    'stench'  
[pʰɐbʒ]    'equal'  
[məbə]    'this'  
[pej]    'rich'  
[pij]    'enemy'  
[pow]    'stable'  
[pzuw]    'fish'  
[psow]    'alive'  
[pʰejʒ]    'correct'

| | |
|---|---|
| [fʼej] | 'filth' |
| [pʰaj] | 'share' |
| [nanuw] | 'kid' |
| [fow] | 'honey' |
| [ʃuχʷ] | 'male horse' |
| [ʔʷoxʷ] | 'work' |
| [maxʷɐ] | 'day' |
| [taɣʷɐ] | 'good' |
| [toʁʷ] | 'thief' |
| [ʃʼuʔʷ] | 'button' |

In the first six words, there are two near-minimal triplets, demonstrating the phonemic status of the three vowels [a, ɐ, ə]. In the remaining forms, four additional vowel qualities [i, e, o, u] emerge. These vowels, however, are limited in the contexts in which they occur. The two back rounded vowels [o, u] occur before rounded consonants, either the labial-velar glide [w] or fricatives associated with a secondary rounding articulation. The two front vowels [i, e], on the other hand, only occur before the palatal glide [j] (see Sidebar LP1.3). This distribution suggests that [o, u, i, e] are allophones of other phonemes. The question then becomes which pairs of vowels belong together as allophones of the same phoneme.

To answer this question, we first observe that the low vowel [a] occurs in the widest range of environments: before [j], before rounded consonants, as well as in the same environments in which [ɐ] and [ə] also occur. We can thus conclude that [a] has no other allophones.

This leaves the six vowels [i, e, u, o, ɐ, ə], which can be grouped into three groups of two, according to the contexts in which they occur. The first two occur only before [j], the next two occur only before rounded consonants, and the last two occur in contexts other than those in which the first four vowels occur, that is, they occur elsewhere. The complication in determining allophonic relationships here lies in the fact that there are two vowels occurring in each of the three contexts, as the diagram in (9) shows.

(9) 

| Before /j/ | Before rounded consonants | Elsewhere |
|---|---|---|
| i | u | ə |
| e | o | ɐ |

This means that [ə] is in complementary distribution with not only both [u] and [i] but also with [o] and [e] (as [ə] never occurs before /j/ or rounded consonants). Likewise, [ɐ] is in complementary distribution with not only [o] and [e] but also [u] and [i]. The question is which vowels stem from the same phoneme and which ones are linked to a different phoneme. Are [u] and [i], or [e] and [o], allophones of [ə]? Are [u] and [i], or [e] and [o], allophones of [ɐ]?

In fact, there are other possible groupings of vowels that maintain the complementary distributions. For example, [u] and [e] could be allophones of [ə], and [o] and [i] could be allophones of [ɐ]. Alternatively, [i] and [o] could be allophones of [ə], and [u] and [e] could be allophones of [ɐ]. To determine the correct pairings, we need to apply the notion of **phonetic similarity** that must be true of allophones. In order to be allophones, not only must two or more sounds be in complementary distribution, they also must be phonetically similar to each other.

To assess phonetic similarity in the case of Kabardian vowels, it is useful to draw a chart depicting the location of vowels in the Kabardian vowel space. This chart is given in (10).

(10)

| | Front | Central | Back |
|---|---|---|---|
| High | i | | u |
| Mid | e | ə | o |
| Mid-low | | ɐ | |
| Low | | a | |

We have determined that [i] and [u] are allophones of one of the central vowels, and that [e] and [o] are allophones of another. Initially, one might be tempted to group [ə] with [e] and [o] since they are all mid vowels. However, this would force us to assume that the mid-low vowel /ɐ/ has the phonetically much higher vowel allophones of [i] and [u], which would violate the requirement that allophones be phonetically similar to each other. Instead, we should group the higher of the vowel pairs, [i] and [u], with the highest of the mid vowels, [ə], as this is phonetically more similar to the high vowels than is [ɐ]. Similarly, the front and the back rounded vowels in Kabardian that are most similar phonetically to [ɐ] are [e] and [o], as these are the lower of the two pairs, and [ɐ] is lower than [ə].

We can thus conclude that [ɐ], [e], and [o] are allophones of the same phoneme, whose base form is /ɐ/. This sound is the base phoneme since it occurs in a wider range of contexts than the other two allophones. This leaves /i/ and /u/ as allophones of the basic phoneme [ə], which may be treated as basic due to its wider distribution compared to the other two variants. The resulting relationship between phonemes and allophones for Kabardian vowels is shown in Figure LP1.5.

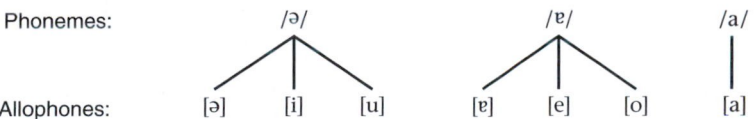

Phonemes: /ə/ /ɐ/ /a/

Allophones: [ə] [i] [u] [ɐ] [e] [o] [a]

**Figure LP1.5** Kabardian vowel phonemes and their allophones

Much more could be said about Kabardian vowels. For example, there are other vowel allophones occurring in various consonantal contexts beyond those we have considered here. Furthermore, the number of vowel phonemes in Kabardian has been a subject of intense debate among phonologists for over fifty years. Analyses of the vowel system have ranged from positing three underlying vowel phonemes, as in the account adopted here based on traditional Russian sources, to assuming only two vowel phonemes, or even a single vowel.

## 1.4   Syllable structure

Kabardian allows a variety of syllable structures ranging from simple to complex. (For a review of terminology related to syllable structure, see Sidebar LP1.4.) The smallest possible syllable consists of a single vowel as in the first syllable of the word *a.nɐ* 'mother.' Closed syllables are quite common, e.g., *pɐn* 'coffin' and *ʃʼɘb* 'back.' Consonant clusters are also widely attested, both in syllable onset and syllable coda position, e.g., *tχʷɐ* 'butter,' *psə* 'water,' *pʃtʰə* 'boil' (milk), *fəzijpɬʼ* 'five women,' and *məɬkʷ* 'property.'

### 1.4.1   Stress

Let's now turn to the positioning of stress in Kabardian words. Recall from Chapter 2 on phonetics that there are pairs of words in English distinguished only on the basis of where stress falls. For example, the noun *import* has stress on the first syllable, whereas the verb *import* has stress on the second syllable. The words in (11) illustrate the location of stress in several Kabardian words. Syllable boundaries are indicated using the IPA symbol for syllable breaks [.] to facilitate examination of the patterns.

(11)   [ˈpʰa.sɐ]        'early'
       [ˈsa.bɐ]        'dust'
       [ˈmə.ʃɐ]        'bear'
       [ʔɐ.ˈda.qʼɐ]        'rooster'
       [χɛɾ.ˈzə.nɐ]        'good'
       [mə.ʔɐ.ˈɾə.sɐ]        'apple'

There are no minimal stress pairs in the Kabardian data in (11). However, when examining stress in a language, it is useful to look not only for minimal stress pairs but also for consistent patterns in the location of stress. For example, in many languages, such as Finnish or Czech, stress falls on the initial syllable of words. In other languages, such as Turkish, stress falls on the final syllable. In the Kabardian data in (11), stress does not consistently fall on either the initial syllable or the final syllable. However, we can still make a generalization about the words: stress falls on the second-to-last syllable. The second-to-last syllable is also known as the **penultimate syllable** (see Textbox LP1.2). Penultimate stress is quite common in languages of the world. For example, it is found in Polish, Mohawk, and Albanian.

Now let's look at several more Kabardian words in (12) to see if they conform to the penultimate stress pattern.

(12)  [sɐ.ˈbən]       'soap'
      [səj.ˈʃʼəb]     'my back'
      [sa.ˈbij]       'baby'
      [na.ˈnuw]       'kid'

The words in (12) all have final (or **ultimate**) stress, unlike those in (11), which had penultimate stress. At this point, there are two different ways we could proceed: we could give up hope of finding any consistent generalization about the location of stress and merely say that each word must be memorized as having either final or penultimate stress; or alternatively, we could compare the two groups of words to see if there is any difference in the shape of the words that might account for their different stress patterns. As it turns out, there is such a difference. All of the words in (12), which have final stress, end in a consonant, whereas those in (11), which have penultimate stress, end in a vowel. We can thus see that stress-assignment depends upon syllable structure.

This is an instance of **weight-sensitive stress**, since the weight or complexity of syllables influences the stress pattern. Textbox LP1.3 gives a brief explanation of syllable weight. In Kabardian, final syllables attract stress if they are complex, or **heavy**; a syllable-final coda consonant makes a syllable heavy. If the final syllable is **light** and contains a vowel without a coda consonant, stress shifts leftward onto the penultimate syllable. Weight-sensitive stress systems are common in the languages of the world. Weight-sensitive stress systems, as well as weight-insensitive stress systems, in which stress predictably falls on a certain syllable regardless of syllable weight, together constitute the class of stress patterns with phonologically predictable – as opposed to phonemic – stress.

## SUMMARY

In this chapter we have surveyed certain basic features of the Kabardian phonological system, including the consonant and vowel phonemes, allophones of these phonemes, syllable structure, and stress. Kabardian phonology is of typological interest for a variety of reasons, including its small vowel and large consonant inventories, which include a twelve-way contrast among voiceless fricatives, and contrasts of ejective and non-ejective fricatives at three places of articulation. There are many additional fascinating aspects of Kabardian phonology – not to mention Kabardian morphology and syntax – that we have left untouched. Many published sources on Kabardian are written in Russian; for more information on Kabardian, the interested reader is referred to the Suggestions for further reading section, which contains references written in English.

## SUGGESTIONS FOR FURTHER READING

**Colarusso, John**. 1992. *The Kabardian language*. University of Calgary Press.

This book provides an overview of key features of the Kabardian language, including the phonology, morphology, and syntax.

**Colarusso, John**. 2006. *Kabardian (East Circassian)*. Munich: LINCOM Europa.

This book is a slightly updated version of Colarusso's (1992) grammar.

**Gordon, Matthew and Ayla Applebaum**. 2006. "Phonetic structures of Turkish Kabardian." *Journal of the International Phonetic Association* **36**.2: 159–186.

This paper provides a detailed phonetic analysis of many features of Kabardian sounds including the vowels, the ejective fricatives, and the stops.

**Gordon, Matthew and Ayla Applebaum**. 2010. "Acoustic correlates of stress in Turkish Kabardian." *Journal of the International Phonetic Association* **40**.1: 35–58.

This paper is a study of the phonetics of the Kabardian stress system.

## EXERCISES

**1.** Natural classes

Examine the following sets of sounds. Indicate whether they form natural classes and, if so, how each class is defined in terms of features.

a. qʰ, q', qʷʰ, qʷ', χ, χʷ, ʁ, ʁʷ
b. ɬ', ɬ, l
c. p, pʰ, b
d. ʃ, ʒ
e. p', t', k', kʷ', q', qʷ'
f. f, s, ʃ, ç, xʷ, χ, χʷ, ħ, h
g. b, v, m, w
h. kʷ, kʷʰ, qʷʰ, qʷ', xʷ, ɣʷ, ʔʷ, χʷ, ʁʷ, w

**2.** Kabardian stress

Based on the description of stress in this language profile, add marks to the following words to indicate where stress falls:

|     |          |               |
|-----|----------|---------------|
| a.  | səjʔʷoxʷ | 'my work'     |
| b.  | japzuw   | 'his fish'    |
| c.  | mɛzeʃ'   | 'new moon'    |
| d.  | tʰane    | 'young bull'  |
| e.  | kʷʰabʒe  | 'gates'       |
| f.  | xʷabe    | 'warm'        |
| g.  | pəsəm    | 'guest'       |
| h.  | pəsəməʃ' | 'good guest'  |
| i.  | səjʃ     | 'my horse'    |

**3.** Allophones

Based on the discussion of allophones in this language profile, convert the following phonemic transcriptions to phonetic ones:

|     |           |                        |
|-----|-----------|------------------------|
| a.  | /paʒe/    | 'fox'                  |
| b.  | /ʃətəʃ'/  | 'good donkey'          |
| c.  | /səsej/   | 'mine'                 |
| d.  | /atew/    | 'father (predicative)' |
| e.  | /ts'əkʷ/  | 'small'                |
| f.  | /pʰejʒ/   | 'truth'                |
| g.  | /ataqe/   | 'rooster'              |
| h.  | /tʰən/    | 'give'                 |
| i.  | /satʰəw/  | 'how'                  |

**4.** Laryngeal alternations

In Kabardian the prefixes meaning 'I' and 'you (plural)' have different allomorphs exemplified by the following forms. Write rules accounting for the alternations.

|     |          |                          |
|-----|----------|--------------------------|
| a.  | zdas     | 'I sewed it'             |
| b.  | vdas     | 'You (pl) sewed it'      |
| c.  | zbʒas    | 'I counted it'           |
| d.  | vbʒas    | 'You (pl) counted it'    |
| e.  | sowʃç    | 'I eat it (habitual)'    |
| f.  | fowʃç    | 'You (pl) eat it (habitual)' |
| g.  | fɬeɣʷas  | 'You (pl) saw it'        |

| | | |
|---|---|---|
| h. | sɬeɣʷas | 'I saw it' |
| i. | stças | 'I wrote it' |
| j. | ftças | 'You (pl) wrote it' |
| k. | s'p'as | 'I educated him' |
| l. | f'p'as | 'You (pl) educated him' |

5. Vowel ~ zero alternations

Kabardian has many words in which there is an alternation between a vowel and zero, as the forms below illustrate. Describe the conditions governing this alternation and write a rule capturing the alternation.

| | | |
|---|---|---|
| a. | ʃə | 'horse' |
| b. | t'ə | 'ram' |
| c. | zəʃ | 'one horse' |
| d. | zət' | 'one ram' |
| e. | fɐ | 'skin' |
| f. | zəfɐ | 'one skin' |
| g. | ʃɐ | 'bullet' |
| h. | zəʃɐ | 'one arrow' |
| i. | ʒə | 'old' |
| j. | ʃəʒ | 'old horse' |
| k. | f'ə | 'good' |
| l. | ʃəf' | 'good horse' |
| m. | ʃəfɐ | 'horse skin' |
| n. | ɬ'ə | 'man' |
| o. | ɬ'əf' | 'good man' |
| p. | sabɐ | 'dust' |
| q. | sɐbɐf' | 'old dust' |
| r. | panɐ | 'thorn' |
| s. | pɐnɐf' | 'good thorn' |

**LANGUAGE PROFILE 2**

# Goemai

## 2.1 Introduction

Goemai (pronounced /gə̀mâi/) is a West Chadic language of Nigeria. As such, it is a member of the large Afroasiatic language family and thus distantly related to Semitic languages, such as Arabic and Hebrew. Within Afroasiatic, Goemai belongs to the Chadic branch, more specifically, to the Southern Angas-Goemai group within the West Chadic sub-branch. Figure LP2.1 summarizes the genealogical position of Goemai within Afroasiatic.

The language is spoken by approximately 150,000 speakers in the lowlands of Central Nigeria, just south of the Jos Plateau and north of the River Benue. The map in Figure LP2.2 gives an indication of the geographical location of the Goemai, showing the three Goemai dialect areas, Duut (including East Ankwe), Dorok, and Kwo.

Over the last century, another Chadic language, Hausa, has emerged as a major language in this area. The use of Hausa is slowly replacing the use of many of the minor languages in the area, including Goemai. Today, most Goemai use Hausa in formal settings (e.g., in contexts involving administration, religion, or education) and when interacting with their many non-Goemai neighbors. Members of the younger generation tend to speak Hausa even to each other; and many children grow up with Hausa as their first, and often only, language.

## 2.2 Basic typological overview

Goemai has a fairly complex phonology. One of the most striking features is a three-way distinction between voiceless aspirated, voiceless non-aspirated, and voiced stops and fricatives. It also has a series of **implosive** stops at the labial and alveolar places of articulation. The language contrasts long and short vowels, and four tones (high, low, falling, rising). Table LP2.1 illustrates some (near-) minimal pairs: (1) exemplifies alveolar stops and implosives, (2) vowel length contrasts, and (3) high and low tones.

**TABLE LP2.1**  (Near-) minimal pairs

| (1) | *tàng* [tʰàŋ] | *t'áng* [táŋ] | *dáng* [dáŋ] | *d'àng* [ɗàŋ] |
|-----|---------------|----------------|--------------|----------------|
|     | 'search'      | 'bat'          | 'tail'       | 'lizard'       |
| (2) | *hàm* [hàm]   | *hààm* [hà:m]  |              |                |
|     | 'carve'       | 'water'        |              |                |
| (3) | *háás* [há:s] | *hààs* [hà:s]  |              |                |
|     | 'flour'       | 'egg'          |              |                |

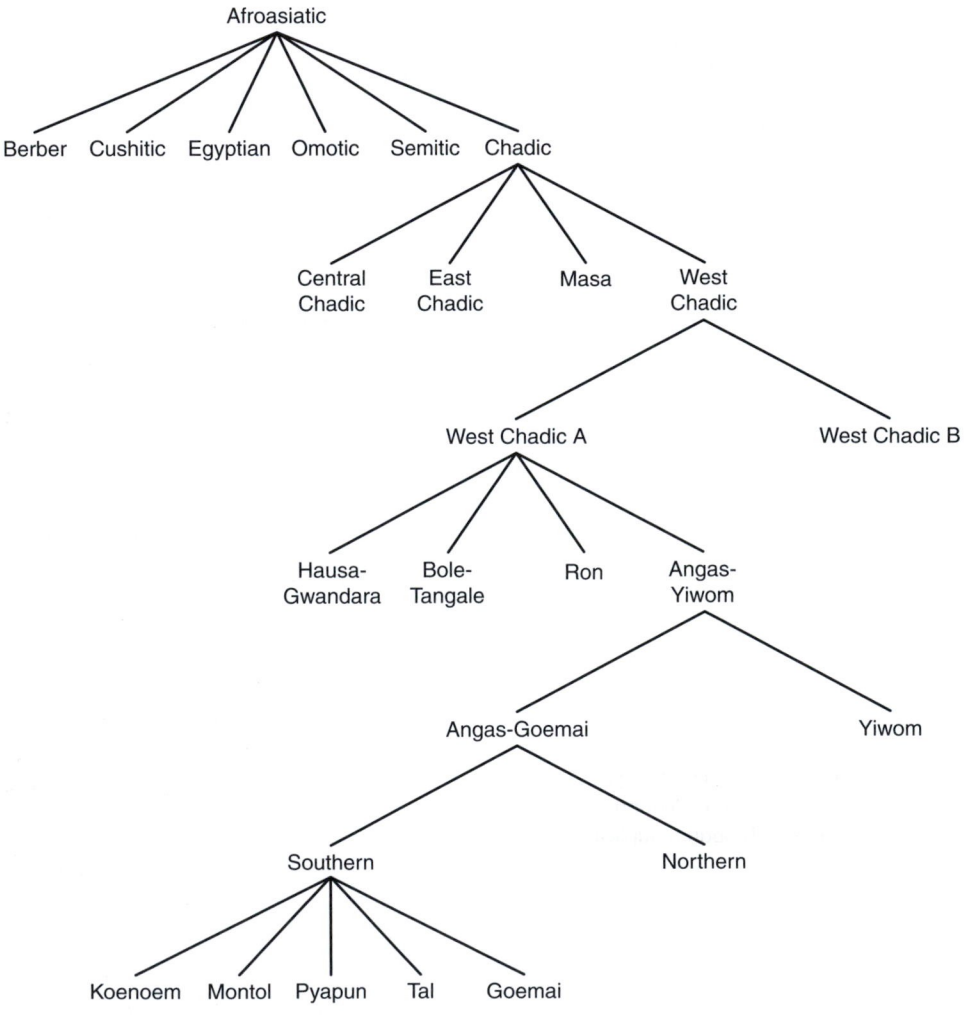

**Figure LP2.1**  Goemai language family tree

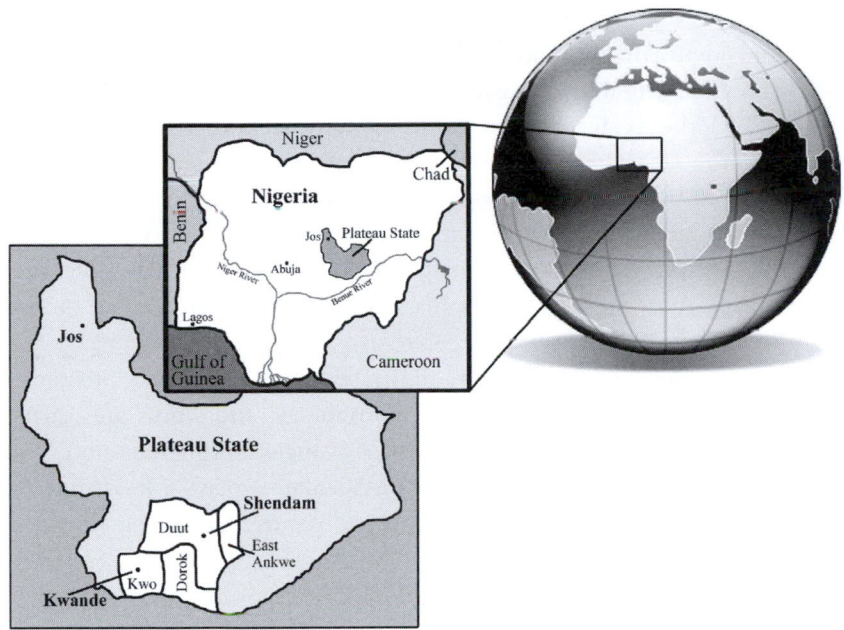

**Figure LP2.2** Map: Nigeria, Plateau State, and the Goemai area (based on Monday 1989; Kurungtiem 1991)

The Goemai people have a way of writing their language called a **practical orthography**, which will be used here. Note that *p*, *t*, *k*, *f*, *s*, and *sh* indicate aspirated obstruents, *p'*, *t'*, *k'*, *f'*, *s'*, and *sh'* indicate non-aspirated obstruents and *b'* and *d'* indicate the two implosives. For the vowels, *oe* indicates [ə], *u̲* indicates [ʉ], and *o̲* indicates [ɔ]. Double letters indicate long vowels, and tones are placed over vowels by means of accents, e.g., *é* indicates a high tone, *è* a low tone, *ê* a falling tone, and *ě* a rising tone.

### SIDEBAR LP2.1

#### IDEOPHONES

Goemai has about eighty **ideophones** that convey a vivid image of a property (such as color or age), a spatial orientation (such as posture or disposition), or a bodily process (such as belching or yawning). Morphologically, the ideophones are often characterized through reduplication, e.g., *sòesák* 'snow white' or *wùwák* 'bright red.' Ideophones have found their way into other word classes, too. For example, many nouns that denote birds reflect the characteristic sound of the bird, e.g., *gòekùk* 'owl, cuckoo,' *kòerè* 'crow,' or *t'íngilíít* 'hornbill.'

Goemai has three open word classes, that is, word classes that easily incorporate new members: nouns, verbs, and adverbs. Notice that Goemai does not have any simple lexical adjectives. While Goemai can use derivational morphology to turn verbs and adverbs into adjectival modifiers, there is no word class of underived adjectives.

Goemai also has closed word classes, such as pronouns, various noun-phrase modifiers, **ideophones**, prepositions, particles, and conjunctions (see Sidebar LP2.1). In most cases, a word occurs in one word class only. Thus, it is uncommon for a word to occur interchangeably as a noun and as a verb, as in English *The table is big* and *He tabled the motion*. Furthermore, there are only a few Goemai derivational morphemes that change the lexical class of words.

As we will see in more detail below, nouns always function as heads of noun phrases and are usually morphologically unmarked. Although Goemai grammar marks number (singular, plural) and classifies nouns based on the posture of referents (see Textbox LP2.1), these categories are – with very few exceptions – not marked on the noun itself.

Verbs in Goemai always function as heads of predicates and are also generally unmarked. There are only two exceptions to this generalization, as will be shown later: about 10 percent of the verbal lexicon distinguishes number; and some subject pronouns can be marked on the verb. Other categories, such as tense or negation, are usually not marked on the verb either, but are expressed through particles.

The brief description above illustrates that Goemai is a predominantly **isolating** language. That is, there is little morphology, and words are usually unmarked and monomorphemic (i.e., they consist of a single morpheme only). While there is some nominal and verbal morphology in Goemai, it plays a lesser role than in other languages. Because of its largely isolating nature, Goemai grammar relies heavily on

---

### TEXTBOX LP2.1

Goemai distinguishes four postural classes (hanging/moving, sitting, standing, and lying) plus one residual class (for all objects that do not fall into one of the postural classes). This classification is based on the typical "posture" of objects. For example, "sitting" objects are all objects that are typically located on their base and that have a usage space. This includes all types of containers (cups, pots, bottles, baskets, etc.), as well as traditional chairs (Figure LP2.3) or woven mats that protect food from flies (Figure LP2.4). This class also includes novel items such as telephones, television sets, radios, and fans.

**Figure LP2.3** A traditional Goemai chair

**Figure LP2.4** A traditional woven mat

syntax. The importance of syntax over morphology can be seen in the structure of its phrases as well as in its grammatical relations, as explained below.

## 2.3   Syntax

Chapter 6 has shown in some detail how languages combine words to form phrases and sentences. This language profile explores some of these syntactic phenomena: the formation of noun phrases and ways of expressing grammatical relations.

### 2.3.1   Noun phrases

Goemai is one of the many languages that show clear evidence for the existence of noun phrases. The Goemai noun phrase (NP) consists of an obligatory head noun and optional modifiers or dependents. These dependents tell us something about the head noun: some help us to identify the referent (e.g., the demonstratives point to a referent in the physical environment, and the articles specify whether or not a referent has been mentioned in the previous discourse), while others offer further descriptive information (e.g., the adjectival modifiers describe a quality of the referent, such as its color or size). All dependents occur in a fixed order, with some of them preceding the head noun (i.e., occurring pre-head) and some following (i.e., occurring post-head). Table LP2.2 summarizes the order of selected pre-head and post-head dependents relative to the head noun and to each other. And Examples (1) to (4) illustrate the depicted order using data from natural discourse.

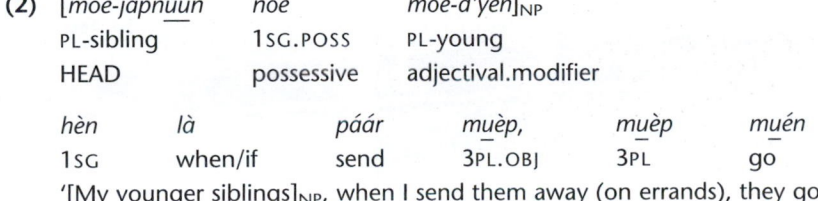

**SIDEBAR LP2.2**

NOTES ON THE GLOSSES

| DEF | definite article |
|-----|------------------|
| EMPH | emphasis |
| F | feminine |
| FOC | focus |
| M | masculine |
| NEG | negation |
| NP | noun phrase |
| OBJ | object |
| PART | particle |
| PL | plural |
| SG | singular |
| SPEC | specific-indefinite article |
| SBJ | subject |
| V | verb |

(1)  *mán*      *yì=kùt*    [*ńdòe=d'uòe*     *gòe-k'ém*]<sub>NP</sub>    *bá*
     do.NEG    2SG=talk    SPEC=voice     SG-different    NEG
                       specific.article=HEAD    adjectival.modifier
     'Don't speak [any other language]<sub>NP</sub>!'

(2)  [*mòe-jàpnúún*    *nóe*     *mòe-d'yén*]<sub>NP</sub>
     PL-sibling       1SG.POSS    PL-young
     HEAD           possessive    adjectival.modifier

     *hèn*    *là*      *páár*    *muèp,*    *muèp*    *muén*
     1SG     when/if    send     3PL.OBJ    3PL     go
     '[My younger siblings]<sub>NP</sub>, when I send them away (on errands), they go.'

**TABLE LP2.2** Order of elements within the Goemai noun phrase

| Pre-head dependent | Head | Post-head dependent | | | |
|---|---|---|---|---|---|
| specific-indefinite article | noun | possessive | adjectival modifier | demonstrative | definite article |

(3)  *mòe=shìn    uh    sh'ít    n-ní    b'ák    góe*
     1PL=do      uh    work    with-it    PROX    in

     [*yíl      mén          ńd'énnòe=hòk*]<sub>NP</sub>              *p'ùùr*
     land     1PL.POSS     PROX.DEM=DEF                    a.lot
     HEAD     possessive   demonstrative=definite.article
     'We do, uh, a lot of work with it here in [the/this our land]<sub>NP</sub>.'

(4)  [*d'à              gòe-b'áng                ńd'énnòe*]<sub>NP</sub>=*hòe*
     calabash         SG-red                   PROX.DEM=exactly
     HEAD             adjectival.modifier      demonstrative
     '[This red calabash]<sub>NP</sub> exactly (...).' (See Textbox LP2.2 on calabashes.)

---

### TEXTBOX LP2.2

Calabashes are plants whose mature fruits are harvested, dried, split lengthwise and then used as utensils – they come in all kinds of shapes and sizes: bottle-shaped (used for transporting drinks and medicine), spoon-shaped (used as cooking spoons), and bowl-shaped (used as vessels for drinking and eating, and as storage containers).

**Figure LP2.5** Calabash bowls

**Figure LP2.6** A Calabash tree

Heads and dependents can occur only in the order illustrated in Examples (1) to (4); any reordering would result in an ungrammatical utterance.

A noun phrase can consist of a head noun only, such as *néng* 'cow' in (5), but can never consist of a dependent element only. However, a dependent element can be turned into a head noun by means of the nominalizing prefixes *gòe–* (SG) or *mòe–* (PL). For example, the dependent demonstrative *ńd'éńnòe* 'this' never occurs without a head noun, as in (4). Its nominalized form, however, does occur as the head of a noun phrase, such as with *gòeńd'éńnòe* 'this one' in (5).

(5)  [*gòe-ńd'éńnòe*]$_{NP}$      *à*          [*néng*]$_{NP}$
     SG-PROX.one           FOC         cow
     '[This one]$_{NP}$ is [a cow]$_{NP}$.'

The head of a noun phrase can be either a noun, as in (5), or a pronoun, as in (6).

(6)  *muép*        *lá*         *kàt*         [*nî*]$_{NP}$
     and.3PL      when/if      find          3SG.OBJ
     'And when they find [him]$_{NP}$ (…).'

With regard to pronominal heads, Goemai displays one very interesting phenomenon. Cross-linguistically, pronouns tend to replace the entire noun phrase. This is also the most common pattern in Goemai. However, it is possible for a pronominal head to replace only the nominal head, and thus co-occur with noun phrase dependents. Example (7) shows a pronoun co-occurring with the definite article.

(7)  *muèp*        *lá*         *k'àòr*       [*ní=hók*]$_{NP}$
     2PL          when/if      instruct      3SG.OBJ=DEF
     'When they instruct [(the) her]$_{NP}$.'

The elements of the noun phrase always form a contiguous group, that is, they cannot be separated by other morphemes such as particles or adverbs. For example, the object noun phrase below is followed by a particle *yì* and an adverb *ńt'ìt* 'well.' It is not possible for either of them to occur anywhere within the noun phrase.

(8)  *mòe=zèm*    *dé*       *kówúròe*   *k'óeléng*   [*d'uòe*   *Gòemâi*]$_{NP}$   *yì*      *ńt'ìt.*
     1PL=like     so.        everyone    hear/        voice.    Goemai          PART     well
                  that                   smell        of
     'We want everyone to understand the Goemai language well.'

So far, we have seen syntactic evidence for the existence of the Goemai noun phrase: the fixed order of head and dependents, and their contiguity. In addition, there is one piece of morphological evidence: the adjectival modifiers (but not the other dependents) change their form in order to agree in number with their head noun. For example, the modifier in (9) takes the singular prefix *gòe–* to agree with the singular head noun *là* 'child,' but takes the plural prefix *mòe–* in (10) to agree with the plural head noun *jáp* 'children.'

(9)  [là          gòe-kyôklók=hók]NP        ńdòe    [núún       múk]NP
     child.SG     SG-small=DEF               and     mother      3SG.POSS

     ńdòe                  [ndá                  múk]NP
     and                   father                3SG.POSS
     '[The small boy]NP, and [his mother]NP, and [his father]NP.'

(10) àkwái         [ńdòe=jáp          mòe-b'àkpê]NP    d'è       d'í
     there.are     SPEC=child.PL      PL-disregard     exist     DIST
     'There were [some disrespectful children]NP.'

### 2.3.2  Grammatical relations

Like English, Goemai is a language where grammatical behavior is shared between the single core argument of an intransitive verb and the more agentive argument of a transitive verb. Thus Goemai, like English, has grammatical subjects that are distinct from objects.

Constituent order is the most obvious piece of evidence for distinguishing Goemai subjects from objects. Goemai constituent order is fixed in that subjects always precede the verb, while objects follow it. Example (11) illustrates the intransitive pattern, with the single core argument preceding the verb. Example (12) illustrates the transitive pattern, with the more agentive argument (i.e., the rabbit as opposed to the stone) being placed before the verb. (This can be contrasted with patterns of argument alignment in Tsez and Bardi; see Textbox LP8.3 in the Bardi Language Profile for discussion.)

(11) fuán         swár
     rabbit        laugh
     'The rabbit laughed.'

(12) fuán         máng     p'áng
     rabbit        take      stone
     'The rabbit took a stone.'

The noun phrase itself is not morphologically marked for its grammatical relation, that is, Goemai does not have any case marking. Pronouns, however, constitute a partial exception to this generalization. Goemai has both free and dependent pronouns. The free pronouns are identical for all core arguments (i.e., for subjects and objects). But the dependent forms can be used only for subjects, not for objects. Table LP2.3 lists the two sets of pronouns.

The dependent pronouns attach to the verb as **clitics** (see Textbox LP3.3 in Language Profile 3 (Manange) for more information on clitics). They can occur with or without any overt noun phrase. Compare (13), where the clitic pronoun is the only reference to the subject, with (14) and (15). In all cases, it is the subject that is marked on the verb, regardless of whether the verb is intransitive (as in 14), or transitive (as in 13 and 15). In contrast, the object argument is never marked on the verb.

**TABLE LP2.3** Personal pronouns

| Category | Free pronoun (all core arguments) | Dependent pronoun (subjects only) |
|---|---|---|
| I (1SG) | *hen* | *n=* |
| You (2SG.M) | *goe* | *goe=* |
| You (2SG.F) | *yoe ~ yi* | *yi=* |
| He, she, it (3SG) | *ni* | *ni= ~ Ø* |
| We (1Pl ) | *men* | *moe=* |
| You (2PL) | *gwen* | *gu=* |
| They (3PL) | *muep* | *muep= ~ uep=* |

(13)  *mòe=màn     ní      b'ák     ńt'ît     bá*
      1PL=know    3SG     PROX     well      NEG
      SBJ=V       OBJ
      'We don't know it well here.'

(14)  *à        nyégòefé      [mòe-gùrùm     muép]      muèp=muáráp      díp*
      FOC      because       PL-person      3PL.POSS   3PL=die          all
                             SBJ                       SBJ=V
      'It is because all their people, they have died.'

(15)  *mèn      mòe=nyàk     yí       bá*
      1PL      1PL=hate     2SG      NEG
      SBJ      SBJ=V        OBJ
      'We, we don't hate you.'

The discussion above has shown that there are three criteria that can be evoked to establish grammatical relations in Goemai: constituent order, pronominal form, and marking of arguments on the verb. While these three criteria clearly distinguish subjects from objects, sometimes core arguments are hard to identify, as it is also possible for all core arguments to be omitted from a clause. This phenomenon is illustrated in (16).

(16)  *[là=ńdòe=gùrùm]ₐ       b'às         [là=ńdòe=shàt         gòe-kyôklók]ₒ*
      little=SPEC=person      cut.off      little=SPEC=porridge   SG-small

      *póe      yì        n-nt'í*
      give     PART      DAT-son.of.rabbit

      *[nt'í]ₐ                láp          yì          s'óe*
      son.of.rabbit          receive      PART        eat
      'Some poor person cut off a little bit of porridge, so that (he) gave (it) to the son of the rabbit. So the son of the rabbit took (it) and ate (it).'

## TEXTBOX LP2.3 GLOSSING CONVENTIONS USED IN THIS LANGUAGE PROFILE

| Convention | Meaning | Convention | Meaning |
|---|---|---|---|
| 1 | first person | FOC | focus |
| 2 | second person | M | masculine |
| 3 | third person | NEG | negation |
| DAT | dative | OBJ | object |
| DEF | definite article | PART | particle |
| DEM | demonstrative | PL | plural |
| DIST | distal | POSS | possessive |
| EMPH | emphatic | PROX | proximal |
| F | feminine | SG | singular |
| | | SPEC | specific-indefinite article |

In (16), the first clause (line 1) introduces two core arguments ('some poor person' and 'a little bit of porridge') by means of lexical noun phrases. In the following clauses, however, they are not referred to by noun phrases or by pronouns. In line 2 both the subject and the object of the verb *póe* 'give (away)' have been omitted, and in line 3 the object of both the verbs *láp* 'receive' and *s'óe* 'eat' is not specified. The practice of omitting noun phrases and pronominal clitics when it is clear who is doing what to whom is common in this language and in many others.

### SUGGESTIONS FOR FURTHER READING

**Hellwig, Birgit**. 2011. *A grammar of Goemai*. Berlin and New York: Mouton de Gruyter.

A description of the Goemai language: a resource for more detailed information on the phenomena discussed in this language profile.

**Corbett, Greville G.** 2000. *Number* (Cambridge Textbooks in Linguistics). Cambridge University Press. Chapter 8.

A discussion of number marking cross-linguistically. The selected chapter describes number-marking on verbs, giving background information to Exercise 2.

**Heine, Bernd and Derek Nurse** (eds.). 2000. *African languages: An introduction*. Cambridge University Press.

**Heine, Bernd and Derek Nurse** (eds.). 2011. *A linguistic geography of Africa*. Cambridge University Press.

These two works are introductory textbooks on Africa, with chapters on different topics to browse; especially recommended: the article by Dimmendaal on morphology in the 2000 volume and – if you've read Chapter 13 of this book on language contact – the article by Creissels et al. on Africa as a linguistic area.

## EXERCISES

1. The following examples contain quantifiers (such as *díp* 'all') and numerals (such as *gòemé* 'one' and *vél* 'two'). Review the arguments in the section entitled "Noun phrases" above, and discuss whether or not quantifiers and numerals belong to the Goemai noun phrase. Note: all examples are taken from natural discourse, and the first translation reflects their intended reading; different contexts can trigger different readings, and this is reflected in the second translation.

a. *gùrùm     díp     muèp=táng     pè     góed'è     s'óe*
   person     all     3PL=search     place     where.there.is     food
   'All the people, they searched for a place where there is food.'
   Or: 'The people, they searched thoroughly for a place where there is food.'

b. *s'óe     muáráp     díp*
   food     die     all
   'All the food had died.'
   Or: 'The food had died completely.'

c. *muèp     fúm     nì     vél*
   3PL     fold     3SG     two
   'They folded it twice.'
   Or: 'They folded the two of them.'

d. *dé     gòe     tù     ńdòe=gùrùm     yì     gòemé*
   so.that     should     kill     SPEC=person     PART     one
   '(…) so that he should kill one person.'
   Or: '(…) so that he should kill a person once.'

2. Goemai displays an interesting phenomenon: a subset of its verbs have distinct singular and plural forms. Table LP2.4 summarizes those verbs that occur in this exercise.

**TABLE LP2.4** Number-marking on verbs: some singular/plural pairs

| Gloss | Singular | Plural |
| --- | --- | --- |
| 'rise (intransitive)' | *yóól* | *yúúl* |
| 'be afraid of (transitive)' | *lúút* | *lwát* |
| 'kill (transitive)' | *tù* | *twò* |
| 'hate (transitive)' | *nyáng* | *nyák* |
| 'set down (transitive)' | *d'ú* | *d'wár* |
| 'gain experience in (transitive)' | *b'óót* | *b'át* |

Verbs agree in number with one (and only one) of the core arguments. In the case of intransitive clauses, the verb unsurprisingly agrees with the subject argument. This pattern is illustrated in

Examples (a) and (b): plural marking on the verb indicates that the subject argument is plural (a), while singular marking on the verb indicates that the subject is singular (b). Notice that the subject noun phrase itself is unmarked for number in both examples: *gùrùm* 'person/people' is interpreted as plural because of the plural verb, and *áás* 'dog/dogs' is interpreted as singular because of the singular verb. Alternatively, it is possible for both the noun phrase and the verb to be marked for the same number (as in c and d).

a. *gùrùm       yúúl        pè        ngàm*
   person      rise.PL     place     much/many
   'People got up (PL) in many places.'

b. *Áás        yóól*
   dog        rise.SG
   'The dog got up (SG).'

c. *muèp       yúúl*
   3PL        rise.PL
   'They (PL) got up (PL).'

d. *ní         yóól*
   3SG        rise.SG
   'It (SG) got up (SG).'

Examples (e) to (j) all feature transitive verbs. Look at these examples, and do the following exercises:

  i. For each transitive verb pair in Table LP2.4 above, determine whether it agrees with the subject or object in number.
 ii. Discuss whether or not it is possible to use verbal number as an additional criterion to argue that Goemai groups subjects together and treats them differently from objects.
iii. Some grammatical patterns in languages are sensitive not only to transitivity but also to the semantic case roles of core arguments (see Chapter 6, section 6.3.5). Write down the semantic case role of each core argument. Can you characterize the distribution of the singular and plural verbs in relation to semantic case roles? If so, describe the distribution succinctly. If not, discuss.

e. *muèp       lwát               hèn        sòsái*
   3PL        be.afraid.of.PL    1SG.OBJ    a.lot
   'They fear me a lot.'

f. *muèp       tú        wò        ńnòe*
   3PL        kill.SG   snake     PROX.DEM
   'They killed this snake.'

g. *tó         ní        twó        muèp       díp*
   okay       3SG       kill.PL    3PL.OBJ    all
   'Okay, he killed them all.'

h. *hèn       nyàng       móe-gòepé    muèp       t'óerép    nt'óerép     ńnòe*
   1SG       hate.SG     PL-that      3PL        lie.PL     lying.PL     PROX.DEM
   'I hate those that are lying there.'

i. *muèp*  *d'ú*  *nì*  *tóe*
   3PL  set.down.SG  3SG.OBJ  EMPH
   'They set him down.'

j. *muèp*  *b'át*  *puér=hók*  *tóe*  *bá*
   3PL  become.experience.in.PL  fishing=DEF  EMPH  NEG
   'They really didn't become experienced in fishing.'

# Manange

## 3.1 Introduction

Manange is a Sino-Tibetan language spoken in Nepal. Sino-Tibetan is very large with over 360 languages, and is itself split into two "sub-families": Sinitic, comprising languages from (mainly) China, and Tibeto-Burman, comprising over 350 languages west-to-east from Pakistan, India, Nepal, Tibet, Bhutan, Bangladesh, Myanmar, Thailand, and China. Manange belongs to the Bodish subgrouping of Tibeto-Burman. This genealogical profile is given in more detail in Figure LP3.1.

Nepal (The Federal Democratic Republic of Nepal since 2007) is a landlocked country of approximately 57,000 square miles (similar in size to the US state of Illinois) located in South Asia, with India bordering the south, east, and west, and Tibet/China to the

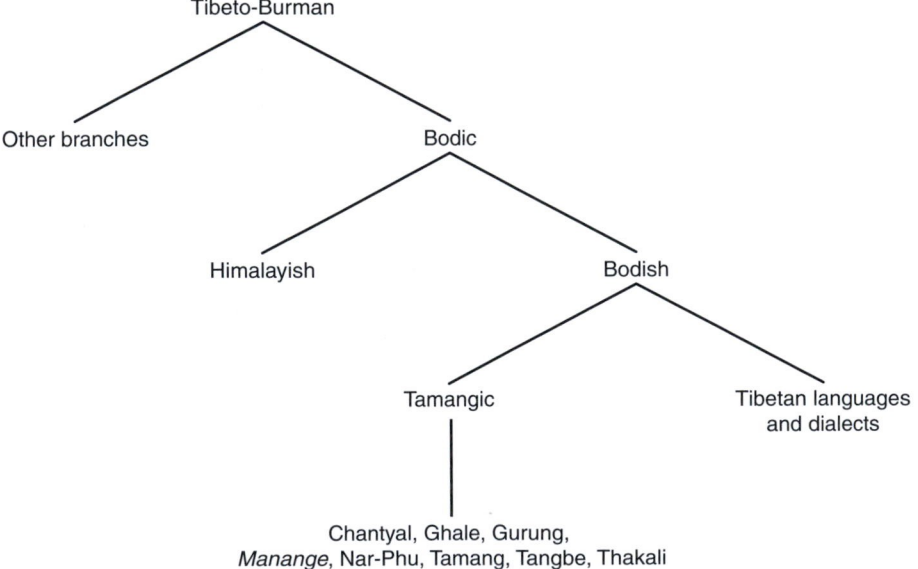

**Figure LP3.1** Genealogical profile of Manange

**SIDEBAR LP3.1**

A **lingua franca** is a language that is spoken within multilingual communities where people do not speak each other's ancestral languages. It usually functions as a language of commerce in a particular nation or region where there is extensive multilingualism. In Nepal, the lingua franca nationwide is Nepali (also the official language of Nepal), but in certain regions within the country, other indigenous languages have lingua franca status, including some dialects of Tibetan in western Nepal.

north. The official language of Nepal, and also its **lingua franca** (see Sidebar LP3.1), is Nepali, an Indo-European language. The capital city of Kathmandu is located in the central part of the country, at an elevation of about 4,400 feet, while the Manang District, the traditional home of Manange speakers, is located to the north and west of Kathmandu. The map in Figure LP3.2 gives a geographic perspective on the location of Manang.

The average elevation of the thirteen Manange-speaking villages is higher than that of Kathmandu, at around 10,000 feet above sea level, with the highest point in Manang at 17,765 feet. The population of Manang is much sparser than that of the rest of Nepal: under 10,000 people live in a district of 867 square miles (the total population of Nepal is currently around 30 million, with over 1 million people in the Kathmandu area). As discussed below, these geographic and human aspects have a significant impact on the linguistic situation in Manang.

The map also shows an important factor in the socioeconomic organization of Manange speakers: the Annapurna Circuit (roughly approximated via the dashed line). This is a footpath of approximately 185 miles in length, which bisects the Manang District as it runs through central Nepal. Traditionally, the Annapurna Circuit was a route for trading foodstuffs and other goods between the Manang region and the rest of

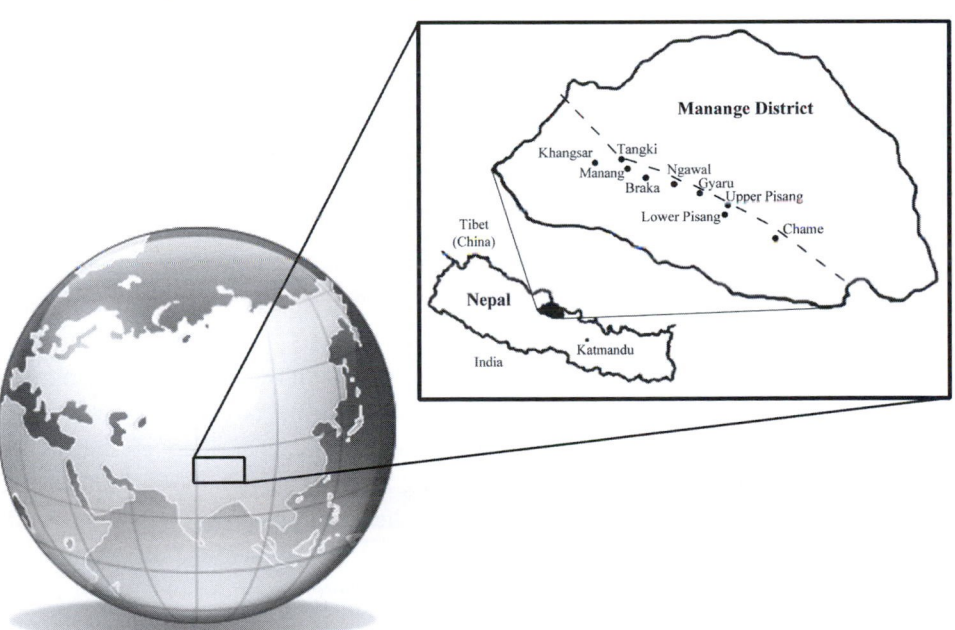

**Figure LP3.2** Map of Manang District: dotted line shows Annapurna trekking route

**Figure LP3.3** A trekking lodge sign in Dharapani, Manang, written in English for tourists

Nepal, Tibet, and India. Nowadays the Annapurna Circuit is famous as a trail for backpackers or "trekkers." As a result, the nearer to the Circuit a Manange settlement is, the more that settlement's economic practices are tailored toward the tourist economy.

Manange villages located right on the Circuit have houses converted into luxury-style lodges, some with German-style bakeries and electricity capabilities operated by small hydro-power generators. There are also numerous small shops selling goods for trekkers. There is a growing predominance of Nepali bilingualism (and to some extent, English), as villagers interact with tourists, porters, and trekking guides, or as city Mananges relocate to Manang to reap the rewards of the trekking industry. The socio-economic situation for inhabitants who live farther away from the Circuit is much different: they engage mainly in yak and goat shepherding, as well as in limited farming, which includes growing buckwheat, potatoes, cauliflower, and garlic in the cooler, drier climates, or corn, millet, and wheat in the warmer southern portions of Manang.

Manange, which has a number of different names (see Textbox LP3.1), is not the only language spoken in Manang; it is one of four Bodish languages in the area, including Gurung, Nar-Phu, and Gyalsumdo, which is a Tibetan variety. In addition to these languages, Tibetan speakers are also represented in Manang; these speakers are

**Figure LP3.4** Sheep Herding along the road, Lower Manang

---

### TEXTBOX LP3.1 **LANGUAGE NAMES**

Many languages have more than one language name. In other words, languages may have one or more **endonyms** or **autonyms** (language names used by the locals or group members themselves) and also one or more **exonyms** (names used by outsiders, and not by group members themselves). Manange is a good example of this: speakers self-report their ethnic group and language name as Nyeshang, Nyeshangte, or Nyangmi (these names are their endonyms). Non-Manange speakers frequently refer to the ethnic group and its speakers as Manange, Manangi, Managkye, Manangba, or Manangbhot (all exonyms). This is not just true for Manange, but for more commonly encountered languages like German (endonym: Deutsch), Dutch (endonym: Nederlands), and Scottish Gaelic (endonym: A' Ghàidhlig). Another example of an endonym/exonym difference within Nepal is that of Newar (endonym: Nepal Bhasa). Interestingly, the term "Manange" has been gradually shifting from a strict exonym to having endonym status, especially for younger speakers.

---

typically migrants who have relocated to Manang due to the lucrative tourist season and better grazing conditions. Additionally, Thakali people, who inhabit the Mustang District to the northwest of Manang, regularly travel through Manang with mule trains.

In recent generations, many Mananges have migrated to Kathmandu, or to lower elevations during winter, to benefit from longer growing seasons and better education and employment opportunities. In winter, many women and children stay in low-elevation villages where Nepali is spoken, while men may travel to other regions for work. Although some Mananges do remain in Manang year round, this number seems to be declining.

Manange has a speaker population of under 5,000; it is thus considered a small but relatively viable language, with some prospect of endangerment. Despite displacement via emigration of some speakers to Kathmandu, there is continued transmission of Manange to younger generations. The primary factor contributing to an observed small-scale shift away from Manange is the rise of access to formal education in Nepali for socioeconomic advancement. However, several factors contribute to the retention of Manange, including positive ethnic-group identity and prestige, and the comparative wealth of Mananges as entrepreneurs. Manange is neither the most nor the least viable language in comparison to other nearby languages: the Gurung dialects Nepal-wide have over 200,000 speakers, while the Phu dialect has perhaps only a couple of hundred.

## 3.2  Typological overview of Manange

Because the Sino-Tibetan family comprises languages covering such a large area, typological descriptions recognize two main types of languages from this family: languages of the "Sinosphere" and languages of the "Indosphere." Languages in the Sinosphere are located mainly in Southeast Asia and are **analytic**, with little inflectional and derivational morphology. This does not mean they lack such traits altogether, but that they tend to show morphological alternations via phonological adjustments (e.g., tone) and tend to rely more heavily on phrasal structures (e.g., compounds and strings of verbs called **serial verbs**) than on affixes. Root morphemes in analytic languages are rarely longer than one syllable. In contrast, languages in the Indosphere, which extends through the Himalayas and into South Asia, have **synthetic** and **agglutinative** morphological patterns, including affixes marking case, honorifics, tense, and aspect. Root morphemes in synthetic languages may be polysyllabic and these languages usually lack tone. However, complicating this division are languages such as Manange, which is geographically located in an Indospheric region, but which shares some features with Sinospheric languages.

### 3.2.1  Manange phonology and morphology

Manange has thirty consonant phonemes, including voiceless plain and aspirated stops and affricates in the bilabial, dental, retroflex, palatal, velar, and glottal places of articulation. Manange also has four nasals (/m, n, ɲ, ŋ/), and three fricatives (/s, ʂ, ʃ/). The consonants also include approximants (/l, j, w/) and an alveolar tap (/ɾ/). In addition, there is a labialized series of consonants, pronounced with lip rounding and a labial-velar off-glide: /pʷ, pʷʰ, mʷ, kʷ, kʷʰ, ŋʷ/. The six vowel phonemes include: /i, u, e, o, ɑ, ʌ/; all vowels except /ʌ/ have a nasalized counterpart.

Manange has four tones, as illustrated by Example (1):

(1) The four tones in Manange (see Sidebar LP3.2 for a
note on the transcription)

| Tone | Melody | Example |
|---|---|---|
| 1 | low level | $\underline{t}u^{22}$ 'stay' |
| 2 | high level | $\underline{t}u^{44}$ 'thread' |
| 3 | very high falling | $\underline{t}u^{52}$ 'cereal' |
| 4 | mid-high falling | $\underline{t}^hu^{42}$ 'six' |

Some words, especially recent loanwords, do not carry a
tone melody. For more on tone, see Textbox LP3.2.

---

TEXTBOX LP3.2 **TONE LANGUAGES**

A language that uses pitch as a primary means for
word or grammatical meaning contrast is said to
be **tonal**, or a **tone language**. While all languages
use pitch in some capacity (e.g., for affective,
interactional, or interrogative functions), tone
languages use pitch to signal meaning
differences. Like many Sino-Tibetan languages,
Manange has a system of several tones that signal
word meaning changes. Manange has four
tones. Some Sino-Tibetan languages have fewer
than four tones (e.g., Meithei, spoken in
northeastern India, which has two tones), and
some have more (e.g., Cantonese, spoken in
Guangdong China, which has six).

---

The morphological profile of Manange is largely analytic, with a small number of
suffixes and clitics, discussed below.

Elements in the noun phrase are structured into a particular order:

DEMONSTRATIVE RELATIVE-CLAUSE **NOUN** ADJECTIVE NUMERAL = CLITIC

**Clitics** (see Textbox LP3.3) are affix-like morphemes that in Manange indicate noun
plurality, definiteness, and case. There are a number of clitic case markers. Of special
importance here is the clitic =*tse*, which marks the more agentive core argument of
a transitive clause; this is called an **ergative** marker (see Textbox LP8.3 in Language
Profile 8 (Bardi) for a fuller discussion of ergativity). The clitic =*ri* marks the object noun
phrase of a transitive clause when the object is both animate and a semantic patient.
Subjects of intransitive clauses are unmarked.

Unlike many other "Indospheric" Tibeto-Burman languages, Manange lacks verbal
affixes that mark number, gender, case, or the honorific status of referents. It also lacks
grammatical markers for tense. There is a small set of verbal suffixes that mark **aspect**
and **mood**, and which are also used to link clauses together in larger complex sentences. There is only one prefix, the negative *a-*.

### 3.2.2 Manange clause and sentence structure

The word order of basic constituents is generally SOV for transitive clauses or
SV for intransitive clauses. Clauses that have markers indicating aspect/mood

## TEXTBOX LP3.3 **CLITICS**

Both **clitics** and affixes are bound morphemes. However, affixes have more restricted distribution than clitics, in that they occur only with words from a single lexical class. A typical example is the past-tense suffix in English, which can only be bound to verbs. Clitics are much less restricted; they may attach to a wider variety of host words. The possessive suffix *'s* in English is considered an **enclitic** (a clitic that follows its host) because it attaches to a variety of hosts (in conveying the grammatical meaning of possession), e.g., to a noun in *the guy's car*; to a verb embedded in a relative clause in *the guy that you know's car*; and to the verb of an adverbial clause embedded into a larger noun phrase in *the guy that you met yesterday while travelling's car*. In Manange, case-markers are analyzed as clitics because they attach to the final element of the noun phrase, regardless of its lexical class. For example, the ergative case clitic, which marks the more agent-like core argument of a transitive or ditransitive verb, attaches to a noun in *mi=tse$^{52}$* (man=ERG) 'man'; to a nominalized verb-like adjective in *mi$^{52}$ mɾe-pʌ=tse$^{44}$* (man fat-NOM=ERG) 'fat man'; and to a numeral in *mi$^{52}$ sẽ=tse$^{44}$* (man three=ERG) 'three men.' All three of these noun phrases are in the ergative case, appropriate for their use as subjects of a transitive clause.

and **evidentiality** are called **finite** and mark the end of a sentence. Some examples are given in (2).

**(2)**  a. Finite, with ergative and patient-marked animate object

nakju=ko=tse$^{22}$        nokor=ko=ri$^{22}$        tʃʰĩ-tsi$^{22}$
dog=DEF=ERG        cat=DEF=P        catch-PRF
'The dog caught the cat.'

b. Finite, intransitive

ale=ko$^{22}$        nu$^{42}$        mo$^{22}$
boy=DEF        sleep        COP
'The boy sleeps.'

The finite markers in these examples are the perfective suffix *-tsi* and the present marker *mo$^{22}$*. You can also see the ergative case-marker on the NP subject of the transitive verb, and the object case-marker on the noun-phrase object of the transitive verb in (2a). The subject of the intransitive verb in (2b) is unmarked.

In addition to finite clauses that are marked for mood, aspect, and/or evidentiality, Manange also has many **non-finite** clauses, which lack marking for these categories. Verbs in non-finite clauses typically have a suffix, *-pʌ*, which is considered a **nominalizer**. This nominalizer is used in the formation of relative clauses, complement clauses, purpose clauses, and clauses that follow a sequential time ordering. Example (3) illustrates *-pʌ* forming a relative clause; note that there is no marking of evidentiality, aspect, or other finite categories.

**(3)**  se-pʌ$^{22}$        mi$^{52}$
kill-NMLZ        person
'murderer' (lit. 'person who kills' or 'killing person')

It is also important to recognize **copula clauses**. In Manange, the **copula** is a verb used to relate a noun (the **copula subject**) with another noun or an adjective (the **copula complement**). In English, the copula is the verb *be*. In (4), the copula relates the copular subject to a following noun, while in (5) it relates the copular subject to a following adjective (see Sidebar LP3.3 for a note on the transcription).

(4)   [My father]$_{CS}$ was [a teacher]$_{CC}$

(5)   [The baby]$_{CS}$ is [tired] $_{CC}$

In Manange the copula is *mo$^{22}$* 'be,' sometimes followed by an additional marker *mu$^{22}$*, which marks the speaker's strength of commitment to the truth or validity of a propositional utterance based on available evidence. Some examples of copula clauses in Manange follow in (6). Practice putting the copula subject and copula complement in parentheses, and then check your answers in Textbox LP3.4 on the next page. In what basic way do copula clauses in Manange differ syntactically from copula clauses in English?

(6)   Copula clauses without bracketing

a. *tsu=ko$^{44}$*     *mi$^{44}$*     *mo$^{22}$*
   this=DEF     eye     COP
   'This is an eye.'

b. *th$\tilde{\imath}$=ko$^{42}$*     *tʃaŋku$^{52}$*     *mo$^{22}$*
   house=DEF     green     COP
   'The house is green.'

c. *pʰolpʌ$^{42}$*     *taŋ=ko$^{52}$*     *thẽ$^{22}$*     *mo$^{22}$*     *mu$^{22}$*
   frog     pot=DEF     empty     COP     EVID
   'The frog pot was empty.'

d. *th$\tilde{\imath}^{42}$*     *naŋ=ri$^{52}$*     *sol-pʌ$^{42}$*     *mo$^{22}$*
   house     inside=LOC     bright-NMLZ     COP
   'The inside (of the) house is bright.'

e. *tsoktʃu$^{22}$*     *siki$^{22}$*     *lʌ-pʌ$^{22}$*     *kʰja=ri$^{42}$*     *mo$^{22}$*
   table     food     do-NMLZ     place=LOC     COP
   'The table is in the kitchen.'

f. *ŋʌ$^{22}$*     *amtsi$^{22}$*     *mo$^{22}$*
   1SG     doctor     COP
   'I am a doctor.'

g. *naraŋ$^{22}$*     *th$\tilde{\imath}$=ko$^{42}$*     *tʃam-pʌ$^{22}$*     *mo$^{22}$*
   before     house=DEF     small-NMLZ     COP
   'The house was small before.'

---

### TEXTBOX LP3.4 ANSWERS: COPULA CLAUSES WITH BRACKETING

(6)    Copula clauses with bracketing

a. [$tsu{=}ko^{44}$]$_{CS}$     [$mi^{44}$]$_{CC}$     $mo^{22}$
     [this=DEF]$_{CS}$     [eye]$_{CC}$     COP
     'This is an eye.'

b. [$t^h\tilde{\imath}{=}ko^{42}$]$_{CS}$     [$t\int a\eta ku^{52}$]$_{CC}$     $mo^{22}$
     [house=DEF]$_{CS}$     [green]$_{CC}$     COP
     'The house is green.'

c. [$p^holp\Lambda^{42}$     $ta\eta{=}ko^{52}$]$_{CS}$     [$t^h\tilde{e}^{22}$]$_{CC}$     $mo^{22}$     $mu^{22}$
     frog      pot=DEF]$_{CS}$     [empty]$_{CC}$     COP     EVID
     'The frog pot was empty.'

d. [$t^h\tilde{\imath}^{42}$     $na\eta{=}ri^{52}$]$_{CS}$     [$sol\text{-}p\Lambda^{42}$]$_{CC}$     $mo^{22}$
     [house     inside=LOC]$_{CS}$     [bright-NMLZ]$_{CC}$     COP
     'The inside (of the) house is bright/well-lit.'

e. [$tsokt\int u^{22}$]$_{CS}$     [$siki^{22}$     $l\Lambda\text{-}p\Lambda^{22}$     $k^hja{=}ri^{42}$]$_{CC}$     $mo^{22}$
     [table]$_{CS}$     [food     do-NMLZ     place=LOC]$_{CC}$     COP
     'The table is in the kitchen.'

f. [$\eta\Lambda^{22}$]$_{CS}$     [$amtsi^{22}$]$_{CC}$     $mo^{22}$
     [1SG]$_{CS}$     [doctor]$_{CC}$     COP
     'I am a doctor.'

g. $nara\eta^{22}$     [$t^h\tilde{\imath}{=}ko^{42}$]$_{CS}$     [$t\int am\text{-}p\Lambda^{22}$]$_{CC}$     $mo^{22}$
     before     [house=DEF]$_{CS}$     [small-NMLZ]$_{CC}$     COP
     'The house was small before.'

The basic way in which copula clauses in Manange differ from copula clauses in English is constituent order. In English, the constituent order is CS COPULA CC, while in Manange it is CS CC COPULA, in accordance with Manange's verb-final constituent ordering.

---

## 3.3 Lexical classes

One of the more interesting properties of Manange is its lexical classes, particularly the class of adjectives. Manange has syntactic and morphological evidence for two classes of adjectives, which are both, in their own ways, distinct from nouns and verbs.

### 3.3.1 Nouns

Nouns represent the largest, most productive lexical class in Manange. Although most words are monosyllabic and monormophemic, new words may be added to the lexicon via compounding and via borrowing (see Textbox LP3.5 on loanwords, as well as Chapter 13). Most commonly loanwords are borrowed from Nepali, but there are also

> ### TEXTBOX LP3.5 **LOANWORDS**
>
> Loanwords are words that enter into a language from another source language. For a full discussion, see Chapter 13, section 13.2. As noted there, the morphological profile of the borrowing language can make incorporating loanwords more complicated, although many languages have strategies to remedy this.
>
> Manange, for example, employs a "dummy" (semantically meaningless) verb $ti^{44}$, which immediately follows the loaned verb (usually borrowed from Nepali) and carries the usual derivational or inflectional morphology in the language (e.g., Nepali *rop* 'plant' → Manange *rop ti-pʌ$^{44}$* plant V-NMLZ 'to plant').

**Table LP3.1** Examples of Manange nouns

| Monomorphemic | Compounds | Loans |
|---|---|---|
| *pa$^{52}$* 'leaf' | *pʰemʷi$^{42}$* 'coin' (metal-money) | *kotʰa* 'pasture' (< Nepali *gotha*) |
| *mi$^{44}$* 'eye' | *meʃʌ$^{42}$* 'beef' (cow-flesh) | *ṣi$^{22}$* 'cotton' (< Nepali *ril*) |
| *tʃoktsu$^{22}$* 'table' | *kjepʰrʌ$^{22}$* 'buckwheat' (barley-flour) | *tauli* 'towel' (< English *towel*) |
| *pʌle$^{52}$* 'leg' | *ʃiɳtuɳ$^{44}$* 'tree' (wood-grove) | *fon* 'phone' (< English *phone*) |

borrowings from English and other languages. Table LP3.1 presents examples of monomorphemic words, compounds, and loanwords from Nepali.

Nouns in Manange show a variety of morphological and syntactic properties that do not apply to other lexical classes. Since nouns are frequently the final element in a noun phrase, they may take enclitics. These include the plural enclitic *=tse*, case enclitics, and the clitics *=ko* (DEF) and *=ri* (INDEF), which mark **definiteness**, the degree to which the entity or concept a noun refers to is already known or has already been introduced in a discourse context. None of these operations is possible for verbs or adjectives in Manange.

(7)  Plural marking
 *nʌkyu=tse$^{22}$*  *nu$^{42}$*  *mo$^{22}$*
 dog=PL  sleep  COP
 'The dogs sleep.'

(8)  Definiteness and case-marking
 *nʌkyu=ko=tse$^{22}$*  *nokor=ri$^{22}$*  *pyu$^{52}$*  *mo$^{22}$*
 dog=DEF=ERG  cat=DAT  chase  COP
 'The dog chases the cat.'

(9)  *ɳʌ=tse$^{22}$*  [*sʌ$^{22}$*  *se-pʌ$^{22}$*  *mi=ko=ri$^{52}$*]  *mʷi$^{42}$*  *pʰrʌ$^{42}$*
 1SG=erg  [goat  kill-NMLZ  person=DEF=DAT]  money  hundred

 *pin-tsi$^{22}$*
 give-PRF
 'I gave one hundred rupees to the man who killed the goat.'

Syntactically, nouns are the only lexical class that can serve as the head of a noun phrase, while neither verbs nor adjectives may perform this function. Therefore, the example in (10a) represents a possible noun phrase in Manange, while those in (10b) and (10c) do not.

(10)   Acceptable and unacceptable NP heads

   a. [nʌkju²²]ₙₚ
      [dog]ₙₚ
      'a/the dog'

   b. *[mleŋkja²²]ₙₚ
      *[black]ₙₚ
      'a/the black one'

   c. *[nu-pʌ⁴²]ₙₚ
      *[sleep-NMLZ]ₙₚ
      'the sleeper/the sleeping one'

### 3.3.2  Verbs

Like nouns, verbs are also an also open class, with additions via compounding or borrowing (although borrowed verbs in Manange are less frequent than borrowed nouns).

Verbs are clearly different from nouns in Manange; there are morphological and syntactic properties that are unique to verbs. For example, verbs may be marked for **aspectual** distinctions (see Textbox LP3.6 for a brief overview of aspect). In (11) **perfective** aspect is marked by a suffix directly on the verb stem and in (12) **progressive** aspect is indicated by both a suffix and the use of the copula as an auxiliary verb (compare English *is running*). In Manange, the auxiliary is placed after the main verb (which is marked with the progressive suffix, similar to *-ing* in English), and therefore occurs at the end of the clause.

---

### TEXTBOX LP3.6 **ASPECT**

Aspect is a grammatical category related to how an event is expressed in temporal terms. Situations expressed as unified completed wholes are in **perfective** aspect, e.g., *they fought*, in contrast to situations expressed from a viewpoint internal to the situation, e.g., *they are fighting* (**progressive**) or *they often fight* (**habitual**). The term **imperfective** includes progressive, habitual, and other types of aspect. Aspect is independent of tense; for example, situations can be expressed in the past progressive (*were fighting*), present progressive (*are fighting*), and future progressive (*will be fighting*).

**(11)** Perfective

| nʌkju=ko²² | kju-tsi⁴⁴ |
|---|---|
| dog=DEF | run-PRF |

'The dog has run.'

**(12)** Progressive

| nʌkju=ko²² | toso⁵² | kju-tse⁵² | mo²² |
|---|---|---|---|
| dog=DEF | now | run-PROG | COP |

'The dog is running right now.'

Another property unique to verbs is that they are the only lexical items that can take the negative prefix *a-*. They are also the last constituent in most clauses.

**(13)**

| kje²² | a-te-ro⁴⁴ |
|---|---|
| voice | NEG-take.out-IMP |

'Don't make a sound.'

In English, many nouns may be treated formally as verbs simply by adding verbal morphology (e.g., *He moved the table* ~ *They tabled the vote*), but this is not possible in Manange. Aspect/mood morphology and the negative prefix apply exclusively to verbs; nouns cannot take these markers.

### 3.3.3 Adjectives

Unlike in many other languages, Manange has not one, but two types of adjectives: those that behave as stereotypical adjectives from the point of view of an English speaker (called "simple adjectives" here), and those that have some properties in common with verbs (called "verb-like adjectives" here). These two types can be distinguished by their formal properties both in the noun phrase, when they have attributive functions, and in the predicate, when they have predicative functions. Both types of adjectives can be used in comparative and superlative constructions (see Textbox LP3.7).

Simple adjectives in Manange constitute a small and closed class, meaning that it is unusual for new items to be added to this class. This class of adjectives includes most color terms and some words expressing semantic dimensions, such as human states and speed or value. Some examples are given in Table LP3.2.

In attributive functions, simple adjectives follow the head noun. These adjectives appear to be able to take inflectional morphology that identifies nouns, including plural, case, and definiteness clitics, as shown in example (14).

**Table LP3.2** Semantic categories of Manange simple adjectives

| Color terms | Human states | Speed/Value |
|---|---|---|
| mleŋkja²² 'black' | kʰjokro²² 'old' | kini⁵² 'fast' |
| olkja²² 'red' | ŋoto⁵² 'true/honest' | kole⁴² 'slow' |
| tʌrkja²² 'white' | | |

(14)  [kʰje⁴²        tʌrkja=ri²²]      ïʌ²²      poɾ⁵²      jʌ²²      mo²²
      [road          white=LOC]        1SG       take       go        COP
      'I take (the prayer scarf) on the white road (to heaven).'

However, because these inflectional markers are clitics (not affixes), they have a freer distribution, attaching to any element that is final in the noun phrase, including adjectives, numerals, nouns, and determiners. Unlike nouns (but like verbs and verb-like adjectives), simple adjectives cannot be the single (head) element of a noun phrase, so a structure like *tʌrkja=ri²² ïʌ²² poɾ⁵² jʌ²² mo²², where the color word tʌrkja²² 'white' is the head of the NP, is not acceptable.

---

### TEXTBOX LP3.7 **COMPARATIVES AND SUPERLATIVES**

In English, adjectives can be placed in **comparative** and **superlative** constructions, either through suffixation, via a "more/most" phrasal structure, or through suppletion of the root (e.g., *red/ redder/reddest, delicious/more/most delicious, bad/worse/worst*). This helps to distinguish adjectives from other lexical classes that cannot do this (e.g., *\*table/tabler/tablest*). In Manange, comparatives and superlatives are formed with the same strategy, a phrasal structure that can be glossed as 'say-comparative.' Examples are shown here with kʰjokro²² 'old (animate).'

a.  u²²              nʌkju²²        kʰjokro²²        mo²²
    DIST.DEM         dog             old              COP
    'That dog is old.'

b.  u²²              nʌkju²²        tsu⁴⁴             nʌkju²²      pi-le⁵²        kʰjokro²²       mo²²
    DIST.DEM         dog             PROX.DEM          dog          say-COMPAR     old             COP
    'This dog is older than that dog.' (lit. 'Compared to that dog, this dog is old.')

c.  tsu⁴⁴           nʌkju=ko²²     tsʰaraŋ⁴⁴        pi-le⁵²        kʰjokro²²       mo²²
    PROX.DEM         dog=DEF         all               say-COMPAR     old             COP
    'This dog is the oldest of all.' (lit. 'Compared to all dogs, this dog is old.')

This structure is not uncommon in languages of South Asia, both in Tibeto-Burman and in Indo-European families.

---

Simple adjectives may be used with the verb 'be' in a copula construction. This is also true of nouns. Adjectives and nouns that occur with a copula are said to be the **copula complements**.

(15)  Noun as a complement of the copula *mo* 'be'
      [u²²             ʃʌ.kʌ=ko⁵²]CS      [toɾe⁵²]CC          [a-ɾe²²            mo²²]PREDICATE
      [DIST.DEM        glacier=DEF]CS      [graveyard]CC       [NEG-COP           COP]PREDICATE
      'That glacier place was not a graveyard (a long time ago).'

(16)  Simple adjective as a syntactic complement of the copula *mo* 'be'
      [pʰolpʌ⁴²         tʰaï=ko⁴⁴]CS      [tʰẽ²²]CC           [mo²²             mu²²]PREDICATE
      [frog             pot=DEF]CS         [empty]COMP         [COP              EVID]PREDICATE
      'The frog pot (pot where the frog lived) was empty.'

Like nouns, but unlike verbs, simple adjectives in the predicate are not directly marked for aspect or mood distinctions, nor do they occur before an evidential marker. Instead, the copula $t\Lambda^{22}$ 'become' is used; it follows the adjective, hosts this morphology, and precedes any evidentials.

(17)  The copula $t\Lambda$ 'become' following a noun
[$kju^{44}$      $tso{=}ko^{44}$]$_{CS}$        [$t^h\tilde{\imath}$]$_{CC}$   [$t\Lambda$-$tsi^{22}$]$_{PREDICATE}$
[water        PROX.DEM=DEF]$_{CS}$   [lake]$_{CC}$   [become-PRF]$_{PREDICATE}$
'This water became a lake.'

(18)  The copula $t\Lambda$ 'become' following a simple adjective
[$k^h\tilde{\imath}^2$]$_{CS}^2$      [$kat^he$]$_{CC}$   [$t\Lambda$-$tsi^{22}$]$_{PREDICATE}$
[3SG]$_{CS}$       [thin]$_{CC}$        [become-PRF]$_{PREDICATE}$
'He became thin.'

In this construction, both adjectives and nouns are acceptable copula complements, and the verb $t\Lambda^{22}$ 'become' is the copula.

Again like nouns, but unlike verbs, simple adjectives do not occur with the negative morpheme prefix. To negate a copula clause, a **suppletive** form of the copula is used, creating a complex copula predicate.

(19)  Suppletive copula following noun
[$u^{22}$]$_{CS}$         [$tore^{52}$]$_{CC}$     [$a$-$re^{22}$      $mo^{22}$]$_{PREDICATE}$
[DIST.DEM]$_{CS}$   [graveyard]$_{CC}$   [NEG-COP     COP]$_{PREDICATE}$
'That (piece of land) was not a graveyard (back then).'

(20)  Suppletive copula following adjective
[$u^{22}$            $n\Lambda kju^2$]$_{CS}^2$   [$mle\ddot{\imath}kja^{22}$]$_{CC}$   [$a$-$re^{22}$      $mo^{22}$]$_{PREDICATE}$
[DIST.DEM     dog]$_{CS}$         [black]$_{CC}$      [NEG-COP     COP]$_{PREDICATE}$
'That dog is not black.'

In contrast to simple adjectives, the class of verb-like adjectives is larger and is open to new membership via compounding. Some examples of verb-like adjectives are provided here, along with some of the semantic dimensions that they can express.

Not surprisingly, verb-like adjectives have some formal properties in common with verbs, but there are also some crucial ways in which they are different. In attributive functions, verb-like adjectives follow the noun; in this way, they are similar to simple adjectives. However, they may not occur as bare stems in this position but must take a suffix -$p\Lambda$, glossed here as NMLZ for "nominalizer," following common practice in

**Table LP3.3** Semantic categories of Manange verb-like adjectives

| Age | Value, human state | Physical property | Dimension |
|---|---|---|---|
| $s\tilde{e}^{22}$ 'young' | $k\tilde{u}^{44}$ 'expensive' | $\int a^{22}$ 'cracked/broken' | $t^hj\Lambda^{22}$ 'big' |
| $ta\eta^{52}$ 'ancient' | $k^he^{44}$ 'cheap' | $t\int\tilde{e}^{52}$ 'soft' | $t\int\tilde{a}^{22}$ 'small' |
| $t\int\tilde{a}^{52}$ 'new' | $n\Lambda^{44}$ 'ill' | $ki^{22}$ 'bitter' | $ru\eta^{52}$ 'long' |
| $\underline{s}u\eta^{44}$ 'brief' | $tsa\eta^{44}$ 'clean' | $k^ha\eta^{44}$ 'cold climate' | $p^hr\Lambda^{44}$ 'thin/fine' |

Tibeto-Burman linguistics. If verb-like adjectives occur in final position in the noun phrase, then like other lexical items, they may host the full range of clitics (plural, case, or definiteness). The following example illustrates an attributive verb-like adjective in NP-final position.

(21) $[kju^{44}$       $t^hj\Lambda\text{-}p\Lambda\text{=}ri^{22}]_{NP}$       $t^h\tilde{e}^{22}$       $t\Lambda\text{-}tsi^{22}$
water       big-NMLZ=LOC       throw       become-PRF
'The ashes were thrown in big water (like a river).'

Verbs can also be used to modify nouns within the noun phrase, in which case they also take the nominalizing suffix. However, while verb-like adjectives follow the noun in the noun phrase, a modifying verb must precede the noun, as in the following example.

(22) $\eta\Lambda\text{=}tse^{22}$       $[k^hol\text{-}p\Lambda^{42}$       $kju\text{=}ko^{42}]_{np}$       $t^hu\eta\text{-}tsi^{42}$
1SG=ERG       [boil-NMLZ       water=DEF]       drink-PRF
'I drank the boiled water.'

In (21) the verb-like adjective $t^hj\Lambda\text{-}p\Lambda^{22}$ 'big-NMLZ' follows the head noun $kju^{44}$ 'water,' while in (22) the nominalized verb $k^hol\text{-}p\Lambda^{42}$ 'boil-NMLZ' precedes the head noun $kju$ 'water.' Thus, although both verb-like adjectives and verbs are marked with the nominalizer suffix $-p\Lambda$, they have distinct NP positions in attributive functions. In this sense, verb-like adjectives are more similar to simple adjectives than to verbs; adjectives of both classes occur in post-nominal position in the noun phrase, while verbs occur in pre-nominal position.

When used as predicate adjectives, verb-like adjectives show some, but not all, of the morphological properties of verbs. Both simple adjectives and verbs are marked with the perfective suffix $-tsi$, as shown in the following examples.

(23) The perfective $-tsi$ suffix marking a verb
$k^hi^{22}$       $k^h\Lambda\text{-}tsi^{22}$
3SG       come-PRF
'He came.'

(24) The perfective $-tsi$ suffix marking a verb-like adjective
$k^hi^{22}$       $t^hj\Lambda\text{-}tsi^{22}$
3SG       big-PRF
'He was big.'

These examples show that verbs and verb-like adjectives can have similar morphological behavior and parallel syntactic structure when they function as predicates. However, this is not always the case. While verbs can be marked by the negative prefix $a$- directly, verb-like adjectives cannot. To negate a verb-like adjective, speakers must use the suppletive negative copula $a\text{-}re^{22}$; the verb-like adjective then occurs as the complement to the copula. This structure is illustrated in the following examples:

(25) Negation-marking on a verb

$kʰi^{22}$       $a-kʰʌ^{22}$       $(mo^{22})$

3SG       NEG-come       (COP)

'He doesn't come.'

(26) Negation marked via suppletive copula for a verb-like adjective

$mi^{52}$       $mile{=}ko^{22}$       $ʂuŋ-pʌ^{44}$       $a-re^{22}$       $mo^{22}$

person       life=DEF       short-NMLZ       NEG-COP       COP

'Man's life is not short.'

We have seen that in some ways verb-like adjectives are structurally identical to verbs: they both are marked with the nominalizer suffix -pʌ in an attributive construction and verb-like adjectives can take a limited range of aspect morphology similar to verbs when used in predicative constructions. However, in other ways verb-like adjectives are different from verbs: they show a different ordering with respect to the head noun in the noun phrase and, when negated in the predicate, they occupy the copula complement position and cannot carry the negative prefix. Other verbs, in contrast, precede the noun in the noun phrase and may host negation morphology. A summary of these main similarities and differences between simple adjectives and verb-like adjectives, along with a comparison to nouns and verbs, is given in Table LP3.4.

This language profile ties in with a point made in Chapter 5 that different languages have different sets of word classes and that in each language it is important to look at the detailed phonological and grammatical properties of words in order to determine which class they fall into. The properties that are used to identify a particular word class in one language may not do so in another; what is true of word classes is also true of many other aspects of the grammar.

**Table LP3.4** Properties of nouns, verbs, simple adjectives and verb-like adjectives

| Property | Nouns | Verbs | Simple adjectives | Verb-like adjectives |
|---|---|---|---|---|
| Position w/respect to noun in NP | N/A | Pre | Post | Post |
| Single head of NP? | Y | N | N | N |
| Hosts perfective aspect? | N | Y | N | Y |
| Hosts imperfective or future? | N | Y | N | N |
| Hosts negative prefix a-? | N | Y | N | N |
| Occurs in complement structures? | Y | N | Y | Some |

## TEXTBOX LP3.8 GLOSSING CONVENTIONS USED IN THIS LANGUAGE PROFILE

| Convention | Meaning | Convention | Meaning |
|---|---|---|---|
| 1 | first person | GEN | genitive |
| 2 | second person | IMP | imperative |
| 3 | third person | INST | instrumental |
| COM | comitative | LOC | locative |
| COMPAR | comparative | NEG | negation |
| COP | copula | NMLZ | nominalizer |
| DAT | dative | P | patientive |
| DEF | definite | PL | plural |
| DEM | demonstrative | PRF | perfect aspect |
| DIST | distal | PROG | progressive aspect |
| ERG | ergative | PROX | proximal |
| EVID | evidential | SG | singular |

## SUGGESTIONS FOR FURTHER READING

**van Driem, George**. 2001. *Languages of the Himalayas: An ethnolinguistic handbook of the Greater Himalayan Region, containing an introduction to the Symbiotic Theory of Language*, 2 vols. Leiden: Brill.

This two-volume book gives a comprehensive overview of the languages and language communities of the Greater Himalayan range, including historical and comparative descriptive data of previously undocumented languages.

**Thomason, Sarah G.** 2001. *Language contact: An introduction*. Edinburgh University Press.

This is a great introductory survey, including many case studies, of the social, political, and historical factors that bring different language communities into contact, as well as the linguistic and societal outcomes of that contact.

**Shopen, Timothy** (ed.). 2007. *Language typology and syntactic description*, 3 vols. Cambridge University Press.

This three-volume edited series is an essential reference for those interested in language documentation and description from a cross-linguistic perspective.

**Grenoble, Lenore A. and Lindsay J. Whaley** (eds.). 1998. *Endangered languages: Current issues and future prospects*. Cambridge University Press.

This edited volume contains proposed frameworks for better understanding the causes, mechanisms, and outcomes of language endangerment, and includes a number of diverse and compelling case studies from endangered language communities around the world.

**Fromkin, Victoria A.** (ed.). 1978. *Tone: A linguistic survey*. New York: Academic Press.

This book is a classic: an engaging survey of the phonetic (acoustic, physiological) dimensions of tone, as well as proposals to deal with tone in formal phonological models. This is a must-read for anyone who wants to study tone and tone-related phenomena in greater depth.

## EXERCISES

1. In the following examples of adjectives in predicative constructions, syntactically analyze the constituent structure of each example, putting each constituent in square brackets and noting the copula subject, the copula complement, and the copula in each example. State the formal evidence present in these examples that supports the distinction between a class of simple adjectives versus a class of verb-like adjectives in Manange.

a. Non-past

| $u^{22}$ | $k^hje{=}ko^{42}$ | $je^{52}$ | $mo^{22}$ | $mu^{22}$ |
|----------|-------------------|-----------|-----------|-----------|
| DIST.DEM | road=DEF | steep | COP | EVID |

'That road is steep.'

b. Future

| $u^{22}$ | $k^hje{=}ko^{42}$ | $je^{52}$ | $t\Lambda\text{-}p\Lambda^{22}$ |
|----------|-------------------|-----------|------------------|
| DIST.DEM | road=DEF | steep | become-NMLZ |

'That road will be steep.'

c. Non-past

| $u^{22}$ | $u\int u{=}ko^{22}$ | $mim\text{-}p\Lambda^{44}$ | $mo^{22}$ | $mu^{22}$ |
|----------|---------------------|----------------|-----------|-----------|
| DIST.DEM | apple=DEF | ripe-NMLZ | COP | EVID |

'That apple is ripe.'

d. Perfective

| $u^{22}$ | $u\int u{=}ko^{22}$ | $min\text{-}tsi^{44}$ |
|----------|---------------------|-------------|
| DIST.DEM | apple=DEF | ripe-PRF |

'That apple was ripe.'

e. Perfective

| $u^{22}$ | $k^hje{=}ko^{42}$ | $je^{52}$ | $mo^{22}$ | $mu^{22}$ |
|----------|-------------------|-----------|-----------|-----------|
| DIST.DEM | road=DEF | steep | COP | EVID |

'That road was steep.'

f. Future

| $u^{22}$ | $u\int u{=}ko^{22}$ | $mim\text{-}p\Lambda^{44}$ | $t\Lambda\text{-}p\Lambda^{22}$ |
|----------|---------------------|----------------|------------------|
| DIST.DEM | apple=DEF | ripe-NMLZ | become-NMLZ |

'That apple will be/become ripe.'

g. Negative

| $u^{22}$ | $u\int u{=}ko^{22}$ | $mim\text{-}p\Lambda^{44}$ | $a\text{-}re^{22}$ | $mo^{22}$ |
|----------|---------------------|----------------|------------|-----------|
| DIST.DEM | apple=DEF | ripe-NMLZ | NEG-COP | COP |

'That apple is not ripe.'

h. Negative

| $u^{22}$ | $k^hje{=}ko^{42}$ | $je^{52}$ | $a\text{-}re^{22}$ | $mo^{22}$ |
|----------|-------------------|-----------|------------|-----------|
| DIST.DEM | road=DEF | steep | NEG-COP | COP |

'That road is not steep.'

2. In the following data, what strategies are used for the modification of nouns within the noun phrase? What do these strategies tell us about the differences between verbs, simple adjectives, and verb-like adjectives in Manange?

a. $\eta\Lambda{=}tse^{22}$    $kju^{44}$    $pla{-}p\Lambda{=}ko^{52}$    $t^hu\eta{-}tsi^{44}$
   1SG=ERG    water    cold-NMLZ=DEF    drink-PRF
   'I drank the cold water.'

b. $\eta\Lambda{=}tse^{22}$    $\eta^wo{-}p\Lambda{=}ko^{52}$    $\int\Lambda^{22}$    $ts\Lambda{-}tsi^{22}$
   1SG=ERG    fry-NMLZ=DEF    meat    eat-PRF
   'I ate the fried meat.'

c. $\eta\Lambda{=}tse^{22}$    $\int\Lambda^{22}$    $k^harkj\Lambda{=}ko^{22}$    $ts\Lambda{-}tsi^{22}$
   1SG=ERG    meat    dry=DEF    eat-PRF
   'I ate the dried meat (like beef jerky).'

3. In the following four sentences, identify the case indicated by each case clitic (currently glossed as "xx"), and provide the appropriate gloss. (Use the glosses found throughout the examples in this language profile.)

a. $ti\eta i^{22}$    $\eta\Lambda{=}l\Lambda^{22}$    $nani{=}tse^{52}$    $\eta\Lambda{=}ju\eta^{22}$    $mo^{22}$
   today    1SG=xx    little.girl=DEF    1SG=xx    COP
   'Today my little sister is with me.'

b. $kj\Lambda^{52}$    $k^hi{=}l\Lambda^{22}$    $t^h\tilde{i}{=}ri^{42}$    $j\Lambda^{22}$    $mi^{22}$
   1SG    3SG=xx    house=xx    go    EVID
   'You went to his house (I think, but I did not witness it).'

c. $mri\eta{=}ko{=}tse^{22}$    $u\int u{=}ko^{22}$    $kola{=}ko{=}ri^{22}$    $p\tilde{i}{-}tsi^{22}$
   woman=DEF=xx    apple=DEF    child=DEF=xx    give-PRF
   'The woman gave the apple to the child.'

d. $\eta\Lambda{=}tse^{22}$    $nakju{=}ko{=}ri^{22}$    $perka{=}tse^{44}$    $p^ho{-}tsi^{44}$
   1SG=xx    dog=DEF=xx    stick=INST    beat-PRF
   'I beat the dog with the stick.'

4. The following four examples have **serial verbs**, sequences of verbs lacking any conjunctions that together form a single complex predicate. In Manange serial verb constructions, one verb is the lexical verb and one (or more) primarily contributes grammatical meaning. For each example, state which verb is the main/lexical verb and which verb is contributing a grammatical meaning? What particular grammatical meaning is it contributing?

a. $net\int el$    $j\Lambda{-}p\Lambda^{22}$    $mi{=}tse^{52}$    $komp\Lambda{=}ri$    $k^h\Lambda t\Lambda$    $pu^{52}$    $k^h\Lambda{-}tsi^{22}$
   religion    go-NMLZ    person=ERG    gompa=LOC    scarf    carry    come-PRF
   'The pilgrim brought the scarf to the temple.'

b. $mri\eta{=}ko{=}tse^{22}$    $k\Lambda p$    $te^{22}$    $l\Lambda^{22}$    $mi^{22}$
   woman=DEF=ERG    cup    fall    do    EVID
   'The woman dropped the cup.'

c. $ale{=}ko^{22}$    $skul{=}ri$    $p^hro^{42}$    $j\Lambda{-}tsi^{22}$
   boy=DEF    school=LOC    walk    go-PRF
   'The boy walked to school.'

d. $t\int^h\tilde{e}^{44}$    $mi{=}ko^{52}$    ten    $mri\eta{=}ko^{22}$    $ts^he^{44}$    $tu^{22}$    $mo^{22}$
   always    person=DEF    and    woman=DEF    fight    stay    COP
   'The man and woman always argue.'

5. For each of the ten clauses below, do the following:

   i. Identify all NPs and underline the head N.
   ii. Identify the main verbs, and indicate whether they are copular, intransitive, transitive, or ditransitive.
   iii. Return to the identified NPs and decide if each NP is functioning as a subject, object, indirect object, copula subject, copula complement, or oblique. What are the grammatical properties of the clause or phrase that helped you to determine this?

a. | $mrin{=}ko{=}la^{22}$ | $kola^{52}$ | $kje\text{-}p\Lambda^{44}$ | $mo^{22}$ | $mu^{22}$ |
   |---|---|---|---|---|
   | woman=DEF=GEN | dress | pretty-NMLZ | COP | EVID |

   'The woman's dress is pretty.'

b. | $mrin{=}ko{=}tse^{22}$ | $kola{=}ko{=}ri^{22}$ | $k\Lambda tti^{22}$ | $upahar{=}tse$ | $p\tilde{\imath}\text{-}tsi^{22}$ |
   |---|---|---|---|---|
   | woman=DEF=ERG | child=DEF=LOC | many | gift=PL | give-PRF |

   'The woman gave many gifts to the child.'

c. | $k^himi{=}jun^{22}$ | $kola^{22}$ | $\eta\Lambda^{22}$ | $mo^{22}$ | $mu^{22}$ |
   |---|---|---|---|---|
   | 3PL=COM | child | five | COP | EVID |

   'They have five children.'

d. | $nakju{=}ko{=}tse^{22}$ | $nokor{=}ko{=}ri^{22}$ | $t\int^h\tilde{\imath}\text{-}tsi^{22}$ |
   |---|---|---|
   | dog=DEF=ERG | cat=DEF=P | catch-PRF |

   'The dog caught the cat.'

e. | $k^hi{=}tse^{22}$ | $siki^{22}$ | $ts\Lambda\text{-}tsi^{22}$ |
   |---|---|---|
   | 3SG=ERG | food | eat-PRF |

   'He ate (the) food.'

f. | $kj\Lambda^{52}$ | $t^han{=}ri^{22}$ | $tu\text{-}tsu^{22}$ | $mo^{22}$ |
   |---|---|---|---|
   | 2SG | floor=LOC | sit-PROG | COP |

   'You are sitting on the floor.'

g. | $\eta\Lambda{=}l\Lambda^{22}$ | $umu{=}tse^{22}$ | $\eta\Lambda{=}ri^{22}$ | $m^w\tilde{\imath}^{42}$ | $p^hr\Lambda^{42}$ | $p\tilde{\imath}\text{-}tsi^{22}$ |
   |---|---|---|---|---|---|
   | 1SG=GEN | mother=ERG | 1SG=LOC | money | hundred | give-PRF |

   'My mother gave me one hundred rupees (unit of money).'

h. | $nakju^{22}$ | $n\Lambda\text{-}p\Lambda{=}ko^{22}$ | $nu\text{-}tsi^{42}$ |
   |---|---|---|
   | dog | sick-NMLZ–DEF | sleep-PRF |

   'The sick dog slept.'

i. | $naran^{22}$ | $lo{=}ri^{52}$ | $\eta\Lambda^{22}$ | $nepal{=}ri$ | $j\Lambda\text{-}tsi^{22}$ |
   |---|---|---|---|---|
   | before | year=LOC | 1SG | Nepal=LOC | go-PRF |

   'Last year I went to Nepal.'

j. | $\eta\Lambda{=}tse^{22}$ | $\eta\Lambda{=}l\Lambda^{22}$ | $kikja{=}ri$ | $m^w\tilde{\imath}^{42}$ | $p^hr\Lambda^{42}$ | $jan\text{-}tsi^{22}$ |
   |---|---|---|---|---|---|
   | 1SG=ERG | 1SG=GEN | pocket=LOC | money | hundred | find/get-PRF |

   'I found one hundred rupees in my pocket.'

**LANGUAGE PROFILE 4**

# Finnish

## 4.1 Introduction

Finnish, called *suomi* by its speakers, is spoken mainly in the country of Finland. There are sizable minorities of speakers of Finnish in Sweden and in western Russia, and smaller groups in other Scandinavian countries, Estonia, Australia, and North America. This area is displayed in Figure LP4.1. There are approximately 6 million speakers of Finnish.

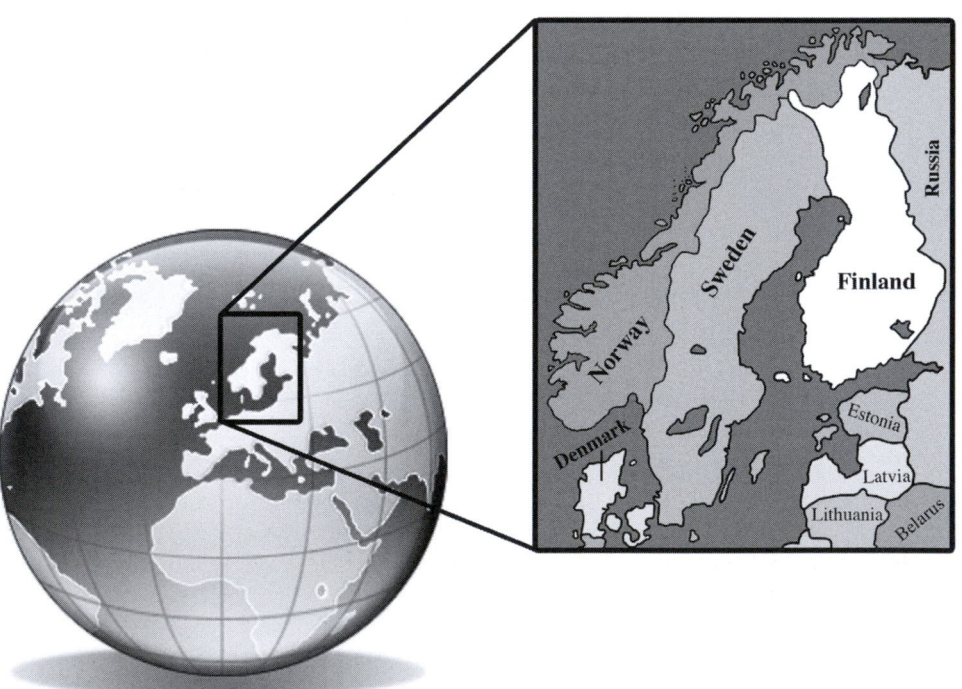

**Figure LP4.1** The geographical area where Finnish is spoken

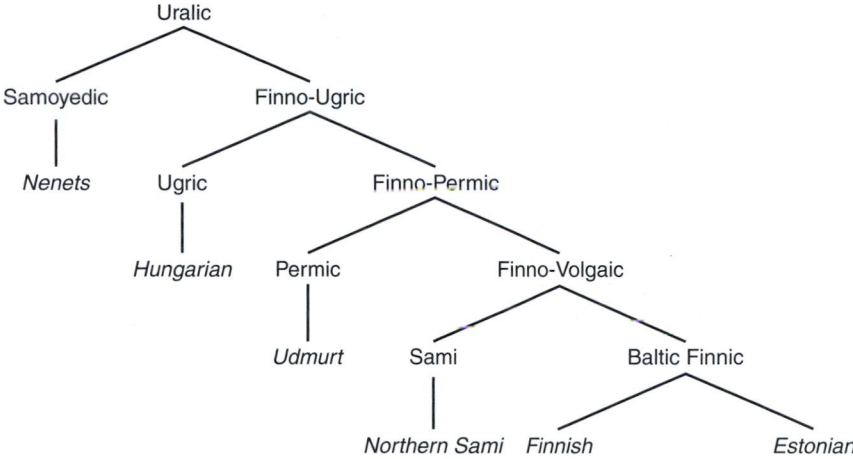

**Figure LP4.2** Uralic family tree (simplified; language listed are examples)

### 4.1.1  Genetic affiliation

Finnish belongs to the Baltic-Finnic branch of the Finno-Ugric family of languages which is in turn a part of the Uralic family. Some of its closest relatives are Meänkieli, a minority language spoken in Sweden, and Estonian. Finnish is also related to the Sami languages spoken in Lapland and to Hungarian, and more distantly to the Samoyed languages, which form the other group of the Uralic languages in addition to the Finno-Ugric languages.

### 4.1.2  Official status and viability

Finnish is one of the two official languages of Finland and is spoken by more than 90 percent of Finns as a first language. The other official language is Swedish, spoken by less than 6 percent of the population (see Textbox LP4.1). Finnish is one of the official languages of the European Union, and it also has official status as

---

TEXTBOX LP4.1 **BILINGUAL STREET SIGNS**

All street signs in Helsinki are in both Finnish and Swedish, with Finnish, the majority language in the municipality, on top, and Swedish, the minority language, on the bottom. In areas where Swedish speakers are in the majority, Swedish is on top.

The sign shown in Figure LP4.3 is on *Yliopistonkatu* 'University Street.' The word *yliopisto* 'university' is formed from native sources, but the word *katu* 'street' is borrowed from Swedish, as you might notice by comparing it to the Swedish name of the street (*Universitetsgatan*). All blocks in downtown Helsinki have names. This block is named for the giraffe, *kirahvi*, although the only giraffes in Finland are at the zoo.

**Figure LP4.3** Bilingual street sign in Helsinki.

a minority language in Sweden. All Finnish-speaking residents of the Nordic countries are entitled to use their language in official contexts. In Finland, education in Finnish is available through the university level, there is a productive literary tradition, and all types of media are available in Finnish. For these reasons, in spite of its relatively small speech community, Finnish is not endangered.

## 4.2 Typological overview

### 4.2.1 Phonology

Finnish has a relatively simple inventory of consonants: it has three voiceless stops [p, t, k], one voiced stop [d] (some dialects, though, lack this sound), three nasals [m, n, ŋ], three fricatives [s, h, v], two liquids [l, r], and the semivowel [j]. Borrowed words can also contain [b] and [g].

Finnish has eight vowels. In the International Phonetic Alphabet these are represented as [i, e, y, ø, æ, a, u, o]. Two of the vowels, [y] and [ø], are front rounded

**TABLE LP4.1** Inessive and allative nouns illustrating vowel harmony patterns

| INESSIVE | | ALLATIVE | | |
|----------|----------|----------|----------|----------|
| Singular | Plural | Singular | Plural | |
| [kylæ-ssæ] | [kyl-i-ssæ] | [kylæ-lle] | [kyl-i-lle] | 'village' |
| [pøydæ-ssæ] | [pøyd-i-ssæ] | [pøydæ-lle] | [pøyd-i-lle] | 'table' |
| [kuva-ssa] | [kuv-i-ssa] | [kuva-lle] | [kuv-i-lle] | 'picture' |
| [koira-ssa] | [koir-i-ssa] | [koira-lle] | [koir-i-lle] | 'dog' |

vowels, which are pronounced with the tongue position of [i] and [e] respectively, but with the lips fully rounded. These sounds are relatively uncommon in the world's languages; however, they may be familiar to you from French (e.g., [y] in *rue* 'street,' and [ø] in *peu* 'few'), German (e.g., [y] in *kühe* 'cows' and [ø] in *schön* 'beautiful'), or Cantonese (e.g., [y] in *syu¹* 'book' and [ø] in *heu¹* 'boots'). English lacks these vowels.

Finnish also has quite a few diphthongs, among them are [yø], [øy], [ie], [æi], [ui], and [iu]. Some of these diphthongs form whole words, e.g., [yø] *yö* 'night' and [ui] *ui* 'swim!'

Finnish has **vowel harmony**; this means that only certain vowels can occur with each other in Finnish words. Three of the front vowels, [y, ø, æ], cannot occur in the same word with any of the back vowels [a, o, u]. However, the other two front vowels, [i, e], are neutral with respect to vowel harmony: they can occur in the same word with either of the other two groups of vowels. These patterns can be seen in Table LP4.1, which provides examples of singular and plural nouns with two case suffixes, the inessive (-*ssA*; where the capitalized vowel symbol indicates that it undergoes harmony) and the **allative** (-*lle*). (More information on Finnish case-marking is given below.) Notice that the vowels in the singular and inessive suffixes are affected by vowel harmony: the front vowel [æ] is found when the root has [y] or [ø]; and the back vowel [a] is found when the root contains [u] or [o]. Contrast this with the vowel in the allative suffix and with the plural [i], which are neutral vowels and so do not change.

Finnish has both long vowels and long consonants; thus, length is phonemic for both consonants and vowels. We can see this in the two minimal sets in Example (1).

**(1)** | [tuli] | 'fire' | [muta] | 'mud' |
| [tu:li] | 'wind' | [mu:ta] | 'other' |
| [tul:i] | 'customs' | [mut:a] | 'but' |

**SIDEBAR LP4.1**

GEMINATE CONSONANTS

Geminate consonants occur only rarely in English, when they arise across morpheme boundaries. For example, there is a geminate /n/ in the word *unnamed* (compare this with *unaimed*). Geminate consonants may also be familiar to you if you have heard native pronunciations of Italian; e.g., there is a geminate stop before the final vowel in *spaghetti*.

Long consonants are also called **geminate** consonants (see Sidebar LP4.1). In addition to having increased duration, they form a bridge across two syllables, closing off one and starting another.

Stress is predictable in Finnish: it always falls on the first syllable of a word.

### 4.2.2 Morphology

Finnish has a relatively complex system of inflectional morphology, especially on nouns, adjectives, and pronouns (referred to as **nominals** in Finnish linguistics). It is especially known for its case-marking; it has one of the largest numbers of cases of any language in the world. A given nominal can have up to fifteen different case forms. Case-marking will be discussed in detail below.

Finnish is predominantly a suffixing language. Number, case, and agreement with a possessor are all suffixed on nominals, while tense, mood, and person are suffixed on verbs. There is also a system of clitics, which occur on various word classes and have a variety of meanings. One example is the question clitic =*kO* (which undergoes vowel harmony; the capital O in the transcription means that one of two vowels, [o] or [ø], can occur there, depending on the harmonic pattern of the root). This can be affixed to a questioned constituent of any word class. Some examples of words with complex morphology are given in (2). A transcription note and the meanings of the morpheme glosses are given in Sidebar LP4.2; use the Sidebar to work through each example and see how the meanings in (2) are composed.

**SIDEBAR LP4.2**

TRANSCRIPTION NOTE

| Finnish orthography | IPA |
| --- | --- |
| ä | [æ] |
| ö | [ø] |

**Glosses**

| | |
| --- | --- |
| AD | adessive ('on') |
| POSS | possessive |
| COND | conditional ('if') |
| CLT | clitic |
| Q | interrogative |
| PST | past |
| PRS | present |
| 3PL | third-person plural |
| PRT | partitive ('part of,' 'some') |
| PTCP | participle |
| NEG | negative |
| ESS | essive ('as,' 'at') |

(2)  Finnish suffixes

   a. *matko-i-lla-ni*
      travel-PL-AD-1SG.POSS
      'on my trips'

   b. *mets-i-ssä-mme*
      forest-PL-INE-1PL.POSS
      'in our forests'

c. *osa-isi-n=ko=han*
   be.able-CONS-1SG=Q=CLT
   'I wonder if I might be able to.'

d. *luk-i-vat=kin*
   read-PST-3PL=CLT
   'They also read.'

e. *keräs-i-mme=kö*
   gather-PST-1PL=Q
   'Did we gather?'

Finnish has two tense suffixes, present and past, as illustrated in (3).

(3)  Finnish tenses

a. *äiti*     *teke-e*     *täs*    *ruoka-a*
   mother  make-3SG.PRS  PROX  food-PRT
   'Mother fixes food here.'

b. *äiti*     *tek-i*      *täs*    *ruoka-a*
   mother  make-3SG.PST  PROX  food-PRT
   'Mother fixed food here.'

Perfect and past-perfect forms can be composed using the verb *olla* 'be' as an auxiliary. The main verb is in a form called a participle. Examples are given in (4).

(4)  a. *äiti*     *on*      *teh-ny*    *täs*    *ruoka-a*
      mother  COP.3SG  make-PTCP  PROX  food-PRT
      'Mother has fixed food here.'

b. *äiti*     *ol-i*     *teh-ny*    *täs*    *ruoka-a*
   mother  COP-PST  make-PTCP  PROX  food
   'Mother had fixed food here.'

Finnish also uses a special auxiliary verb to mark negation. This verb has limited inflection. It does have person marking; however, it does not inflect for tense. The tense is indexed by the different forms of the main verb, as can be seen by comparing (5) and (6).

(5)  *e-n*     *ol-e*    *nyt*    *koto-na*
   NEG-1SG  COP-PRS  now   home-ESS
   'I am not at home now.'

(6)  *e-n*     *ol-lut*    *eilen*     *koto-na*
   NEG-1SG  COP-PTCP  yesterday  home-ESS
   'I was not at home yesterday.'

### 4.2.3  Syntax

#### Adpositions

Finnish has both prepositions and postpositions, although postpositions are more common. The dependent noun phrases that occur with prepositions are most commonly in the partitive case, while those that occur with postpositions are most commonly in the genitive case. (The cases are discussed below.) You can see this difference in case on the pronoun that occurs with the preposition in (7), and that which occurs with the postposition in (8).

(7)    *ilman*        *sinu-a*
       without       2SG-PRT
       'without you'

(8)    *sinu-n*       *kanssasi*
       2SG-GEN       with
       'with you'

   Some adpositions can be used as both prepositions and postpositions, and may accordingly co-occur with noun phrases which are either partitive or genitive. For these adpositions, there may be a difference in meaning in postpositional and prepositional use, as illustrated below for *ympäri* 'around.'

(9)    *talo-n*                   *ympäri*
       house-GEN                 around
       'around the (circumference of) house'

(10)   *ympäri*       *talo-a*
       around        house-PRT
       '(scattered) around the house'

#### Constituent order

Constituent order in Finnish can said to be flexible, as there is no arrangement of S, V, and O in a basic sentence that is ungrammatical; that is, all the orders in (11) are grammatical in Finnish. However, when the language is used, SVO is the overwhelmingly most common word order, a fact that can be determined by quantitative analysis of both written and spoken Finnish discourse.

(11)   Possible constituent orders in Finnish
       *Marja*        *syö*          *omenoit-a*
       Marja.NOM      eat.3SG        apple.PL-PRT
       'Marja is eating apples.'

|       |       |       |
|-------|-------|-------|
| *syö* | *Marja* | *omenoita* |
| *omenoita* | *Marja* | *syö* |
| *omenoita* | *syö* | *Marja* |
| *Marja* | *omenoita* | *syö* |
| *syö* | *omenoita* | *Marja* |

## 4.3  Case in Finnish

As noted above, Finnish is rich in case morphology. In a study of 261 languages, only 24 were found to have more than ten cases (Iggesen 2011). The largest number of cases that has been found in a single language is twenty-one. These were in Hungarian, a language related to Finnish. Finnish itself has fourteen productive cases. These are presented in Table LP4.2 below, which shows the inflection of the noun *talo* 'house.' The names of the cases (taken from Latin) are also given. The meanings of the cases and uses of the cases will be discussed below.

The nominative, partitive, accusative, and sometimes also the genitive are the core cases in Finnish; they are used to mark core arguments such as subjects and objects. The rest of the cases are the oblique cases, which mostly code a variety of locational semantic roles (these expand the inventory given in Chapter 6, section 6.3.5).

### 4.3.1  Core cases

Most subjects in Finnish are in nominative case. The Finnish verb agrees with the subject when it is nominative, as in Example (12) below. Objects can be in the

**Table LP4.2** The fourteen Finnish cases, illustrated with the noun *talo* 'house'

| | | |
|---|---|---|
| NOMINATIVE | talo | |
| GENITIVE/ACCUSATIVE | talo-n | core cases |
| PARTITIVE | talo-a | |
| INESSIVE | talo-ssa | |
| ELATIVE | talo-sta | |
| ILLATIVE | talo-on | |
| ADESSIVE | talo-lla | |
| ABLATIVE | talo-lta | |
| ALLATIVE | talo-lle | oblique cases |
| TRANSLATIVE | talo-ksi | |
| ESSIVE | talo-na | |
| ABESSIVE | talo-tta | |
| INSTRUCTIVE | talo-in | |
| COMITATIVE | talo-ineen | |

accusative case or the partitive case. Objects are in the accusative case if the referent of the object is affected by the action of the verb. If the referent is not affected, then the object is in partitive case. For example, objects in negated sentences, in which, of course, the object is not affected at all, are in the partitive, as in (12).

(12)  *minä         e-n          juo          kahvi-a*
      1SG.NOM    NEG-1SG    drink      coffee-PRT
      'I'm not drinking coffee; I don't drink coffee.'

In addition, the object is in partitive case when the referent of the object NP is indefinite, when it is only partially affected by the action expressed by the verb, or when the verb does not refer to specific events with completed endpoints. Hence the partitive case is found in (13).

(13)  *äiti            tek-i          täs          ruoka-a*
      mother.NOM    make-PST    here      food-PRT
      'Mother fixed food here.'

This clause does not express a particular instance of Mother cooking, with a clear endpoint, or particular food being prepared, but rather a generic process of food-making without a clear endpoint. Contrast this with Example (14), where the accusative case occurs.

(14)  *mummo=kin         aina          laitta-a          se-n          laakeese-en*
      grandma.NOM=CLT    always      put-3SG        3SG-ACC    shallow-ILL
      'Grandma also always puts it in a shallow [dish].'

Here, the action has a clear endpoint of the food being in the shallow dish. Also, after Grandma puts the food in the shallow dish, it has been affected by being transferred into a location.

   Recipients in ditransitive clauses are also core arguments; they are in the allative case as exemplified in (15).

(15)  *minä         osta-n          sinu-lle          kahvi-n*
      1SG.NOM    buy-GEN       2SG-ALL        coffee-ACC
      'I'm buying/will buy you a (cup of) coffee.'

### 4.3.2  Oblique cases

The oblique cases convey a wide range of meanings, which are roughly summarized in Table LP4.3.

   As you can see, the majority of the meanings are concerned with spatial arrangement and movement trajectories; these are termed "local cases" (similar to the locative case in other languages) as they indicate different types of location.

**Table LP4.3** The Finnish oblique cases (also called "local cases") and their meanings

| Latin term | Inflection of *talo* 'house' | Approximate meanings |
| --- | --- | --- |
| INESSIVE | talo-ssa | 'in, inside' |
| ELATIVE | talo-sta | 'from (the interior of)' |
| ILLATIVE | talo-on | 'into' |
| ADESSIVE | talo-lla | 'on, at, near' |
| ABLATIVE | talo-lta | 'from the outside/surface/vicinity of' |
| ALLATIVE | talo-lle | 'onto' |
| TRANSLATIVE | talo-ksi | 'for, (transformed) into' |
| ESSIVE | talo-na | 'as, at' |
| ABESSIVE | talo-tta | 'without' |
| INSTRUCTIVE | talo-in | 'with, by means of' |
| COMITATIVE | talo-ine-en | 'accompanied/equipped with' |

**SIDEBAR LP4.3**
**REGIONAL DIFFERENCES IN PRONOUNS**
You may have noted that the first-person singular pronoun here is *mää*, while in previous examples it was *minä*. This represents regional variation (see Chapter 11). The presence of socially determined variation is frequently a feature of examples taken from naturally occurring discourse, such as these.

Finnish has both an "internal" and an "external" set of local cases. To simplify slightly, the basic meaning of the internal local cases (the inessive, elative, and illative) is to express movement to or from, or location *on the inside of* some reference point. The external cases (adessive, ablative, and allative) express movement to or from, or location *on the outside of* something. Consider the following examples. (Sidebar LP4.3 contains a note on regional variation.)

(16) 1. *ja      si-in        puu-hella-lla*
         and    there-LAT    wood-stove-AD
         'and there on the wood stove'

     2. *kerran     ni*
         once       PTC
         'one time'

     3. *mää      illa-lla        paisto-i-n*
         1SG      evening-AD      fry-PST-1SG
         'I was frying [mushrooms] in the evening.'

In line 1, the noun *puuhellalla* 'on the wood stove' is in the adessive case; the choice of case here could be thought to be motivated by the fact that frying happens on the outside surface of the stove, with the stove providing support. Compare this with the next example.

(17)  1 *kana*      *tul-i*        *sisä-än*      *ja*
      chicken    come-PST    inside-ILL    and
      '[A] chicken came in and'

    2 *hyppä-s*       *kiisseli-vati-in*
      jump-PST      pudding-dish-ILL
      'jumped into [a] pudding dish'

In line 2, the word *kiisselivatiin* 'into the pudding dish' is in the illative case. Here, the case can be thought to express the movement of the chicken to the inside of the pudding dish. Notice also that the adverb *sisään* in line 1 is in the illative case as well. It is not uncommon for locational adverbs and even adpositions to have partial paradigms in the locative cases; this is the case with the adverb *sisä-*, which has forms for all the local cases. See Textbox LP4.2 for a note on the historical development of cases in Finnish.

---

**TEXTBOX LP4.2  A HISTORICAL NOTE ON THE DEVELOPMENT OF FINNISH CASES**

The internal and external local cases developed relatively recently, perhaps from postpositions. Before that, the partitive, the essive, and the lative cases expressed location. They expressed, respectively, movement from, location in, and movement to a reference point. These cases are still used in connection with some adverbials. For example, the partitive is used to express motion away in *ulko-a* 'from the outside' and *koto-a* 'from home.' We find the essive used in expressions indicating static location, such as *ulko-na* 'outside' and *koto-na* 'at home.' With most nouns in modern Finnish, the partitive is a core case, marking objects (as discussed above), and the essive expresses a state or role, e.g., *opettaja-na* 'as a teacher,' *sairaa-na* '(while being) sick.' The lative shows up in certain adverbs such as *ulo-s* 'out, to the outdoors.'

---

## 4.4  A syntactic conundrum: the habitive construction

The local cases are a considerable resource in the Finnish language. They are also used to express more abstract relations than mere location. An important use of the adessive case is in a particular type of possessive construction called the habitive. This construction is one way that Finnish indicates possession, a function accomplished in English by the verb *to have*.

(18)  1 *mä*      *muista-n*        *sillon*    *ku*
      1SG       remember-1SG    then      when
      'I remember then when'

2  ***mei-ll***    ***ol-i***     ***se***    *Hirvensalo-n*       *saunakamari*
   1PL-AD      COP-PST     DEM     Hirvensalo-GEN      sauna.room.NOM
   'we had the Hirvensalo sauna room'

3  *ol-i*      *viel*    *semmose-s*     *asuttava-s*          *kunno-ssa*
   COP-PST    still    such-INE       live.PASS.PTCP-INE    condition-INE
   '(We) had (it) in a liveable condition'

In the Finnish habitive construction, the possessor NP (in this example *mei-ll(ä)*) is in the adessive case, and the head noun of the possessed NP is in either the nominative (e.g., *Hirvensalon saunakamari* 'the Hirvensalo sauna room' in this example), the partitive, or (if the possessed NP is a pronoun) the accusative case. (See Textbox LP4.3 for more on *saunakamari* in Finland.)

---

### TEXTBOX LP4.3  **THE SAUNAKAMARI IN FINLAND**

The sauna (steam bath) is an important part of traditional Finnish culture. The term *saunakamari* literally means 'sauna room,' but this is not a very satisfactory translation. The word refers to a room in a sauna building. Traditionally this room was separate from the room with the sauna itself and could be used as a dressing room. In earlier times, a sauna was often built on a new farm before the main living building was built, and in that case, the *saunakamari* could be used as an initial living space with cooking and sleeping facilities. The photograph in Figure LP4.4 shows a modern *saunakamari*. It is used as a sauna dressing room, but it also serves as an extra sleeping area. There is also a hot plate – suitable for simple cooking – on top of the wood stove, with which the room can be heated during the cold time of the year.

---

This causes problems for the constituency analysis of the possessive construction. What should be considered the subject of the expression? Most Finnish subjects are nominative, are clause-initial, and trigger agreement in the verb. An example is the first clause in line 1, *mä muista-n* 'I remember,' where the clause-initial subject is a nominative first-person pronoun and the verb is accordingly in the first-person singular form.

The possessive construction has two core arguments: the possessor and the possessed. Which is the subject? The possessor argument is not a very good candidate, since it is in an oblique case (the adessive), and the verb does not agree with it in either person or number; the possessor is a first-person plural pronoun, but the verb is in the third-person singular form.

On the other hand, the possessed noun phrase is not a very typical subject either. It is clause-final and although it can be in the nominative case, as in Example (18) above, it can also be in the partitive or even the accusative case. As the partitive and accusative cases are typically found on objects (see Textbox LP4.4), there is an inherent contradiction between the possessed noun carrying these case-markers and the grammatical relation of subject.

**Figure LP4.4.** A modern *saunakamari* (photo by Raimo Hyvönen)

---

TEXTBOX LP4.4 **WHY PARTITIVE CASE FOR OBJECTS?**

As we have seen, Finnish shows clear historical evidence of a dynamic interaction between core and oblique cases. Oblique cases have been recruited into more grammatical uses and so now mark core arguments.

How might a noun phrase carrying an oblique case-marker – such as the partitive – be reanalyzed as a grammatical object? Consider Example (a), which has a partitive noun phrase.

a. *söimme          kala-a*
   eat-PST-1PL      fish-PRT
   'We ate (some) fish'

In modern Finnish, this clause, with its partitive noun phrase, means 'we ate (some) fish,' where *kala-a* is a partitive-marked object. Earlier, however, it might have meant something like 'we ate from the fish,' where the partitive noun phrase would have been oblique. Of course, a person eating *from* a fish logically entails a person eating fish, so semantically it makes sense to reinterpret the oblique locational noun phrase as a (core) object. Some of the semantics of the partitive expression remain, including the implication that only a partial, indefinite amount of the fish was eaten.

This example shows that there is a dynamic interplay between core and oblique cases, with the semantics of specific cases allowing for reinterpretation of the grammatical nature of arguments.

---

There is further evidence that the possessed noun phrase has the syntactic behavior of an object. This is found in the negation of the habitive construction, which necessarily puts the possessed noun phrase in the partitive case, as in (19), which is the negated counterpart of (18).

(19)  *mei-ll*      *ei*       *ol-lut*           *si-tä*
     1PL-AD     NEG      be-PST.PTCP     DEM-PRT

     *Hirvensalo-n*           *sauna-kamari-a*
     Hirvensalo-GEN           sauna-room-PRT
     'We didn't have that Hirvensalo sauna room.'

Compare this with the marking of the object in the affirmative and negative versions of the simple transitive clause in (20) and (21).

(20)  *toinen*       *on*       *laitta-nu*        *se-n*          *vielä*
     another      COP      fix-PST.PTCP     3SG-ACC       even
     'Someone else has even fixed it.'

(21)  *toinen*       *ei*       *oo*       *laitta-nu*        *si-tä*         *vielä*
     another      NEG      COP      fix-PST.PTCP     3SG-PRT       even
     'Someone else hasn't even fixed it.'

In these examples, the object *se-n* is in the accusative case in the affirmative version in (20), yet in the partitive case, *si-tä*, in the negative version in (21). The shift to partitive under negation shows an exact syntactic parallel between the possessed noun phrase in the habitive construction and the object noun phrase of a transitive clause.

We may thus want to say that in the habitive construction, there is not very good evidence at all for the existence of a subject constituent, even though ordinary Finnish transitive and intransitive clauses give clear evidence of subject and object constituents. Thus, it is reasonable to consider Finnish a nominative-accusative language (see Textbox LP8.3 in the Bardi Language Profile for a brief discussion of nominative-accusative versus other types of alignment systems), but to recognize that the grammatical relations of subject and object are not relevant in every type of construction. (This is also true for English; consider cases such as *There is a boat* or *It is raining*.)

---

TEXTBOX LP4.5 **GLOSSING CONVENTIONS USED IN THIS LANGUAGE PROFILE**

| Convention | Meaning | Convention | Meaning |
|---|---|---|---|
| 1 | first person | ESS | essive |
| 2 | second person | GEN | genitive |
| 3 | third person | ILL | illative |
| ACC | accusative | IMPRS | impersonal |
| AD | adessive | INE | inessive |
| ALL | allative | INF | infinitive |
| CLT | clitic | LAT | lative |
| CONS | mutual consent | NEG | negation |
| COP | copula | NOM | nominative |
| DEM | demonstrative | PASS | passive |

| Convention | Meaning | Convention | Meaning |
|---|---|---|---|
| PL | plural | PST.PTCP | past participle |
| POSS | possessive | PTC | particle |
| PROX | proximal | PTCP | particple |
| PRS | present tense | Q | interrogative |
| PRT | partitive | SG | singular |
| PST | past tense | | |

## SUGGESTIONS FOR FURTHER READING

**Cambell, Lyle and Marja-Liisa Helasvuo**. 2006. *Grammar from the human perspective: Case, space, and person in Finnish*. CILT 277. Amsterdam: John Benjamins.

This book has a number of interesting articles on various aspects of Finnish, especially on case-marking.

**Huumo, Tuomas**. 2010. "On directionality and its motivation in Finnish expressions of sensory perception." *Linguistics* **48**.1: 49–97.

This article concerns the use of local cases with verbs of perception. This would be interesting reading for those who might be intrigued by Exercise 3.

**Karlsson, Fred**. 2008. *Finnish: An essential grammar*, 2nd edn. London and New York: Routledge.

This is a complete and easily approachable reference grammar of Finnish.

## EXERCISES

1. Finnish exhibits a series of alternations in consonants referred to as 'lenition.' This can be seen in the examples below, which show the regular consonant realization that is found in both the nominative and partitive forms, and the 'lenited' consonant realization that is found in the genitive forms.

   a. List each change exemplified in the data (e.g., t > d).
   b. Which natural classes of sound are affected by the lenition process?

   Can you write any general rules that apply to more than one example?

   c. What would you predict would be the genitive form of *kukka* 'flower'?

   |  | NOM | PRT | GEN | |
   |---|---|---|---|---|
   | i. | mato | matoa | madon | 'worm' |
   | ii. | tapa | tapaa | tavan | 'manner' |
   | iii. | ratti | rattia | ratin | 'steering wheel' |
   | iv. | tauko | taukoa | tauon | 'pause' |
   | v. | tappi | tappia | tapin | 'plug' |
   | vi. | vaara | vaaraa | vaaran | 'danger' |
   | vii. | kello | kelloa | kellon | 'bell' |
   | viii. | runo | runoa | runon | 'poem' |

2. Finnish local cases. On the basis of what you have read about the Finnish local cases, try to determine which local case the boldfaced NP should be in.

   a. Laitoin lasit **kaappi**___     'I put the glasses in the cupboard.'
   b. **Pöydä**___ on kukkia.     'There are flowers on the table.'
   c. Istahdin **terassi**___     'I sat down on the patio.'
   d. Unohdin laukkuni **bussi**__     'I left my purse on the bus.'
   e. Poika liukastui **jää**___     'The boy slipped on the ice.'
   f. Polka liukastui **jää**___     'The boy slipped (and fell) on the ice.'
   g. **Metsä**__ on pimeää     'It's dark in the forest.'
   h. Näin paraatin **terassi**___     'I saw the parade from the patio.'
   i. Liimasin tarran **puskuri**__     'I glued the sticker on the bumper.'
   j. Kiinnitin koukun **seinä**__     'I fastened the hook onto the wall.'

3. Explain these unconventional uses of English prepositions made by Finnish speakers, based on what you know about Finnish cases. Can you make a guess as to why there is no preposition before 'lost articles' in (b)?

   a. Sign seen in a University of Helsinki bathroom:
      No hand towels **into** the toilet bowl

   b. Sign seen at the indoor food shopping hall, Kauppahalli, in Helsinki:
      Ask your lost articles **from** the hall supervisor

4. Consider the case of the subject in the following examples. When are subjects marked as genitive? What happens with verb agreement with genitive subjects?

   a. *vielä=kö*    *te*    *leiki-tte*    *täällä*
      still=Q    2PL    play-2PL    PROX
      'Are you still playing here?'

   b. *teidä-n*    *pitä-ä*    *nyt*    *menn-ä*    *nukku-ma-an*
      2PL-GEN    must.3SG.PRS    now    go-1.INF    sleep-3.INF-ILL
      'You must go and sleep now.'

   c. *on=ko*    *meidä-n*    *pakko*
      COP=Q    1PL-GEN    force
      'Do we have to?'

   d. *me*    *halua-mme*    *vielä*    *leikki-ä*
      1PL    want-1PL    still    play-1.INF
      'We still want to play.'

   e. *no*    *ei*    *teidä-n*    *ihan*    *heti*    *tarvitse*    *menn-ä*
      PTC    NEG.3SG    2PL-GEN    quite    immediately    need    go-1.INF
      'Well, you don't need to go right away.'

   f. *e-mme*    *me*    *enää*    *kaua-a*    *leiki*
      NEG-1PL    1PL    any.more    long-PRT    play
      'We won't play for a long time.'

5. Finnish object case. In this exercise, objects are marked either as accusative, with the suffix *-n*, or as partitive, with the suffix *-a*, or they are nominative, with no suffix. Determine under what conditions objects are nominative in Finnish. (Note: Examples h–j have a suffix glossed 'impersonal' which is used in a syntactic construction where the subject is unexpressed.)

   a. *lu-i-n*    *kirja-n*
      read-PST-1SG    book-ACC
      'I read a/the book.'

b. *lu-i-n*              *kirja-a*
   read-PST-1SG       book-PRT
   'I was reading a/the book.'

c. *osta*                *auto*
   buy.2SG.IMP        car
   'Buy a car!'

d. *\*osta*      *auto-a*

e. *\*osta*      *auto-n*

f. *e-n*              *osta*      *auto-a*
   NEG-1SG          buy        car-PRT
   'I won't buy a/the car.'

g. *osta-n*              *auto-n*
   buy-1SG             car-ACC
   'I'm buying/going to buy a car.'

h. *oste-taan*                  *auto*
   buy-IMPRS                 car
   '(Some people) buy a car/let's buy a car.'

i. *juo-daan*                  *olut-ta*
   drink-IMPRS               beer-PRT
   '(Some people) drink beer/let's drink beer.'

j. *juo-daan*                      *olut*
   drink-IMPRS                   beer
   '(Some people) drink a beer/let's drink a beer.'

k. *halua-n*      *osta-a*          *auto-n*
   want-1SG      buy-INF          car-ACC
   'I want to buy a car.'

l. *minu-n*      *pitää*      *osta-a*          *auto*
   1SG-GEN      must        buy-1.INF      car
   'I must buy a car.'

m. *minu-lla*      *on*      *ajatus*      *osta-a*      *auto*
   1SG-AD        COP      thought      buy-1.INF    car
   'I have an idea to buy a car.'

**LANGUAGE PROFILE 5**

# Nuuchahnulth (Nootka)

## 5.1 Introduction

Nuuchahnulth [nu:tʃa:ʔnuɬ] is spoken on the west coast of Vancouver Island in south-western British Columbia, Canada. The language and the people were formerly known as *Nootka*, a name used since the time of contact by Captain Cook. However, since the name *Nuuchahnulth* (meaning '[those who live] all along the mountains') was adopted as the official designation by the Nuuchahnulth people in 1978, it has been the preferred designation for themselves and their language.

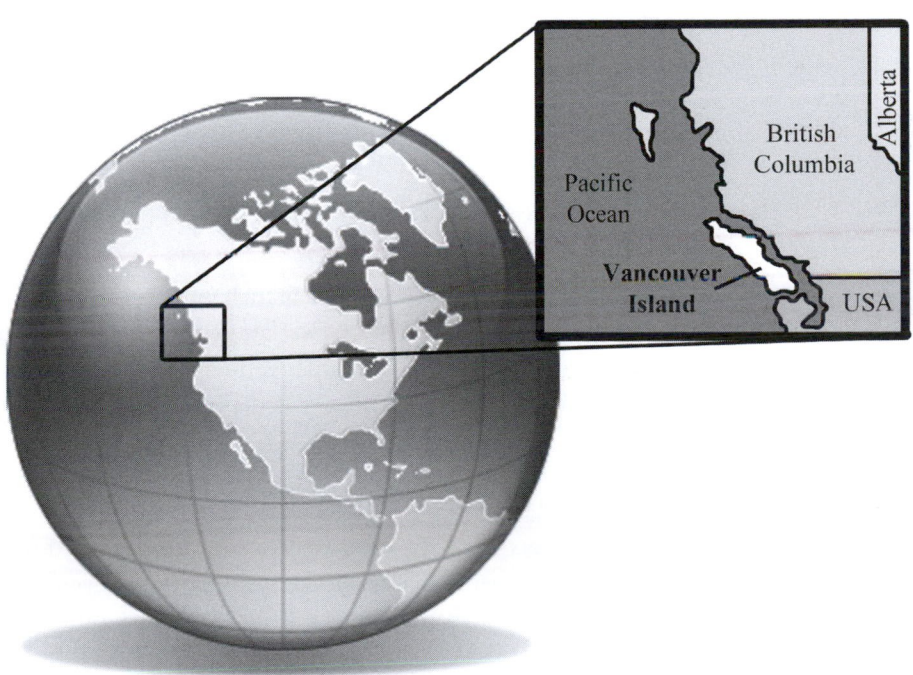

**Figure LP5.1** Vancouver Island

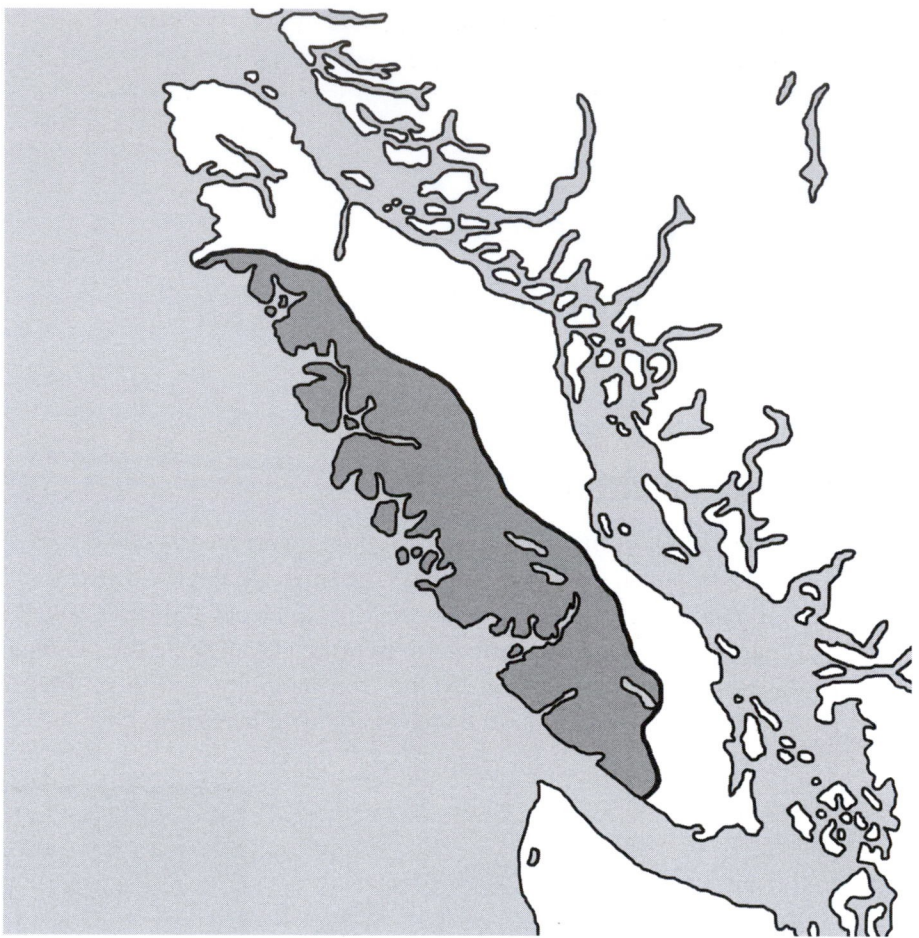

**Figure LP5.2** Map of Nuuchahnulth area on Vancouver Island

Nuuchahnulth belongs to the southern branch of the Wakashan language family. There is a significant amount of dialectal variation within the language, especially in phonology. However, due to language endangerment and amalgamation among various groups that were previously distinct, the dialectal differences are being lost to a certain degree.

### 5.1.1   Speech community

The number of speakers has been estimated to be a few hundred, but the number is decreasing very rapidly. Most fluent speakers are in their seventies and higher and are also very fluent in English. Younger Nuuchahnulth community members are monolingual English speakers. Everyday communication within the local communities is conducted almost exclusively in English, and Nuuchahnulth is heard only occasionally, for example, in ceremonial speeches. Consequently, English is becoming the primary language of communication even for fluent Nuuchahnulth speakers, and Nuuchahnulth is not actively acquired by children. In these respects Nuuchahnulth can be characterized as a highly endangered language. Efforts to revitalize the traditional language have been made with varying degrees of success. Generally speaking, however, they have yet to make a measurable impact on the endangerment of the language.

## 5.2  Typological overview

### 5.2.1  Sound system

Nuuchahnulth, like other languages from the Pacific Northwest Coast region of North America, has a well-developed consonant system. Among the notable features are the following: some relatively uncommon sounds, most significantly **ejectives** and **pharyngeals**; a rich set of lateral consonants; and a contrast between rounded (i.e., pronounced with rounded lips and a labial-velar off-glide) and unrounded obstruents in the velar and uvular places of articulation. (Similar consonants are found in Tsez and Kabardian and discussed in those language profiles; for discussion of ejectives, see also Chapter 2, Textbox 2.3.) Nuuchahnulth lacks a voicing contrast in consonants. Instead, the primary contrast in obstruents is in **glottalized** (ejective) vs. non-glottalized (plain) consonants. The inventory of consonant phonemes in Nuuchahnulth is given in Table LP5.1; phonetic forms are given in square brackets when different from the standard Nuuchahnulth orthography. (Textbox LP5.1 discusses why orthographic practice frequently differs from the IPA. Sidebars throughout this profile provide notes on the conventions of the Nuuchahnulth writing system and on transcription.)

**TABLE LP5.1**  Nuuchahnulth consonants

| Stops/Affricates | p | t | c [ts] | ƛ [tɬ] | č [tʃ] | k | kʷ | q | qʷ | ʕ [ʔ] | ʔ |
|---|---|---|---|---|---|---|---|---|---|---|---|
| Ejectives | ṗ | t̓ | c̓ [ts̓] | ƛ' [tɬ'] | č̓ [tʃ'] | k̓ | k̓ʷ | (q̓) | (q̓ʷ) | | |
| Fricatives | | | s | ł [ɬ] | š [ʃ] | x | xʷ | (x)[χ] | (xʷ)[χʷ] | h [ħ] | h |
| Sonorants | m | n | | | y | | w | | | | |
| Glottalized sonorants | ṁ | ṅ | | | ẏ | | ẇ | | | | |

**TABLE LP5.2** Nuuchahnulth vowels

|        | Front | Center | Back  |
|--------|-------|--------|-------|
| High   | i, ii |        | u, uu |
| Low    |       | a, aa  |       |

**SIDEBAR LP5.2**

TRANSCRIPTION CONVENTION

Vowel length is indicated by the doubling of the vowel symbol, e.g., *ii* for [iː].

Glottalized sonorants, such as those found in Nuuchahnulth, are comparatively rare in the world's languages. In this language they are produced with a glottal closure preceeding the production of the sonorant. Note that orthographic conventions for Nuuchahnulth place apostrophes indicating glottalization above (not to the right of) the affected segment.

Compared to the elaboration found in the consonant system, the vowel system in Nuuchahnulth is rather simple, consisting of three vowels, *i*, *a*, and *u*, with a two-way length distinction.

Given how different the phonological inventories of English and Nuuchahnulth are, examining how English words are adapted into Nuuchahnulth is especially interesting; see Textbox LP5.2.

## TEXTBOX LP5.2 **LOANWORDS**

When words are borrowed from a foreign language, sounds and word shapes that are foreign to the language are usually modified to fit to the native morphophonological structure (this phenomenon is referred to as **adaptation** as discussed in Chapter 13, section 13.2.1). The pattern of modifications found in loanwords, therefore, provides us with an interesting perspective on the way the sound and word structures vary among languages.

The following are examples of Nuuchahnulth words borrowed from English. From the way original sounds are modified in these words, we can see the differences between Nuuchahnulth and English sound systems. Notice what happened to the consonants that are not part of the Nuuchahnulth sound system, i.e., [b], [d], and [f].

*muut* < *boat*
*taana* < *dollar*
*kʷapi* < *coffee*

More interestingly, the borrowed words began to follow the morphological patterns of the language once they started to be felt as part of the lexicon of the language. In Nuuchahnulth, free roots ending in /n/ have separate connecting forms for use with suffixes:

*saasin* 'humming bird' > *sasitq-*
*kaaʔin* 'crow' > *kaʔitq-*
*ċiitin* 'money given away at potlach' > *ċititq-*

The rule is (i) to shorten the first vowel if it is long and (ii) to replace the final /n/ with /tq/. See what happens with loanwords that end in /n/:

*saamin* 'salmon' > *samitq-* as in *samitq-ašt* 'dried salmon' (*-ašt* 'dried food')
*taawin* 'town' > *tawitq-*

Although these words originated in English, they now behave like native Nuuchahnulth words.

## 5.2.2 Word formation

Word formation in Nuuchahnulth can be very complex. The complexity is introduced exclusively through the attachment of affixes, most of which are suffixes. There is no compounding (combining of multiple roots) in Nuuchahnulth. The richest word formation is found in verbs. The suffixes involved in verb formation in Nuuchahnulth include not only those indicating grammatical relations and configurations, such as moods, persons of the subject, aspects, possessive, and causative, but also those expressing concrete lexical meanings. The suffixes of the latter kind are rather unusual cross-linguistically. Affixes commonly encode grammatical functions rather than lexical meanings.

The suffixes expressing concrete lexical meanings (sometimes called "lexical suffixes") give the word formation in Nuuchahnulth a very different feel than that in European languages. Notice the amount of information that can be packed into a single Nuuchahnulth word:

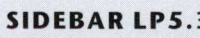

**SIDEBAR LP5.3**

NOTES ON EXAMPLES

Examples in this chapter are presented in the following four-line format:

*example as pronounced*
*morpheme breakdown of the example*
morpheme-by-morpheme glosses
Free translation

Note that the = indicates a **clitic** as opposed to a suffix. Clitics are bound morphemes with freer distribution than suffixes; see Textbox LP3.3 in Language Profile 3 (Manange) for fuller discussion.
The following abbreviations are used in the examples below:

| | |
|---|---|
| CAUS | causative |
| IND | indicative (assertion) |
| 1PL | first-person plural subject |

(1) *t̓iiʕaaqstiɬmaḥsapniš*
*t̓iqʷ-'a·qsta-'iɬ-maḥsa='ap=ni·š*
sit.down-amongst-on.the.floor-desiring.to=CAUS=IND.1PL
'We want you to sit among us.'

(2) *ʕupqswiiʕaqƛn̓uk*
*ʕupq-swi·q-'aqƛ-n̓uk*
flow.through-go.through-inside-in.hand
'He (grabbed some sand off the beach and) ran it through his fingers.'

In the above examples, each expression constitutes a single formal unit of one word and yet each expresses a rich meaning that needs to be translated as a sentence in English. Because of this characteristic, Nuuchahnulth is classified as a **polysynthetic** language (see Chapter 4, section 4.8). We will take a deeper look at the nature of the polysynthesis in Nuuchahnulth below.

### 5.2.3 Word classes

In many familiar languages, words can be divided into relatively clear word classes, as discussed in Chapter 5. In modern linguistics, the classification of words is made on the basis of the kinds of morphophonological processes they undergo (inflection or the ability to take case-markers) and of the roles they can play in a sentence (e.g., as the predicate or the subject). The word-class distinction, especially that between noun and verb, is often considered universal, that is, a feature that one should expect to find in every human language. When we examine inflected words that are being used in sentences and utterances, we can find a similar distinction in Nuuchahnulth. For example, in (3) below *hawiɬčaqšiƛuks* is functioning as a verb, whereas *maḥt̓ii* is functioning as a noun. We can determine this on the basis of the morphosyntactic characteristics of these words: for *hawiɬčaqšiƛuks* the verbal inflection and the fact that it functions as a predicate; and for *maḥt̓ii* the lack of verbal inflection and its syntactic role as an argument.

> **SIDEBAR LP5.4**
> GLOSSES
> PFV perfective aspect
> POSS possessive

(3) *hawiɬčaqšiƛuks* *maḥt̓ii*
*hawiɬ-čaq-ši(ƛ)=uk=s* *maḥt̓ii*
finish-having.done-PFV=POSS=1SG house
'I finished making my house.'

> **SIDEBAR LP5.5**
> GLOSSES AND TRANSCRIPTION NOTE
> DEF definite
> 3 third-person subject
>
> The symbol *i·*, with a "middle dot" represents a variable-length vowel, where length is dependent on the context. For more details, see Exercise 4.

Similarly, in (4) *haʕicxšiƛʔiš* and *ta:ktaʔi* can be characterized as a verb and a noun, respectively. Notice that *haʕicxšiƛʔiš* takes the verbal inflection (the third-person indicative mood=*ʔi·š*) and functions as the main predicate, and that *ta:ktaʔi* takes nominal inflection (definite =*ʔi·*) and functions as an argument.

(4)  *haʕicxšiƛʔiš*          *taaktaʔi*
     *haʕicx-ši(ƛ)=ʔi·š*     *taakta=ʔi·*
     sneeze-PFV=IND.3        doctor=DEF
     'The doctor sneezed.'

However, while it is possible to classify Nuuchahnulth words into noun and verb on the basis of their morphosyntactic behavior in sentences, this classification cannot easily be extended to lexical roots. The difficulty can be illustrated in the following set of examples:

(5)  *nunuukʔiš*            *łuucmaʔi*
     *nunuuk=ʔi·š*          *łuucma=ʔi·*
     singing=IND.3          woman=DEF
     'The woman is singing.'

(6)  *łuucmaʔiš*            *nunuukʔi*
     *łuucma=ʔi·š*          *nunuuk=ʔi·*
     woman=IND.3            singing=DEF
     'The one who is singing is a woman.'

Above we see that the same root can be put into different functions, either as a verb or a noun. The root *nunuuk* 'singing' has a verbal inflection (third-person indicative =*ʔi·š*) and is functioning as the main predicate in (5), but it has a nominal inflection (definite =*ʔi·*) and is functioning as an argument in (6). The root *łuucma* 'woman,' on the other hand, shows the opposite characteristics in the respective examples. To view this from another angle, we could say that most of Nuuchahnulth roots can be part of a verb or a noun. It is therefore not an obvious task in Nuuchahnulth to classify roots on the basis of the kinds of affixes they can take or the kinds of roles they can play within a clause.

Because of this difficulty, Nuuchahnulth is sometimes cited as a language without a word-class distinction. However, that characterization is rather misleading. First, the difficulty is concerned only with the classification of lexical roots. As stated before, we can identify verbs and nouns with respect to words in a sentence. Secondly, we can see some behavioral classes even among Nuuchahnulth roots. In particular, there seems to be a relatively clear division between roots denoting entities and those expressing actions, events, and states. The entity-like roots are more closely associated with the noun: they occur as nouns frequently and freely, but their use as verbs is very restricted in terms of frequency and meaning. The opposite is true for roots expressing actions, events, and states: they can form a verb frequently and without much restriction, but they must be attached with a definite morpheme to be used as a noun.

Thus, the apparent issue of (the lack of) the word-class distinction in Nuuchahnulth has to do with the traditional conception of the word-class distinction that often fails to sort out root-level and word-level classifications.

### 5.2.4  Basic constituent order

In Nuuchahnulth sentences, the predicate is usually placed first, followed by the subject and/or the object. The subject is more likely to precede the object when a speaker produces a sentence out of context – for example, when translating a sentence from English – but the order between the two can easily be reversed when speakers are producing natural, continuous speech.

The initial placement of the predicate is fairly rigid. A nominal argument (either subject or object) can be placed before the predicate for special emphasis, but in such cases there is an intonational break separating the preposed argument from the rest of the sentence.

A noun phrase referring to the subject or object may be omitted when its identity is already known. In natural discourse (especially in conversation), one would rarely find a sentence with both the subject and the object overtly mentioned.

### 5.2.5  Word order within NPs

A noun phrase is formed with a nominal head and its modifying elements. It is relatively rare to have a noun phrase with more than one modifying element in naturally occurring discourse. When modifiers do co-occur, they appear in a fixed order. To see this, however, one has to first understand another important aspect of Nuuchahnulth noun phrases.

When suffixes are semantically associated with a noun phrase, they are invariably attached to the first constituent of the phrase, regardless of the position of the head noun. This is illustrated in (7)–(9) below: the lexical suffix *-i·ł* 'making' is attached to the first constituent of the phrase regardless of the position of the noun *čapac* 'canoe' in these examples.

**(7)**  *čaapaciił*
čapac-i·ł
canoe-making
'He made a canoe.'

**(8)**  *ƛutiił*           *čapac*
ƛut-i·ł           čapac
nice-making     canoe
'He made a nice canoe.'

**(9)**  *ʔiiḥiił*           *ƛut*     *čapac*
ʔi·ḥ-i·ł           ƛut     čapac
greatly-making     nice     canoe
'He made a very nice canoe.'

The fact that the suffix *-i·ł* 'making' shifts its host in Examples (7)–(9) suggests that it is associated with the noun phrase as a whole rather than with any individual element within the phrase. This type of "migratory" attachment pattern is sometimes found with sentence-level inflectional elements such as mood and person morphemes, but it is uncommon to find such behavior in suffixes with rich lexical content.

Once this fact is understood, it can be seen that the order of noun-phrase elements is fixed: quantifier/numerals > property concepts > nominal. Examples (10) and (11) illustrate some complex noun phrases, which were elicited (i.e., speakers produced them as translations of English sentences). Lexical suffixes are attached to the first element in each case.

(10)  *ʔayiips*        *ʔaʔiih*        *muwač*
      *ʔaya-i·p=s*     *ʔuʔiiḥ*        *muwač*
      many-getting=1SG   large          deer
      *quantifier*      *property*       *nominal*
      'I got many big deer.'

(11)  *ʔaƛciqisʔiš*                                          *tupqumɬ*        *čapac*
      *ʔaƛ-ciq-'is=ʔi·š*                                     *tup-qumɬ*       *čapac*
      two-being.on.the.shore-being.on.the.beach=IND.3        black-rounded    canoe
      *number*                                               *property*       *nominal*
      'There are two black canoes on the beach.'

### 5.2.6  Complex meanings marked by clause combinations

Clause structure in Nuuchahnulth is comparatively simple. In other languages, a common grammatical means of introducing complexity into a clause is to use adpositions, which can introduce locational or temporal noun phrases, or relate additional participants to the main predicate. For example, in English a basic clause *John built the canoe* can be expanded with prepositional phrases: *John built the canoe with his friends on the beach*. Nuuchahnulth does not have any adpositions, so the expression of such an expanded event description involves the combination of clauses. In (12) below, the meaning expressed in English by a prepositional phrase *with the sea lion* is encoded in Nuuchahnulth as a clause *tukuuk ʔukʷink* 'being together with the sea lion' combined to the main clause *ɬaapsʔatu qawiqaaɬ* 'Qawiqaalth dove into the water.'

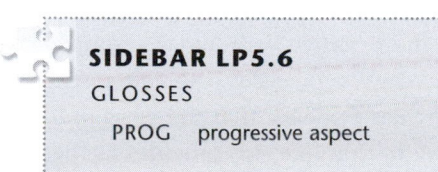

**SIDEBAR LP5.6**

GLOSSES

PROG     progressive aspect

(12)  [*ɬaapsʔatu*      *qawiqaaɬ*]       [*tukuuk*     *ʔukʷink*]
      *ɬaps-ʔatu*       *qawiqaaɬ*        *tukuuk*      *ʔu-kʷink*
      dive-sinking.     Qawiqaalth        sea.         3SG-being.
      into.water                          lion         together.with
      *main clause*                       *combined clause*
      'Qawiqaalth dove into the water with the sea lion.'

Again, in (13), what would be expressed in English as a prepositional phrase *for her grandchildren* is expressed in Nuuchahnulth as a combined clause *ʔuuʔatup kʷakuucuk* 'doing it for her grandchildren.'

(13)    *[šišaa]*      *[ʔuuʔatup*      *kʷakuucuk]*
       *šiš-(y)a·*      *ʔu-ʿatup*      *kʷakuuc=uk*
       clean-PROG      3SG-doing.for      grandchild=POSS
       *main clause*      *combined clause*
       'She would peel them for her grandchildren.'

## 5.3   Formation of negation and questions

The formation of non-declarative sentences, i.e., negation and questions, involves two different syntactic constructions in English (see Chapter 6, section 6.4). Nuuchahnulth also has separate constructions for negation and question formation, but they are quite different from those in English.

### 5.3.1   Negation

In a Nuuchahnulth negative sentence, negation is expressed through complementation (see Chapter 6, section 6.5.3). A special negative verb serves as the verb of the matrix clause, and the negated content is expressed as a complement clause. Thus, in (14), the first verb *wik* 'not' expresses negativity and the complement clause *haʔukšiƛ* 'eat' expresses the action to be negated. Since English does not negate sentences this way, it is difficult to come up with a literal translation. It is something like 'it is not that he ate,' although this conveys a strong sense of speaker assertion (compared to 'he didn't eat') that is not part of the semantics of Nuuchahnulth.

(14)    *[wikaƛ]*      *[haʔukšiƛ]*
       *wik=ʿaƛ*      *haʔuk-ši(ƛ)*
       NEG=EVENT      eat-PFV
       *negative verb*      *complement clause*
       'He did not eat.'

> **SIDEBAR LP5.7**
> GLOSSES
>    QUOT    quotative

The relative order between the negative verb and its complement is fixed: the former always precedes the latter; the predicate-initial position provides evidence that the word indicating negation is indeed a verb. Example (15) provides further evidence in that it demonstrates the ability of the word indicating negation to take verbal morphology, specifically the past-tense marker.

(15)    *[wiiẏimtwaʔiš]*      *[wiiqhap*      *maaɬuuʔisʔatḥ*    *qʷayaciik]*
       **wiiẏa**=imt=wa·ʔi·š      *wiiq-ḥap*      *maaɬuuʔisʔatḥ*    *qʷayaciik*
       <u>never</u>=PST=QUOT.3      unpleasant-      Manhousat    wolf
                               acting.like
       *negative verb*      *complement clause*

'It was said that Manhousat people never did harm to wolves.'

> ## TEXTBOX LP5.3 **POLAR VERSUS CONTENT QUESTIONS**
>
> There are two types of questions in the world's languages: polar questions (discussed in Chapter 6), which can be answered by a simple "yes" or "no" response, and content questions (sometimes called "WH questions"), which query a specific piece of information. Thus, in English the question "Did you finish the ice cream?" is a polar question and can be answered by a simple affirmative or negative response, while "When will you buy more?" is a content question, as it requests that the interlocutor supply a specific piece of information.

### 5.3.2  Question formation

**SIDEBAR LP5.8**

GLOSSES

Q    interrogative

**Polar questions** (see Textbox LP5.3) are expressed in Nuuchahnulth with an interrogative clitic attached to the verb.

(16)  ʔuuqḥ ƚimtḥin
      ʔuuqḥƚ=imt=ḥin
      tell.about=PST=Q.1PL
      'Did we tell about it?'

(17)  mamuukḥ
      mamuuk=ḥ
      work=Q.3
      'Is he working?'

It is also very common, especially with the second-person subject, to express polar questions using only a rising intonation contour, without the interrogative marker.

(18)  haw̓iiqƛk
      haw̓iiqƛ=k
      hungry=2SG
      'Are you hungry?'

(19)  ḥaw̓iƚk.
      ḥaw̓iƚ=k
      wealthy/chief=2SG
      'Are you wealthy?; Are you a chief?'

**Content questions**, on the other hand, can be expressed – like negation – with a complement construction where the question word functions as the verb of the matrix clause. The event or state with respect to which the question is asked is expressed either with a lexical suffix or with a complement clause. The main predicate built around the question word can carry the interrogative clitic, although the predicate without the clitic is also very common. There are thus a variety of possible strategies for this function, and they can combine to produce a range of related constructions, as illustrated in the following examples.

(Note that the morphological gloss INC.CAUS indicates **inceptive** aspect + causative, while the gloss PASS indicates passive.)

**(20)** question word+lexical suffix; without interrogative clitic
*ʔaaqičiiɫk*
*ʔaqi-{č}iiɫ=k*
what-make=2SG
'What you you making?'

**(21)** question word+lexical suffix; with interrogative clitic
*ʔunistumtḥsuu*
*ʔuna-ista=umt=ḥsuu*
that.much-persons.onboard=PST=Q.2PL
'How many of you were on the canoe?'

**(22)** with complement clause; without interrogative clitic

| [*ʔačaʕanitk*] | [*quʔiiẏaṗat*] |
|---|---|
| *ʔačaq='at=it=k* | *qu-'i·ẏa·p='at* |
| who=PASS=PST=2SG | person-INC.CAUS=PASS |
| *question word* | *complement clause* |
| 'Who raised you?' | |

**(23)** with complement clause; with interrogative clitic

| *ʔaqishẇitasʔaƛitḥ* | *šiiƛuk* |
|---|---|
| *ʔaqish=it=ḥsuu* | *šiiƛuk* |
| why=PST=Q.3 | move |
| *question word* | *complement clause* |
| 'Why did you move?' | |

### 5.3.3 Nuuchahnulth morphology and polysynthesis

In this section we will take a detailed look at the complex word formation in Nuuchahnulth. As mentioned above (see Examples 1 and 2), what sets Nuuchahnulth word formation apart from that in familiar languages like English are the facts that it allows (a) the packing of complex meanings within a word through the combination of many morphemes and (b) for a single word to contain all the information necessary to serve as an independent sentence. This type of word formation is known as polysynthesis (introduced in Chapter 4, section 4.8; see also Language Profiles 6 and 12 on South Concucos Quechua and Seneca, respectively).

Polysynthesis in Nuuchahnulth is based on the affixation of **lexical suffixes**. The lexical suffix is a cross-linguistically unusual type of affix in that it expresses a concrete lexical meaning rather than an abstract grammatical function, and in that the inventory is large. (There are between 400 and 500 suffixes of this type in Nuuchahnulth.) Despite their semantic richness, lexical suffixes are purely dependent elements morphologically: they must always be attached to some stem and can never stand alone to form a word.

The meanings expressed by lexical suffixes span across a wide range (see, e.g., Textbox LP5.4). The following is a sample list of lexical suffixes:

| Actions/Events | | States | |
|---|---|---|---|
| -ḥẇaɫ | 'using . . .' | -yuʔaaɫ | 'being aware of . . .' |
| -ʼi·c | 'eating . . .' | -maḥsa | 'desiring to . . .' |
| -ṅaaḥ | 'seeking . . .' | -ḥtin | 'being made of . . .' |
| -ʔatu | 'sinking into the water' | –ḥta | 'being apart' |

| Entities | | Locations | |
|---|---|---|---|
| -ʔaq | 'animal hide' | -ʼis | 'being on the beach' |
| -mapt | 'plant' | -ʼas | 'being on the ground' |
| -qimɫ | 'round object' | -ʼa· | 'being on the rock' |
| -ʼaqsup | 'female from . . .' | -ʼiɫ | 'being in the house' |

---

### TEXTBOX LP5.4 **LEXICAL SUFFIXES FOR FEASTING**

Lexical suffixes express conventionalized actions and concepts that are highly entrenched in everyday life. Consequently, the inventory of lexical suffixes can tell us something about the everyday life of the people who have been using the language. For example, feasting and the gift-giving festival known as a *potlatch* are central rituals in Nuuchahnulth culture (and indeed in many indigenous communities of the Pacific Northwest Coast). It may at first look curious to the outsider to find suffixes like -ʼinɫ 'giving feast of . . ., distributing . . . in feast,' -ʼimcu 'feasting, entertaining,' or -ṫuuɫa 'potlatch for,' but this shows how important potlatch and feast-giving are in Nuuchahnulth culture and social life.

---

The semantic range of lexical suffixes overlaps with that of roots, but there are some notable differences between the two. Locative concepts are almost exclusively expressed by lexical suffixes. In contrast, nominal concepts (entities) are predominantly expressed by roots. Although there are lexical suffixes expressing nominal concepts, the meanings expressed are limited to conventionalized, generic notions.

In most cases there is no clear etymological link between a lexical suffix and a root. There are a few pairs of lexical suffixes and roots that do share a similar form and meaning, e.g., the verb root *wa·* 'say' and the lexical suffix -*wa·* 'say,' but they are very limited exceptions.

Lexical suffixes, because of their rich semantics, play a significant role in shaping the semantic and syntactic characteristics of the word. Particularly interesting are those that become the semantic head of the word (i.e., convey the word's primary semantic content). In Example (24) a verbal lexical suffix -*(č)iiɫ* 'make' is attached to a nominal root *čapac* 'canoe' to form a word 'to make a canoe.'

(24)  *čaapaciiɫ*
      *čapac-(č)iiɫ*
      canoe-make
      'make a canoe'

The nominal root is the head: it is an independent morpheme and it serves as the base of word formation. The lexical suffix, on the other hand, is a bound morpheme that

needs to be attached to the base, thus making it dependent on the root. However, this dependency relationship seems to be reversed semantically. The verbal lexical suffix determines the basic meaning of the word, whereas the nominal root is supplementing the meaning expressed by the lexical suffix. Thus, this word formation is an interesting case of a mismatch between the morphological relationship and the semantic relationship. (25) is an additional example.

**(25)**  *kɬatʃinɬʔaqƛs*
*kɬatq-'inɬ=ʔaqƛ=s*
hairseal-giving.a.feast.of=FUT=1SG
*root    lexical suffix*
'I will give a feast of hair seal; I will serve hair seal at a feast.'

### 5.3.4  Functions of polysynthetic words in discourse

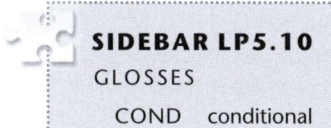

Thanks to the unusually powerful word-formation mechanism involving lexical suffixes, a word in Nuuchahnulth can encode a meaning as rich as that of a multi-word English sentence. Thus, the same information can sometimes be encoded either morphologically or syntactically. In the following examples, the participant *child* is expressed as a root with a lexical suffix in one case (26) but as a separate independent word in another (27).

**(26)**  *ɬaatńanakšiƛʔaƛquuk*
*ɬaatńa-na·k-ši(ƛ)='aƛ=quuk*
child.PL-having-PFV=EVENT=COND.2SG
'when you have children'

**(27)**  *ʔunaakʔaɬ          ɬaatńa.*
*ʔu-na·k=ʔa·ɬ        ɬaatńa*
3SG-having=PL        child.PL
'They had children.'

This flexibility raises an interesting question: why does the speaker choose one strategy of encoding over the other? The choice has to do with whether the speaker is referring to a particular person or entity. The compact expression generally expresses habitual, institutionalized activities rather than particular ones. For example, the predicate in (26) expresses a general activity of having children rather than a particular activity bound in time and place (e.g., having a particular child). Thus, a nominal element combined with a lexical suffix within a complex word, like *ɬaatńa* 'children' in (26), is not **referential** in discourse (i.e., not used for introducing a referent into a discourse that will subsequently be discussed or "tracked" as an activated referent; see Chapter 9). In contrast, when the speaker refers to a particular entity (e.g., the children in (27)), the nominal and verbal elements are expressed as separate words. Observe the contrast between (a) and (b) in Example (28).

(28)  a. *čaapaciiłwitas.*
       *čapac-iił-witas*
       canoe-making-about.to
       'He is going to make a canoe.'

       b. *6 months*     *hił*          *paačiina*     *čapac*     *ʔusiik*
          *hił*          *paačiina*     *čapac*        *ʔu-siik*
          six.months    be.there       pachina        canoe       3SG completing
          'For six months, I was at Pachina completing the canoe.'

Sentence (28a) was produced at the beginning of a narrative in which the speaker explained how a canoe used to be built. Here the root *čapac* 'canoe' does not refer to a particular entity: the notion of *canoe* is part of a generic action of *canoe-making*. In (28b), on the other hand, the same root *čapac* is used referentially to make reference to a particular canoe that the speaker was requested to build, and it is expressed in a word separate from the verbal element.

A similar contrast is observed in (a) and (b) of example (29) (the parts of the translation in square brackets present information known from the broader discourse context):

(29)  a. *ʕuyiičapat*                        *hitaaqλîλ.*
         *ʕuyi-ˈiˑc=ˈap=ˈat*                 *hita-ˈaˑqλi(λ)*
         medicine-consuming=CAUS=PASS        get.there-being.in.the.woods
         'They had me take medicine in the woods [so that I could have sons].'

      b. *sukʷiʔaλ*                          *ʕuyaakʔi*
         *sukʷi(λ)=ˈaλ*                       *ʕuyi=ʔaˑk=ʔiˑ*
         take=EVENT                           medicine=POSS=DEF
         'He [Mink] took out his medicine [to create a lake].'

In (29a) *ʕuyi* 'medicine' is part of a general activity of *medicine-taking* and therefore does not refer to a particular medicine. In contrast, *ʕuyi* in (29b) does refer to a particular medicine owned by Mink, as indicated by the possessive and definite suffixes.

Lexical suffixation and compounding in languages like English show a great deal of functional similarity in this aspect, although these two processes are very different in structural terms. Compare the above examples with morphological complexes like *berry-picking* and *bird-watching* in relation to *pick the berry* and *watch the bird*. The compact expression is only possible when the nominal does not refer to a specific entity.

Polysynthesis complicates our cross-linguistic understanding of the nature of words. Languages of this type show that the layout of the major domains of structural formation (i.e., word-level structure vs. clause-level structure) can differ significantly among languages.

## TEXTBOX LP5.5 GLOSSING CONVENTIONS USED IN THIS CHAPTER

| Convention | Meaning | Convention | Meaning |
|---|---|---|---|
| 1 | first person | NEG | negative |
| 2 | second person | PASS | passive |
| 3 | third person | PFV | perfective |
| CAUS | causative | PL | plural |
| COND | conditional | POSS | possessive |
| DEF | definite | PROG | progressive |
| EVENT | event | PST | past tense |
| FUT | future tense | Q | interrogative |
| INC | inceptive aspect | QUOT | quotative |
| IND | indicative | SG | singular |

## SUGGESTIONS FOR FURTHER READING

**Nakayama, Toshihide**. 2001. *Nuu-chah-nulth (Nootka) morphosyntax*. Berkeley: University of California Press.

This book gives an overview of word and sentence formation in Nuuchahnulth.

**Thompson, Laurence C. and M. Dale Kinkade**. 1990. "Languages." In Sturtevant, W. C. (ed.), *Handbook of North American Indians,* Vol. VII: *Northwest Coast*. Washington, DC: Government Printing Office. 30–51.

This article surveys languages of the Pacific Northwest Coast area of North America where Nuuchahnulth is located.

**Mithun, Marianne**. 1999. *The Languages of Native North America*. Cambridge University Press.

This book contains an overview and rich discussion of structural characteristics of the indigenous languages of North America.

**Croft, William**. 2000. "Parts of speech as language universals and as language-particular categories." In Vogel, P. M. and B. Comrie (eds.), *Approaches to the typology of word classes*. Berlin: Mouton de Gruyter. 65–102.

This paper contains some good discussion about issues and difficulties in word classification.

**Fortescue, Michael**. 1994. "Polysynthetic morphology." In Asher, R. E. et al. (eds.), *Encyclopedia of language and linguistics*. Oxford: Pergamon Press. 2601–2602.

This article gives a good overview of the characteristics and types of polysynthesis.

### EXERCISES

1.  Perfective aspect allomorphs
    The perfective aspect suffix *-šiƛ* in Nuuchahnulth has three allomorphs, *-šiƛ* ~ *-čiƛ* ~ *-kʷiƛ*. This problem will focus on the allomorphs *-šiƛ and -čiƛ*. (This alternation is represented in the top line of the transcription.) Compare the phonological environments in which each occurs. Determine the distribution pattern of these two allomorphs and write a clear statement about the conditions under which each appears.

    a.  *ḥamipšiƛ*
        *ḥamip-šiƛ*
        recognize-PFV
        'he recognized'

    b.  *tu:kšiƛ*
        *tu:k-šiƛ*
        cover.with.sand-PFV
        'he covered (it) up with sand'

    c.  *ta:čiƛ*
        *ta:-šiƛ*
        poke-PFV
        'he poked (it)'

    d.  *ƛ̓ĩtšiƛ*
        *ƛ̓ĩt-šiƛ*
        split-PFV
        'he split (it)'

    e.  *t̓ičiƛ*
        *t̓i-šiƛ*
        throw-PFV
        'he threw (it)'

    f.  *yacšiƛ*
        *yac-šiƛ*
        step-PFV
        'he stepped on'

    g.  *maḥšiƛ*
        *maḥ-šiƛ*
        collapse-PFV
        'it collapsed'

    h.  *ƛ̓apxšiƛ*
        *ƛ̓apx-šiƛ*
        slam-PFV
        'he slammed'

    i.  *qačiƛ*
        *qa-šiƛ*
        pierce-PFV
        'he pierced'

2. Word analysis
   Each of the following words is composed of two morphemes. Create a mini-glossary with a gloss for each morpheme.

   a. ẏak-i·ʔiƛ
      'looked into the house'

   b. kamatqʷ-i·ʔiƛ
      'running into the house'

   c. kamatqʷ-wa·s
      'running out'

   d. ʕup-wa·s
      '(water) flowing out'

   e. mat-wa·s
      'flying out'

   f. tuxʷ-wa·s
      'jumping out'

   g. tuxʷ-ʕaʔatu
      'jumping down'

   h. ti-ʕaʔatu
      'falling down'

   i. mat-ʕaʔatu
      'flying down'

   j. ha·tk-ʕaʔatu
      'rolling down'

   k. ti-ʼi·ƛ
      'falling on the ground'

3. Vowel contraction
   In Nuuchahnulth, when two vowels meet across a morpheme boundary, they contract into one. The quality of the resulting vowel is predictable. Using the following set of data, succinctly state in English prose the pattern that determines the quality of the contracted vowel. Note: you can ignore the length of the resulting vowel for this exercise.

   a. sučii ̵ɫ
      suča-i· ɫ
      five-fathoms
      'five fathoms'

   b. ʔukči·s
      ʔu-kči-a·s
      3SG-be.with-in.chair
      'sitting beside (someone) on the chair'

c. *huʔin*
*huʔa-in·*
back-come
'come back'

d. *n̓upuuɫ*
*n̓upu-i·ɫ*
six-fathoms
'six fathoms'

e. *ʔukčumyiɫ*
*ʔu-kči-umɫ-ʿiɫ*
3SG.M-be.with-be.in.a.group-be.in.the.house
'being on the floor with him'

f. *c̓aawumɫ*
*c̓awa-umɫ*
one-be.in.a.group
'There is only one in a group.'

g. *ʔuyii*
*ʔu-ayi·*
3SG-give
'give it (to him)'

h. *ḥaʔuyi*
*ḥaʔu-ayi·*
exchange-give
'give in exchange'

i. *ʔayuʔa:ɫ*
*ʔaya-uʔa:ɫ*
many-perceive
'find many (of them)'

4. Variable-length vowels
   Nuuchahnulth has so-called variable-length vowels that are realized as long vowels in some
   contexts and as short vowels in others. Note: variable-length vowels are indicated by a "middle
   dot," i.e., /V·/ where V stands for any vowel letter, in the morphemic (second) line of each
   example.

   Compare the forms in the text (top) line and those in the morphemic (second) line to see whether
   the variable-length vowel is pronounced as long (as in (a)) or short (as in (b)). Formulate a statement
   that distinctly states the conditions under which a variable-length vowel will be realized as short and
   realized as long.

   (Hint: Notice that the same morpheme [e.g., *-a·s* 'on a board/platform'] is sometimes pronounced
   with a long vowel and sometimes with a short vowel. What does this tell you about where to look for
   the conditions that trigger the rule?)

   a. *kiɫaas*
      *kiɫ-a·s*
      carry.a.canoe-on.platform
      'He is carrying a canoe on a board.'

    b. *hatkkʷisas*
      *hatkʷ-kʷis-a·s*
      roll-away.from-on.platform
      'roll off of the platform'

    c. *ɬučnaakšiƛ*
      *ɬuč-na·k-šiƛ*
      woman-have-PFV
      'He got married.'

    d. *ʕiɬčnaakšiƛ*
      *ʕiɬč-na·k-šiƛ*
      dog-have-PFV
      'She had dogs.'

    e. *ƛuḥiičas*
      *ƛuḥ-i-č-a·s*
      press.against-cover-on.platform
      'slap on something on the table'

    f. *ʔaƛaċasqi*
      *ʔaƛa-ċa·s-qi·*
      two-at.the.crown.of.the.head-on.the.head
      'He had two (of them) at the crown of the head.'

    g. *ʕaasiqnakšiƛ.*
      *ʕa·siq-na·k-šiƛ*
      plan-have-PFV
      'He got a plan.'

    h. *suqii*
      *su-qi·*
      hold-on.the.head
      'He is holding it on the head.'

    i. *ʔuʔiipas*
      *ʔu-ʔiip-a·s*
      3SG-give.to-on.platform
      'He put it on the table.'

    j. *ṫaatṅanaḱaƛ*
      *ṫaatṅa-na·k=ʼaƛ*
      children-have=EVENT
      'She had a child.'

**5.** Change-inducing suffixes
Some of the suffixes in Nuuchahnulth cause various changes in the shape of the root. For each of the examples below, compare the underlying (second line) and combined (top line) shapes of each root and note any changes that have occurred (don't worry about changes in the suffixes themselves). Make a list of the suffixes that do instigate changes and those that do not. For those that do, state the phonological change that the root undergoes.

a. *ma:ḥtiqi:ł*
   *maḥtiq-(č)i:ł*
   house-make
   'making a house'

b. *wiwiḱap*
   *wik-a·p*
   NEG-understand
   'not understanding'

c. *ʔi:qšaḥap*
   *ʔiq-šaḥap*
   the.same-do
   'doing the same thing'

d. *wi:ki:ł*
   *wik-(č)i:ł*
   NEG-make
   'barren; (woman) not producing a child'

e. *ʔa:qiḥćik*
   *ʔaqi-ḥći·=k*
   what-hold.over.fire=2SG
   'what are you cooking?'

f. *ʔiʔiqḥwa*
   *ʔiqḥ-wa·*
   the.same-keep.saying
   'keep saying the same thing'

g. *ṅi:ƛ́yaki:ł*
   *ṅiƛ́yak-(č)i:ł*
   oar-make
   'making an oar'

h. *ƛułṕu:qs*
   *ƛuł-ṗu·qs*
   good-smell
   'good smell'

i. *ʔa:qiči:łk*
   *ʔaqi-(č)i:ł=k*
   what-make=2SG
   'what are you making?'

j. *wiḱaqƛ*
   *wik-aqƛ*
   NEG-worth
   'cheap; worthless'

k. *wiku:s*
   *wik-u:s*
   NEG-at.home
   'there is nobody at home'

l. *wi:kšaḥap*
   *wik-šaḥap*
   NEG-do
   'doing nothing'

m. *ƛu:ɫšaḥap*
   *ƛuɫ-šaḥap*
   nice-do
   'act nicely; doing nice things'

n. *ƛuɫsu:qƛ*
   *ƛuɫ-su·qƛ*
   good-have.emotion
   'feeling good'

o. *wikʔa:ta*
   *wik-ʔa·ta*
   NEG-lack
   'sufficient; not lacking anything'

p. *wi:kmaʕuk*
   *wik-maʕuk*
   NEG-one.skilled.in
   'a person without skills'

# South Conchucos Quechua

## 6.1 Introduction

The South Conchucos Quechua language is spoken in the Andes mountains of central Peru. The name *Quechua* derives from the native word *\*qitṣwa* meaning 'temperate zone,' which translates to an elevation ranging from 9,000 to 13,000 feet. South Conchucos Quechua villages are traditionally located on steep, rugged slopes at these lofty altitudes.

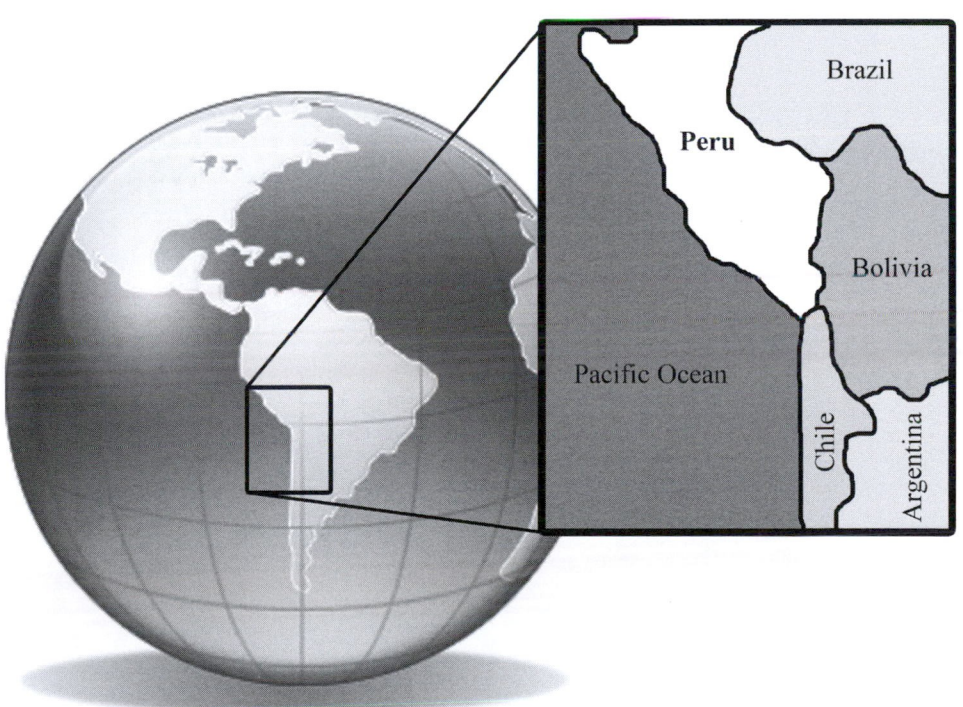

**Figure LP6.1** Location of Peru

### 6.1.1   Genetic affiliation

South Conchucos Quechua is a member of the Quechua language family. These languages, native to western South America, developed long before the Inca Empire was established (Torero 1964: 477). According to the *Ethnologue*, forty-four varieties of Quechua are currently spoken by over 9 million people throughout much of the Andean highlands and to a lesser extent in the Amazonian lowlands (Lewis, Simons, and Fennig 2013).

Torero locates the Quechua homeland along the coast and mountains of central Peru. From a linguistic point of view, this region is heavily fragmented, with "no full mutual intelligibility between the different dialects" (Adelaar 2006: 121). Twenty modern varieties, including South Conchucos Quechua, are spoken in this "Central Quechua" region, which is roughly a fifth of the size of California or twice the size of Switzerland (see Figure LP6.2). The other shaded areas correspond to all other

**Figure LP6.2** Map: The Quechua language family (Hintz 2011: 12, adapted from Landerman 1991: 37)

Quechuan varieties extending north and south of the original Central Quechua homeland. The distance between where Inga Quechua (Colombia) and Santiago del Estero Quechua (Argentina) are spoken is approximately 2,160 miles, which is nearly the distance from Los Angeles to Washington, DC.

### 6.1.2 Location and size of speech community

South Conchucos Quechua is spoken by approximately 250,000 people in the eastern Ancash and western Huánuco regions of central Peru (see Figure LP6.3). This area is bounded on the west by the glacier-covered Cordillera Blanca, with many peaks towering over 20,000 feet. The South Conchucos Quechua language area extends northeastward across the Marañón River gorge. Some large communities have up to 3,000 residents, but the vast majority of people live in smaller settlements scattered across this remote Andean region. Major population centers include Huari, Chavín de Huantar, Llamellín, San Luis, and Huacaybamba.

### 6.1.3 Language viability, society, and culture

Traditional Andean agricultural practices are the norm in the communities of South Conchucos. Small fields etched into rugged slopes produce potatoes (*papa*), corn (*hara*), wheat (*tri:gu*), beans (*tawri*, *a:ba*), and other crops. (See Sidebar LP6.1 for a brief note on transcription conventions.) Families typically own one or more cows (*wa:ka*) and donkeys (*ashnu*), and raise a few pigs (*kuchi*), chickens (*wallpa*), and guinea pigs (*haka*), as well as sheep (*u:sha*) for wool. The community-based production of alpaca wool sold to the national government is a recent innovation.

> **SIDEBAR LP6.1**
>
> The symbol : is often used to represent lengthening of the preceding sound and thus can indicate a long vowel sound, as in the word *tri:gu* 'wheat.'

South Conchucos Quechua speakers are not shy about their language. Quechua is the language of everyday life for people of all ages, the language of understanding and connection. A small percentage of the population are monolingual Quechua speakers, who are generally older women and men, as well as preschool children. Most adults and school-age children can also communicate to varying degrees in the local variety of Spanish, but there is a definite preference for Quechua. Children play together in Quechua. School teachers often speak and joke around in Quechua. In fact, people almost always speak among themselves in Quechua, but switch to Spanish to accommodate outsiders.

Native-authored literature is another recent innovation. There are over one hundred titles published in South Conchucos Quechua, including books of traditional stories, songs, riddles, a health manual, literacy materials, a translation of the novel *Heidi*, and a translation of the New Testament. Thousands have learned to read in their native language through community-based literacy efforts.

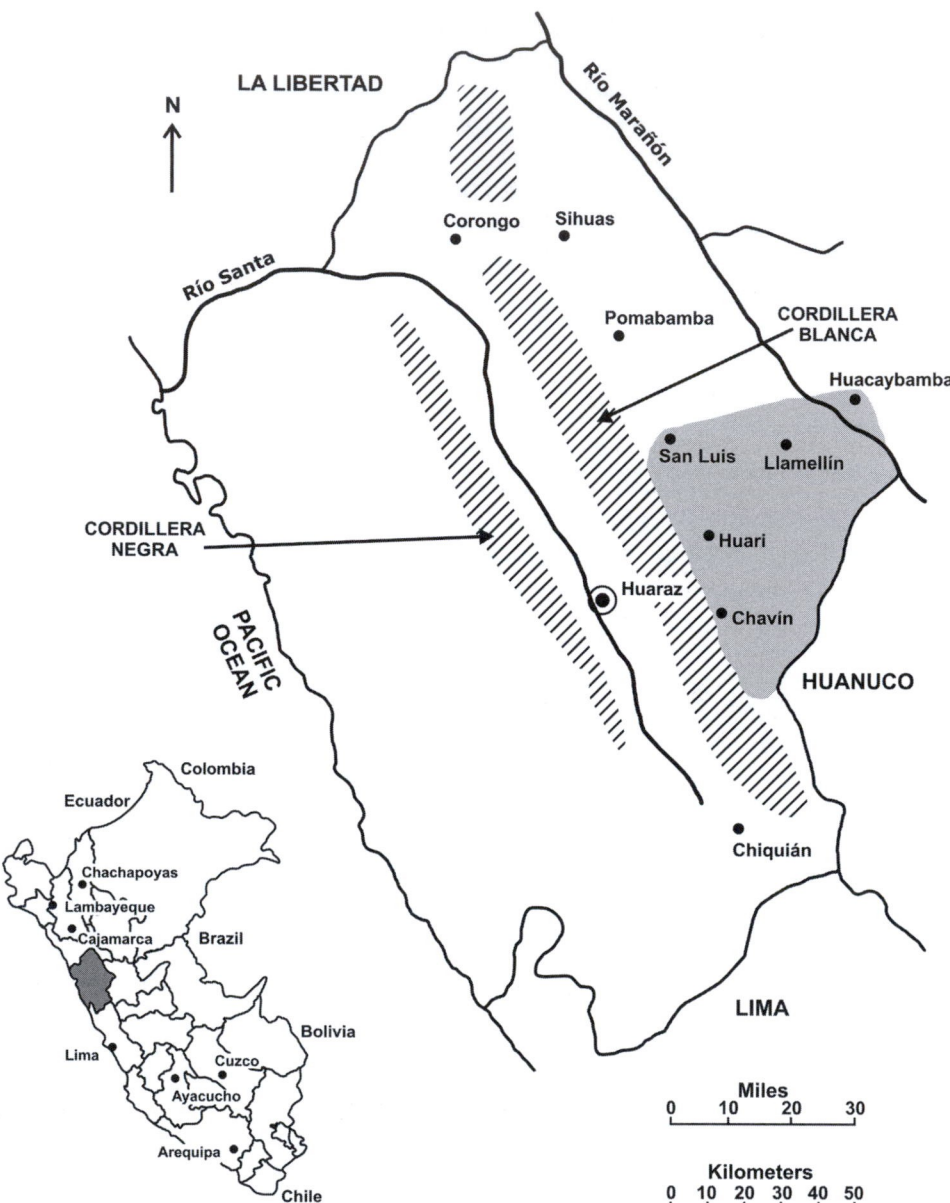

**Figure LP6.3** Map: The South Conchucos Quechua language area

## 6.2 Typological overview

### 6.2.1 Segmental sound system

The native sound system of South Conchucos Quechua has seventeen consonants, three short vowels, and three long vowels. IPA symbols for these sound segment **phonemes** are shown in Table LP6.1. Among those listed in rows 1–3, only /ɢ/ is

**TABLE LP6.1** Native phonemes of South Conchucos Quechua

| Consonants | Bilabial | Alveolar | Postalveolar/Palatal | Velar | Uvular | Glottal |
|---|---|---|---|---|---|---|
| Oral stops | p | t | | k | ɢ | |
| Affricates | | ts | tʃ | | | |
| Nasal stops | m | n | ñ | | | |
| Flap (tap) | | ɾ | | | | |
| Fricatives | | s | ʃ | | | h |
| Central approximants | w | | j | | | |
| Lateral approximants | | l | ʎ | | | |

| Vowels | Front | Central | Back |
|---|---|---|---|
| High | i i: | | u u: |
| Mid | | | |
| Low | | a a: | |

**voiced**. Spanish loans have introduced the consonants /b/, /d/, /g/, /f/, and trilled /r/, as well as the vowels /e/ and /o/ along with their lengthened counterparts /e:/ and /o:/. Some examples of loanwords from Quechua to English are given in Textbox LP6.1. Examples in this language profile use the following alphabetic symbols in place of the corresponding IPA symbols: q for ɢ, y for j, r for ɾ, ch for tʃ, sh for ʃ, and ll for ʎ.

---

**TEXTBOX LP6.1 QUECHUA WORDS USED IN ENGLISH (TYPICALLY FROM QUECHUA TO SPANISH TO ENGLISH)**

| English | Quechua | |
|---|---|---|
| puma | *puma* | 'mountain lion, cougar' |
| jerky | *tṣarki* | 'dried meat strips' |
| llama | *llama* | 'domestic animal related to the camel' |
| condor | *kuntur* | 'large vulture' |
| quinine | *kina* | 'malaria treatment from cinchona tree bark' |
| quinoa | *kinwa* | 'edible grain high in protein' |
| guano | *wanu* | 'fertilizer from dried seabird dung' |
| pampa | *pampa* | 'grass-covered plain' |
| coca-cola | *kuka* | 'coca plant or leaves' |

**Figure LP6.4** Endangered Andean *puma*

## 6.2.2 Word classes

Major word classes in South Conchucos Quechua include the following:

| | | |
|---|---|---|
| NOUN ROOTS: | *haka* | 'guinea pig' |
| | *papa* | 'potato' |
| PERSONAL | *noqa* | 'I' |
| PRONOUNS: | *qam* | 'you' |
| | *pay* | 's/he' |
| | *noqantsik* | 'we (inclusive), you and I' |
| DEMONSTRATIVE: | *kay* | 'this (near)' |
| PRONOUNS: | *tsay* | 'that (distant)' |
| | *taqay* | 'that (more distant)' |
| VERB ROOTS: | *apa-* | 'take' |
| | *aywa-* | 'go' |
| ADVERBS: | *alla:pa* | 'very' |
| | *ras* | 'fast' |
| PARTICLES: | *ma:* | 'let's see' |
| | *ama* | 'do not' |

Words that describe attributes, such as *puka* 'red' and *hatun* 'large,' take the same suffixes and serve the same grammatical functions as nouns.

---

**TEXTBOX LP6.2 HAKA 'GUINEA PIG'**

A corner of the kitchen is ideal for raising *haka* 'guinea pig.' In the Andes mountains hotly spiced *haka* (Spanish *picante de cuy*) is a favorite dish prepared for special celebrations, such as birthdays and festivals.

**Figure LP6.5** *Haka* 'Guinea pig'

---

## 6.2.3 Word formation

South Conchucos Quechua is a **polysynthetic** language, that is, words are formed by combining several **morphemes** together. Words typically consist of a single root form plus a sequence of **suffixes** and **enclitics**. There are a total of 95 suffixes: 64 used in verbs and 31 used in nouns (or pronouns). In addition, 19 enclitics are common to both verbs and nouns. There are no **prefixes**.

This language is also **agglutinative**. In other words, most suffixes and enclitics express a single component of meaning and generally do not change form across morpheme boundaries (though final vowels may change). This agglutinative tendency makes South Conchucos Quechua words relatively easy to divide into individual morphemes. (A list of all the bound morphemes used in the examples, together with their glosses, can be found at the end of this language profile.)

## TEXTBOX LP6.3 **QUECHUA PUT THE "COCA"** IN COCA-COLA

The *kuka* (coca) plant is native to the highlands of western South America. Its pungent leaves are traditionally chewed with lime powder (calcium hydroxide) to increase the release of alkaloids. Coca serves as a stimulant to overcome fatigue, hunger, thirst, and altitude sickness. It is also used as an anesthetic. Coca has been a vital part of the religious cosmology of Andean people from the pre-Inca period through the present. Extract of coca leaves has been cited as an ingredient in the original Coca-Cola recipe.

**Figure LP6.6** Sun-dried coca leaves

Let's identify each morpheme in the two words given in (1).

(1)  *haka-n-kuna-pa:*          *apa-ra-mu-sha*
     guinea.pig-3-PL-PURP     take-BRIEF-TO-PST
     'She brought (food) for her guinea pigs.'

The first word is the noun *hakankunapa:*, which means 'for her guinea pigs.' This word begins with the noun root *haka* 'guinea pig' followed by three noun suffixes. The first suffix *-n* marks third-person possessive 'her,' followed by *-kuna* 'noun plural' and *-pa:* 'purpose.'

The second word in (1) is the verb *aparamusha* which means 'she brought it.' This word consists of the verb root *apa-* 'take' followed by three verbal suffixes. The first suffix *-ra* reports the brief duration of the event. The suffix *-mu* shifts the meaning from 'take (there)' to 'bring (here).' The suffix *-sha* indicates a past event. We will explore South Conchucos Quechua verb formation in greater detail in section 6.3 below.

## 6.2.4  Possession in nouns

Four suffixes are used to indicate possession in nouns. First-person **possessive** is marked by the suffix *-:*, that is, the final vowel of the noun stem is lengthened (*haka* 'guinea pig' versus *haka:* 'my guinea pig'). Second-person possessive is marked by the suffix *-yki*. As we saw in (1), third-person possessive is marked by the suffix *-n*. South Conchucos Quechua has an additional possessive suffix, *-ntsik*, which marks first-person inclusive, meaning 'yours and mine.'

(2)  Possessive suffixes

|        |                      | *papa*      | 'potato'                      |
|--------|----------------------|-------------|-------------------------------|
| *-:*   | 1st person           | *papa-:*    | 'my potato'                   |
| *-yki* | 2nd person           | *papa-yki*  | 'your potato'                 |
| *-n*   | 3rd person           | *papa-n*    | 'his/her potato'              |
| *-ntsik* | 1st person inclusive | *papa-ntsik* | 'our potato' (yours and mine) |

## 6.2.5  Word order within clauses

A **main clause** consists of a verb, plus an optional **subject** noun phrase, an optional **object** noun phrase, and various other optional elements. In English the subject (S), verb (V), and object (O) most often occur in the order S-V-O, where the subject precedes the verb and the verb precedes the object. By contrast, the order of these elements in South Conchucos Quechua is relatively free. A study by Diane Hintz (2003) found that fewer than 7 percent of main clauses in connected speech have both subject and object noun phrases expressed. In those that do, no single order is significantly more frequent than others. Examples of the two most frequent orders, S-O-V (35 percent) and S-V-O (32 percent), are given in (3) and (4). Though S most frequently occurs in the clause-initial position, pragmatic factors also motivate S in the clause-final position.

(3)  **S**                    **O**                        **V**
*Maria=pis*          *shinqiru-ta=m*              *rantiku-sh*
Maria=EVEN          hot.drink-OBJ=AFFIRM          sell-PST
'Maria also sold hot drinks.'

### TEXTBOX LP6.4 **WHERE DOES THE POTATO COME FROM?**

Potatoes are native to the highlands of South America where they have been consumed for more than 8,000 years. Spanish explorers brought the plant to Europe in the late sixteenth century. The International Potato Center, headquartered in Peru, seeks to reduce poverty and achieve sustainable food security in developing countries.

The English word *potato* derives from Spanish *patata*. According to the Spanish Royal Academy, *patata* derives from a combination of Quechua *papa* 'potato' and Taino *batata* 'sweet potato.'

**Figure LP6.7** Varieties of *papa* (potato)

(4)  S            V                    O

| *noqa* | *wanu-tsi-:=mi* | *tsay* | *kuru-ta* |
|---|---|---|---|
| 1SG | die-CAUS-1=AFFIRM | that | worm-OBJ |

'I (will) kill that worm.'

Although word order is variable in main clauses, **adverbial clauses** are almost always verb-final. The main clause in (5) is *Wachullash aywakusha* 'Lorenzo went up there.' The final three words (within brackets) constitute an adverbial clause.

(5)  **S**                    **V**            **O**          **V**

*Wachu-lla=sh*            *aywa-ku-sha*    [*tsay chi:na-ta apa-rku-r*]
Lorenzo-JUST=REPORT    go-MIDDLE-PST  that  girl-OBJ  take-CONSENT-ADV.SS
'Lorenzo went there (they say), taking along that girl.'

The two-word object *tsay chi:nata* 'that girl' is followed by the verb *aparkur* 'taking along.' Two types of adverbial clauses in South Conchucos Quechua are described in Sidebar LP6.2.

## 6.2.6  Case and grammatical relations

The association between a noun (or pronoun) and a verb is referred to as a **grammatical relation**. Core grammatical relations in South Conchucos Quechua are subjects and objects. As seen above in (3)–(5), objects are marked by the case suffix *-ta* (e.g., *shinqirutam, kuruta, chi:nata*). Subjects, on the other hand, are marked by the absence of any case suffix (e.g., *Mariapis, noqa, Wachullash*).

At least fifteen additional case suffixes mark non-core, or peripheral, grammatical relations, also known as **obliques**. For example, in (1), the case suffix *-pa:* marks 'purpose' in the word *haka-n-kuna-pa:* 'for her guinea pigs.' Other obliques include *-cho:/-chu* 'location,' *-man* 'toward,' *-pita* 'from,' *-no:/-nuy* 'like,' and *-yaq* 'until.'

## 6.2.7  Evidentials

South Conchucos Quechua has a small, yet very important, set of six word-final enclitics that report the speaker's source of information and the degree of certainty the speaker holds toward that information. These enclitics are known as **evidentials**. They can attach to almost any word, but their use is generally restricted to only one per sentence. The most frequent evidentials in everyday speech are =*mi*, =*chir*, and =*cha:*. The least frequent are =*chi*, =*shi*, and =*ran*.

We have seen examples of =*mi* (or =*m*) in the words *shinqirutam* in (3) and *wanutsi:mi* in (4). This enclitic means 'I affirm ...' Affirmative =*mi* reports information that the individual speaker has acquired personally and is willing to endorse. In contrast, the reportative enclitic =*shi* (or =*sh*), illustrated in *Wachullash* in (5), reports second-hand information that the speaker does not necessarily endorse. =*shi* adds the sense 'They say ...'. The conjectural enclitic =*chi* reports information acquired via deduction, meaning 'I suppose ...'

**(6)** atska     wa:ka=chi          pe      sha-ya:-mu-n=si
many     cow=CONJECTURE     well    come-PL-TO-3=EVEN
'Many cows also came along (I suppose).'

Evidential enclitics in this language also express contrasts along the interpersonal dimension. For example, individual knowledge reported by =mi contrasts with mutual knowledge reported by =cha:, which could be translated as 'We (inclusive) all know ...'

**(7)** tsay-pa=cha:              qati-ya-ra-n              mama-yki-kuna
that-GEN=MUTUAL          follow-PL-PST-3          mother-2-PL
'In that place your mothers [your ancestors] pastured animals (as we all know).'

## 6.3  Verb formation

A total of sixty-four suffixes and nineteen enclitics are used in the formation of South Conchucos Quechua verbs. Normally, a verb root must have at least one suffix to mark the person of the subject. The actual number of verbal suffixes and enclitics tends to range from three to six in a given verb, though eight to ten is not uncommon.

A simplified view of South Conchucos Quechua verb structure is presented in Table LP6.2. The verb root is followed by a sequence of suffixes and enclitics. A set of six OPTIONAL suffix slots is followed by three OBLIGATORY suffix slots, and finally the ENCLITIC slots. The enclitics can attach to either verbs or nouns.

In Table LP6.2, the verb shoqatsimaruykicha: is divided into its individual morphemes. The verb root shoqa- 'comfort' is followed by one suffix or enclitic in each general position of the verb. The causative suffix -tsi fills one of the OPTIONAL slots. This is followed by the suffixes -ma: (allomorph -ma) 'first-person object,' -ru 'past tense,' and -yki 'second-person subject' in the three OBLIGATORY slots. The final verbal element, the evidential enclitic =cha: 'mutual knowledge,' fills an ENCLITIC slot. We will now examine some of these verb slots in more detail.

**TABLE LP6.2** Verb structure

| VERB ROOT | OPTIONAL VERB SLOTS (6) | OBLIGATORY VERB SLOTS (3) | | | ENCLITIC SLOTS |
|---|---|---|---|---|---|
| | | OBJECT | TENSE-DEVERBAL | SUBJECT | |
| shoqa- | -tsi | -ma | -ru | -yki | =cha: |
| comfort | CAUS | 1.OBJ | PST | 2 | MUTUAL |
| 'You made me feel comforted.' | | | | | |

### 6.3.1   Subject slot

As shown in Table LP6.2, the OBLIGATORY slot set consists of the TENSE-DEVERBAL slot, preceded by the OBJECT and followed by the SUBJECT. The subject in present tense is specified by one of four suffixes. First-person subjects are marked by the suffix -:, which lengthens the final vowel of the verb stem. Second person is marked by the suffix -nki and third person by the suffix -n. The suffix -ntsik marks first-person inclusive, meaning 'you and I.'

(8)   Subject suffixes in present tense

|  |  |  |  |
|---|---|---|---|
|  |  | rika- | 'see' |
| -: | '1' | rika-: | 'I see' |
| -nki | '2' | rika-nki | 'you see' |
| -n | '3' | rika-n | 's/he sees' |
| -ntsik | '1.INCL, first person inclusive' | rika-ntsik | 'we see' (you and I) |

The suffixes in (8) also mark the person of the subject in past tense, with the exception of second person, which is marked by -yki rather than -nki (rika-nki 'you see' versus rika-ra-yki 'you saw').

### 6.3.2   Tense-deverbal slot

The TENSE-DEVERBAL slot can be filled by any one of twenty-seven different suffixes. Nearly half of these indicate **tense**, or the location of an event in time. Present tense is marked by the absence of an overt suffix in the TENSE-DEVERBAL slot, as illustrated in (8) and (10). South Conchucos Quechua also has five past-tense suffixes: -sha in (1), (5), (11), and (14), -ru in (Table LP6.2) and (13), -na: 'narrative past,' -ra in (7), and -q in (4a) (in the Exercises).

Why does South Conchucos Quechua have so many past-tense suffixes? We can answer this question by examining how each is used in connected speech. For example, either -ru or -ra can report a past event, whether it took place recently or many years ago. The contrast is that events marked by -ru are usually more recent than events marked by -ra. In other words, recent past -ru and remote past -ra specify relative degrees of pastness.

Surprisingly, recent past -ru is used only with first-person, second-person, and first-person inclusive referents. Recent past in third person is marked by the suffix -sha instead.

Habitual past -q in (4a) (in the Exercises Section) reports a situation that is customarily repeated in the past. In contrast, the past-tense suffixes -ra, -ru, and -sha report past situations that are not ongoing, but bounded in the past.

The past-tense suffixes -ru and -ra are followed by a separate suffix that marks the subject. In contrast, each suffix in (9) marks both future tense and the person of the subject, rather than marking these with two separate suffixes. (Textbox LP6.5 gives an example sentence using the suffix –shayki.)

**(9)**   Future-tense suffixes

|  |  |  | rika- | 'see' |
|---|---|---|---|---|
| -sha: | '1.FUT' |  | rika-sha: | 'I will see' |
| -nki | '2.FUT' |  | rika-nki | 'you will see' |
| -nqa | '3.FUT' |  | rika-nqa | 's/he will see' |
| -shun | '1.INCL.FUT' |  | rika-shun | 'we will see' (you and I) |
| -shayki | 'FUT1>2, first-person subject with second-person object' |  | rika-shayki | 'I will see you' |

---

**TEXTBOX LP6.5 ONE SUFFIX, THREE COMPONENTS OF MEANING**

The suffix -shayki conveys three components of meaning. It marks not only future tense and first-person subject, but also second-person object:

tsay-kaq-ta=ra:           willa-yku-shayki=qa
that-DEF-OBJ=yet          tell-OBLIGATE-FUT1>2=TOP
'I will tell you about that.'

---

Some suffixes that fill the TENSE-DEVERBAL slot produce an adverbial clause and have a special function of specifying its subject. The adverbial suffix -r, illustrated in (5), indicates that the subject of the adverbial clause is the same as the subject of the main clause. In contrast, -pti indicates that the subjects of the two clauses are different. For example, the subject of the main clause in (10) is mamantsik 'our mother' and the subject of the adverbial clause is first person 'I.' Because the two subjects are different, the speaker uses the adverbial suffix -pti in the TENSE-DEVERBAL slot of the verb shakamupti:pis (in brackets).

**(10)**   mama-ntsik          waqa-n          feyupa          [sha-ka-mu-pti-:=pis]
mother-1.INCL          cry-3          much          come-MIDDLE-TO-ADV.DS-1=EVEN
'Our mother cries a lot, even though I come home often.'

## 6.3.3   Optional verb slots

Twenty-eight additional suffixes may fill the six OPTIONAL slots close to the verb root. Speakers use these suffixes to express a variety of functions not available in the OBLIGATORY slots discussed above. We will now examine suffixes that adjust valency and express social functions.

First, certain suffixes affect the **valency** of a verb by increasing or decreasing the number of arguments it controls. For example, the verb root wanu- 'die' normally takes only one argument: the subject. When the **causative** suffix -tsi is added, however, the resulting verb stem *wanu-tsi-* 'kill' takes two arguments: a subject and an object. The valency has been increased.

(11)  *wanu-sha*          'she died'
      *wanu-tsi-sha*      'he killed her' (caused her to die)

The **passive** suffix *-ka:* (allomorph *-ka*) decreases valency. The verb root *rura-* 'do' normally can take two arguments: a subject and an object. When the passive suffix *-ka* is added, the resulting verb stem controls only one argument: the subject. The valency has been decreased.

(12)  *rura-n*        'he does it'
      *rura-ka-n*     'it happens'

Other suffixes in the OPTIONAL verbal slots systematically express social functions, such as **stance**. For example, in (13) the suffix *-rku* indicates both parties' willingness to stay together by mutual consent. The stances of the participants converge. By contrast, in (14) the suffix *-yku* (allomorph *-yka*) conveys the unwillingness of the children to be put to sleep by their mother. The stances of the participants diverge.

(13)  *ta:ra-ya-ru-:*      *ishke:*    *tsakay*    *punu-rku-r=yan*
      stay-PL-PST-1        two         night       sleep-CONSENT-ADV.SS=DISTR
      'We stayed together, sleeping there for two nights.'

(14)  *rantiku-sha*        *wamra-n-kuna-ta*       *punu-yka-tsi-r*
      sell-PST             child-3-PL-OBJ          sleep-OBLIGATE-CAUS-ADV.SS
      'She sold (drinks) after putting her unwilling children to sleep.'

The South Conchucos Quechua language is beautiful and complex, a reflection of shared concepts distilled through generations of human experience. Language documentation makes these ideas accessible to others and helps motivate the speech community to increasingly value their language and to pass it on to future generations.

---

### TEXTBOX LP6.6 **GLOSSING CONVENTIONS USED IN THIS LANGUAGE PROFILE AND THEIR CORRESPONDING MORPHEMES**

**Suffixes**

| | | |
|---|---|---|
| 1 | *-:* | first person |
| 1.INCL | *-ntsik* | first-person inclusive |
| 1.OBJ | *-ma(:)* | first-person object |
| 2 | *-yki* | second-person possessive or second-person in past tense |
| 2, FUT.2 | *-nki* | second-person subject in present or future tense |
| 3 | *-n* | third person |
| ABL | *-pita* | case: ablative |
| ADV.DS | *-pti* | adverbializer, different subjects |
| ADV.SS | *-r* | adverbializer, same subjects |

## TEXTBOX LP6.6 *(cont.)*

| | | |
|---|---|---|
| BRIEF | *-ri/-ra* | punctual aspect (brief duration) |
| CAUS | *-tsi* | causative |
| CONSENT | *-rku/-rka* | mutual consent, aligned stance, perfective aspect |
| DEF | *-kaq* | definite |
| FUT.1 | *-sha:* | future tense, first-person subject |
| FUT.2 | *-nki* | future tense, second-person subject |
| FUT.3 | *-nqa* | future tense, third-person subject |
| FUT.1.INCL | *-shun* | future tense, first-person inclusive subject |
| FUT.1>2 | *-shayki* | future tense, first-person subject, second-person object |
| GEN | *-pa* | case: genitive |
| JUST | *-lla* | delimitative, courtesy, just |
| MIDDLE | *-ku/-ka* | middle voice, reflexive |
| OBJ | *-ta* | case: direct or indirect object |
| OBLIGATE | *-yku/-yka* | obligation, non-aligned stance, perfective aspect |
| PASS | *-ka(:)* | passive |
| PST | *-ra* | past tense, general |
| PST | *-ru* | past tense, recent |
| PST | *-sh(a)* | past tense, recent, involving third person |
| PST.HABITUAL | *-q* | past habitual aspect |
| PL.N | *-kuna* | plural noun |
| PL.V | *-ya(:)* | plural verb |
| PURP | *-pa:* | case: purpose |
| TO | *-mu* | cislocative, translocative (directional affix) |

### Evidential enclitics

| | | |
|---|---|---|
| AFFIRM | *=m(i)* | evidential: affirmed individual knowledge |
| APPEAL | *=chir* | evidential: unaffirmed mutual knowledge |
| CONJECTURE | *=ch(i)* | evidential: unaffirmed individual knowledge |
| EPISODE.YET | *=ran* | evidential: episodic individual knowledge |
| MUTUAL | *=cha:* | evidential: affirmed mutual knowledge |
| REPORT | *=sh(i)* | evidential: reportative, nonpersonal knowledge |

### Other enclitics

| | | |
|---|---|---|
| DISTR | *=yan* | distributive |
| EVEN | *=pis/=si* | additive, even, too |
| TOP | *=qa* | topic |
| YET | *=ra:* | yet |

## SUGGESTIONS FOR FURTHER READING

**Adelaar, Willem F. H.** with **Pieter Muysken**. 2004. *The languages of the Andes*. Cambridge University Press.

This book documents in a single volume the wide variety of languages and language families native to the Andes region of South America.

**Bode, Barbara**. 1989. *No bells to toll: Destruction and creation in the Andes*. New York: Scribner.

This book gives insight into the minds of Quechua and Spanish speakers in an Andean valley who tell their own stories in the aftermath of a devastating earthquake and massive avalanche.

**Hintz, Daniel J.** 2011. *Crossing aspectual frontiers: Emergence, evolution, and interwoven semantic domains in South Conchucos Quechua* (University of California Publications in Linguistics 146). Berkeley: University of California Press. PDF available online at: www.escholarship.org/uc/item/6wb842zj.

Based on naturally occurring speech in South Conchucos Quechua, the author describes the remarkable aspect system and its relation to tense, modality, and other semantic domains.

**Spyri, Johanna**. 2010. *Heidi*. Trans. Reida Valenzuela, Edilberto Valenzuela and Diane Hintz. Huaraz, Peru: Instituto Lingüístico de Verano. PDF available online at: www.sil.org/americas/peru/pubs/Heidi.pdf.

A translation of the classic Swiss novel *Heidi* into South Conchucos Quechua, with watercolors contextualized for the Andes by native artist Tobías Mendoza.

**Weber, David John**, and others. 1998. *Rimaycuna, Quechua de Huánuco: Diccionario del quechua del Huallaga con índices castellano e inglés*. Lima, Peru: Instituto Lingüístico de Verano. PDF available online at: www.sil.org/americas/peru/pubs/slp48.pdf.

This trilingual dictionary (Huallaga Quechua – Spanish – English) is the most comprehensive available for any Quechuan language.

## EXERCISES

1. "Peruvian death pepper"

   South Conchucos Quechua speakers refer to the local variety of hot pepper as *utsu*. These aromatic peppers are also known as *gringu wanutsiy*, which means '(will) kill a gringo.' Garfield's colorful term is "Peruvian death pepper."

   Carefully examine (a) and then answer the following questions.

   a. *utsu-ta=qa*          [*alla:pa*      *aya-pti-n=pis*]                    *miku-ya-nki=ra:*
      hot.pepper-OBJ=TOP   very      be.spicy-ADV.DS-3=EVEN   eat-PL-2=YET
      'Even though they are very spicy, you still eat hot peppers.'

   i. Identify each affricate and nasal consonant.
   ii. How many long vowels are there?
   iii. What is the word class of *alla:pa*?

**Figure LP6.8** Garfield strip featuring the "Peruvian Death Pepper"

    iv. There is only one noun in (a). Can you identify it?

    v. The two-word adverbial clause *alla:pa ayaptinpis* (within brackets) is embedded within the main clause *utsutaqa mikuyankira:*. What is the translation of the adverbial clause? What is the translation of the main clause?

    vi. What is the grammatical relation (subject, object or oblique) that links *utsutaqa* to the main clause verb *mikuyankira:*? What case suffix indicates this?

    vii. What is the order of these two main clause elements?

**2.**  Object-Tense-Subject

    a. Divide each verb on the left into separate morphemes (verb root plus suffixes).

    b. List the form and meaning of each verb root and suffix.

    c. Fill in the blanks.

| | |
|---|---|
| *apan* | 's/he takes' |
| *apa:* | 'I take' |
| *aparan* | 's/he took' |
| *apara:* | 'I took' |
| *muruntsik* | 'we (inclusive) plant' |
| *mururantsik* | 'we (inclusive) planted' |
| *murunki* | 'you plant' |
| *mururayki* | 'you planted' |
| _____ | 'I plant' |
| _____ | 'you take' |
| _____ | 'you took' |

d. Challenge: Identify the meaning of the verbal suffix -*ma(:)*. (You already know the meanings of the suffixes -*n*, -*nki* and -*yki* and the past-tense suffix -*ra*.) Fill in the blanks.

| | |
|---|---|
| *willan* | 's/he tells' |
| *willaman* | 's/he tells me' |
| *willamanki* | 'you tell me' |
| *apamaran* | 's/he took me' |
| *apamarayki* | '___ took me' |
| _____ | 'you told me' |
| *qatiman* | 's/he follows ___' |
| *qatimaq* | 's/he used to follow me' |
| *qatimaran* | '_____' |

3. Parsing

   Divide the word *papantsikkunapa:* 'for our potatoes' into separate morphemes. How many suffixes does this word have? What does each suffix mean? Compare with the word *hakankunapa:* in (1).

4. Past habitual

   Which two English words below are the translation of the habitual past suffix -*q*?

   (a) *qocha-pita=qa*      *pe*      *sha-ka-ya:-mu-q*              *kiki-n-kuna-lla*
       lake-ABL=TOP   then   come-MIDDLE-PL-TO-PST   self-3.POSS-PL-JUST

   'From the lake (the cows) used to come all by themselves.'

5. Adverbial

   If the speaker in (10) above had used the adverbial suffix -*r* in place of -*pti*, as in (a), how would this change the meaning? Fill in the appropriate two English words below.

   (a) *mama-ntsik*        *waqa-n*    *feyupa*    [*sha-ka-mu-r=pis*]
       mother-1.INCL   cry-3   much   come-MIDDLE-TO-ADV.SS=EVEN

   'Our mother cries a lot, even though _____ _____ home often.'

## LANGUAGE PROFILE 7

# Tsez

## 7.1 Introduction

Tsez, also known as Dido, is spoken in the North Caucasus, more specifically in the Republic of Daghestan (also spelled Dagestan), the southernmost constituent republic of the Russian Federation. Tsez is spoken by about 15,400 people, according to the 2002 census of the Russian Federation. Most speakers of Tsez live in their traditional territory in western Daghestan, against the main range of the Caucasus mountains and close to

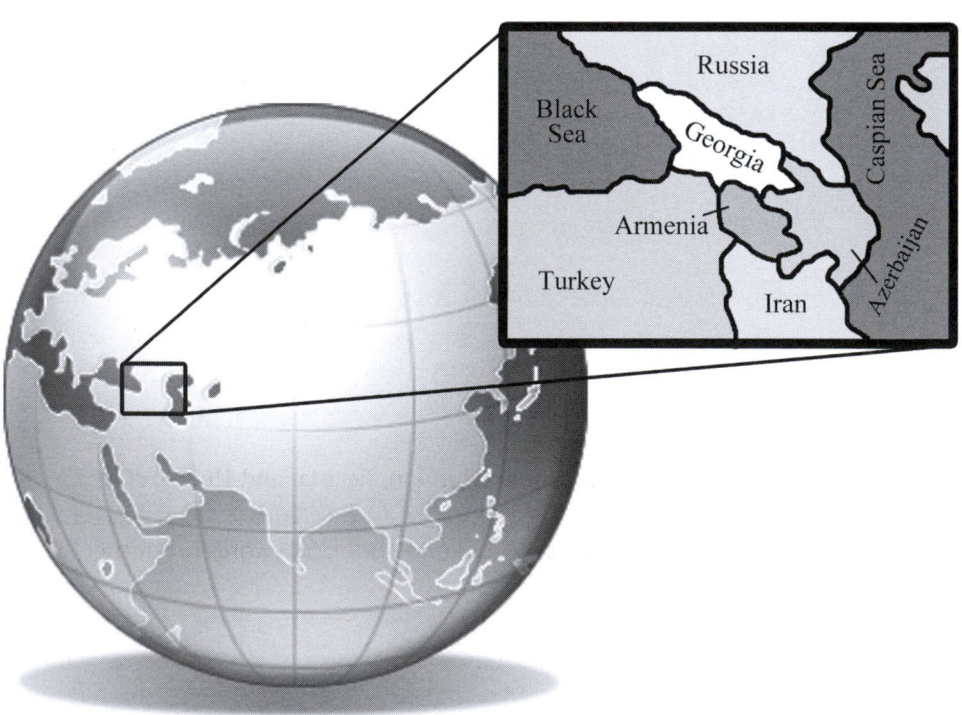

**Figure LP7.1** Area of Russia bordering Georgia; the location of Daghestan

**Figure LP7.2** Location of the Tsez-speaking area

the frontier with the Republic of Georgia. ("Dido" is, incidentally, the Georgian name for the Tsez.) However, a substantial number, perhaps about 45 percent, have migrated to lowland areas of Daghestan. In the traditional territory, Tsez is the usual language of spoken communication and is acquired as a first language by all children. As such, the language is not currently endangered, although there are some recent changes that could jeopardize its status in the not too distant future: the frontier between Russia and Georgia has been increasingly militarized, and the traditional Tsez area is now home to a military presence whose members either are native speakers of Russian or use Russian as their lingua franca and who neither know nor can be expected to learn Tsez.

Tsez is one of five languages belonging to the Tsezic group of languages, which also includes Khwarshi, Hinuq (Ginukh), Bezhta, and Hunzib (Gunzib). The languages are about as distinct from one another as the Germanic languages, so that speakers of one Tsezic language can easily recognize individual words in another – the word for 'girl,' for instance, is *kid* in both Tzez and Bezhta, just as 'hand' is *hand* in both English and German. However, as with Germanic languages, speakers of one language have to take the trouble to learn another if they want to speak it fully and not just recognize individual words. The Tsezic group of languages in turn is part of a larger language family called Nakh-Daghestanian (also called East Caucasian or Northeast Caucasian), which includes most but not all of the indigenous languages of Daghestan. (For

**Figure LP7.3** The author, Bernard Comrie, with Arsen Abdulaev, a native speaker of Tsez

example, Kumyk, a major language of the Caspian seaboard, is a Turkic language.) Some Nakh-Daghestanian languages are also spoken in northern Azerbaijan as well as further to the west. These include Chechen and Ingush, which are spoken in the like-named republics of the Russian Federation, as well as Tsova Tush (also called Bats and Batsbi). The latter is an endangered language spoken by perhaps 3,000 speakers in Georgia and is undergoing rapid linguistic assimilation to Georgian. The internal diversification of the Nakh-Daghestanian family is comparable to that of Indo-European, despite the much smaller area it covers and its much smaller number of languages and speakers.

The North Caucasus is an area of extreme linguistic diversification. The Nakh-Daghestanian family includes both large (by local standards) languages like Chechen, with well over a million speakers, and Avar, with almost 800,000 speakers, as well as some smaller languages. Some of these smaller language have even fewer speakers than Tsez (e.g., Hinuq is the language of a single village, with about 600 speakers). As a general rule, the larger languages are characterized by exogamic marriage practices, that is, members of these speech communities are encouraged not to marry close relatives, which over time has probably led to the assimilation of smaller speech communities and the development of larger ones. The smaller languages are characterized by endogamic marriage practices, that is, members of the speech community are encouraged to marry within a very restricted geographical area and kinship network, including, for instance, cousins. In general, endogamic practices characterize the more mountainous areas, but the small speech communities should not be seen as a direct result of the difficulties in population movement caused by mountainous terrain – in New Guinea, for instance, it is precisely in the Highlands that the larger speech communities are found. Rather, endogamy is a response to the shortage of agricultural land in the mountains and the fear that marriage to outsiders might give the latter rights to this scarce land.

Tsez is basically an unwritten language. Avar, a distant relative within the Nakh-Daghestanian language family, is the traditional lingua franca of western Daghestan, including the area where the Tsezic languages are spoken. More recently, however, Russian has encroached on this role, not least because it is the language of instruction in local schools (and more recently of television), although Avar is still taught as a school subject. In general, those who grow up in the traditional Tsez-speaking area speak Tsez, Avar, and Russian, though younger people usually feel more at home with Russian as their primary non-native language, and older speakers with Avar. There is no standard Tsez language; each village has its own dialect. However, there is rarely any difficulty for inhabitants of one village to understand those of another, with the possible exception of the dialect of the village of Sagada (Tsez: soX'o), the most divergent Tsez dialect. Tsez speakers speak the dialect of their home village and there is no single prestigious variety that other speakers assimilate to. The dialectal diversification of the language can be seen as another effect of endogamy, strengthening relations within the village and setting each village apart from its neighbors.

As might be expected from the status of Avar as a lingua franca, Tsez has borrowed a lot of vocabulary from Avar, including many vocabulary items that ultimately come from Persian, Turkic languages, or Arabic. (The Tsez, like most populations of Daghestan and the North Caucasus more generally, are Muslims, in contrast to the Christian Georgians across the main range of the Caucasus.) Although the frontier with Georgia is now closed, there was regular contact across the main range of the Caucasus going back at least two millennia. Not surprisingly, Tsez also has some loanwords from Georgian, mainly words denoting concrete items that were also acquired initially from Georgia, such as certain foodstuffs, agricultural implements, and elements of house building and furnishing. Nowadays, Russian is the main source of loanwords referring to aspects of the modern world.

## 7.2  Phonology

Although phonetics and phonology is not the main thrust of this chapter, it will be necessary to explain some of the unusual properties of the Tsez phoneme inventory, especially as it relates to consonants, so that the examples can be appreciated not only morphologically and syntactically, but also phonetically and phonologically.

**TABLE LP7.1** The vowel inventory of Tsez

|  | Front | Back | Front | Back |
|---|---|---|---|---|
| High | i | u |  |  |
| Mid | e | o |  |  |
| Low | a |  | ā |  |
|  | Short vowels | | Long vowels | |

**TABLE LP7.2** The consonant inventory of Tsez

|  | Bilabial | Dental | Lateral | Palatal | Velar | Uvular | | Pharyngeal | Glottal |
|---|---|---|---|---|---|---|---|---|---|
|  |  |  |  |  |  | Plain | Pharyngealized |  |  |
| Plain stop | p | t |  |  | k |  |  |  |  |
|  | p' | t' |  |  | k' | q' | q'ˤ |  |  |
|  | b | d |  |  | g |  |  |  |  |
| Affricate |  | c | ƛ | č | q | qˤ |  |  |  |
|  |  | c' | ƛ' | č' |  |  |  |  |  |
| Fricative |  | s | ɬ | š | x |  |  | ħ | h |
|  |  | z |  | ž | ɣ | ɣˤ |  | ʕ |  |
| Nasal | m | n |  |  |  |  |  |  |  |
| Liquid |  | r | l |  |  |  |  |  |  |
| Semivowel | w |  |  | y |  |  |  |  |  |

All Tsez dialects have five short vowels, indeed the usual set of five vowels that is the single most frequent vowel inventory across the languages of the world. Different dialects have differing numbers of long vowels, though the Asakh (Tsez: asaq) dialect of the village of Mokok, on which this chapter is based, has one long vowel. (Orthographically, this is represented as [ā], rather than IPA [aː].) See Table LP7.1.

The consonant system, by contrast, is very rich (as in other languages of the region; see Textbox LP7.1). The symbols are in general those of the International Phonetic Alphabet, although [š, ž] are used to indicate the palato-alveolar fricatives [ʃ, ʒ], [y] is used rather than [j] for the palatal glide, and the symbols [x] and [ɣ] (rather than [χ] and [ʁ]) are used for the **uvular** fricatives. For the affricates, which are very frequent in Tsez, the IPA **digraphs** (two-character symbols) have

**SIDEBAR LP7.1**

The IPA symbol [q] typically represents a voiceless uvular stop. In Tsez, it is phonetically the voiceless uvular affricate [qχ] hence its position in the consonant chart. Since there is no voiceless uvular stop in the language, the symbol *q* is used to represent this sound throughout this chapter.

been abandoned in favor of the symbols [c] for dental, [ƛ] for lateral (see below), and [č] for palatal.

Like many languages spoken in the Caucasus region and belonging to different families (including Indo-European), Tsez has a three-way opposition among its plain stops. In addition to voiced [b], for instance, there are two voiceless correspondents, slightly aspirated [p] and **ejective** [p']. The ejective is formed by closing the vocal cords, closing the lips, raising the larynx to increase pressure within the oral cavity, and then releasing the closure at the lips (and releasing the closure of the vocal cords at the same time or just

---

### TEXTBOX LP7.1 **EVIDENCE OF A LINGUISTIC AREA**

You might notice that the consonant inventory of Tsez shares a number of features with that of Kabardian, another language of the Caucasus. For example, both languages have a series of ejective stops, many velar and uvular stops and fricatives, and a voiceless pharyngeal fricative. These features, together with others, are found in many languages of the region and suggest that the Caucasus is a **linguistic area** (see Chapter 13, section 13.6).

---

after). The release of the compressed air creates the "popping" sound that is characteristic of ejective consonants. The vocal cord (glottal) closure is what is crucial to ejective sounds; this contrasts them with all other phonemes of the language, which use air directly from the lungs. There is only a two-way opposition among the affricates and uvulars, with no voiced counterparts. Despite the richness of their consonant system, speakers of Tsez may experience difficulties with the [ʤ] sound at the beginning of *John*, which is absent from their phoneme inventory (and also, incidentally, with the [f] at the beginning of *fish*, which Tsez also lacks). The **lateral affricate** ƛ consists of a [t] opening out into an [l], much as in English *bottle*. The uvulars are pronounced further back in the mouth than the velars, with the back of the tongue against the uvula. The **pharyngeals** involve compressing the larynx to give a hoarse sound. It should be noted that the uvulars also have pharyngealized counterparts, which are distinct phonemes, and which involve compressing the larynx at the same time as making the uvular sound. Indeed, in word-initial position some other consonants also have phonemically distinct pharyngealized counterparts. A rich set of consonant phonemes pronounced in the back of the mouth (uvulars, pharyngeals) is typical of languages of the North Caucasus, as well as a number of other Middle Eastern languages, including Arabic. Finally, most (though not all) consonants can also occur with phonemically distinct labialization, i.e., simultaneous lip rounding.

## 7.3  Clause structure

In order to explain the basic structure of clauses in Tsez, I will use some illustrative sentences taken from a folk tale, "The Hen and the Rooster," collected by Isa Abdullaev. In this story the rooster cheats on the hen by visiting a frog, after which the hen gets her revenge by beating up the frog. Eventually, the hen and rooster are reconciled, although the long-term fate of the frog remains, alas, unknown. Since sentences in Tsez narratives have a tendency to be rather long, incorporating several clauses (a point to which I return below), some material (in particular, dependent clauses) has been omitted from the sentences as they appear in the original story.

### 7.3.1  Intransitive verbs

Consider the first example (1):

(1)  *hudāyziko*        *mamalay*       *b-ik'i-n*              *łoħro-de-r.*
      on.third.day      rooster.ABS     III.SG-go-PST.UNW       frog-APUD-LAT
      'On the third day the rooster went to the frog.'

**SIDEBAR LP7.2**
GLOSSES
These terms, their meanings, and uses will be presented below.

| Term | Meaning | Gloss |
|------|---------|-------|
| adessive | location near | AD |
| possessive | possession | POSS |
| lative | motion towards | LAT |
| ablative | motion away from | ABL |
| sub | location under | SUB |
| super | location above, on top of | SUPER |
| Latin *apud* | location beside | APUD |
| witnessed | directly witnessed event | WIT |
| unwitnessed | event not witnessed | UNW |

The core of this clause is *mamalay bik'in* 'the rooster went'; indeed, this could be a well-formed clause and sentence in isolation. The verb *-ik'i-* 'go' is an intransitive verb, like its English counterpart, and requires only a single argument, the one that goes. In Tsez, the noun phrase referring to this argument, *mamalay* 'rooster,' is in its **citation form**, that is, the form that would be given if one were to ask a speaker of Tsez: "What is the word for *rooster* in your language?" For reasons that will become clear below, I will call this form of a noun the **absolutive** case, abbreviated ABS. So a Tsez intransitive verb takes a single argument in the absolutive case.

The word *łoħroder* 'to the frog' is not an obligatory constituent of the clause, but nonetheless it paves the way for a discussion of one of the most fascinating aspects of Tsez morphology. The absolutive case of this word is *łoħro*; so in order to express the idea 'the frog went,' a Tsez speaker would say *łoħro bik'in*, as one would predict from the preceding discussion. But in Example (1), the word for 'frog' is in a different case. In fact, the word *łoħroder* includes two case suffixes in succession, *-de*, which I have glossed as APUD, and *-r*, which I have glossed as **lative** (abbreviated LAT). **Apud** is a Latin preposition meaning 'beside, at the house of, in the presence of,' and is used as a convenient gloss for a Tsez case suffix that expresses location beside an entity, especially an animate (including human) entity, The expression *łoħro-de* on its own is well-formed in Tsez and simply means 'beside the frog,' referring to a static location near the frog. Other case suffixes can express different kinds of location in Tsez, as in *łoħro-λ'* 'frog-SUPER,' i.e., 'on the frog,' or *łoħro-λ* 'frog-SUB,' i.e., 'under the frog,' where I again use Latinate glosses for convenience (Latin SUPER 'above, on top of'; SUB 'under'). Note that the suffix for SUPER has an ejective lateral affricate (λ'), while that for SUB has a plain lateral affricate (λ).

The addition of lative -*r* expresses motion to(ward), so *łoħro-de-r* 'frog-APUD-LAT' means 'to beside the frog.' In English we would probably be content with just 'to the frog,' but Tsez requires greater explicitness. We can now form words meaning 'onto the frog' and 'to under the frog' by adding the lative, although some vowel insertion is needed in Tsez to avoid consonant clusters not tolerated by the language: *łoħro-λ'o-r* 'frog-SUPER-LAT'; *łoħro-λ-er* 'frog-SUB-LAT.' In addition to the lative suffix indicating motion to(ward), Tsez also has an ablative suffix -*āy*, indicating motion (away) from. We can now form *łoħro-d-āy* 'frog-APUD-ABL,' i.e., 'away from beside the frog' (though again English would probably be content with just 'from the frog'); *łoħro-λ'-āy* 'frog-SUPER-ABL,' i.e., 'from on the frog' (more idiomatically in English, 'off the frog'); and *łoħro-λ-āy* 'frog-SUB-ABL,' i.e., 'from under the frog' (which in this case is also idiomatic English).

Stringing cases together in this way to express a combination of a specific location type (beside, on, under) and location versus motion (at, to, from) is very unusual among the languages of the world, although it happens to be typical of Nakh-Daghestanian languages. These languages are often said to have huge case inventories, with scores of cases, but this is rather misleading: instead, the languages have a rather restricted number of cases and a general rule for combining these cases, thus giving rise to a large number of case combinations. Note that English can sometimes combine prepositions in this way (e.g., 'from under'), although this is relatively rare in languages with prepositions (or postpositions), and as we saw above with literal and idiomatic English translations, not all of the logically expected combinations are possible or idiomatic in English, in contrast to Tsez.

Let us now turn to the verb in Example (1). The suffix -*n* (with a variant -*no* after a consonant) on the verb is a tense suffix, expressing the so-called past unwitnessed, abbreviated PST.UNW. The "past" part of this is unsurprising, since Tsez, like English, has a set of past-tense forms that are used not only for real events that happened in the past but also conventionally in stories that are told as if they had happened in the past. But what about "unwitnessed"? It turns out that Tsez has two past tenses, past witnessed (PST.WIT) and past unwitnessed, distinguished according to whether or not the speaker witnessed the event in question or not. In Example (1), as is typical for a traditional tale, the speaker, in this case the narrator, did not witness the events in question, so the past unwitnessed is used. If, however, the same sentence were to occur not in a traditional tale but as a report on a strange incident I witnessed in the yard, then I would say (2), using the past witnessed suffix -*s*.

(2)  *mamalay*          *b-ik'i-s*                        *ɬoħro-de-r.*
     rooster.ABS       III.SG-go-PST.WIT       frog-APUD-LAT
     'The rooster went to the frog.'

The grammatical category that indicates the speaker's source of the information expressed in a sentence is called **evidentiality**. Tsez has a rather restricted evidential system: evidentiality is distinguished only with past time reference – the present-tense verb form *bik'ix* 'goes,' with the present-tense suffix -*x*, contains no information as to whether or not the speaker is witnessing the event – and there is only a binary opposition between witnessed and unwitnessed. Many other languages of the world have a richer set of oppositions, distinguishing, for instance, between information obtained from a visual versus an auditory source.

Finally, what about the prefix *b-* on the verb with its mysterious gloss 'III'? In English, regular verbs agree with their subjects in person and number in the present tense, with a distinction between the third-person singular form (*he/she/it sings*), and the form used for all other person–number combinations (*I/we/you/they sing*). In Tsez, verbs do not agree in person, but they do agree in number, and also in gender. The gloss III.SG in (1) indicates that the verb is agreeing with a noun of gender III and in the singular. Incidentally, only verbs beginning with a vowel can show gender–number agreement, while verbs beginning with a consonant simply show no agreement, so 'the rooster crowed' shows up simply as *mamalay q'oq'oλi-n* 'rooster.ABS crow-PST.UNW.'

Tsez has a system of four genders, each of which triggers a distinct consonant prefix on vowel-initial verbs in the singular; in the plural, there is a distinct prefix for gender I, while the other three genders merge into a single corresponding prefix. The forms of the prefixes are shown in Table LP7.3. These are, incidentally, the only prefixes in the language.

A relatively large number of genders is typical for Nakh-Daghestanian languages, with three to five being common and larger numbers rarer but clearly attested. For languages with such large numbers of genders, there is a tradition of using the term "noun class" rather than gender, but there is really no principled basis for this distinction. Just as an adjective in Spanish has to agree in gender (and number) with its noun (masculine -*o* in *hombre delgado* 'thin man,' but feminine -*a* in *mujer delgada* 'thin woman'), in Tsez a vowel-initial verb must agree in gender and number.

**TABLE LP7.3** Tsez gender prefixes

|      | I   | II  | III | IV  |
| ---- | --- | --- | --- | --- |
| SG   | Ø-  | y-  | b-  | r-  |
| PL   | b-  | r-  | r-  | r-  |

There is little in the form of a Tsez noun to tell what gender it belongs to (unlike Spanish, for instance, where nearly all nouns ending in *-o* are masculine), although there are some semantic correlates to the various genders. This is clearest with gender I, which includes all and only nouns denoting male humans (and assimilated supernatural beings). Gender II includes all nouns denoting female humans, but also a fair number of inanimate nouns. Gender III includes all nouns denoting animals, but also a large number of nouns denoting inanimates. Gender IV contains only inanimates, including abstract nouns. Thus, for nouns denoting humans and animals, gender is predictable, but inanimate nouns can belong to any of genders II, III, and IV. The precise factors determining gender assignment remain to be worked out, and there may be a large element of purely conventional assignment, but semantic analogy and formal analogy (e.g., initial or final consonants that are similar to the singular gender prefix) both seem to play a role. Given this information about Tsez gender–number prefixes on verbs, *mamalay b-ik'i-n* 'the rooster went' could be changed to: *uži ik'i-n* 'the boy went,' *kid y-ik'in* 'the girl went,' *uži-bi b-ik'i-n* 'the boys went,' or *mamalay-bi r-ik'i-n* 'the roosters went,' where *-bi* is the absolutive plural suffix. It should be noted that the absence of a prefix on a vowel-initial verb specifically indicates gender I singular and is in no sense a neutral form.

Before leaving gender, we may note one difference between English and Tsez with regard to the conventions for gender of personified animals. In English, the tendency is to treat personified animals as humans, and to refer to them as *he* and *she*. In Tsez, personified animals remain animals, and therefore take gender III agreement. This is absolutely consistent through all such tales I have encountered, even in an example like "The hen and the rooster" where the participants have such gender-stereotyped roles (e.g., errant husband, betrayed wife, "the other woman").

### 7.3.2 Transitive verbs

Let us now consider a transitive verb, that is, one having an agent or agent-like argument and a patient or patient-like argument, as in (3). The English translation of (3) contains a verb *break* that can be both transitive (as here) and intransitive (*The leg broke*), but Tsez has no verbs of this kind, and the verb *-ecur-* is unequivocally transitive, requiring two arguments. (The Tsez equivalent to English intransitive 'break' is the related verb *-ecu-*.)

(3)  *onoč-ā*       *y-ecur-no*              *k'onču.*
     hen-ERG      II.SG-break-PST.UNW      leg.ABS
     'The hen broke [the frog's] leg.'

Let us first consider the case-marking in (3). In English, most noun phrases appearing as core arguments of intransitive or transitive verbs show no case-marking, but some personal pronouns do. As can be seen in Examples (4) and (5), in English the single argument of an intransitive verb (abbreviated as S), and the agent-like argument of a transitive verb (abbreviated A) are in the so-called **nominative** (NOM) case, while the patient-like argument of a transitive verb (abbreviated P) is in the so-called **accusative** (ACC) case.

**(4)**  *He          went.*
    S
    NOM

**(5)**  *He        hit      me.*
    A                   P
    NOM              ACC

Tsez has a different system, which holds for nearly all noun phrases in the language. Compare examples (6) and (7) below to (4) and (5) above. In a transitive clause, it is the P that appears in the same case as the S of an intransitive clause, while the A appears in a different case. Conventionally, the case used for S and P is called the absolutive (ABS), while the case used for A is called the **ergative** (ERG).

**(6)**  *mamalay        b-ik'i-s*
    rooster.ABS       III.SG-go-PST.WIT
    S
    ABS
    'The rooster went.'

**(7)**  *onoč-ā        y-ecur-no              k'ončus*
    hen-ERG       II.SG-break-PST.UNW     leg.ABS
    A                                P
    ERG                              ABS
    'The hen broke the leg.'

In (7), the citation form of the word 'leg' is *k'ončus*, and as with all Tsez nouns this is the form used as absolutive. The citation form and absolutive for 'hen' is *onoču*. The ergative suffix in Tsez is *-ā*. As A of its clause in (7), the word for 'hen' must appear in the ergative, i.e., as *onoč-ā*. (The final vowel of the stem is dropped before the ergative suffix to avoid vowel hiatus.) The case-marking system of Tsez is thus an ergative-absolutive system, in contrast to the nominative-accusative system found (albeit only with some personal pronouns) in English. Ergative-absolutive case-marking is widespread among the indigenous languages of the Caucasus.

But what about verb agreement in (7)? The word for 'hen,' like all animal nouns, belongs to gender III. The word for 'leg' belongs to gender II. Clearly, in (7) the verb agrees with 'leg,' i.e., with the P of its clause, not the A. More generally, Tsez verbs agree with their absolutive argument, i.e., like case-marking, verb agreement operates on an ergative-absolutive basis. In English, by contrast, verb agreement, just like case-marking of pronouns, operates on a nominative-accusative basis, so that in *The dogs chase the cat* or *The cat chases the dog*, the verb agrees with the A, just as it agrees with the S of an intransitive verb.

The scope of this profile has enabled us to examine only a few of the linguistic features of Tsez, concentrating on those that can be introduced in a concise manner without presupposing other information about the language's structure. Many relevant features, such as word order, have gone untreated. (For the record, depending on the specific discourse contexts, any rearrangements of the words in the Tsez sentences cited would be possible.) But I hope to have shown how one can gain at least some insight into cross-linguistic diversity by examining a language with a very different typological profile from those which are familiar to us.

---

### TEXTBOX LP7.2 **GLOSSING CONVENTIONS USED IN THIS LANGUAGE PROFILE**

| Convention | Meaning | Convention | Meaning |
|---|---|---|---|
| ABL | ablative | NOM | nominative |
| ABS | absolutive | POSS | possessive |
| ACC | accusative | PST | past |
| AD | adessive | SG | singular |
| APUD | location beside | SUB | location under |
| ERG | ergative | super | location above; on top of |
| I/II/III/IV | gender classes | UNW | unwitnessed |
| LAT | lative | WIT | witnessed |

---

### SUGGESTIONS FOR FURTHER READING

**Alekseev, M. E. and R. N. Radžabov**. 2004. "Tsez". In Michael Job (ed.), *Indigenous languages of the Caucasus*, Vol. III, Part 1. Ann Arbor: Caravan Books.

This is the only published general account of Tsez in English.

**Comrie, Bernard**. 2008. "Linguistic diversity in the Caucasus." *Annual Review of Anthropology* **37**: 131–148.

This source is valuable for more general information on linguistic diversity in the Caucasus.

---

### EXERCISES

1. Verb morphology

In this language profile, we noted that Tsez verbs can change their form by adding both prefixes and suffixes. The only prefixes are those indicating agreement in gender. Suffixes include those indicating tense, in particular the past witnessed and past unwitnessed tenses that were introduced in the profile.

Below, you are given examples of intransitive clauses with various verbs and subjects, in both of the past tenses. You will notice that there is some variation across different verbs. For instance, some verbs in the past witnessed end in -*si*, while others end in -*s*; likewise, the past unwitnessed shows variation between -*no* and -*n*. Also, some verbs agree with the subject, as noted in the language profile, while other verbs do not.

a. What determines whether a verb undergoes agreement, like *ik'is/yik'is/bik'is*, or fails to undergo agreement, like *gugis*?

(i) a. *uži č'ariłsi.*
    *uži č'ariłno.*     'The boy woke up.'

   b. *kid č'ariłsi.*
     *kid č'ariłno.*     'The girl woke up.'

   c. *łoħro č'ariłsi.*
     *łoħro č'ariłno.*     'The frog woke up.'

(ii) a. *uži exus.*
    *uži exun.*     'The boy died.'

   b. *kid yexus.*
     *kid yexun.*     'The girl died.'

   c. *łoħro bexus.*
     *łoħro bexun.*     'The frog died.'

(iii) a. *uži gugis.*
    *uži gugin.*     'The boy disappeared.'

   b. *kid gugis.*
     *kid gugin.*     'The girl disappeared.'

   c. *łoħro gugis.*
     *łoħro gugin.*     'The frog disappeared.'

(iv) a. *uži ik'is.*
    *uži ik'in.*     'The boy went.'

   b. *kid yik'is.*
     *kid yik'in.*     'The girl went.'

   c. *łoħro bik'is.*
     *łoħro bik'in.*     'The frog went.'

(v) a. *uži izis.*
    *uži izin.*     'The boy got up.'

   b. *kid yizis.*
     *kid yizin.*     'The girl got up.'

   c. *łoħro bizis.*
     *łoħro bizin.*     'The frog got up.'

(vi)   a.  *uži kecsi.*      'The boy slept.'
          *uži kecno.*

        b.  *kid kecsi.*      'The girl slept.'
          *kid kecno.*

        c.  *ɬoħro kecsi.*      'The frog slept.'
          *ɬoħro kecno.*

(vii)   a.  *uži ƛexsi.*      'The boy stayed.'
          *uži ƛexno.*

        b.  *kid ƛexsi.*      'The girl stayed.'
          *kid ƛexno.*

        c.  *ɬoħro ƛexsi.*      'The frog stayed.'
          *ɬoħro ƛexno.*

(viii)   a.  *uži oqsi.*      'The boy became.'
          *uži oqno.*

        b.  *kid yoqsi.*      'The girl became.'
          *kid yoqno.*

        c.  *ɬoħro boqsi.*      'The frog became.'
          *ɬoħro boqno.*

   b.  What is the relevant factor governing the choice between -*si* versus -*s* for the past witnessed? What governs the choice between -*no* versus -*n* for the past unwitnessed?

   c.  Some verbs show dialect variation, with different dialects of Tsez preferring one or other of the alternative forms given below. Under what circumstances is this variation permitted?

(ix)   a.  *užɪ aysi/ays.*      'The boy came.'
          *uži ayno/ayn.*

        b.  *kid yaysi/yays.*      'The girl came.'
          *kid yayno/yayn.*

        c.  *ɬoħro baysi/bays.*      'The frog came.'
          *ɬoħro bayno/bayn.*

(x)   a.  *uži zowsi/zows.*      'The boy was.'
          *uži zowno/zown.*

        b.  *kid zowsi/zows.*      'The girl was.'
          *kid zowno/zown.*

        c.  *ɬoħro zowsi/zows.*      'The frog was.'
          *ɬoħro zowno/zown.*

**TABLE LP7.4** Complex case inflections for two Tsez nouns (*besuro* 'fish' and *halmaɣ* 'friend')

|        | SUPER        | AD         | APUD       | POSS        |
|--------|--------------|------------|------------|-------------|
|        | *besuroλ'*   | *besurox*  | *besurode* | *besuroq*   |
| +ABL   | *besuroλ'āy* | *besuroxāy*| *besurodāy*| *besuroqāy* |
| +LAT   | *besuroλ'or* | *besuroxor*| *besuroder*| *besuroqor* |
|        | *halmaɣλ'o*  | *halmaɣxo* | *halmayde* | *halmaɣqo*  |
| +ABL   | *halmaɣλ'āy* | *halmaɣxāy*| *halmaɣdāy*| *halmaɣqāy* |
| +LAT   | *halmaɣλ'or* | *halmaɣxor*| *halmaɣder*| *halmaɣqor* |

2.  Noun morphology

    In this language profile, an introduction was given to the interesting system of Tsez cases expressing location (see Sidebar LP7.2). In addition to the location types discussed in the profile, two more are introduced here, namely location *near* and location *at*. The latter is also used in the expression of possession. For this reason it is glossed POSS 'possessive.' When used by itself, the simple possessive form of a noun indicates that the noun is in someone's possession (thus the meaning is similar to that of the verb 'have'). When the possessive is combined with the lative suffix, it indicates movement into someone's possession (as with the verb 'give'). When the possessive is combined with the ablative, it indicates movement out of someone's possession (as with the verb 'take away').

    The examples in Table LP7.4 give the various case combinations possible for two nouns, *besuro* 'fish' and *halmaɣ* 'friend.'

    The system is very logical: one combines a suffix for a type of location from the horizontal axis with a suffix for location or motion on the vertical axis.

    a.  Divide the suffixes from the stems. Do you observe variation in the stems or in the suffixes?

    b.  Begin the morphological analysis by focusing on the forms with the single suffix only (i.e., the first and fourth row). List the forms of the SUPER, AD, APUD, and POSS suffixes. You will notice that three of these suffixes each have two allomorphs. The allomorphs with the final vowel are found only on stems that end with consonants, such as *halmaɣ*. Suggest a motivation for the additional vowel on just consonant-final stems, i.e., why should this be? (Hint: try pronouncing the forms with and without the vowel.)

    c.  Next address the ablative suffix. What is its form? Why do we not find the *-o* allomorphs of the SUPER, AD, APUD, and POSS suffixes co-occurring with the ablative case-marker? For example, why do we find *halmaɣqāy*, rather than *\*halmaɣqoāy*? Also, consider the APUD-ABL forms *besurodāy* and *halmaɣdāy*. State in prose the phonetic process that has occurred, and then write a rule.

    d.  Now consider the lative forms. What is the form of the lative suffix? Here we find the *-o* allomorphs of the suffixes reappearing (as you saw in b). Why should this be?

    e.  Another set of forms, those with the sub ('under') suffix, follows:

|       | SUB          |
|-------|--------------|
|       | *besuroƛ*    |
| + ABL | *besuroƛāy*  |
| + LAT | *besuroƛer*  |

|       |              |
|-------|--------------|
|       | *halmaγeƛ*   |
| + ABL | *halmaγƛāy*  |
| + LAT | *halmaγƛer*  |

You will notice the vowel /e/ occurring in *halmaγeƛ*, but in none of the other forms. Is it best to analyze this /e/ as part of the stem, part of the suffix, or as a vowel inserted by rule? Explain your reasoning for your answer. What about the /e/ in the lative forms? Write a single rule that applies in both cases and discuss its phonetic motivation.

f. Two further Tsez nouns are *ziru* 'fox' and the man's name *idris* 'Idris.' Using everything you have learned about the phonology so far, determine the correct Tsez forms for each of the following. (The English versions are sometimes unidiomatic.)

| i.    | 'from under the fox' | SUB-ABL    |
|-------|----------------------|------------|
| ii.   | 'from near Idris'    | AD-ABL     |
| iii.  | 'on the fox'         | SUPER      |
| iv.   | 'by Idris'           | APUD       |
| v.    | 'to by the fox'      | APUD-LAT   |
| vi.   | 'to under Idris'     | SUB-LAT    |
| vii.  | 'from by the fox'    | APUD-ABL   |
| viii. | 'under Idris'        | SUB        |
| ix.   | 'to on the fox'      | SUPER-LAT  |
| x.    | 'near Idris'         | AD         |

3. Pronoun morphology and agreement

Nearly all nouns and most pronouns in Tsez distinguish an absolutive case and an ergative case, as in the examples in the profile. However, first- and second-person singular pronouns are exceptions, since they have an invariable form, *di* (first-person singular) and *mi* (second-person singular), used for all of S, A, and P. Below, you are given some examples of intransitive and transitive clauses with first- and second-person singular pronoun arguments.

| i.    | *di ik'is.*      | 'I went (man speaking).'                    |
|-------|------------------|---------------------------------------------|
| ii.   | *di yik'is.*     | 'I went (woman speaking).'                   |
| iii.  | *di bik'is*      | 'I went (frog speaking, e.g., in a story).'  |
| iv.   | *mi ik'is.*      | 'You went (speaking to man).'                |
| v.    | *mi yik'is.*     | 'You went (speaking to woman).'              |
| vi.   | *mi bik'is*      | 'You went (speaking to animal).'             |
| vii.  | *di mi egirsi*   | 'I sent you (woman speaking to man).'        |
| viii. | *di mi egirsi*   | 'I sent you (man speaking to man).'          |
| ix.   | *di mi yegirsi*  | 'I sent you (woman speaking to woman).'      |
| x.    | *di mi yegirsi*  | 'I sent you (man speaking to woman).'        |
| xi.   | *di mi begirsi*  | 'I sent you (woman speaking to animal).'     |
| xii.  | *di mi begirsi*  | 'I sent you (man speaking to animal).'       |

The focus of this problem is on verb agreement. State which argument(s) the verb agrees with in (a) intransitive and (b) transitive clauses. Is the agreement pattern the same as, or different from, that for full noun phrases?

**LANGUAGE PROFILE 8**

# Bardi

## 8.1 Introduction

Bardi is one of Australia's 320 or so Indigenous languages. The name of the language is pronounced ['bɐː|ɖi] (see Sidebar LP8.1). Bardi is one of several dialects of a language that is also (confusingly!) called Bardi. Other dialects include Jawi [ɟaːwɪ] (which begins with a voiced palatal stop) and Bard (or Baard) [bɐːɖ]. Bardi is also an **ethonym** (the name of the people of the area).

Most Bardi people live in the northwest of Western Australia, in an area called the Kimberley region. The main Bardi communities are One Arm Point and Lombadina. Bardi people also live in towns such as Broome and Derby, and in outstations (outposts from the communities). Bardi people are sea people; Bardi and Jawi traditional territories included not only the tip of the Dampier peninsula but also the neighboring islands. See Textbox LP8.1 for a related note.

The number of Bardi speakers is quite small. It is not certain exactly how many speakers there are. As of 2013, only about five people speak the language fluently, but many more can understand it and some can speak it a bit. There are about one thousand Bardi people in total.

Although only the oldest people in Bardi communities speak Bardi fluently, some young Bardi children are interested in their language and culture and there is a language program at One Arm Point school. While the Bardi language is in a fragile state, Bardi people are taking action to make sure their language continues and that their culture is strong.

Bardi is a member of the *Nyulnyulan* language family. This family has about eight languages in it. They are all spoken in the Western Kimberley region of Western Australia. Nyulnyulan is one of twenty-eight language families that are indigenous to the Australian mainland and the Torres Strait.

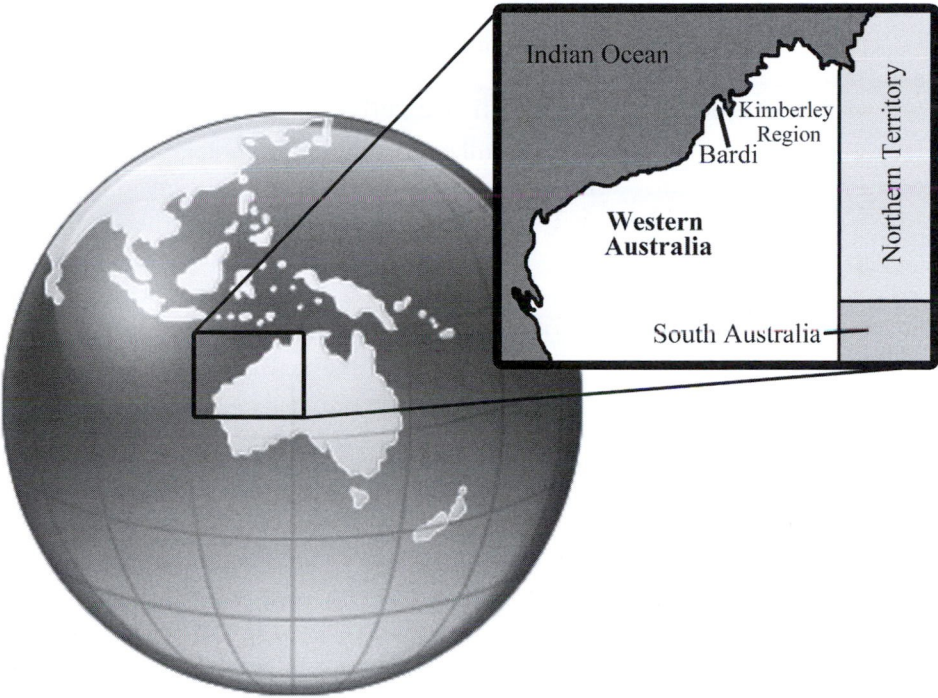

**Figure LP8.1** Map of the region where Bardi is spoken

---

**TEXTBOX LP8.1 WHAT SHOULD WE CALL THE FIRST PEOPLES OF AUSTRALIA?**

There are several terms used to describe Australia's First Peoples. The term "native" is offensive in Australia, and "First Nation" is not used. The most widely used terms are "Aboriginal" and "Torres Strait Islander" or "Indigenous." However, some people don't like the term "Indigenous," because they feel it has been imposed on them by Europeans, and that it serves to remove Aboriginal people from public discourse.

---

## 8.2  Basic typological overview

### 8.2.1  Phonetics and phonology

The Bardi phonemic inventory has seventeen consonants and seven vowels. As in roughly half of Australian languages, Bardi has five places of articulation for stops and nasals. These include a set of **retroflex** consonants, as well bilabial, dental, palatal, and velar ones. Bardi also has a distinction between two types of r-sounds, a feature which is common in Australian languages. For example, *ara* (with an approximant, somewhat like English [ɹ]) means 'other,' but *arra* (with a trill [r]), means 'no' or 'don't.' There are also three different laterals: retroflex /ɭ/, palatal /ʎ/, and alveolar /l/. There is no phonemic voicing contrast in consonants. Bardi distinguishes between long and short vowels.

## 8.2.2 Argument marking on the verb

Bardi has extensive morphological marking of grammatical relations, found in both verb agreement and case-marking. Within the verb, the subject, object (if there is one), oblique argument (e.g., benefactive), and possessor are all indexed morphologically. The subject argument is indicated by a prefix, while other NPs (as well as some types of adjuncts) are indicated by **clitics**, which follow the verb root and tense marking. Example (1) has a third-person prefix *i-* which indexes the subject argument *Jibaji*. See Sidebar LP8.4 for a note on the glossing.

(1)  *Jibaji*     *aarl-on*        ***i**-na-ng-gala-na-na*
     Jibaji       fish-LOC         3-TR-PST-wander-CONT.REM.PST
     'Jibaji was fishing.'

This example also shows that tense can be marked in two places in the Bardi verb. Here it is marked both by the prefix *ng-*, which indicates past tense, and again by the suffix *-na*, which indicates that the action of the verb occurred a while ago, hence in the remote past rather than the recent or immediate past. The other suffix *-na* marks the action as continuous. This is a type of **aspect**, a grammatical category independent of tense that indicates, for example, whether an event is continuous, completed, or habitual. Since Example (1) has both the past and continuous, the verb translates into English as 'was fishing'. Also of note here is the prefix *na-* which explicitly marks the verb root as being transitive (we'll come back to this below).

Example (2) illustrates a clitic on the verb that indicates that the indirect object is first-person plural (i.e., 'us'):

(2)  *Way*        *i-n-nya-na=**jard***          *oola*  *janjali*  *nyalab.*
     come.toward  3-TR-catch-REM.PST=1PL.IO      rain    cyclone    this.way
     'A cyclone came toward us.' (Bessie Ejai: janjal.wav)

This example contains two other interesting features of Bardi. First, it contains a **complex predicate**, two or more words that act as a single predicate of a single clause, with one set of arguments. Each word in a complex predicate contributes to the overall meaning. In (2) the sequence *way innyanajard* is a complex predicate constructed of the preverb *way* and the verb *innyanajard*; these structures will be discussed in more detail below. Secondly, this clause illustrates a type of classification that is quite common in Australia. A general noun (in this case, *oola* '(fresh) water, rain') is juxtaposed with a more specific item (*janjali* 'cyclone').

The verb in Example (3) carries both a prefix *nga-*, indicating a first-person singular subject, and the clitic =*rri*, which marks the second-person singular object:

(3) *Ngay-**nim***     *loorrboo*     **nga**-*n-k-i-ya*=*rri*.
    1SG-ERG     ignore     1SG-TR-FUT-do-FUT=2SG.P
    'I won't listen to you.'

This is also a good example of double future-tense marking; the *verb ngankiyarri* has both a future-tense prefix *k-* and a future-tense suffix *-(y)a*. Just as in Example (1), this verb has a prefix (here *n-*) that marks it as being transitive.

Finally, Example (4) shows oblique agreement in addition to the marking of subject and direct object. The verb has the third-person-singular subject marker *i-*, the object marker =*irr* (which is coreferential with *aarli* 'fish'), and the oblique clitic =*jin*, which could indicate either a possessor argument (i.e., his fish), or a beneficiary (i.e., cooked a fish for him).

(4) *Ginyinggon*     *i-na-marra-na-n*=*jin*=*irr*           *aarli*.
    then     3-TR-cook-CONT-REM.PST=3SG.OBL=3PL.P     fish
    'Then he cooked his fish/then he cooked the fish for him.'

The examples in (1)–(4) give you a lot of information about how Bardi works. We can see that the marking of grammatical relations on the verb is a salient element of Bardi morphology. We have also seen that Bardi grammar has extensive marking of tense and aspect, as well as complex predicates.

### 8.2.3   Case-marking

Another important feature of Bardi is case-marking. It has quite a few different cases, including ergative (illustrated in (3) above) and absolutive on core arguments (these will be discussed more fully below), but also locative (roughly 'at'), allative ('to'), ablative ('from'), semblative ('like'), comitative ('with'), and a few others. Many of these cases provide information about the location of an item, whether someone is going with someone else or using something as an instrument, or whether something looks like something else. Some of these grammatical cases are illustrated in the following examples.

In (5), Bessie Ejai is describing how an animal was made in the shape of a house. She uses the semblative case to describe how something is similar to something else.

(5)

| I-nga-rr-a-m | awoojoo-**marr** | ni-mara | ngirray-**marr** |
|---|---|---|---|
| 3-PST-PL-TR-make | house-SEMBL | 3SG-chest | hut-SEMBL |

| moorrooloo-ngarr | ni-many. |
|---|---|
| little-INTENSIFIER | 3SG-throat |

'They made the chest-part like a house, like a hut, and there's a little opening [a 'throat'].'

Sentence (6) has an example of the comitative case, which indicates a person or thing that accompanies someone or something else:

(6)

| I-ng-arr-ala-n | aeroplane | arr | i-n-joo-na-na |
|---|---|---|---|
| 3-PST-PL-see-REM.PST | plane | come | 3-TR-do-CONT-REM.PST |

| nyalab | goonkoordoo-**nyarr** | gala. |
|---|---|---|
| this.way | smoke-COM | COMPL |

'They saw the plane coming towards them with smoke [coming from the engines].'

Example (7) has a locative case; here indicating that one thing is on another. This case can also be used for other spatial relationships (e.g., 'at,' 'in'; see Textbox 23.2), combined with a spatial adverb (e.g., 'under,' 'above'), or used for certain types of motion.

(7)

| Mooloo | boor | i-n-jal=jin | ara-nim | oorany |
|---|---|---|---|---|
| louse.PL | look | 3-TR-look=3SG.OBL | other-ERG | woman |

| ara | oorany | n-alm-onon. |
|---|---|---|
| other | woman | 3SG-head-LOC |

'One woman was looking for lice on another woman's head.'

---

### TEXTBOX LP8.2 **DESCRIBING SPACE**

Bardi case-marking can be combined with spatial adverbs to allow speakers to make more precise descriptions of space. For example, in (7) one could also say *garndi nalmonon* 'on top of the woman's head,' using *garndi* 'on top' in addition to the case-marking on *nalmonon*.

---

(8)

| Joo-nim | jooroorr | a-ni-wi=jirri. |
|---|---|---|
| 2SG-ERG | sand | 2.IMP-tr-poke=3PL.OBL |

'You poke the sand.'

Examples (8) and (9) illustrate one of the cases that is used on core arguments; the ergative. (For further discussion of ergative **alignment**, see Textbox LP8.3.) In Bardi, ergative case-marking is consistently found on subject arguments of transitive clauses. In (8), an example appears on the second-person pronoun, the subject of the transitive verb *aniwijirri* 'you poke it,' while in (9) it is found on the noun phrase *aamba* 'man,' the subject of *injalajarrmoordoo* 'he is looking at us.'

(9)   *Aamba-nim*        *i-n-jala=jarrmoordoo.*
      man-ERG          3-TR-look.at=1PL.P
      'A man's looking at us!'

The ergative case-marker can be also found in Examples (3) and (7) above, as well as in (10):

(10)  *Ginyinggi-nim*    *baawa*    *boor*    *i-n-jala=jin*       *bordog-on*    *arrijin.*
      3SG-ERG          child      look      3-TR-look=3SG.IO    tree-LOC      nothing
      'This child was looking for his on the tree, but he didn't find it.'

You might notice something unusual in (10) concerning the placement of the case-marker. Many languages have case-marking that goes on every item in a noun phrase; examples are Russian and Latin. Other languages have case-marking which goes only on the final item in the phrase; Japanese and Turkish are languages like this. Bardi is different: in Bardi, the case-marker goes on only the first item in the phrase.

---

## TEXTBOX LP8.3 **ERGATIVE-ABSOLUTIVE VERSUS NOMINATIVE-ACCUSATIVE ALIGNMENT**

Grammatical phenomena such as agreement and case-marking can group arguments in different ways. Sometimes the single core argument of an intransitive verb (abbreviated as S) is treated in the same way as the more agentive core argument of a transitive or ditransitive verb (abbreviated as A), thus defining the subject grammatical relation. Bardi verb agreement is of this type. In the examples below, the verb takes the third-person prefix *I-* In agreement with the S argument in (a) and with the A argument in (b). An entirely different marker is used for the non-agentive core argument (abbreviated as P) in example (b).

a.   *Boonyja*     *aarli*     ***i-ng-arr-jimbi-na.***
     all           fish        3-PST-PL-die-REM.PST
              S
     'All the fish died.'

b.   *Aamba-nim*      ***i-n-jala=jarrmoordoo.***
     man-ERG         3-TR-look.at=1PL.P
     A                              P
     'A man's looking at us!'

However, case-marking in Bardi groups arguments in a different way. The A argument is singled out with a special marker (*-nim*, called the **ergative**) while both S and P arguments receive no marking. An unmarked S can be seen in example (a); an unmarked P can be seen in (c):

c.   *Joo-**nim***      *jooroorr*      *a-ni-wi=jirri.*
     2SG-ERG          sand            2.IMP-TR-poke-3PL.OBL
     A                P
     'You poke the sand for them.'

When grammatical phenomena group S and P in this way, the category is called **absolutive**, which is a type of grammatical relation.

These different grammatical relations are called **alignment patterns** because the single intransitive argument sometimes aligns grammatically with the more-agentive transitive argument, and sometimes with the less-agentive transitive argument. These patterns are illustrated in Figure LP8.2.

TEXTBOX LP8.3   (*cont.*)

**Intransitive**      $\begin{pmatrix} S \\ A \end{pmatrix}$

**Transitive**                       P

Pattern A: Nominative-accusative alignment

**Intransitive**                       $\begin{pmatrix} S \\ P \end{pmatrix}$

**Transitive**        A

Pattern B: Ergative-absolutive alignment

**Figure LP8.2** Alignment patterns

## 8.2.4  Constituent order

In English and many other languages, as you've seen, the order of constituents is fixed in such a way as to indicate grammatical relations. Since English is an SVO language, with the subject argument consistently preceding the verb, which precedes the object, sentences like *The dog bit Dorothy* and *Dorothy bit her dog* have critically different meanings. Bardi constituent order is not fixed in this way; the order of constituents in a sentence is much more free than it is in more familiar languages (in fact, Bardi can also omit arguments much more than English can, so it is quite common to find Bardi sentences which only have verbs in them, and no nouns, pronouns, or adjectives). This does not mean that there is no information provided by the order of words in Bardi. The order of constituents in Bardi is used to structure information for the hearer. For example, the first item in the clause is the grammatical focus; it is the most important piece of information in the clause. Here "important" means something like "what the speaker most wants the hearer to focus on." For example, answers to content questions appear in the first position in the clause. Similarly, the choice between using a full noun phrase or omitting it provides a way for the speaker and hearer to keep track of the participants in the discourse. Constituent order will be the focus of more extensive discussion below.

## 8.2.5  Word classes

Bardi has nouns and verbs, just like all other languages. There are both distributional and morphological reasons for distinguishing between nouns and verbs in this language. Nouns in Bardi can appear as the subjects of transitive sentences (where they take ergative case-marking and verbal agreement). That is, nouns can be arguments of verbs, but verbs can't be arguments of verbs. Nouns can be replaced by pronouns, such as *ginyinggi* 'he, she, it' or *irr* 'they'; however, no other word class can replace a verb. Bardi nouns take case-marking, while verbs take a lot of other, different morphology. Verbs are marked for tense and aspect, for the person and number of their subject (and object, if present), and for transitivity. Examples of nouns in Bardi include *oorany* 'woman,' *aarli* 'fish,' *liyan* 'heart, spirit,' *mayi* 'food,' and many others. Nouns form an open word class. Examples of verbs in Bardi include *-joogooloo-* 'break,' *-ni-* 'be, sit,' and *-booloo-* 'come.' Verbs in Bardi are not an open word class. There are about 250 of them in the language, but they are a closed set. Bardi does not borrow inflecting verbs, and there are no word-formation processes that create new inflecting verbs out of other material.

Although Bardi verbs are a closed class, there is another word class: preverbs, which combine with verbs to provide verbal meanings (see Sidebar LP8.4). Preverbs are an open word class in Bardi. They never appear on their own in a sentence; preverbs can be identified by the fact that they occur immediately before the (inflecting) verb, and they are the only type of word that can appear between the negative marker *arra* and the inflecting verb.

(11)  *Arra      booroo     oo-la-la-n-in                      mara~mara.*
      NEG       look       3.IRR-IRR-see-CONT-REM.PST         far
      'He didn't look around very far.'

(11')  *\*Booroo      arra      oo-la-la-n-in       mara~mara.*

**SIDEBAR LP8.4**

Preverbs are the mechanism by which Bardi borrows verbs. A verb borrowed from English, Kriol, or another language becomes a preverb and occurs with an additional inflecting verb that carries the agreement, tense, aspect, and mood information. Here are some examples (the inflecting verb is given in its root form):

*wajim -ma-*   'wash'
*loojim -joo-*  'die' (from lose'im)
*gadim -ma-*   'cut'

All of these verbs have *-im* on the end of the loaned preverb. This is the Kriol transitivity marker; it attaches to all transitive verbs. For more on loanwords and processes of borrowing, see Chapter 13.

Bardi also has a class of adjectives. However, it is not a very clearly defined class, as Bardi adjectives share many properties with Bardi nouns, much more so than in languages like English. For example, like nouns, Bardi adjectives can be heads of noun phrases. Adjectives also have some behaviors that are not shared with nouns. Adjectives can be used as preverbs, where they have a systematic relationship with their inflecting verb. This is a very productive patterns for adjectives, but does not occur with nouns. For example, consider the adjective *boordiji* 'big' in the following sentences:

(12)  *Boordiji   i-ni-n.*
      big        3-sit-CONT
      'it's big'

      *Boordiji    i-n-ma-n.*
      big         3-TR-make-CONT
      'he/she/it made it big'

      *Boordiji    i-n-joo-n.*
      big         3-TR-do/say-CONT
      'it got big'

These adjectives are functioning as preverbs. Evidence for this is that the adjective can occur between the negative marker *arra* and the verb:

(13)  *Arra      boordiji    oo-l-i-n.*
      NEG       big         3-IRR-do/say-CONT
      'it is not big'

Nouns cannot occur in these constructions; the sentence *\*arra iila oolin* – with *iila* 'dog' in the position of a preverb – is ungrammatical and cannot express the meaning 'it's not a dog.' Remember from the previous example that the order of elements in a negative verb phrase is *arra* + preverb + verb; the ungrammaticality of sentences like *\*arra iila oolin* is good evidence that nouns can't productively derive preverbs, but adjectives can. Thus, nouns and adjectives can be distinguished by their behavior in Bardi. Another property that distinguishes adjectives from nouns is that adjectives, but not nouns, can be modified by *giija* 'very'; so that you can say *boordiji giija* 'very big,' but not *\*iila giija* 'very dog.'

Bardi has only four numbers: 'one,' 'two,' 'three,' and 'four' (*arinyji, gooyarra, irrjar, and gooyarragooyarra*). For the most part, numbers behave like adjectives in their syntax, with a few exceptions: numbers take derivational morphology that other adjectives can't. For example, 'three' is *irrjar* and you can use a 'times' suffix, *-nan*, to say *irrjar-nan* 'three times,' but not *\*loogal-nan* 'bad times.'

(14)  *Irrjar-nan*      *i-n-jaybi-gal=jarrngay*         "*jan*         *i-n-joo-gal*
      three-times      3-TR-ask-REC.PST=1SG.P         where         3-TR-do-REC.PST

      *jan*                *baawa?*"
      1SG.POSS         child
      'Three times he asked, "where's my child?"'

Bardi has two conjunctions: *agal* 'and' and *gorror* 'or.' It doesn't have adpositions or articles. The functions of English prepositions, like *to*, *at*, and *beside*, are split between Bardi case-markers and adverbs. Bardi does not have a morpheme like the English article *the*, which indicates when a noun phrase is **definite** (identifiable). Instead, Bardi speakers use demonstratives like *jarri* 'this' and the presence or absence of a full noun to give information about the definiteness of the noun phrase. For example, if a noun is omitted in discourse, then it is usually identifiable, and known to the speaker and hearer. The first time something is mentioned, it is represented with a noun phrase, but in subsequent mentions, noun phrases are typically omitted and the argument is represented only by agreement marking.

Bardi has a class of personal pronouns with three singular and five non-singular members (see Textbox LP8.4 for discussion of the non-singular categories). The full set of personal pronouns is given in Table LP8.1.

Bardi pronouns have different behaviors from those in languages such as English. For example, the third-person pronouns can be used to modify nouns; in this use, they function a bit like demonstratives, as in *ginyinggi aamba* 'that man' or *ginyinggi-nim baawa* 'that child' (in ergative form). They are not frequently used, since the functions of pronouns like English *he* and *you* are mostly taken up by Bardi verbal agreement marking, as seen in examples like (11) and (14).

**TABLE LP8.1** Bardi pronouns

| Person | Singular | | Non-singular | |
|--------|----------|---|--------------|---|
| 1st | *ngayoo* | 'I' | *ayoo* | 'we two (me and you)' |
| | | | *arroodoo* | 'we all but not you' |
| | | | *arridil* | 'we all including you' |
| 2nd | *joo* | 'you (singular)' | *goorr* | 'you (plural)' |
| 3rd | *ginyinggi* | 'he, she, it' | *irr* | 'they' |

---

TEXTBOX LP8.4 **CATEGORIES OF NON-SINGULAR PRONOUNS**

Table LP8.1 illustrates the fact that Bardi has more plural pronouns than singular pronouns. These extra forms are found in the first-person category, that is, references that include the speaker. There is a special first-person **dual** form, which refers to the speaker and hearer both (you (sg.) and I). The first-person-plural forms distinguish between references that include the hearer ('we all including you'), and references that exclude the hearer ('we but not you'). Such **inclusive** and **exclusive** distinctions are found in the pronoun systems in many languages.

Bardi has a number system that is described in the literature as an "Ilocano" or "minimal/augment" system. In languages with such systems, there is only one dual pronoun (the first-person dual inclusive *ayoo* in Bardi). There are no other dual pronouns; the first-person dual exclusive is signaled by *arroodoo*, which also marks plural exclusive.

## 8.2.6  Constituency

One of the key diagnostics for word classes in many languages is the use and positioning of words in different types of phrases. For example, in English only prepositions can function as heads of prepositional phrases and auxiliary verbs must precede verbs in a verb phrase. We also saw in Chapter 4 that constituency and morphological structure together provide the main evidence for different types of word classes. In the previous section, most of the evidence presented for Bardi word classes was morphological (e.g., verbs take agreement morphology while nouns take case-marking), although there was also some evidence regarding syntactic structure (e.g., preverbs occur between the negative particle and the verb, while nouns do not). Constituent order plays a somewhat limited role for identifying word classes in Bardi. This is because constituent order in this language is quite a bit more flexible than in some other more familiar languages, and this makes the use of constituent structure as a diagnostic for word classes a bit more subtle.

As an example, consider the following English sentence:

(15)    *I ate two fish yesterday.*

One piece of evidence that *two* and *fish* are in the same phrasal constituent (here the object noun phrase) is that they cannot be separated by other elements of the sentence:

(16)    *\*I two ate fish yesterday.*
        *\*Two I ate fish yesterday.*

Here are two Bardi sentences, both equivalent in meaning to (15):

(17)    a.  *Nga-n-arli-gal*        *gooyarra*    *aarli*    *bardi.*
            1SG-TR-eat-REC.PST      two          fish       yesterday

        b.  *Gooyarra*    *nga-n-arli-gal*        *aarli*    *bardi.*
            two          1SG-TR-eat-REC.PST       fish       yesterday

Both orderings are perfectly acceptable and used by speakers. In Bardi, it is grammatical to split numerals from their associated nouns; the two sentences (one with the numeral separate, the other with it adjacent) highlight different aspects of the situation. Example (17a) is the usual – or unmarked – way of expressing this situation, while (17b) implies that the number was different than expected, i.e., 'It was two!' (e.g., as opposed to three).

Does this mean that Bardi "has no grammar" or "has no evidence for phrasal constituency?" No, although it does mean we need to look beyond the obvious diagnostics for phrasal constituency and find Bardi-specific evidence that words combine into phrases.

The first piece of evidence for a noun-phrase constituent is that case-markers are suffixed to the first word of the noun phrase (as noted above; see, e.g., Example (10)). This tells us that nothing to the left of that word belongs in the phrase.

Secondly, nouns (and noun phrases, by implication) in Bardi have dependents, just as English noun phrases do. There are possessors, adjectives, and relative clauses. They obey the same restriction that the case-marker goes on the first word of the phrase. (See Sidebar LP8.5 for a note on the glossing.)

(18)    [*Ngay-nim*      *jan*          *gooloo*    *jina-rr*                      *irrmoorra*]
        1SG-ERG          1SG.POSS       father      3SG.POSS-3PL.POSSEE            paternal.aunt

        *baanigarr*      *gorna*        *balab*     *i-ngi-rr-i-na-na.*
        when             good           there       3-PST-PL-do-CONT-REM.PST
        'My father's aunties were really happy about it then [that my father got back safely].'

In this sentence, the subject is the complex noun phrase *ngaynim jan gooloo jinarr irrmoorra* 'my father's aunties.' The ergative marker *-nim* goes on the first word of the phrase, the first-person singular pronoun *ngay*. (A standard way of marking possession in Bardi is to denote the possessor by a noun or pronoun followed by a possessive pronoun. So the complex noun phrase in (18) would be more literally translated as 'I my father his aunties.' The third-person possessive pronoun *jinarr* cross-references the person and number of both the possessor and the possessed.)

A third type of evidence for a noun-phrase constituent is that we can replace a noun phrase with a pronoun. So in the previous example, we can replace *ngaynim jan gooloo jinarr irrmoorra* 'my father's aunties' with *irrnim* 3PL-ERG 'they (ergative).'

Noun-phrase elements don't have an absolutely fixed order, but they do have a set of strong tendencies. For example, noun heads tend to be final in their phrases. So, adjectives, possessors, locational phrases, and quality phrases (e.g., *the man with a beard*) all usually precede the noun.

### 8.2.7   Constituent order

Throughout this book, languages have been commonly described as having a dominant constituent order, such as SVO, SOV, VSO. Bardi word order is not easily described in this way. Consider Table LP8.2, which shows the numbers and percentages of different constituent orders occurring in two Bardi narratives.

There are many things to note from Table LP8.2. The first is that almost half the clauses in the Bardi narratives contain no free noun-phrase arguments at all (as indicated by the V-only examples in the last row before the totals), and only three clauses contained both a noun-phrase subject and a noun-phrase object (two VSO and one OVS). Secondly, there is a preference for the nominal argument to follow the verb, independently of whether it is an S-argument or an O-argument. Thirdly, almost 10 percent of the clauses contain more than one verb with a common argument (VOV, VSV), or contain a discontinuous argument (OVO, SVS).

From the range of orders found in Bardi, one can conclude that Bardi constituent order does not signal the grammatical relations of the arguments. The following sentences describe the same event, but note that the constituent order varies:

(19)  [*Mooloo*]     *boor*     *i-n-jal=jin*              [*ara-nim*      *oorany*]
      louse.PL       look       3-TR-look=3SG.OBL          other-ERG      woman
      [*ara*         *oorany*]   *nalm-onon.*
      other          woman       3SG-head-LOC
      'One woman was looking for lice on another woman's head.'

(20)  [*Mooloo*]     *boor*     *i-n-jal=jin*              [*ara*        *oorany*].
      louse.PL       look       3-TR-look=3SG.OBL          other        woman
      'One woman was looking for lice on another woman's head.'

**TABLE LP8.2** Constituent orders occurring in two Bardi narratives (Bowern 2008)

| Order | Number | Percentage |
| --- | --- | --- |
| SVO | 0 | 0% |
| SOV | 0 | 0% |
| OVS | 1 | 0.6% |
| OSV | 0 | 0% |
| VOS | 0 | 0% |
| VSO | 2 | 1.2% |
| SV | 13 | 7.6% |
| VS | 22 | 12.9% |
| OV | 10 | 5.8% |
| VO | 26 | 15.2% |
| OVO | 10 | 5.8% |
| VOV | 4 | 2.3% |
| SVS | 1 | 0.6% |
| VSV | 1 | 0.6% |
| V | 81 | 47.4% |
| Total: | 171 | 100% |

So, if word order doesn't tell us anything about grammatical relations between arguments and verbs, how do we get that information? It is communicated by a combination of three things: case-marking, verb agreement, and real-world knowledge. You've already seen a few examples of verb agreement in action, where subjects have person and number morphemes, and objects have person/number clitics. You've also seen some examples of ergative case-marking, e.g., (8), (9), and elsewhere.

In summary, we've seen that there is evidence for word classes and constituency in Bardi, although the tests are a little more complex than in languages with rigid constituent order. Constituent order does not provide information about the grammatical roles of arguments in the clause. It does, however, provide us with discourse information about the relative prominence and importance of participants in the sentence.

> ## TEXTBOX LP8.5 **GLOSSING CONVENTIONS USED IN THIS LANGUAGE PROFILE**
>
> | Convention | Meaning | Convention | Meaning |
> |---|---|---|---|
> | 1 | first person | **LOC** | locative |
> | 2 | second person | NEG | negation |
> | 3 | third person | OBL | oblique |
> | COM | Comitative | p | patient |
> | COMPL | Completive | PL | plural |
> | CONT | Continuous | POSS | possessive |
> | COP | Copula | POSSEE | possessed |
> | ERG | ergative | PST | past tense |
> | FUT | future tense | REC.PST | recent past |
> | IMP | imperative | REM.PST | remote past |
> | INTENSIFIER | intensifier | SEMBL | semblative |
> | IO | indirect object | SG | singular |
> | IRR | irrealis | TR | transitive |

## SUGGESTIONS FOR FURTHER READING

**Aklif, Gedda**. 1999. *Ardiyooloon Bardi Ngaank: One Arm Point Bardi dictionary*. Halls Creek: Kimberley Language Resource Centre.

The first and only published dictionary of Bardi, with an English–Bardi finder list and maps of Bardi country.

**Bowern, Claire**. 2012. *A grammar of Bardi*. Berlin: Mouton.

A reference grammar of Bardi that contains extensive information about Bardi phonology, morphology, and syntax.

**McGregor, William**. 2004. *The languages of the Kimberley*. London: Routledge.

This book gives a summary of languages of the Northwest of Australia. It is designed for students who are unfamiliar with Australian languages.

## EXERCISES

1.  Consider again the discussion of Bardi preverbs. In what ways are they similar to auxiliary verbs and in what ways are they different? Do you agree with the author that preverbs are not auxiliaries? You may want to review the discussion of auxiliary verbs in Chapter 6 in formulating your answer.

2.  Examine the following Bardi words (in IPA), along with their English translations:

    | | | | |
    |---|---|---|---|
    | ŋijambalə | my foot | ŋimiŋgar | my shadow |
    | nijambalə | his foot | nimiŋgar | his shadow |
    | irɟambalə | their feet | irmiŋgar | their shadow |
    | gurɟambalə | your feet | gurmiŋgar | your shadow |

a. What are the root morphemes in these words?

b. Which morpheme means 'my'?

c. Do any of the morphemes alternate? If so, which one(s), and what is the environment for alternation?

d. If ɟalaŋgun means 'elbow,' how would you say *his elbow*?

3. Put the ergative case on the correct Bardi word. In each of the following Bardi sentences, one of the words is missing the ergative case. Use the interlinear glosses and the free translations to figure out which word should be marked.

a.  *Liinygoorr* *i-n-arli-gal*   *jan*  *iila.*
 crocodile 3SG-TR-eat-REC.PST 1SG.POSS dog
 'A crocodile ate my dog.'

b.  *Gaanyji* *i-n-arli-gal*   *jan*  *iila.*
 bone  3SG-TR-eat-REC.PST 1SG.POSS dog
 'My dog ate a bone.'

c.  *Jiidi-nyarr* *aamba* *nyoongoorl* *oorany* *i-n-jala-na.*
 beard-COM man  old   woman 3SG-TR-see-REM.PST
 'The old woman saw a man with a beard.'

4. Causal ergatives

The suffix *-nim*, in addition to marking ergative case, also appears in special sentences to mark an argument that is a semantic cause. It is attached to the noun that denotes the cause, as in:

> *Aalga-nim*   *nga-nga-marra.*
> sun-ERG    1SG-PST-burn
> 'I am burnt.' (lit. I burnt because of the sun.)

Note that the verb does not agree with this argument, but instead agrees with the semantic patient.

A set of verbs in Bardi use this frame (ergative-marked CAUSE; patient as a subject of the verb). Here are two more examples:

a.  *liga-nim*  *alig* *nga-n-da-n.*
 sickness-ERG hurt 1SG-TR-do-CONT
 'I'm sick.'

b.  *Banyjoordoo-nim* *boonyja* *aarli* *i-nga-rr-jimbi-na.*
 fish.poison-ERG all  fish 3-PST-PL-die-REM.PST
 'All the fish died from the fish poison.'

Is it best to analyze these examples as transitive or intransitive? Provide an analysis that

 i. specifies whether these clauses are intransitive or transitive

 ii. specifies arguments as either core or oblique

 iii. explains the agreement and case-marking facts

**LANGUAGE PROFILE 9**

# Lowland Chontal

## 9.1 Ethnographic profile

Oaxaca Chontal (wah-HA-kah chone-TAL) is a small, genetically unclassified language family of southern Mexico. There are two surviving varieties: Highland Chontal, in the Sierra Madre del Sur mountains, and Lowland Chontal, along the Pacific coast. A third

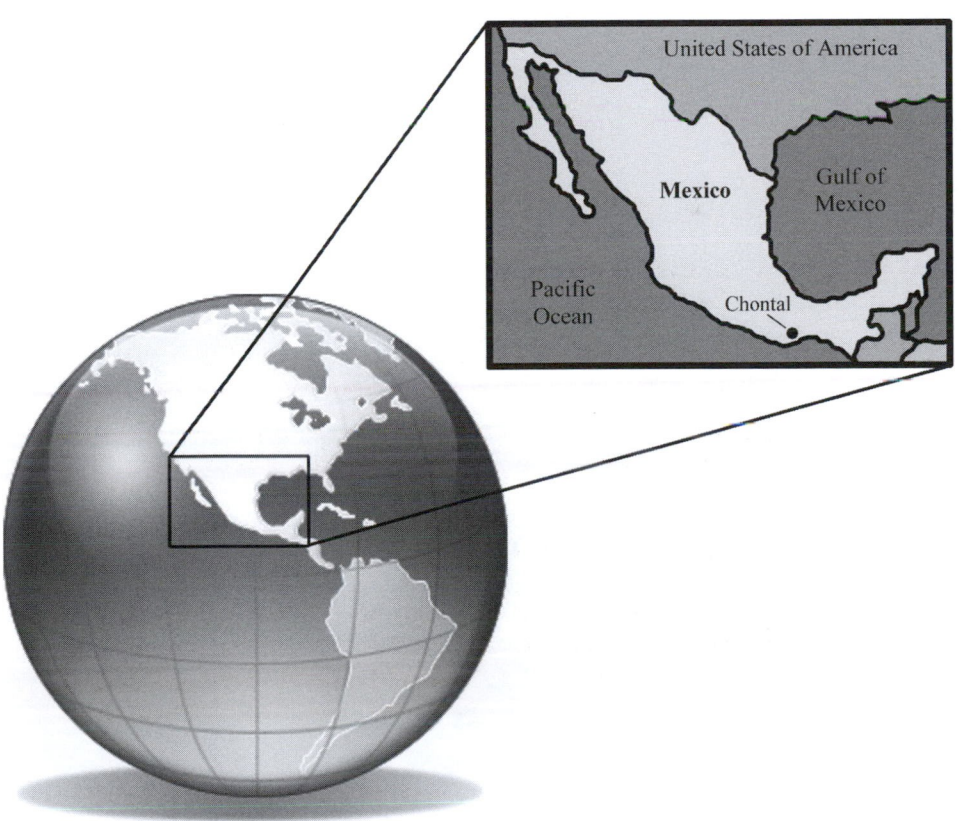

**Figure LP9.1** Region where Chontal is spoken

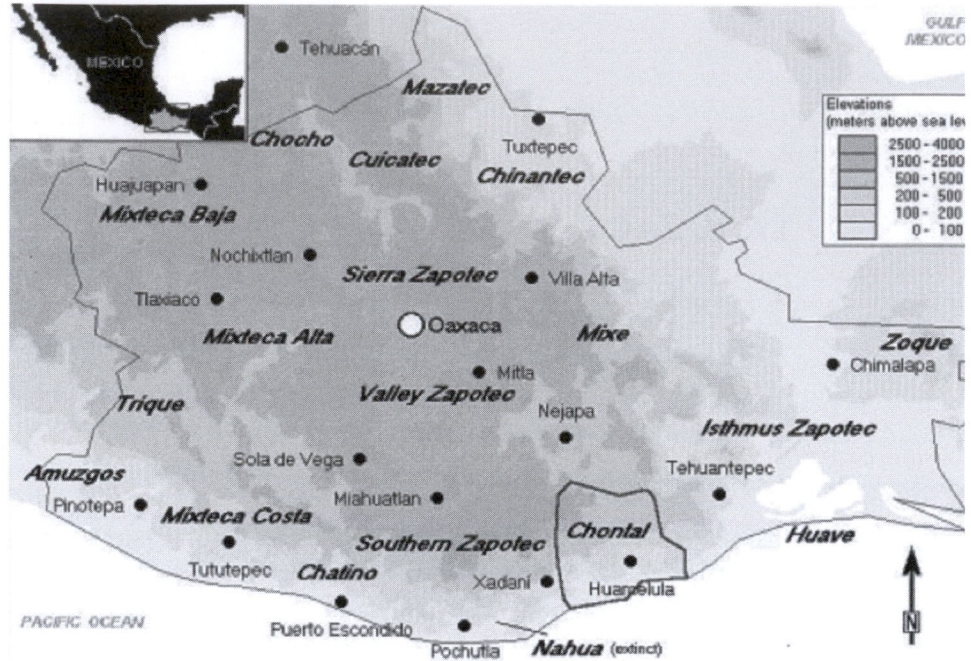

**Figure LP9.2** Map of ethnolinguistic families in Oaxaca, Mexico (P. Kroefges)

**Figure LP9.3** View from a hilltop of San Pedro Huamelula, Oaxaca, Mexico

---

TEXTBOX LP9.1 **WHAT'S IN A NAME?**

The ethnic designation "Chontal" derives from a word in the Nahuatl language, *chontalli* 'stranger,' used by the Aztecs to refer to any unfamiliar ethnic group in ancient Meso-America. As a result, there are or were a number of groups, speaking unrelated languages, all called Chontal. Within Mexico, these are distinguished by naming the state where the people live today. Chontal of Tabasco is a Mayan language still spoken in Tabasco, while Chontal of Guerrero is no longer spoken by ethnic Chontal people in Guerrero. Although there are "Chontal people" in all three states, we have no reason to think they were once a single community.

In the Chontalpa of Oaxaca, people refer to themselves as Chontales and call their language *latyaygi*, 'the word.'

In Spanish, many people refer to the language as *el dialecto*, 'the dialect,' a term which can carry a pejorative sense. At first, many people I met in Mexico responded with patient amusement to my insistent corrections that Chontal is a language and not a dialect. I unintentionally convinced even the most skeptical by sending people postcards from the United States written in Chontal. Friends reported that this simple act was greeted with amazement and the realization that Chontal is a real language.

---

sister language died out in the past century. These are the mother tongues of the Chontalpa, a region in the Mexican state of Oaxaca.

No one knows exactly where Chontal speakers came from. (Textbox LP9.1, which discusses the language name, explains in part why this is so.) Our best estimates indicate they arrived in Oaxaca sometime between 300 and 1000 AD. Today there are some 4,600 speakers of Oaxaca Chontal among the nearly 13,000 ethnic Chontals, according to the 2000 census.

The language described in this profile is Lowland Chontal. It is a highly endangered language, with perhaps a hundred fluent first-language speakers who are quite elderly, and a much larger number of semi-speakers, aged fifty and above. No children learn Chontal as a first language and very few have access to any type of bilingual education. The highland and lowland varieties of Chontal are not mutually intelligible. There is relatively little contact between speakers of the two varieties, due in part to social prejudice and in part because the two groups are no longer major markets for each other.

 **SIDEBAR LP9.1**

For an idea of what this part of the world is like, and to hear from people about their own experiences, see the *How Languages Work* companion website.

## 9.2  Typological profile

### 9.2.1  Morphological type

Chontal is a predominantly **synthetic** language in that derivational and inflectional morphemes bind to roots to form single words. The morphology is **agglutinative**, and most words are easily analyzable into recognizable morphemes, which include roots, affixes, and **clitics**. Nominal morphology is mostly prefixing, and verbal morphology is mostly suffixing.

For example, the noun phrase 'my little burro' in (1) is a single word in Chontal, with four prefixes before the noun root: a determiner, analogous to 'a' or 'the' in English, a possessive prefix, a linker morpheme, and a diminutive. (Abbreviations used in the glosses are listed at the end of the chapter.)

**(1)**  *l-ay-ñe-'wa-buru*
DET-1SG.POSS-LINKER-DIM-burro
'My little burro.'

The only obligatory affix on a Chontal verb is an inflectional suffix that describes the verb action in such terms as perfective (complete), imperfective (incomplete), durative (ongoing or habitual), or imperative (as a command). There are ten categories of verbal inflection in Chontal. Suffixes have different shapes for singular vs. plural subject, and the durative suffix takes different forms according to the verb root. With the stem *sago-* 'eat,' the suffixes for a singular subject are *-pa* 'perfective,' *-'ma* 'imperfective,' and *-duy* 'durative,' as in (2).

**(2)**  *sago-* 'eat'     *sagopa*     'ate'       completed action
                          *sago'ma*    'eats'      incomplete action
                          *sagoduy*    'eating'    ongoing or habitual action

There are fourteen optional derivational suffixes that occur between the verb root and the inflectional morphology. These include suffixes that signal the presence or absence of certain participants and suffixes that describe qualities of the verb action, such as repeated, distributed, or intensive. The clause 'We heard it again' can be expressed as a single word in Chontal, as in (3).

**(3)**  *tay-ko-kom-pa=yang*
hear-APPL-ITR-PFV=1PL.A
'We heard it again.'

The applicative suffix indexes the 'it' that we heard; the iterative suffix indicates that the hearing was repeated, and the perfective suffix tells us the hearing was completed. The final linguistic element in (3), marking the subject person 'we,' is a clitic. There are many clitics in Chontal; these attach to nouns, verbs, and very often to other clitics. Morpheme boundaries for clitics are marked with an equal sign rather than a hyphen.

## 9.2.2  Syntactic type

Chontal is a verb-initial language with variable constituent order. Most sentences in conversation and narrative begin with the verb. If subjects (S) and objects (O) are mentioned, these follow the verb, and usually the subject precedes the object. Example (4) has two clauses, in VSO and VS order.

**(4)**

| **V** | **S** | **O** | **V** | **S** |
|---|---|---|---|---|
| *'oy'mi-'me'* | *sayang* | *lam-buru'* | *may-gom-'me'* | *sayang* |
| pack-IPFV.PL | 1PL.A | DET.PL-burro | go-ITR-IPFV.PL | 1PL.A |

'We would pack the burros and get on the road again.'

However, VSO and VS word orders are not obligatory. Any subject or object can precede the verb if a speaker wants to highlight a certain participant. See how the speaker plays with the focus in the excerpt in (5). The deer and the child are introduced in (a), then the child is highlighted and the deer is not mentioned in (b), and the conclusion of the action is described using the basic VS word order in (c).

(5)  a.          **S**                    **V**              **S**              **V**
     *ñulyi  el   venado  joypa    ñulye-pa    pero   l-a-'wa        jolaf'-a*
     one    DET  deer    already  run-PFV.SG  but    DET-NOM-CHILD  sitting.above-
                                                                    STAT.SG

     'A deer ran with the child on its head (sitting above).'

  b. **O**                                          **V**
     *l-a-'wa-mulyi          joypa       chasa    tye-'e-pa*
     DET-NOM-DIM-boy        already     now      fall-CAUS-PFV.SG
     'Now it (the deer) dropped the little boy.'

  c.          **V**              **S**
     *joypa       tye-pa       l-a-'wa-mulyi*
     already     fall-PFV.SG  DET-NOM-DIM-boy
     'And the little boy fell.'

A final important feature of Chontal morphosyntax is the case-marking system. In this language, subjects and objects are marked according to semantics of **agentivity**. To be *agentive* is to act with control and intention; to be *non-agentive* is to experience something beyond your control or intention. The relevant semantic case roles are those of AGENT and PATIENT, and in every clause, core participants are marked as agentive (A) or patientive (P), according to the perceived level of control or intention of the participant over the event encoded by the verb.

This is easiest to illustrate with transitive and ditransitive clauses that involve multiple participants. In (6) and (7), note how the person markers change in the two clauses, as I (A) eat you (P), or you (A) give me (P) some bread.

(6)  *iya'       te-'m-o'*
     1SG.A      eat-IPFV-2SG.P
     'I'm going to eat you.'

(7)  *jl-pay-pa=yma'          l-ay-'i*
     1SG.P-give-PFV=2SG.A    DET-1SG.POSS-bread
     'You gave me bread.'

We see the same types of differences with plural first- and second-person participants, in (8) and (9). We (A) see you (P), and you (A) say something to us (P).

(8)  *sim-p-olwa'       sa=yang*
     see-PFV-2PL.P     DM=1PL.A
     'We saw you.'

(9) *mi-p-onga'*          *sa=ymang*
    tell-PFV-1PL.P     DM=2PL.A
    'You told us.'

The semantic differences are fairly transparent in multi-participant events, as one can judge the relative agentivity of each participant with respect to the others. In each clause above, one participant (the grammatical subject) was more agentive, marked as A, and another participant (the grammatical direct or indirect object) was less agentive, and marked as P. The complete paradigm of agent–patient morphology is shown in Table LP9.1, with allomorphs in parentheses. Markers in the A column can occur as independent pronouns or as clitics, and these clitics can attach to verbs or to other clitics. Markers in the P column are strictly verbal affixes.

The lack of person markers for third persons, represented by zeroes in Table LP9.1, has certain consequences. Look back at the excerpt in Example (5), and notice that none of the verbs carry person-marking morphology. When all the participants are third-person singular, the distinction between agents and patients is not expressed. We say the agent–patient distinction is *neutralized* for this grammatical person/number. The distinction is not neutralized for third-person plural, as shown in (10), with two clauses about burros. The verb in (a) shows only that the subject is plural, seen in the infix *-jl-* and the plural form of the imperfective suffix *-'me'*, while the verb in (b) explicitly indicates that the subject is both third-person plural and non-agentive, with the suffix *-ilya'*.

(10) a. *tyijpe*     *sa*     *ñaño-jl-'me'*     *lam-buru*
        DIST     DM     pass-PL-IPFV.PL     DET.PL-burro
        'There the burros would pass through,

   b. *pero*     *paychu-g-ilya'*     *chasa*     *lam-buru*
      but     be.afraid-DUR-3PL.P     now     DET.PL-burro
      'but now they were afraid.'

**Table LP9.1** Agent–patient morphology in Chontal

| Person | A | P |
|---|---|---|
| 1SG | *iya' (=ya')* | *jl-* |
| 2SG | *ima (=yma')* | *-o'* |
| 3SG | Ø | Ø |
| 1PL | *iyank' (=yang)* | *-onga' (-inga')* |
| 2PL | *imank' (=ymang)* | *-olwa' (-ilwa')* |
| 3PL | Ø | *-ola' (-ilya')* |

Notice something unusual about Example (10): both clauses are intransitive, with just one participant, yet the verbal person-marking morphology is different. This is a key feature of the agentive system in Chontal: the single participant of an intransitive clause will be marked as an agent or a patient according to the perceived level of control or intention of the participant over the event encoded by the verb. In Examples (11)– (14), all the events in (a) are controlled by the participants, while all the events in (b) are not.

(11) a. *kas-pa=ya'*
stand-PFV=1SG.A
'I stood up.'

b. *jl-ma-'ma*
1SG.P-die-IPFV.SG
'I will die.'

(12) a. *may-pa=yma'*
go-PFV=2SG.A
'You went.'

b. *te-p-o'*
fall-PFV-2SG.P
'You fell.'

(13) a. *sago-pa=yang*
eat-PFV=1PL.A
'We ate.'

b. *paychu-p-onga'*
be.afraid-PFV-1PL.P
'We were afraid, we became afraid.'

(14) a. *soy-pa=ymang*
dance-PFV=2PL.A
'You danced.'

b. *'i-'m-olwa'*          *alegre*
become-IPFV-2PL.P      happy
'You will be happy.'

### 9.2.3 Phonological type

The sound system of Chontal is composed of five vowels and thirty-three consonants. The vowel inventory is quite simple, with five distinct phonemes *a, e, i, o, u*. **Vowel length** is not phonemic, but it occurs in certain words, especially in **penultimate** stressed syllables. These longer sounds are written with two vowels. There is one diphthong /ai/, written {ay}.

The consonant inventory is more complex, characterized by series of plain and glottalized segments (see Sidebar LP9.2). In the practical orthography used here, the apostrophe represents both a glottal stop and **glottalization**: *k', ts', ch', f', s', x', jl'* are glottalized obstruents, and *'m, 'n, 'ñ, 'l, 'w* are glottalized sonorants. The letter *j* represents both velar and glottal voiceless fricatives, following a common orthographic practice from Spanish, and the letter *x* represents an postalveolar voiceless fricative. Dialectal variants of the lateral fricative *jl, jl'* are written *tl, tl'*. (See Textbox LP9.2 for another note on Chontal pronunciation.)

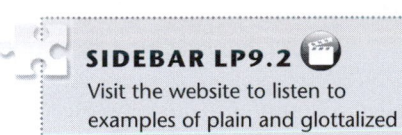

**SIDEBAR LP9.2**
Visit the website to listen to examples of plain and glottalized segments in Chontal.

**Figure LP9.4** Women on their way to a town dance

---

### TEXTBOX LP9.2 **PALATALIZATION**

Most speakers of Lowland Chontal palatalize alveolar segments before or after a high or front vowel /i, u/ or the palatal approximant /y/. See Example (a), with possessed forms of the body part *anepo'* 'back,' and notice how the vowel of the possessive prefix determines the shape of the determiner and the first consonant of the root.

a. *l-o-nepo'*
   DET-2SG.POSS-back
   'your back'
   *ly-i-ñepo'*
   DET-3SG.POSS-back
   'his/her back'
   *l-ay-ñepo'*
   DET-1SG.POSS-back
   'my back'

Furthermore, when a verb root begins with an alveolar consonant, that initial alveolar is palatalized in third-person inflections, singular and plural. This process creates alternations *l~ly, n~ñ, s~x, ts~ch,* and *t~ty*, as in (b).

b. *toj'me-duy=ya'*          *tyoj'me-duy*
   speak-DUR.SG=1SG.A       speak-DUR.SG
   'I'm speaking'             'he/she is speaking'

The result is rampant palatalization, which is mostly predictable, although it should be noted that some speakers seem to palatalize alveolars in all words, regardless of phonetic environment.

---

## 9.3 Compound-stem predicates

Chontal has a special complex verb construction called a compound-stem predicate. These compound stems have one inflectional suffix and one set of core participants, and they can predicate single- and multi-participant events.

All compound-stem predicates encode change: change of location, change of position, or change of state. When we talk about change, we talk about **figures** and **grounds**, terms adapted from psychology. A **figure** is an entity that changes with respect to a **ground**, a reference point or reference situation. In linguistics, the semantic case roles corresponding to figures include *actor, patient, experiencer,* and *theme.* The semantic roles corresponding to a ground include *source* and *goal.*

Compound stems are formed of two types of verbal elements, each making an individual contribution to the meaning of the construction. The basic template is as follows; VE stands for "verbal element":

### VE1 – VE2 – (DERIVATION) – INFLECTION

Each type of element will be introduced separately, and then we will look at some examples of elements in combination, as compound stems. The initial verbal element, here called **VE1**, specifies one of the following:

- Something about the figure
  - its size, shape, type, position, or configuration
- Something about the type of goal
- Something about the change event itself
  - the process or cause that leads to change, or
  - the shape of the path taken by the figure in motion

These VE1 verbal elements fall into four semantic classes:

I.  A "classificatory" VE1 identifies the shape, size, or identity of the figure as:

*ch'u-* 'grain (especially corn)'    *k'e-* 'liquid (especially water)'
*le-* 'animate' or 'long and thin'    *pe-* 'small'
*soy-* 'shallow plate'    *wa-* 'container'

The final morpheme *wa-* 'container' can refer to the figure, such as a glass or a plate that is moved, or it can also refer to the goal, as 'into a container.'

II. A "dispositional" VE1 identifies the posture, spatial disposition, or configuration of the figure with respect to the ground, as, for example:

*jojl/jol/jola-* 'sit, sitting'    *kas-* 'stand, standing'
*ñaj-* 'lie, lying'    *kuch'-* 'huddle, huddled over'
*ño-* 'cross, crosswise'    *k'o-* 'mouth (mouth-ward)'
*spe-* 'spread, scattered'    *sk'ing-* 'items in a circle'

III. A "means" VE1 describes something about the manner of how the change takes place. This is a large category that includes:

*cho-* 'spill'    *te-* 'fall'    *sk'wi-* 'stab'
*fa-* 'plant'    *fuj-* 'blow'    *jas-* 'split, slice, tear'
*jlay-* 'bend, break'    *jli-* 'slide, slip'    *jlo-* 'scoot'
*kej-* 'cut, chop'    *k'wa-* 'insert'    *pes-* 'force'

IV. A "trajectory" VE1 depicts the specific shape of the path taken by the figure in motion:

| | | |
|---|---|---|
| *'oy-* 'flat arc' | *s'wi-* 'arc back' | *spa-* 'high arc' |
| *ki-* 'straight, horizontal' | *go-* 'back and forth' | |

The second element, the **VE2**, specifies:

- the direction of motion;
- the endpoint of motion or position in space;
- the end-state of a change of state, as "apart, in two pieces."

| | | | |
|---|---|---|---|
| *-f'* | 'up' | *-ay* | 'across' |
| *-ayj* | 'down' | *-ñi* | 'across' |
| *-'mi* | 'in' | *-f'i* | 'upon' |
| *-gi, -ki* | 'out' | *-may* | 'down in' |
| *-k'oy* | 'inside' | *-way, -we* | 'down on' |

There are approximately a hundred VE1 elements and about a dozen VE2 elements. Not all combinations of VE1 and VE2 are allowed: there are about 175 compound-stem predicates attested in the current corpus. It is difficult to understand why some meanings can combine but others cannot. For example, one can combine *jway-* 'jump' and *-ñi* 'across' into the compound stem *jwayñi-* 'jump across,' but we cannot make similar constructions to express 'run across,' 'swim across,' or 'dance across.' Speakers simply know that those combinations do not make real words. Without written records of the language, we have few clues as to the **diachronic** processes that produced compound stems. For now, we have to assume that these constructions reflect meaningful combinations that have been used more frequently and have somehow been more useful to speakers over time. Some of this "usefulness" is suggested in the description of compound-stem predicates below.

### 9.3.1 Means predicates: manner of motion, manner of change

Details of how a change happens can be provided with a "means" construction, based on a means VE1. Examples (15) and (16) both talk about ways to put seed into the earth: the same figure, and the same goal. The difference between the two is the manner of moving the seeds. In (15), the farmer will broadcast (i.e., loosely throw) the seeds into the field, and the verb begins with *faj-* 'plant, sow.'

(15) *faj-'mi-'ma*      *sa*      *layñega*
plant-in-IPFV.SG      DM      cornfield
'He will sow the cornfield.'

In contrast, in (16), the motion is more controlled, as a few kernels of corn are carefully dropped into the prepared ground.

(16)  *tye'-'mi-'ma*          *sa*      *fane*      *la'wa-kosak'*
      drop-in-IPFV.SG         DM        three       little-corn
      'He will trickle in three corn kernels (into the furrow).'

The 'planting' examples demonstrated different manners of motion. A means VE1 can also distinguish a particular type of state change, including the different qualities of the result of a stage change. The next three examples all describe ways to separate an object into more than one piece. The VE1 *jas-* 'tear, split' is used when the figure is cloth or paper.

(17)  *jas-ñi-pa=yma'*            *el*       *je'e*
      tear-across-PFV.SG=2SG.A    DET        paper
      'You ripped the paper apart.'

The VE1 *ski-* means to 'split or divide something cleanly in two,' whether a piece of kindling or a crowd of people or, as in (18), a piece of fruit.

(18)  *ski-ñi-pa=yma'*            *el*       *mangu*
      split-across-PFV.SG=2SG.A  DET        mango
      'You split the mango in two.'

And the VE1 *pay-* 'break, shatter' is used when the figure is hard or brittle and therefore likely to break into more than one piece.

(19)  *pay-ñi-pa=yma'*            *la'i*     *pedazo*    *pedazo*    *pedazo*
      break-across-PFV.SG=2SG.A  bread      piece       piece       piece
      'You broke apart the bread into pieces.'

### 9.3.2  Classificatory predicates: referent introduction and tracking

Compound verbs can do more than just create new verbs with more detailed meaning. They can also be used in discourse to clarify the identity of **referents**. For example, in (20), the classificatory element indexes the size of the figure (the bag), clarifying that the speaker is referring to the small backpack, as opposed to another bag.

(20)  *tyinchi*    *maa=yma'*     *p-ayj-pa*            *l-o-bolsa*
      why          NEG=2SG.A      small-down-PFV.SG     DET-2SG.POSS-bag
      'Why don't you take off your backpack?'

In (21), the classificatory element identifies the figure as a grain, likely corn or rice.

(21)  *ch'uj-'mi-'ma=yma'*      *ten*       *sa=yma'*      *majkoda*
      grain-in-IPFV=2SG.A      what        DM=2SG.A       cook
      'You put in whatever grain you want to cook.'

In Example (22), from conversation, the classificatory element indicates to the addressee which item in the shared context should be picked up.

(22) *wa-f'-jla'*                            *jay*
container-up-IMP.SG                 female.friend
'Pick that up, girlfriend (a plate, a glass, a bowl, a basket).'

Argument omission or **ellipsis** is very common in Chontal, and the use of classificatory compound-stem predicates is a useful strategy for introducing referents, tracking referents in discourse, and maintaining a background participant in the discourse frame without using a noun phrase.

### 9.3.3  Dispositional predicates: spatial precision and referent tracking

Dispositional predicates, with dispositional VE1s, can give rich detail about the spatial configuration of the figure after a change of position, as, for example, 'mouthward upon' (23) or 'sitting down in' (24).

(23) *k'o-ma-f'i-yuy*            *iya'*       *l-i-tapadera*         *l-ay-k'ejwa'*
mouth-X-up.on-DUR.SG      1SG.A     DET-3SG.POSS-lid     DET-1SG.POSS-well
'I put/am putting a lid on my well.'

(24) *jojl-may-pa*                   *lapixu'*     *maj-lixpantalek-'ej*
sitting-down.in-PFV.SG      pot          LOC-forked.branch-tree
'The pot was sitting in the crotch of the tree.'

Other dispositional VE1s depict a more abstract arrangement of the figure. The element *sk'ing-* 'items in a circle' describes the placement of multiple figures into a circle, such as when dealing cards or doling out food, drink, or money. In (25), the speaker related how workers would come in from the fields and sit down around big bowls of food for the midday meal.

(25) *xago-'me'*         *lakujlwe',*      *xk'ing-we-'me'*                         *lamats'*
eat – IPFV.PL       man.PL        items.in.circle-down.on-IPFV.PL     earth
'The men are going to eat, so they sit in a circle on the ground.'

In addition, dispositional predicates play a minor role in referent tracking. Example (26) illustrates this function. There is no noun phrase that mentions the figure argument, the body of the deceased. Instead, the dispositional element *ñaj-* 'lying' tracks the figure as 'a lying thing' that is moved from the small mat used during a visitation into a casket for burial.

(26) *tyijpe*     *sa*       *ñaj-f'-'mi-pa'*         *jaape*     *li-kaja*
DIST        DM        lying-up-in-PFV.PL      where      3SG.POSS-coffin
'There they picked him up and put him in his coffin.'

**Figure LP9.5** Scene from a Chontal sugar cane parade

Example (26) also demonstrates that some compound stems combine two VE2 elements to depict an elaborated trajectory of motion, here, 'up' and then 'in.'

### 9.3.4 Trajectory predicates: elaborated path of motion

Only a few compound-stem predicates in my corpus depict an elaborated path of motion by stacking VE2 elements as a series of endpoints, as in (26). More commonly, a trajectory VE1 is used to describe different shapes of the trajectory of movement.

In (27), a figure is placed on top of a ground by moving it in a flat arc: here, a person places a saddle on the back of a burro.

**(27)**  *'oy-f'i-'ma*                *sa=ya'*        *l-ay-buru*
flat.arc-up.on-IPFV.SG       DM=1SG.A      DET-1SG.POSS-burro
'I will saddle my burro.'

In (28), chili seedlings (the figure) are removed from a bucket, moving in a different type of arc up over the edge of the bucket, and planted in a field.

**(28)**  *xpa-gi-'ma*       *sage=l*     *kasi*    *para*    *sa*    *fa-'ma*
high.arc-out-IPFV    DM=DET      chili     to        DM     plant-IPFV
'He would transplant the chili to plant it.'

And finally, the trajectory element *ki-* depicts a path that projects in a straight line, as in (29).

(29) 

| *joypa* | *sa=yma'* | *ki-ñi-pa* | *el* | *puente* | *de* | *Piña* |
|---------|-----------|------------|------|----------|------|--------|
| already | DM=2SG.A | straight-across-PFV | DET | bridge | GEN | Piña |

'Now you've crossed the Piña bridge.'

This overview of compound-stem predicates in Lowland Chontal gives a taste of the complex meanings they convey. The same types of verb are found in Highland Chontal, although these have not been described. Intriguingly, the compound stem may provide a window into the prehistory of the Chontal people. This construction is not found in southern Mexico outside the Oaxaca Chontal family but is well attested in languages that are or were spoken in present-day Oregon, California, Arizona, and northwestern Mexico. A thorough comparison of compound stems in all of these languages may help us understand any areal or genetic connections between the languages and among the people who spoke them.

Lowland Chontal is a marvelous language with rich resources for encoding change, giving precise detail of spatial disposition, physical qualities of the figure, the manner of change, and the perception of agentivity. The endangered status of the language and the difficulties of revitalization mean that the scope and nuance of the grammar of change in Chontal may disappear with the last fluent speakers. Documentation of endangered languages is vital to our understanding of the diversity of the human mind and the record of human history.

---

TEXTBOX LP9.3 **GLOSSING CONVENTIONS USED IN THIS LANGUAGE PROFILE**

| Convention | Meaning | Convention | Meaning |
|------------|---------|------------|---------|
| 1 | first person | IPFV | imperfective |
| 2 | second person | ITR | iterative |
| 3 | third person | LINKER | linking affix |
| A | agent | LOC | locative |
| APPL | applicative | NEG | negation |
| CAUS | causative | NOM | nominal |
| DET | determiner | P | patient of transitive |
| DIM | diminutive | PFV | perfective |
| DIST | distal | PL | plural |
| DLOC | dislocative | POSS | possessive |
| DM | discourse marker | SG | singular |
| DUR | durative | STAT | stative |
| IMP | imperative | | |

## SUGGESTIONS FOR FURTHER READING

**DeLancey, Scott**. 1999. "Lexical prefixes and the bipartite stem construction in Klamath." *International Journal of American Linguistics* **65**: 56–83.

**González, Alicia María**. 2002. *The edge of enchantment: Sovereignty and ceremony in Huatulco, México*. National Museum of the American Indian, Smithsonian Institute. Distributed by Fulcrum Publishing.

This is a beautifully photographed ethnographic study with a slightly dated social perspective.

**Levinson, Stephen C. and Wilkins, David P.** (eds.). 2006. *Grammars of space: Explorations in cognitive diversity*. Cambridge University Press.

A cross-linguistic study of how languages encode spatial relationships.

**Merlan, Francesca**. 1985. "Split intransitivity: functional oppositions in intransitive inflection." In Nichols, J. and A. C. Woodbury (eds.), *Grammar inside and outside the clause*. Cambridge University Press. 324–362.

This article gives more information on how languages mark agentive systems.

**Mithun, Marianne**. 1991. "Active/agentive case marking and its motivations." *Language* **67**.3: 510–546.

A study of active/agentive systems and how they develop.

**Mithun, Marianne**. 2007. "Grammar, contact and time." *Journal of Language Contact -THEMA* **1**: 144–167.

**O'Connor, Loretta M.** 2007. *Motion, transfer, and transformation: The grammar of change in Lowland Chontal*. Amsterdam and Philadelphia: John Benjamins.

A grammar of Lowland Chontal with a special emphasis on motion and change.

**O'Connor, Loretta M.** 2014. "Una huella del contacto? Verbos de movimiento en el chontal de la Baja de Oaxaca." In L. Guerrero (ed.), *Verbos de movimiento en lenguas de América: léxico, sintaxis y pragmática*. Ciudad México: UNAM.

These three articles are additional studies on compound stem verbs and their role in tracing language contact.

**Waterhouse, Viola**. 1967. "Huamelultec Chontal." In *Handbook of Middle American Indians*, Vol. V: *Linguistics*, ed. N. A. McQuown. Austin: University of Texas Press. 349–367.

A sketch grammar of Chontal.

## EXERCISES

1. Agent–patient systems, sometimes called agentive or active-static systems, are found in languages all over the world. This grammatical system represents a type of "semantic alignment" because core participants are marked according to a semantic motivation.

   Agentive languages and active-static languages differ with respect to what motivates the different types of marking. Agentive languages like Chontal tend to respond to semantic features of agentivity, understood as control, volition, or intention, while active-static languages tend to use one set of markers for events (active) and one set for states (static).

What these grammatical systems have in common is that, formally, they treat the single argument of intransitive verbs (S) sometimes like the subject of transitive verbs (A) and sometimes like the object (O) of transitive verbs. Therefore, we say that agentive and active systems treat some S arguments like A arguments and other S arguments like O arguments.

A speaker of an agentive language like Chontal answers several questions in each description of change (e.g., did the participant cause the change? Did he or she control it, or did it happen involuntarily? Was the change a surprise?). Some languages permit both types of marking on individual verbs, to encode differences such as *drinking* vs. *getting drunk* and *falling asleep* vs. *fainting*.

Consider each of the following pairs of sentences. In each case, the (a) member of the pair is in agentive form, while the (b) member of the pair is in patientive form. What is the likely difference in meaning or implication between each pair? Give an example of situations in which a speaker might use each one. Explain your reasoning.

1  a. *xuxkixpa=yma'*
      be.late=2SG.A
      'You took a long time, you're arriving late.'

   b. *xuxkixp-o'*
      be.late-2SG.P
      'You took a long time, you're arriving late.'

2  a. *xyoo-day'*          *'ñi*
      laugh-DUR.PL(A)      nothing.more
      'They just laugh.'

   b. *xyoo-go-p-ola'*
      laugh-APPL-PFV-3PL.P
      'They burst out laughing.'

3  a. *tyay-kay'*              *la'way'*
      understand-DUR.PL(A)     children
      'The children understand.'

   b. *joypa*        *tya-lay-t-olwa'*
      already       understand-PL-DLOC-2PL.P
      'Now you understand.'

4  a. *iyang=sa*       *styulye-pa'*
      1PL.A=DM        get.angry-PFV.PL
      'We got angry.'

   b. *iyang=sa*       *paychuj-p-onga'*
      1PL.A=DM        be.afraid-PFV-1PL.P
      'We got scared.'

(Note that a different lexical verb is used here. Explain why the S of *styulye-pa'* takes the agentive form, while that of *paychuj-p-onga'* takes the patientive form.)

5  a. *jak'-pa=ya'*
      disappear-PFV.SG=1SG.A
      'I disappeared.'

b. *jak'-p-ola'*        *la'way'*
disappear-PFV-3PL.P     children
'The children disappeared.'

2. Each of the following stems is composed of two parts: one initial verbal element (VE1) and one secondary verbal element (VE2). Identify the two verbal elements in each stem, noting that there are some allomorphs. Create a mini-glossary with a gloss for each VE1 or VE2 element, and indicate which of the four classes (i.e., classificatory, dispositional, means, or trajectory) each VE1 falls into.

    a. *k'ejway-*           'form a puddle'
    b. *k'ejmay-*          'be left over, like soup in the bottom of the pan'
    c. *k'ejk'oy-*          'form a blister'
    d. *k'ef'i-*             'water the flowers'
    e. *k'aygi-*           'draw water from a well'
    f. *k'ej'mi-*          'pour liquid'

    g. *lef'-*              'pick up a child or a rifle'
    h. *layj-*             'help an old lady out of a car'
    i. *legi-*             'pull a branch from the fire'
    j. *leñi-*             'receive people in your home'

    k. *pef'-*             'pick up a ball, rock, spoon, or envelope'
    l. *payj-*            'take off your backpack'
    m. *pef'i-*          'set an egg on the shelf'
    n. *pej'mi-*         'jump into the water (usually refers to a child)'
    o. *pek'oy-*         'stick your hand between the rocks'
    p. *peñi-*           'send a letter in the mail'
    q. *pay-*             'give someone a loaf of bread'

    r. *spaf'-*           'whip, spank'
    s. *spaf'i-*          'pull apart the outer leaves on an ear of corn (without removing them)'
    t. *spagi-*          'transplant tomato plants from your bucket into the field'
    u. *spak'oy-*        'lock the door with a wedged branch'
    v. *spañi-*         'shuck corn completely'

# Manambu

## 10.1 Introduction

The island of New Guinea is probably the most linguistically diverse and complex area in the world, with over 1,000 languages spoken in an area of 900,000 square kilometers. About 300 to 400 languages belong to the Austronesian language family.

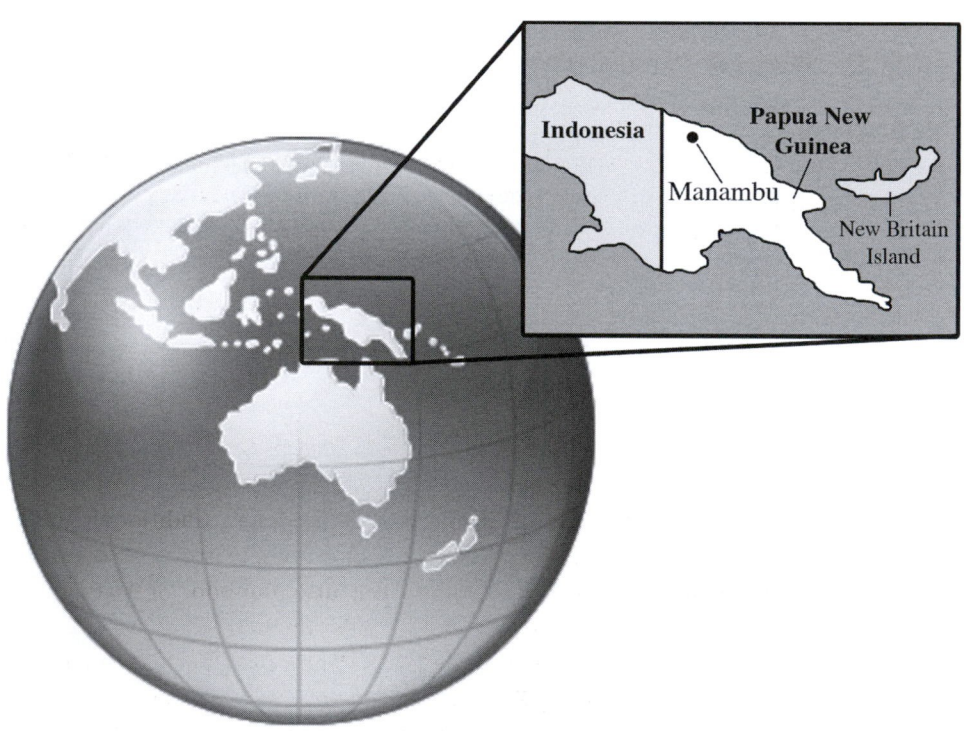

**Figure LP10.1** Location of Manambu speakers in New Guinea

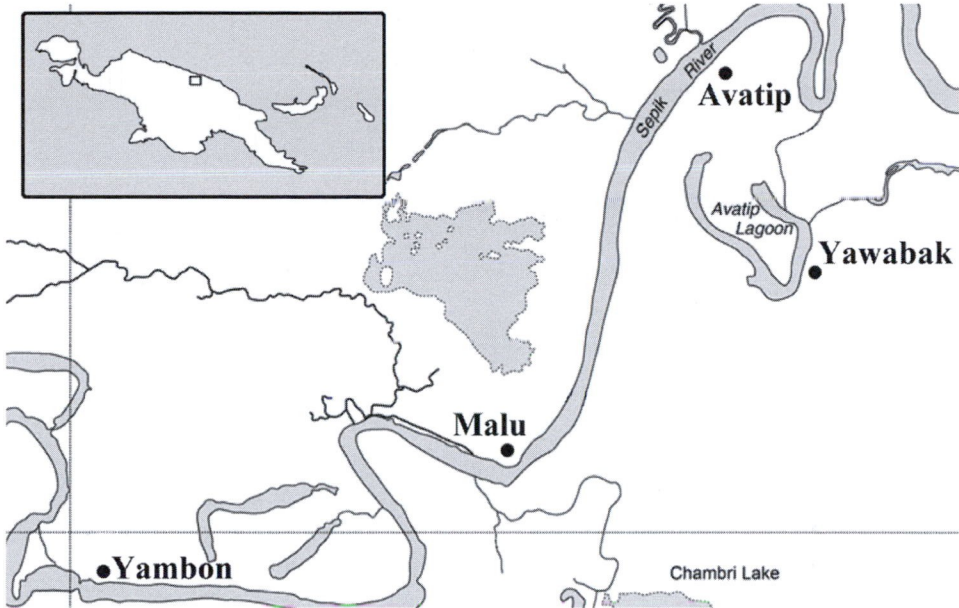

**Figure LP10.2** The Manambu-speaking villages Yawabak, Avatip, Malu, and Yuanab (Yambon)

Other, non-Austronesian, languages are called "Papuan" (Foley 1986: 1; Aikhenvald and Stebbins 2007). This rough denomination covers over sixty linguistic families and a fair number of linguistic isolates spoken in the area. Within New Guinea itself, the Sepik River basin (which includes East Sepik and West Sepik, or Sandaun, provinces), with its 200 languages, is the most linguistically diverse. Of the several language families of the Sepik (including the Lower Sepik, Ramu, Sepik Hill, Kwoma-Nukuma, and Tama families), the Ndu family is the largest in terms of both the number of speakers and the territory over which it extends, from the Sepik river itself northwards to the coast (Roscoe 1994).

Manambu is a member of the Ndu language family. About 2,500 people speak Manambu in four villages in the East Sepik Province (Ambunti district) along the Sepik River: Avatip, renowned as the most traditional village and a sort of Manambu "metropolis"; Malu, the place where the first contact with Europeans took place early in the twentieth century; Yambon, or Yuanab; and Yawabak (see Figure LP10.2). Not more than 200–400 Manambu speakers live in scattered expatriate communities in major cities of Papua New Guinea including Port Moresby, Wewak, Lae, Madang, Kokopo and Mount Hagen. Because of the complex language contact situation, the Manambu language is considered to be endangered (see Textbox LP10.1).

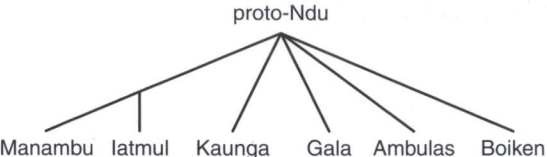

**Figure LP10.3** The Ndu language family

---

### TEXTBOX LP10.1 **HOW VITAL IS MANAMBU?**

Just like many other indigenous languages in Papua New Guinea, Manambu has hardly any monolingual speakers. Most children acquire Tok Pisin, the local lingua franca, as their first language, using it in their day-to-day communication. School education is conducted in Papua New Guinea English. The Manambu language can therefore be considered endangered.

Both Tok Pisin and Manambu are used at home and also in those rituals which are still performed, albeit in a reduced form (compared to what was documented earlier). Tok Pisin is dominant in village meetings, parent–teacher meetings at school, and in church (where Manambu is also used, but to a limited extent). That is, Tok Pisin and Manambu are in a partially diglossic situation. The necessity for proficiency in Tok Pisin is enhanced by the number of outsiders living in the villages, mostly as the result of mixed marriages.

However, the prospects for Manambu's survival may not be that dismal. The role models of returning urban Manambu – and the power and enduring value of cultural knowledge conceived as the knowledge of important words and totemic and personal names – are what may ensure that the language lives on. Tok Pisin and Papua New Guinea English are there to stay, as languages of the outside power and authority conceptualized as attributes of the "white man's" world. But neither of these intruders appears to shatter the position of Manambu as the language of spiritual and symbolic power, which, in this Sepik culture, is most valued. Manambu remains an emblematic language for the people it "belongs" to, and the traditional owners are determined to pass it on.

---

In terms of its grammatical structure, Manambu is one of the most complex languages in the Ndu family. The relative complexity of Manambu can be partially accounted for by language contact (see Chapter 14). The Manambu incorporated into their community members of neighboring tribes whom they had conquered as a result of inter-tribal warfare (Harrison 1993; Aikhenvald 2009). These outsiders spoke different languages and as they learned Manambu they did so imperfectly, bringing in features of their own native speech. Some of these features eventually spread through the entire Manambu community, creating a **substrate** effect.

We now turn to a few salient features of the language. First we present a brief snapshot of the Manambu's linguistic type, and some typological features. We then discuss one of the key issues in Manambu grammar: the marking of grammatical relations on verbs, and on nouns.

## 10.2 The linguistic features of Manambu

### 10.2.1 Phonology

Manambu has twenty-one consonants and nine vowels, more than any other language of the Ndu family. These are shown in Tables LP10.1 and LP10.2. An interesting Ndu phonological feature is discussed in Textbox LP10.2.

Stress is contrastive: it may distinguish words with different meanings. Minimal pairs are *ákəs*, a particle indicating habitual negation, and *akə́s* 'catch!', *gə́ñə̄r* 'to tail, with 'tail' and *gə̄ñə̄r* 'later.'

**TABLE LP10.1** Consonants in Manambu

|  | Bilabial | Labiodental | Dental | Alveolar | Palato-alveolar | Palatal | Velar | Glottal |
|---|---|---|---|---|---|---|---|---|
| Voiceless non-labialized stops | p |  | t |  |  |  | k |  |
| Voiceless labialized stops | p<sup>w</sup> |  |  |  |  |  | k<sup>w</sup> |  |
| Voiced non-labialized stops | b |  | d |  |  |  | g |  |
| Voiced labialized stops | b<sup>w</sup> |  |  |  |  |  | g<sup>w</sup> |  |
| Voiced fricative |  | v |  |  |  |  |  |  |
| Voiceless fricatives |  |  |  | ʒ |  |  |  | h |
| Voiced affricate |  |  |  |  | j [dʒ] |  |  |  |
| Lateral |  |  | l |  |  |  |  |  |
| Trilled rhotic |  |  | r |  |  |  |  |  |
| Nasals | m |  | n |  |  | ñ [ɲ] |  |  |
| Glides | w |  |  |  |  | y [j] |  |  |

**TABLE LP10.2** Vowels in Manambu

|  | Short vowels | | | Long vowels | | |
|---|---|---|---|---|---|---|
|  | front | central | back | front | central | back |
| high | i |  | u | iː |  | uː |
| middle |  | ə |  |  |  |  |
| low | æ | a |  | æː |  | aː |

---

**TEXTBOX LP10.2 PRENASALIZED STOPS**

Manambu shares an interesting phonological feature with many Papuan and Austronesian languages of this area: voiced stops and the voiced affricate are prenasalized in syllable-initial position. So, the word for 'man' /du/, is pronounced as [ⁿdu]. Incidentally, this root is shared by all the Ndu languages and is the name given to the whole family.

---

## 10.2.2  Morphology

As discussed in Chapter 4, languages can be classified based on their degrees of fusion and degrees of synthesis. Manambu can be described as **synthetic**, that is, allowing many morphemes per word. The language is also **agglutinating**, so it is relatively easy to determine the boundaries between morphemes, although there is some fusion. Most grammatical morphemes are suffixes. There are just two prefixes: the valency-increasing *kay-*, which will be discussed below, and the second-person imperative *a-*.

## 10.2.3  Word classes: nouns

The major word classes in Manambu, nouns and verbs, are both open classes. The two are clearly distinguished, as they have different grammatical categories and different inflectional possibilities.

**SIDEBAR LP10.2**

CLASSIFICATORY FATHERS

Each Manambu person has more than one man whom they address as *asa:y* 'father.' One uses this term for a biological father, and also for one's father's brothers – that is, 'paternal uncles.' These are called "classificatory fathers." A child belongs to the same clan as their classificatory father. A son would learn traditional lore and family history from one of his fathers and listen to their advice. In addition, names – which are considered a prized possession among the Manambu – are inherited from one's classificatory fathers.

**SIDEBAR LP10.3**

In Example (1), you will notice that the associative non-singular and the dual marker in Manambu are homonyms. This is accidental; they are not etymologically related, as each has a different proto-Ndu etymology (see Aikhenvald 2008: 594–595).

Beginning with nouns, nominal categories include two genders (masculine and feminine), three numbers (singular, dual, and plural), nine case forms, and a number of derivations.

Number is usually realized through agreement on modifiers and on the verb. For example, consider the noun phrase *kə-di ya:p* (PROX.DEM-PL rope) 'these ropes,' which is taken from Example (7) below. The proximal demonstrative stem *kə* 'this' takes a plural suffix reflecting the plurality of the head noun. (Similarly, the demonstrative *these* is plural in English.) Number marking is found on only some nouns. Kinship terms, including the word for 'child' *ñan*, and a handful of nouns from other semantic groups (such as *kudi* 'mouth'), are marked for number, e.g., *asa:y* 'father,' *asay-vəti* (father-DU) 'two classificatory fathers' (see Sidebar LP10.2), *asay-ugw* (father-PL) 'many classificatory fathers.' The noun *ñan* 'child' has a semi-suppletive form *ñədi* for the dual number, and a plural *ñan-ugw* 'children.'

A special type of plural can be marked on personal names. This is referred to as an **associative plural**. It refers to a group of two or more people associated with the person who is named. Thus, *Tanina-bər*

(Tanina-ASSOC.NSG) may mean 'Tanina and one other person,' or two altogether, in which case this form requires dual agreement on modifiers and on the verb. In Example (1), agreeing elements are underlined (see Sidebar LP10.3 for an additional note on this example).

(1)  *a-bər*　　　　　*Tanina-bər*　　　　　*wakuna-bər*
　　DIST.DEM-du　　Tanina ASSOC.NSG　　go.out-3DU
　　'Those two, Tanina and one other person, are going out'

The same form *Tanina-bər* can refer to Tanina and more than one person, i.e., more than two altogether. In such cases, plural agreement markers appear on the modifiers – such as the demonstrative *a-di* 'DIST.DEM-PL' in Example (2) – and on the verb:

(2)  *a-di*　　　　　*Tanina-bər*　　　　　*wakuna-di*
　　DIST.DEM-PL　　Tanina-ASSOC.NSG　　go.out-3PL
　　'Those several/many, Tanina and other people, are going out'

Gender is marked in independent pronouns and in pronominal suffixes on the verb. But it is only distinguished for the second- and third-person singular categories; the distinction is **neutralized** (not made) in the non-singular numbers – the dual and the plural. Each noun is assigned masculine or feminine gender. In the noun phrase, modifiers (including demonstratives, interrogatives, possession markers, and three of the adjectives) agree with the gender of the head noun; there is gender agreement in the verb as well.

For the majority of nouns, gender is not expressed on the noun itself, that is, one cannot determine the gender of a noun simply by looking at its form (as is true with much of the vocabulary of Romance languages). The only exception is personal names – a highly salient subgroup of nouns in Manambu that are also considered tantamount to monetary valuables, those whose ownership is disputed in name debates (see Textbox LP10.3). Most personal names have masculine and feminine counterparts, which are distinguished morphologically; for example, the male name *Kiginəbək* has a female counterpart *Kiginəbəkə-bər*. Some male personal names contain the morpheme *du* 'man,' e.g., *Kawi-du*, while some female personal names contain *ta:kw* 'woman,' e.g., *Ñamamayra-ta:kw.*

Nouns are assigned genders according to the sex of a human referent, and to the shape and size of a referent of any other semantic group. That is, men are assigned to the masculine, and women to the feminine gender. A large dog or a large house is treated as masculine, and a small dog or a small house as feminine. Many speakers are aware of the correlation between gender assignment and size: *a-də wuna-də wi*

## TEXTBOX LP10.3 **THE VALUE OF NAMES**

Manambu culture differs dramatically from those of western societies. For example, the Manambu people place particular importance on ownership of personal names, and totemic names belonging to the major clan groups and their subclans. Possessing multiple names is viewed as a major asset. Ritual debates concerning name ownership are, traditionally, the main political forum and the center of village life. For a detailed ethnographic study of the Manambu, see Harrison (1990, 1993).

**Figure LP10.4** A ritual name debate

(DIST.DEM-SG.M 1SG-SG.M house) 'that (masculine) house of mine' – referring to a big house I own – may be translated as 'that big man-type house of mine.'

Conversely, *a-Ø wuna-Ø wi* (DIST.DEM-SG.F 1SG-SG.F house) 'that (feminine) house of mine' – referring to a small house I own – may well be translated as 'that small woman-type house of mine.' Round objects, such as *ab* 'head,' *gwas* 'turtle,' or *ya:l* 'belly,' are normally feminine. But a belly of an unusually large size can be referred to with the masculine form of a modifier.

Assigning a gender to a mass noun depends on the amount of the referent: money can be referred to as masculine if we are talking of a large sum; a small sum will be referred to with feminine gender. A not-too-dark night is feminine; if a night is completely dark, it becomes masculine. The word *ka:m* 'hunger' is treated as masculine if one is very hungry, and as feminine if one is only a bit peckish. A further important function of gender is to distinguish polysemous nouns.

For instance, *ma:m* 'older sibling' can refer either to an elder brother or an elder sister; gender is instrumental for disambiguating the reference.

By semantic extension, an unusually big or bossy woman can be treated as masculine, and a squat fattish man as feminine. The word *ab* 'head' typically requires feminine agreement, due to its round shape. But if one is suffering from a severe headache, one can say 'my-masculine head is hurting' – this is because the head then feels unusually big and heavy.

### 10.2.4  Word classes: verbs

Some Manambu verbs are either strictly intransitive or strictly transitive. Strictly intransitive verbs include motion verbs, e.g., *yi-* 'go,' *ya-* 'come,' *gəp-* 'run,' and a few others, such as *pərki-* 'be torn.' A few verbs can be used only transitively, e.g., *yi-* 'say, speak' and *kur-* 'do, make, get.' There are few ditransitive verbs, e.g., *kwatiya-* 'give to a non-third person,' *kui-* 'give to this person,' and derivations based on this. However, over 80 percent of verbs in Manambu are **ambitransitive**: they can be used either transitively or intransitively, in a similar way to English *eat*: in its transitive use, it requires an object (e.g., *I have eaten dinner*); in its intransitive use, no object appears (e.g., *I have eaten already*).

Ambitransitive verbs in Manambu include ingestive verbs *kə-* 'consume (food, drink, smoke)' and *jə-* 'chew,' and verbs of cognition *wukə-* 'hear, obey, understand' and *laku-* 'know, understand.' The verb *rali(na)-* 'untie, be untied' is among the few ambitransitive verbs of the type similar to English *break*, as in *I have broken a glass* and *A glass broke*. This represents one of two types of ambitransitive verbs, where the subject of the intransitive clause (*glass* in *a glass broke*) corresponds to the object of the transitive clause (*I have broken a glass*). We will call this type of ambitransitive S.of.I = O.of.T. The other type of ambitransitive verb is exemplified by English *eat*. Here the subject of the intransitive clause (*I ate.*) corresponds to the subject of the transitive (*I ate a sandwich*). This type will be referred to as S.of.I=S.of.T. Moving back to Manambu *rali(na)*, Examples (3) and (4) illustrate that this is the S.of.I=O.of.T type.

(3)  Intransitive

    [*wun-a*        *kwa:r*]<sub>SUBJ</sub>    (*ka:p*)      *ralina*
    POSS.1SG.F    grass.skirt    (by.itself)    untie.3SG.F.NPST
    'My grass skirt comes/has come untied (by itself)'

(4)  Transitive

    [*wuna-ø*     *kwa:r*]<sub>OBJ</sub>    *ralina-wun*
    1SG.SG.F     grass.skirt    untie-1SG.F.NPST
    'I untied/have untied my grass skirt'

The prefix *kay-* derives a transitive verb from an intransitive verb. The intransitive verb *pərki(na)-* 'be torn' is shown in Example (5).

(5) Intransitive

[*wuna-ø*    *ku-su-wapwi*]_S
1SG-SG.F    put-UP-clothes

*bəta:y*    *pərkina*
already    tear(INTR).3SG.F.NPST
'My clothing (lit. 'clothing to put on/wear') is already torn'

In Example (6), the verb 'be torn' is transitivized.

(6) Causativized transitive

[*kə*    *kuprapə*    *ñan*]_A    [*wuna-ø*    *ku-su-wapwi*]_O
PROX.DEM.SG.F    bad    child    1SG-SG.F    put-UP-clothes

**kay**-*pərkina*
CAUS-tear(INTR).3SG.F.NPST
'This naughty girl (fully) tore my clothing'

---

### TEXTBOX LP10.4 **CAUSATIVE CONSTRUCTIONS**

**Causative constructions** are ways of expressing a caused event. The causative construction illustrated in (6) represents the most common type: morphological causation. In morphological causatives there is a causative morpheme, like *kay-* in Manambu, that is affixed to the verb. Most commonly in the world's languages causative constructions increase the valence of the verb by one degree, so that intransitive verbs become transitive, and transitive verbs become ditransitive. They thus involve the introduction of a new core argument, the semantic causer, which is treated as the agentive core argument (i.e., the A). The single core argument of the corresponding intransitive clause (S) becomes the O of the derived transitive, as with the argument *wuna ku-su-wapwi* 'my clothing' in Examples (5) and (6).

---

This prefix *kay-* occurs with about a hundred verbs referring to states and processes (the most frequently used ones are listed in Aikhenvald 2008: 407). Derived transitive verbs containing *kay-* are strictly transitive.

The prefix *kay-* can also occur on several dozen ambitransitive and transitive verbs, all of them verbs of manipulation. With these verbs, it does not function as a causative (see Textbox LP10.4) and does not increase valency. Instead, its effects are as follows:

1. It converts any ambitransitive verb into a strictly transitive one. That is, the transitivity status of the verb is affected. However, *kay-* does not make such a verb into a causative, i.e., it does not introduce a new "causer."

2. The semantic effect of *kay-* on transitive and ambitransitive verbs implies an increase in manipulative effort, intentionality, volitionality, and control on the part of the subject (A), and may also imply that the object (O) is multiple or large.

Consider the ambitransitive verb *rali(na)*- 'untie, be untied,' which was introduced in examples (3) and (4). In (7), the same verb is used with the prefix *kay-*. The ropes are tangled, and untying them requires special effort:

(7) ya:n        kə-di          ya:p      a-rali       a-kay-rali
    come.SEQ    PROX.DEM-PL    rope      IMP-untie    IMP-MANIP-untie
    'Come and untie these ropes; untie them with special effort' (since they are entangled)'

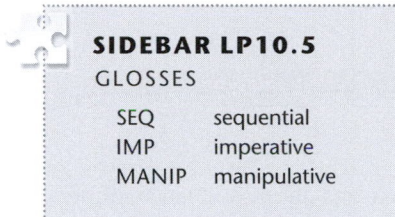

**SIDEBAR LP10.5**

GLOSSES

| | |
|---|---|
| SEQ | sequential |
| IMP | imperative |
| MANIP | manipulative |

This causative-manipulative polysemy is rather uncommon cross-linguistically. It is reminiscent of similar patterns described for Oceanic languages (Harrison 1982; Dixon 1988), which are also spoken in the Pacific region.

Verbal inflectional categories cover three persons, two genders (distinguished in second and third person), three numbers, and a variety of aspects. Among the various modal meanings are the "frustrative" ('intend but fail to do'), the purposive 'intend' and the desiderative 'want,' as shown in Example (8).

(8) wun      kami:     kə-kər
    1SG      fish      consume-DESIDERATIVE
    'I want to eat fish'

A verb in the declarative mood can cross-reference the person, number, and gender of the subject. If a clause contains a constituent that is more topical than the subject, this constituent can also be cross-referenced alongside the subject. This will be discussed more fully below.

As we will see, past and non-past tenses are fused with person-marking suffixes, while future and irrealis are marked with suffixes. Most verbs take directional markers, specifying whether the movement follows an upward, a downward, or an outward direction, toward the speaker or away from them. A verbal root can be reduplicated to express intensive, continuous, or repeated action.

Verbs are productively combined with each other to specify the manner or a sequence of actions, such as *væsə-piñə*- (step-slip) 'slip stepping,' or *gəpə-wula*- (run-go.inside) 'go inside by running.' Some verbs have taken on grammatical meanings when combined with other verbs (i.e., they have become grammaticalized; see Chapter 13): the verb *təp*- 'to be closed' acquired the meaning of 'do for the last time,' as in *və-təp*- (see-be.closed) 'see for the last time,' and the verb *wa*- 'say, speak' developed into a causative marker, as in *yaga*- 'be scared,' *wa-yaga*- 'make (someone) scared.'

### 10.2.5 Adjectives

Manambu has two subclasses of adjectives. Both are closed classes that do not admit new members. One subclass consists of just three members: *kwasa* 'small,' *numa* 'big,' and *yara* 'fine.' These adjectives always agree with the noun in gender and in number, e.g., *numa-də du* (big-SG.M man) 'big man,' *numa ta:kw* (big-SG.F woman) 'big woman,'

| TABLE LP10.3 Manambu personal pronouns | | | |
|---|---|---|---|
| PERSON/GENDER | SG | DU | PL |
| 1 | *wun* | *an* | *ñan* |
| 2.M | *mən* | *bər* | *gwur* |
| 2.F | *ñən* | | |
| 3.M | *də* | | *dəy* |
| 3.F | *lə* | | |

*numa-di du* (big-PL man) 'big men.' The other subclass has about sixteen members, covering meanings of value (e.g., *vyakətə* 'good', *kuprapə* 'bad'), size (e.g., *gərgər* 'tiny,' *səmi* 'long'), and color (e.g., *gla* 'black,' *wama* 'white,' *ñiki* 'red'). These adjectives do not agree with the noun they modify but have a single form, regardless of the gender and number of the noun, e.g., *vyakətə du* 'good man,' *vyakətə ta:kw* 'good woman.' Many of these adjectives are transparently related to nouns: for instance, *ñiki* 'red' is also the word for blood, and *wama* 'white' is derived from *wa:m* 'white cockatoo' (a type of bird).

## 10.2.6 Personal pronouns

Personal pronouns are a closed word class (the full set is given in Table LP10.3). The categories of number (singular, dual, plural), gender (masculine, feminine), and person (first, second, third) are all distinguished. However, they are not maximally distinguished; there are not distinct forms for every logically possible combination of these three categories. We can analyze the distribution of categories as follows:

- Number is distinguished in all forms. One can always tell from the pronoun whether the referent is singular, dual, or plural.
- Gender is only distinguished in the second- and third-person singular. Gender distinctions are neutralized (i.e., not made) in the first-person singular and in all non-singular (dual and plural) categories.
- Three persons are distinguished in the singular and plural. The distinction between second person and third person is neutralized in the dual; i.e., there is only one marker for all non-first persons in the dual.

## 10.2.7 Demonstratives

Demonstratives are the most complex of the closed word classes. They distinguish five directions – up, down, across, outwards, and inside or away from the Sepik River – in addition to three additional degrees of distance.

The three demonstrative stems are *kə-* 'this, close to speaker,' *wa-* 'this, close to hearer,' and *a-* 'that, far from both speaker and hearer.' Each of these stems can

> ### TEXTBOX LP10.5 **THE CULTURAL RELEVANCE OF COUNTING**
>
> The Manambu language has a decimal counting system. Proficient speakers can count up to a hundred using Manambu terms. In traditional times, counting was an established cultural practice: male prowess was estimated on the basis of how many enemies a man had killed, and so it was customary to count the victims, as a matter of competition. Nowadays, Tok Pisin and English numbers are used more and more often, especially in counting money.

combine with one of five directional suffixes, *wur* 'up, upstream,' *-d(a)* 'down, downstream,' *-aki* 'across,' *-aku* 'outwards' or *-wula* 'inside, away from the Sepik River towards the shore.' For example, a Manambu speaker refers to stars, which are far up in the sky, as *kə-di-a-wur kugar* (PROX.DEM-PL-LINKER-UP-star) 'those stars (up),' and a village close to the speaker away from the Sepik River is referred to as *kə-d-a-wula təp* (PROX.DEM-SG.M-LINKER-AWAY.FROM.RIVER-village) 'this village away from the Sepik River.'

## 10.2.8  Clause combining and switch reference

Similar to many other languages of New Guinea, Manambu has extensive **clause-chaining**, a construction that creates chains of clauses by using a special set of suffixes on the verbs in the non-final clauses in the chain, then fully inflecting the verb in the final clause of the chain. In addition, and again like many other languages of the area, Manambu has a complex system of **switch-reference**, whereby the clause-chaining suffixes indicate whether the subject of the clause is the same as, or different from, that of the main clause. Example (9) illustrates a chain of two clauses. The suffix *-ku* on the verb of the first clause is a clause-chaining suffix. In addition to forming the chain, it marks two other grammatical meanings: that the action of the non-main clause is completed, and that its subject is the same as that of the main clause. Note that in same-subject chained clauses (e.g., the first clause of (9)), the person of the subject is not marked on the verb. Clause boundaries are indicated with square brackets.

(9)  [*a-di*         *jəb*       *kur-ku*]           [*ata*     *ya:d*]
     DIST.DEM-PL   design     make-COMPL.SS       then     go.3SG.M.PST
     'Having made those designs, he went off'

**SIDEBAR LP10.6**
GLOSSES

| | |
|---|---|
| COMPL | completed action |
| SS | same subject (switch reference) |
| DS | different subject (switch reference) |

In contrast, in Example (10) the subjects of the chained clause and the main clause are different. The predicate of the non-main clause contains a person marker (*-də-*, which indicates third-person masculine singular) followed by the clause-chaining suffix *-k*, which indicates both that the action of the chained clause is completed, and that we are to expect a different subject from the following main clause.

(10)  [a-di            jəb          kur-də-k]
      DIST.DEM-PL      design       make-3SG.M-COMPL.DS

      [ata      ya:d]
      then     go.3SG.M.PST
      'After he (Iraman) had made those designs, he (Kawidu) went off'

The verb always occurs at the very end of a chained clause. In a main clause, the order is more flexible: the verb-final principle is a tendency rather than a steadfast rule.

## 10.3  Grammatical relations

Understanding grammatical relations in Manambu is pivotal for getting a grasp of its structure. Grammatical relations are marked in two ways: by case-marking on nouns, and by agreement on verbs. Although these are common ways of indicating grammatical relations cross-linguistically, the way these are realized in Manambu are typologically unusual.

### 10.3.1  Verb agreement

Verbs in Manambu can be inflected by two sets of suffixes that mark the person, gender, and number of arguments. Verbs can be 'fully' or 'partially' inflected. Fully inflected verbs agree with (or "cross-reference") two arguments: the subject and any other argument (except the copula complement or quoted speech) that is more topical than the subject, i.e., the **topic**. (See Textbox 10.6 for a discussion of topicality.) Partially inflected verbs agree with only the subject; an example of this is the non-final verb in (10). Some verbs are uninflected and don't take person agreement at all; we saw this with the desiderative verb in (8) and the non-final same-subject verb in (9).

If there is no constituent more topical than the subject and the verb is a fully inflected verb, the subject (A or S) is cross-referenced as the topic. This is done with one of the set of 'topic' agreement suffixes (glossed TOP). The full paradigm of suffixes that cross-reference the most topical argument is given in Table LP10.4.

---

### TEXTBOX LP10.6 **TOPICALITY**

Many languages are like Manambu in having grammatical means – such as morphemes or separate constructions – that indicate whether or not the people or entities referred to by arguments are important to the surrounding discourse. If they are, they are likely to come up repeatedly. Such referents are considered to be **topical** in the discourse. In English the passive construction is used when the patient is more topical than the agent; the passive allows the topic to be the subject of the clause. For example, in the sentence *Elizabeth was hit by a car*, Elizabeth (the patient) is the topic, and is thus put into subject position via the passive construction. We expect subsequent conversation to revolve around Elizabeth ("Oh no! Is she okay?") and not the car. (Therefore "Oh no! I hope the car is alright!" would be a distinctly odd reply.)

**TABLE LP10.4** Agreement paradigm for topical arguments

| PERSON/GENDER | SG | | DU | | PL | |
|---|---|---|---|---|---|---|
| | NPST | PST | NPST | PST | NPST | PST |
| 1.F | -wun | -l-wun | -bər-an | | -diy-an | |
| 1.M | -də-wən | | | | | |
| 2.F | -ñən | -lə-ñən | -bər-bər | | -di-gwər | |
| 2.M | -də-mən | | | | | |
| 3.F | -ø | -l | -bər | | -di | |
| 3.M | -d | | | | | |

**SIDEBAR LP10.7**

GLOSSES

TOP   topic

Consider Example (11). The ambitransitive verb 'know' is used intransitively, i.e., without any object. The subject, 'he,' is cross-referenced on the verb as the most topical argument.

(11)   *bu*          *lakuna-d*
       already       know-3SG.M.TOP.NPST
       'He knows (already); he is knowledgeable'

This same verb can be used transitively, with an object. In (12) the object is not topical, that is, it is not something that is likely to be further discussed in the discourse. Since the subject is the most topical argument in the clause, again it is the only participant cross-referenced on the verb.

(12)   [*kə*              *ma:j*]ₒ    *lakuna-d*
       PROX.DEM.SG.F    story      know-3SG.M.TOP.NPST
       'He knows/understands this story'

A non-subject argument can also be cross-referenced by these suffixes if it is more topical than the subject. This is true regardless of the verb's transitivity. In Example (13) the object is topical (the conversation revolves around the road) and is thus indexed by a suffix from the paradigm in Table LP10.4, the same set used for the subject in (11) and (12). The subject is also cross-referenced on the verb, but now with a *different* suffix from an independent set, given in Table LP10.5. Thus the verb in (13) agrees with two arguments: the topic and the subject.

**TABLE LP10.5** Cross-referencing paradigm for non-topical subjects

| PERSON/GENDER | SG | | DU | | PL | |
|---|---|---|---|---|---|---|
| | NPST | PST | NPST | PST | NPST | PST |
| 1.F/M | -tua- | -tuə | -ta- | -tə- | -bana- | |
| 2.F | -ñəna- | -ñənə- | | | | |
| 2.M | -məna- | -mənə- | -bra | -brə- | -gwura- | |
| 3.F | -la- | -lə- | | | | |
| 3.M | -da- | -də- | | | -dana- | -da |

(13)  [lə]ₐ      a-də          [yabə-m]ₒ
      3SG.F    DIST.DEM-SG.M    road(M)-ACC/LOC

laku-*la*-d
know-3SG.F.SBJ.NPST-3SG.M.TOP.NPST
'She knows the road (fully)'

Arguments other than the subject or object can also be topics and cross-referenced on the verb. In (14) it is the addressee that is marked, since it the topic.

(14)  dəkə-k        ata      wa-*tuə*-d
      3SG.M-DAT    thus    say-1SG.SBJ.PST-3SG.M.TOP.PST
      'I said to him thus'

In (15) the topical argument refers to a time (note that 'time' is usually feminine, being conceived of as round and cyclic; hence the feminine form of the demonstrative 'that' is used).

(15)  [a                   səkər]ₜₑₘₚₒᵣₐₗ      ya-də-*l*
      DIST.DEM.SG.F      time              come-3SG.M.SBJ.PST-3SG.F.TOP.PST
      'He came at that time'

The choice between cross-referencing one or two arguments on a Manambu verb is largely independent of the verb's transitivity: both transitive and intransitive verbs can cross-reference one or two arguments.

The Manambu system of verb agreement is typologically unusual in two ways. First, the number of cross-referenced arguments (one of which has to be the subject) depends on the discourse properties of the non-subject constituent, rather than on the transitivity, or other lexical properties, of the verb.

Secondly, the subject can be cross-referenced by one of two sets of suffixes, as opposed to just one. But note that the subject is the only argument that *must* be marked on the verb in one way or the other. Thus, the verbal agreement system constitutes evidence for the grammatical relation of subject, despite the fact that two sets of suffixes are involved. The system also provides evidence for the grammatical relation of topic in Manambu, as the topic is the argument cross-referenced by the paradigm in Table LP10.4.

## 10.3.2  Case-marking on nouns, and grammatical relations

In addition to verb agreement, grammatical relations are also indicated by case-marking, with subjects being marked one way, and non-subjects being marked differently. Nouns distinguish nine case forms:

  i.   Subjects do not take any case-markers.
 ii.   Objects can either not be case-marked or take the case-marker *-Vm*. This pattern will be discussed further below.
iii.   Oblique arguments take case-markers based upon their semantics. The oblique cases are as follows.
   a.   locative case ('at', 'to') *-Vm*
   b.   dative-aversive ('to', 'for fear of') *-Vk*
   c.   comitative ('with' as in 'do something with someone') *-wa*
   d.   terminative ('up to a point') *-Vb*
   e.   transportative ('via transport') *-say, -sap*
   f.   allative-instrumental ('to' or 'with (an instrument)') *-Vr*
   g.   substitutive 'instead of' *-yæy*

The object of a transitive verb takes no case-marker if it is either indefinite, or non-referential and non-topical, or not completely involved in the activity. An example is in (12) above: 'this story' is not topical and thus is not case-marked. (Similar examples are 'grass skirt' in (3), 'clothing' in (6), and 'ropes' in (7)). See Textbox LP10.7 for a comparison of this type of case-marking pattern to that found in Spanish.

---

### TEXTBOX LP10.7 **DIFFERENTIAL OBJECT MARKING IN SPANISH**

This type of pattern, where objects take a case-marker only if they have certain semantic or discourse properties, is common cross-linguistically. The technical name for this in linguistics is differential object marking. An example of another language with differential object marking is Spanish. In the sentence *Esta mañana he visto a la hermana de María* 'This morning I saw Maria's sister,' the object is obligatorily marked with the accusative preposition *a*. Contrast this with *Esta mañana he visto la nueva iglesia* 'this morning I saw the new church,' where the object is unmarked, due to the semantic and discourse properties of the noun phrase (i.e., it is inanimate and non-topical). The factors that determine the presence or absence of *a* with objects in Spanish are famously subtle, and there is a large literature on this subject.

In contrast, the noun 'male children' in (16) is the topic of a stretch of discourse, and so it acquires case-marking, in addition to being cross-referenced on the verb. That is, agreement on verbs and case-marking on nouns follow different principles.

(16)  *a*            *kuprapə*    *wapi*    *dua-ñan-ugw-a:m*
      DIST.DEM.SG.F    bad        bird      man-child-PL-ACC

      *kə-la-di*
      eat-3SG.F.SBJ.PST-3PL.TOP.PST
      'That bad bird ate up the male children (we are talking about)'

- Verb agreement: subjects are always cross-referenced; non-subjects are only cross-referenced if they are topical.
- Case-marking: subjects are never case-marked; objects are only case-marked if definite, referential, and/or topical. Non-core arguments are case-marked in accordance with their semantic role.

## 10.4  Conclusions

We have seen that the grammatical structures of Manambu are typologically interesting and unique. However, even though the grammar may seem exotic, the pieces are familiar and the language follows the same core principles on which other grammatical systems are based. This universality across languages attests to the common cognitive make-up of our species, and the common needs of speakers in daily communication within societal structures. We've also seen hints at the relationship between the Manambu language and culture, as the language simultaneously reflects and transmits the Manambu worldview.

---

**TEXTBOX LP10.8 GLOSSING CONVENTIONS USED IN THIS LANGUAGE PROFILE**

| Convention | Meaning | Convention | Meaning |
|---|---|---|---|
| 1 | first person | DAT | dative |
| 2 | second person | DEM | demonstrative |
| 3 | third person | DESIDERATIVE | desiderative |
| ACC | accusative | DIST | distal |
| ASSOC | associative | DS | different subject |
| AWAY.FROM.RIVER | directional affix | DU | dual |
| CAUS | causative | F | feminine |
| COMPL | completive | FUT | future tense |

## TEXTBOX LP10.8 (*cont.*)

| | | | |
|---|---|---|---|
| HABITUAL | habitual | PL | plural |
| IMP | imperative | POSS | possessive |
| INTR | intransitive | PROX | proximal |
| LINKER | linking morpheme | PST | past tense |
| LOC | locative | SBJ | subject |
| M | masculine | SEQ | sequential |
| MANIP | manipulative | SG | singular |
| NPST | non-past tense | SS | same subject |
| NSG | non-singular | TOP | topic |
| OBL | oblique | UP | directional affix |

## SUGGESTIONS FOR FURTHER READING

**Aikhenvald, Alexandra Y.** 2008. *The Manambu language of East Sepik, Papua New Guinea.* Oxford University Press.

This is a comprehensive study of the Manambu language.

**Harrison, Simon**. 1990. *Stealing people's names: History and politics in a Sepik River cosmology.* Cambridge University Press.

1993. *The mask of war.* Manchester University Press.

These two books are detailed ethnographic studies of the Manambu and their culture.

**Roscoe, Paul**. 1994. "Who are the Ndu? Ecology, migration, and linguistic and cultural change in the Sepik Basin." In Strathern, Andrew J. and G. Stürzenhofecker (eds.), *Migrations and transformations: Regional perspectives on New Guinea.* University of Pittsburgh Press. 49–84.

This article discusses the history and expansion of the Ndu-speaking people.

## EXERCISES

1. The discussion of the Manambu personal pronouns provided an analysis of the distribution of the grammatical categories person, gender, and number, stating where they are marked and where they are neutralized. Construct a similar paradigm for English personal pronouns. Analyze the categories and write a similar set of statements that accurately characterizes the distribution of grammatical categories. Then provide a set of statements on how the English and Manambu paradigms are similar and how they are different.

2. Review the discussion on the semantic basis of gender assignment and the effect of gender on lexical meanings. Given this discussion, consider each pair of expressions below. Of the two meanings given, which is likely to be signaled by the masculine form of the expression, and which is likely to be signaled by the feminine form?

a. *numa səkal*
   'big distance'
   'enormous distance'

b. *trausis* (loanword from English)
   'trousers'
   'trousers for a baby'

c. *vaey*
   'spear'
   'gun'

d. *wi*
   'house'
   'palace'

e. *ta:b*
   'finger'
   'hand/arm'

f. *ab*
   'head'
   'headache'

g. *gəl*
   'raincloud'
   'clouds covering whole sky'

h. *numa*
   'man'
   'fat round man'

i. *ga:n*
   'somewhat dark night'
   'completely dark night'

3. The following pairs of clauses each exemplify ambitransitive verbs in Manambu. For each pair, determine whether the verb is of the S.of.I=O.of.T type (where the subject of the intransitive clause corresponds to the object of the transitive) or the S, of.I=S.of.T type (where the subject of the intransitive corresponds to the subject of the transitive). See section 10.2.4 of this profile to review this distinction.

   a. *kaykwa-* 'spill' (transitive); 'capsize' (intransitive)
   b. *rali-* 'untie' (transitive); 'come untied' (intransitive)
   c. *laku-* 'know' (transitive); 'be knowing' (intransitive)
   d. *kaja-* 'move (something) apart' (transitive); 'disperse; move apart' (intransitive)
   e. *səluku-* 'forget something' (transitive); 'be forgotten' (intransitive)
   f. *jə-* 'chew something' (transitive); 'chew' (intransitive)

4. Each of the Manambu sentences below consists of multiple clauses in a clause chain. For the purposes of this exercise, verbs with clause-chaining morphology are in boldface, although the suffixes have not been separated and glossed. Based on the meanings of each example, state which of the following clause-chaining forms would be most appropriate for each boldfaced verb:

Sequential action, same subject
Sequential action, different subject
Simultaneous action, same subject
Simultaneous action, different subject

a. [*nak*      *aki-taba:r*    **vœki:n**]    [*nak*     *mapa-taba:r*     *vœrad*]
  one      left-hand    go.off      one     right-hand    come.in.3SG.M.TOP
  'One (road) goes off to the left; one comes in from the right.'

b. [**kar-dan**]              [*taka-u*]
  bring-down          put.down-1SG.IMP
  'Shall I bring it downstairs and put it down?'

c. [*ata*    **rəta:y**]    [**kəta:y**]    [*ata*     *wata:y*      *tabu-dian*]
  then    live        eat       then    that.way    escape-1PL.TOP
  'Then living and eating, in that way we escaped (the invaders).'

d. [*dəkədə*       *ñan*     *gu*     *kəku*      **kiya-dək**]      [*ata*      *gra:d*]
  POSS.SG.M    child    water    consume    die-3SG.M     then    cry.3SG.M
  'After his son had drowned, then (the father) cried.'

e. [**kusuta:y**]           [*vœra-kna-dəmən*]
  wear            go.to.speaker-FUT-2SG.M.TOP
  'You will come to us wearing (the shirt).'
  (Context: mother telling a boy to try on a new shirt)

5. In Example (4d) above, the expression translated as 'drown' in English is actually a clause chain *gu kə-ku kiya-dək*, literally 'consumed water and died.' The verb *kə-ku* has the suffix for sequential, same-subject clause chains. This implies a conceptualization of drowning as involving events in sequence (drink water, then die). Does this match your conceptualization of drowning? Why or why not? You may want to consider how drowning is expressed in English or other languages that you speak in addressing this. (For a larger project, look up expressions for drowning in other languages and compare.)

6. In each of the examples below, the final inflection of the verb has been replaced by a series of Xs. Using the paradigms in Tables LP10.4 and LP10.5, provide the appropriate cross-referencing suffix or suffixes for each of the following Manambu sentences. In each case, the topical argument is given in bold.

*kə*              **wiyakə-də**              *ki*     *ada*               *kwatiya-kə-XXXX*
PROX.DEM      house-POSS.SG.M    key    DIST.DEM    give.to.you-FUT-
'I will give you that house key (lit. that key of this house).'

Answer: *tua-d* (SG.SBJ-3SG.M.TOP)

a. **kami:**      *də*        *kə-kwa-XXXX*
  fish      3SG.M    eat-PST.HABITUAL-
  'He used to eat fish.'

b. *yigən*           *və-kəna-XXXX*
  dream      see-FUT-
  'She will have (lit. see) a dream.'

c. ***na:gw***          *vya-wuta-tu-XXXX*
   sago.palm          hit-break-many-
   'She broke all the (branches) of the sago palms.'

d. ***bəgam***          *ku-sada-k-XXXX*
   bag.SG.F.LOC          put-down-FUT-
   'She will put (the purse) inside the bag.'

e. ***brəkədə***      *ñaj*          *kəda*          *wa-XXXX*
   3DU.OBL      paternal.uncle      PROX.DEM      say-
   'This paternal uncle said to them.'

**LANGUAGE PROFILE 11**

# Indonesian

## 11.1  Introduction

### 11.1.1  Location and history

The population of the Republic of Indonesia is historically, culturally, ethnically, and linguistically diverse. With more than 240 million people, present-day Indonesia boasts the distinction of being the fourth most populated nation in the world, after China, India, and the United States. Its heterogeneous population consists of hundreds of native ethnic groups, who are estimated currently to speak at least 300 distinct languages. The creation of the Republic of Indonesia involved a host of complex socio-political factors, one of the most important of which has been the development, standardization, and promotion of Indonesian as the official, national language of unification (see Textbox LP11.1 on the language's name).

The Republic of Indonesia is geographically located within the largest archipelago on Earth, consisting of more than 17,000 equatorial islands, only about one-third of which are inhabited. Indonesia is located between mainland Southeast Asia and Australia and provides a crucial seafaring link between the Indian and Pacific oceans. Because of its strategic location, the archipelago has been characterized by extensive trade, colonization, and contact, which has led to a rich and diverse cultural history. The first inhabitants of the archipelago were Melanesians, followed by a migration of Austronesian people, the earliest evidence of which dates back to around 2000 BCE. The next millennia saw the flourishing of various Hindu kingdoms, Buddhist kingdoms, alliances between islands, and Sultanates. Between the thirteenth and sixteenth century, the population gradually began to convert to Islam, and, outside of Bali, which is still predominantly Hindu, Islam is now the majority religion. In the early sixteenth century, the Portuguese colonized parts of the archipelago, known popularly in those times as the "Spice Islands." The Dutch colonized much of the region beginning in the early seventeenth century and continued to occupy and govern the islands until shortly after Indonesia declared independence on August 17, 1945, and began promoting Indonesian as the official, national language.

## TEXTBOX LP11.1 **WHAT TO CALL LANGUAGES**

An **autoglossonym** is a linguistic term meaning "the name of a language in that language" (lit. self-tongue-name). For example, *Deutsch* is the autoglossonym of the language that English speakers call German, *español* is the autoglossonym for the language known in English as Spanish, and so on. Indonesian speakers call their own language *bahasa Indonesia* (lit. language of Indonesia). Many foreigners mistakenly refer to Indonesian simply as "Bahasa," as in: "Oh, I learned a little Bahasa when I went surfing in Bali." However, the word *bahasa* is a common noun that simply means 'language,' originating from the Sanskrit word *bhaṣa*. It is used productively in Indonesian to derive names for all languages, e.g., *bahasa Jepang* (lit. language of Japan) 'Japanese,' *bahasa Perancis* (lit. language of France) 'French,' *bahasa Jawa* (lit. language of Java) 'Javanese,' *bahasa Bali* (lit. language of Bali) 'Balinese,' *bahasa Inggeris* (lit. language of England)

'English,' and so forth. A foreigner who refers to Indonesian as "Bahasa" is misanalyzing the autoglossonym.

When writing about the Indonesian language in an English context, it is generally not appropriate to refer to it as *bahasa Indonesia*. Just as this textbook refers to other major world languages using English names such as German or Spanish (rather than the autoglossonyms *Deutsch* or *español*), I will consistently use the English name Indonesian throughout this profile. However, especially for speakers of endangered and minority languages, use of an autoglossonym can be seen as a sign of respect and solidarity – and it is always best for field linguists to be sensitive to the desire of communities of speakers, and to refer to languages by the names which its speakers prefer to have used in a particular context.

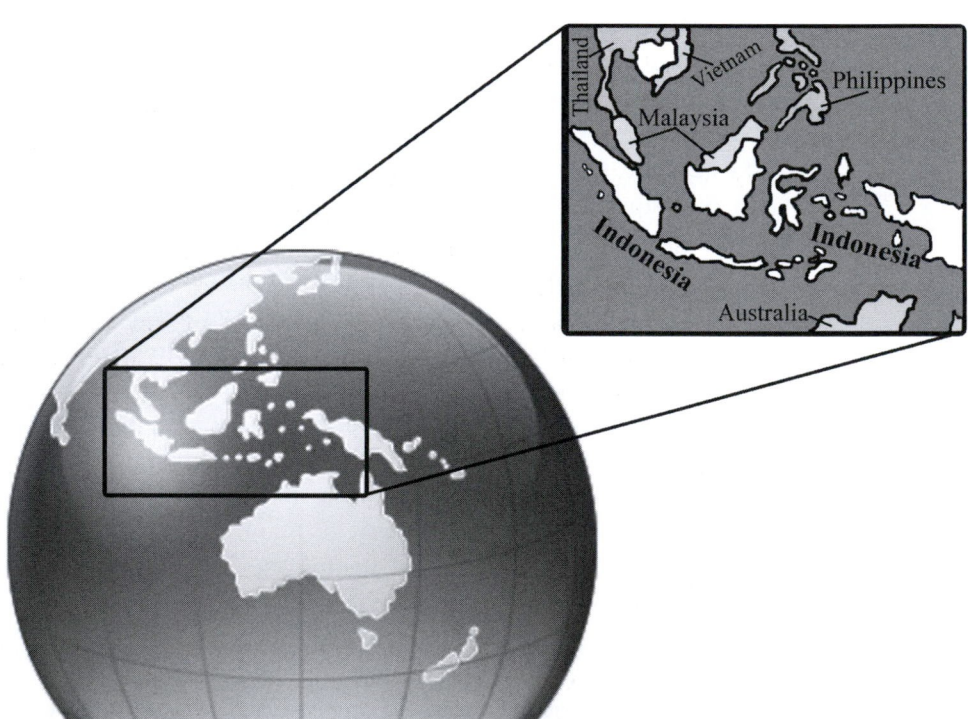

**Figure LP11.1** Map showing location of Indonesian Archipelago

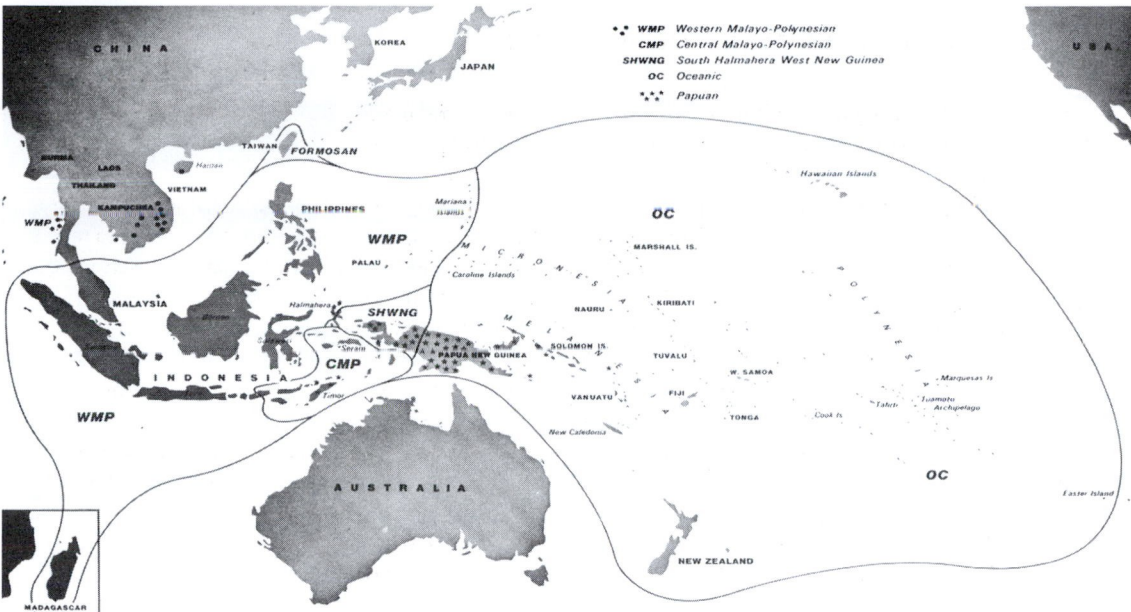

**Figure LP11.2** Map of the Austronesian language area

### 11.1.2   Genetic affiliation

Indonesian is a member of the Western Malayo-Polynesian branch of the Austronesian language family. The Austronesian family is the largest language family in the world, including approximately 1,300 languages – nearly 20 percent of all languages on earth. Austronesian languages are widely spoken along a 10,000 mile geographic range from Easter Island to Madagascar. Indonesian is a variety of Malay, and is, to a large extent, mutually intelligible with the varieties of Malay spoken in Malaysia, Brunei Darussalam, and Singapore. The development and standardization of formal Indonesian, used in education, the media, and in public official settings, was achieved primarily through government-sponsored **language planning**, an issue to which we will return in section 11.4 of this profile. Alongside Indonesian, numerous local and colloquial Malay varieties are also spoken, as are numerous local languages.

## 11.2  **Speech community and viability**

Unlike many of the other languages profiled in this volume, Indonesian is quite robust, with approximately 250 million speakers worldwide, including an estimated 17 million people classified as native speakers. Recent estimates of the literacy rate in Indonesia claim that upwards of 90 percent of the population can read Indonesian. The language serves as the medium of instruction for most education, and is the

**Figure LP11.3** A documentation training workshop in Maluku (photo courtesy Michael Ewing)

primary language in broadcast and print media. Many Indonesians speak a local language as well: the three most widely spoken are Javanese, Sundanese, and Madurese. As the urban populations of Indonesia increase, and as people of different linguistic backgrounds move to the cities and intermarry – which generally results in their children growing up speaking Indonesian at home – the number of people who are competent in formal written Indonesian, and the number of those who speak a colloquial variety of Indonesian in their daily lives, will continue to increase even further. While this is a boon for the status and use of Indonesian, it has the unfortunate side effect that many local languages are declining, and some are disappearing altogether; much of the population has shifted to Indonesian as a language of economic opportunity and wider communication. Linguists, both in Indonesia and abroad, are concerned about this situation and are working with members of smaller speech communities to document and describe many of these local languages.

## 11.3  Structural overview

The purpose of this section is to offer a brief glimpse of Indonesian phonology, morphology, and syntax, in order to give a general flavor of its structure. I will focus on features that may be of particular interest to English-speaking students with no prior exposure to Indonesian.

### 11.3.1   Phonology

The pronunciation of Indonesian differs slightly from region to region, and varies considerably based on whether the speaker is using formal or colloquial varieties. From a typological perspective, and from the perspective of English-speaking learners of Indonesian, there is nothing terribly "exotic" or "difficult" about pronouncing Indonesian. Like English, there is no phonemic tone, and vowel length is not contrastive.

Owing primarily to the history of Portuguese and Dutch colonization, Indonesian is written in the Latin alphabet, and there is a high grapheme to phoneme correspondence. In other words, with only a few exceptions, non-speakers of Indonesian can pronounce it fairly accurately simply by knowing which letter represents which phoneme. Most letters have a pronunciation fairly close to the corresponding IPA symbols. The following are a few exceptions: the letters *c* and *j* represent the voiceless and voiced alveo-palatal affricates [tʃ] and [dʒ] respectively, e.g., *baca* [batʃa] 'read' and *meja* [medʒa] 'table'; the letter *y* is used for the voiced palatal approximant [j], e.g., *yakin* [jakin] 'sure'; the letter *r* represents the alveolar tap [ɾ], which for some speakers and in some words may be realized as a trill [r], e.g., *baru* [baɾu] 'new'; *rata-rata* [ɾataɾata] 'on average'; and the letter *e* is pronounced either as [e] or [ə], e.g., *bebek* [bebeʔ] 'duck,' *selesai* [sələsai] 'finished,' *jendela* [dʒəndela] 'window.'

Syllable-final [p] and [t] are unreleased, e.g., *map* [map̚] 'folder' and syllable-final [k] is pronounced as a glottal stop [ʔ], e.g., *baik* [baiʔ] 'good,' *pak* [paʔ] 'sir/Mr.' Moreover, sequences of two identical vowels are usually broken up by the insertion of a glottal stop, e.g., *maaf* [maʔaf] 'pardon/excuse me,' *saat* [saʔat̚] 'moment.' Primary stress generally falls on the penultimate (next-to-last) syllable – although there are some exceptions.

Three aspects of phonotactics may strike English speakers as both interesting and tricky: (1) syllables may begin with [ŋ], e.g., *ngeri* [ŋəri] 'scary'; (2) syllable onsets may consist of a sequence of a nasal followed by a voiced stop, e.g., *mbak* [mbaʔ] 'sister (term of address)', *ndak* [ndaʔ] or *nggak* [ŋgaʔ] 'no/not' (colloquial); and (3) syllables may end with [h], e.g., *rumah* [ɾumah] 'house,' *contoh* [tʃontoh] 'example,' *jatuh* [dʒatuh] 'to fall.'

### 11.3.2   Morphology

Indonesian is primarily an **isolating** language, with very little in the way of inflectional morphology. There is no verbal morphology for tense, aspect, or mood, and no noun morphology for case, gender, or number. This has led to a common misconception about Indonesian that it is a "simplified" language that is particularly easy to learn – a false belief that James Sneddon, a noted scholar of Indonesian, refers to as the "myth of simplicity" (Sneddon 2003: 14–17). Indonesian makes productive use of reduplication, and has morphology for voice and valence (see below), as well as derivational morphology for nominalization and other processes. For example, among its many functions, the suffix *-an* may be used to derive nouns from (some) verbs:

e.g., *makan* 'eat' > *makanan* 'food'; *minum* 'drink (v.)' > *minuman* 'drink (n.)'; *baca* 'read' > *bacaan* 'reading material.'

**Reduplication** is a word-formation process found in many languages of the world (see Textbox LP11.2). In Indonesian reduplication is quite frequent, highly productive, and has various meanings. Some words consist of a lexicalized reduplicated form – one that cannot be further broken down into parts. For example, *labah-labah* is the word for 'spider,' and the form *\*labah* does not exist singly on its own to derive this word. (A roughly analogous example from English is the word *dodo*, as in dodo bird, which is not derived from the stem [do].) Other examples include *kupu-kupu* 'butterfly,' *kura-kura* 'turtle,' *pura-pura* 'pretend,' and *tiba-tiba* 'suddenly' (although the verb *tiba* means 'arrive'). In current Indonesian orthography, reduplication is written out in full, with a hyphen between the reduplicated elements (e.g., *labah-labah* 'spider'). In older orthographies, and currently in online communication such as internet chat and text messages, reduplication is often written using the digit "2" to represent the reduplicated element (e.g., *labah2* 'spider'). Full reduplication of a noun stem indicates something like a distributed plural – an uncounted group of objects, e.g., *bunga* 'flower' > *bunga-bunga* '(lots of) flowers.' A reduplicated verb stem tends to indicate repeated or non-directed action, e.g., *jalan* 'walk' > *jalan-jalan* 'stroll; go for a walk.' When combined with other derivational morphology, reduplication can have a number of idiomatic

---

## TEXTBOX LP11.2 **REDUPLICATION**

**Reduplication** is a morphological process found in many languages, which creates words by repeating all or part of a stem. In languages that make use of **full reduplication**, the entire stem is repeated, as in the Indonesian examples presented above. Another example of full reduplication comes from Kayardild, a Tangkikc language of Australia: *kandu* 'blood' > *kandukandu* 'red.' In languages that employ **partial reduplication**, only a portion of the stem is repeated; examples of partial reduplication from other languages include other Austronesian languages such as Pangasinan from the Philippines, which uses reduplication for plurals: *manók* 'chicken' > *manómanók* 'chickens'; *toó* 'man' > *totoó* 'people.' Some languages have both full and partial reduplication.

Reduplication can convey both lexical and grammatical meaning. Examples of reduplication with lexical meaning include the Indonesian words presented above: *labah-labah* 'spider,' *kupu-kupu* 'butterfly,' *kura-kura* 'turtle,' *pura-pura* 'pretend,' and *tiba-tiba* 'suddenly.' The grammatical meanings encoded by reduplication

cross-linguistically include continuous or repeated action (already illustrated above by the Indonesian word *jalan-jalan* 'to stroll; go for a walk'), plurality (similar to the above Indonesian word *bunga-bunga* 'lots of flowers'), and augmentation in size and intensity (e.g., in color or manner of action). Some examples of reduplication from a number of languages follow:

Nez Perce, a Sahaptian language of the Northwestern United States:

*té:mul* 'hail' > *temulté:mul* 'sleet'

Tigak, an Austronesian language of Papua New Guinea:

*giak* 'send' > *gigiak* 'messenger'

Choctaw, a Muskogean language of the Southern United States:

*tonoli* 'to roll' > *tononoli* 'to roll back and forth'

Mokilese, an Austronesian language of Micronesia:

*roar* 'give a shudder' > *roarroar* 'be shuddering' > *roarroarroar* 'continue to shudder'

meanings. For example, reduplicating a noun stem and adding the *-an* nominalizing suffix (mentioned above) indicates that the noun is a toy: *rumah* 'house' > *rumah-rumahan* 'toy house, dollhouse'; *tikus* 'mouse' > *tikus-tikusan* 'toy mouse'; *ayam* 'chicken' > *ayam-ayaman* 'toy chicken, weather vane'; *mobil* 'car' > *mobil-mobilan* 'toy car.'

## 11.3.3 Syntax

The order of Indonesian's major sentence constituents is typically SVO (the subject, followed by the verb, followed by the object), although in natural conversation, both subjects and objects are often unexpressed and inferred from context. Within the noun phrase, adjectives, relative clauses, determiners, and quantifiers follow the nouns they modify, while numerals precede them. Indonesian also uses prepositions.

One of the more interesting facts about Indonesian morphosyntax has to do with the marking of voice on verbs (Textbox LP11.3 provides a general overview of **voice**

---

### TEXTBOX LP11.3 **VOICE CONSTRUCTIONS**

The term **voice** refers to two or more syntactic constructions that provide alternative mappings between arguments and grammatical relations. Chapter 6 briefly discussed active and passive voice in English. Recall that in English the active voice is the neutral construction, prototypically with the agent of a transitive clause as the subject and the patient of a transitive clause as the object:

| [*The kids*] | *ate* | [*all the cookies*] |
|---|---|---|
| subject | transitive verb | object |
| agent | | patient |

English passive voice differs from the active grammatically in three ways: the verb is intransitive and changes form (occurs with the auxiliary *be* and is in the past participle form); the patient argument is realized as the subject of the intransitive clause; and the agent is either unexpressed or is an oblique object of the preposition *by*:

| [*All the cookies*] | *were eaten* | (*by* [*the kids*]) |
|---|---|---|
| subject | intransitive verb | (oblique) |
| patient | | agent |

There are other types of voice beyond active and passive that are found in languages of different typological profiles. (On the other hand, many languages don't have voice constructions at all.) The different voice constructions are generally used to move arguments that have important or given referents into the prominent position of subject, or to move unimportant or unknown referents out of the subject position. (See also Textbox LP10.6.)

---

**SIDEBAR LP11.1**
The three forms *mem-* [məm], *men-* [mən], and *meng-* [məŋ] are allomorphs of a single morpheme. To determine the rules that condition the appearance of each allomorph, see Exercise 1 of this language profile.

constructions). In formal Indonesian, transitive verbs take a prefix that marks them as being either **active voice**, where the **agent** (the doer of the action) is the grammatical subject, or **passive voice**, where the **patient** (the undergoer of the action) is the grammatical subject. The Indonesian active-voice prefix (glossed AV) has several allomorphs: *mem-* [məm], *men-* [mən], or *meng-* [məŋ] (see Sidebar LP11.1). The Indonesian passive prefix (glossed PASS) is *di-* [di] with no allomorphs. Consider the simple active sentence in Example (1).

(1)  | Ali | mem-beli | tiga | sepeda | baru | itu | di | Jakarta |
     |-----|----------|------|--------|------|-----|-----|---------|
     | Ali | AV-buy | three | bike | new | DEM | LOC | Jakarta |

'Ali bought those three new bicycles in Jakarta.'

Here, *Ali* is the agent. The verb *beli* 'buy' is prefixed with *mem-* (active voice), which tells us that the agent (*Ali*) is also the grammatical subject of the sentence. The object noun phrase consists of the head noun *sepeda* 'bicycle' preceded by the numeral *tiga* 'three' and followed by the adjective *baru* 'new' and the demonstrative determiner *itu* 'that/those.' The sentence concludes with the locative prepositional phrase *di Jakarta* 'in Jakarta.' Contrast this with the passive sentence in Example (2).

(2)  | Tiga | sepeda | baru | itu | di-beli | Ali | di | Jakarta |
     |------|--------|------|-----|---------|-----|-----|---------|
     | three | bike | new | DEM | PASS-buy | Ali | LOC | Jakarta |

'Those three new bicycles were bought by Ali in Jakarta.'

Here, the prefix *di-* on the verb *beli* 'buy' indicates that the sentence is passive – that the patient ('those three new bicycles') is the grammatical subject.

Indonesian voice and valence categories are far more complex and nuanced than can possibly be illustrated in this language profile. Despite some apparent similarities to English active and passive clauses, these Indonesian constructions actually encompass a broader range of discourse functions and semantic meanings, and it is often quite challenging for English speakers to learn to use them with native-like fluency and **idiomaticity**. See the Suggestions for further reading section for reference grammars that provide a more thorough discussion and additional examples.

## 11.4  Language planning

One of the most remarkable aspects of Indonesian has been its ascendance from being a marginal "outside" language, spoken by less than 5 percent of Indonesia's population in 1928, to its adoption as a high-status national language, with over 90 percent literacy among Indonesia's current population. Along with this dramatic increase in use, Indonesian has also attained a symbolic status as a key part of the identity and soul of Indonesia itself – part of being an Indonesian person is speaking the Indonesian language. This has come about through well-organized **language planning**, in conjunction with sociopolitical circumstances that have led Indonesian people to adopt and legitimize it. Language planning refers to the deliberate and systematic development of a language, usually through government-sponsored institutions and policies. It is usually categorized into two types: (1) **corpus planning**, that is, planning the body of the language – its writing system, its vocabulary (usually through publishing an official dictionary), and its grammar – and (2) **status planning**, that is, propagating the language via education and media, shaping public attitudes toward the language, and prescribing its role in society and the domains in which it is used. This section will provide a cursory discussion of the history of

Indonesian language planning and will focus on **spelling reform** to illustrate key sociopolitical factors that influence corpus planning. Interested readers should consult sources in the Suggestions for further reading section for a more in-depth and thorough discussion than is possible here.

As explained earlier in this profile, the Indonesian archipelago is inhabited by several hundred ethnic groups, who speak an estimated 300 distinct languages. When attempting to bring this diversity together into the new Republic of Indonesia, leaders of the Indonesian independence movement strongly believed that one single language should be chosen to facilitate the unification process and to foster a united "Indonesian" identity. But considerable debate emerged as to which language this should be. In terms of numbers of native speakers, Javanese would have been the clear choice, since the majority of the population lived on Java, and the Javanese were (and still are) the politically dominant and largest ethnic group within Indonesia. However, had Javanese been chosen as the national language, other ethnic groups would have been disadvantaged and felt further isolated, which would likely have undermined the entire unification process itself. Another suggestion was Dutch, which many people viewed as a "modern" language, and which some educated Indonesians could already speak. However, since Indonesia had been a Dutch colony for nearly 400 years, choosing the language of the colonizers, at the same time as fighting for independence from them, would have had clear, negative, symbolic and ideological consequences for the newly independent nation. A third suggestion was English, which was also considered a "modern" world language, and, in the context of Indonesian independence at least, did not have the colonial baggage of Dutch. However, English was seen as too "foreign," had no history of use within Indonesia, and would not have been able to serve the founders' goals of developing a uniquely Indonesian identity.

Ultimately, at a 1928 meeting known as the Second Indonesian Youth Congress, leaders of the Indonesian independence movement passed a resolution calling for the adoption of a variety of Malay to serve as the national language of unification. They named this language Indonesian. The choice of a variety of Malay was successful for several reasons. First, since less than 5 percent of the Indonesian population were speakers, no single ethnic group was privileged; everyone had to learn it. Secondly, it did not bring with it the ideological baggage of Dutch or other European languages that were associated with colonization and oppression. Thirdly, since Malay is an Austronesian language genetically related to many of the languages of the archipelago, it did not seem as "foreign" as Dutch or English would have been. Finally, this variety of Malay, which was primarily descended from literary Classical Malay, had already been used as an administrative language under the Dutch, and so was already familiar among native educators and government officials.

After independence, government-sponsored agencies oversaw both corpus and status planning, including the creation of new vocabulary to foster the use of Indonesian in modern scientific and technological contexts, publishing an official dictionary and

**Figure LP11.4** High school students at an exhibit on biography at a provincial government library in Ambon. The banner reads: "Get to know the biography collection as an expression of the identity and quality of prominent people" (photo courtesy Michael Ewing)

grammar, developing teaching materials, and conducting regular radio and television programs to promote its use. Currently, the official Indonesian language planning body is known as *Pusat Bahasa* 'language center' (prior to 2001, its name was *Pusat Pembinaan dan Pengembangan Bahasa* 'center for language cultivation and development'). The most recent editions of the official dictionary and grammar are listed in the Suggestions for further reading section.

One issue that the Indonesian language planning situation clearly illustrates is that the form and status of a language is intimately bound up with its political, cultural, and social environment. Whether a language thrives (as with Indonesian) or, unfortunately, loses speakers (as with many indigenous languages of Indonesia and all over the world) strongly depends on macro-level factors such as politics, power, and economics. Indonesian – and other world languages like English, for that matter – owes its status and success not to language-internal or structural factors, but rather to the political forces that shape and promote it at an official level, and to the economic and social factors at the individual level that cause people to adopt or reject it. In the case of Indonesian, these have led to its acceptance and adoption by a culturally, ethnically, and linguistically diverse group of people. Understanding the sociopolitical situation of a language and its speakers is a crucial component of understanding how languages work, and of understanding why some languages may thrive while others may become endangered.

The remainder of this profile presents a case study of Indonesian spelling reform, in order to provide a concrete illustration of how corpus planning works, and to demonstrate a basic linguistic fact about spelling systems more generally – namely, a language's orthography is a social convention that can be changed for political, linguistic, and practical reasons.

### 11.4.1  Spelling reform

Nothing typifies prescriptive language ideologies better than social attitudes toward spelling. From our earliest schooling, we are taught that there is generally only one "correct" way to spell a word. American schoolchildren tend to have to take weekly spelling tests throughout elementary and middle school, are penalized for not spelling words correctly, and are rewarded for good performance in school-wide and national spelling bee contests. Society tends to sanction misspelling, treating it as a sign of ignorance or lack of intelligence. We often think of a word's spelling as immutable and final. However, linguists recognize that orthography is simply a social convention, and, like all social conventions, can be changed.

**Figure LP11.5** Sign at an archaeological site in Bali written in Indonesian with Latin script and in Balinese with Balinese script (photo courtesy Michael Ewing)

Spelling reform refers to a systematic change in the orthography for a given language. It is an example of language planning, generally taking place in society from the top down; in other words, educational or government institutions design and promote a new orthography for a language, which publishers, print media, and individuals then adopt. Reasons for spelling reform chiefly include ideological goals (to affiliate or disaffiliate with other nations or political groups who may write the language in a certain way), linguistic or pedagogical principles (to more closely reflect one **grapheme** per phoneme in an attempt to make the written language more transparent and easier to learn; see Textbox LP11.4), or practical reasons (to make the language easier to type or print given the current technology). Indonesian spelling reform in the twentieth century reflects all three of these concerns.

Malay has a long written history, with stone inscriptions dating back to the seventh century. The earliest Malay writing system was based in a Pali script (related to the script used for Sanskrit), which was later replaced by the Arabic alphabet. Starting in the Dutch colonial era, local officials began to write Malay using the Latin alphabet, which is the alphabet still used today for writing Indonesian. However, during this period, spelling differed from region to region, was not uniform, and was generally quite idiosyncratic. Then, in 1902, the Dutch education scholar Charles van Ophuijsen

---

### TEXTBOX LP11.4 **WHY ONE GRAPHEME PER PHONEME?**

We have seen earlier (in Chapter 2, Phonetics), that there are many limitations of using orthographic representations, or spelling, to represent the sounds of spoken language. In English, many written letters can represent more than one possible sound. For example, the English grapheme "c" can be used to represent two different sounds: [k] as in *cat* and [s] as in *ceiling*. In contrast, the single voiced velar nasal [ŋ] at the end of the word *ring* is represented by a combination of two letters, or graphemes: "ng." In fact, some sounds of English, such as the velar nasal [ŋ], are simply not represented by single graphemes in the Roman alphabet.

Clearly, the English system is not ideal for those learning to read and write English. It is more efficient for learners to have an orthographic system that uses one grapheme per phoneme, i.e., to use a single written symbol to represent each sound. The orthographic systems of some languages (such as written Spanish, or the *hiragana* syllabary in Japanese) nearly approximate this one-grapheme-per-phoneme model, making them easier to learn to read and write, whereas other languages (such as English and French) do not.

Why don't all writing systems have one grapheme per phoneme? Orthographic systems tend to be more stable than spoken pronunciations over time. In other words, whereas a language may undergo historical sound changes, the orthography of the language is more likely to stay the same, with the result that the pronunciation begins to stray more and more from the original written representation over time. For example, the grapheme "r" is preserved in postvocalic environments in written English even in dialects where the corresponding phoneme hasn't been pronounced in that environment for years.

This exemplifies yet another complication that arises from representing spoken language in writing: regional dialects of a language may vary widely in pronunciation. However, there are obvious advantages to adopting a single conventionalized orthographic system of writing even when there is regional variation, e.g., the graphemes "ll" in Spanish can be pronounced as a voiced palatal lateral or a voiced palatal glide, depending on the region.

Think about other languages (and writing systems) that you are familiar with: do they approximate one grapheme per phoneme or not?

published the first standardized national orthography for Indonesian Malay. This orthography was based primarily on the pronunciation of literary Malay found in the Riau-Johor Sultanate (Riau is now a province in Indonesia and Johor is now a state in the present-day Republic of Malaysia) and was based in rules of spelling for the Dutch language. For example, in Dutch, the high back rounded vowel [u] is spelled by the sequence of letters *oe*; and van Ophuijsen prescribed *oe* to spell [u] in Indonesian as well.

After Indonesian independence, two large-scale spelling reforms took place. The first, in 1947, formally known as *Ejaan Republik* 'Republic spelling,' clearly illustrates the political, linguistic, and practical reasons for spelling reform. One major change was to abandon the use of *oe* to spell [u], instead spelling it simply with the letter *u*. For example, the spelling of the Indonesian word pronounced [buku] 'book' changed from *boekoe* (pre-1947) to *buku* (current spelling); similarly, the spelling of [baru] 'new' changed from *baroe* (pre-1947) to *baru* (current spelling) and [rumah] 'house' from *roemah* (pre-1947) to *rumah*. This spelling reform was both a clear symbolic statement of independence from the Netherlands – no more would Indonesian be bound by the idiosyncratic Dutch spelling of the vowel [u] – and also an attempt to simplify spelling based on the principle of one grapheme per phoneme. While this spelling change systematically applied to all Indonesian words containing [u], it raised an interesting problem as to what to do about the spellings of names. Some people whose name contained this vowel chose not to change the spelling of their name, while others did. The print media sometimes kept the old spelling for the names of famous people, and sometimes adopted the new spelling. For example, sometimes the names of Indonesia's first two presidents are written *Soekarno* and *Soeharto* respectively, following the old spelling, while other times they appear in print as *Sukarno* and *Suharto*, following the new system.

A second change brought about by the 1947 spelling reform was the abandonment of the letter *é* to write the vowel [e]. Prior to 1947, *é* was used for [e] and *e* was used for [ə]. After 1947, both vowels are now written with the letter *e*. For example, [dʒəndela] 'window' is currently spelled *jendela*, where the *e* in the first syllable represents [ə] and the *e* in the second syllable represents [e]. The main reason for the loss of the letter *é* was primarily due to a desire to make the orthography easier to type using standard typewriters, and the fact that this was the only letter in Indonesian written with an accent mark.

The second major spelling reform, known as *Ejaan yang Disempurnakan* 'perfected spelling,' took place in 1972. This was a collaborative effort between Indonesia and Malaysia, to unify the orthographies of both nations. On a political level, this reflected closer international relations between these two nations; on a linguistic level, unifying the spelling systems meant that literature published in Malaysia could easily be read in Indonesia, and vice versa. From the Indonesian perspective, major spelling changes took place at the level of several consonants. For example, the pre-1972 spelling of [dʒ] and [tʃ] were *dj* and *tj* respectively, which were then changed to *j* and *c*. Prior to 1972, the capital of Indonesia [dʒakarta] was spelled *Djakarta*, and after 1972, the official spelling changed to *Jakarta*. Pre-1972 *medja* 'table' and *batja* 'read' became *meja* and *baca*. Other consonant spelling changes included changing the spelling of [j] from *j* to *y*, and changing the spelling of [x] (a voiceless velar fricative) from *ch* to *kh*.

In sum, Indonesian spelling reform provides a case study of corpus planning at work, as large-scale, systematic changes were implemented that affect the writing system for the entire language. Note that these changes apply to all Indonesian words containing the given letters. For this reason, spelling reform is often expensive, as it requires the printing of new signs, new maps, new dictionaries, and new textbooks, etc. Indonesian spelling reform clearly illustrates that a language's orthography is a social convention and can change in response to political, linguistic, practical, and ideological concerns.

## TEXTBOX LP11.5

| Convention | Meaning | Convention | Meaning |
|---|---|---|---|
| AV | active voice | LOC | locative |
| DEM | demonstrative | PASS | passive |

## SUGGESTIONS FOR FURTHER READING

**Wolff, John U., Dede Oetomo, and Daniel Fietkiewicz**. 1992. *Beginning Indonesian through self-instruction*. Ithaca, NY: Cornell University, Southeast Asia Program.

A three-set volume that teaches Indonesian through the intermediate level, if you are interested in learning the language. A set of CDs to accompany the textbook is also available.

**Soderberg, Craig and Kenneth Olson**. 2008. "Illustrations of the IPA: Indonesian." *Journal of the International Phonetic Association* **38**: 209–213.

A detailed phonetic illustration of Indonesian as spoken by one person from Jakarta.

**Sneddon, James, Alexander Adelaar, Dwi Noverini Djenar, and Michael C. Ewing**. 2010. *Indonesian: A comprehensive grammar*, 2nd edn. London: Routledge.

A comprehensive and user-friendly grammar of formal Indonesian written in English.

**Ewing, Michael**. 2005. "Colloquial Indonesian." In Adelaar, A. and N. Himmelmann (eds.), *The Austronesian languages of Asia and Madagascar*. London: Routledge. 227–258.

**Sneddon, James**. 2006. *Colloquial Jakartan Indonesian*. Pacific Linguistics, Research School of Pacific and Asian Studies. Canberra: The Australian National University.

Both of these texts provide an overview of the grammar of colloquial Indonesian.

**Sneddon, James**. 2003. *The Indonesian language: Its history and role in modern society*. Sydney: University of New South Wales Press.

A thorough overview of the history of Indonesian, including discussion of language planning.

**Sebba, Mark**. 2007. *Spelling and society: The culture and politics of orthography around the world*. New York: Cambridge University Press.
A comprehensive study of the social, cultural, and political aspects of orthography, as well as the history and debate surrounding spelling reform in various countries (including a section on Indonesia and Malaysia).

**Alwi, Hasan, Soenjono Dardjowidjojo, Hans Lapoliwa, and Anton Moeliono**. 1998. *Tata Bahasa Baku Bahasa Indonesia*, 3rd edn. Balai Pustaka.

**Departemen Pendidikan Nasional**. 2008. *Kamus Besar Bahasa Indonesia*, 4th edn. Jakarta: Gramedia Pustaka Utama.
These two texts are the official grammar and dictionary of formal Indonesian.

## EXERCISES

1. Spelling in computer-mediated communication
   This profile described spelling reform as a top-down process, in which educational or government institutions systematically design and promote a new orthography for a language. Another aspect related to spelling change, not discussed in this chapter, comes about through innovative spellings originating in certain types of media and/or socially defined groups of people. One aspect of contemporary society stereotypically associated with spelling innovations is computer-mediated communication (CMC), such as text messages and chats. Find fifteen examples of recent CMC that you have sent or received. In this body of data, identify each instance where the spelling is different from standard written English. Succinctly characterize the differences between the CMC spelling and the standard spelling. What generalizations can you make about the differences? What do you think motivates these innovative spellings? In your answer, consider the medium of communication, as well as the social group(s) you most closely identify yourself with.

2. Spelling reform
   In this profile, we saw that Indonesian underwent two major spelling reforms during the twentieth century, and we reviewed the reasons for some of these changes. For this exercise, consider the situation of English orthography. Write an essay in which you propose a large-scale spelling reform for English. What would you change from the current orthography, and why would you change it? Conclude your essay by carefully discussing both the advantages and the disadvantages of implementing such a proposal for English on an international scale.

3. Morphophonemics
   In section 11.3.3 of this profile above, we saw that a verb stem often takes a prefix to mark it as active voice. The active voice prefix has several allomorphs. Examine the following list of Indonesian verb stems and their active forms, written in Indonesian orthography, and answer the questions that follow. (The sequence *ng* represents IPA [ŋ], *c* is IPA [tʃ], *j* is [dʒ], and *e* in the prefix is always [ə])

|   | Stem | Active | Gloss |
|---|------|--------|-------|
| a. | *ajar* | *mengajar* | 'teach' |
| b. | *antar* | *mengantar* | 'deliver (something)' |
| c. | *baca* | *membaca* | 'read' |

| | | | |
|---|---|---|---|
| d. | *bakar* | *membakar* | 'burn' |
| e. | *cari* | *mencari* | 'search' |
| f. | *curi* | *mencuri* | 'steal' |
| g. | *dengar* | *mendengar* | 'hear' |
| h. | *dorong* | *mendorong* | 'push' |
| i. | *gebuk* | *menggebuk* | 'beat (a drum)' |
| j. | *gonggong* | *menggonggong* | 'bark (of a dog)' |
| k. | *hilang* | *menghilang* | 'disappear' |
| l. | *isi* | *mengisi* | 'fill' |
| m. | *jual* | *menjual* | 'sell' |
| n. | *ulang* | *mengulang* | 'repeat' |

   i. Based on the above data, list all the allomorphs of this Indonesian verbal prefix.

  ii. Write a general rule to account for the distribution of these allomorphs. Be sure to do this in terms of natural classes of sounds, rather than specific phonemes.

 iii. Which is the basic allomorph? Justify your answer.

 iv. What phonological process does this illustrate?

Now consider the additional Indonesian data in (o–t) below:

| | Stem | Active | Gloss |
|---|---|---|---|
| o. | *kacau* | *mengacau* | 'stir up (trouble)' |
| p. | *kenal* | *mengenal* | 'know (someone)' |
| q. | *panggil* | *memanggil* | 'call' |
| r. | *pukul* | *memukul* | 'hit' |
| s. | *tulis* | *menulis* | 'write' |
| t. | *tunggu* | *menunggu* | 'wait' |

  v. Compare (o–t) with (a–n) above. Without doing anything to the rule you wrote in (ii) above, what additional statement needs to be made about the phonology of Indonesian verb stems and prefixes to account for these new data? Again, be sure to think in general terms of natural classes of sounds.

 vi. The rules you wrote in (ii) and (v) must occur in a certain order with respect to one another. State which rule must go first and which rule must go second, and explain how you know this. (Hint: Explain specifically what would happen if you put the rules in a different order.)

4. Language planning

The purpose of this exercise is to give you the chance to do some original library research of your own on a language not presented in this volume. Do some in-depth reading about language planning, and find out about it in places other than Indonesia. Three excellent cases to research are: Modern Hebrew in Israel, Irish in Ireland, or Hawaiian in the state of Hawaii. Some efforts at language planning have been highly successful, such as with Indonesian, and others have not. For one of the three languages listed above, write a paper in which you outline some of the reasons for the successes or failures of language planning policies. Be sure to consider how corpus planning and status planning were implemented; also consider why, in what domains of life, and to what extent, speakers chose to adopt or reject the use of the language.

# Seneca

## 12.1 Introduction

At the end of the fifteenth century, when Europeans began a serious invasion of the Western Hemisphere, it was home to hundreds of distinct languages. North of the Rio Grande alone, there were approximately 300 languages belonging to about fifty separate language families. The first of these languages to be recorded in writing was spoken on the St. Lawrence River near the present site of Quebec City. The French explorer Jacques Cartier made three voyages to what is now eastern Canada beginning in 1534, and from those voyages we know something about a language that was spoken in a place the French called Stadacona. Among the words of the Stadaconan language was the name of a place, which the French spelled *canada*, which meant simply 'town' or 'settlement.'

Stadaconan turned out to be a language that was related to others within the Iroquoian language family, named after the five (later six) nations of the Iroquois. All of those languages are believed to be descended from a common ancestor that must have been spoken several thousand years ago. Linguists refer to that ancestor language as Proto-Iroquoian. In addition to a number of languages in northeastern North America, many of which disappeared before the eighteenth century, the only other known member of the Iroquoian language family is Cherokee, which was spoken by a large number of people in the southeastern part of the United States. Most of the Cherokees were forced to move to Indian Territory (now Oklahoma) during the administration of Andrew Jackson, although a few of them escaped to the hills and managed to remain in western North Carolina. Figure LP12.1 is a diagram of the Iroquoian language family.

The term Lake Iroquoian covers the six languages spoken in the vicinity of the Great Lakes. At the time of first European contact, the Tuscaroras lived in the eastern part of North Carolina. Early in the eighteen century they moved north to join their ancestors in the area of present-day New York State, where they were adopted by the Five Nations to become the sixth Iroquois nation. Huron lost its speakers in the nineteenth century, except that a divergent dialect known as Wyandotte survived in Oklahoma until the 1960s.

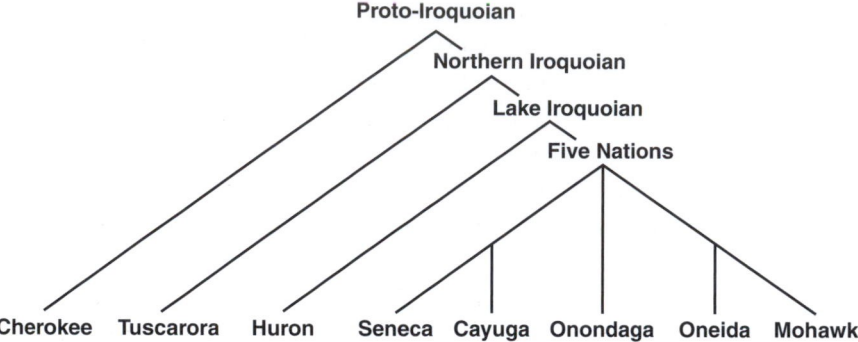

**Figure LP12.1** The Iroquoian language family

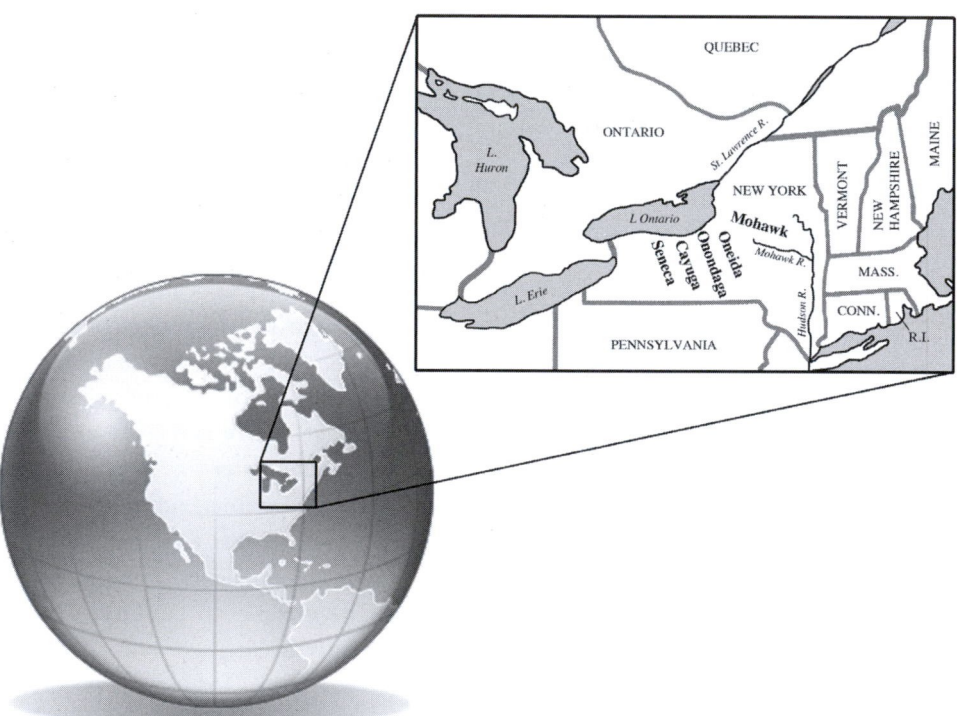

**Figure LP12.2** Map: The Iroquoian languages

The focus of this language profile is Seneca, which is spoken now by fewer than fifty people on three reservations (often now called territories) in western New York: Cattaraugus, Allegany, and Tonawanda. *Seneca* is a name for these people that was adapted from the Dutch name *Sinneken*. The Dutch applied that name to all the Iroquois nations west of the Mohawks, the immediate neighbors of the Dutch in Fort Orange (now Albany). The English who succeeded the Dutch were fond of classical references, as demonstrated by the many New York State place names like Rome and Ithaca, not to mention small towns like Homer and Virgil. It was thus not surprising that Dutch *Sinneken* was reinterpreted as *Seneca*, the name of two ancient Roman writers.

The Iroquois group just west of the Mohawks were the Oneidas, whose name refers to a standing stone. It is possible that *Sinneken* began with an element *sinn-* meaning 'stone' in some Algonquian (non-Iroquoian) language, to which the Dutch added their own diminutive suffix *-ken*. In any case, as Europeans extended their knowledge of the Iroquois ever farther west – to the Oneidas, Onondagas, Cayugas, and Senecas – the name *Sinneken* or *Seneca* was eventually restricted to the westernmost Iroquois group to which it is applied today. The languages are closely related, to the extent that neighboring groups – the Mohawks and Oneidas, or the Senecas and Cayugas – have little difficulty understanding each other. On the other hand, the languages that are more distantly separated – for example, the Mohawks on the east and Senecas on the west – are not mutually intelligible. Mohawk, Oneida, Onondaga, Cayuga, and Seneca thus form what is known as a **dialect continuum**.

## 12.2    The status of unwritten languages

When Europeans first arrived in the Western Hemisphere, only some of the Maya and Aztec languages of Central America had their own writing systems. Hundreds of other languages had no written tradition. One sometimes encounters the naive view that unwritten languages are inferior to those that are written, but writing is at best a recent addition even to those languages that have such a system. This is not to say that writing is unimportant; its ability to conquer time and space has produced revolutionary changes in human history. But a language is a language, regardless of whether or not it is written. People have been speaking for as long as they have been people, and until very recently in human history, writing – if it existed at all – was confined to a small group of specialists.

Seneca was first written toward the end of the seventeenth century by a French Jesuit missionary named Julien Garnier. He had a "good ear" and wrote with considerable accuracy, although like other Jesuits he failed to recognize the glottal stop, an important Seneca consonant. Living among the Senecas between 1671 and 1709, he compiled French–Seneca and Seneca–French dictionaries. Parts of them were lost, but other parts have survived. During the remainder of the eighteenth century, the language underwent a number of changes in its sounds, the effect of which was to create a language that is so different from its seventeenth-century ancestor that modern Seneca speakers would have difficulty understanding it. For example, the word for 'bread' in Garnier's time was *ohráhkwa'*, which corresponds to modern *á:hgwa'* (see Sidebar LP12.1 for a note on the writing system).

**SIDEBAR LP12.1**

ORTHOGRAPHIC NOTE

The Seneca data will be given in the standard Seneca orthography. Corresponding IPA symbols are overtly noted in the text or are indicated in subsequent sidebars.

## 12.3    **Seneca phonology**

### 12.3.1    Vowels

Seneca has eight vowels, which are often written today as shown in Table LP12.1. Two of the vowels are nasalized, as indicated by the dieresis – *ë* and *ö* – the two dots above the letters. The low front vowel *ä* is marked in the same way, but is not nasalized. The

**Table LP12.1** Seneca Vowels

|                          | Front    | Back     |
|--------------------------|----------|----------|
| High                     | i [i]    | u [u]    |
| Mid                      | e [e]    | o [o]    |
| Low-mid and nasalized    | ë [ẽ]    | ö [õ]    |
| Low                      | ä [æ]    | a [a]    |

vowel *u* is limited to serving as a replacement for *a* in words indicating that something is tiny; compare *niyága'à:h* 'small girl' and *niyúgu'ù:h* 'tiny girl.'

Vowels in Seneca occur with three degrees of length. There is a short *a* in the last syllable of *ni:ga'* 'how big I am,' while in the same word, the colon indicates a long *i* in the first syllable. There are also extra long vowels, written *a:a* as in the word *gaga:a'* 'story.' Vowels may also be pronounced with either a low or a high pitch. High-pitched or accented vowels are written with an acute accent, as in *gagá'da'* 'white oak.' Some long vowels have a falling pitch, written with a grave accent as in *à:hge:d* 'he might come.'

## 12.3.2  Consonants

Seneca has fifteen consonants, as shown in Table LP12.2. The affricates *ts*, *tš*, and *dz* are written with two letters, but they function as single sounds. It would be more consistent to write the voiced palatal affricate as *dž*, but *j* is preferred because it reflects the usual English spelling of the same sound. The apostrophe, ', is used for the glottal stop. Whereas in English *h* occurs only before a vowel, in Seneca it can also occur after a vowel, as in the word *à:hge:d* at the end of the previous paragraph.

**SIDEBAR LP12.2**

ORTHOGRAPHIC NOTE

The transcription of postalveolar consonants here follows the orthographic tradition typically used for Native American languages.

| Seneca  | IPA   |
|---------|-------|
| š       | [ʃ]   |
| č       | [tʃ]  |
| ǰ or j  | [dʒ]  |
| y       | [j]   |
| '       | [ʔ]   |

**Table LP12.2** Seneca consonants

|                           | Alveolar | Postalveolar | Velar | Laryngeal |
|---------------------------|----------|--------------|-------|-----------|
| Voiceless aspirated stops | t        |              | k     |           |
| Voiced stops              | d        |              | g     |           |
| Fricatives                | s        | š            |       |           |
| Voiceless affricates      | ts       | č            |       |           |
| Voiced affricates         | dz       | j            |       |           |
| Sonorants                 | n        | y            | w     |           |
| Laryngeals                |          |              |       | h, '      |

## 12.4  A Seneca narrative

The following is a story that was told by Mrs. Elsie Jacobs, a Seneca woman who was eighty-six years old at the time (See Textbox LP12.1 for more on Mrs. Jacobs). She prefaced the story by asking her listener whether he had ever been haunted,

---

### TEXTBOX LP12.1  **MRS. ELSIE JACOBS**

Mrs. Jacobs was born in 1908 on the Cattaraugus Reservation, the oldest of six children. Not long after the incident described here, her mother died during the birth of her sixth child and Elsie was raised by her grandparents, Ida and John Bluesky. Ida was Seneca and spoke to Elsie in that language, but John, who is mentioned in the story, was Cayuga and spoke to her in English. She thus grew up fluent in both languages, an advantage in a school where some of the children entered speaking only Seneca.

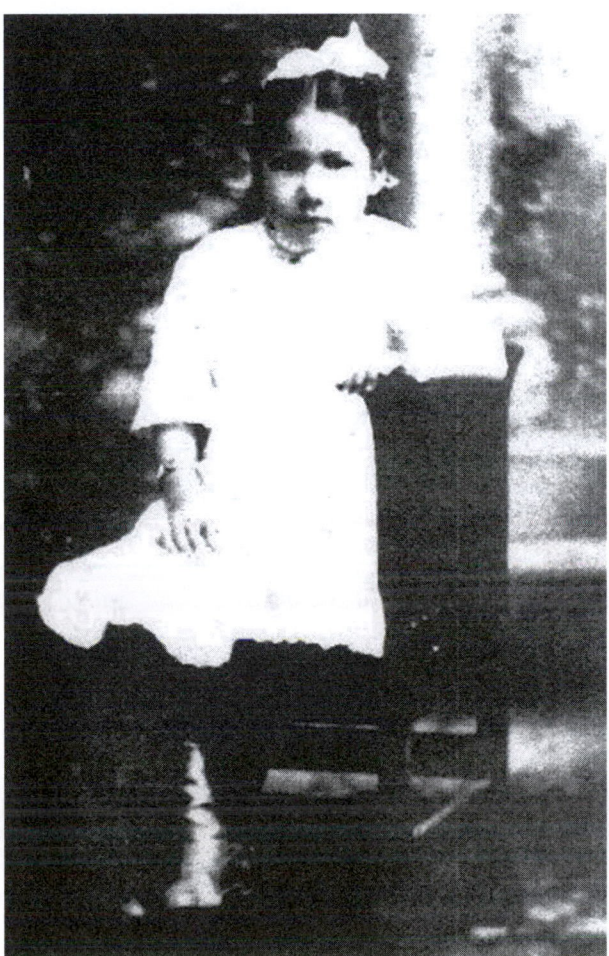

**Figure LP12.3** Mrs. Jacobs as a young girl

**SIDEBAR LP12.3**

The audio recording for this story is available on the website.

and she proceeded to describe what seemed to have been a supernatural event she had experienced when she was seven years old. At that time she was living with her grandmother, but she frequently visited the home of her mother, where this incident occurred.

The story is presented here with separate numbered lines for each sentence, as defined by a falling pitch at the end. Each of these sentences is presented in three lines. The first line is what Mrs. Jacobs said, the second contains an English translation for each Seneca word, and the third is a free translation of the entire sentence.

(1) Dza:dak    tšiwágoshíya'göh,             o'dwagajëönyö:s    no'yě́:neh.
    seven       when I had crossed winters    I got haunted       at mother's
    'When I was seven years old, I got haunted at my mother's.'

(2) Akso:d          i:  ' koh   wa'agyajö̌'se:nö',   ho 'ka:'   koh   neh   nyagwai'   gayá'da'.
    grandmother   I   and    we two went          I took it    and    the    bear        doll
                               visiting             there
    'Grandma and I went visiting, and I took the teddy bear.'

(3) Hosgě́'ëgéhdöh      hohšö:ni:h.
    soldier             he was dressed
    'He was dressed as a soldier.'

(4) That John      hotgwe:nyö:h at      Indian Fair.
                   he had won it
    'That John had won at the Indian Fair.'

(5) Da:h   o:nëh   nä:h   wa'ágwatgá:nye:'   gayá'da'shö̌'öh,   he'tgëh   wa'a:gwe:'.
    so     then    !      we played          dolls             above     we went there
    'So then we played dolls, we went upstairs.'

(6) Ga:nyo'   nä:h   wa'ögwagě̀:'dë',      wa'ákiyáshë:',     trúnkgeh     wa'ákíá'dë'.
    when      !      we got tired of it    we laid them       on the        we put them
                                           down               trunk         on it
    'When we got tired of it we laid them down on the trunk.'

(7) Da:h   o:nëh   nä:h   wa'ágwatgá:nye:',   dayagwajë:'        gë:s at the top of the steps.
    so     then    !      we played          we sat down there   repeatedly
    'So then we played, we sat down there at the top of the stairs.'

(8) Dayágwatéyo'dzën     gë:s.
    we slid down there    repeatedly
    'We slid down there.'

(9) *Ta'gë:'öh    nä:h    ne'hoh    dödà:da't    neh    nyágwai'    gǎ:'tëshǎgë:ya:d.*
after a    !    there    he stood there    the    bear    at the top of the
while    stairs
'After a while the bear stood there at the top of the stairs.'

(10) *Da:h    o:nëh    nä:h    wa'ǒgwahjö'.*
so    then    !    we got scared
'So then we got scared.'

(11) *Wa'áki:nö:g    neh    no'yëh,    wa'ǒtgato'    hǎ:'gwah    waöwögë'.*
we called to her    the    mother    she looked    also    she saw him
'We called mother, she looked and she saw him too.'

(12) *Da:h    o:nëh    wa'ödadí:nö:g    né:wa'    neh    Gram,    wa'e:gë'    hǎ:'gwah.*
so    then    she called to her    this time    the    she saw it    too
'So then she called Gram, she saw it too.'

(13) *Da:h    o:nëh    nä:h    wa'agwadé'go'    wa'agwajë:'    gasdò:shǎk'ah.*
so    then    !    we ran away    we sat down    next to the stove
'So then we ran away and sat down next to the stove.'

(14) *O:nëh    da'sayagyáhdë:di'    neh    akso:d,    niyǒgyahjǒ'öh.*
then    we didn't go home    the    grandmother    how scared we were
'Then we didn't go home with my grandmother, we were so scared.'

(15) *Heh    niyo:we'    sa:ayö'    neh    ha'nih.*
there    how far    he came back    the    father
'Until Father came back.'

(16) *Da:h    o:nëh    nä:h    o'shágwa:owi',    wá:tgato'    hǎ:'gwah.*
so    then    !    we told him    he looked    too
'So then we told him, he looked too.'

(17) *O:nëh    gyö'öh    de'ta:d    neh    nyagwai'.*
then    hearsay    he isn't standing any more    the    bear
'Then (he told us) the bear isn't standing there any more.'

(18) *Da:h    o:nëh    nä:h,    wa'ékö:ni'    neh    no'yëh,    ëdzǒki'jǒ:nö'    shö:h.*
so    then    !    she cooked    the    mother    she will take us back    just
'So then mother cooked, she was just going to take us back.'

(19) *Da:h    o:nëh    nä:h    wa:ayö'    neh    John    shökí:nöke'.*
so    then    !    he arrived    the    John    he was there to get us
'So then John came to get us.'

(20) *Da:h    o:nëh    nä:h    dödayagwáhdë:di'.*
so    then    !    we went home
'So then we went home.'

**(21)** 

| Da:h | ne'hoh | shö:h | neh | gagais, | do:gës | nä:h | ne'hoh | niyáwë'öh. |
|------|--------|-------|-----|---------|--------|------|--------|-----------|
| so   | there  | just  | the | length of story | really | ! | there | how it happened |

'So that's just the end of the story, that's what really happened.'

### 12.4.1   The influence of English

When this story was recorded, everyone in the community spoke English most of the time and there were very few people who held extended conversations in Seneca. Mrs. Jacobs showed the influence of English in several places. Line 4 contains an example of what linguists call code-switching (see Chapter 11). The beginning and end of the sentence were in English but the verb in the middle was in Seneca:

**(4)**   *That John hotgwe:nyö:h, at Indian Fair.*
                    he has won it
'That John had won at the Indian Fair.'

The English at the end of Line 7 is another example:

**(7)**   

| Da:h | o:nëh | nä:h | wa'ágwatgá:nye:', | dayagwajë:' | gë:s | at the top of the stairs. |
|------|-------|------|------------------|------------|------|----------------------------|
| so   | then  | !    | we played        | we sat down there | repeatedly | |

'So then we played, we sat down there at the top of the stairs.'

Two sentences later, however, in Line 9, the same idea was expressed with a Seneca word:

**(9)**   

| Ta'gë:'öh | nä:h | ne'hoh | dödà:da't | neh | nyágwai' | gä̌:'tëshä̌gë:ya:d. |
|-----------|------|--------|-----------|-----|----------|--------------------|
| after a while | ! | there | he stood there | the | bear | at the top of the stairs |

'After a while the bear stood there at the top of the stairs.'

In Line 12, Mrs. Jacobs said *Gram* rather than *Akso:d*, the Seneca word for grand-mother that she used elsewhere:

**(12)**   

| Da:h | o:nëh | wa'ödadí:nö:g | né:wa' | neh | Gram, | wa'e:gë' | hä̌:'gwah. |
|------|-------|---------------|--------|-----|-------|----------|-----------|
| so   | then  | she called to her | this time | the | Gram | she saw it | too |

'So then she called Gram, she saw it too.'

Code-switching may also occur within a single word. In Line 6, the English *trunk* was followed by the Seneca suffix *-geh*, translatable as 'on': *trunkgeh* 'on the trunk.' In Line 13, the influence of English is more obscure in the word *gasdò:shǎk'ah* 'next to the stove,' but in fact *-sdò:-* in the middle of that word was borrowed from English *stove*. The Seneca word for 'stove' alone is *gasdò:shä'*, with the neuter prefix *ga-* and the noun-forming suffix *-shä'*. Here it was followed by the verb root *-k'ah* 'be next to'. There is an alternative, entirely Seneca word for 'stove' – *ganö̌hsodáia'shä'*, literally 'that which heats the house,' but Mrs. Jacobs chose the half-English version. (See Textbox LP12.2 for a note about Seneca's influence on English.)

## 12.5 Polysynthesis and fusion

Europeans who first encountered polysynthetic languages like Seneca liked to say that they could express within a single word a thought that in English or another European language would require an entire phrase or even an entire sentence. The second word in Line 1 above, *tšiwágoshíya'göh*, means literally 'when I have crossed winters' – five words in English. Its parts include:

(1)  | *tši-* | *wág-* | *-osh-* | *-íya'g-* | *-öh* |
     | when- | I- | -winter- | -cross- | -PERFECT |

Crossing winters is the idiomatic way Seneca expresses the idea of being a certain age; hence the free translation 'when I was seven years old.' Winters in the Northeast were severe, and surviving one was a salient achievement by which the passage of years was measured. The "perfect" suffix locates the crossing of winters as an event that occurred in the past but was still relevant, as when we would say in English *I have crossed (a certain number of winters)*.

As we have seen in these types of examples, Seneca words can contain a large number of morphemes. Moreover, the language has undergone a large number of sound changes whose effect has often been to obscure the boundaries between those morphemes. Languages of this type are called not only **polysynthetic** but also **fusional**, with separate morphemes fused together.

This process is evident in the word *gá:těshágë:ya:d* 'at the top of the stairs' in Line 9 above, which is difficult to segment into discrete morphemes because the morphemes have been fused together through processes of historical sound change, as discussed in Textbox LP12.3.

Some shorter words in Seneca hide more complexity than is evident on the surface. In Line 2 above *ho'ka:'* 'I took it there' is the modern pronunciation of a word that was once pronounced *\*hwa'khaw'*. Over time, the first syllable, *hwa'-*, was replaced by *ho'-*, the *kh* sequence was reduced to *k*, and the *w* in the last syllable was dropped with compensatory lengthening of the preceding *a*; thus today we have *ho'ka:'*.

---

### TEXTBOX LP12.3 **SOUND CHANGE LEADING TO FUSION**

Several centuries ago, the word *gá:tëshágë:ya:d* 'at the top of the stairs' would have been pronounced *garáʼdëshrágëhyad*; the asterisk shows that this is a reconstructed pronunciation from the past. At that time, under certain conditions, vowels in even-numbered syllables were accented – in this case syllables 2 and 4. The sequence *ra* in the second and fourth syllables was replaced by *rä*, producing *garáʼdëshrágëhyad*, and later the *r* dropped out, leaving *gaáʼdëshágëhyad*. The vowel sequence *aä* at the beginning of that word coalesced into a long *ä:*, leaving *gá:ʼdëshágëhyad*. At some point the *h*

in the next-to-last syllable also dropped out with compensatory lengthening of the preceding vowel, and the *a* in the final syllable was lengthened as well. Thus, today we have the pronunciation *gá:ʼdëshágë:ya:d*.

| Original pronunciation | *garáʼdëshrágëhyad* |
| ra -> rä | *garáʼdëshrágëhyad* |
| r deletes | *gaáʼdëshágëhyad* |
| aä -> ä: | *gá:ʼdëshágëhyad* |
| h deletes; vowels lengthen | *gá:ʼdëshágë:ya:d* |

---

### 12.5.1 The predominance of verbs

As with the other Northern Iroquoian languages, Seneca uses verbs to a far greater extent than English and other European languages. In fact, exaggerating only slightly, a nineteenth-century missionary among the Mohawks wrote, "In their language almost everything is a verb" (Cuoq 1866). Perhaps the most salient feature of Seneca verbs is their inclusion within a single word of both an event and a participant in the event. Such a word can then be used to refer either to the event itself or to the participant. Thus, one possible translation of the verb *hayë:twas* is 'he plants', a habitual event, but the same word can also be used to refer to a man who does the planting: a 'planter,' 'gardener,' or 'farmer.'

Not only do Seneca verbs include information on the participants in events, they are also subject to modifications of the basic meaning that are expressed by derivational suffixes following the verb base. The element meaning 'plant' appeared as the base *-yëtwa-* of the word *hayë:twas*. But this base itself is composed of the root *-yët-* with the meaning 'be set in place' followed by a derivational suffix *-w-* that means 'cause to.' Thus, the meaning 'plant' is derived from 'cause to be set in place.' To this base can be added a number of further modifications, which at the same time trigger changes in the form of the habitual aspect suffix at the end. These are given in Table LP12.3.

### 12.5.2 Noun incorporation

Another feature of polysynthetic languages that adds to their complexity is **noun incorporation**: the addition of a noun root to modify the meaning of the verb root (see Textbox LP12.4). In Line 1 in the story above, we saw the incorporation of *-osh-* 'winter' with the verb root *-iyaʼg-* 'cross' to express the idea of crossing winters. Another example of incorporation occurred at the very end of the story in Line 21, in the word *gaga:is*, either 'it's a long story' or 'the length of the story.' Here the noun root *-gar-*

**Table LP12.3** Modifications on the word base -yëtwa- 'plant'

| Word base | Meaning | Modifications through derivational suffixes |
|---|---|---|
| -yëtwahs- | 'go planting' | with the 'dislocative' suffix -ahs- and habitual -e's in hayétwahse's 'he goes planting' |
| yëtwat | 'use for planting' | with the 'instrumental' suffix -at- and habitual -a' in hayétwata' 'he uses it for planting' |
| -yëtwahse- | 'plant for someone' | with the 'benefactive' suffix -hse- and habitual -h as well as the 'he for me' prefix hag- in hagyétwahseh 'he plants for me' |
| -yëtwahsö- | 'plant things' | with the 'distributive' suffix -hsö- and habitual -h in hayétwahsöh 'he plants things' |
| -yëtwagw- | 'harvest' | with the 'reversive' suffix -gw- (harvest interpreted as the reverse of plant) and habitual -as in hayétwagwas 'he harvests' |
| -yëtwagwaö- | 'harvest things' | with both the 'reversive' suffix -gw- and the 'distributive' suffix -ö- and habitual -h in hayétwagwaöh 'he harvests things' |

---

### TEXTBOX LP12.4 **NOUN INCORPORATION**

Noun incorporation is similar to compounding in that two separate roots, stems, or words are combined into one; however, in this case, a noun root is used to modify a verb root, resulting in a verb. Often the modification of the verb by the noun serves to make the meaning of the verb more specific.

Noun incorporation occurs only rarely in English, but can be seen in verbs such as *bartend* (which incorporates the noun *bar*), and *babysit* (incorporating the noun *baby*).

---

'story' was incorporated with the verb root -*is* 'be long.' The earlier form *\*gagaris* acquired a long vowel in the next to last syllable, *\*gaga:ris*, and then the *r* was lost to produce *gaga:is*. This word illustrates how the same word can be used for a state, 'it's a long story,' or for something that is in that state, 'the length of the story.'

## 12.5.3 Pronominal prefixes

All of the verbs in Seneca, and many of the nouns, include a so-called pronominal prefix that specifies the gender, number, and role of one or more participants in an event or state, or (with a noun) the possessor of an object. In Line 1 above, both of the verbs, *tsïwágoshíya'göh, o'dwagajëönyö:s* 'when I had crossed winters, I got haunted' contain a prefix -*wag*- that corresponds to the English pronoun *I*. In Line 2, the verb *ho'ka:'* 'I took it there' also contains an element translated 'I,' but in this case the prefix is -*k*- rather than -*wag*-. This -*k*- is the form taken by a first-person prefix that specifies

**Table LP12.4** Some first-person prefixes in Seneca

|         | Singular      | Dual        | Plural      |
| ------- | ------------- | ----------- | ----------- |
| Agent   | *-g-* or *-k-* | *-(y)agya-* | *-(y)agwa-* |
| Patient | *-wag-*       | *-(y)ögya-* | *-(y)ögwa-* |

someone who performs an action, called an agent. The *-wag-* prefix in the first two verbs, on the other hand, is used when someone is affected by an event, called a patient. Someone who has 'crossed winters' is regarded as affected by the experience, as is a person who gets haunted.

In Lines 5 and 6, we have the verbs *wa'ágwatgá:nye:'* 'we played' and *wa'ögwagè:'dë'* 'we got tired.' The first-contains the 'first-person plural *agent*' prefix *-agwa-*: the agent of the playing. The second contains the 'first-person plural *patient*' prefix *-ögwa-*. Someone who gets tired is assigned to the patient role. We can line up the four prefixes described so far as in Table LP12.4.

In the upper left cell of Table LP12.4, *-g-* appears before vowels and *-k-* before (most) consonants. Although the *k* in *ho'ka:'* 'I took it there' appears to be followed by a vowel, we saw that this word was earlier pronounced *\*hwa'khaw'*, where the *k* was followed by an *h* and hence pronounced *k* rather than *g*. In the dual and plural columns, the initial *y* was dropped after a glottal stop, as in the examples above. We can see this *y* in Line 14, *da'sayagyáhdë:di'* 'we (dual) didn't go home'; in Line 7, *dayagwajë:'* 'we (plural) sat down there'; and with a patient prefix in Line 14, *niyö́gyahjö'öh* 'how scared we were.'

It is also possible for an agent to be combined with a patient within a single transitive prefix. In Line 16, *o'shágwa:owi'* 'we told him' contains the transitive prefix *-shagwa-*, which combines a first-person plural agent with a masculine singular patient: 'we (did something to or for) him.' With the same verb root, a few other possibilities are: *o'shǒ́gwa:owi'* 'he told us' and *o'ké:owi'* 'I told her.' In all there are sixty-seven of these pronominal prefixes, including intransitive agents and patients and transitive combinations of them. The following are some combinations with a masculine singular *agent*, 'he,' attached to the verb stem *-nöe's* 'like.' Dual means 'two' and plural means 'three or more.'

| | |
| --- | --- |
| *haknöe's* | 'he likes me (singular)' |
| *shökninöe's* | 'he likes us (dual)' |
| *shögwanöe's* | 'he likes us (plural)' |
| *yanöe's* | 'he likes you (singular)' |
| *shesninöe's* | 'he likes you (dual)' |
| *sheswanöe's* | 'he likes you (plural)' |
| *honöe's* | 'he likes him' |
| *shagónöe's* | 'he likes her' |
| *hagónöe's* | 'he likes them' |

The following combinations have a masculine singular *patient*:

| | |
|---|---|
| *henŏe's* | 'I like him' |
| *shehnínöe's* | 'we (dual inclusive) like him' |
| *shedwánöe's* | 'we (plural inclusive) like him' |
| *shaknínöe's* | 'we (dual exclusive) like him' |
| *shagwánöe's* | 'we (plural exclusive) like him' |
| *hesnŏe's* | 'you (singular) like him' |
| *shesnínöe's* | 'you (dual) like him' |
| *sheswánöe's* | 'you (plural) like him' |
| *höwŏnöe's* | 'she or they like him' |

**SIDEBAR LP12.4**
ORTHOGRAPHIC NOTE
In the combination [*sh*] the [s] and [*h*] are pronounced separately, not as the single sound spelled *sh* in English.

There are two things to notice in this last set. In one respect Seneca makes more distinctions than English does, but in another respect it makes fewer. There are four different ways of translating the English pronoun *we* when it combines an agent with a masculine singular patient. The group covered by 'we' may be dual or plural, and it may be **inclusive** or **exclusive**. An inclusive 'we' includes the person being talked to, the listener. Inclusive dual is like saying 'you and I,' and inclusive plural includes 'you and I and some other people.' An exclusive 'we' excludes the person being talked to: 'we' but not including 'you.'

The other thing to notice is that in the last word, *höwŏnöe's* 'she or they like him,' no distinction is made between a single female, 'she,' and plural third person, 'they.' This absence of a distinction between 'she' and 'they' appears in other transitive prefixes as well. It exemplifies the manner in which cultural practices sometimes influence language. In ancient Iroquois society men and women had very different roles. Writing of the Hurons, one anthropologist wrote that:

> the most basic distinction in Huron society was that made between the sexes . . . Almost every task was considered to be either exclusively men's work or exclusively women's work, and every Huron was expected to be familiar with all or most of the tasks appropriate to his or her sex. For the most part, men engaged in tasks that required considerable physical strength, or which took them away from home for long periods. Women performed tasks of a more routine nature that kept them in, or close to, their villages . . . In addition to hunting and fishing, clearing land, building houses, and manufacturing tools, the major activities that men engaged in were trading, waging war, and government.
>
> (Trigger 1976: 34, 45)

Gender roles were distributed in Iroquois society in such a way that men were conspicuous and flamboyant, while women stayed in the background. Their position, however, was one from which women influenced what men did in fundamental ways. Rather than being unimportant or undervalued, women were responsible for keeping life going, both from day to day and from generation to generation.

Descent was traditionally traced through the women, land belongs to the women, and chiefs are appointed by the women – who theoretically can depose them at will. This means that female children are important to a family, the opinions of women carry weight, and women have some legal and political power.

(Richards 1974: 401)

The foregrounded role of men and the backgrounded but powerful role of women is mirrored in a pronominal prefix system that elaborates masculine gender while it integrates women with people in general.

## 12.5.4   Verbs, nouns, and particles

Viewed in terms of their internal structure, Seneca words fall into three major classes: verbs, nouns, and particles. Verbs consist minimally of a pronominal prefix, a verb base, and an aspect suffix, but there are many ways in which that simple structure may be expanded, as we saw above. Nouns usually consist of little more than a pronominal prefix, a noun base, and a noun suffix. Mrs. Jacobs' story contained only one example of a morphological noun: *gayáʼdaʼ* 'doll' (line 2). It is built on the noun root *-yaʼt-*, which refers more generally to a 'body' but is also used for a doll. It is preceded by the neuter prefix *ga-* and followed by the generalized noun suffix *-aʼ*. In Line 5, this word occurred in its **distributive** version *gayáʼdaʼshöʼöh* 'dolls.' The *-shöʼöh* suffix is called distributive rather than plural because it implies not only that there were several dolls, but also that these dolls were of different types, one being a teddy bear and others of other kinds.

Mrs. Jacobs' story contained 128 words, of which 13 were English. Of the 115 Seneca words, only two were nouns as described in the paragraph above. One word, *haʼnih* 'father' belongs to a small subset of kinship terms that have their own unique structure, contrasting in that respect with *akso:d* 'grandmother,' which is actually a verb. That leaves 42 verbs and 70 words that belong to the diverse class of particles: words with no internal structure or, in a few cases, a very simple and often idiosyncratic structure. Particles perform a number of different functions, which can be assigned to the following rough categories:

- *Numerals:* the first word in Mrs. Jacobs' story was the numeral *dza:dak* 'seven.' (See Sidebar LP12.6 for other numerals in Seneca.)
- *Kinship terms:* also in Line 1 was *noʼyéːneh* 'at mother's,' composed of *noʼyëh* 'mother' (in lines 11 and 18) plus the locative suffix *-neh*.
- *Animals:* a number of animal names, such as *nyagwaiʼ* 'bear' (lines 2, 9, and 17) have no obvious internal structure, as is the case with *jiːyäh* 'dog,' *gwaʼyòːʼ* 'rabbit,' and others.
- *Pronouns:* Line 2 contains the first-person pronoun *iːʼ*, which can mean 'I,' 'we,' 'me,' or 'us.' The second-person pronoun is *iːs* 'you.'
- *Temporal adverbs:* conspicuous in this text is the adverbial particle *oːnëh* 'then' (lines 5, 7, 10, 12–14, and 16–20) expressing succession in time. A more specific temporal location is provided by *néːwaʼ* 'this time' (line 12). An event that occurs a number of times is signaled by *gëːs* 'repeatedly' (lines 7 and 8). A passage of intervening time is signaled by *taʼgëːʼöh* 'after a while' (line 9).

- *Spatial adverbs:* the most general indicator of a specific location is *ne'hoh* 'there' (lines 9 and 21). The little word *heh* 'there' (line 15) is limited to particular expressions. Vertical location is signaled by *he'tgëh* 'above' (line 5).
- *Article:* the particle *neh* (lines 2, 9 11, 12, 14, 15, 17–19, and 21) can often be translated as the English definite article 'the,' although it has more uses as well.
- *Epistemics:* Native American languages tend to be more concerned than European languages with the source and evaluation of the knowledge that is being communicated. There are two epistemic particles in Mrs. Jacobs' account. When one is telling about something one has not witnessed directly, it is common to insert the hearsay particle *gyö'öh* (line 17), absolving oneself of direct responsibility for the information. The other particle in this category is *do:gës* 'really' (line 21), expressing certainty about what happened.
- *Limiter:* the particle *shö:h* 'just' (lines 18 and 21) indicates that the information conveyed was the only possibility.
- *Intensifier:* the particle *nä:h* (lines 5–7, 9, 10, 13, 16, and 18–21), which is translated here with an exclamation point (!), corresponds to saying something in English with greater emphasis. Here it appeared most often in the fixed expression *Da:h o:nëh nä:h* 'so then,' which began many of the sentences (lines 5, 7, 10, 13, 16, and 18–20). It corresponds to pronouncing the word 'then' with higher pitch and greater loudness.
- *Connectives:* finally, there are several particles that logically connect what preceded with what follows. The most common is *da:h* 'so' (lines 5, 7, 10, 12, 13, 16, and 18–21). The particle *koh* 'and' (line 2) is placed after the connected item rather than before, as in English: *akso:d i:' koh* 'grandmother and I.' Similar in function is *hä́:'gwah* 'also' (lines 11, 12, and 16). Finally, there is the temporal conjunction *ga:nyo'* 'when' (line 6), which is less tightly integrated with the event than the prefix *tsï-* in *tsïwágoshíya'göh* 'when I had crossed winters' (line 1).

## SUMMARY

We have seen something of the history of the Seneca language and the features that assign it to the polysynthetic and fusional language type. Mrs. Jacobs' narrative provided a basis for illustrating some of the basic elements of Seneca structure, especially the predominant role of verbs and the way verbs can be expanded to modify the nature of events and states. Although complex verbs are the principal means of expressing ideas, the last section described some of the variety found in the ubiquitous particles that modify the flow of discourse.

## SUGGESTIONS FOR FURTHER READING

**Chafe, Wallace**. 1996. "Sketch of Seneca, an Iroquoian language." In Goddard, Ives (ed.), *Handbook of North American Indians*, Vol. XVII: *Languages*. 225–253. Washington, DC: Smithsonian Institution.

This sketch covers many aspects of Seneca phonology, morphology, and discourse, as well as a selected vocabulary of Seneca words.

**Mithun, Marianne**. 1999. *The languages of Native North America*. Cambridge University Press.

The chapter in this book on the Iroquoian language family provides an overview of research on each of the Iroquoian languages along with a more detailed discussion of Cayuga, whose relation to Seneca is very close.

**Morgan, Lewis Henry**. 1851. *League of the Ho-De´-No-Sau-Nee, Iroquois*. Rochester: Sage & Brother, with numerous reprintings.

This book is a classic description of traditional Iroquois culture as viewed by an outsider who had expert help from contacts on the Tonawanda Seneca Reservation. The chapter titled "Language of the Iroquois" unfortunately repeats misguided prejudices regarding the nature of "primitive" languages.

## EXERCISES

1. In Line 1, Mrs. Jacobs said *no'yë́:neh* 'at mother's (house).' How would she have said 'at father's (house)'?
2. If *o'shögwagë'* means 'he saw us (plural),' how would a Seneca person say 'we (plural) saw him'?
3. How would Mrs. Jacobs have said 'when I was five years old'?
4. The word *ganö́hsagë́:ya:d* means 'at the top of the house.' How would this word have been pronounced three hundred years ago? Which part of it carries the meaning 'house'?
5. A Seneca woman was talking about a new restaurant in town. She said, 'It's very expensive gyö'öh.' Why did she insert the Seneca word *gyö'öh* into a sentence that was otherwise in English? What is this type of phenomenon called?

# Akkadian

## 13.1 Historical background

Akkadian is a Semitic language that is no longer spoken, but which is related to the living Semitic languages Arabic, Amharic, Hebrew, and Aramaic. Akkadian is one of the earliest attested languages, surpassed in this respect only by Sumerian and Ancient Egyptian. It was spoken in ancient Mesopotamia (a term which refers to the land "between the rivers," or between the Euphrates and the Tigris), in an area roughly corresponding to today's Iraq.

The first written records in Akkadian date from around 2500 BC, and the language continued to be spoken until around 500 BC, when it was displaced by Aramaic. Nevertheless, texts in Akkadian continued to be written for several more centuries. The Akkadian language thus has a written history spanning more than two thousand years, almost twice as long as that of English. During this period, the language underwent considerable changes. However, some of the basic traits of its grammar, such as the remarkable root-and-template architecture of the verbal system, which we shall explore in more detail below, have characterized Akkadian throughout its history.

The name of the language derives from the city of *Akkade* which was founded in the twenty-third century BC as the imperial capital of the first "world conqueror," King Sargon. After 2000 BC, Akkadian diverged into two main varieties: Babylonian, which was spoken in the south of Mesopotamia in an area dominated by the city of Babylon (today south of Baghdad), and Assyrian, which was spoken in the north. The Babylonians and Assyrians dominated the political and cultural horizon of the Ancient Near East up until the sixth century BC. Their political dominance may have waxed and waned, but for a good part of 2,000 years, Mesopotamian emperors would rule over "the four corners" (of the earth). From Sargon in the third millennium BC to Sennacherib and Nebuchadnezzar in the first, these emperors would lay claim to the title "King of the Universe." More stable than the power of the sword, however, was the cultural hegemony of Mesopotamia over the whole region. The Akkadian language shaped the dominant canon for much of the Near East in terms of religion, the arts, science, and

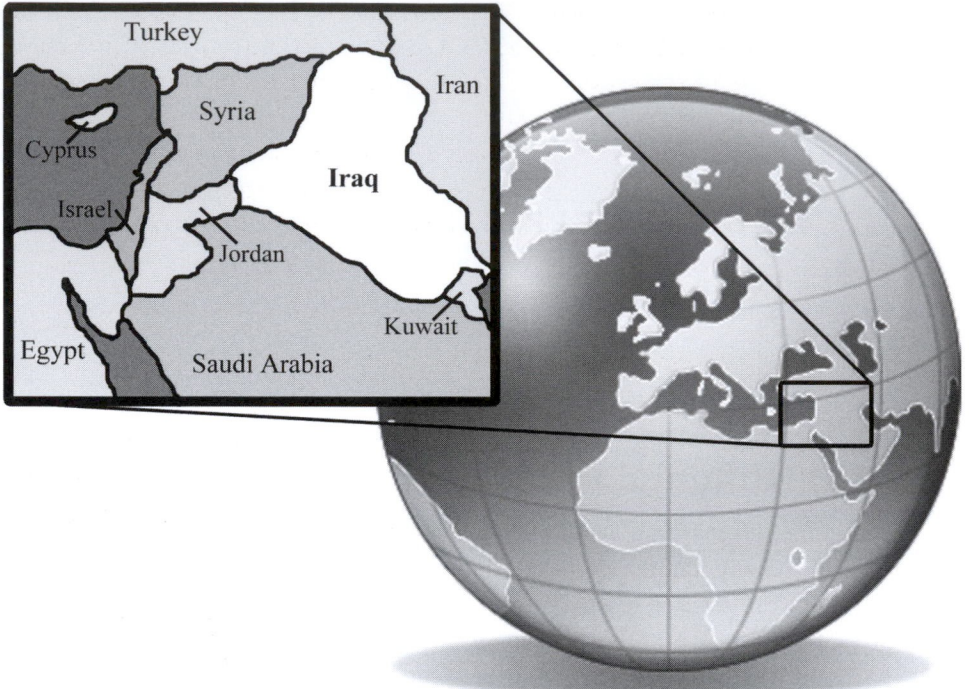

**Figure LP13.1**  Map of Mesopotamia

law. And the **cuneiform** ('wedge-shaped') writing system, which Akkadian speakers had originally borrowed from their Sumerian neighbors, was exported far and wide, and adapted as the script of many diverse languages, from Hittite to Elamite, and from Hurrian to Ancient Persian. Akkadian itself was used as a **lingua franca** throughout the Near East, and was the means of diplomatic correspondence. Languages across the Near East also borrowed many scientific and cultural terms from Akkadian, a few of which may even be recognized by English speakers today. For instance, the first word in the Jewish expression *mazel tov* ('luck good' in Hebrew) is a borrowing from the Akkadian astrological term *mazzaltu*, which meant the position of a star in the sky.

After millennia of cultural supremacy, however, Assyria was defeated and Babylon soon followed suit, finally finished off by the Persians. The sixth century BC ushered in an age of rapid decline, so that within a few centuries both the Akkadian language and its writing system fell into oblivion. Hundreds of thousands of clay tablets, the product of 2,000 years of civilization, lay forgotten in the desert sands for two more millennia, to be rediscovered and deciphered only in the nineteenth century. Since then, an incredible wealth of texts has been recovered from the soil of Iraq and neighboring countries and has opened up a unique perspective into one of history's greatest civilizations. The texts encompass many genres, including poetry (such as the Epic of Gilgamesh), legal documents (such as the Code of Hammurabi), religious incantations, royal inscriptions of heroic deeds, diplomatic correspondence, everyday letters between individuals, monolingual and multilingual dictionaries, mathematical and astronomical texts, medical treatises, school exercises, and a seemingly endless quantity of administrative documents, from real estate contracts to lists of workers' food rations. One reason for such an abundance of surviving materials is that the texts were written not on paper, but on wet clay tablets, using a triangular shaped wedge. And clay, once dried, is highly durable; thus, there are hundreds of thousands of tablets that have been recovered, and thousands more yet to be unearthed.

## 13.2  The writing system

The **cuneiform** writing system was developed toward the end of the fourth millennium BC by the Sumerians, the earlier inhabitants of southern Mesopotamia. In the middle of the third millennium BC, Akkadian speakers borrowed the script and adapted it to write their own language. Figure LP13.2 is a hand copy of a clay tablet from the British Museum, which contains a letter from around 1800 BC. The letter begins, "Tell my lord, this is what your maid Tatūr-mātum said: May (the gods) Šamaš and the bride Aya keep you well forever for my sake. Concerning the fish and the locusts that I told you about, don't forget them. Bring them with you."

The cuneiform script is rather complex, because it used both **syllabograms** (phonetic signs that represent syllables or parts of syllables, represented in modern transliterations by small letters, e.g., *ma, an, nam*, etc.) and **logograms** (whole-word signs, represented in modern transliterations by capitals, e.g., GÉME – 'maid'). In the first line of the text in Figure LP13.2, for example, all the signs are to be read phonetically (see Textbox LP13.1 for a transcription note). But in line 3, the third sign from the right is the logogram GÉME. Since the logograms were borrowed from Sumerian, modern transliterations represent these logograms according to their Sumerian rather than Akkadian pronunciations. The Akkadian pronunciation of the word 'maid' was actually *amat*, so the word transliterated as GÉME-*ku-ma* was actually pronounced *amatkama* 'your maid.' A further complication is that some logograms were not meant to be

---

### TEXTBOX LP13.1  **TRANSCRIPTION NOTES**

- The symbol š represents a voiceless palato-alveolar fricative, IPA [ʃ].
- The symbol ṭ illustrates a voiceless retroflex stop, typically pronounced with contact between the bottom of the tongue and the postalveolar region.
- Vowels with a macron (horizontal line) over the top are phonetically lengthened.

- There are two **pharyngeal** consonants made by retracting the tongue root towards the back of the **pharynx**. The symbol ḥ represents a voiceless pharyngeal fricative, while ʕ represents a voiced pharyngeal fricative or approximant.

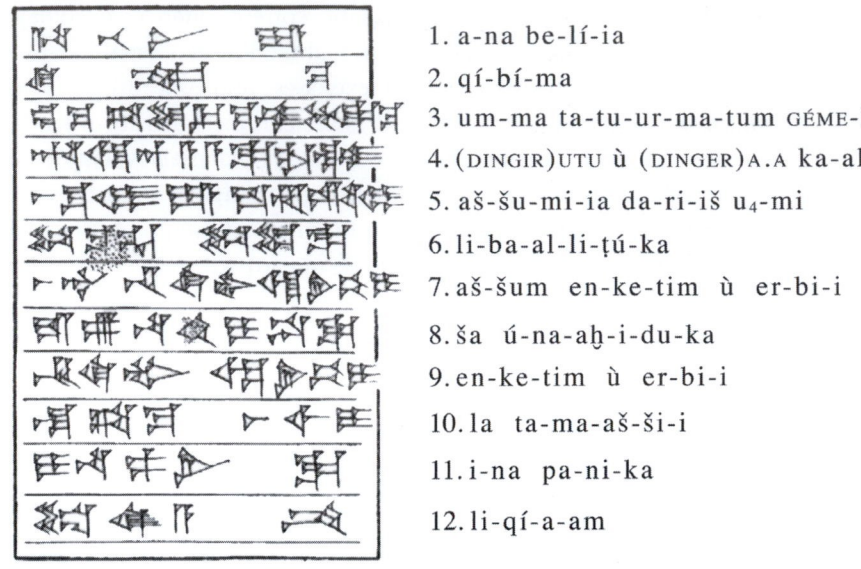

1. a-na be-lí-ia
2. qí-bí-ma
3. um-ma ta-tu-ur-ma-tum GÉME-ka-ma
4. (DINGIR)UTU ù (DINGER)A.A ka-al-la-tum
5. aš-šu-mi-ia da-ri-iš u₄-mi
6. li-ba-al-li-ṭú-ka
7. aš-šum en-ke-tim ù er-bi-i
8. ša ú-na-aḫ-i-du-ka
9. en-ke-tim ù er-bi-i
10. la ta-ma-aš-ši-i
11. i-na pa-ni-ka
12. li-qí-a-am

**Figure LP13.2** Clay tablet from the British Museum: letter, circa 1800 BC

pronounced at all, but were 'determinatives' that specified which type of noun followed them. The first sign in line 4 (DINGIR) is a logogram for 'god,' showing that a god's name is to follow (in this case the Sun god, called *Utu* in Sumerian and *Šamaš* in Akkadian).

In (1) through (8), you can see how to "decode" the first few lines of the letter in Figure LP13.2. Each line is given in sign-for-sign transliteration, as well as a normalization, which attempts to reproduce what the Akkadian actually sounded like (how this was determined is an interesting but complicated story beyond the scope of the current chapter), followed by both a gloss and a translation:

(1)  a-na      be-lí-ia
     *ana*      *bēli-ya*
     to        lord-POSS.1SG
     'to my lord

(2)  qí-bí-ma
     *qibī-ma*
     say.IMP-FOC
     say:

(3)  um-ma      ta-tu-ur-ma-tum      GÉME-ka-ma
     *umma*      *tatūr-mātum*         *amat-ka-ma*
     QUOT       Tatūr-mātum          maid-POSS.2SG-FOC
     (this is what) your maid Tatūr-mātum said:

(4)  ᵈUTU      ù      ᵈA.A     ka-al-la-tum
     *šamaš*    *u*    *Aya*    *kallātum*
     Šamaš     and     Aya     bride
     Šamaš and the bride Aya

(5)  aš-šu-mi-ia        da-ri-iš       u₄-mi
     *aššum-iya*        *dāriš*        *ūmī*
     sake-POSS.1SG      eternity.GEN   day.PL
     forever for my sake

(6)  li-ba-al-li-ṭú-ka
     *liballiṭ-ū-ka*
     COND.keep.alive-3PL-2SG
     may keep you well

(7)  aš-šum        en-ke-tim     ù      er-bi-i
     *aššum*       *enkētim*     *u*    *erbī*
     concerning    fish          and    locusts
     concerning the fish and the locusts

(8)  ša       ú-na-aḫ-i-du-ka
     *ša*     *una'idu-ka*
     which    1SG.instruct.PST-2SG
     that I instructed you (about)'

## 13.3  The consonantal roots of Akkadian (and other Semitic languages)

In Chapter 4, we saw that morphemes do not always have to be pieces of words such as prefixes or suffixes. In the English nouns *man/men* and *goose/geese*, for example, plurality is not marked by a suffix but rather by a change of vowel inside the word itself. Similarly, English verbs such as *drink/drank* mark the past tense not by a suffix *-ed*, but by an internal vowel change. In English, such marking of grammatical categories in this way is restricted to a few odd nouns and a few irregular verbs. (There are also some relics of a causative pattern marked by an internal vowel alternation, e.g., *fall–fell* 'make fall,' *sit–set* 'make sit,' *rise–raise*, etc.) But there are languages where such internal vowel alterations are far more widespread and far more systematic. The Semitic verb offers one of the most elaborate and sophisticated examples of such vowel alterations among the world's languages. The vowels change so much, in fact, that they are not deemed to be a part of the verbal root at all. The verbal root in the Semitic languages is generally described as consisting only of consonants. The Akkadian root for 'to put' or 'to place' is š-k-n, and the root for 'to cut' or 'to block' is p-r-s. This consonantal root is an abstract notion, of course, because it is not pronounceable as such, and never appears in this way in practice. The consonantal root comes to life only when it is superimposed on a **template**, which is a pattern of vowels (and sometimes additional consonants) that has three empty slots for the three consonants of the root. To take one example, the Akkadian template *i*○○*u*○ denotes the past tense in the third-person masculine, so if we insert the root š-k-n into the template, we get:

Root:     š-k-n

Template: i○○u○  (past tense, third-person masculine)

i ⓢ ⓚ u ⓝ  ('he placed')

A different template *i*○*a*○○*a*○ forms the present tense. Here, in addition to the vowels that appear between the root consonants, the second root consonant is also doubled, or **geminated**. So if we insert the root p-r-s into the template, we get:

Root:     p-r-s

Template: i ○a○○a○  (present tense, third-person masculine)

i ⓟa ⓡⓡa ⓢ  ('he blocks')

There are a very large number of such templates in Akkadian (and in other Semitic languages), and they are used to mark all manners of verbal distinctions. For example, different templates denote the different tenses, aspects, moods, and other inflectional categories of the verb. Here are a few examples of templates:

| Template | Function | meaning |
|---|---|---|
| i○○u○ | PST.3SG.M | he X-ed |
| i○a○○a○ | PRS/FUT.3SG.M | he X-s/will X |
| i○ta○a○ | PRF.3SG.M | he has X-ed |
| ○u○u○ | IMP.2SG.M | X! |
| ○ā○i○um | PTCP.3SG.M | someone who X-s |
| ○a○○um | VERBAL.ADJ.3SG.M | (an) X-ed (thing) |
| ○a○ā○um | INF | to X |

Notice that in addition to different vowels between the root consonants and gemination (doubling of a consonant, as in the present-tense template above), sometimes there are consonants which are included as part of the templates themselves. The perfect tense, for instance, has a *t* infix as part of the template.

This algebraic-seeming template system is not just an artifice of our description. Experiments have shown that both the consonantal roots and the templates have psychological reality for speakers of Semitic languages. To put it simply, while to English ears, forms which have no vowels in common, such as *parsum* (verbal adjective), *iprus* (past), or *iparras* (future) all sound quite dissimilar, for speakers of Semitic

**TABLE LP13.1** Partial network of possible Akkadian 3-consonant templates

| | PAST | PRESENT | PERFECT | INFINITIVE | IMPERATIVE |
|---|---|---|---|---|---|
| BASIC | i○○u○ | i○a○○a○ | i○ta○a○ | ○a○ā○um | ○u○u○ |
| ITERATIVE | i○ta○○a○ | i○tana○○a○ | i○tata○○a○ | ○ita○○u○um | ○ita○○a○ |
| PASSIVE | i○○a○i○ | i○○a○○a○ | itta○○a○ | na○○u○um | na○○i○ |
| CAUSATIVE | uša○○i○ | uša○○a○ | ušta○○i○ | šu○○u○um | šu○○i○ |

languages, such forms are perceived as closely related variations on a theme: the consonants p-r-s.

The template system is far richer than what has been presented so far, because in addition to the basic distinctions of tense, mood, and aspect presented above, different templates are also used to mark other nuances of the action such as passive, causative, reflexive, intensive, iterative (repeated or habitual action). Here are several examples of these:

This dimension of variation is perpendicular to the tense-mood-aspect templates.

| | | |
|---|---|---|
| i○ta○○a○ | ITR.PST.3SG.M | he continually X-ed |
| i○○a○i○ | PASS.PST.3SG.M | he was X-ed |
| uša○○i○ | CAUS.PST.3SG.M | he caused to X |

For example, there are separate passive templates for the past, the present, the perfect, and so on, resulting in a complex two-dimensional network of templates. Several of these are shown in Table LP13.1, but in reality there are nearly a hundred such templates.

As if this weren't enough, the two-dimensional mesh in Table LP13.1. needs to be combined with yet another dimension: subject agreement, or the different persons that are also marked on the verb. However, these markings for person are not indicated by further internal vowel alterations, but rather in a somewhat more typical fashion, using prefixes and suffixes. Here are a few examples for the simple past tense:

| | |
|---|---|
| I blocked | a-Ⓟ Ⓡu Ⓢ |
| you (male singular) blocked | ta-Ⓟ Ⓡu Ⓢ |
| you (female singular) blocked | ta-Ⓟ Ⓡu Ⓢ-ī |
| you (plural) blocked | ta-Ⓟ Ⓡu Ⓢ-ā |
| he/she cuts | i-Ⓟ Ⓡu Ⓢ |

Finally, in addition to subject agreement, there are also suffixes that mark pronominal direct and indirect objects. So, for instance, *aṭrud* means 'I sent,' and *aṭrud-akkuš-šu* 'I sent him to you,' where *-akkuš* means 'to you' and *-šu* means 'him.'

## 13.4  Messiness due to sound changes

The system as presented so far may seem to be the paragon of regular perfection, but in reality, there are many exceptions that make the situation on the ground look much less neat. In the third millennium BC, Akkadian underwent several drastic sound changes as a result of intense contact with Sumerian, a non-Semitic language. This is one major source of untidiness in the language's verbal system. Sumerian speakers evidently had difficulty with the many glottal and **pharyngeal** consonants of the Semitic languages (sounds that can still be heard in Arabic today), and during the centuries of intense contact with Sumerian, Akkadian lost most of these "difficult" consonants. However, since many three-consonantal roots originally contained such consonants, the drastic sound changes in Akkadian often obscured the three-consonantal nature of the roots. For instance, the original Semitic root ʕ-r-b ('enter') had as the first root consonant the pharyngeal fricative ʕ. When inserted into the template for the simple past, i⊕⊙u⑤, it originally resulted in the form iʕrub 'he entered.' But by the end of the third millennium, the pharyngeal had disappeared, so the sequence iʕ was reduced to a long vowel ī, to give the form īrub, where the three-consonantal pattern is no longer so apparent.

While these irregularities, which developed in Akkadian due to contact-induced sound changes, are of fairly late origin, there are other exceptions in the system which are in fact far older, and which, as we shall see in a moment, are actually relics of very early stages in the evolution of the Semitic verbal system.

## 13.5  Historical development

How can a system like that of the Semitic verb have come into being? Research on **grammaticalization** has shone much light on the origin of affixes, even on the emergence of complex paradigms of affixes. At first sight, the abstract idea of a purely consonantal root and the algebraic template system seem to defy historical explanation through the blind mechanisms of change, as they appear to have been designed on the table of a gifted architect. In Deutscher (2005: chapter 6), however, I tried to show how such a system could nevertheless have emerged through entirely normal diachronic processes, in particular, through cycles of sound change and **analogy**. While a full presentation of the detailed argument goes beyond the scope of this chapter, the following discussion presents some of the basic principles of this claim. Interestingly, the clues for understanding how the notion of a consonantal root system could have emerged are all found in various types of exceptions in the verbal system.

The most important of these exceptions can be called the "quirk vowel" (in traditional grammars it is called the "root vowel"). I explained above that vowels are not part of the root and only determine the grammatical nuance. While this is true in general, two of the simplest templates (simple past and simple imperative) flout this rule, since they have an arbitrary vowel between the last two root consonants, that is, an unmotivated vowel which depends on each root itself. Thus, while some roots, like p-r-s, adhere to the template i○○u○ in the simple past (*iprus* 'he cut'), other roots, such as p-t-l 'twist,' have a different vowel between the last root consonants. The past form of p-t-l is not *iptul* but *iptil*. The difference in the vowel does not play any grammatical role. Rather, when you learn the language, you simply have to memorize the "quirk vowel" of each root just as you have to memorize the vowels of every English verb.

While the quirk vowel seems like an unmotivated irregularity from the synchronic perspective of the mature Semitic system, there are various indications that this quirk vowel is in fact an extremely old feature, a relic from the time *before* the root-and-template system had started to develop. The simple past tense thus points to a period when the ancestor language still had more "normal" roots, like *prus* or *ptil*, that consisted of both vowels and consonants.

There are further revealing exceptions in the verbal system that suggest how such normal roots were transformed into the purely consonantal design. The first step seems to have been the development of a single internal vowel alteration that came to mark a distinction in tense, a situation rather similar to English verbs such as *sit–sat* or *drink–drank*. I mentioned earlier that the future tense is formed with the template i○a○a○. This is true of regular verbs, but there are some verbs that disobey this rule. They are called "hollow," because they have only two consonants in their root instead of three (e.g., m-t 'die,' *imūt* 'he died'). The hollow verbs don't follow the regular future-tense template, and instead simply change their vowel to *a*: *imūt – imât* 'he died' – 'he will die.' In the attested stages of Akkadian, such hollow verbs amount to only a few exceptions, but various factors indicate that there were many more of them in earlier stages of the language. Indeed, it seems that the pattern shown by hollow verbs – a single internal vowel mutation – was the earlier pattern that marked the future tense of *all* verbs. So originally the corresponding future form to the past tense *iprus* ('he blocked') would have been just *ipras* (see Textbox LP13.2).

---

**TEXTBOX LP13.2**

It is not difficult to imagine how an internal vowel mutation (*iprus – ipras*) could have emerged, because there are parallel developments in other languages, from more recent times. The most famous is the *i*-mutation of Germanic, which is responsible for the vowel alteration between English nouns such as *man – men*, as well as causative English verbs such as *to fall – to fell*. The original plural of *mann* in Germanic would have been formed regularly, with a suffix *-iz*: *\*mann-iz*. But by a process of assimilation (specifically vowel harmony), the vowel *i* of the suffix colored the preceding *a* to

*e*, resulting in *menn-iz*. The final *-iz* was later reduced, leaving only *men*.

Similarly, the causative form 'to fell' goes back to a Proto-Germanic suffix *-ian* (originally from a Proto-Indo-European verb *\*yo* 'make'). *\*fall-ian* 'fall-make' originally became *\*fell-ian* because of the *i* of the suffix, with the ending entirely eroding later on, leaving only *fell*. The Semitic vowel alteration to *a* would not have developed through an assimilation to an *-i* suffix, of course, but perhaps through the effect of a laryngeal. At any rate, the basic principles could have been fairly similar.

The earlier stage of the verbal system which we have so far reconstructed had only one internal vowel alteration to mark tense (*iprus-ipras*), had "normal" roots with both consonants and vowels, and was not even dominated by roots with three consonants. How could this system have metamorphosed into the mature Semitic system, with purely consonantal roots of predominantly three consonants? A relatively easy part of the question is how more three-consonant roots emerged. There are various indications that one of the main paths for this process involved cycles such as the English ones below, where verbs become longer through piling up of word-class-changing affixes:

| VERB | > | NOUN | > | ADJECTIVE | > | VERB |
|------|---|------|---|-----------|---|------|
| (to) tail (=cut) | | tailor | | | | (to) tailor |
| (to) profess | | profess-ion | | profess-ion-al | | (to) profess ion-al-ize |

In the Semitic languages, such augmentations mainly involved prefixes rather than suffixes. So a root that started out with two consonants, e.g., *kun* 'to be firm,' was turned into an adjective *ša-kun* 'firm/durable,' and then (through functional shift) back to a verb *šakun* 'to place, to establish.' At some stage, as more and more such augmented verbs emerged, roots with three consonants came to dominate the scene.

The trickier question is to understand how one simple vowel alteration (*iprus–ipras*) could have led to the idea of a purely consonantal root. The details are complex, but in order to understand the consonantal root, we actually only need to investigate how one further vowel alteration emerged, this time between the first two root consonants. There are two possible places for internal vowels between three consonants: $Ov_1Ov_2O$, or Position 1 and Position 2, for short. The vowel alteration in Position 1 could have emerged through a combination of sound change and analogical **back-formation**. The following discussion roughly describes the process. Augmented verbs (verbs like *šakun*, which had acquired their third consonant through a prefix) had a vowel in Position 1 (the vowel of the original augment prefix). But at some stage, a regular type of sound change deleted this vowel in *some* phonetic environments. In particular, this sound change (called **syncope**) deleted the middle vowel from any sequence of three short vowels in a row. In verbal forms with prefixes, like the past-tense *i-šakun*, the middle short vowel was in Position 1: *i-šakun > i-škun*. But in verbal forms with suffixes, like the verbal adjective *šakun-um*, the middle vowel of the three was in Position 2: *šakun-um > šakn-um*. This is illustrated in Figure LP13.3.

This process was a "blind" sound change, conditioned only by the phonetic environment, not by meaning. But the result of this purely phonetic change created a pattern in which one verbal form (*šakn-um*) had a vowel in Position 1, whereas another form (*i-škun*) had none (with the situation reversed in Position 2). For speakers in later generations, who were no longer familiar with the phonetic motivation for the sound change, this pattern could have come to be perceived as a bearer of a meaningful grammatical distinction. And once it was perceived as such, it could have been

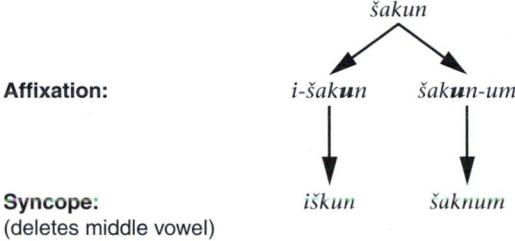

**Affixation:**       *i-šakun*       *šakun-um*

**Syncope:**          *iškun*        *šaknum*
(deletes middle vowel)

**Figure LP13.3**   The effects of syncope on forms with prefixes (left) and suffixes (right)

extended by analogical back-formation to roots like *prus* (which never had an augmented prefix to begin with), to produce a verbal adjective *pars-um*, effectively inserting a vowel into Position 1 that had never originally been there.

Once this pattern had been generalized to all verbs, it resulted in a system where the different verbal forms no longer shared any vowels: *iprus* ('he blocked'), *ipras* ('he will block'), *pars-um* ('blocked'). The root's original vowel (the *u* in Position 2) appeared in only one verbal form, so it no longer seemed to be the "default" vowel, but rather merely the vowel of one particular tense. Moreover, vowels were not shared between all verbal forms in either position, so both positions were seen to participate in the variation according to grammatical function.

For a new generation of speakers, all that remained as a uniting factor between the different verbal forms were the three consonants, or the consonantal root. For example, what now bears the core meaning 'to block' is no longer a pronounceable chunk *prus*, but the three consonants p-r-s. So the consonantal root system is simply based on the emergence of verbal forms that share the same consonants, but no longer share any vowels, and where both vowel positions are grammatically variable. The templates such as iOOuO, iOOaO, OaOOum, are really just a way of representing this pattern, whereby the internal vowels are primarily determined by the grammatical nuance, and not by the whim of the root.

The system we have arrived at through this description of prehistoric changes is still very simple, and is worlds away from the dozens of templates in the attested stages of the language. Deutscher (2000) shows how some of the more elaborate templates could have emerged (such as passive, causative, reflexive, intensive) through relatively straightforward paths of grammaticalization. Once a few such templates begin to emerge, speakers can start forming higher-level analogies, by superimposing existing templates onto one another (e.g., if a passive template emerged in the past tense, it could have been superimposed on the future tense, to give a future passive template). Thus, the complexity of the system is a self-amplifying process, in which the templates can interact by analogy in a grid-like way. A small number of templates might therefore have proven enough of a "critical mass" to trigger an explosion in the number of new templates, leading to the breathtaking sophistication of the attested system.

> ### TEXTBOX LP13.3 **GLOSSING CONVENTIONS USED IN THIS LANGUAGE PROFILE**
>
> | Convention | Meaning | Convention | Meaning |
> |---|---|---|---|
> | 1 | first person | M | masculine |
> | 2 | second person | PASS | passive |
> | 3 | third person | PL | plural |
> | CAUS | causative | POSS | possessive |
> | COND | conditional | PRF | perfect aspect |
> | FOC | focus | PRS | present |
> | FUT | future tense | PST | past tense |
> | GEN | genitive | PTCP | participle |
> | IMP | imperative | QUOT | quotative |
> | INF | infinitive | SG | singular |
> | ITR | iterative | VERBAL.ADJ | verbal adjective |

### SUGGESTIONS FOR FURTHER READING

**Benett, Patrick**. 1998. *Comparative Semitic linguistics*. Winona Lake, Ind.: Eisenbrauns.

This is a useful introduction to Semitic linguistics aimed at beginning students.

**Deutscher, G.** 2005. *The unfolding of language*. New York: Henry Holt.

Chapter 6 of this book gives a fuller account of the diachronic development outlined above.

**Huehnergard, J.** 1997. *A grammar of Akkadian*. Atlanta, Ga.: Scholars Press.

This book is a study grammar of Akkadian, suitable for self-study.

**Kouwenberg, N. J. C.** 2010. *The Akkadian verb and its Semitic background*. Winona Lake, Ind.: Eisenbrauns.

This book is an advanced magisterial history of the Akkadian and Semitic verbal system.

**Oppenheim, A. L.** 1964. *Ancient Mesopotamia: Portrait of a dead civilization*. University of Chicago Press.

This book is an introduction to the history and culture of Mesopotamia.
Web resource: http://knp.prs.heacademy.ac.uk/cuneiformrevealed/
An introduction to the world of Akkadian and the cuneiform writing system, as well as many other useful links.

### EXERCISES

1. Based on the information about different templates given in the chapter, and using the root š-ṭ-r, which means 'write' or 'inscribe,' find out how to say in Akkadian: *you (pl.) wrote, he writes, write!* (imperative or command form), *he made (someone) write, (something) is written*.

**Figure LP13.4** Word Written in Cuneiform Script (for Exercise 4)

2. The verb *liballiṭ* is a precative form (i.e., a wish form) of the root b-l-ṭ 'be well/healthy,' and means 'may he make (someone) well.' Can you identify the template on which the root was superimposed? In the letter quoted at the beginning of the chapter, there is a form *liballiṭūka*. What elements have been added to the form and how do they change the meaning?
3. The form *iztanammar* means 'he keeps singing.' Based on the templates in the chapter, can you identify the consonants of the Akkadian root 'sing'?
4. In the following word written in the cuneiform script, the first sign stands for *ḫa*, the third for *mu*, the fourth for *ra*. You can discover what the second and the fifth signs stand for based on the transcription of the letter in Figure LP13.2. Can you figure out what name is written here?

# GLOSSARY

**absolutive**: denotes both a case and a grammatical relation based on morphosyntactic behavior where the less agentive core argument of a transitive verb (the P) shares grammatical behavior with the single core argument of an intransitive verb (the S); opposed to ergative.

**abstraction**: a shift in meaning from more concrete to more abstract, e.g., the English adverb *besides* was used earlier for concrete spatial location, but is now used with the more abstract meaning 'in addition, moreover.'

**accent**: the phonological characteristics of a speaker's variety.

**accessible activation state**: an idea that is not currently actively focused on in a discourse, but which has been mentioned earlier and/or is in the periphery of the addressee's consciousness.

**accusative**: a grammatical **case** that marks noun phrases that occur as objects of clauses.

**acoustic phonetics**: the study of the physical characteristics of speech sounds, such as duration, frequency, and intensity.

**activation state**: an assumption that a particular referent or idea is **given**, **new**, or **accessible** in the mind of the interlocutor.

**active articulator**: an articulator which moves in the production of a sound; contrasts with **passive articulator**.

**active (voice)**: a construction in which the semantic agent of a transitive verb is the grammatical subject; contrasts with **passive (voice)**.

**adaptation**: the replacement of a foreign phoneme in a loanword with the nearest phonetic equivalent in the native language.

**addressee**: the person to whom an utterance is addressed (i.e., the person one is speaking to); sometimes referred to as "the hearer."

**adjective**: a word class whose members can occur either modifying a noun in a noun phrase or within a predicate; adjectives specify attributes of the referent of the associated noun.

**adposition**: a word class that occurs with a noun phrase and that indicates the grammatical, spatial, temporal, or logical relationship of the noun phrase to another element of the clause; may be a preposition (which occurs before the noun) or a postposition (which occurs after the noun); adpositions are typically **particles**.

**adpositional phrase**: a syntactic constituent headed by an adposition; includes prepositional phrases and postpositional phrases.

**adverb**: a cover term for words that are not lexical nouns, verbs, or adjectives, but that still have lexical (as opposed to grammatical) content.

**adverbial clause**: a dependent clause that is linked to a matrix clause by an adverbial conjunction or affix that specifies the semantic relationship between clauses, most commonly manner, time, location, quantity, condition, or cause.

**adverbial conjunction or affix**: a free word or affix that specifies the semantic relationship between clauses, e.g., conditional (English *if*), causal (*because*), temporal (*when*).

**affective filter**: the emotional component of an L2 learner's conscious learning process, which involves how comfortable or uncomfortable he or she is when speaking an L2.

**affix**: a morpheme attached to a root, e.g., the English plural -*s*.

**affricate**: a sound produced by combining a stop with a following fricative in rapid succession.

**African American English** (AAE): a variety of English spoken primarily by African Americans; it is overwhelmingly similar to other varieties of English but contains a number of distinctive grammatical, phonological, and lexical features.

**agent**: a semantic case role denoting the volitional instigator (the "do-er") of an activity or event.

**agentivity**: the degree of volition, control. or intention of an agent or potential agent.

**agglutinative**: a morphological structure in which the boundaries between morphemes are clear-cut and generally encode a one-to-one morpheme-to-meaning ratio; contrasts with **fusional**.

**agreement**: a type of inflection in which one word indexes semantic categories of another word.

**alignment patterns**: different grammatical relations based on whether the single core argument of an intransitive verb (also called the S) receives the same grammatical treatment (i.e., aligns with) the more agentive core argument of a transitive verb (the A) or the less agentive core argument of a transitive verb (the P). S/A versus P alignment is referred to as nominative-accusative alignment with the S/A defining subject and the P defining object; A versus S/P alignment is referred to as ergative-absolutive alignment with the A being the ergative and the S/P the absolutive.

**allomorph**: a phonetic variant of a morpheme, often motivated by the same phonetic forces that govern the occurrence of allophones; allomorphs of the English plural suffix include /s/, /z/, and /əz/.

**allophone**: two or more sounds that occur predictably in mutually exclusive environments, i.e., in **complementary distribution**.

**alternation (i)**: multiple forms of a phoneme, morpheme, syntactic construction, etc.

**alternation (ii)**: in sociolinguistics, code-switching that occurs between clauses.

**alveolar**: a sound made by placing the tip of the tongue against the alveolar ridge.

**alveolar ridge**: the hard ridge just behind the teeth before the upper surface of the mouth becomes more domed in shape.

**ambitransitive**: a verb that can be used both transitively (with two core arguments) and intransitively (with a single core argument); e.g., English *he tore his clothes, his clothes tore*.

**analogy**: a process by which speakers seek to repair perceived irregularities in their language; speakers remodel "exceptions" by analogy to other patterns.

**analytic**: see **isolating**.

**antepenultimate syllable**: the third-to-last syllable of a word, the syllable preceding the **penult**; sometimes called the **antepenult**.

**antonyms**: broadly, two or more lexemes or other expressions with opposite meanings; narrowly, two or more lexemes that are gradable **contraries**, so denote opposite ends of a spectrum, such as *short/tall* (the relation among antonyms is called **antonymy**).

**applied linguistics**: the field that considers how linguistics can be applied to situations in the world; includes language teaching, computational linguistics, forensic linguistics, language documentation, speech pathology, and speech and hearing sciences.

**approximant**: a sound produced through a slight narrowing of the vocal tract, but not enough to cause noise or a complete obstruction.

**argument**: a noun phrase holding a particular grammatical status in relation to a verb; can be **core** or **oblique**.

**articles**: a small class of grammatical particles that obligatorily occur in some noun phrases in some languages; often index the definiteness (identifiability) of a noun, e.g., *the* and *a(n)* in English.

**articulatory effort**: the degree of muscular effort required for the articulation of a particular sound.

**articulatory phonetics**: the study of how the vocal organs produce speech.

**aspect**: a grammatical category that signals the temporal consistency of an event or state, e.g., ongoing, completed, or habitual; often (but not always) marked on verbs or indicated by auxiliaries.

**aspiration**: the puff of air created by a delay in the onset of voicing upon the release of a stop.

**assimilation**: the process whereby one sound comes to share some phonetic property or cluster of properties with another sound in its environment; the most common type of phonological process; can involve voicing, nasalization, or point of articulation.

**associative plural**: a grammatical category typically marked by an affix on personal names; most commonly it refers to two or more people associated with the person who is named; e.g., Nepali *manoj-haru* 'Manoj and his group/kin/friends.'

**auditory phonetics**: the study of perception of phonetic properties of speech by the auditory system.

**autoglossonym**: (lit. "self-tongue-name") the name by which speakers of a language refer to that language; for example, *Deutsch* is the autoglossonym of the language that English speakers call German, *español* is the autoglossonym for the language known in English as Spanish, and *English* is the autoglossonym for English.

**automaticity**: the ability to process (linguistic) input and output quickly, unconsciously, and effortlessly, i.e., automatically, without having to think about each word or step in the process.

**autonym**: see **endonym**.

**auxiliary verbs**: a small subclass of verbs with fixed positions and abstract meanings; typically appear along with or instead of a main verb.

**back-formation**: a word-formation process based on an **analogy** in which the structural interpretation of one word is applied to a different word; frequently involves applying a morpheme boundary to a word that did not originally contain one, e.g., *ham-burger* from original *Hamburg*.

**backness**: a parameter for describing vowel sounds based on how far back the raised part of the tongue is during articulation; one of three main dimensions for describing vowels; may be *front, back,* or *central.*

**behaviorism**: a theory from psychology suggesting that if an L2 learner hears a stimulus in an L2 and repeats the word or sentence enough times, it will become a habit and can then be used to communicate successfully.

**beneficiary**: a semantic case role denoting an entity who benefits from an action.

**bidialectal**: able to speak two dialects.

**bilabial**: sound that involves a narrowing or complete closure of the upper and lower lip.

**bilingual**: a person who speaks two different languages or a society where primarily two languages are spoken; contrasts with **monolingual** and **multilingual**.

**borrowing**: the incorporation of a word or grammatical element from one language into another.

**bound morpheme**: a morpheme that cannot stand on its own as a word, e.g., English *un-*.

**broad phonetic transcription**: a level of phonetic transcription where detailed nuance (such as nasalization of vowels before nasal consonants) is not transcribed; contrasts with **narrow transcription**.

**calque**: a word or expression created via morpheme-by-morpheme translation from a source language.

**case**: the morphological marking of the syntactic and (in some cases) semantic relations that hold between the noun phrases and the verb of a sentence.

**causative**: a construction type that typically increases by one the number of core arguments in a clause; in a causative clause an agent typically causes a patient to perform some action; also used to refer to an affix that adds the meaning 'cause' or 'make,' e.g., the English *en-* of *en-able*.

**central**: a sound produced so that air flows through the center of the mouth rather than over the sides of the tongue; contrasts with **lateral**.

**Child-Directed Speech (CDS)**: a special register with distinctive linguistic properties that is used in certain societies for addressing very young children.

**CHILDES** (Child Language Data Exchange System): an online system of resources on language acquisition, including an archive of children's speech from various languages, programs for data analysis, and instructional materials.

**circumfix**: an affix that surrounds the root, with one part before it and another after it; circumfixes add meanings beyond those of the components.

**citation form**: the common, "dictionary" form of a word, with little or no inflection.

**classifier**: a word class whose members serve to classify a noun by shape, animacy, function and/or other criteria.

**clause**: a syntactic unit typically consisting of a verb (in some languages within a verb phrase), its noun phrase arguments, and adverbial elements (usually adverbs and adpositional phrases).

**clause chain**: a syntactic construction made up of one or more non-final clauses followed by a final clause; verbs in non-final clauses are marked by special suffixes, sometimes indicating switch reference.

**climax**: the culmination of a narrative plot, typically at the end of a **narrative**; something unusual or unexpected which makes the narrative worth listening to and telling.

**clitic**: a morpheme which is phonologically bound but which is able to combine with a broader range of stems than an **affix**; clitics frequently are not restricted to attaching to words from a single lexical class and have semantic scope over phrases as opposed to words; an **enclitic** is bound to the end of a word while a **proclitic** is bound to the beginning of a word.

**closed syllable**: a syllable that ends in a consonant.

**closed word class**: a word class, whose members are often small in number, which is resistant to new members.

**co-articulation**: an articulatory overlap between sounds in actual speech so that speech organs are preparing to produce the next sound while still producing the first.

**co-construction**: the process by which a linguistic unit, such as an utterance, conversation, or narrative, is produced by more than one person.

**coda**: a consonant or consonant cluster that follows the nucleus within the syllable.

**coded content**: the meanings conventionally associated with a linguistic form; contrasts with **utterance meaning**.

**code-switching**: the use of two or more languages in the same interaction or utterance, while conforming to the phonological and grammatical system of each language.

**cognates**: words in genetically related languages that are descended from the same word in a common parent language, e.g., Breton *dek*, Irish *deich*, Latvian *desmit*, Czech *deset*, Greek *déka*, Farsi *dah*, Hindi *das*, Dutch *tien*, Frisian *tsien*, Norwegian *ti*, Icelandic *tíu*, and English *ten*.

**cognition**: the mental processes that take in information from the environment, use it to form **mental representations**, and apply this stored knowledge in activities such as learning, thinking, speaking, and remembering.

**cognitive linguistics**: the study of how language is related to how humans learn and process information.

**collocations**: pairs of words that are frequently used together, and may be learned, processed, and produced as a chunk, e.g., *light lunch, pretty much, right now*, etc.

**communicative competence**: the knowledge of grammatical rules as well as the ability to use them in culturally appropriate ways; includes grammatical and sociolinguisitic competence.

**community of practice**: a social group that jointly engages in culturally meaningful activities and often develops distinctive ways of speaking.

**comparative**: an adjective, adverb, or similar morpheme that compares one thing to another; for example, the *-er* suffix in *an elephant is bigger than a mouse*, or the word *more* in *she has more money now*; see also: **superlative**.

**comparative method**: a procedure by which sounds, morphemes, and vocabulary of an earlier language can be reconstructed by comparing forms in the daughter languages.

**complement clauses**: dependent clauses that function as noun-phrase arguments of verbs.

**complementary antonyms** (aka **complemetaries**): a pair of expressions that make systematically and absolutely opposite contributions to the meaning of an expressed proposition: e.g., *on/off, once/never, real/imaginary*; can neither both be true nor both be false at any time; one is always true, and the other false.

**complementary distribution**: in phonology, a distributional pattern that occurs when two phonetically similar sounds do not occur in the same phonetic environment; indicates that the two sounds are allophones of a single phoneme.

**complex predicate**: two or more words that act as a single predicate of a single clause; the clause has only one set of arguments.

**complex sentence**: a sentence with more than one clause.

**complicating action**: a sequence of events in a **narrative** which are told after the introduction and which lead to the climax.

**compositionality (principle of)**: the idea that the meaning of a complex expression should be a regular function of the meanings of its parts.

**compositional semantics**: the study of how the meanings of complex expressions are built up from, or otherwise related to, the senses of their individual parts; also see **lexical semantics**.

**compound**: a word composed of two roots, stems, or words.

**computational linguistics**: the study of language and computers; includes speech recognition (computers recognizing human speech) and speech synthesis (computers producing speech).

**conceptual metaphor**: a figure of thought that allows one complex frame to be conceptualized in terms of another frame; e.g., UP is GOOD (the evaluative frame associated with *good* is conceptualized in terms of the spatial frame associated with *up*).

**concordance**: an index of all the words in a corpus along with their immediate linguistic contexts and some information about the frequency and location of each.

**conditioned sound change**: a sound change that occurs only in certain environments, for example, Old English *k* has been lost in present-day English, but only at the beginning of words before *n*, as in *knight* or *knuckle*.

**conjunctions**: a class of words, typically particles, which conjoin two or more words, phrases, or clauses at the same level of structure.

**connotation**: any effect or association arising from the use of a meaningful expression, aside from its reference; contrasts with an expression's **denotation**, that is, its effects on reference.

**consonant harmony**: a type of assimilation in which one consonant is produced with the same place or manner of articulation as a nearby consonant; see **vowel harmony**.

**constituent**: a subpart of a higher unit.

**constituent structure**: the constituents of a unit and their structural relationships.

**construal**: the process of understanding an expressed meaning; the imaginative enactment of propositional contents in the mind of a language user.

**constructed dialogue**: a stretch of speech which intends to quote or reproduce the speech of another person, but does not necessarily repeat the exact words of the quoted person.

**constructions**: fixed grammatical patterns associated with particular functions.

**contact**: see **language contact**.

**content question**: a question that requires informative content in the answer, rather than a simple 'yes' or 'no' (e.g., *where did you go?*); also known as 'wh-questions' based on the spelling patterns of the English interrogative pronouns *who, what, where, when, which,* and *why*.

**context**: the interactional, physical, cultural, and social environment in which utterances are produced.

**continuity hypothesis**: the hypothesis in nativist acquisition theory that children have the same syntactic categories and rules as adults from the outset.

**contrary antonyms** (aka **contraries**): a pair of lexemes or other expressions that denote opposite ends on a scale of alternatives: e.g., *short/tall, quiet/loud, eager/shy*; cannot both be true at any time, but both may be false.

**contrastive distribution**: the situation in which two or more sounds occur in the same position in otherwise identical words and the words have different meanings (i.e., the sounds occur in **minimal pairs**); sounds that are in contrastive distribution are separate phonemes; e.g., the English words *pat* and *bat* illustrate that /p/ and /b/ are in contrastive distribution and so constitute separate phonemes in English.

**convention**: a customary way of doing something in a community; an arbitrary behavior that people adhere to because they expect others to do the same.

**conversational topic**: a sequence of related ideas expressed through substantive intonation units.

**converse antonyms** (aka **converses**): a pair of lexemes or other expressions that denote the same situation from differing or "opposite" perspectives, e.g., *give/take, learn/teach, above/below*.

**coordination**: the combination of two independent elements of the same type using a conjunction; in clause-combining, refers to the formation of a complex sentence by linking two clauses using a conjunction; contrasts with **subordination**.

**copula**: a special type of verb, such as *be* in English, which denotes a relation between two noun phrases (e.g., *he is a teacher*) or between a noun phrase and an adjective (e.g., *he is tall*).

**copula clause**: a clause which relates a copula subject to a copula complement, usually using a copula verb.

**copula complement**: a noun or adjective which is related to the subject in a copula clause.

**copula subject**: the subject noun phrase of a copula clause, which is related to another noun or an adjective.

**core argument**: an argument that has a direct grammatical relationship with a verb.

**coreference/coreferential**: two or more morphemes, words, or other linguistic forms that index (i.e., point to, refer to) the same entity (i.e., the referent, thing referred to).

**corpora**: see *corpus*.

**corpus**: (pl. *corpora*) a database containing collected recordings of spoken or written language.

**corpus linguistics**: a methodology for linguistic analysis which examines statistically significant patterns over very large sets of discourse data with the help of computers.

**corpus planning**: a phase of **language planning** in which the "body" of the language is developed, such as its writing system, vocabulary, and grammar.

**creaky voice**: irregular relaxed vibrations superimposed on normal voicing, often evident at the ends of spoken sentences.

**creole**: a pidgin which is learned by children as a native language and in the process undergoes significant development in order to meet the communicative needs of native speakers; e.g., Tok Pisin.

**Critical Period Hypothesis (CPH)**: the view that there is a biologically determined period for language to be learned naturally and perfectly; also referred to as the "sensitive period."

**cross-sectional research**: in first language acquisition, research which compares children in different age groups at a single point in time, either in their spontaneous speech or in their performance of an experimental task.

**cuneiform**: a writing system used in ancient Mesopotamia; the word cuneiform means 'wedge-shaped' and refers to signs made with a stylus on wet clay.

**dative**: a nominal case used with semantic recipient noun phrases of ditransitive verbs.

**death**: see **language death**.

**decategorialization**: a process by which a word from a major lexical class, such as a noun, verb, or adjective, loses characteristics typical of that class, particularly inflection, e.g.,

English modals, which have developed from full verbs, but no longer show agreement: *He will have run*, not *He will-s ha-s run*.

**declension**: a traditional grammar term for the phonological forms that result from morphological case inflections.

**definite**: grammatical marking on a noun phrase which indicates identifiability, i.e., the speaker believes the addressee will be able to identify the referent; can be marked using an article (e.g., English *the*); contrasts with **indefinite**.

**deictic expressions**: words or constructions that point to some aspect of an utterance context, e.g., the place and time of an utterance (*here*, *now*), speaker (*I*), addressee (*you*).

**deixis**: a symbolic pointing relation between a linguistic sign and its context of utterance.

**deletion**: the phonological process by which a sound is lost (i.e., deleted).

**demonstrative**: a small closed class of words that occur in the noun phrase and that have a deictic ("pointing") function; typically differentiates **proximal** (e.g., *this*) and **distal** (e.g., *that*), in addition to other categories.

**demonstrative pronoun**: a demonstrative that occurs in the syntactic position of a pronoun, e.g., *that* in *That bothers me*.

**denotation**: the thing, state, or event that a linguistic expression refers to in the real world, or, more precisely, in some large set of possible worlds; the potential referents of an expression.

**dense sampling**: in language acquisition research, obtaining more frequent samples of child speech than is customary, e.g., at least five hours per week.

**dental**: a sound made by placing the tip of the tongue against the back of the upper teeth.

**dependent**: an element that modifies and is structurally subordinate to a head; can refer to words, phrases, and clauses.

**derivation**: a morphological process that creates new lexemes; derivational processes may change the word class of the stem they are added to, e.g., *govern/govern-ment* (verb → noun), though this is not always the case.

**descriptive**: an approach to language that describes how people actually use language without evaluating language use as either "right" or "wrong"; contrasts with **prescriptive**.

**determiner**: a cover term for a set of word classes that can occupy a single slot in a noun phrase; in English these include articles, demonstratives, and possessives.

**diachrony**: referring to two (*dia-*) or more points in time (*-chrony*); an example of a diachronic description would be a comparison of the vowel system of Old English with the vowel system of English today; contrasts with **synchrony**.

**dialect**: a variety of a language that is characteristic of a group defined on the basis of geographic or social factors, and that is mutually intelligible with other dialects of the same language despite differences in phonology or grammar.

**dialect continuum**: a situation in which speakers of adjacent language varieties can understand each other, but speakers of geographically separated varieties cannot.

**dictionary**: a standard way of representing a mental or social **lexicon** as a list of lexemes ordered alphabetically by spelling, each with information about its uses, its senses, and its pronunciations.

**diffusion**: the spread of linguistic features from one language to another.

**diglossia**: a multidialectal or multilingual situation in which two varieties of speech (either dialects or languages) are used in different social domains; if three or more languages or dialects are involved, the term **multiglossia** is used.

**digraph**: an orthographic representation of a single sound with two orthographic characters (letters or symbols); e.g., *ng* for the English velar nasal consonant.

**diphthong**: a combination of vowels that functions as a single unit in the sound system; contrasts with **monophthong**.

**direct object**: a grammatical relation based on morphosyntactic behavior shared by the object of transitive verbs and the non-recipient object of ditransitive verbs.

**discourse**: a stretch of language larger than a phrase or sentence, such as a narrative or conversation; (the study of) spontaneous speech in its natural context.

**discourse analysis**: analysis of how speakers use linguistic structures in stretches of language larger than the sentence for the purposes of communication; includes language and interaction, conversational analysis, information structuring, etc.

**discourse marker**: a lexical item that is independent of the grammar of the clause but performs discourse-level or interactional functions.

**discourse-marker switch**: code-switching that occurs at a discourse marker.

**discourse particle**: a **particle** with discourse-interactional functions, such as *oh, hmm*, or *yeah*.

**dissimilation**: the phonological process by which one sound becomes less like another nearby sound.

**distal demonstrative**: a demonstrative word that indicates things farther from the speaker and hearer (e.g., English *that*).

**distributive**: a grammatical category (typically in the verb) that indicates that an action occurs repeatedly across multiple individual participants.

**ditransitive**: verbs that take three core arguments.

**double-object construction**: a construction in English and some other languages in which the two objects of a ditransitive verb are positioned directly following the verb, with the semantic recipient first; e.g., *John gave Fred the book*.

**dual**: a grammatical number category specifying two; contrasts with **singular** (one) and **plural** (many).

**ejective**: an obstruent (usually a stop) made with glottal closure accompanying closure in the oral cavity; the glottis is raised to compress the trapped air, producing a characteristic "popping" sound upon release.

**ellipsis**: this is when a linguistic unit, such as a word, phrase, or clause, is not uttered; the unexpressed unit can be understood in the speech context by the listener without explicit mention.

**embed**: in syntax, the positioning of a phrase, clause, or sentence as a constituent of another element of lesser or equal complexity; e.g., a clause that functions as a constituent of a noun phrase (such as a relative clause) is said to be embedded within the noun phrase.

**emotive content**: those aspects of an expression's meaning that reflect a speaker's attitude toward or evaluation of what is spoken about.

**empirical**: based on observable or experimental data.

**enclitic**: a **clitic** which occurs on the right edge of the word that it is bound to.

**encyclopedias** and **encyclopedic knowledge**: the mental encyclopedia contains knowledge that supplements the lexicon and includes information ***not*** included in a lexeme's semantic contents; more generally, encyclopedic knowledge encompasses both general and expert knowledge about the world.

**endangerment**: when a language begins to lose speakers, often from population loss or **language shift**, and becomes threatened with obsolescence or death.

**endonym**: a name for a language used by speakers of that language; also called an autonym; contrasts with **exonym**.

**entailment**: a relation between two propositions, P and Q, such that if P is true and P entails Q, then Q must also be true.

**ergative**: a grammatical relation based on morphosyntactic behavior (frequently case) unique to the more agentive argument of transitive and ditransitive verbs; ergative case thus marks the more agent-like argument of a transitive verb; opposed to **absolutive**.

**ergative-absolutive**: a language system organized on the basis of ergative and absolutive grammatical relations; see also: **nominative-accusative**.

**ethnonym**: the name applied to the people of a given ethnic group.

**evaluative device**: in narrative research, the particular linguistic and non-linguistic strategies, such as repetition, that the narrator uses to highlight the significance or point of the story, i.e., why it is worth telling.

**evaluative function**: in narrative research, the function of conveying the significance or point of the story, i.e., why it is worth telling.

**evidential**: a grammatical category (sometimes a word class) whose members indicate the source and/or certainty of knowledge communicated in a statement.

**exclusive**: a category used in first-person plural reference to include the speaker and at least one other, but not the hearer; contrasts with **inclusive**.

**exonym**: a name for a language used by outsiders, not by speakers of that language; contrasts with **endonym**.

**expansion**: in language acquisition, a caregiver utterance that provides a fuller, more grammatical version of a preceding child utterance that is incomplete or ungrammatical.

**experiencer**: a semantic case role denoting an entity that experiences a physical or emotional state.

**experimental research**: a type of study in which the researcher manipulates linguistic or contextual features to observe the effects on the performance of a particular task.

**explicated inferences**: a type of pragmatic inference that is required in order to determine the explicit message of an utterance.

**explicature**: the linguistic code enriched by **explicated inferences** in order to "fill in the blanks" and obtain the full message of an utterance.

**expression**: a reusable linguistic form.

**extralinguistic competence**: the ability to use knowledge of the world (not included in the linguistic system) to interpret the meaning of utterances.

**family tree** or **Stammbaum**: a schematic representation of the relationships among languages in a family, that is, all of those languages descended from a common ancestral language; typically represented in a branching "tree" structure.

**fictive motion**: the depiction of a static situation – like a road over some terrain, or a sloping roof – as a path that one imaginatively travels; e.g., *The road winds through the mountains*, *The roof slopes gently (up/down)*.

**figure**: an entity that is profiled with respect to a **ground**.

**finite**: a clause or verb with marking that indicates tense, aspect, mood, and/or evidentiality; contrasts with **non-finite**.

**first language acquisition**: the process by which young children come to know and use the language(s) of their caregivers.

**first person**: refers to the speaker; *I*.

**flap**: a sound produced with extremely short complete closure at the alveolar ridge; differentiated from an alveolar stop by the extreme shortness of the closure for the flap; sometimes also referred to as a **tap**.

**forensic linguistics**: the examination of linguistic evidence in legal proceedings.

**formal theory**: linguistic theories that analyze structures independently of function, instead constructing a formal model of linguistic knowledge based on abstract categories, structures, and principles; the model is posited to represent a single Universal Grammar taken to be part of humankind's genetic endowment.

**fortition**: the phonological process by which consonants take on greater obstruction or become "stronger," as when a fricative becomes a stop.

**fossilization**: in second language acquisition, an end-state of acquisition in which the learner's L2, still not native-like in certain respects, does not develop further; this state can apply to linguistic items or to subsystems of the learner's L2, such as the phonological system; that is, other subsystems, such as syntax, may continue to develop.

**fragmentary intonation units**: an intonation unit which is not completed, such as when interrupted or when restarting a word or phrase; also known as fragmentary phrases.

**frame, semantic**: the background knowledge associated with an expression, distinct from its **profile**.

**frame elements**: the participants and relations in a semantic frame.

**free morpheme**: a morpheme that can stand on its own as a word, e.g., English *house* or *of*.

**free variation**: the situation in which two or more allophones of a phoneme may occur in the same word without creating a difference in meaning.

**fricative**: a sound in which the two articulators are close together, but not so tightly occluded that no air can escape through the mouth.

**fronting**: a **phonological error pattern** in which a child moves consonants forward in the mouth; e.g., pronouncing car [kaɹ] as [da] by replacing velar [k] with alveolar [d].

**full reduplication**: see **reduplication**.

**function**: the purpose for which a linguistic structure is used in context.

**functional continuity**: the persistence of the same function (e.g., direct listener's attention) over time, even though that function may be expressed by different non-linguistic or linguistic forms as time passes.

**functional discourse-based theories of first language acquisition**: theories that attribute the process of first language acquisition to general cognitive abilities such as learning and analogy; contrast with **nativist theories**.

**functional discourse-based theory**: linguistic theories based on the premise that language is shaped by its role as a tool of human communication, including its embedding in general human cognition and its role in human social, cultural, and communicative interaction; focuses on both formal and functional properties of language; takes naturally occurring discourse as the primary source of data that has bearing on the central questions of the field.

**fundamental frequency**: the rate of vocal fold vibration, perceived as pitch.

**fusional**: a morphological structure in which the boundaries between morphemes are no longer clear-cut; the English plural noun *feet* shows fusional structure: it is difficult to separate the root 'foot' from the plural suffix (see the Seneca Language Profile for an excellent example of a fusional language).

**gemination**: the process by which a consonant is doubled or lengthened; the consonant is referred to as a **geminate**.

**generalization**: a gradual process of change in which a particular linguistic form is applied in an increasing number of cases, so that the frequency of the form increases and its function/meaning becomes more general; used in discussing language change and language acquisition.

**genetic relationship**: the relationship among all languages and dialects descended from the same parent language; English and German are genetically related, but not English and Japanese.

**genitive**: a nominal case used when the noun is a possessor (*brother's book*) or when the noun holds a similar relationship with another noun.

**genre**: a variety of discourse; includes written or spoken, fiction, nonfiction, storytelling, conversation, interviews, e-mail, text messaging, newspaper articles, etc.

**gerund**: a noun derived from a verb; frequently gerunds serve as verbal complements, as in *I enjoy learning languages*, where the gerund *learning* is part of the object complement, or *Swimming laps can be tiring*, where *swimming* is the verb of the subject complement.

**given information**: information that is activated in the listener's mind because it has just been mentioned or is obvious in context; therefore it is information that the speaker assumes to be already in the focal consciousness of the addressee.

**gliding**: in language acquisition, a **phonological error pattern** in which a child substitutes the glides [j] or [w] for liquids [l] and [ɹ], e.g., pronouncing *lap* [læp] as [jæp]; see **phonological error pattern**.

**gloss**: the translated representation of a morpheme's meaning; frequently won't capture the full meaning of a morpheme, due to translational issues.

**glottal**: referring to the glottis or vocal folds; a sound made with the glottis as the place of articulation.

**glottalization**: a secondary articulation involving the production of a glottal constriction in conjunction with one or more non-glottal segments.

**glottal stop**: a stoppage of voicing created by blocking off all airflow through the larynx by closing the **glottis**.

**glottis**: within the larynx, the space between the vocal cords which opens and closes when the vocal cords vibrate; controls **voicing** and other aspects of phonation.

**goal**: a semantic case role denoting the endpoint of a motion trajectory.

**grammar**: the morphology and syntax of a language, also known as morphosyntax. (Note: this is a complex term used in a number of ways in linguistics; this definition is the one used most frequently within this book.)

**grammatical borrowing**: a borrowing of grammatical elements such as syntactic structures, derivational affixes, or lexemes from a grammatical word class.

**grammatical relations**: relationships between core arguments and verbs and that are marked by particular grammatical behaviors, such as agreement, case-markers, or constraints on ordering.

**grammatical word classes**: those classes whose words have more abstract meanings; often grammatically obligatory; contrasts with **lexical word classes**.

**grammaticalization** (also known as **grammaticization**): the development of a lexical item, such as a noun or verb, into a grammatical morpheme, or the shift of a grammatical morpheme into a more grammatical morpheme.

**grapheme**: a single written character used in the orthographic system of a language; does not necessarily correspond to a single phoneme.

**Great Vowel Shift**: a series of changes in English beginning around 1400 by which originally long vowels were raised, that is, pronounced with the tongue rising higher in the mouth.

**Grice's Maxims**: the set of four maxims (rules) that Grice claims interactional participants follow in order to cooperatively reach understanding; includes the maxims of **Quantity** (speakers should provide just enough information, neither too much nor too little), **Quality** (speakers must assert truthful and well-supported information), **Relevance** (speakers must make their contributions relevant to the ongoing interaction), and **Manner** (speakers must be brief, clear, unambiguous, and orderly).

**ground**: a reference point or reference situation against which a **figure** is profiled.

**habitual**: an **aspect** indicating that an event occurred, occurs, or will occur repeatedly and with some regularity.

**habitual *be***: in African American English, the use of uninflected *be* as an aspectual marker indicating habitual or repeated activity, rather than as a copula.

**hard palate**: the hard portion of the upper surface of the mouth behind the alveolar ridge.

**harsh voice**: irregular vibrations superimposed on normal voicing by a tense larynx.

**head**: the element that determines the syntactic function of a phrase (e.g., a phrase headed by a noun is called a *noun phrase* and occupies the syntactic position of a noun within a clause); must be present for its modifiers or **dependents** to appear.

**head noun**: the noun in a noun phrase; typically mentioned in contrast to its **dependents**; sometimes specifically refers to the noun modified by a dependent relative clause.

**heavy syllable**: a complex syllable in a **weight-sensitive stress** system; depending on the language, syllables are heavy when they have a syllable-final coda consonant, a long vowel, or a diphthong; contrasts with light syllable.

**height**: a parameter for describing vowel sounds based on height of the tongue during articulation; one of three main dimensions for describing vowels; may be *high*, *low*, or *mid*.

**historical linguistics**: the study of how languages change over time, how languages are related, and how they have descended from a language spoken in the past; includes the study of language contact.

**homonyms**: lexemes or expressions that share the same form (in spelling, in pronunciation, or in both) but have different senses; e.g., *sea* and *see*.

**hypernym**: a term, *a*, which is less specific than some other term, *b*, and which therefore has a broader denotation; thus *move* is a hypernym of *walk*, and *cook* is a hypernym of *fry*.

**hyponym**: a term, *a*, which is more specific than some other term, *b*, and which therefore has a narrower denotation; thus, *amble* is a hyponym of *walk*, and *mumble* is a hyponym of *speak* (the relation among hyponyms is called **hyponymy**).

**iambic feet**: units composed of a sequence of two syllables, the second of which is stressed.

**icon**: a type of sign for which the signifier somehow resembles its signified; contrasts with **index** and **symbol**.

**identifiability**: whether the speaker assumes an idea is given, accessible, or new to the addressee.

**identity**: the social positioning of self and other, including demographic categories, styles, relational roles, interactional roles, stances, and personas.

**ideology of language acquisition**: the beliefs held by an individual or social group about how children acquire language, e.g., by imitating adult speech.

**ideophone**: a word class where the words convey a sensory perception of a color, a smell, a shape, an action, etc.; often exhibits phonological and morphological peculiarities; a well-known subset of ideophones are **onomatopoeic** words, i.e., words that imitate a sound.

**idiom**: a multi-word expression whose meaning cannot be simply constructed from the meaning of its parts.

**idiomaticity**: relating to one or more idioms, complex expressions with conventional senses (meanings) that cannot be predicted from the senses of their parts, i.e., where the sense is not entirely compositional.

**imagery**: any visual, auditory, tactile, olfactory, or somato-sensory associations that a linguistic expression may have.

**imperfective**: an **aspect** used to present a situation from an internal viewpoint, so that it is portrayed as though in progress, repeated, or habitually recurring; contrasts with perfective.

**implicature**: a type of pragmatic inference that the speaker intends the addressee to infer based on a set of contextually available assumptions; unlike logical inferences, implicatures are only plausible, but do not follow necessarily; also referred to as particularized conversational implicature.

**implosive**: a type of voiced stop consonant produced by moving the glottis downward (thus creating a vacuum) before releasing the stop; implosives are written in the IPA by adding a hook to the top of the letter, e.g., [ɓ], [ɗ], [ɠ].

**inceptive**: an **aspect** indicating the beginning of an activity or entrance into a state.

**inclusive**: a category used in first-person plural reference to include the speaker, hearer, and perhaps others; contrasts with **exclusive**.

**indefinite**: grammatical marking on a noun phrase that indicates non-identifiability, i.e., the speaker does not believe the addressee will be able to identify the referent; can be marked using an article (e.g., English *a*); contrasts with **definite**.

**index (i)** (noun): in semantics, a type of sign for which the **signifier** and the **signified** are somehow physically or causally connected; contrasts with **icon** and **symbol**.

**index (ii)** (verb): in sociocultural linguistics, to use language symbolically to convey a social meaning.

**indexicality**: the use of language to convey a context-specific meaning.

**indirect object**: a grammatical relation pertaining only to the recipient object of ditransitive verbs.

**infix**: an affix that appears inside of the root (not just inside of the word).

**inflection**: morphological processes that do not create new lexemes (mental dictionary entries), but simply add grammatical meaning such as past tense, plural number, or case.

**insertion (i)**: the phonological process by which a sound is added (i.e., inserted).

**insertion (ii)**: code-switching of a lexical item within a single clause.

**instrument** (or **instrumental**): a semantic case role denoting an entity that is used to perform an action.

**intensity**: the strength of a sound wave, perceived as loudness.

**interactional meaning**: those aspects of an expression's meaning that serve to build the flow of discourse or to manage relations among the discourse participants.

**interactional role**: a role within social interaction that performs a specific linguistic activity such as narrating, asking a question, etc.

**Interaction Hypothesis**: a hypothesis proposed by Long (1996) which claims that language development is promoted by the interactions between speakers through

**negotiation for meaning**, particularly the types of negotiation that trigger interactional adjustments by the L1 (or more competent) speaker.

**interdental**: a consonant sound made by placing the tip of the tongue between the upper and lower teeth.

**interference**: in language contact, changes to a language made due to incomplete acquisition by speakers of other languages.

**interlanguage**: the L2 language system created by a learner; the combination of structural elements of a language learner's first and second languages that results from the learner's incomplete mastery of the second language.

**interrogative pronoun**: an interrogative word ("question word") that occurs in the syntactic position of a pronoun, e.g., *who* in *Who came to the house?*

**intersubjective**: occurring across separate conscious minds through shared experience and consensus.

**intonation**: the changes in fundamental frequency (perceived as pitch) that occur during a phrase or utterance; adds meaning to spoken discourse.

**intonation unit**: a segment of speech characterized by a single coherent pitch contour, often by declining pitch, volume, and/or rapidity, as well as by preceding and following pauses; also called **prosodic phrase**.

**intransitive**: verbs that take at most one core argument.

**isolating** or **analytic**: a morphological structure in which each word has very few morphemes, usually just one, i.e., there are no or only several affixes or clitics; common in a number of Southeast Asian languages, such as Vietnamese; contrasts with **synthetic** or **polysynthetic**.

**item and arrangement**: a type of morphological description that specifies the environment where each of two or more allomorphs occurs.

**item and process**: a type of morphological description that posits a basic form of each allomorph and then states a set of processes (phonological rules) that derive each of the non-basic allomorphs.

**L1**: one's first language, often called one's native language or mother tongue.

**L2**: one's non-native second language, learned as an adolescent or adult.

**labeled tree diagram**: a schematic representation of the hierarchical structure of a phrase, clause, or sentence; includes a labeled node for each phrase and labels for word classes.

**labiodental**: a sound that involves a narrowing or complete closure between the upper teeth and the lower lip.

**language**: a mode of communication used by humans, usually spoken but also written or signed; distinguished from a **dialect** by **mutual intelligibility**: speakers of two separate languages are unable to understand each other.

**language acquisition**: (the study of) how language is learned, includes **first language acquisition** (the study of how children learn their native language) and **second language acquisition** (the study of how speakers learn a language that is not their native tongue).

**language and the brain**: the field that examines the neurological basis of language.

**language change**: a language innovation that spreads throughout a speech community to become a regular feature of the language.

**language conservation**: efforts to keep a language alive within a speech community through finding ways to promote its use; often includes development of materials to be used in education, as well as activities leading to language documentation.

**language contact**: the situation in which speakers of two or more distinct languages interact with each other, leading to changes in one or more of the languages.

**language death**: the loss of a language that occurs when the last speaker of the language dies and the language ceases to be a symbolic marker of identity for the community.

**language documentation**: the creation of an extensive record of a language and how it is used by the speech community; typically involves creation of an analyzed archive of recordings of authentic speech and frequently the production of a dictionary and grammar.

**language family**: all of the languages and dialects that have developed from a single, common ancestral language.

**language ideology**: a culturally shared belief or attitude about language and its users.

**language of thought**: the building blocks of (pre-linguistic) human conceptual structure, which allow us to imagine and think about the world in general, and which constitute the ultimate source for the semantic content of linguistic expressions.

**language planning**: the deliberate and systematic development and promotion of a language, usually through government-sponsored institutions and policies.

**language revitalization**: efforts on the part of communities whose languages have been entirely lost or significantly reduced to increase the number of speakers and domains of use.

**language shift**: the process in which members of a speech community adopt a different language and discontinue speaking their original language.

**language transmission**: the passing on of a language from one generation to the next.

**larynx**: the part of the vocal tract that contains the vocal folds; located behind the thyroid cartilage (or Adam's apple).

**lateral**: a sound produced with a closure only in the center of the mouth so that air flows over the side(s) of the tongue; contrasts with **central**.

**lative**: a grammatical case that indicates motion toward a location.

**lax**: a phonetic property of vowels produced with tongue positioned toward the center of the vowel space; contrasts with **tense**; tense vowels tend to be shorter than lax vowels.

**lenition**: the phonological process by which consonants become less consonant-like and more vowel-like, e.g., shifts from voiceless to voiced stops (such as p > b), stops to fricatives (b > v), and fricatives to glides (v > w); also known as "weakening."

**leveling**: the use of identical inflection across different forms of the same lexical item.

**lexeme**: a vocabulary item in the mental lexicon; a single lexeme, e.g., English *freeze*, might have several word forms, such as *freeze, freezes, freezing, froze*, and *frozen*.

**lexical borrowing**: (verb) the phonological and grammatical integration of a lexical item from one language into another language; (noun) a loanword from a lexical word class.

**lexical bundles**: expressions that recur; sometimes idiomatic; may have a range of structures.

**lexical collocations**: particular lexemes or expressions which are common throughout a given **linguistic area**.

**lexicalization**: the addition of a morphological formation to the mental lexicon as a single unit, or a recognizable vocabulary item (lexical item); e.g., *inappropriateness* is lexicalized, whereas *inelegantness* is not, though it could become lexicalized if it were used often enough.

**lexically conditioned**: allomorphs whose occurrence (distribution) cannot be predicted on the basis of the sounds around them, but simply must be learned with the individual word, e.g., the plurals *mice* and *alumni*.

**lexical overextension**: in language acquisition, a type of error in which a word is applied to a larger number of referents than is appropriate in adult speech; see **referent** and **overextension**.

**lexical semantics**: the study of the kinds of meanings associated with individual expressions, including morphemes, lexemes, and idioms; contrasts with **compositional semantics**.

**lexical suffix**: a suffix that expresses a concrete lexical meaning rather than an abstract grammatical function.

**lexical underextension**: in first language acquisition, a type of error in which a word is applied to a smaller set of referents than is appropriate in adult speech; see **referent** and **underextension**.

**lexical word classes**: those classes whose words typically convey a wide range of concrete and often specific meanings; contrasts with **grammatical word classes**.

**lexicon**: the mental dictionary; the speaker's knowledge of the words of a language and how they are used.

**lexifier**: in a situation of creolization, a language that provides vocabulary used in the pidgin that becomes a creole; see also: **superstrate**.

**light syllable**: a type of syllable in a **weight-sensitive stress** system; typically if a syllable ends in a short vowel without a coda consonant, it is considered light; contrast with **heavy syllable**.

**lingua franca**: a language used as a frequent means of communication between speakers of multiple other languages; frequently used in commerce.

**linguist**: a person who examines the structures of languages and the principles underlying those structures; one who practices linguistics.

**linguistic analysis**: the process of recognizing and analyzing systematic patterns in languages.

**linguistic area**: a geographic region with languages from two or more different language families that have shared linguistic features due to borrowing or diffusion; also known as a Sprachbund.

**linguistic exogamy**: marriage to a person who speaks a different language.

**linguistic feature**: a specific form used by a speaker at any linguistic level, including the pronunciation of a specific vowel or consonant, the use of a particular grammatical structure, a certain lexical choice, or a particular interactional practice.

**linguistic paleontology**: the reconstruction of aspects of the life and culture of the speakers of a proto-language based on reconstructed vocabulary.

**linguistic repertoire**: the range of linguistic varieties available to a speaker.

**linguistic typologist**: a linguist who studies the classifications of languages based on structure and looks for relationships between structural types.

**linguistic typology**: a subfield of linguistics concerned with describing and classifying linguistic structures in the world's languages, with finding correlations between structures, and with classifying languages based on their structural types.

**linguistic variety**: a cover term for any type of linguistic system with characteristic phonological, grammatical, and lexical features, including languages, dialects, registers, and styles.

**linguistics**: the scientific study of language.

**lip rounding**: a parameter for describing vowel sounds based on whether the lips are rounded during articulation; may be *rounded* or *unrounded*.

**liquid**: a category of sounds which includes lateral approximants and r-type sounds.

**loanword**: a word that has been borrowed into one language from another language; see **borrowing**.

**local process**: a phonological process governed by an adjacent environment; contrasts with **non-local** or **long-distance process**.

**locative**: a semantic relation of location and/or the grammatical marking of location by case; refers to static location when contrasting with categories of source and/or goal.

**logogram**: a written character which represents a whole word.

**long-distance process**: a phonological process governed by a non-adjacent environment (e.g., **vowel harmony**); also called a **non-local process**; contrasts with **local process**.

**longitudinal research**: in first language acquisition, a type of research which follows the language development of one or more individual children over time.

**main clause**: a grammatical structure that consists of an independent verb plus optional elements such as noun phrases, adverbs, and particles; compare **matrix clause**.

**main verb**: the **verb** that carries the more concrete semantic information about the action, state, or relation described in a clause.

**manner of articulation**: the degree of narrowness of the constriction in the vocal tract involved in producing sound; can vary from slight narrowing (for approximants) to complete blockage (for stops).

**matrix clause**: the grammatically primary clause in a complex sentence; the head clause upon which other clauses are dependent; similar to a **main clause**, but also implies a relationship with a dependent clause.

**mean intensity**: the arithmetic average of intensity measurements over a phrase.

**Mean Length of Utterance (MLU)**: the average number of morphemes per utterance in a sample of speech; used in language acquisition research as a measure of linguistic development.

**mental representation**: forms of stored information/knowledge in the mind, including imaginal forms such as mental images, symbolic forms such as words and grammatical constructions, and physiological forms such as patterns of neural activation in the brain.

**merger**: the merger of two phonemes into one, e.g., the vowels of English *beat* and *beet* were originally separate phonemes that underwent merger.

**metaphor**: the extension of an expression typically used in one semantic domain to use in another, e.g., the term *leap*, which refers to a kind of jump, is now often used metaphorically in such expressions as *a leap of faith*; based on analogical reasoning.

**metathesis**: the phonological process by which two sounds are transposed.

**metonymy**: a kind of semantic shift whereby the meaning of a word, expression, or construction comes to refer to an associated object or situation; e.g., *be going to* shifting from denoting a motion event to denoting future tense or purpose.

**minimal pair**: a pair of words with different meanings, which differ in only one sound occurring in the same environment; used to determine whether two sounds are phonemes in a language.

**minimal set**: a set of more than two words with different meanings that differ in only one sound occurring in the same environment.

**monitor**: a cognitive process of an L2 learner; the learner's cognitive "watchdog" that consciously reviews what the learner has said in the L2 and monitors it for correctness.

**monolingual**: a person who speaks one language, or a society in which only one language is spoken (the latter situation is rare); contrasts with **bilingual** and **multilingual**.

**monophthong**: a vowel produced with a single articulatory configuration; contrasts with **diphthong**.

**mood**: a grammatical category marking the probability or reality of an utterance (e.g., declarative, subjunctive, interrogative, etc.).

**morpheme**: the smallest meaningful part of a word; includes roots, affixes, clitics, and particles.

**morphology**: the study of the internal structure of words and the principles underlying such structuring.

**morphosyntactic behavior**: the patterns of morphological and syntactic occurrence and positioning of a word; can be used to determine word class.

**morphosyntax**: the morphology and syntax of a language and their interaction; also known as grammar.

**multilingual**: a person who speaks three or more languages or a society in which multiple languages are spoken; contrasts with **monolingual** and **bilingual**.

**mutual intelligibility**: the ability of speakers of two or more language varieties to understand each other (a possible criterion for distinguishing language from dialect).

**narrative**: the relation of a sequence of events, traditionally following a **narrative schema**.

**narrative co-construction**: the production of a narrative by more than one person; see **co-construction**.

**narrative schema**: a pattern of storytelling that introduces characters, places elements in space and time, and progresses through events toward the climax.

**narrow phonetic transcription**: a phonetic transcription that seeks to record as much detail as possible, for example, transcribing nasalized vowels before nasal consonants where a **broad phonetic transcription** might not.

**nasal**: a sound produced with air passing through the nose; contrasts with **oral**.

**nativist theories**: theories of first language acquisition based upon the view that innate grammatical structures (**Universal Grammar**) are required to explain the process of first language acquisition; contrast with **functional discourse-based theories of first language acquisition**.

**natural class**: a group of sounds sharing one or more phonetic features that pattern together in a phonological system; to be a natural class, a group of sounds must share one or more phonetic features and must include all of the sounds in that language which share those features.

**near-minimal pair**: a pair of words that differ in more than one sound, but in which the sounds immediately adjacent to the target sounds are the same in both words; used to determine whether two sounds are phonemes in a language when no minimal pair can be found.

**negation**: syntactic or morphological marking of negative meaning (i.e., 'not').

**negative concord**: the marking of negation in more than one possible grammatical position.

**negotiation for meaning**: a type of linguistic interaction to facilitate communication; L2 learners signal difficulty in understanding their interlocutor, using conversational strategies to seek clarification or elaboration.

**neurology**: the study of the nervous system; for linguistics, the primary neurological domain of relevance is the brain.

**neutralization** (verb: **neutralize**): when a linguistic distinction that is made in one context is not made – i.e., is neutralized – in another; for example, in German the phonemic distinction between /t/ and /d/ is neutralized in word-final position (only /t/ is found), and in Spanish the distinction between masculine and feminine gender is neutralized (not made) in first-person and second-person pronouns.

**new activation state**: an idea which the addressee is unlikely to be focused on and which the speaker introduces into the discourse, thus activating it.

**new information**: information a speaker assumes is not already in the focal consciousness of the addressee, since it is being mentioned for the first time or is not obvious in context.

**nominal**: a cover term for nouns and noun-like expressions; in Finnish, these include nouns, pronouns, and adjectives.

**nominalizer**: an affix that creates nouns; the English suffixes *-ness*, *-ity*, and *hood* are all nominalizers: *sweet/sweet-ness*, *scarce/scarc-ity*, *woman/woman-hood*.

**nominative**: a grammatical **case** that marks noun phrases that occur as subjects of clauses.

**nominative-accusative**: a language system which treats the subjects of both transitive and intransitive verbs similarly, and distinguishes them from objects of transitive verbs; see also: **ergative-absolutive**.

**nonce formation**: the first innovative production of a new word through compounding or derivation.

**non-finite**: a clause or verb that lacks marking for tense, aspect, mood, and/or evidentiality that is found in other clauses in the same language; contrasts with **finite**.

**non-inverted question**: in English, a *wh*-question in which the subject precedes the verb.

**nonrestrictive relative clause**: a relative clause that does not aid in the identification of the referent of the head noun, but provides further information about it.

**nonrhotic**: relating to the pronunciation of the English phoneme /r/ as a vowel.

**noun**: a grammatically defined word class, whose members can function as the heads of **noun phrases**; typically denote entities or concepts.

**noun incorporation**: the addition of a noun root to modify the meaning of the verb root.

**noun phrase**: a syntactic constituent headed by a noun or pronoun; optionally includes one or more dependent modifiers.

**nucleus**: the most prominent (or loudest) part of the syllable; typically filled by a vowel; also called the **syllable peak**.

**number**: a grammatical category which differentiates **singular**, **plural**, and sometimes **dual** or other number categories.

**numeral**: a word class often distinct from other quantifiers whose members indicate an exact quantity.

**numeral classifier**: a **classifier** that occurs in expressions with numerals and sometimes other **determiners**.

**object**: a grammatical relation based on morphosyntactic behavior pertaining to the less agentive arguments of transitive and ditransitive verbs; includes **direct objects** and **indirect objects**.

**object complement**: a complement clause that functions as the grammatical object of a verb.

**object of an adposition (preposition/postposition)**: a noun phrase dependent on an adposition in an adpositional phrase.

**objective**: unbiased; independent of preconceptions or evaluative judgments.

**obligatory context**: a linguistic context in which the use of a particular morpheme is required in order for the utterance to be grammatically correct.

**oblique argument**: an argument that does not have a direct grammatical relationship with a verb; oblique arguments typically convey information external to the strict verbal semantics (such as spatial, temporal, or logical relations), so are often "optional" elements of the clause.

**observational study**: in language acquisition research, a type of study in which the researcher makes a written, audio, or video record of children's naturally occurring communicative behaviors.

**obsolescence**: an extreme state of language endangerment.

**obstruent**: a category of sounds which includes oral stops, affricates, and fricatives.

**online creation of natural discourse**: the process in which conversation partners articulate their thoughts and navigate social interaction in real time.

**onomatopoeia**: sound symbolism in words; terms for birds and certain other animals, whose names in some way mimics their calls, as well as terms for various actions and sounds effects.

**onset**: a consonant or consonant cluster that precedes the nucleus within the syllable.

**open syllable**: a syllable that ends in a vowel.

**open word class**: a class into which one can easily incorporate new members through borrowing or other word-formation processes.

**Optimal Relevance**: in pragmatics, when a relevant utterance achieves a balance between the quantity of contextual cues informing the utterance and the mental effort necessary to process those cues.

**oral**: a sound produced with air passing through the mouth only; contrasts with **nasal**.

**orthography**: writing system; see also **practical orthography**.

**overextension**: in language acquisition, a type of error in which a linguistic form or construction is used in a larger number of contexts than is appropriate in adult speech; see **lexical overextension**.

**overregularization**: in language acquisition, a type of error in which the regular form of a morpheme is used in cases that require an irregular form, e.g., *goed* instead of *went*.

**palatal**: a sound made with the tongue contacting the center of the hard palate.

**palatalization**: a phonological process by which a non-palatal consonant takes on a palatal or palato-alveolar articulation; typically triggered by high vowels, front vowels, or the palatal approximant.

**palato-alveolar**: a sound made with the tongue contacting the area just behind the alveolar ridge; also known as **postalveolar**.

**paradigm**: the set of forms that includes all possible morphological variants of a single word.

**paradox**: a sentence that expresses two propositions both of which cannot be simultaneously true; a useful device for testing the entailments of lexemes.

**partial reduplication**: see **reduplication**.

**particle**: an independent word which does not inflect (i.e., which has only a single morphological form).

**particle verb**: in English, compound verbs containing a verb plus a particle that historically developed from a preposition but no longer functions as one.

**passive (voice)**: a construction which allows the semantic patient to function as the grammatical subject of an intransitive clause; agentive arguments are either unexpressed or placed in an adpositional phrase; contrasts with **active (voice)**.

**passive articulator**: an articulator which remains stationary in the production of a sound; contrasts with **active articulator**; includes teeth, upper surface of the vocal tract, etc.

**patient**: a semantic case role denoting an entity that undergoes a change of state as the result of an activity or event.

**penultimate syllable**: the second to last syllable in a word; also called the **penult**.

**perceptual salience**: an explanatory factor for phonological processes, based on the observation that phonologies tend to be constructed in a way that increases the perceptual distinctness of sounds from one another.

**perfective**: an aspect that presents a situation as a bounded and completed whole; contrasts with imperfective.

**persona**: a social type that may be associated with particular personal attributes or with a broader social group.

**personal pronoun**: a word class whose members refer to a first-person referent (the speaker), a second-person referent (the addressee), or a third-person referent (someone other than the speaker and addressee, but not semantically specific); typically distinguishes singular and plural (e.g., *I, we*); constitutes the sole element of a noun phrase.

**perspective**: one of several ways of construing a situation.

**pharyngeal**: a consonant articulated with the root of the tongue against the back wall of the pharynx.

**pharynx**: the part of the vocal tract above the larynx and behind the oral cavity (roughly the throat above the larynx).

**phoneme**: a sound that is used in a language to contrast words with different meanings.

**phonetics**: the physical properties of sounds in language and the study of those properties.

**phonological error pattern**: in language acquisition, a consistent difference between the adult and child pronunciation of a phonological unit such as a syllable or speech sound.

**phonologically conditioned**: allomorphs whose occurrence (distribution) can be predicted on the basis of the sounds around them, e.g., occurrence of the English plural allomorphs /-s/, /-z/, and /-əz/ can be predicted based on their phonological environment.

**phonological process**: an alteration in phonetic structure due to the phonological properties of the form or its environment (e.g., deletion of a vowel that is adjacent to another vowel; devoicing of a consonant word-finally).

**phonology**: the systematic patterns of sounds in language and the study of those patterns.

**phrasal accent**: the most prominent part of a phrase.

**phrasal constituent**: a grammatically coherent subpart of a sentence, consisting of a head and any dependent modifiers; the phrase as a whole acts as a single syntactic unit; the lexical category of the head determines the phrase type, e.g., a phrasal constituent with a noun at its head is a noun phrase.

**phrase**: a structurally defined subpart of a sentence, including a head and optional dependents; used in Chapter 10 for a sequence of words within a single intonation unit.

**pidgin**: a simplified form of linguistic communication used for limited communication between adult speakers of two (or more) mutually unintelligible languages; consists of grammatical and lexical elements from both languages.

**pitch**: the perception of a sound on a scale of low to high; correlates with **fundamental frequency**.

**pitch contour**: in prosody, a pitch pattern characterized by rises and falls.

**place of articulation**: the location within the vocal tract at which air flow is obstructed to produce a sound; refers to the articulator(s) involved in producing the sound (e.g., bilabial, dental, alveolar, etc.).

**plural**: a grammatical number category indicating many; contrasts with singular and sometimes with dual.

**polar question**: a question that one could answer with a simple "yes" or "no" response; contrasts with content questions (also known as wh-questions) that ask for a specific piece of information, such as when something will or did occur.

**polyglot**: a person who speaks many languages.

**polysemy**: the property of having multiple, distinct, and incompatible senses.

**polysynthetic**: a morphological structure in which words tend to have large numbers of morphemes; characteristic of many languages of North America and the Caucasus; contrasts with **isolating**.

**possessive**: a grammatical case or construction that indicates possession.

**postalveolar**: a sound made with the tongue contacting the area just behind the alveolar ridge; also known as **palato-alveolar**.

**postposition**: see **adposition**.

**postpositional phrase**: see **adpositional phrase**.

**postvocalic /r/**: the pronunciation of /r/ after a vowel; in American English, the *r*-less variant is found in African American English and in the Southern and Eastern United States.

**poverty of the stimulus**: in nativist linguistic theory, the argument that the speech children hear does not provide sufficient evidence for them to acquire fundamental aspects of linguistic structure through learning; it is therefore assumed that the necessary syntactic information must be innately available as part of **Universal Grammar**.

**practical orthography**: a set of conventions for writing a particular language (including rules for spelling, word division, punctuation, etc.).

**pragmatic interpretation**: the process of applying contextual information to draw inferences, in order to arrive at the intended meaning of a linguistic utterance.

**pragmatics**: the study of how context shapes our use and interpretation of linguistic expressions; the competence to draw from context plausible inferences, which complement linguistic meanings.

**predicate (i)** (noun): (syntax) the central structural element of a clause, typically a verb, that determines the number and type of core arguments of the clause; (traditional) the portion of the clause that conveys information about the subject (e.g., the state or activity), typically consisting of the verb, its objects, adverbials, adjectives, or other modifiers.

**predicate (ii)** (verb): (semantics) the part of a proposition that is actually proposed, "put forth," i.e., predicated about a subject.

**predicate adjective**: an adjective that occurs as the primary element of the predicate, e.g., *He is tall*.

**predicate nominal**: a noun phrase that occurs as the primary element of the predicate, e.g., *He is a millionaire*.

**prefix**: an affix that occurs before the root, e.g., the English negative *un-* 'not.'

**preposition**: see **adposition**.

**prepositional phrase**: see **adpositional phrase**.

**prescriptive**: an approach to language that sets out rules for "proper" grammar and classifies the use of particular linguistic features as "right" or "wrong"; contrasts with **descriptive**.

**presupposition**: a background proposition that comes embedded in the use of a construction, and which gets expressed without being asserted.

**primary stress**: the syllable in a word that has the most acoustic prominence; contrasts with **secondary stress** and **unstressed**.

**principle of compositionality**: the meanings of complex expressions depend on the meanings of their parts, and individual expressions have stable meanings that combine in regular ways.

**principle of language variation**: within a single language, variability is inherent based on social, situational, and other factors.

**principle of linguistic diversity**: many different languages are spoken around the world, and often more than one language is used in a single community or in interactions between communities.

**Principle of Relevance**: the principle proposed by Sperber and Wilson to replace Grice's Maxims; states that people are automatically geared toward searching for maximally relevant information and that linguistic acts specifically come with a presumption of relevance.

**productivity**: in morphology, the degree to which a particular morphological formation is used by speakers to create new words; the English suffix *-hood* of *mother-hood* is no longer very productive, but the suffix *-ness* of words like *happi-ness* is highly productive.

**profile**: the primary figure, or focus of attention within a larger conceptual structure, or **frame**; the profile is what an expression designates within a frame.

**progressive**: an **aspect** that indicates an event is in-progress or ongoing.

**prominence**: the effect of causing a portion of speech to stand out because of its higher pitch, volume, lengthening, and/or special voice quality.

**pronoun**: a word class whose members constitute the sole element of a noun phrase, and so do not co-occur with modifiers.

**proposition**: a basic unit of thought; something which one could believe or know, which could be true or false.

**propositional content**: those aspects of an expression's meaning that affect the truth conditions of an expressed proposition.

**propositional schema**: an abstract representation of the detailed meaning of a lexical item, presented as a set of propositions that the word contributes to an utterance.

**propositional semantics**: the study of how meanings of individual elements combine in clauses and sentences.

**prosodic phrase**: see intonation unit.

**prosodic styles**: particular prosodic patterns associated with particular individuals or with particular speech usages such as oratory or acting.

**prosody**: the variations in pitch, volume, timing, and voice quality that overlay linguistic utterances.

**Proto-Indo-European**: a reconstruction of the Indo-European language; the language ancestral to English and all other languages genetically related to it.

**proto-language**: a reconstruction of the common parent language ancestral to a group of related languages.

**prototype**: a salient exemplar or subtype of a category.

**prototype effect**: a way of reasoning about a category based on one or a few especially salient models or exemplars.

**pro-verb**: a verb that can substitute for a verb phrase; e.g., English *do*.

**proximal demonstrative**: a demonstrative that indicates things closer to the speaker (e.g., English *this*); contrasts with **distal demonstrative** that indicates things closer to the addressee (e.g., English *that*).

**psycholinguistics**: a branch of both linguistics and psychology that studies the relationship between language behavior and psychological processes, especially the process of language acquisition.

**recipient**: a semantic case role denoting an entity that receives a theme.

**recursion**: the ability for a phrasal constituent to embed another phrasal constituent of the same type within it; e.g., the English prepositional phrases in *the cat on the pillow in the corner of the room*.

**reduplication**: a morphological process, found in many languages, in which all (**full reduplication**) or part (**partial reduplication**) of a morpheme is repeated to signal a certain meaning.

**reference**: the relation between a linguistic expression and its potential referents.

**referential**: a term used to describe noun phrases that refer to a particular entity. For example, *My sister wants to marry a lumberjack* has both a referential interpretation (she wants to marry a particular lumberjack) and a non-referential or generic interpretation (she wants to marry someone with that occupation, but doesn't have anyone specific in mind).

**referential function**: a term used in narrative research for the function of recounting who did what to whom, i.e., the sequence of events that constitute the plot of the narrative (its primary referential content); contrasts with **evaluative function**.

**referents**: the "real-world" objects of thought and language; people, objects, and situations that exist independently of human language, but toward which human language may be directed.

**register**: a variety that is associated with the specialized activities of a particular group.

**regulatory intonation unit**: an intonation unit containing an utterance that regulates the flow of information in discourse, such as *okay*, *yeah*, and *hm*; also known as regulatory phrases; contrasts with **substantive intonation unit**.

**relational role**: a social or cultural role that carries with it a set of social rights, obligations, relationships, and areas of expertise.

**relative clause**: a dependent clause embedded in a noun phrase that modifies a noun.

**renewal:** the refreshment of language through the replacement of words and grammatical constructions whose impact has faded through frequent use.

**retroflex**: a place of articulation for consonants, produced with the tip of the tongue curled backwards toward the roof of the mouth behind the alveolar ridge.

**reversive antonyms** (aka **reversives**): lexemes or constructions denoting motion or change in opposite directions; e.g., *melt:freeze*, *come:go*, *buy:sell*.

**rhotic**: relating to the pronunciation of /r/.

**root**: the main morpheme of a word, the foundation to which other morphemes may be added; roots typically carry the core meaning of the word, e.g., *late* in English *be-late-d-ly*.

**scaffolding**: in language acquisition, caregiver behaviors that support young children's use of language before they are capable of performing independently, e.g., adult questions that support a child's telling of a story.

**schwa**: a mid central lax unrounded vowel, closest to the neutral position of the tongue at rest, as in the first vowel of *apart*; represented in the IPA as [ə].

**script**: in semantics, a dynamic frame, consisting of a series of events or scenarios that unfold through time.

**secondary articulations**: articulations of consonants that include an additional articulatory gesture overlapping the primary consonant articulation, e.g., the labial gesture causing lip rounding in $k^w$.

**secondary stress**: one or more syllables in a word that are less prominent than the syllable with primary stress, but more prominent than unstressed syllables.

**second language acquisition (SLA)**: (the study of) the processes by which people (children and adults) learn any language in addition to their first language.

**second person**: refers to the addressee; *you*.

**segments**: a term used in phonetics to indicate individual speech sounds such as vowels, consonants, and syllables; contrasts with **suprasegmentals**.

**semantic case roles**: semantic (meaning) relationships between verbs and arguments; distinct from grammatical relationships.

**semantic content**: the meaning of an expression, i.e., its sense.

**semanticization**: the process by which the meaning of an expression changes from pragmatic status (i.e., contextually inferred) to semantic status (i.e., conventionally encoded and accessed even in the absence of a supporting context).

**semantics**: the study of how linguistic forms make sense (have meaning); the relation between morphosyntactic forms and their coded semantic content.

**sense**: the conventional significance (i.e., meaning) of a linguistic sign (such as a word).

**sensitive period**: a biologically programmed period of time during which, it is hypothesized, young children are able to acquire language most easily and successfully.

**sentence**: an integrated syntactic unit consisting of at least one clause and optionally adverbials that have scope over the sentence as a whole.

**serial verbs**: sequences of verbs lacking any conjunctions or affixes that together form a single complex predicate; certain verbs in serial constructions tend to recur and convey grammatical meanings such as aspect, direction, or case.

**sibilant**: an apical 'hissing' fricative or affricate, such as s, z, ts, dz, ʃ, ʒ, tʃ and dʒ; sibilants are also described with the feature [+strident].

**sign**: a linguistic expression, drawing, or other representation associated with a meaning or conception; a sign has two parts: a formal part, that is the **signifier**, and a conceptual part, that is the **signified**.

**signified**: the content of a **sign**; the conceptual content conventionally associated with a **signifier**.

**signifier**: the form of a **sign**; that aspect of a sign that expresses a meaning.

**singular**: a grammatical number category indicating exactly one.

**slang**: a set of rapidly changing lexical items often associated with youth and casual social contexts.

**sociocultural linguistics** (*also* **sociolinguistics**): the study of the interactional, social, and cultural uses and meanings of language.

**sociolinguistic variable**: a linguistic feature that varies either across speakers or in the speech of a single speaker.

**sociolinguistic variant**: one of the alternate forms of the same sociolinguistic variable, conditioned by linguistic and/or social factors.

**soft palate**: the soft portion of the upper surface of the mouth located behind the hard palate; also known as the **velum**.

**sonorant**: a category of sound that includes nasals and all approximants, both lateral and central.

**sound substitution**: in language acquisition, a type of **phonological error pattern** in which speech sounds that are difficult to perceive or produce are replaced with ones that are easier to perceive or produce.

**source**: a semantic case role denoting the beginning point of a motion trajectory.

**spectrogram**: a visual display of the acoustic properties of speech in which variations in intensity through time are shown with degrees of shading.

**speech act**: a social action that a speaker intends to perform by producing an utterance, such as a command, greeting, or request.

**speech and hearing sciences**: the study of the anatomy and physiology of hearing and communication, including development of speech and language.

**speech community**: a group of people who share a common language or dialect and cultural practices.

**speech pathology**: the study and treatment of speech disorders.

**speech timing**: distribution of speech elements through time, including acceleration, deceleration, and pausing.

**spelling reform**: a systematic change in the **orthography** for a given language, usually designed and promoted by educational or government institutions, which publishers, print media, and individuals then adopt.

**Sprachbund**: see **linguistic area**.

**stabilization**: in second language acquisition, a plateau stage in a learner's L2 development; unlike **fossilization**, stabilization does not represent an end-state of acquisition but rather a temporary cessation in language development for one or more subsystems.

**Stammbaum**; see **family tree**.

**stance**: an interactional position that linguistically indicates the speaker's attitude toward the talk and toward his or her interlocutors at a given moment.

**standard (language)**: a prestige variety of a language that is implicitly or explicitly recognized as being the norm within a nation, often deliberately engineered and given legal status, and usually taught in schools and used in print and broadcast media.

**status planning**: a phase of **language planning** to promote the use of a language in society by propagating the language via education and media, shaping public attitudes toward the language, and prescribing its role in society and the domains in which it is used.

**stop**: a consonant sound that involves a complete closure of the vocal tract.

**stopping**: in language acquisition, a type of a **phonological error pattern** in which a child replaces a fricative or other type of consonant with a stop, e.g., pronouncing English *see* [si] as [di].

**stress**: the relative prominence of different syllables in a word; typically measured in terms of duration, intensity, and/or fundamental frequency; includes **primary stress** (the syllable that carries the main stress in the word) and **secondary stress** (stress that is not as strong as the primary stress but stronger than completely unstressed syllables).

**strident**: a noisy sound (typically a fricative or affricate) which involves the funneling of air against the back of the teeth.

**structural isomorphism**: the similarity in structure that emerges through the gradual convergence of the grammars and lexicons of two languages which coexist in a situation of intensive language contact.

**style**: a socially distinctive way of doing things, including a distinctive way of using language.

**style shifting**: an individual speaker's alternation between different varieties of the same language based on social context.

**subglottal system**: the parts of the vocal tract which provide the air that the upstream articulators manipulate to produce sound; includes the lungs and the trachea.

**subject**: a grammatical relation based on morphosyntactic behavior shared by the single argument of an intransitive verb and the more agentive argument of a transitive or ditransitive verb, but not shared by other arguments.

**subordinating conjunction**: a word or affix that marks an adverbial subordinate clause by specifying the specific semantic relationship between the adverbial clause and the matrix clause (e.g., English *if, because, when, although*).

**subordination**: in clause combining, the structure that results from having one clause (the **subordinate clause**) inside of and/or dependent on another.

**substantive intonation unit**: an intonation unit where the utterance conveys referential information, i.e., ideas of events, states, people, or objects; also known as substantive phrases; contrasts with **regulatory intonation unit**.

**substrate**: the minority language or languages in a situation of intense language contact and typically shift; contributes the grammar and some vocabulary to the creation of a pidgin and creole; contrasts with **superstrate**.

**substratum interference**: in a situation of language contact, changes to a **target language** that arise from the incomplete acquisition by speakers of minority languages; speakers transfer features of their native languages to the target language and the changes are adopted by the target-language community.

**subtopic**: a new **topic of conversation** which is related to or slightly shifted from a previous topic.

**suffix**: an affix that occurs after the root, e.g., the English plural *-s*.

**superlative**: an adjective, adverb, or similar morpheme that compares one thing to all others in a designated group; for example, the English *-est* suffix in *the elephant is the biggest land mammal*, or the word *most* in *she has the most money of anyone in this room*. See also **comparative**.

**superstrate**: the dominant language in a situation of intense language contact; in situations with pidgins and creoles, it usually contributes most of the vocabulary; in the latter sense also known as the **lexifier** language; contrasts with **substrate**.

**suppletive**: highly irregular allomorphic variation where two (or more) morphological forms of a single root are phonemically unrelated; for example, English *was, am*, and *is* are suppletive forms of the verb *to be*, and *went* is the suppletive past-tense form of the verb *to go*.

**supralaryngeal vocal tract**: the portion of the vocal tract located above the larynx; contains most of the physiological structures that are manipulated in speech.

**suprasegmental**: phonetic properties that extend across multiple sounds; includes syllables, stress, tone, intonation, etc.

**surface allophones**: the phonetic realizations of a phoneme; may be identical to the underlying phoneme or derived by a phonological process.

**switching**: see **code-switching**.

**switch-reference**: a system of verbal affixes that indicate whether the subject of the following clause is the same as, or is different from, the subject of the current clause.

**syllabic consonant**: a consonant that functions as a syllable peak; e.g., the second syllable of 'little,' [l̩], or the second syllable of 'butter,' [ɹ̩].

**syllable**: a linguistic grouping that consists of a single peak, which may be flanked on one or both sides by consonants.

**syllable weight**: a classification of syllables by the structure of the coda; **light syllables** typically have only a single vowel in the coda; **heavy syllables** typically have either a long vowel, a diphthong, or a vowel followed by one or more consonants.

**syllable peak**: the most prominent (or loudest) part of the syllable; typically filled by a vowel; also called the **nucleus**.

**syllabogram**: a written character that represents a syllable, e.g., *ma, an, nam*.

**symbol**: a type of sign for which the relation between the **signifier** and the **signified** is a matter of convention; contrasts with **icon** and **index**.

**synchrony**: a single point in time (typically the present) for which a language is described; contrasts with **diachrony**.

**syncope**: the loss of an unstressed vowel in the middle of a word.

**synonym**: two or more lexemes or other expressions that make the same or similar contributions to the sense of a sentence (the relation among synonyms is called **synonymy**).

**syntax**: the set of grammatical structures that allow for the combination of words into phrases and sentences; the study of such structures and the principles underlying them.

**synthetic**: morphological structure in which each word has several morphemes, usually more than **isolating** languages but fewer than **polysynthetic languages**; characteristic of many Romance languages, as well as Finnish (see Language Profile 4).

**tag switching**: code-switching that occurs at a discourse marker.

**tap**: a sound produced with extremely short complete closure at the alveolar ridge; differentiated from an alveolar stop by the extreme shortness of the closure for the tap; sometimes also referred to as a **flap**.

**target language**: in a situation of language contact, a dominant language which a minority population acquires.

**taxonomy**: a lexical field in which lexemes are arranged in a branching hierarchy of inclusion relations; for example, the lexical field of animals includes a branch of dogs which includes a branch of poodles.

**template**: a schematic representation of a structure; in syntax, used to indicate the possible elements that occur in a phrase, the order in which they may appear, and the optionality of elements; in phonology, typically refers to the possible orderings of consonants and vowels in a syllable.

**temporal**: a semantic case role denoting a location in time.

**tense (i)**: a grammatical category which differentiates time (e.g., past, present, future); often (but not always) marked on verbs.

**tense (ii)**: a phonetic property of vowels produced with tongue positioned in the periphery of the vowel space; contrasts with **lax**; tense vowels tend to be longer than lax vowels.

**tenseness**: with **backness** and **height**, one of three main dimensions for describing vowels, based on peripherality of tongue position and length; encompasses **tense** and **lax**.

**terminal pitch contour**: a pitch contour associated with the final portion of an intonation unit.

**theme**: a semantic case role denoting an entity undergoing motion or being located.

**third person**: refers to an entity other than the speaker or addressee; *he, she, it, they.*

**timing**: see **speech timing**.

**tone (tonal) language**: a language in which fundamental frequency (or its perceptual correlate, pitch) plays an important part in distinguishing between words with different meanings; i.e., languages where pitch is phonemic.

**topic** (adjective **topical**): a referent that is important to the surrounding discourse, so is likely to be referred to repeatedly.

**transitive**: verbs that take two core arguments.

**transitivity (i)**: the property of a verb to take a particular number of arguments.

**transitivity (ii)**: the extent to which a verb expresses an action that affects a participant.

**truth conditions**: what must be the case for a **proposition** to be true.

**typology**: see **linguistic typology**.

**typology and universals**: the study of how the world's languages are similar and different; includes classification of languages based on structure as well as positing relationships between structural types.

**U-shaped learning**: a process of language development involving the learning of irregular forms; learners first produce a correct form, then an incorrect form (based on analogy from learning the grammatical system), and finally the correct form again upon learning exceptions to the rules.

**ultimate syllable**: the last syllable in a word; also called the **ultima**.

**uncooperative pragmatic inference**: a type of pragmatic inference that is not intended but could be inferred from the context.

**underextension**: in first language acquisition, a type of error in which a linguistic form or construction is applied to a smaller set of referents than is appropriate in adult speech.

**underlying phoneme**: the allophone of a phoneme that occurs in the widest array of environments; the allophone taken to be the "basic" form, from which other allophones are derived via phonological processes.

**Universal Grammar (UG)**: in formal linguistic theories, a set of innate linguistic categories, structures, principles, and constraints that form the basis for the grammars of all languages; in nativist theories of language acquisition, UG is hypothesized to account for children's first language acquisition.

**utterance**: a single instance of speech.

**utterance meaning**: what a speaker intends to express by his or her use of language in a particular context.

**uvular**: consonant produced by the back of the tongue coming into contact with or approximating the uvula (the appendage which hangs down in the back of the oral cavity).

**vagueness**: the quality of having a relatively broad – or broadly undefined – **sense**, and thus encompassing a relatively wide range of possible referents.

**valency**: the number of core arguments of a verb.

**variable**: see **sociolinguistic variable**.

**variant**: see **sociolinguistic variant**.

**variety**: see **linguistic variety**.

**velar**: a consonant produced by contact between the back of the tongue and the **velum** (soft palate).

**velum**: the soft portion of the upper surface of the mouth located behind the hard palate; also known as the **soft palate**.

**verb**: a member of a class of words which function as the grammatical centers of **predicates**; typically denote actions, events, activities, or states.

**verbalizer**: a derivational affix that creates verbs, e.g., English *-ize*, as in *real-ize* 'make real.'

**verb phrase**: a syntactic constituent consisting of a verb as the **head** of the phrase, and optional dependents including adverbs, prepositional phrases, object noun phrases, and indirect objects in prepositional phrases.

**vernacular**: the linguistic variety used in everyday speech in casual settings.

**voice**: a grammatical construction providing alternate mappings between semantic roles and grammatical relations; includes **active** and **passive**.

**voiced consonant or vowel**: any consonant or vowel sound produced with vibration of the vocal folds.

**voiceless consonant or vowel**: any consonant or vowel sound produced without vibration of the vocal folds.

**voice quality**: a cover term for various modifications of a normal speaking voice.

**voicing**: the effect produced by the vibration of the vocal folds.

**volume**: see **intensity**.

**vowel harmony**: a type of long-distance assimilation in which all vowels in a word must share a feature (e.g., height or backness).

**vowel length**: the temporal duration of a vowel, phonemic in some languages.

**vowel reduction**: the phonological process by which unstressed vowels are converted to schwa-like allophones.

**waveform**: a visual representation of sound based on its acoustic properties.

**weight-sensitive stress**: a stress system in a language where the weight or complexity of syllables influences the **stress** patterns; contrasts with **weight-insensitive stress**, where stress is predictably assigned to a given syllable (e.g., initial, final, penultimate) in a word; also referred to as quantity-(in)sensitive stress.

**whispering**: a voice quality in which the vocal folds in the larynx do not come together as closely as in normal voicing.

**"women's language"**: a language ideology regarding how women are expected to speak.

**word**: an independent, phonologically coherent linguistic unit containing one or more morphemes, which can fill a particular slot in a sentence.

**word class**: a set of words that share morphological and syntactic behavior, e.g., **nouns**, **adjectives**, or **adpositions**.

**working memory**: a cognitive system for temporarily storing and processing information that has just been experienced or recalled; enables performance of tasks such as language comprehension and production, learning, and problem-solving.

**zero auxiliary**: the absence of an auxiliary verb that is typically overtly expressed.

**zero copula**: the absence of a copula verb that is typically overtly expressed.

# REFERENCES

Adelaar, Willem F. H. 2006. "The vicissitudes of directional affixes in Tarma (Northern Junín) Quechua." In Rowicka, G. I. and E. B. Carlin (eds.), *What's in a verb: Studies in the verbal morphology of the languages of the Americas*. Utrecht: LOT. 121–41.

Aikhenvald, Alexandra Y. 2004. "Language endangerment in the Sepik area of Papua New Guinea." In Sakiyama, O. and F. Endo (eds.), *Lectures on endangered languages: 5, From Tokyo and Kyoto conferences, 2002*. Endangered Languages of the Pacific Rim Project. Suita, Osaka. 97–142.

2008. *The Manambu language from East Sepik, Papua New Guinea*. Oxford University Press.

2009. "Language contact along the Sepik River." *Anthropological Linguistics* **50**: 1–66.

Aikhenvald, Alexandra and Pauline Agnes Luma Laki. 2006. "Manambu." In Brown, Keith (ed.), *Encyclopedia of language and linguistics*, Vol. VII, 2nd edn. (article 4491). Elsevier: Oxford. 475–476.

Aikhenvald, Alexandra and Tonya N. Stebbins. 2007. "Languages of New Guinea." In Miyaoka, O., O. Sakiyama, and M. Krauss (eds.), *Vanishing languages of the Pacific*. Oxford University Press. 239–266.

Alim, H. Samy. 2006. *Roc the mic right: The language of hip hop culture*. New York: Routledge.

Anttila, Raimo. 1972. *An introduction to historical and comparative linguistics*. New York: Macmillan.

Appel, René and Pieter Muysken. 2005. *Language contact and bilingualism*. Amsterdam: Academic Archive.

Applegate, Richard. 1998. "Learn Inezeño Chumash workbook for the Inezeño Chumash Revitalization Project." Unpublished manuscript.

Ariel, Mira. 2008. *Pragmatics and grammar*. Cambridge University Press.

2010. *Defining pragmatics*. Cambridge University Press.

Bamberg, Michael and Alexandra Georgakopoulou. 2008. "Small stories as a new perspective in narrative and identity analysis." *Text & Talk* **38**: 377–396.

Barnhart, Robert K. (ed.). 2008. *Chambers dictionary of etymology*. Edinburgh: Chambers.

Barrett, Marilyn. 1986. "Early semantic representations and early word usage." In Kuczaj, Stan and Marilyn Barrett (eds.), *The development of word meaning*. New York: Springer-Verlag. 39–67.

Baxter, Alan N. 1988. *A grammar of Kristang (Malacca Creole Portuguese)*. Canberra: Pacific Linguistics.

Beebe, Leslie and Hansun Zhang Waring. 2005. "Pragmatic development in responding to rudeness." In Frodesen, Jan and Christine Holten (eds.), *The power of context in language teaching and learning*. Boston: Heinle Thomson. 67-76.

Biber, Douglas, Stig Johansson, Geoffrey Leech, Susan Conrad, and Edward Finegan. 1999. *Longman grammar of spoken and written English*. Harlow: Pearson.

Bird, Charles and Timothy Shopen. 1979. "Maninka." In Shopen, Timothy (ed.), *Languages and their speakers*. Cambridge, MA: Winthrop Publishers. 59-112.

Blake, Rée and Meredith Josey. 2003. "The /ay/ diphthong in a Martha's Vineyard community: What can we say 40 years after Labov?" *Language in Society* **32**.4: 451-85.

Blake, Robert J. 2000. "Computer mediated communication: A window on L2 Spanish interlanguage." *Language Learning & Technology* **4**.1: 120-136.

Blakemore, Diane. 1992. *Understanding utterances* (Blackwell Textbooks in Linguistics 6). Oxford: Blackwell.

Bloom, Lois. 1970. *Language development*. Cambridge, Mass.: MIT Press.
  1973. *One word at a time*. The Hague: Mouton.

Bonfiglio, Thomas Paul. 2002. *Race and the rise of Standard American*. Berlin: Mouton de Gruyter.

Bowerman, Melissa. 1978. "The acquisition of word meaning: An investigation into some current conflicts." In Waterson, Natalie and Catherine E. Snow (eds.), *The development of communication*. New York: Wiley. 263-287.

Braine, Martin. 1976. "Children's first word combinations." *Monographs of the Society for Research in Child Development* **41**.1, serial no. 164.

Broen, Patricia A. 1972. "The verbal environment of the language-learning child." *Monographs of the American Speech & Hearing Association* 17.

Brown, Roger. 1973. *A first language: The early stages*. Cambridge, Mass.: Harvard University Press.

Bunte, Pamela A. and Martha B. Kendall. 1981. "When is an error not an error? Notes on language contact and the question of interference." *Anthropological Linguistics* **23**: 1-7.

Burridge, Kate. 2006. "Language contact and convergence in Pennsylvania German." In Aikhenvald, Alexandra Y. and R. M. W. Dixon (eds.), *Grammars in contact*. Oxford University Press. 179-200.

Campbell, Lyle. 1999. *Historical linguistics: An introduction*. Cambridge, Mass.: MIT Press.

Campbell, Lyle, Terrence Kaufman, and Thomas Smith-Stark. 1986. "Meso-America as a linguistic area." *Language* **62**: 530-570.

Chafe, Wallace. 1996. "Sketch of Seneca, an Iroquoian language." In Goddard, Ives (ed.), *Handbook of North American Indians,* Vol. XVII: *Languages*. Washington, DC: Smithsonian Institute. 551-579.

Chen, Katherine Hoi Ying. 2008. "Positioning and repositioning: Linguistic practices and identity negotiation of overseas returning bilinguals in Hong Kong." *Multilingua* **27**.1-2: 57-75.

Chirikba, Viacheslav. 2008. "The problem of the Caucasian Sprachbund." In Muysken, Pieter (ed.), *From linguistic areas to areal linguistics*. Amsterdam: John Benjamins. 25-93.

Choi, Soonja. 2000. "Caregiver input in English and Korean: Use of nouns and verbs in book-reading and toy-play contexts." *Journal of Child Language* **27**: 69-96.

Choi, Soonja and Alison Gopnik. 1995. "Early acquisition of verbs in Korean: A cross-linguistic study." *Journal of Child Language* **22**: 497-529.

Chomsky, Noam. 1965. *Aspects of the theory of syntax*. The Hague: Mouton.

Clancy, Patricia. 2007. "Discourse-functional correlates of argument structure in Korean acquisition." In McGloin, Naomi (ed.), *Japanese/Korean linguistics 15.* Stanford, Calif.: CSLI Publications. 1-20.

Clark, Eve. 1973. "What's in a word? On the child's acquisition of semantics in his first language." In Moore, T. E. (ed.), *Cognitive development and the acquisition of language.* New York: Academic Press. 65-110.

  2009. *First language acquisition,* 2nd edn. New York: Cambridge University Press.

Clark, Eve and Barbara, Kelly, (eds.). 2005. *Constructions in acquisition.* Stanford, Calif.: CSLI Publications.

Comrie, Bernard. 1979. "Russian." In Shopen, Timothy (ed.), *Languages and their status.* Cambridge, MA: Winthrop Publishers. 91-152.

Corbett, Greville. 2004. "The Russian adjective: a pervasive yet elusive category." In Dixon, R. M. W. and Alexandra Y. Aikhenvald (eds.), *Adjective classes: A crosslinguistic typology.* Oxford University Press. 199-222.

Corominas, Joan. 1961. *Breve diccionario etimologico de la lengua castellana.* Madrid: Editorial Gredos.

Craig, Collette Grinevald 1977. *Structure of Jacaltec.* Austin: University of Texas Press.

Cross, Toni G. 1977. "Mothers' speech adjustments: The contributions of selected child listener variables." In Snow, Catherine E. and Charles Ferguson (eds.), *Talking to children: Language input and acquisition.* New York: Cambridge University Press. 151-188.

Crystal, David. 2003. *English as a global language,* 2nd edn. Cambridge University Press.

Cuoq, Jean-André. 1866. *Études philologiques sur quelques langues sauvages de l'Amérique.* Montreal: Dawson Brothers.

Curnow, Timothy J. 2001. "What language features can be 'borrowed'?" In Aikhenvald, Alexandra Y. and R. M. W. Dixon (eds.), *Areal diffusion and genetic inheritance: Problems in comparative linguistics.* Oxford University Press. 412-436.

Daiute, Colette and Katherine Nelson. 1997. "Making sense of the sense-making function of narrative evaluation." *Journal of Narrative and Life History* **7**.1-4: 207-215.

Denison, Norman. 1971. "Some observations on language variety and plurilingualism." In Ardener, E. (ed.), *Social anthropology and language.* London: Tavistock Publications. 157-183.

Derwing, Tracey M., Murray J. Munro, and Grace F. Wiebe. 1998. "Evidence in favor of a broad framework for pronunciation instruction." *Language Learning* **48**: 393-410.

Derwing, Tracey M. and Marian J. Rossiter. 2003. "The effects of pronunciation instruction on the accuracy, fluency, and complexity of L2 accented speech." *Applied Language Learning* **13**: 1-17.

Deutscher, Guy. 2000. *Syntactic change in Akkadian: The evolution of sentential complementation.* Oxford University Press.

  2005. *The unfolding of language.* New York: Henry Holt.

de Villiers, Jill G. and Peter A. de Villiers. 1973. "A cross-sectional study of the acquisition of grammatical morphemes." *Journal of Psycholinguistic Research* **2**: 267-278.

Diessel, Holger. 2004. *The acquisition of complex sentences.* New York: Cambridge University Press.

Diessel, Holger and Michael. Tomasello. 2000. "The development of relative clauses in spontaneous child speech." *Cognitive Linguistics* **11**.1-2: 131-151.

Dixon, R. M. W. 1988. *A grammar of Boumaa Fijian.* University of Chicago Press.

  1994. *Ergativity.* Cambridge University Press.

  2004. *The Jarawara language of Southern Amazonia.* Oxford University Press.

Dodd, Barbara, Allison Holm, Zhu Hua, Sharon Crosbie, and Jan Broomfield. 2006. "English phonology: Acquisition and disorder." In Hua, Zhu and Barbara Dodd (eds.), *Phonological development and disorders in children: A multilingual perspective*. Tonawonda, NY: Multilingual Matters. 25-55.

Doke, C. M. 1935. *Bantu linguistic terminology*. London: Longmans, Green.

Du Bois, John W. 1987. "The discourse basis of ergativity." *Language* **63**.4: 805-855.

Du Bois, John W., Wallace L. Chafe, Charles Meyer, and Sandra A. Thompson. 2000. *Santa Barbara Corpus of Spoken American English*, Part 1. Philadelphia: Linguistic Data Consortium, University of Pennsylvania.

Du Bois, John W., Wallace L. Chafe, Charles Meyer, Sandra A. Thompson, and Nii Martey. 2003. *Santa Barbara Corpus of Spoken American English*, Part 2. Philadelphia: Linguistic Data Consortium, University of Pennsylvania.

Du Bois, John W. and Robert Englebretson. 2004. *Santa Barbara Corpus of Spoken American English*, Part 3. Philadelphia: Linguistic Data Consortium, University of Pennsylvania.

2005. *Santa Barbara Corpus of Spoken American English*, Part 4. Philadelphia: Linguistic Data Consortium, University of Pennsylvania.

Eckert, Penelope. 2000. *Linguistic variation as social practice*. Oxford: Blackwell.

Eckert, Penelope and Sally McConnell-Ginet. 1995. "Constructing meaning, constructing selves: Snapshots of language, gender, and class from Belten High." In Hall, Kira and Mary Bucholtz (eds.), *Gender articulated: Language and the socially constructed self*. New York: Routledge. 469-507.

Ellis, Nick C. 2002. "Frequency effects in language processing." *Studies in Second Language Acquisition* **24**: 143-188.

Emeneau, Murray B. 1956. "India as a linguistic area." *Language* **32**: 3-16.

Ervin-Tripp, Susan. 1979. "Children's verbal turn-taking." In Ochs, Elinor and Bambi Schieffelin (eds.), *Developmental pragmatics*. New York: Academic Press. 391-414.

Fenson, Larry, Philip S. Dale, J. Steven Reznick, Elizabeth Bates, Donna J. Thal, and Steven J. Pethick. 1994. "Variability in early communicative development." *Monographs of the Society for Research in Child Development* **59**.5, serial no. 242.

Fernald, Anne, Traute Taeschner, Judy Dunn, Mechthild Papousek, Benedicte De Boysson-Bardies, and Ikuko Fukui. 1989. "A cross-language study of prosodic modifications in mothers' and fathers' speech to preverbal infants." *Journal of Child Language* **15**: 477-501.

Fillmore, Charles J. 1985. "Frames and the semantics of understanding." *Quaderni di Semantica* **6**.2: 222-254.

Filppula, Markku. 2003. "The quest for the most 'parsimonious' explanations: Endogeny vs. contact revisited." In Hickey, Raymond (ed.), *Motives for language change*. Cambridge University Press. 161-173.

Fodor, István. 1984. "Language reforms of the past and in the developing countries." In Fodor, I. and Claude Hagège (eds.), *Language reform: History and future*, Vol. III. Hamburg: Buske Verlag. 441-44.

Foley, William A. 1986. *The Papuan languages of New Guinea*. Cambridge University Press.

Fought, Carmen. 2003. *Chicano English in context*. New York: Palgrave Macmillan.

Fortescue, Michael, Steven Jacobson, and Lawrence Kaplan. 1994. *Comparative Eskimo dictionary with Aleut cognates*. Fairbanks: University of Alaska, Alaska Native Language Center.

Fortson, Benjamin W. 2004. *Indo-European language and culture*. Oxford: Blackwell.

Friedman, Victor. A. 2006. "Balkanizing the Balkan Sprachbund." In Aikhenvald, Alexandra Y. and R. M. W. Dixon (eds.), *Grammars in contact*. Oxford University Press. 201-219.

Fries, Charles C. and Kenneth L. Pike. 1949. "Coexistent phonemic systems." *Language* **25**: 29–50.

Gabas, Nilson. Jr. 1999. "A grammar of Karo, Topi (Brazil)." Ph.D. dissertation, University of California, Santa Barbara.

Gastambide Arrillaga, Carlos. 1990. *El idioma indígena taíno en las Antillas* (Serie Gaztambide Arrillaga de historia y linguística). Estudio de Investigación Filológica, Vol. XXII. Puerto Rico: Ramallo Bros.

Gerken, LouAnn. 1991. "The metrical basis of children's subjectless sentences." *Journal of Memory & Language* **30**: 431–451.

Girard, Victor J. 1971. *Proto-Takanan phonology* (University of California Publications in Linguistics **70**). Berkeley: University of California.

Goldberg, Adele and Devin Casinhiser. 2006. "Learning argument structure generalizations." In Clark, Eve and Barbara Kelly (eds.), *Constructions in acquisition*. Stanford, Calif.: CSLI Publications. 185–204.

González, Alicia María. 2002. *The edge of enchantment: Sovereignty and ceremony in Huatulco, México*. Washington, DC: National Museum of the American Indian, Smithsonian Institute. Distributed by Fulcrum Publishing.

Green, Georgia M. 1989. *Pragmatics and natural language understanding*. Hillsdale, NJ: Lawrence Erlbaum.

Grice, H. Paul. 1975. "Logic and conversation." In Cole, Peter and Jerry L. Morgan (eds.), *Syntax and semantics*, Vol. III: *Speech acts*. New York: Academic Press. 41–58.

1989. *Studies in the way of words*. Cambridge, Mass.: Harvard University Press.

Grundy, Peter. 1995. *Doing pragmatics*. London: Edward Arnold.

Gumperz, John J. and Robert Wilson. 1971. "Convergence and creolization: A case from the Indo-Aryan/Dravidian Border in India." In Hymes, Dell (ed.), *Pidginization and creolization of languages*. Cambridge University Press. 151–168.

Hajek, John. 2006. "Language contact and convergence in East Timor." In Aikhenvald, Alexandra Y. and R. M. W. Dixon (eds.), *Grammars in contact*. Oxford University Press. 163–178.

Hakuta, Kenji, Ellen Bialystok, and Edward Wiley. 2003. "Critical evidence: A test of the critical period hypothesis for second language acquisition." *Psychological Science* **14**.1: 31–38.

Harrison, Sheldon. 1982. "Proto-Oceanic *aki(ni) and the Proto-Oceanic periphrastic causatives." In Halim, Amran, Lois Carrington, and S. A. Wurm (eds.), *Papers from the Third International Conference on Austronesian Linguistics*, Vol. I: *Currents in Oceanic*. Canberra: Pacific Linguistics. 179–230.

Harrison, Simon. 1990. *Stealing people's names: History and politics in a Sepik river cosmology*. Cambridge University Press.

1993. *The mask of war*. Manchester University Press.

Haspelmuth, Martin. 1993. *A grammar of Lezgian*. Berlin: Mouton de Gruyter.

Heine, Bernd, and Tania Kuteva. 2002. *World lexicon of grammaticalization*. Cambridge University Press.

Heine, Bernd and Heiko Narrog (eds.). 2010. *The Oxford handbook of grammaticalization*. Oxford University Press.

Hilbert, Michaela. 2008. "Interrogative inversion in non-standard varieties of English." In Siemund, Peter and Noemi Kintana (eds.), *Language contact and contact languages*. Amsterdam: John Benjamins. 261–289.

Hill, Jane and Kenneth C. Hill. 1986. *Speaking Mexicano: Dynamics of syncretic language in Central Mexico*. Tucson: The University of Arizona Press.

Hintz, Daniel J. 2008. "Aspect and aspectual interfaces in South Conchucos Quechua: The emergence of grammatical systems." Ph.D. dissertation, University of California, Santa Barbara.

2011. *Crossing aspectual frontiers: Emergence, evolution, and interwoven semantic domains in South Conchucos Quechua* (University of California Publications in Linguistics 146). Berkeley: University of California Press.

Hintz, Diane M. 2003. "Pragmatics of word order in South Conchucos Quechua." MA thesis, University of California, Santa Barbara.

Hock, Hans Henrich. 1991. *Historical linguistics.* Berlin: Mouton de Gruyter.

Hock, Hans Henrich and Brian Joseph. 1996. *Language history, language change, and language relationship.* Berlin: Mouton de Gruyter.

Hoff, B. J. 1968. *The Carib language.* The Hague: Martinus Nijhoff.

Hoff, Erika. 2009. *Language development*, 4th edn. Belmont, Calif.: Wadsworth.

Hoff-Ginsberg, Eirka. 1987. "Topic relations in mother–child conversation." *First Language* **7**: 145-158.

Hopper, Paul J. and Elizabeth Closs Traugott. 2004. *Grammaticalization*, 2nd edn. Cambridge University Press.

Horn, Laurence R. 1984. "A new taxonomy for pragmatic inference: Q-based and R-based implicatures." In Schiffrin, Deborah (ed.), *Meaning, form, and use in context: Linguistic applications* (Georgetown University Round Table on Languages and Linguistics). Washington, DC: Georgetown University Press. 11-42.

Hua, Zhu and Barbara Dodd. 2006. "Towards developmental universals." In Hua, Zhu and Barbara Dodd (eds.), *Phonological development and disorders in children: A multilingual perspective.* Tonawonda, NY: Multilingual Matters. 431-449.

Huang, Yan. 2007. *Pragmatics.* Oxford University Press.

Huehnergard, John. 1997. *A Grammar of Akkadian.* Atlanta, Ga.: Scholars Press.

Hyams, Nina. 1986. *Language acquisition and the theory of parameters.* Dordrecht: Reidel.

2011. "Missing subjects in early child language." *Studies in Theoretical Psycholinguistics* **41**: 13-52.

Iggesen, Oliver A. 2011. "Number of cases." In Dryer, Matthew S. and Martin Haspelmath (eds.), *The World Atlas of Language Structures Online.* Munich: Max Planck Digital Library, feature 49A. Available online at: http://wals.info/.

Ingram, David. 1986. "Phonological development: Production." In Fletcher, Paul, and Michael Garman (eds.), *Language acquisition*, 2nd edn. New York: Cambridge University Press. 71-92.

Iverson, Jana and Susan Goldin-Meadow. 2005. "Gesture paves the way for language development." *Psychological Science* **16**.5: 367-371.

Jacobson, Steven. 1985. *Yop'ik Eskimo dictionary.* Fairbanks: Alaska Native Language Center.

Jahr, Ernst H. and Ingvild Broch (eds.). 1996. *Language contact in the Arctic: Northern pidgins and contact languages.* Berlin: Mouton de Gruyter.

Kelly, Barbara. 2003. "The emergence of an argument structure framework from gesture to speech." Ph.D. dissertation, University of California, Santa Barbara.

2005. "The development of constructions through early gesture use." In Clark, Eve and Barbara Kelly (eds.), *Constructions in acquisition.* Stanford, Calif.: CSLI Publications.

Kim, Young-Joo. 1987. "The acquisition of relative clauses in English and Korean: Development in spontaneous production." Ph.D. dissertation, Harvard University.

2000. "Subject/object drop in the acquisition of Korean: A cross-linguistic comparison." *Journal of East Asian Linguistics* **9**.4: 325-351.

Kouwenberg, N. J. C. 2010. *The Akkadian verb and its Semitic background.* Winona Lake, Ind.: Eisenbrauns.

Krashen, Stephen D. 1989. "We acquire vocabulary and spelling by reading: Additional evidence for the Input Hypothesis." *The Modern Language Journal* **73**: 440–464.

Kurungtiem, Casmir Toekwap. 1991. *"Impact of colonialism on the Goemai land."* Unpublished B.Sc. thesis, University of Jos.

Kyratzis, Amy. 2000. "Tactical uses of narratives in nursery school same sex groups." *Discourse Processes* **29**.3: 269–299.

Labov, William. 1963. "The social motivation of a sound change." *Word* **19**: 273–309.

1973. *Language in the inner city: Studies in the Black English Vernacular.* Philadelphia: University of Pennsylvania Press.

1997. "Some further steps in narrative analysis." *Journal of Narrative and Life History* **7**: 395–415.

Lakoff, Robin Tolmach. 2004. *Language and woman's place: Text and commentaries,* revised and expanded edn., ed. Mary Bucholtz. New York: Oxford University Press.

Lamb, Sidney. 1958. "Mono grammar." Ph.D. dissertation, University of California, Berkeley.

Landerman, Peter N. 1991. "Quechua dialects and their classification." Ph.D. dissertation, University of California, Los Angeles.

Lehiste, Ilse. 1988. *Lectures on language contact.* Cambridge, Mass.: MIT Press.

Levinson, Stephen C. 1983. *Pragmatics.* Cambridge University Press.

Levinson, Stephen C. and David P. Wilkins (eds.). 2006. *Grammars of space: Explorations in cognitive diversity.* Cambridge University Press.

Lewis, M. Paul, Gary Simons, and Charles D. Fenning (eds.). 2009. *Ethnologue: Languages of the world,* 17th edn. Dallas, TX: SIL International. Available online at: www.ethnologue.com/.

Lieven, Elena. 2009. "Developing constructions." *Cognitive Linguistics* **20**.1: 191–199.

Lieven, Elena, Julian M. Pine and Gillian Baldwin. 1997. "Lexically-based learning and early grammatical development." *Journal of Child Language* **24**: 187–219.

Lieven, Elena and Heiki Behrens. 2012. "Dense sampling." In Hoff, Erika (ed.), *Research methods in child language: A practical guide.* New York: Wiley. 226–239.

Lightbown, Patsy M. and Nina Spada. 2006. *How languages are learned,* 3rd edn. Oxford University Press.

Liszkowski, Ulf. 2006. "Infant pointing at 12 months: Communicative goals, motives and social-cognitive abilities." In Enfield, Nicholas J. and Stephen C. Levinson (eds.), *Roots of human sociality: Culture, cognition and interaction.* New York: Berg. 153–178.

Long, Michael. 1996. "The role of the linguistic environment in second language acquisition." In Ritchie, W. and Bhatia T. (eds.), *Handbook of second language acquisition.* San Diego: Academic Press. 413–468.

Lorimer, D. L. R. 1935. *The Burushaski language.* Institutet for Sammenligende Kulturforskning. Leipzig: Otto Harrowsowitz, Vol. I.

Maddieson, Ian. 1984. *Patterns of sounds.* Cambridge University Press.

Mallory, J. P. 1989. *In search of the Indo-Europeans: Language, archaeology and myth.* London: Thames and Hudson.

Masica, Colin. 1976. *Defining a linguistic area: South Asia.* University of Chicago Press.

2001. "The definition and significance of linguistic areas." In Bhaskararao, Peri and K. V. Subbarao (eds.), *South Asia yearbook 2001: Papers from the Symposium on South Asian Languages: Contact, convergence, and typology.* Delhi: SAGE Publications. 205–267.

McCabe, Allyssa. 1997. "Developmental and cross-cultural aspects of children's narration." In Bamberg, Michael (ed.), *Narrative development: Six approaches.* Mahwah, NJ: Lawrence Erlbaum. 137-174.

McKay, Sandra Lee. 2000. "Teaching English as an international language: Implications for cultural materials in the classroom." *TESOL Journal* **9**.4: 7-10.

Miller, Peggy and Linda Sperry. 1988. "Early talk about the past: The origins of conversational stories of personal experience." *Journal of Child Language* **15**: 293-315.

Miller, Wick. 1972. *Newe Natekwinappeh: Shoshoni stories and dictionary* (University of Utah Anthropological Papers 94). Salt Lake City: University of Utah.

1988. "Computerized database for Uto-Aztecan cognate sets." Unpublished monograph. Salt Lake City: Anthropology Dept., University of Utah.

Mithun, Marianne. 1991. "Active/agentive case marking and its motivations." *Language* **67**.3: 510-546.

Monday, Binlak Benson. 1989. "A study on the development of western education in Shendam Local Government Area of Plateau State." Unpublished Ph.D. thesis, College of Education (Gindiri) and Ahmadu Bello University (Zaria).

Montgomery-Anderson, Brad. 2008. "A reference grammar of Oklahoma Cherokee." Ph.D. dissertation, University of Kansas.

Munro, Pamela and William E. Mace. 1995. *A new Tübatulabal dictionary,* revised preliminary version. University of California, Los Angeles.

Murane, Elizabeth. 1974. *Daga grammar.* Glendale, Calif.: Summer Institute of Linguistics.

Murray, J. A. H. (ed.). 1971. *Compact edition of the Oxford English Dictionary.* Oxford University Press.

Nadkarni, M. V. 1975. "Bilingualism and syntactic change in Konkani." *Language* **51**: 672-683.

Nation, I. S. P. 2001. *Learning vocabulary in another language.* Cambridge University Press.

Nelson, Katherine. 1973. "Structure and strategy in learning to talk." *Monographs of the Society for Research in Child Development* **38**.1-2, serial no. 149.

Newman, Stanley. 1965. *Zuni grammar.* Albuquerque: University of New Mexico.

Ochs, Elinor. 1988. *Culture and language development: Language acquisition and language socialization in a Samoan village.* New York: Cambridge University Press.

Ochs, Elinor, Bambi Schieffelin, Martha L. Platt (eds.). 1979. "Propositions across utterances and speakers." In Ochs, Elinor and Bambi Schieffelin, *Developmental pragmatics.* New York: Academic Press. 251-268.

Ochs, Elinor and Bambi Schieffelin. 1984. "Language acquisition and socialization: Three developmental stories." In Shweder, Richard A. and Robert A. LeVine (eds.), *Culture theory: Essays on mind, self, and emotion.* New York: Cambridge University Press. 276-320.

O'Connor, Loretta M. 2007. *Motion, transfer, and transformation: The grammar of change in Lowland Chontal.* Amsterdam and Philadelphia: John Benjamins.

Oppenheim, A. Leo. 1964. *Ancient Mesopotamia: Portrait of a dead civilization.* University of Chicago Press.

Owens, J. 1996. "Grammatisierung, semantisierung und sprachkontakt: Arabischim Tschad-See-Gebiet." In Haase, Martin and Nicole Nau (eds.), *Sprachkontakt und Grammatikalisierung.* Special issue of *Sprachtypologie und Universalienforschung* **49**.1: 79-85.

Owens, Robert E. Jr. 2012. *Language development: An introduction,* 8th edn. Upper Saddle River, NJ: Pearson.

Phillips, Juliet R. 1973. "Syntax and vocabulary of mothers' speech to young children: Age and sex comparisons." *Child Development* **44**: 182-185.

Phinney, Archie. 1934. *Nez Perce texts.* New York: Columbia University Press.

Pine, Julian and Elena Lieven. 1997. "Slot and frame patterns and the development of the determiner category." *Applied Psycholinguistics* **18**: 123-138.

Pinker, Steven. 1984. *Language learnability and language development.* Cambridge, Mass.: Harvard University Press.

Pitkin, Harvey. 1985. *Wintu dictionary* (University of California Publications in Linguistics 95). Berkeley: University of California.

Podesva, Robert J. 2007. "Phonation type as a stylistic variable: The use of falsetto in constructing a persona." *Journal of Sociolinguistics* **11**.4: 478-504.

Pujolar, Joan. 2000. *Gender, heteroglossia, and power: A sociolinguistic study of youth culture.* Berlin: Mouton de Gruyter.

Pye, Clifton. 1996. "'Kiche' Maya verbs of breaking and cutting." *Kansas Working Papers in Linguistics* **21**: 87-98.

Radford, Andrew, Martin Atkinson, David Britain, Harald Clahsen, and Andrew Spencer. 2009. *Linguistics: An introduction*, 2nd edn. Cambridge University Press.

Refsing, Kirsten. 1986. *The Ainu Language: The morphology and syntax of the Shizunai dialect.* Aartius University Press.

Rescorla, Leslie A. 1980. "Overextension in early language development." *Journal of Child Language* **7**: 321-335.

Richards, Cara B. 1974. "Onondaga women: Among the liberated." In Matthiasson, Carolyn J. (ed.), *Many sisters: Women in cross-cultural perspective.* New York: Free Press. 401-419.

Rickford, John R. and Faye McNair-Knox. 1994. "Addressee- and topic-influenced style shift: A quantitative sociolinguistic study." In Biber, Douglas and Edward Finegan (eds.), *Sociolinguistic perspectives on register.* New York: Oxford University Press. 235-275.

Roscoe, Paul. 1994. "Who are the Ndu? Ecology, migration, and linguistic and cultural change in the Sepik Basin." In Strathern, Andrew J. and G. Stürzenhofecker (eds.), *Migrations and transformations: Regional perspectives on New Guinea.* University of Pittsburgh Press. 49-84.

Rowling, J. K. and Mary GrandPré. 2000. *Harry Potter and the goblet of fire.* New York: Arthur A. Levine Books.

Rubino, Carl Ralph Balvez. 1977. "A reference grammar of Ilocano." Ph.D. dissertation, University of California, Santa Barbara.

Sachs, Jacqueline. 1983. "Talking about there and then: The emergence of displaced reference in parent-child discourse." In Nelson, Katherine (ed.), *Children's language*, Vol. IV. Hillsdale, NJ: Lawrence Erlbaum. 1-28.

Sapir, Edward. 1930. *The Southern Paiute language.* Proceedings of the American Academy of Arts and Science 65.

Schieffelin, Bambi. 1990. *The give and take of everyday life: Language socialization of Kaluli children.* New York: Cambridge University Press.

Schlesinger, Itzak M. 1974. "Relational concepts underlying language." In Scheifelbusch, Richard L. and Lyle L. Lloyd (eds.), *Language perspectives: Acquisition, retardation, and intervention.* Baltimore: University Park Press. 129-151.

Schwartz, Richard. 1988. "Phonological factors in early lexical acquisition." In Smith, Michael and John L. Locke (eds.), *The emergent lexicon: The child's development of a linguistic vocabulary.* New York: Academic Press. 185-222.

Seidlhofer, Barbara. 2005. "English as a lingua franca." *ELT Journal* **59**.4: 339-341.

Shepherd, Alice. 2006. *Proto-Wintun* (University of California Publications in Linguistics 137). Berkeley: University of California Press.

Shibatani Masayoshi. 1990. *The language of Japan* (Cambridge Language Surveys). Cambridge University Press.

Slobin, Dan I. 1970. "Universals of grammatical development in children." In Flores D'Arcais, Giovanni B. and Willem J. Levelt (eds.), *Advances in psycholinguistics*. Amsterdam: North Holland. 174–186.

   1979. *Psycholinguistics*, 2nd edn. Glenview, Ill.: Scott Foresman.

   1986. "Crosslinguistic evidence for the Language-Making Capacity." In Slobin, Dan I. (ed.), *The crosslinguistic study of language acquisition,* Vol. II: *Theoretical issues*. Hillsdale, NJ: Lawrence Erlbaum. 1029–1067.

Smith, Neilson V. 1973. *The acquisition of phonology: A case study*. New York: Cambridge University Press.

Snow, Catherine E. 1977a. "Mothers' speech research: From input to interaction." In Snow, Catherine E. and Charles Ferguson (eds.), *Talking to children: Language input and acquisition*. New York: Cambridge University Press. 31–49.

   1977b. "The development of conversation between mothers and babies." *Journal of Child Language* **4**: 1–22.

   1986. "Conversations with children." In Fletcher, Paul and Michael Garman (eds.), *Language acquisition,* 2nd edn. New York: Cambridge University Press. 69–89.

Snow, Catherine E., Barbara Alexander Pan, Alison Imbens-Bailey, and Jane Herman. 1996. "Learning how to say what one means: A longitudinal study of children's speech act use." *Social Development* **5**.1: 56–84.

Sperber, Dan and Deirdre Wilson. 1986/1995. *Relevance*. Oxford: Blackwell.

Stolz, Thomas. 1986. *Gibtes das kreolischeSprachwandelmodell? Vergleichende Grammatik des Negerholländischen* (Linguistik 46). Frankfurt, Bern, and New York: Lang.

Stonham, John. 2005. *A concise dictionary of the Nuuchahnulth language of Vancouver Island*. Lewiston, NY: Edwin Mellen.

Sun, Chaofen. 1996. *Word order change and grammaticalization in the history of Chinese*. Stanford, Calif.: Stanford University Press.

Suppes, Patrick. 1974. "The semantics of children's language." *American Psychologist* **29**: 103–114.

Tauli, Valter. 1984. "The Estonian language reform." In Fodor, István and Claude Hagège (eds.), *Language reform: History and future,* Vol. III. Hamburg: Buske Verlag. 309–330.

Taylor, Ann, Tandy Warnow, and Don Ringe. 1998. "Character-based reconstruction of a linguistic cladogram." In Smith, John Charles and Delia Bentley (eds.), *Historical linguistics 1995*. Amsterdam: John Benjamins. 393–408.

Thomas, Elaine. 1978. *A grammatical description of the Engenni language*. Arlington, TX: Summer Institute of Linguistics and the University of Texas at Arlington.

Thomas, Jenny. 1995. *Meaning in interaction: An introduction to pragmatics*. London: Longman.

Thurston, W. R. 1987. *Processes of change in the languages of northwestern Britain*. Canberra: Pacific Linguistics.

Tomasello, Michael. 1992. *First verbs*. New York: Cambridge University Press.

   2006. "Acquiring constructions." In Siegler, Robert and Deanne Kuhn (eds.), *Handbook of child psychology: Cognition, perception and language*. New York: Wiley. 255–298.

   2008. *Origins of human communication*. Cambridge, Mass.: MIT Press.

Tomasello, Michael and Patricia Brooks. 1999. "Early syntactic development: A construction grammar approach." In Barrett, Martyn (ed.), *The development of language*. Hove, Sussex: Psychology Press. 161–189.

Torero, Alfredo. 1964. "Los dialectos quechuas." *Anales científicos de la Universidad Agraria* **2**: 446-478.

Tosco, Mauro. 2001. *The Dhaasanac language: Grammar, texts, vocabulary of a Cushitic language of Ethiopia.* Cologne: Köppe.

Trigger, Bruce. 1976. *The children of Aataentsic: A history of the Huron people to 1660.* Kingston and Montreal: McGill-Queen's University Press.

Ullrich, Jan. 2008. *New Lakota Dictionary: Lak□ótiyapi-English/English-Lak□ótiyapi & Incorporating the Dakota dialects of Yankton-Yanktonai & Santee-Sisseton.* Bloomington, Ind.: Lakota Language Consortium.

Waterhouse, Viola. 1967. "Huamelultec Chontal." In Wauchope, R. and N. A. McQuown (eds.), *Handbook of Middle American Indians,* Vol. V: *Linguistics.* Austin: University of Texas Press. 349-367.

Watkins, Calvert. 1981. "Indo-European and the Indo-Europeans." *The American heritage dictionary of the English language.* Boston: Houghton Mifflin. 1496-1502.

Widdowson, Henry G. 1988. "Grammar, and nonsense, and learning." In Rutherford, William E. and Michael Sharwood Smith (eds.), *Grammar and second language teaching.* New York: Newbury House. 146-155.

Zahar, Rick, Tom Cobb, and Nina Spada. 2001. "Acquiring vocabulary through reading: Effects of frequency and contextual richness." *Canadian Modern Language Review* **15**.4: 541-572.

Z'graggen, John A. 1980. *A comparative word list of the Mabuso languages, Madang Province, Papua New Guinea* (Pacific Linguistics, Series D 32). Canberra: The Australian National University Department of Linguistics, Research School of Pacific Studies.

Zhang, Qing. 2005. "A Chinese yuppie in Beijing: Phonological variation and the construction of a new professional identity." *Language in Society* **34**: 431-466.

Zhurinskij, Alfred N. 1995. *Lingvistika v zadachakh: Uslovija, reshenija, kommentarii* (Linguistics in problems: statements, solutions, comments). Moscow: Indrik.

# INDEX